meroitica

Schriften zur altsudanesischen Geschichte und Archäologie
Humboldt-Universität zu Berlin

Herausgegeben von
Steffen Wenig

Band 22

2005

Harrassowitz Verlag · Wiesbaden

Afrikas Horn

Akten der Ersten Internationalen
Littmann-Konferenz
2. bis 5. Mai 2002 in München

Herausgegeben von
Walter Raunig und Steffen Wenig

2005
Harrassowitz Verlag · Wiesbaden

Redaktion und Druckvorlage: Karin Lippold und Petra Andrássy.
Die Bände 1–14 erschienen im Akademie-Verlag Berlin.

Die Herausgabe dieses Werkes wurde ermöglicht durch Spenden von:
ORBIS AETHIOPICUS, Gesellschaft zur Erhaltung und Förderung
der äthiopischen Kultur e.V.
Gesellschaft für asiatische Kunst und Kultur
Deutsche Bank AG
Dr. Hans Peter Linss, Berg, Starnberger See

Bibliografische Information Der Deutschen Bibliothek:
Die Deutsche Bibliothek verzeichnet diese Publikation in der Deutschen
Nationalbibliografie; detaillierte bibliografische Daten sind im Internet
über http://dnb.ddb.de abrufbar.

Bibliographic information published by Die Deutsche Bibliothek:
Die Deutsche Bibliothek lists this publication in the Deutsche
Nationalbibliografie; detailed bibliographic data is available in the
internet at http://dnb.ddb.de.

Informationen zum Verlagsprogramm finden Sie unter
http://www.harrassowitz.de/verlag
Gedruckt auf alterungsbeständigem Papier.
Druck und Verarbeitung: Memminger MedienCentrum AG
Printed in Germany

ISSN 0138-3663
ISBN 3-447-05175-2

Enno Littmann begrüßt den Gouverneur von Tigray, Gabre-Selassie.
Rechts im Bild D. Krencker, links Th. von Lüpke und E. Kaschke.

Konferenz und Publikation
sind dem Andenken
des großen Orientalisten
Enno Littmann (1875 – 1958)
gewidmet.

Inhalt

I. The Archaeology of the Horn of Africa

II. The History of the Horn of Africa

III. The Ethiopian Church

IV. Enno Littmann und die Deutsche Aksum-Expedition

V. Recent Research and New Discoveries

Vorwort

Es war wohl einer der stillen Spätnachmittage im November des Jahres 1997, als wir im bescheidenen Garten unserer einfachen Unterkunft in Adi Käyeh, Eritrea, im Gespräch über den Fortgang der Forschungsarbeiten der Humboldt-Universität auf dem Plateau von Qohaito ganz automatisch wieder auf die großartigen Leistungen der Deutsche Aksum-Expedition von 1906 zu sprechen kamen. Dabei entstand die Idee, in Erinnerung an diese große Forschungsreise in bestimmten zeitlichen Abständen wissenschaftliche Konferenzen durchzuführen und dies unter dem Namen des Leiters der Deutschen Aksum-Expedition, des berühmten Orientalisten Enno Littmann (1875-1958). Diese Idee wurde dann von allen in Adi Käyeh anwesenden Teilnehmern sofort positiv aufgenommen. Dem Inhalt nach sollten diese Konferenzen der Archäologie und Kulturgeschichte Nordostafrikas, speziell des Horns von Afrika, gewidmet sein, also Gebieten, die auf den internationalen Äthiopisten-Kongressen nur eine untergeordnete Rolle spielen. Wir waren und sind der Ansicht, dass auf wenige Themenkomplexe begrenzte und damit kleinere Konferenzen wissenschaftlich ergiebiger sind als die großen Mammuttagungen, auf denen tiefer gehende Diskussionen von vornherein ausgeschlossen sind. Als Muster für diese "First International Littmann Conference" dienten die 1971 von F. Hintze (1915-1993) ins Leben gerufenen Internationalen Meroitisten-Konferenzen, die bis 1996 sehr erfolgreich verliefen.

Im Vorfeld wurden vier Hauptreferenten gebeten, sich zu aktuellen Themen vorzubereiten. Nach Möglichkeit sollten diese Hauptreferate einige Zeit vor Beginn der Tagung an die Teilnehmer verteilt werden, damit sich diese mit schriftlichen oder mündlichen Kurzbeiträgen zu den entsprechenden Themen äußern könnten. In unserem Fall lag dann vor Konferenzbeginn allerdings nur ein Hauptreferat, das von Stuart Munro-Hay, rechtzeitig vor und wurde den angemeldeten Teilnehmern zugesandt. Das Echo darauf war sehr positiv. Herr Munro-Hay bekam eine Reihe von Stellungnahmen, die er in der hier abgedruckten Form seines Hauptreferates eingearbeitet hat. Wir sind davon überzeugt, dass die für die Konferenzen gewählte Veranstaltungsform auf die Dauer effektiv ist und zu umfassenden Diskussionen zu bestimmten Themen führt. Dabei wird auch die Möglichkeit geboten, über neueste Forschungen in der Arbeitsgruppe "Recent Research and New Discoveries" sprechen zu können.

Es verging einige Zeit, bis für die erste der Konferenzen Termin, Ort, Organisation, Finanzierung und Referentenliste festgelegt werden konnten. Als Veranstalter traten auf: Die Humboldt-Universität zu Berlin, das Staatliche Museum für Völkerkunde München und die Eberhard-Karls-Universität Tübingen. Sie führten die Konferenz mit Unterstützung von Orbis Aethiopicus und der Gesellschaft für Asiatische Kunst und Kultur, München e.V. durch. Als Tagungsort bot sich das Staatliche Museum für Völkerkunde München an, da sich diese Institution – wenn auch in bescheidenem Umfang – nicht nur am aktuellen Forschungsunternehmen der Humboldt-Universität beteiligte, sondern schon seit rund einem Vierteljahrhundert in vielfältiger Hinsicht dem genannten Raum und dabei besonders Äthiopien und Eritrea seine Aufmerksamkeit widmete. Als Termin für die "Erste Internationale Littmann-Konferenz" wurde das Jahr 2002 gewählt, denn vier Jahre später könnte dann erneut eine Littmann-Konferenz stattfinden und dies wäre das Jahr 2006, also das Jahr der hundertsten Wiederkehr der berühmten Deutschen Aksum-Expedition.

Dank der finanziellen Unterstützung durch eine Reihe von Institutionen und der Privatwirtschaft, so durch den Deutschen Akademischen Austauschdienst, die Allianz-Kulturstiftung, die Gerda Henkel Stiftung, die HypoVereinsbank und Augustiner-Bräu München war es möglich, eine ganze Reihe von namhaften Wissenschaftlern nicht nur aus europäischen Ländern, sondern auch aus Afrika, Asien und Amerika zur Teilnahme an der Konferenz einzuladen. Sie kamen aus Äthiopien, Deutschland, Eritrea, Finnland, Frankreich, Großbritannien, Italien, Kanada, den Niederlanden, Österreich, Polen, Russland, der Schweiz und den USA. So gilt unser Dank nicht nur allen Teilnehmern für ihre Referate, ihre rege Mitarbeit und für den Gedankenaustausch, sondern auch allen Institutionen und Firmen, die dies ermöglicht haben. Unser Dank gilt ebenso Herrn Direktor Dr. Claudius C. Müller und Frau Karin Guggeis M.A. vom Staatlichen Museum für Völkerkunde München für die Unterstützung und Hilfe bei der Ausrichtung des Kongresses. Herrn Prof. Dr. Rainer Voigt, Berlin, danken wir in besonderer Weise, da er kurzfristig aus einem vorgesehenen Beitrag ein Hauptreferat machte.

Im Rahmen der ersten Internationalen Littmann-Konferenz wurde in 80 Beiträgen der aktuelle Forschungsstand auf den Gebieten Geschichte, Archäologie, Ethnologie, Soziologie, Linguistik, Religionswissenschaft und Ökonomie in Nordostafrika behandelt. Etwa die Hälfte dieser Beiträge sind nun im vorliegenden Band zusammengefasst.

Die Konferenz begleitend wurde am Abend des 2.5.2002 in Anwesenheit von vier Botschaftern die Ausstellung „Enno Littmann und die deutsche Aksum-Expedition (Äthiopien – Eritrea)" eröffnet, die in Objekt, Bild und Text über dieses bedeutende Forschungsunternehmen vor nun bald 100 Jahren berichtete. Hier danken wir besonders Herrn Hans von Lüpke, dem Enkel des Fotografen der Deutschen Aksum-Expedition Theodor von Lüpke, der archäologisches Material zur Verfügung stellte.

Frau Karin Lippold vom Seminar für Archäologie und Kulturgeschichte Nordostafrikas der Humboldt-Universität zu Berlin hat sich der mühevollen Aufgabe unterzogen, das Layout am Computer herzustellen und mehrere Beiträge, die nur in gedruckter Form vorlagen, abzuschreiben. Für ihren großartigen Einsatz gilt unser herzlichster Dank.

Wir danken ebenso Frau Dr. Petra Andrassy von der Humboldt-Universität für ihre Unterstützung bei der Layout-Gestaltung sowie für umfangreiche und uneigennützige Hilfe bei der Herausgabe der Publikation.

Herrn Langfeld vom Verlag Harrassowitz Wiesbaden gilt unser Dank für die verlegerische Begleitung der vorliegenden Publikation und seine Zustimmung zur Aufnahme der Tagungsakten in die Reihe *Meroitica*.

Dem Leser wünschen wir beim Studium der Beiträge dieser neuen Tagungsreihe viel Erkenntnisgewinn – und wir hoffen auf ein Wiedersehen zur "Second International Littmann Conference" 2006 in Berlin.

Ein Hinweis an die Leser: Besonders bei der Schreibung von Eigennamen gibt es in den einzelnen Beiträgen gravierende Unterschiede. Die Herausgeber haben sich entschieden, diese nicht zu vereinheitlichen, so dass die Autoren die Verantwortung für ihre Beiträge auch in dieser Hinsicht selbst tragen.

Berlin und München im Frühjahr 2004

Steffen Wenig   Walter Raunig

Statement by the Ethiopian Ambassador

Hiruy Amanuel

Distinguished members of the Organizing Committee
Distinguished participants of this conference
Ladies and Gentlemen,

I am deeply honored to be amongst you here today in Munich, and to attend the First Littmann Conference dedicated to the Archaeology and History of the Horn of Africa. I thank you for the invitation.

It is very obvious why we are all here. We have come together because of our interest in the history of the Horn of Africa. Some of you have spent a major part of your professional lives in research and the study of our part of the world. Others are here because for them, the Horn of Africa is their home. I am here, not just because I come from Ethiopia at the center of the Horn, but also to demonstrate the respect and recognition that we in Ethiopia accord to the scholarship and dedicated study made by many on the subject of our country with its ancient and fascinating history. Noteworthy among them is none other than Enno Littmann who led what is known as the German Expedition to northern Ethiopia in the first decade of the last century.

I would like to take this opportunity to express our appreciation for the initiative taken by the Organizing Committee of this conference to make this important gathering a success.

Dear Participants,

You are all aware that it is not in the realm of history and antiquity that the Horn of Africa is known in the larger community here in Europe and in other parts of the world. Our region is unfortunately known for other and less positive attributes; the prevalence of famine and the persistence of conflict. That is, of course, not the whole story. But the better story of our country is often not told, and it is therefore refreshing and encouraging when distinguished academics come together to share views on what is one of the most positive features of our subregion – its long and remarkable history and its rich culture.

But the past has relevance to the present and the future. One subject to be taken up at this conference, for instance, is that of the Ethiopian Orthodox Church, an ancient and at the same time living community of millions that has made and continues to make a central impact on the region in which we live.

Archaeology – another matter you will touch upon – is very much alive in the Horn of Africa. Over the past decade, improved access to many parts of Ethiopia has resulted in growing interest and activity of an archaeological nature. Although it may not be the most popular concept to archaeologists and historians we have begun to hear in Ethiopia the terms 'Archaeological tourism' and 'pale ontological tourism' to describe a new form of activity to that is based on encouraging international visitors to see the important sites for themselves and to experience at first hand the panorama of antiquity. We have 'Lucy' or 'Dinkinesh' and other no less impressive discoveries to thank for the reputation as the Cradle of Humanity.

The conference will also examine the Red Sea dimension. The focus on the two shores of the Red Sea at this conference has its present day echo as well. For a number of reasons, the Horn of Africa is once again attracting greater international political attention that would benefit from a more in-depth analysis of the historical developments that have shaped and continue to shape the events in our part of the world.

I am confident that with the significant number of distinguished participants that are present, and many from my country, this conference would take scholarship an important step forward through the sharing of ideas and the examination of new developments. At the same time I would hope that some of your discussions would revolve around how best to build the capacities of the countries in the sub-region to conserve their heritage while building knowledge and consciousness among their citizens. In reference to Ethiopia many would speak of Lalibela, Gondar and Axum. But you all know that the country has much more. But then, how many more really know about how much is out there. Within the current effort to speed up the economic transformation and development of Ethiopia must be included a strong element aimed at building national capacity, in human, material and financial terms to enable us to understand and also present ourselves to the world as a whole. Among the many challenges we face today is the continued Italian reluctance regarding the return of the Axum obelisk. We need the support of all as we seek to return the Axum Obelisk now in Rome to Ethiopia despite the many obstacles that continue to be placed in our way. We believe that the Littmann Conference should add its voice to the international call for the return of this cultural treasure. After all, it was the Littmann Expedition that provided the actual photographs of the location of the obelisks in Axum, those standing and fallen, including the one that currently stands in Rome. We are also working hard to ensure the return to the extent possible of other looted objects of historical value. We have been encouraged by the recent return of the tabot spirited away to Scotland in 1865.

At the same time, however, we need to protect what is in the country from modern day looting. That is easier said than done and the more support we get, the better. We also need to ensure that the present and coming generations develop with greater understanding and respect for their heritage – a real challenge in the rapidly globalising world, so that they and not just tourists and the select few see and appreciate what they have. We will share with the those concerned back in Ethiopia your suggestions and contributions in this regard.

Dear members of the Organizing Committee
Ladies and Gentlemen,

In conclusion I wish to draw your attention to the next congress of Ethiopian studies that will be held in Hamburg in the summer of 2003. It will be an important event for which preparations have already begun.

I wish also to remind you, if you have forgotten, that in three years time, in 2005, Ethiopia and Germany will mark the 100 years of diplomatic relations. The year will be marked with events both in Ethiopia and Germany and we invite you to join us both here and in Ethiopia.

May this conference be crowned with success.
I thank you.

Statement by the Eritrean Ambassador

Zemede Tekle Woldetatios

Mr. Chairman
Distinguished members of the Organizing Committee
Ladies and Gentlemen,

Allow me to congratulate the Organizing Committee for its relentless effort to make such conference a reality. I would also like to thank it for giving me the opportunity to be part of this historic conference and say some few words.

"The early history of Eritrea and Northern Ethiopia will have to be rewritten in the light of dramatic new discoveries. And they have relevance to the worldwide demand for balanced historical and cultural studies freed from arrogance, prejudice and racism". These are the words of Prof. Richard Greenfield in his article, "New Discoveries in Africa, Change Face of History", in New African Magazine of Nov. 2001.

I chose to quote him because, to my understanding, his statement ushers the future, it anticipates the true history of our ancestors and their civilization based on scientific studies and concrete facts. It also adds to the famous phrase of Mr. Basil Dawidson "Liberated History will out" to be tangible.

Ladies and Gentlemen,

Prominent archaeologists from universities of Europe and U.S. have already visited Eritrea. Some have got a birds eye view and others substantial information of the importance of archaeological sites that the country possess. And have testified that the country has potential on this matter. But archaeology is still uncharted and I am sure the archaeologists who are acquainted with such resources of the country are eager to dig deep down to discover what is not discovered.

The University of Asmara and its young Department of Archaeology is also working very hard and I believe has already established good relationships with different departments of archaeology to work with them and accommodate the eagerness of the interested partners. And in the near future, I hope all the ambitions to make Eritrea play a part on the fulfilment of the remaining gaps in the chain of history of our region to be a reality.

Ladies and Gentlemen,

With peace everything is possible. The peace that our people have fought and eager to attain and attained, I can say it is in good shape.

Taking advantage of this conductive atmosphere to development a change for the best to all the people in the region is possible.

Thank you!

Teilnehmerverzeichnis

H.E. Hiruy Amanuel, Berlin
H.E. Tekle Zemede, Berlin
S.E. Hubert Kolb, Asmara
S.E. Werner Daum, Kuwait

Amborn, Hermann, München
Asfa-Wossen Asserate, Frankfurt/Main

Becker, Heinrich, Seefeld
Best, Renate, Frankfurt/Main
Billig, Daniela, Berlin
Bokrezion Zera Yohans, Neu-Isenburg
Bombeck, Stefan, Bottrop
Braukämper, Ulrich, Göttingen
Breyer, Francis, Tübingen
Brunner, Ueli, Pfäffikon
Buder, Walter, Stuttgart
Buffa, Vittoria, Rom

Chernetsov, Sevir, St. Petersburg
Chojnacki, Stanisław, Sudbury
Cohen, Leonard, Jerusalem
Crummey, Donald, Urbana

Daum, Gisela, Kuwait
Deska, Dagmara, Warschau
Diesfeld, Jens-Jochen, Starnberg
Dima Noggo Sarbo, Frankfurt/Main
Dornisch, Klaus, Nürnberg

Eisenhofer, Stefan, München

Fattovich, Rodolfo, Neapel

Georgieff, Dorothea, Oftersheim
Gerlach, Iris, Berlin/Sana
Girma Fisseha, München
Gonschior, Thomas, Emmering
Gossage, Carolyn M., Toronto

Gräber, Gerd, Mannheim
Guggeis, Karin, München

Haefner, Harald, Zürich
Hahn, Wolfgang, Wien
Hani, Hayajneh, Irbid
Heide, Martin, Germering
Henze, Martha H., Washington
Henze, Paul B., Washington
Heyer, Friedrich, Heidelberg
Higel, Thomas, Garmisch-Partenkirchen
Hiß, Reinhard, Mainz
Hussein Ahmed, Addis Abeba

Kaplan, Steven, Jerusalem
Karberg, Tim, Berlin
Kellermann, Petra, Mainz
Kleiner, Michael, Hamburg
Krafft, Walter, Berlin
Kriss, Hubert, Berchtesgaden
Kropp, Manfred, Beirut/Mainz
Krüger, Manfred, Frankfurt/Main

Lang, Franz, München
Lepage, Claude, Benquet
Littmann, Gert, München
von Lüpke, Hans, Nürnberg
Lusini, Gianfrancesco, Pisa

de Maigret, Alessandro, Neapel
Marcus, Cressida, Okemos
Marcus, Harold G., East Lansing
Markt, Silke, München
Martínez d'Alòs-Moner, Andreu, Hamburg
Marx, Annegret, Aachen
May, Reinhard, Bad Reichenhall
Melchers, Konrad, Brachtal

Melchers, Nina, Brachtal
Meyer, Ronny, Mainz
Morin, Didier, Bordeaux
Mucha, Rebekka, Berlin
Müller, Claudius C., München
Munro-Hay, Stuart, Mézin

Pascher, Lothar, München
Peltz, Christian, München
Persoon, Joachim, Ipendam
Petros Berga, Edam
Phillips, Jacke, Cambridge
Phillipson, David W., Cambridge
Pietruschka, Ute, Halle/Saale
Priess, Maija, Hamburg

Raunig, Walter, München
Rezene Russom, Asmara
Ritler, Alfons, Jegenstorf
Roenpage, Peter, Hattstedt
Roenpage, Dorothea, Hattstedt
Rubinkowska, Hanna, Warschau

Scheibner, Thomas, Berlin
Scheubel, Ursula, München
von Schnurbein, Rüdiger, Berlin
Scholler, Heinrich, München
Sedov, Alexander, Moskau
Senait Mesgina, Mainz
Sievertsen, Uwe, Tübingen
Six, Veronika, Hamburg

Smidt, Wolbert, Hamburg
Sokolinskaia, Evgenia, Hamburg
Stache-Weiske, Agnes, Grafing
Stehmann, Kurt, Bickenbach
Stehmann, Raimund, Dingsdorf
Strebel, Eberhard, Friedrichshafen

Taddia, Irma, Bologna
Timkehet Teffera, Berlin
Trellenkamp, Michael, Berlin

Uoldelul Chelati, Asmara

Vogel, Friedrich, Linden
Vogel, Susanne, Linden
Vogt, Burkhard, Bonn
Voigt, Rainer, Berlin
Volker-Saad, Kerstin, Berlin

Wagner, Ewald, Gießen
Weigel, Anne, München
Wenig, Ingrid, Berlin
Wenig, Steffen, Berlin
Weninger, Stefan, Augsburg
Witakowski, Witold, Warschau
Woube Kassaye, Joensuu

Zelleke, Adelheid, Aachen
Zewde Gabre-Selassie, Addis Abeba
Ziegler, Susanne, Berlin
Ziethen, Gabriele, Worms

I. The Archaeology of the Horn of Africa

The Archaeology of the Horn of Africa

Rodolfo Fattovich

Introduction

The Horn of Africa includes the modern states of Eritrea, Ethiopia, Djibuti and Somalia.The region is characterized by a strong contrast between temperate highlands up to 3000-4000 m in elevation and arid or semiarid lowlands, and is cut by a rift generating the Danakil depression. The environment exhibits a great variety of climatic and ecological conditions, that may sharply change in contiguous regions.[1] The Horn of Africa is also exposed to environmental hazard, such as climatic fluctuations, causing droughts and famines, geo-dynamic activity with volcanic eruptions and earthquakes, invasions of desert locust swarms, and epidemics.[2]

People include Semitic, Cushitic, Omotic, and marginally Nilo-Saharan and Bantu speaking groups, which are divided into many linguistic sub-groups. These populations developed different adaptive strategies and territory occupation patterns, ranging from nomadic or semi-nomadic pastoralism in the lowlands to sedentary vege-culture, hoe farming, and ox-plow agriculture on the highlands, as well as different social and economic organizations, from acephalous societies in the western lowlands to highly centralized states on the highlands.[3] Moreover, populations with different adaptive strategies and social and economic organizations are often very close to each other, with a complex system of interaction at a small and middle regional scale.

The history of the region was greatly affected by this environmental and ethnic diversity, and was complicated by the location of the Horn at the interface of the Mediterranean world, Indian Ocean world, and African world. The historical dynamics in the Horn of Africa were thus characterized by:

1. A progressive interaction between the single populations at a different regional scale.
2. Their inclusion into larger networks of trade and cultural contacts with the Mediterranean regions, Middle East, and African hinterland.

---

1 See e.g., Dainelli 1935.
2 Ethiopian Mapping Authority 1988: pl. 19-21; Gouin 1979; Zein - Kloos 1988.
3 See e.g., Almagià 1935; Conti Rossini 1937; Zanetti 1996.

3. The constant re-adjustment of the single social and economic organizations to environmental hazard and political or economic pressure from the outside, in order to maintain their basic cultural identity.

The very complicated history of the Horn of Africa is well reflected in the archaeological record, which is very rich and covers the whole time span from the beginning of the Early Stone Age to the 19th century AD.[4]

In Eritrea and northern Ethiopia, including the Mareb/Gash and Barka lowlands along the border between Eritrea and the Sudan, the archaeological evidence includes lithic industries of the Early, Middle and Late Stone Age; neolithic and protohistorical sites; rock-pictures; ancient urban settlements and cemeteries; medieval built and rock-hewn churches; ancient Islamic cemeteries; and cemeteries of uncertain age.

In central, western and southern Ethiopia there are lithic industries dating to all periods of the Stone Age; protohistorical stelae fields and settlements; rock-pictures; medieval rock-hewn churches and settlements.

In eastern Ethiopia there are lithic industries similar to those of East Africa and northern Africa; dolmens and settlements with ciclopic walls; rock-pictures; tumuli; and early Islamic sites.

In Djibuti and Somalia there are lithic industries of the Early, Middle and Late Stone Age; neolithic sites; tumuli and cemeteries of late prehistoric and historical age; coastal sites with artifacts of Hellenistic-Roman age; early Islamic sites.

Despite this rich evidence, the Horn of Africa is still largely unexplored from the archaeological point of view. Investigations focussed mainly on a few specific topics, such as early prehistory, rock-art, megaliths, and early historical and medieval periods, and provided only a fragmentary reconstruction of the past of the region.

This situation is aggravated by the almost total absence of local professionals to manage the cultural heritage. A Department of Archaeology has been recently established at the University of Asmara in Eritrea with the technical support of the University of Florida, Gainsville. Since 1991 the organization of a M.A. program in archaeology is in progress at Addis Ababa University in Ethiopia with the technical support of the University of Naples "L'Orientale", Naples (Italy), as part of the Italian-Ethiopian University Cooperation Program.

4   Fattovich 1993.

1. The Archaeology in the Horn of Africa: An Historical Outline

Archaeological investigations in the Horn of Africa have a long history, beginning in the 16th century, when Francisco Alvarez described the church of Mary of Tsion at Aksum and the rock-hewn churches at Lalibela in northern Ethiopia.[5]

In the 17th to 19th centuries travellers and scholars recorded the occurrence of ancient monuments in northern Ethiopia and Eritrea, particularly at Aksum. In the late 19th century G. Révoil recorded for the first time ancient sites in northern Somalia.

A proper archaeological investigation began in the early 20th century when professional scholars conducted excavations and surveys in Eritrea and Tigray, as well as in the Omo Valley. In particular, the *Deutsche Aksum Expedition* led by E. Littmann, D. Krencker and Th. von Lüpke in 1905-1906 exhaustively recorded the ancient monuments at Aksum in Tigray, and at Qohaito, Kaskase, Tokonda, and Matara in Eritrea, as well as the church at Dabra Damo in Agamè and the so-called Old Church at Asmara, which no more exists. On this basis, the German scholars provided a detailed analysis of the Aksumite architecture, and laid the foundations of Aksumite archaeology.[6]

Investigations in the 1920s and 1930s provided new evidence about the Stone Age in southern and eastern Ethiopia and Somalia, rock-art in eastern Ethiopia, and megalithic monuments (dolmens, tumuli, and stelae) in eastern, central and southern Ethiopia. In the 1930s and 1940s systematic excavations were conducted at Aksum, and a particular attention was paid to the medieval rock-hewn churches in Ethiopia and Islamic sites in Somalia. This research expanded the knowledge of past in the Horn, but was mostly descriptive and no real effort to build cultural sequences was made. Only C. Conti Rossini published in the 1928 an account of the available archaeological evidence in a coherent historical context.[7]

In 1952 the Ethiopian Institute of Archaeology was established in Addis Ababa, with the support of French scholars (J. Leroy, J. Leclant, J. Doresse, H. de Contenson, F. Anfray, R. Schneider). Excavations were conducted at Aksum, Hawlti, Melazo, Yeha (northern Ethiopia), and Matara (Eritrea), and provided the basic evidence to outline the early historical cultural sequence in these regions.[8]

Beginning in the mid-1960s, the Stone Age was more systematically investigated at Melka Konture (central Ethiopia), in the Omo valley, the Rift Valley, and Afar. In the mid-1970s human palaeontology became a major area of research. In the 1960s and 1970s more attention was paid to the late prehistory, in particular the megaliths of eastern, central and southern Ethiopia and rock-art.

---

5 For more detailed outlines of the history of archaeological research in the Horn of Africa see Anfray 1963; Mussi 1974-75; Michels 1979; Brandt - Fattovich 1990; Fattovich 1992, 2001.
6 Littmann - Krencker - von Lüpke 1913; see also Phillipson 1997.
7 Conti Rossini 1928.
8 See de Contenson 1961, 1963; Anfray 1968, 1990.

In the early 1970s large scale excavations and surveys were conducted at Aksum (northern Ethiopia) and its immediate surroundings by British, Italian and American expeditions. These investigations provided further evidence about the Aksumite and Post-Aksumite periods in northern Ethiopia and Eritrea.

In the 1980s archaeological research was practically suspended in Ethiopia. Only some palaeoanthrological fieldwork was conducted in the Omo Valley.

In the late 1960s and 1980s, systematic surveys and excavations were conducted in the middle Atbara valley and the Gash Delta, on the Sudanese side of the Eritrean-Sudanese lowlands by American, Sudanese and Italian scholars. These investigations made evident the crucial role of the lowlands in the diffusion of food production towards the plateau and in the process of state formation in northern Ethiopia and Eritrea.

In the 1970s and 1980s archaeological investigations were conducted in the territory of Djibuti by French scholars, who enlarged the knowledge of the Stone Age, rock-art and late prehistory, and on early historical times. In Somalia, archaeological research was resumed in the 1960s and 1970s by British, Russian, Swedish, American, and Italian scholars, who investigated prehistoric, early historical, and Islamic sites.

The most important contribution of the research in the 1960s to 1980s was the reconstruction of the past of the region in a culture-historic and/or processual perspective.[9]

In the 1990s archaeological and palaeoanthropological fieldwork was resumed in Ethiopia and Eritrea, while it was interrupted in Somalia because of the deterioration of the political situation in the country.

In Ethiopia, K. A. Bard and R. Fattovich, D. W. Phillipson, and H. Ziegert resumed the archaeological investigation at Aksum in Tigray;[10] Hirsh and Poissonier, J. Chavaillon and M. Piperno, R. Joussaume, X. Gutherz, D. Boukhaze-Khan and B. Poisblaud, and J.-L. Quellec continued fieldwork in central and southern Ethiopia;[11] S. A. Brandt and V. Fernandez began some investigations in southwestern Ethiopia; and J. D. Clark, D. Johanson, and T. White conducted research in the Afar region. In Eritrea, archaeological research was resumed by G. Calegari, S. Wenig, S. Brandt, P. Schmidt and M. Curtis, G. Sagri and R. C. Walter.[12] In Djibuti research was continued by R. Joussaume.[13]

In these years local scholars also conducted excavations and surveys in Ethiopia and Eritrea. In Ethiopia we can remember the contributions of B. Assefa, Y. Beyene, and Z. Almeseged in the area of human paleonthology and early prehistory; A. Tare-

9   See Anfray 1968, 1990; Clark 1988; Brandt 1984, 1986; Fattovich 1988, 1990b, 1990c, 1994; Michels 1994; Begashaw 1994.
10 See Fattovich - Bard - Petrassi et al. 2000; Phillipson 2000; Ziegert 2001.
11 Hirsh - Poissonnier 2000; Bouville, Cros - Joussaume 2000; Ghuterez 2000; Boukhaze-Khan - Poisblaud 2000; Le Quellec - Abegaz 2001.
12 Wenig 1997; Curtis - Lisbekal 1999; Calegari 1999; Walter *et al.* 2000; Schmidt - Curtis 2001.
13 Gutherz - Joussaume - Amblard et al. 1996.

kegn, A. Negash, T. Hagos and G. Tesfay in the area of late prehistoric and historical archaeology.[14] In Eritrea, we can remember the work of Y. Libsekal.[15]

Environmental, political, cultural and ideological factors greatly affected the archaeological research in the Horn of Africa.[16] The result was a very unbalanced picture in terms of explored areas and investigated periods. The Early and Middle Stone Age in the Rift Valley and Somali plateau, and the Pre-Aksumite and Aksumite periods (c. 1000 BC-AD 1000) on the northern Ethiopian and Eritrean highlands were more systematically investigated. The late prehistory (c. 10,000-1000 BC), and the later periods (ca. AD1000-1600) on the plateau have been almost completely neglected by scholars, except for rock-art, megaliths, and rock-hewn churches. Islamic archaeology has been practically ignored.

2. The Archaeology of the Horn of Africa: A Theoretical Approach

In my opinion, the aim of archaeology in the Horn of Africa is to reconstruct on the material evidence the historical processes, which caused the origins and development of the single populations and their interaction, from prehistory to the present at a local and regional scale, for a more careful explanation of the present and an interpretation of possible future trends.[17]

Actually, archaeology has a crucial role in reconstructing the cultural developments in the region from prehistory to the early 19th century. The textual evidence – including inscriptions, oral traditions, royal chronicles, hagiographical texts, and external sources – provides the skeleton of the history of the region with a partial and strongly ideologically oriented view of the real conditions of the ancient populations. In turn, linguistics provide a sketchy picture of the dynamics of peopling in ancient times, and needs the archaeological evidence to support its historical inferences.

The reconstruction of historical processes in the region requires a long-term perspective, over centuries or millennia, abandoning the traditional distinction between prehistory and history. Therefore, archaeology must be integrated with history, anthropology, and historical linguistics, as well as the environmental sciences in a wide-ranging diachronic analysis of these processes.

Environmental archaeology is a particularly promising area of research for analysis of the historical processes in the Horn of Africa. This approach, dealing with changes in the Man-Environment interaction through time, can contribute to a more detailed explanation of recurrent phenomena, such as draughts and famines. Environmental archaeology can also provide a more complete record of catastrophic events (e.g.,

---

14 Negesh 1997a, 1997b; Almeseged 2000; Hagos 2000, 2001; Tesfay 2000
15 Libsekal 1995.
16 See Fattovich 2001.
17 See Fattovich 1990a, 1997a; Hayden 1993.

volcanic eruptions and earthquakes), which occurred in the past, for a better understanding of their possible periodicity. In such a way, archaeology may contribute not
only to outlining historical dynamics, but also to developing regional planning programs.[18]

In this perspective, the main topics of archaeological research in the Horn of Africa are:

1. The peopling of the Horn in the early to middle Holocene (c. 10,000-4000 BC) to
   make evident the ethnic and cultural background to the later societies of the region.
2. Origins of food production and its consequences on the dynamics of peopling in
   the region.
3. The emergence of social complexity in the northern Horn in the middle to late
   Holocene (c. 3000-500 BC).
4. The origins and development of the Ethio-Semitic Christian state and the diffusion
   of Christianity in the Horn.
5. The spread of Islamic communities and the rise of Islamic states.
6. The dynamics of peopling and socio-economic developments in southern and
   western Ethiopia and in Somalia.

Early prehistoric archaeology and human paleontology, dealing with the human bio-
logical and cultural evolution in the region is another area in the archaeological research in the Horn of Africa. However, they are more directly related to the study of
general prehistory and human evolution rather than to the reconstruction of the history of the populations of the Horn of Africa.

3.   State of Art

A.   The peopling of the Horn in the early to middle Holocene (c. 10,000-4000 BC)

Later Stone Age microlithic industries dating to the Early-Middle Holocene (ca.
10,000-4000 B.C.) were recorded in Ethiopia, Eritrea and Somalia. They suggest that at
this time hunting-gathering populations with different lithic traditions occupied the
region.[19]

These industries include the Eibian and Doian industries in southern Somalia, the
Wilton industries on the highlands and along the coast in Ethiopia, Eritrea, and northern Somalia, the industry of Logghia in Afar, and an industry similar to the "Capsian
of Kenya" in the Rift Valley. The latter one most likely emerged from a industrial com-

---

18 See e.g., Dramis - Fattovich 1994; Bard - Coltorti - DiBlasi et al. 2000.
19 Clark 1954; Faure et al. 1976; Brandt 1986.

plex with backed blades, which was identified in the southern Afar and dated to ca. 9000-2000 BC.[20]

The industry of Logghia (7th-6th millennia BC) might be intrusive in the Afar region, as it shows some similarities to epipaleolithic industries of the 12th millennium BC in the Nile Valley and northern Africa.[21]

Most likely, networks of exchanges between the highlands and the coastal regions emerged in the early Holocene, when the coastal regions were more intensely occupied.[22] The earliest evidence of these contacts was recorded at Lake Besaka in the middle Awash valley, about 500 km from the sea. This evidence consists of marine shells (*Oliva* cf. *bulbosa*, *Engina mendicaria*) widely spread in the Red Sea, Persian Gulf and along the East African coast. They were found associated with some burials, tentatively dated to the 5th-4th millennia BC.[23]

B   *Origins of food production and its consequences on the dynamics of peopling in the region*

Food production appeared in the Horn of Africa in the Middle Holocene (c. 4000-1000 BC).[24] Domestic cattle and possibly wheat and barley were introduced into the highlands from the western lowlands between ca. 3500 and 1500 BC.[25] Most likely some populations in eastern Ethiopia were already pre-adapted to food production in the Late Pleistocene, but no evidence of an independent domestication of plants was found so far in the Horn.[26] Ensete (false banana) may have been domesticated in southern Ethiopia at an early date, and may have been cultivated on the northern highlands before the introduction of cereals.[27]

Two major centers of peopling emerged as a consequence of the new adaptative strategy of food producion along the western Eritrean-Sudanese lowlands and in eastern Ethiopia. Pastoral and agro-pastoral people with an indigenous cultural tradition, partly related to those of the middle Nile Valley, occupied the Eritrean-Sudanese lowlands.[28] Pastoral populations with Afro-Arabian traditions occupied the eastern Ethiopian plateau, as it is suggested by the Ethiopian-Arabian rock drawings. Begin-

20 See Graziosi 1940; Clark 1954; Hivernel-Guerre 1972; Clark - Williams 1978; Brandt 1980, 1986, 1988; Coltorti - Mussi 1987.
21 Faure et al. 1976; see also Fattovich 1988.
22 See Blanc 1955; Franchini 1953; Anfray 1968; Roubet 1970; Faure, Gasse, Roubet - Taieb 1971.
23 See Clark - Williams 1978; Brandt 1980.
24 See Phillipson 1993; Barnett 1999.
25 Clark 1988; Fattovich 1988.
26 Clark - Prince 1978.
27 Brandt 1984; Smeds 1955, n.d.
28 Fattovich 1990b.

ning in the late 3rd millennium BC these people spread to southern Ethiopia, northern Somalia, and Eritrea.[29]

The archaeological evidence, though scarce, suggests that food production appeared in the northern Horn (Eritrea, Tigray and western Eritrean-sudanese lowlands) in the Middle Holocene (c. 4000-2000 BC). Domestic cattle and possibly wheat and barley were introduced onto the plateau from the western lowlands between c. 3500 and 1500 BC.[30]

The earliest evidence of food-production has been traced in the lowlands, along the middle Atbara valley (*Butana Group*, c. 3800-2700 BC). The economy relied on hunting and fishing with possible cultivation of cereals, and, since the late 4th millennium BC, livestock breeding.[31]

Beginning in the mid-3rd millennium BC, herders spread over the western lowlands, most likely as far as the Red Sea coast and southern Red Sea hills (*Gash Group*, c. 2700-1500/1400 BC). They practiced the cultivation of barley, along with hunting and fishing, and were included in an interchange circuit from Egypt to the Horn of Africa and Southern Arabia.[32]

In the mid-2nd millennium BC people, culturally related to those of Nubia and possibly Eastern Desert, mixed with the local Gash Group people and occupied the lowlands from the Atbara to the Barka valley (*Jebel Mokram Group*, c. 1400-800 BC). They were an agro-pastoral population, cultivating sorghum and breeding cattle, with marginal contacts with the Middle Nile Valley.[33]

Rock-art suggests that pastoral people occupied the eastern plateau in Eritrea in the 2nd millennium BC.[34] Longhorn cattle herders with an Afro-Arabian cultural tradition, coming from eastern Ethiopia, were moving on the plateau as far as the Rore (*Ethiopian-Arabian Style*).[35] Longhorn and shorthorn cattle herders with a possible Saharan origin were moving in the upper Mareb valley and in the Akkele Guzay (*Naturalistic Style, Iberic Style*).[36]

A sedentary culture was located on the Hamasien plateau (Eritrea) in the late 2nd to early 1st millennia BC (*Ona Group A*, with red ware).[37] The sites include cemeteries and settlements, which are sometimes very large in size. The ceramics of this culture include bowls and necked jars decorated with geometric motifs similar to those of Kerma and Sihi along the rim and/or the shoulder, as well as black-topped vessels.

29 Cervicek 1971, 1979.
30 See Clark 1988; Fattovich 1988; Phillipson 1993; Barnett 1999.
31 Fattovich, Marks - Ali 1984; Marks, Ali - Fattovich 1986; Marks - Sadr 1988; Sadr 1991; see also Arkel 1954.
32 Fattovich, Sadr & Vitagliano 1988-89; Fattovich 1991a, b, 1993b; Sadr 1991; see also Arckel 1954.
33 Fattovich 1991b; Fattovich, Sadr - Vitagliano 1988-89; Sadr 1991.
34 See Graziosi 1964a, b; Joussaume 1981; Calegari 1999.
35 See Cervicek 1971, 1978-79.
36 See Graziosi 1964a, b; Clark 1976a, b.
37 Tringali 1978-79, 1981; Munro-Hay & Tringali 1993; Schmidt & Curtis 2001.

The occurrence of large residential settlements points to plant cultivation. Some possible stone bull-heads might suggest a ceremonial role of cattle.

At the same time a sedentary population was located near the Gulf of Zula.[38] They were part of a coastal cultural complex, which included the Arabian coast from the southern Saudi Tihama to Aden.[39] The occurrence of ceramics similar to those from the Tihama in the deepest levels at Matara in Akkele Guzai might suggest that this population also occupied the plateau.[40]

Scarce archaeological evidence suggests that hunter-gatherers occupied Tigray up to the Middle Holocene.[41] Pottery, pointing to a more sedentary life-style, appeared in the 4th-2nd millennia BC, but no evidence of food production is associated with it.[42]

At present, it seems that people with ceramics in a different style occupied the region of Aksum, the massif of Temben to the east of Aksum, and the edge of the plateau near Mekele. Ceramics and lithic tools dated to the 3rd-2nd millennia BC have been recorded in a few rock-shelters near Aksum. They included thin coarse ware decorated with combed, impressed, incised and grooved patterns, undecorated thin fine ware, and microlithic tools, associated with coarser flint tools. These materials may reflect a local tradition. The lithic tools, in particular, suggests a cultural continuity in the region since the early Holocene.[43] The evidence from Temben has not yet been exhaustively published and the correct date of the finds is uncertain.[44] The ceramics can be ascribed to two groups, apparently not related to those from the Aksum area. One of these groups might show some similarities to the pottery of the Gash Group of the western lowlands.[45] Finally, the ceramics from Quiha, near Mekele, tentatively dated to 3rd-2nd millennia BC, include vessels which show some stylistic affinities with those of the Gash Group in the western lowlands.[46]

The earliest direct evidence of domestic cattle in eastern Horn was found at Lake Besaka and dates to the mid-2nd millennium BC.[47] Rock-art suggests that pastoral people with cattle and fat-tail sheep occupied this region, as far as northern Somalia, and were moving along the Rift Valley, as far as the Sidamo region, since the late 3rd-mid-2nd millennia BC (*Ethiopian-Arabian Style*).[48] Sedentary people were probably settled

38 Paribeni 1908.
39 Zarins 1990; Fattovich 1996c.
40 See Anfray 1966.
41 Fattovich 1988a; see also Bard, Corltorti, Di Blasi, Dramis - Fattovich 2000.
42 Phillipson 1977, 1990; Fattovich 1985, 1988a.
43 Phillipson 1977, 2000: 22-26; Fattovich - Beyene - D'Andrea et al. 2000; see also Fattovich 1988a; Finneran 2001.
44 See Negash 1997.
45 Negash *pers. com.* (June 2000).
46 Clark 1954: 324; Barnett 1999: 127-146.
47 Brandt 1980.
48 Clark 1954; Anfray 1967a; Cervicek 1971; Joussaume 1981; Brandt - Carder 1987; Brandt - Brooke 1984.

on the plateau near Harrar in the mid-2nd millennium BC, as we can infer from some cemeteries with dolmes and the remains of villages with cyclopic walls.[49]

In the Afar region some evidence of food producing people was recorded at Asa Koma (Djibuti).[50] The ceramics from this site, dating to the 2nd millennium BC, can be related to those of the Tihama and exhibit some similarities to the pottery of the Gash Group in the Eritrean-Sudanese lowlands.

C.   The emergence of social complexity

The emergence of complex societies and states in northern Ethiopia and Eritrea depended on the progressive inclusion of the region into the exchange circuit between the Mediterranean Sea and the Indian Ocean from the 5th-4th millennia BC to the 1st millennium AD.[51]

This inclusion was due to the occurrence of prized natural resources (such as gold, aromatic gums, animal skins, etc.) in the region, and her strategic location at the interface of two circuits: a) the *Nile Valley and Red Sea circuit*, connecting Egypt with the southern Red Sea, and b) the *Afro-Arabian circuit*, connecting the Horn of Africa with southern Arabia and India.[52]

In mid-3rd to mid-2nd millennia BC a complex society with a clearly cut settlement hierarchy arose in the Gash Delta (*Gash Group*). At this time the Gash Delta was an important node in a regional circuit stretching from the middle Nile Valley to the Red Sea coast, southern Atbai Mountains, southern Arabia and probably Afar.[53]

So far, five main phases of development of the Gash Group have been recognized: Proto-Gash Group Phase (c. 3000-2700 BC); Early Gash Group Phase (c. 2700-2300 BC); Middle Gash Group Phase (c. 2300-1900 BC); Classic Gash Group Phase (c. 1900-1700 BC); Late Gash Group Phase (c. 1700-1500/1400 BC).[54]

The social complexity of the Gash Group can be inferred from the settlement pattern, administrative devices, funeral evidence, architecture, and increasing standardization in the manufacture of pottery.

On the site size, the Gash Group settlement pattern suggests the occurrence of local service centers and perhaps a regional center, and may reflect a centralized economy of chiefdom type. The administrative devices include clay stamp seals, tokens, and clay sealings.[55]

The funeral evidence suggests that the Gash Group people was divided into three main segments, represented by three different types of burials associated with three

49 Azais - Chambard 1931; Joussuame 1980.
50 Gutherz - Joussaume - Amblard et al. 1996.
51 See Fattovich 1996, 1997b, 1997c, 1999.
52 Fattovich 1996b, 1997c, 1997d; Manzo 1999.
53 Fattovich, Sadr - Vitagliano 1988-89.
54 Fattovich 1991.
55 Fattovich 1991.

types of stelae. The great amount of pottery and faunal remains, and the occurrence of fire places near the monoliths points to a elaborated ritual with funeral banquets, and difference in rank and status of the individuals was probably emphasized with the number of animals sacrificed for the banquet. Moreover, the stelae were erected to indicate the funeral meaning of the area, not single tombs.

The remains of two large rectangular mud-brick buildings dating to the *Late Gash Group* were discovered at the major site of Mahal Teglinos. The high frequency of fragments of storage jars in the rooms suggests that they were used as a magazine. This evidence supports a complex social organization in the Gash Delta in Late Gash Group times. In turn, the ceramics at Mahal Teglinos shows a progressive standardization in the manufacture of pottery, with a progressive increase in frequency of coarse ware and closed pots, including storage jars, and a decrease in decoration variability through the time.[56] The progressive standardization and increase in pottery manufacture, as well as the increase in closed forms (storage jars) also suggest the emergence of a society at a chiefdom scale in Classic and Late Gash Group.

In the mid-2nd millennium BC the Eritrean-Sudanese lowlands were isolated from the exchange network with Nubia and Egypt, but small-scale complex societies survived in the region (*Jebel Mokram Group*).[57]

A network of exchanges based on the circulation of obsidian emerged between the northern Horn of Africa (Eritrea, Tigray, and Eritrean-Sudanese border lowlands) and southern Arabia in the 5th millennium BC.[58] These contacts consolidated in the 3rd-2nd millennia BC, as we can infer from a comparison between the ceramics from sites in Eastern Sudan, Ethiopia, Djibouti and Yemen dating to ca. 2500-1500 BC. In particular, the ceramics of the "Gash Group" (ca. 2700-1500/1400 BC) from Mahal Teglinos near Kassala, suggest that the western Eritrean-Sudanese lowlands were included into a network of contacts with the southern regions of the Horn of Africa and southern Arabia, as well as with Eastern Sudan, Nubia and Egypt.[59]

Beginning in the late 3rd to mid-2nd millennia BC the people living along the coast of the southern Red Sea and the Gulf of Aden had a relevant role in the development of the Afro-Arabian circuit.[60]

The archaeological evidence from the sites at Sihi to the south of Jizan in the Saudi Tihama and Adulis near the Gulf of Zula in the Eritrean Sahel suggests that these sites were part of a coastal cultural complex in the late 3rd to mid-2nd millennium BC.[61] This complex was characterised by bowls and pots with a rounded base and geometrical decorations. Some similarities between the ceramics from Sihi and Adulis, and the Nubian ones of C-Group and Kerma (late 3rd to mid-2nd millennia BC), although not

56 See Fattovich - Vitagliano 1987.
57 Fattovich - Sadr - Vitagliano 1988-1989; Sadr 1991.
58 Zarins 1989, 1990, 1996.
59 Fattovich 1991, 1997b.
60 See Fattovich 1997a, 1997b; Phillips 1998; Manzo 1999; Buffa - Vogt 2001.
61 See Zarins - Al-Jawarad Murad - Al-Yish 1981; Zarins - Zaharani 1985; Zarins - Al-Badr 1986; Paribeni 1908: 446-451.

yet conclusive, may point to contacts with the Nile Valley, when the state of Kerma (ca. 2500-1500 BC) controlled the trade between Egypt and the regions of the Horn of Africa, and the Upper Nile. These contacts are also supported by the occurrence of circular structures with vertical slabs at the edge, similar to Kerma graves, at Aqiq, on the coast to the south of the Barka delta.[62]

Beginning in the mid-2nd millennium BC, a new cultural complex appeared along the southwestern coast of Arabia (*Sabir Culture*, ca. 2000-600 BC).[63] The ceramics of the Sabir Culture were characterized by big jars and bowls with vertical or horizontal handles, pots in the shape of a tulip, and bowls with a ring base, and represent an indigenous tradition. Despite the scarce evidence, contacts and possibly exchanges between the Arabian and African regions of the southern Red Sea continued in the 2nd millennium BC. This is suggested by some similarities in the ceramics of the Terminal Gash Group (ca. 1500-1400 BC) at Mahal Teglinos and at Wadi Urq' in the Yemeni Tihamah.[64] A few potsherds with geometric motifs comparable to specimens of the Pan-Grave Culture (ca. 1700-1500 BC) and/or Jebel Mokram Group (ca. 1400-1000 BC) of the Eastern Desert have been also found at Sabir.[65]

A complex society arose on the Hamasien plateau, near Asmara, in the late 2nd to early 1st millennia BC (*Ona Group A*), as at least one settlement at Sembel-Cuscet, close to the upper Anseba valley, occupied an area of about 25 ha, with evidence of a massive building and possible clay stamp seals.[66] The people of the *Ona Culture* in central Eritrea were also part of a network of contacts with the coastal regions of the southern Red Sea. The range of contacts of the Ona Culture is still uncertain. Some similarities in the ceramics point to contacts with the western lowlands in the mid-2nd millennium BC. Some chipped stone bull-heads and some types of pottery suggest contacts with the Arabian Peninsula, as well. In particular, a clay artifact similar to the stone "bull-heads" of the Ona Culture was collected at Sabir.[67]

In the 1st millennium BC the interaction between the populations of the opposite shores of the southern Red Sea become more intense and culminated with the rise of a pre-Aksumite state (*Kingdom of Daamat*, ca. 700/600-400 BC) on the highlands, in Eritrea and central Tigray. The location of the pre-Aksumite sites points to an expansion of the pre-Aksumite state along a restricted area from Qohaito in Eritrea to the Takaze River in Tigray. This expansion was marked by the foundation of ceremonial centers, such as Kaskase, Addi Gerameten and Fikiya in Eritrea, and Yeha in Tigray. A town was located at Matara.[68]

At present two phases in the development of pre-Aksumite state can be distinguished: a) an initial penetration of South Arabs, possibly coming from different regions

---

62 See Cremaschi - D'Alessandro - Fattovich et al. 1986; Fattovich 1995.
63 See Phillips 1998; Buffa - Vogt 2001.
64 Fattovich - Sadr - Vitagliano 1988-89; Fattovich 1996a.
65 Buffa - Vogt 2001.
66 See Tringali 1965, 1967, 1969, 1978-79, 1981, 1986; Fattovich 1988; Schmidt - Curtis 2001.
67 See Buffa - Vogt 2001.
68 See de Contenson 1981; Anfray 1990: 17-61; Fattovich 1990; Robin - de Maigret 1998.

of southern Arabia, into the Eritrean and Tigrean highlands; b) the consolidation of a proper state as a consequence of the inclusion of the highlands into the area of direct political and economical influence of the Sabeans.

Rock inscriptions in the Akkele Guzay (central Eritrea) suggest that South Arabs were settled on the plateau in the early 1st millennium BC.[69] The use of the Sabean monumental script and language in the royal inscriptions, and the construction of large ceremonial centers at sites such as Kaskase in Akkele Guzay and Yeha in Tigray characterized the second phase of the Pre-Aksumite Period.

The Ethio-Sabean state declined and/or collapsed in the late 4th-3rd centuries BC. A pre-Aksumite urban society apparently survived in the Akkele Guzai up to the early 1st millennium AD, at least at Matara. In Tigrai, an Ethio-Sabean complex society perhaps survived at Yeha, but the ceramics suggest that a local cultural tradition emerged in the region.

D.   *The origins and development of the Kingdom of Aksum and the diffusion of Christianity in the Horn*

In the late 1st millennium BC a new state (*Kingdom of Aksum*, c. 150 BC-AD 700) arose in Tigrai, as a consequence of the inclusion of the region into the Roman exchange circuit of the Erythrean Sea.[70] In the 1st millennium AD the kingdom was the most important African intermediary between the Roman/Byzantine Empire and India, East Africa and Central Africa.

The kingdom originated from a local proto-Aksumite polity that emerged at Aksum in the 4th-2nd centuries BC.[71] This polity distinguished itself from the former Ethio-Sabean one, focusing ideologically on platforms with stelae and pit-graves for the funeral cult of the elite rather than on monumental cult temples of the gods. The remains of a monumental building, constructed in a technique reminiscent of Ethio-Sabean architecture, at the site of Ona Nagast (Bieta Giyorgis) may suggest that some symbols of the earlier state were maintained in proto-Aksumite time.

Possible cultural links with late prehistoric cultures in the Eritrean-Sudanese lowlands are suggested by the style and symbolism of the funeral stelae, which are comparable to those of the Gash Group in the lowlands. In both contexts votive offerings were placed close to the stelae. Some similarities can also be demonstrated in the ceramics.[72]

In the 1st century BC-early 3rd century AD Aksum was a regional petty kingdom with a "tribal" identity. Other petty kingdoms were located at Henzat to the south of Adwa, Anza in the Agamè, and Matara in the Akkele Guzai. In the 3rd-early 4th centu-

---

69 Ricci 1994.
70 Fattovich 1988, 1999; Munro-Hay 1993.
71 Fattovich - Bard 2001.
72 Fattovich - Bard 2001; Bard - Fattovich - Manzo et al. 2002.

ries AD, the Aksumites dominated the highlands in northern Ethiopia and Eritrea. They also controlled the western Eritrean-Sudanese lowlands, the regions to the west of the Tekeze river, southwestern Arabia, and made raids in the Nile Valley as far as Meroe. Coinage was minted beginning in the late 3rd century AD. Christianity was introduced into the kingdom in the 4th century, and consolidated as a State religion in the 5th century AD. In the 6th-7th centuries the Christian State controlled the trade with the African hinterland as far as northern Somalia, western Ethiopia, and eastern Sudan. The decline of Aksum begun in the late 7th century, when the kingdom was isolated from the Red Sea trade because of the spread of Islam. The decline may have accelerated in the 8th-9th centuries by environmental degradation and epidemics. Arab sources record that in the late 9th century the Christian kingdom was still powerful, but the capital was no longer located at Aksum.

So far, no real effort has been made to investigate the expansion of the Christian state in the Middle Ages, and scholarly interest focused mainly on the rock-hewn churches.[73] These monuments suggest a cultural continuity between the Aksumite and post-Aksumite periods, up to the 13th century AD. Their distribution provide evidence about the progressive expansion of Christianity southwards in the first half of the 2nd millennium AD. The later developments of the Ethiopian state, during the 14th-17th centuries, are still unexplored archaeologically, and the investigation was limited to the description of some palaces and churches of the Gondarine period.[74]

E.   The spread of Islamic communities and the rise of Islamic states

Archaeological investigation on the early Islamic period is practically nonexistent. The scarce, available evidence suggests that Islamic communities were settled along the Red Sea coast, the western Ethio-Sudanese lowlands, and the southeastern plateau between the 8th and 12th centuries AD.[75]

At present, the earliest evidence of an Islamic sultanate dating to the late 1st millennium AD has been recorded at Dahlac Kebir and possibly at Er-Rih, near Aqiq.[76] Muslim communities were also settled on the highlands in Tigray in the early 10 century AD.[77] In turn the occurrence of Islamic coins in tumuli dating to the 8th century AD in the region of Harrar suggests that Muslims traders were already penetrating into the Ethiopian highlands at this time.

The occurence of monumental tombs, identifiable with early *qubbas*, dating to the early 2nd millennium AD along the Barka and Anseba valleys and the Red Sea coast

---

73 Monti della Corte 1938; Buxton 1946, 1947, 1971; Bianchi Barriviera 1962, 1963; Lepage 1975; Anfray 1990.
74 See e.g., Monti Della Corte 1938; Anfray 1988; Di Salvo 1999.
75 Cuoq 1981.
76 Crowfoot 1911; Puglisi 1969; Oman 1976, 1987.
77 Schneider 1967.

suggests that Islamic communities penetrated into the northern highlands from the northwest.[78]

Remains of ancient Islamic settlements have been also recorded along the Rift Valley, and confirm that this region was densely populated by Muslims in the Middle Age.[79]

F.   Socio-economic developments in southern and western Ethiopia and in Somalia

The peopling in the southern and western plateau before the mid-2nd millennium AD are still uncertain.

Up to now, only the funeral megalithic stelae with carved decorations in central and southern Ethiopia have been investigated in a more systematic way. This research has shown that these stelae go back to the late 1st-early 2nd millennia AD. In the Shoa these megaliths include stelae decorated with swords and other symbols, stelae decorated with masked anthropomorphic figures; anthropomorphic stelae; stelae representing a schematic human figures with all the elements of clothes; and hemispheric or conical stones. In Sidamo phallic or anthropomorfic monoliths were recorded. The origins of these monuments are uncertain. Most likely, they represent local traditions which will be better understood when the associated settlements will be investigated in a greater detail.[80]

The origins of the Nilo-Saharan peoples living along the Sudanese border are unknown. The archaeological research conducted along the western Eritrean-Sudanese lowlands suggests that the Kunama in western Eritrea may belong to a very ancient indigenous population that occupied the area since the 5th millennium BC.[81] The origins of the Somali people are completely unknown from the archaeological point of view.[82]

The available evidence suggests that nomadic or seminomadic people occupied northern Somalia, at least since the 1st millennium BC. They are represented by thousands of stone cairns visible in this region.[83] These cairns included stone circles, conical cairns, cubic cairns, and cairns in the shape of a truncated pyramid. Some of the people, living along the coast, were also also included into a network of exchanges with Roman traders.[84]

78 Crowfoot 1911; Fattovich 1990b.
79 Curle 1937; Wilding 1980.
80 Neuville 1928; Azais - Chambard 1931; Joussaume 1980, 1995; Anfray 1982.
81 Fattovich 1994.
82 See Jönsson 1983.
83 Rèvoil 1982; Cerulli 1931.
84 Chittick 1975; Labrousse 1978; Desanges 1994; Desanges, Stern - Ballet 1993.

Finally, archaeological investigations along the coast from Berbera to Benadir made evident that the people living in these regions were included into the Muslim interchange circuit of the northern Indian ocean since the 9th-10th centuries AD.[85]

Conclusion

Archaeology can greatly contribute – and already contributed – to a reconstruction of the history of the Horn of Africa in the last seven millennia. Nevertheless, much work must be still conducted before an exhaustive picture of the past of the region will emerge from the archaeological record.

In particular, a priority for the archaeological research in the Horn of Africa is to intensify the investigation of unexplored regions with systematic surveys and test excavations. In fact, present programs of economic development are menacing the heritage in many regions of the Horn, as most of this heritage is not monumental and may easily excape to an unaccurate assessment.

Finally, another priority is to sustain the training of local professionals for the research, study, and management of the archaeological heritage.

Bibliography

Alemseged, Z.
2000   Les Hominidés plio-pléistocenes de la basse vallée de l'Omo (Éthiopie) et leurs environnements. *Annales d'Ethiopie 16:* 1-9.

Almagià, R.
1935   Geografia antropica ed economica. *L'Africa Orientale,* Roma: 195-283.

Anfray, F.
1963   Histoire de l'archéologie Ethiopienne. *Tarik 1:* 17-21.
1967   Les sculptures rupestres de Chabbè dans le Sidamo. *Annales d'Ethiopie 7:* 19-24.
1968   Aspects de l'archéologie Ethiopienne. *Journal of African History 9:* 345-366.
1982   Les steles du sud: Shoa et Sidamo. *Annales d'Ethiopie 12:* 43-221.
1988   Les Monuments Gondariens des XVIIe et XVIIIe Siécles. Un Vue d'ensemble. In: *T. Beyene (ed.), Proceedings of the Eighth International Conference of Ethiopian Studies - Addis Ababa 1984.* Addis Ababa: 9-45.

---

85 Chittick 1969; Jama 1996.

1990   *Les anciens Ethiopiens*. Paris.

Anonymous
1988   *National Atlas of Ethiopia*. Ethiopian Mapping Authority. Addis Ababa.

Arkell, A. J.
1954   Four Occupation Sites at Agordat. *Kush 2:* 33-62.

Azais, F. and R. Chambard
1931   *Cinq années de recherches archéologiques en Ethiopie*. Paris.

Bard, K. A., Coltorti, M., di Blasi, M. C. et al.
2000   The Environmental History of Tigray (Northern Ethiopia) during the Holoce-
        ne: a Preliminary Outline. *The African Archaeological Review 17 (2):* 65-86.

Bard, K. A., Fattovich, R., Manzo, A. et al.
2002   Aksum Origins, Kassala and Upper Nubia: New Evidence from Bieta Giyorgis,
        Aksum. *Archéologie du Nil Moyen 9:* 31-40.

Barnett, T.
1999   *The Emergence of Food Production in Ethiopia*. Oxford.

Begashaw, K.
1994   The Evolution of Complex Societies in North Western Ethiopia along the
        Ethio-sudanese Border. In: *B. Zewde, R. Pankhurst and T, Beyene (eds.), Pro-
        ceedings of the Eleventh International Conference of Ethiopian Studies - Addis
        Ababa 1991, I*. Addis Ababa: 47-62.

Bianchi Barriviera, G.
1962   Le chiese in roccia di Lalibela ed altri luoghi del Lasta. *Rassegna di Studi Etio-
        pici 18:* 5-77.
1963   Le chiese in roccia di Lalibela ed altri luoghi del Lasta. *Rassegna di Studi Etio-
        pici 19:* 5-118.

Blanc, A. C.
1955   L'industrie sur obsidienne des iles Dahlac (Mer Rouge). *Actes du IIe Congrés
        Panafricain de Préhistorie - Algier 1952*. Paris: 355-357.

Boukhaze-Khan, D. and Poisblaud, B.
2000   Art rupestre et Nèolithique de l'Éthiopie. Découvertes récentes. *Ananles
        d'Ethiopie 16:* 39-53.

Bouville C., Cross, J.-P. and Joussaume, R.
2000   Étude anthropologique du site à stèles du Tuto Fela en pays Gedeo (Éthiopie). *Annales d'Ethiopie 16:* 15-24.

Brandt, S. A.
1980   Archaeological Investigations at Lake Besaka, Ethiopia. In: *R. E. Leakey and B. A. Ogot (eds.), Proceedings of the 8th Panafrican congress of Prehistory and Quaternary Studies - Nairobi 1977.* Nairobi: 239-243.
1984   New Perspectives on the Origins of Food Production in Ethiopia. In: *J. D. Clark and S. A. Brandt (eds.), From Hunters to Farmers.* Berkeley: 173-190.
1986   The Upper Pleistocene and early Holocene prehistory of the Horn of Africa. *The African Archaeological Review 4:* 41-82.
1988   Early Holocene mortuary practices and hunter-gatherer adaptations in southern Somalia. *World Archaeology 20 (1):* 40-56.

Brandt, S. A. and Brooke, G. A.
1984   Archaeological and Palaeoenvironmental Research in Northern Somalia. *Current Anthropology 25 (1):* 119-121.

Brandt, S. A. and Carder, N.
1987   Pastoral rock art in the Horn of Africa: making sense of udder cahos. *World Archaeology 19 (2):* 194-213.

Brandt, S. A. and Fattovich, R.
1990   Late Quaternary Archaeological Research in the Horn of Africa. In: *P. Robertshaw (ed.), A History of African Archaeology.* London: 95-108.

Buffa, V. and Vogt, B.
2001   Sabir – Cultural Identity between Saba and Africa. In: *R. Eichmann and H. Parzinger (eds.), Migration und Kulturtransfer. Der Wandel vorderer- und zentralasiatischer Kulturen im Umbruch vom 2. zum 1. vorchristlichen Jahrtausend.* Bonn: 437-450.

Buxton, D.
1946   Ethiopian Rock-hewn Churches. *Antiquity 20:* 60-69.
1947   The Christian antiquities of Northern Ethiopia. *Archaeologia 92:* 1-42.
1971   The Rock-hewn churches of Tigre Province (Ethiopia). *Archaeologia 102:* 33-100.

Calegari, G.
1999   *L'arte rupestre dell'Eritrea.* Repertorio ragionato ed esegesi iconografica. Milano.

Cerulli, E.
1931   Tradizioni storiche e monumenti della Migiurtinia. *Africa Italiana 4:* 153-169.

Cervicek, P.
1971   Rock paintings of Laga Oda (Ethiopia). *Paideuma 17:* 126-136.
1979   Some African Affinities of Arabian Rock Art. *Rassegna di Studi Etiopici 27:* 5-12.

Chittick, N. H.
1969   An Archaeological Reconnaissance of the Southern Somali Coast. *Azania 4:* 115-130.
1976   An Archaeological Reconnaissance in the Horn: the British-Somali Expedition 1975. *Azania 11:* 117-134.

Clark, J. D.
1954   *Prehistoric Cultures of the Horn of Africa.* Cambridge.
1976a   The Domestication Process in sub-Saharan Africa with special reference to Ethiopia. In: *E. Higgs (ed.), Origine de l'élevage et de la domestication.* IXe Congrés UISPP, colloque XX, prétirage. Nice: 56-115.
1976b   Prehistoric Populations and Pressures Favoring Plant domestication in Africa. In: *J. R. Harlan, J. M. J. De Wet and A. Stemler (eds.), Origins of African Plant Domestication.* The Hague: 67-105.
1988   A Review of the Archaeological Evidence for the Origins of Food Production in Ethiopia. In: *T. Beyene (ed.), Proceedings of the Eighth International conference of Ethiopian Studies – Addis Ababa 1984.* Addis Ababa: 55-70.

Clark, J. D. and Prince, G. R.
1978   Use-wear on Later Stone Age Microliths from Laga Oda, Haraghè, Ethiopia, and Possible Functional Interpretations. *Azania 13:* 101-110.

Clark, J. D. and Williams, W. A.
1978   Recent Archaeological Research in Southeastern Ethiopia (1974-1975). *Annales d'Ethiopie 11:* 19-42.

Coltorti, M. and Mussi, M.
1987   Late Stone Age hunter-gatherers of the Juba Valley. *Nyame Akuma 28:* 32-33.

Conti Rossini, C.
1928   *Storia d'Etiopia.* Bergamo.
1937   *Etiopia e genti d'Etiopia.* Firenze.

Cremaschi, M., D'Alessandro, A., Fattovich, R. et al.
1986   Gash Delta Archaeological Project: 1985 Field Season. *Nyame Akuma 27:* 45-48.

Crowfoot, J. W.
1911   Some Red Sea Ports in the Anglo-Egyptian Sudan. *The Geographical Journal*
        37: 523-550.

Cuoq, J.
1981   *L'Islam en Éthiopie des origines au XVIe siècle.* Paris.

Curle, A. T.
1937   The ruined towns of Somaliland. *Antiquity 11:* 315-327.

Curtis, M. C. and Libsekal, Y.
1999   Archaeological Survey in the Adi Qeyeh Area, Eritrea. *Nyame Akuma 51:* 25-
        35.

Dainelli, G.
1935   Le condizioni fisiche dell'Africa Orientale. *L'Africa Orientale.* Roma: 69-191.

de Contenson, H.
1961   Les prinipales étapes de l'Ethiopie antique. *Cahiers d'Etudes Africaines:* 12-
        13.à
1963   Les subdivisions de l'archéologie éthiopienne: état de la question. *Revue Ar-*
        chéologique: 189-191.
1981   Pre-Aksumite Culture. In: *G. Mokhtar (ed.), General History of Africa, II. An-*
        cient Civilizations of Africa. Berkeley: 341-361.

Desanges, J.
1994   La cote africaine du Bab el-Mandeb dans l'antiquité. *Hommages à Jean Leclant*
        3. Paris: 161-194.

Desanges, J., Stern, E. M. and Ballet, P.
1993   *Sur le routes antiques de l'Azanie et de l'Indie.* Paris.

Di Salvo, M.
1999   *Churches of Ethiopia.* Milano.

Dombrowski, J.
1970   Preliminary Report on Excavations in Lalibela and Natchabiet Caves. *Annales*
        d'Ethiopie 10: 21-29.

Dramis, F. and Fattovich, R.
1994   From Past to Present: Research Perspectives in Environmental Archaeology
        on the Ethiopian Plateau. In: *B. Zewde, R. Pankhurst and T. Beyene (eds.),*
        Proceedings of the Eleventh International Conference of Ethiopian Studies I.
        Addis Ababa: 9-14.

Fattovich, R.

1988   Remarks on the Late Prehistory and Early History of Northern Ethiopia. In: *T. Beyene (ed.), Proceedings of the Eighth International Conference of Ethiopian Studies – Addis Ababa 1984.* Addis Ababa: 85-104.

1990a   Processi storici e microevoluzione umana: riflessioni sulla possbile integrazione tra discipline storiche ed antropologiche. *Rivista di Antropologia 68:* 5-35.

1990b   The peopling of the northern Ethiopian-Sudanese borderland between 7000 and 1000 BP: a preliminary model. *Nubica 1/2:* 3-45.

1990c   Remarks on the Pre-Aksumite Period in Northern Ethiopia. *Journal of Ethiopian Studies 23:* 1-33.

1991   Ricerche archeologiche italiane nel delta del Gash (Kassala), 1980-1989: un bilancio preliminare. *Rassegna di Studi Etiopici 33:* 89-130.

1992   *Lineamenti di storia dell'archeologia dell'Etiopia e della Somalia.* Napoli.

1993   L'archeologia in Etiopia ed Eritrea: Aspetti, Problemi e Prospettive. *Africa 48 (3).* Roma: 464-469.

1994a   The Contribution of the Recent field Work at Kassala (Sudan) to Ethiopian Archaeology. In: *C. Lepage (ed.), Etudes éthiopiennes I.* Paris: 43-51.

1994b   Sulle origini dei Baria e dei Cunama. In: *Y. Beyene, R. Fattovich, P. Marassini, A. Triulzi (eds.), Etiopia e oltre. Studi in onore di Lanfranco Ricci:* 27-67.

1995   L'archeologia del Mar Rosso: problemi e prospettive. Note in margine alla recente pubblicazione di due siti costieri della Somalia settentrionale. *Annali dell'Isituto Universitario Orientale di Napoli 55 (2):* 158-176.

1996   The Afro-Arabian circuit: contacts between the Horn of Africa and Southern Arabia in the 3rd-2nd millennia BC. In: *L. Krzyzaniak, K. Kroeper and M. Kobusiewicz (eds.), Interregional Contacts in the Later Prehistory of Northeastern Africa.* Poznan: 395-402.

1997a   Archaeology and historical dynamics: The case of Bieta Giyorgis (Aksum), Ethiopia. *Annali dell'Istituto Universitario Orientale di Napoli 57:* 48-79.

1997b   The Near East and Eastern Africa: Their Interaction. In: *J. Vogel (ed.), Encyclopedia of Precolonial Africa.* Walnut Creek: 479-484.

1997c   Northeastern States. In: *J. O. Vogel (ed.), Encyclopedia of Precolonial Africa.* Walnut Creek: 484-489.

1997d   The Contacts between Southern Arabia and the Horn of Africa in Late Prehistoric and Early Historical times: A View from Africa. In: *A. Avanzini (ed.), Profumi d'Arabia.* Roma: 273-286.

1999   The development of urbanism in the northern Horn of Africa in ancient and medieval times. In: *P. Sinclair (ed.), The Development of Urbanism in Africa from a Global Perspective,* Uppsala (electronic publication: www. arkeologi. uu.se).

2001   Horn of Africa. In: *T. Murray (ed.), Encyclopedia of archaeology: history and discoveries I (A-D).* Oxford: 35-43.

Fattovich, R. and Bard, K. A.

2001   The Proto-Aksumite Period: An Overview. *Annales d'Ethiopie 17:* 3-24.

Fattovich, R., Bard, K. A., Petrassi, L. et al.
2000   *The Archaeological Area of Aksum: A Preliminary Assessment*. Napoli.

Fattovich, R., Marks, A. E. and Ali, A. M.
1984   The Archaeology of the Eastern Sahel, Sudan: Preliminary Results. *The African Archaeological Review 2*: 173-188.

Fattovich, R., Sadr, K. and Vitagliano, S.
1988-89 Society and Territory in the Gash Delta (Kassala, Eastern Sudan), 3000 B.C.-A.D. 300/400. *Origini 14*: 329-357.

Fattovich, R. and Vitagliano, S.
1987   Gash Delta Archaeological Project: 1987 Field Season. *Nyame Akuma 29*: 56-59.

Faure, H., Gasse, F., Roubet, C. et al.
1976   Les formations lacustres holocènes (argilles et diatomées) et l'industrie epipaléolithique de la region de Logghia (basin du Lac Abbè). In: *B. Abebe et al. (eds.), Proceedings of the 7ᵗʰ Pan-African Congress of Prehistory and Quaternary Studies – Addis Ababa 1971*. Addis Ababa: 391-403.

Franchini,V.
1953   Stazioni litiche in Eritrea. *Bollettino dell'Istituto di Studi Etiopici 1*. Asmara: 25-30.

Fleagle, J. G., Yirga, S., Brown, Th. M. et al.
1994   New Palaeontological Discoveries from Fejej, Southern Omo, Ethiopia. In: *B. Zewde, R. Pankhurst and T. Beyene (eds.), Proceedings of the eleventh International Conference of Ethiopian Studies - Addis Ababa 1991 I*. Addis Ababa: 15-22.

Gouin, P.
1979   *Earthquake History of Ethiopia and the Horn of Africa*. Ottawa.

Graziosi, P.
1940   *L'Età della Pietra in Somalia*. Firenze.
1964   New Discoveries of Rock Paintings in Ethiopia, I-II. *Antiquity 38*: 91-98, 187-190.

Gutherz, X.
2000   Sondages dans l'abri sous-roche de Moche Borago Gongolo dans le Wolayta (Éthiopie). *Annales d'Ethiopie 16*: 35-38.

Gutherz, X., Joussaume, R., Amblard, S. et al.
1996   Le site d'Asa Koma (République de Djibouti) et les premeirs producteurs dans la Corne de l'Afrique. *Journal des africanistes 66 (1-2):* 253-297.

Hagos, T.
2000   Preliminary notes on the Stelae of Efrata and Gidim of northern Shoa. *Annales d'Ethiopie 16:* 55-58.
2001   New Megalithic sites in the vicinity of Aksum, Ethiopia. *Annales d'Ethiopie 17:* 35-41.

Hayden, B.
1993   *Archaeology. The Science of Once and Future Things.* New York.

Hirsh, B. and Poissonnier, B.
2000   Recherches historiques et archéologiques à Meshalä Maryam (Mänz, Ethiopie): résultats préliminaires. *Annales d'Ethiopie 16:* 59-87.

Hivernelle-Guerre, F.
1972   Les industries du Late Stone Age dans la région de Melka-Kontouré. *Travaux de la R.C.P. 230 (CNRS) 3:* 27-37.

Jama, A. D.
1996   *The Origins and Development of Mogadishu AD 1000 to 1850.* Uppsala.

Jönsson, S.
1983   *Archaeological Research Co-Operation between Somalia and Sweden.* Stockholm.

Joussaume, R.
1980   *Le mégalithisme en Ethiopie.* Addis Ababa.
1981   L'art rupestre de l'Ethiopie. In: *C. Roubet, H.-J. Hugot and G. Souville (eds.), Préhistoire Africaine.* Paris: 159-175.
1988   *Mission Archélogique en Republique de Djibuti.* Paris.
1995   *Tiya – L'Éthiopie des mégalithes.* Chauvigny.

Labrousse, H.
1978   Enquestes et decouvertes d'Obok a Doumeira. *Annales d'Ethiopie 11:* 75-77.

Le Quellec and Abegaz, G.
2001   New sites of South Ethiopian rock engravings: Godan Kinjo, Ejersa Gara Gallo, Laga Harro, and remarks on the Šappe-galma school. *Annales d'Ethiopie 17:* 205-224.

Libsekal, Y.
1995 *Archaeological Prospect in the Region of Akkele-Guzay (Eritrea): a Preliminary Report.* Asmara.

Lepage, C.
1975 Le premier art chrétien d'Ethiopie. *Les Dossiers de l'Archéologie 8:* 34-57.

Littmann, E., Krencker, D. and von Lüpke, Th.
1913 *Deutsche Aksum Expedition I-IV.* Berlin.

Manzo, A.
1999 *Echanges et contacts le long du Nil et de la Mer Rouge dans l'époque protohistorique (IIIe et IIe millénaires avant J.-C.).* Oxford.

Marks, A. E. and Sadr, K.
1988 Holocene Enviroments and Occupations in the Southern Atbai, Sudan: a Preliminary Formulation. In: *J. Bower and D. Lubbel (eds.), Prehistoric Cultures and Enviroments in the Late Quaternary of Africa.* Oxford: 69-90.

Michels, J. W.
1979 Aksumite Archaeology: An Introductory Essay. In: *Y. M. Kobishchanov, Axum.* University Park: 1-34.
1994 Regional Political Organization in the Aksum-Yeha Area during the pre-Aksumite and Aksumite Eras. In: *C. Lepage (ed.), Etudes éthiopiennes I.* Paris: 61-80.

Monti Della Corte, A. A.
1938 *I Castelli di Gondar.* Roma.
1940 *Lalibela.* Roma.

Munro-Hay, S.
1993 State development and urbanism in northern Ethiopia. In: *Th. Shaw, P. Sinclair, B. Andah and A. Okpoko (eds.), The Archaeology of Africa: Food, Metals and Towns.* London: 609-621.

Munro-Hay, S. and Tringali, G.
1993 The Ona sites of Asmara and Hamasien. *Rassegna di Studi Etiopici 35:* 135-170.

Mussi, M.
1974-75 Etat des connaissances sur le Quaternaire de la Somalie. *Quaternaria 18:* 161-183.

Negash, A.
1997a Temben's place in the Neolithic of Northern Ethiopia. In: *Fukui E., Kurimoto and M. Shigeta (eds.), Ethiopia in Broader Perspective I.*.Kyoto: 389-398.
1997b Preliminary results of an archaeological reconnaissance of Tigrai, Northern Ethiopia. *Nyame Akuma 47*: 27-32.

Neuville, H.
1928 Contribution à l'étude des mégalithes abyssins. *L'anthropologie 38*: 255-288.

Oman, G.
1976 *La necropoli islamica di Dahlac Kebir I-II*. Napoli.
1987 *La necropoli islamica di Dahlac Kebir III*. Napoli.

Paribeni, R.
1908 Ricerche sul luogo dell'antica Adulis. *Monumenti antichi 17*: 497-523.

Phillips, C.
1998 The Tihamah c. 5000 to 500 BC. *Proceedings of the Seminar for Arabian Studies 28*: 233-237.

Phillipson, D. W.
1977 The Excavations of Gobedra Rock-Shelter, Axum. *Azania 12*: 53-82.
1993 The antiquity of cultivation and herding in Ethiopia. In: *Th. Shaw, P. Sinclair, B. Andah and A. Okpoko (eds.), The Archaeology of Africa. Food, Metals and Towns*. London: 344-357.
1997 *The Monumnets of Aksum*. London.
2000 *Archaeology at Aksum, Ethiopia 1993-1997*. London.

Puglisi, G.
1969 Alcuni vestigi dell'isola di Dahlac Chebir e la leggenda dei Furs. In: *Proceedings of the Third International conference of Ethiopian Studies – Addis Ababa 1966*. Addis Ababa: 35-47.

Révoil, G.
1882 *La Vallée du Daror*. Paris.

Ricci, L.
1994 On both sides of al-Mandab. In: *H. G. Marcus (ed.), New Trends in Ethiopian Studies. Papers of the 12th International Conference of Ethiopian Studies I*. Lawrenceville: 409-417.

Robin, Ch. and de Maigret, A.
1998   Le grand temple de Yéha (Tigray, Éthiopie), après la premiere campagne de
        fouilles de la Mission Française (1998). *Compte Rendus de l'Académie des
        Inscriptions et Belles-Lettres*. Juillet-Octobre 1998: 737-798.

Roubet, C.
1970   Prospection et découvertes de documents préhistoriques en Dankalie (Ethio-
        pie septentrionale). *Annales d'Ethiopie 8:* 13-20.

Schmidt, P. R. and Curtis, M. C.
2001   Urban precursors in the Horn: early 1st millennium BC communities in Eritrea.
        Antiquity 75: 849-859.

Schneider, M.
1967   Stélels funèraires arabes de Quiha. *Annales d'Ethiopie 7:* 107-118.

Smeds, H.
1955   The Ensete Planting culture of Eastern Sidamo (Ethiopia). *Acta Geographica
        13 (4):* 1-39.
n.d.   *Some view-points on the origin of ensete cultivation in Ethiopia.* Ms. in file,
        Institute of Ethiopian Studies. Addis Ababa.

Tesfay, G.
2000   Rock Art around the Zalambesa Area in the Eastern Zone of Tigrai (Ethiopia).
        Annales d'Ethiopie 16: 89-92.

Tringali,G.
1965   Cenni sulle 'ona' di Asmara e dintorni. *Annales d'Ethiopie 5:* 143-152.
1967   Necropoli di Curbacaiehat (Asmara). *Journal of Ethiopian Studies 5 (1):* 109-
        114.
1969   Varietà di asce litiche in 'ouna' dell'altopiano eritreo. *Journal of Ethiopian
        Studies 7 (1):* 119-122.
1978   Necropoli di Cascassè e oggetti sudarabici (?) della regione di Asmara (Eri-
        trea). *Rassegna di Studi Etiopici 26:* 49-66.
1981   Note su ritrovamenti archeologici in Eritrea. *Rassegna di Studi Etiopici 28.*
        1980-1981 (1981): 101-113.
1986   Elenco commentato dei reperti archeologici custoditi nel museo del Collegio
        'La Salle' in Asmara. *Quaderni di Studi Etiopici 6-7.* 1985-1986 (1986): 143-
        157.

Walter, R. C., Buffler, M. T., Brugemann, J. H. et al.
2000   Early human occupation of the Red Sea coast of Eritrea during the last inter-
        glacial. *Nature 405:* 65-69.

Wenig, St.
1997   German Fieldwork in Eritrea. *Nyame Akuma 48:* 20-21.

Wilding, R.
1980   The desert trade of eastern Ethiopia. In: *R. E. Leakey and B. A. Ogot (eds.),*
        Proceedings of the 8ᵗʰ Panafrican congress of Prehistory and Quaternary Stu-
        dies – Nairobi 1977. Nairobi: 379-380.

Zanetti, U. s.j.
1996   Les Langues de l' Ethiopie et de la Corne de l'Afrique. In: *X. Van der Stappen*
        (ed.), Aethiopia. Pays, Hisotire, Populations, Croyances, Art and Artisanat.
        Tervuren: 214-219.

Zarins, J.
1989   Ancient Egypt and the Red Sea Trade: the case for Obsidian in the Predynastic
        and Archaic Periods. In: *A. Leonard and B. B. Williams (eds.), Essays in An-*
        cient Civilization Presented to Helene Kantor. Chicago: 339-368.
1990   Obsidian and the Red Sea Trade Prehistoric Aspects. In: *M. Taddei and P.*
        Gawen (eds.), South Asian Archaeology 1987 I. Napoli: 507-541.
1996   Obsidian in the Larger Context of Predynastic/Archaic Egyptian Red Sea Tra-
        de. In: *J. Reade (ed.), The Indian Ocean in Antiquity.* London: 89-106.

Zarins, J. and Al-Badr, H.
1986   Archaeological Investigations in the Southern Tihama Plain II. *Atlal 10:* 36-57.

Zarins, J., Al-Jawarad Murad, A. and Al-Yish, K. S.
1981   The Comprensive Archaeological Survey, a: The Second Preliminary Report
        on the Southwestern Province. *Atlal 5:* 9-37.

Zarins, J. and Zaharani, A.
1985   Recent Archaeological Investigations in the southern Tihama Plain,
        1404/1984. *Atlal 9:* 65-107.

Zein, Z. A. and Kloos, H. (eds.)
1988   *The Ecology of Health and Disease in Ethiopia.* Addis Ababa.

Ziegert, H.
2001   Preliminary report on the Hamburg Archaeological Mission to Aksum 2000.
        Annales d'Ethiopie 17: 25-33.

Water Management and Settlements in Ancient Eritrea

Ueli Brunner

The Red Sea is the result of the divergent movement of the African and Arabian plate thus forming a large *graben*. The two sides are almost identical: Eritrea seems to be the mirror image of Yemen or vice versa. On both sides a dry coastal plain with hot and humid air stretches along the seashore (Brunner 1999: 10). The edge of the plain is marked by an uplifted landmass forming a steep ascent for more than 2000 m to a fertile plateau with lush vegetation due to summer rains which surpass 300 mm/year. According to a Government Report[1] 30% of the country were still covered with forest in 1900. There is a small area to the north of Asmara, where the summer rains of the Intertropical Convergence Zone overlap with the winter rains of depressions moving southward along the Red Sea, which are reactivated at the mountain slopes. Here the annual precipitation sums up to about 1000 mm. The drainage pattern shows short and steep intermittent rivers from the high plateau to the Red Sea and long gentle rivers flowing westward towards Sudan.

The agricultural practices are in accordance with the climatic conditions. In the highland plateau rainfed agriculture prevails whereas irrigation is common along the rivers in the arid coastal plain. Rainfed agriculture differs quite a lot between the two countries on either side of the Red Sea. In Yemen over 90% of the fields are totally levelled, horizontal and bordered by a small wall to retain all the rainwater. In the semiarid areas rainwater harvesting is applied. Rainwater is collected on the rocky surface of gentle slopes and conducted by small walls running transverse to the slope into the fields (Eger 1987). This improved system of rainfed agriculture is absent in Eritrea and terraced fields may only be encountered in Akeleguzay south of Adi Keyh.[2]

Irrigation in the lowlands is practised in the same way as in Yemen. A diversion dam built of mud and gravel leads a part of the flood water into a large channel. The slope of the channel is slightly inferior to the river bed so it gains in height and reaches the lateral embankments. Here the spate flow is divided into several smaller canals that conduct the water to large fields. The further irrigation ensues from field to field but only if the upper one is flooded by half a metre of water. This single irrigati-

---

1   Government of Eritrea, National Environmental Management Plan for Eritrea. Asmara, 1995, p. 59.
2   The writing of the place names are according to: Government of the State of Eritrea, Eritrea National Map 1:1,000,000. Compilation and Cartography by the Representatives of the Eritrean Government Offices, and the Institute of Geography, Group for Development and Environment, University of Berne, Switzerland, 1995.

on gives sufficient moisture to the soil to grow a yield. The similarity of the technical terms indicates their Arabic origin. The diversion dam is locally called *agim* whereas in Yemen it is *ʿaqm*. The main channel in Eritrea is a *musqa* and in Yemen a *saqîa*. In Eritrea canals and diverting structures are often supported by Acacia branches: "Every year thousands of trees and shrubs are cut for this purpose, devastating the surrounding areas."[3]

The South Arabian culture is shaped by irrigation and related water management systems. It can therefore be characterized as a hydraulic culture. The people of Southern Arabia developed themselves a well adapted usage of water in different natural environments (Brunner - Kohler 1997: 171-195). In the plains the fields were watered by flood irrigation and the households got their water from wells. In the highlands rainwater harvesting by side walls was the assurance for a safe yield on the terraces whereas the water for domestic use was collected in cisterns. Both agricultural systems were not really dependent on fertile soil; they rather produced it themselves. Flood water irrigation leads to a continuous accumulation of silt in the fields. The soil on the terraces is either brought by men or by the collected water on the nearby slopes. It is a matter of fact that agriculture is preferably begun on fertile soil, but it is not a necessity.

If we believe that Southern Arabia once influenced Eritrea with its hydraulic culture, where are the places for colonization? How can they be found? The most valuable sign for ancient irrigation are fine grained sediments. In three regions of Eritrea such sediments were observed on the occasion of a short visit in the autumn of 1997. The following account is not a scientifically based research; it is rather a description of signs from ancient irrigation.

The Gulf of Zula

The Gulf of Zula is like the signpost of the Red Sea to the Danakil Depression. The climate of Massawa, lying a mere 50 km to the northwest, serves quite well to characterize the atmospheric conditions of this region although the temperature may be higher due to its location inland. Humid air, missing rain and high temperature make it an unpleasant region. Nevertheless the agricultural potential is excellent thanks to a river system which debouches from the west into the Gulf of Zula (Fig. 1). The catchment area may sum up to about 3000 km². Its tributaries collect mostly the water from summer rains; however the western ones reach into the area with supplement winter rains.[4] The discharge at the confluence is still not perennial but it shows two peaks, a small one in winter and the main flow in summer.

---

3   State of Eritrea, Eastern Lowlands Wadi Development Project. Vol. II, p. 65.
4   Eritrea National Map 1:1,000,000. Cf. footnote 2.

The sediment load of the riverwater is high. The best example to indicate this is a modern dam, built about 50 years ago, whose reservoir behind the at least 10 m high dam is totally filled up with silt. This explains the fact that the city of Adulis, which was an important port at Aksumite time, is nowadays located 4 km from the sea shore (Anfray 1990: 51, 125f.). The river that flows along the town built up a large delta into the shallow Gulf of Zula. All around Adulis silty sediments with structures of canals and field walls indicate the former flood irrigation in this region (Fig. 2). Thus a lush oasis formed the economic background of this busy port. North of the town the ancient irrigation sediments are untouched whereas to the south these fertile accumulations are still used by modern farmers as their fields. A local informant reported the existence of many old dams in the region. Unfortunately, there was no time to visit them. The Gulf of Zula is an area worth investigating closer as to the ancient farming. In the lower reaches of Wadi Haddas local people still profit from the knowledge of ancient times while irrigating by diversion dams. For the understanding of the ancient agricultural practices it would be very useful to study the present situation.

Keren

Three of the largest rivers of Eritrea carry a name that sounds very familiar to people accustomed to the geography of Southern Arabia. First of all and well known is the Mereb which corresponds to the Sabean capital Ma'rib. The river Haddas finds its equivalent in the village of Hadda near Sana'a and the Anseba is closely related to the ancient town of Nisâb in the Wâdî Hammâm southeast of Ma'rib (Robin - Brunner 1997). The pronunciation of the term Nisâb, as it is commonly written, can be various. If locals speak carefully they pronounce N'sâb. If it is spoken rapidly one either understands Nisâb or also Ansâb. This version is definitely close to the Eritrean term "Anseba".

Keren, the capital of the province Senhit, is located at a tributary of the Anseba. About 2 km outside the town to the north on the edge of the river there is a well known shrine in a large baobab tree. This is St. Mariam Dearit, whose festival takes place May 21, that is just before the beginning of the summer rains, so its origin may be a worship of fertility. This sacred place lies on a fertile silt terrace high above the river and it is worth having a closer look at the cliff (Figs. 3 and 4).

The river bed shows the firm rock. The base of the section is made up of a slightly cemented conglomerate. It is overlain by a thick layer of reddish brown material that could be interpreted as fossil soil. The vast majority of the profile consists of monotonous silt with little fine sand. There is absolutely no coarse material such as gravel or pebbles as one would expect in natural accumulations. At two places structures were detected that are common in South Arabian irrigation sediments and which are relicts of canals for irrigation (Brunner 1997: 196). The surface of this silt terrace is partly covered by fertile fields but at some spots kilns were installed to bake bricks from local material. This is the very best proof of a really fine grained sediment.

The preliminary interpretation of this sequence may be as follows: The slightly solidified conglomerate at the base may belong to the Upper Pleistocene when a harsh climate deprived the surrounding slopes of vegetation, which resulted in heavy erosion (Bard et al. 2000: 72). The fossil soil developed under more humid conditions than today. A thick vegetation cover protected the hill slopes from being eroded. So the reddish brown horizon seems to correspond to the Middle Holocene. The present day environmental conditions with a mere 400 mm of precipitation a year only began in the second millenium BC (Bard et al. 2000). This means that from this time onward a safe agriculture depended on irrigation. The region around Keren was suited for irrigation due to the gentle slope of the small rivers. A clear dating of the sediment and therefore of irrigation cannot be given. The time of observation was not enough to take samples. However there are indications to narrow the time span. The earliest possible date for this irrigation will be the second millenium BC. Before there was no need for irrigation. A recent dating can be excluded by the baobab flourishing on the surface. Its diametre of almost 10 m indicates a rather old age of a thousand years or more. The thickness of the silt material can be taken as a hint for a rather long irriga- tion period of even more than a thousand years (Brunner 1997: 196). So the begin- ning may have taken place in the time period of the Kingdom of Daamat, an urban society with strong South Arabian, especially Sabean, characteristics (Bard et al. 2000: 70). Its centre was in Yeha e.g. North Tigray but so far no relicts of this culture have been found in the middle course of the Anseba river. Irrigation in this region may have persisted till the Aksumite period in the first millenium AD. Relicts of the Ona- culture around Asmara don't indicate irrigated agriculture (Schmidt - Curtis 2000: 853).

Akeleguzay

Regarded superficially the environmental conditions in the provinces of Senhit and Akeleguzay seem to be similar. A closer look reveals two important differences. The fertile valley floors in Senhit lie about 1500 m a.s.l. whereas the altitude of the major agricultural areas in Akeleguzay is mostly over 2000 m a.s.l. The mean annual rainfall in both regions is around 400 mm. It is even a little bit higher in Akeleguzay. But the total amount of rainfall may give a wrong idea of the agricultural potential of a region. In the Senhit area most of the rainfall is concentrated in the rainy season that starts in June and goes till September. In Akeleguzay it is more complicated. The local Saho farmers distinguish between three rainy seasons (Strebel 1979: 21):

sugum rains between March and May
karma rains between June and September
barit rains between October and December

In normal years *sugum* rains are not sufficient for the growing of crops, so farmers seldom use it for rainfed agriculture. Relevant for them are the *karma* rains whereas barit rains are unpopular. As the term "*barit*" suggests – in Arabic it means cold – they are even called killing rains because they can damage the yield. About two thirds up to three fourths of the precipitation seem to fall as *karma* rains. In certain years they may not be sufficient to produce a yield, even if the total amount of the whole year is more than 300 mm. A stabilization of the yield can only be reached by irrigated agriculture. Here already the *sugum* rains can be used to flood a few fields and even small *karma* rains will produce another yield. It is this safety of agricultural production in drought periods that mark out a highly developed society as the hydraulic culture that existed and still exists in Southern Arabia. On the African side of the Red Sea irrigated agriculture is not as elaborate but there still exist good examples in Ethiopia (Stitz 1974: 340) and Eritrea (Schmidt - Curtis 2000: 64f.). Straube calls this improved land use "agrarian intensified complex" (1967: 198). He found it with some tribes of northeastern and eastern Africa as well as in Sudan. The agrarian intensified complex implies different measures such as building of cultural land, conservation of soil, regulating the water household, improvement of the soil structure, conservation or improvement of the soil fertility, protection of crops and improvement of the productivity of the labourers.

In Akeleguzay signs that this important step from extensive to intensive farming had been taken are widespread. Many of the modern fields and also deserted ones lie totally horizontal. On these levelled fields the suspended fine sediment is accumulated with every flooding resulting in rich soils with a high capacity in water retention.[5] This intensive work of terracing the slopes or accumulating silt plains along rivers has changed the natural relief into a man-made landscape (Fig. 5). Further signs of this effort to give the agricultural production a safer basis are the remains of old dams and canals that could be found in many places. If the inscription DAE 34 of Matara supports this effort, as Littmann's translation suggests, or if it has nothing to do with water management, as Drewes thinks, is not definitely clear.[6] A further hint for the high standard of water management are the cisterns. The most prominent one is the cistern of Safira on the Qohaito plateau. It is located at the beginning of a shallow valley that falls down into a gorge after a few hundred metres. The catchment area of the cistern is rather small, only about 0.5 km² and covers a relatively flat rocky surface. The high altitude of 2600 m a.s.l. leads to more rainfall, lower temperatures and less evaporation than elsewhere.

The cistern has natural borders on three sides whereas the downstream side is made up of a 67 m long wall built of masonry that is enforced on the air side by earthen material. Altogether this structure implements the idea of a dam. That is the reason why it is often called dam of Safira. But the term dam often evokes irrigation and this cannot be the case here, because the area suited for fields is missing. Furthermore the stone wall on the waterside is such an excellent masterwork that it is more apt to speak of a wall (Fig. 6). This wall is divided into three parts, these three sections

---

5 According to Bosshart the main concentration of suspended sediments in small rivers is about 4g/l. It is much higher during a flood. Cf. Bosshart 1995: part III, 27.

6 Informal information from Prof. Weninger, University of Marburg.

forming a straight line only at the base. Regarding the top of the wall the middle part steps back in downstream direction. Only this section seems to be totally original. The outer ends are partly renovated in a simple manner. Early travellers reported these parts as ruins (Littmann 1913: pl. XXIII) or they interpreted the missing walls as sluices (Bent 1893: 220; Schoeller 1895: 17). Normally sluices are well defined, but Bent and Schoeller list two different sizes, so it is unlikely that they really found sluices.

The western part of the wall starts at the firm rock and has a length of 23.6 m. The well hewn ashlars were taken from the basin thus enlarging it by a few cubic metres. Nine layers, each between 25 cm and 40 cm build up the entire wall. Its height is about 3.50 m. The layers can easily be seen because every one steps back by about 3 cm. The ashlars fit very well so no mortar was used to make the wall watertight.

The central section is the nicest part of the wall and with almost 30 m also the longest one. It demonstrates in all its elements that a decorative architecture was more relevant than its function. The main building material are again ashlars. It is a sandy limestone. Every layer of ashlar is covered by thin plates of slate. The upper ashlars step back by about 20 cm so the wall gives the impression of a steep staircase. Thus all three elements of Aksumite architecture are found at this central section of the wall: It is not in a line with the rest of the wall, every layer steps back and the layers are marked by slate plates (Anfray 1990: 121). The impression that the central part of the wall is the product of different stairs is underlined by long ashlars which jut out on the water side, always four to one layer. If you look from the basin these single steps form two isosceles triangles. Their basis lies at the bottom and the two points at the top of the wall. Hence there are altogether four lofty stairs mounting the central wall transversally.

The eastern section of the wall is mostly rebuilt with small ashlars put together with mortar. It is the shortest part, only 14 m long, because it ends at a crosswall that serves as the foundation for a platform. Here the German Aksum Expedition mapped the outline of a large structure of 22 m x 20 m which cannot be seen anymore (Littmann 1913: pl. XXIII). One member of the expedition presumed that it could be a sanctuary.

Small rock-strips border the basin to the north. It is obvious that here lay the quarry for the ashlars of the wall. The inlet to the cistern is about 1 m higher than the top of the wall. Just behind the inlet lies another, smaller depression (Fig. 7). It serves as a sedimentation basin, so only more or less clean water can flow into the cistern. The layout is very much the one of many in Yemen (Figs. 8a+b). Nevertheless it is not of Sabean origin. It seems that the knowledge for the arrangement of the cistern came from Yemen but the architecture of the wall is definitively Aksumite. Yemenite cisterns are waterproof whereas this cistern is leaking although it is reinforced by the earthen dam. The drainage water permanently irrigates the valley floor downstream. This pasture is visited by sheep, goats, donkeys, horses and cattle.

What was the use of the cistern? The location of the settlement of Qohaito is similar to many Yemenite villages. It lies on top of a plateau where rainwater is abundant but where springs are scarce. The springs only exist in lower altitudes, either at the outer cliff or in chasms within the plateau. Both locations of the springs are hard to reach. By collecting the rainwater in a cistern, water for domestic use is within easy reach. In Yemen cisterns often form the informal social centre for the female population during daytime. In the evening the livestock gathers at its border hoping that it will be watered soon. Normally animals haven't access to the basin because they would infect the water. So the cistern of Safira seems to be an ordinary cistern that may have been constructed at the edge of an ordinary folk's house as there are a hundred examples in Yemen. The refinement of the wall shows the status of the Aksumite settlement. Qohaito must have been quite important.

Conclusions

The examples of Adulis, Keren and Qohaito discussed show three different locations of settlements. Adulis is situated on a vast plain at the border of a large river. The agricultural background consisted of an oasis that was man-made; flood irrigation made it bloom and accumulated fertile silt. The same system was in use near Keren, but here a shallow valley served as the nucleus of a fertile oasis. On the semihumid plateau of Qohaito there is no need for irrigation but there is need for domestic water. This need was fulfilled by building a cistern.

　All three examples can be found, multiplied by the factor one hundred, in Southern Arabia where the hydraulic culture has been studied for two decades. The research of water management systems has helped to answer the many questions concerning the location of settlements, the economic basis of civilizations or even the number of people living in a certain place. Eritrea has almost identical geographical conditions. It would therefore be useful to transfer the developed methods of geoarchaeological research from Yemen to Eritrea as the farmers transferred the hydraulic knowledge in the first millenium BC.

Bibliography

Anfray, F.
1990   *Les Anciens Éthiopiens*. Paris.

Bard, K. A., Coltroti, M., DiBlasi, M. C., Dramis, F. and Fattovich, R.
2000   The Environmental History of Tigray (Northern Ethiopia) in the Middle and Late Holocene: A Preliminary Outline. *African Archaeological Review 17,2:* 65-96.

Bent, J. T.
1893   *The Sacred City of the Ethiopians being a Record of Travel and Research in Abyssinia in 1893*. London.

Bosshart, U. P.
1995   *Catchment Discharge and Suspended Sediment Transport in the Highlands of Ethiopia and Eritrea*. Ph.D. Thesis, University of Berne, Switzerland.

Brunner, U.
1997   Geography and Human Settlements in Ancient Southern Arabia. *Arabian Archaeology and Epigraphy 8:* 190-202.
1999   *Jemen – Vom Weihrauch zum Erdöl*. Wien.

Brunner, U. and Kohler, S.
1997   Bewässerung im Jemen. *Mare Erythraeum 1*. München: 171-195.

Eger, H.
1987   *Runoff Agriculture: A Case Study About the Yemeni Highlands*. Jemen-Studien 7. Wiesbaden.

Littmann, E.
1913   *Deutsche Aksum-Expedition*. Berlin.

Robin, Chr. and Brunner, U.
1997   *Map of Ancient Yemen – Carte du Yémen Antique*. München.

Schmidt, P. R. and Curtis, M. C.
2000   Urban precursors in the Horn: early 1st-millenium BC communities in Eritrea. *Antiquity 75:* 849-859.

Schoeller, M.
1895   *Mittheilungen über meine Reise in der Colonia Eritrea (Nord-Abyssinien)*.
        Berlin.

Stitz, V.
1974   *Studien zur Kulturgeographie Zentraläthiopiens*. Bonner Geographische
        Abhandlungen 51. Bonn.

Straube, M.
1967   Der agrarische Intensivierungskomplex in Nordost-Afrika. *Paideuma XIII*:
        198-222.

Strebel, B.
1979   *Kakteenbauern und Ziegenhirten in der Buknaiti Are (Nordaethiopien)*.
        Ph.D. Thesis, University of Zurich.

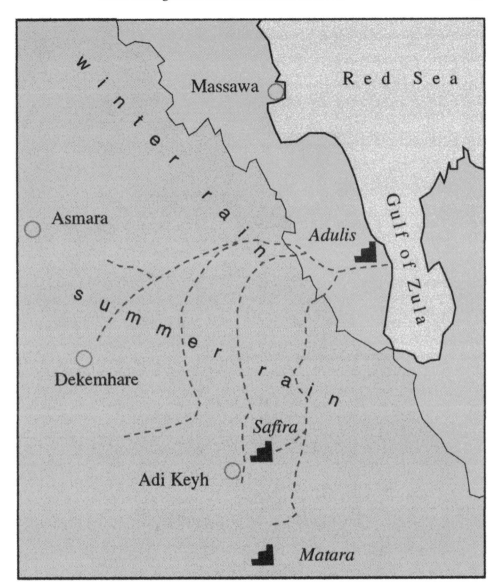

Fig. 1   Sketch map of the Gulf of Zula.

Fig. 2   Irrigation sediments in Adulis.

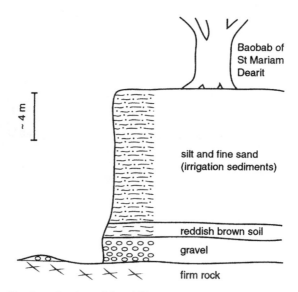

Fig. 3   Section of the cliff at St. Mariam Dearit, Keren.

Fig. 4   A cliff near St. Mariam Dearit showing discordant layers.

Fig. 5   Terracing near Tokonda, Akeleguzay.

Fig. 6   The central wall of the cistern of Safira on the Qohaito plateau.

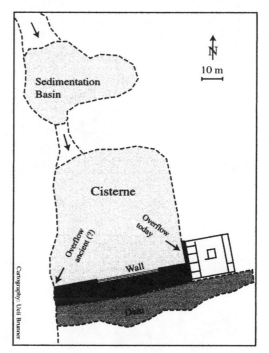

Fig. 7   Sketch map of the cistern of Safira.

Fig. 8a+bComparison of cisterns: Safira in Eritrea and Kawkaban in Yemen.

New Discoveries in Ethiopian Archaeology
Dabr Takla Hāymānot in Dāwnt and Enṣo Gabre'ēl in Lāstā[1]

Stanislaw Chojnacki

The purpose of this presentation is to draw to your attention two early architectural monuments which recently came to light. The first of these discoveries was Dabr Takla Hāymānot in Dāwnt in June 1996, and the second was Enṣo Gabre'ēl discovered on April 7, 1997 in Lāstā.

In June 1996, accompanied by my assistants, *Ato* Tamasgēñ Gētāhun and *Ato* Kafeyālew Tolosā, who was our photographer, I travelled to Dāwnt to photograph the 15th-century paintings in Dabra Abunā Musē, also known as Yadebba Māryām (Wright 1957: 10-11). This cave church contains well preserved 15th-century wall paintings (Buxton 1970: 146-147, figs. 84-85). We journeyed from Addis Ababā to Waldyā in order to see the bishop there and obtain the necessary written authorization to photograph them. From there we travelled on the road to Dabra Tābor to Gašanā – a distance of 116 km from Waldyā. Here we turned south on a road under construction. We passed the town of Kon and continued on the unfinished section of the road down to the River Gētā. After fording it we started climbing on the old Italian track.

At about the 55 km mark from Gašanā, we found that the track was washed out and we had to spent the rest of the night in the car. At dawn of the next day, June 6, we left the car nearby and climbed the steep cliffs up to the high Dāwnt plateau. By 9 a.m. we had arrived at Ayda Mikā'ēl and here we were able to hire a horse for me. We then proceeded across a large plain with scattered villages and, as might be expected, in each one there was a church. According to local custom, on each occasion, one had to stop, dismount and make a bow towards the church.

Towards mid-day we arrived at Dačā Iyasus and met *Maggābi sera'āt* Fantāhun Gētāhun, head of the local ecclesiastical office. He gladly agreed to accompany us to Yadebba Māryām and also suggested visiting another church on the way. As he explained, we would find 'big ruins' there.

During the early afternoon of the same day, we walked some six km across a wide plain and reached the Dabra Amin commonly known as Dabr Takla Hāymānot, the place with the big "ruins" promised by *Maggābi sera'āt*. What I found there was far beyond my expectations – namely the remnants of large and obviously very ancient

---

1 Paper presented at the First International Littmann Conference held in Munich on 2nd to 5th May, 2002.

structures. They were built in a completely different manner than any other buildings which I had previously encountered during my journeys to remote places in Ethiopia. I therefore made a preliminary exploration of the site and Kāfeyalew took excellent photographs. Then we moved to Yadebba Māryām situated a half an hour's of walking distance from Dabr Takla Hāymānot. Since the fifteenth century the royal script provided *debr* or support for royal churches (Crummey 1999: 218).

I decided to revisit the place at the earliest possible date and, indeed, in April 1997 I travelled again to Yadebba Māryām, this time with my friend Paul Henze, enthusiastic traveller and a supreme amateur photographer, *Ato* Mulugētā Hayla Māryām originating from Wāg, *Ato* Wudu Tāfētē, lecturer at the Addis Ababā University and *Ato* Mohāmmad Danbobā our always helpful driver. We reached Waldyā on April 7 and during the next day we travelled on the same road that had been under construction the year before until we arrived at the place where we had spent the night on our previous visit. From there we climbed the steep cliffs of high plateau. This time, however, due to a recent rainfall, the black soil of Dāwnt had changed into sticky mud, and it was only after six hours of painful trekking, completely exhausted, we reached Dačā Iyasus late in the evening. We were already aware that Dāwnt is known as a difficult region for travellers and this time it lived up to its reputation, however we were graciously invited to spent the night at the hospitable house of our old friend *Maggābi sera'āt* Fantāhun.

On the morning of the 9th of April, we first went to Yadebba Māryām and after having finished the photography, in the late afternoon we began our return journey intending to revisit Dabr Takla Hāymānot on the way. Due to the fading light and heavy rain we decided to pass the night in the village where Dabr Takla Hāymānot is located, and the villagers very kindly invited us into their homes. Purely by chance I was led to the house of a farmer who remembered my first visit to Yadebba Māryām more than twenty years earlier in 1974.

The next morning, April 10, the sky was again clear and we could inspect the ruins thoroughly taking their measurements while Paul Henze photographed them. He also photographed a 14th or 15th-century processional copper cross of a circular frame type. The church, however, did not appear to possess any old manuscripts. In conjunction with the good photographs taken by Kafyālew and the slides by Paul Henze I fortunately acquired sufficient documentation to write a preliminary paper on the ruins, but in-depth exploration is still needed in order to fully assess the importance of this discovery.

Having completed our task, we hired horses and rode along the ridge of the high plateau passing a great many Gelada baboons which were collecting food in the adjacent fields. When disturbed we observed them running quickly towards the cliffs in search of protection.

The church of Dabr Takla Hāymānot, also named Dabr Amin Takla Hāymānot, and the surrounding village is situated at a distance of two hundred metres from the western edge of the Dāwnt plateau where steep cliffs drop off into the wide Dibbān valley

joining the Gēṭā River basin (Fig. 1). The Yadebba Māryām cave church is situated on
the northern slopes of the same valley.

The ruins consist of three groups of structures each having a different form and
apparently serving different purposes. The main structure is enclosed by the walls of
the recently constructed round church, the external walls of which were fashioned
using a mixture of chaff and mud – a widely used building material in Ethiopia (Fig.
2). The neatly trimmed thatched roofing is supported with slender Eucalyptus poles
forming a narrow gallery around the church. During our first visit we had found the
church still under construction, which, in turn, made it possible for us to see and take
a picture of the chest or stand for keeping the *tābot*, wooden tablet, primarily meaning 'ark' (Beckingham 1961: 543-550). It was a crudely-made and fairly recent piece of
church furniture (Fig. 3). Within this modest country church, however, there was also
a much older structure in fairly good condition which now serves as a *maqdās* or holy
of holies for the new church.

On this occasion we found that the east wall of the *maqdās* has been newly constructed using mud and some broken pieces of stone probably taken from the original
structure. The wall on the north side has been partly repaired in the same manner and
a small wooden window was added (Fig. 4). During the reconstruction, openings
were made to the *maqdās* complete with the makeshift doors (Fig. 5). They do not,
however, correspond to the original construction. The structure used for the *maqdās*
is almost square measuring ten metres by twelve and was built in an east-west direction (Fig. 6). On its west side the wall was extended indicating that what we were
now seeing was probably only a part of the original structure. In the south wall, there
is an opening narrowing outwards, which appears to be a defence device similar to
those in Mediaeval Europe and the Near East. It was recently blocked with stones
(Fig. 7). The walls were constructed of blocks of limestone neatly cut to form smooth
walls without the use of either mud or mortar. There are two pilasters with slanting
edges (Fig. 8). The west wall is in good condition and still measures about five metres
which presumably was the height of the original structure. At the corners there are
extensions protruding approximately 35 cm with a width of about one metre. In the
same wall, at 50 cm from the ground, there is a rectangular niche measuring 47 cm by
52 cm which is roughly 40 cm deep and its bottom is hollowed. It obviously belonged
to the original structure but its purpose is not immediately obvious (Fig. 9). There
were no openings for entrance in the western and southern walls.

For the construction large blocks were used, the biggest measured being 2 m wide
and 86 cm high. We could not measure their thickness, but we presume that the
blocks were roughly 40 cm thick and cut to fit closely to one another. Some were
shaped at one end to form an extended attachment at an angle to the adjacent block
(Fig. 10).

In front of the new church there is an elongated structure about 12 m long and 3 m
wide of which only the south tower-like end is relatively well-preserved. It is made of
huge square or rectangular blocks of stones perfectly adjusted at the corners and still
extending to the original height (Fig. 11). The base of the north end consists of chis-
elled blocks, however, it has partially lost the outer layer of its face-stones thereby

exposing the inner layer which consisted of rough stones and a kind of mortar (Fig. 12). Between both ends, the wall was constructed with similar blocks but the middle part of it was mostly gone. At present the structure in the church and the one outside it are completely separate, however at some juncture there must have been some architectural connection between the two.

At a distance of about 100 m from the main building, there are the remnants of the wall surrounding the extensive area of the original enclosure. This wall is made of irregular stones, except for the bottom portion where stone blocks were used. There is also a gate 2 m 50 cm wide with the remnants of two pillars on either side (Fig. 13). Cut stones formed the base and top of each and the remaining part of the column was composed of a mixture of rough stones and mortar (Fig. 14). In the north pillar was a rectangular opening 60 cm long and 32 cm wide, into which a wooden bar used for blocking the gate had once been inserted. According to local tradition, however, the space was believed to have served as lion's cage.

These constructions clearly indicate an advanced knowledge of the art of building and stone cutting. They also suggest a substantial concentration of power and economic means on the part of the unidentified individual who ordered the construction of these buildings. Who was this and who were his subjects? An answer to the first part of the question was put forward by the local residents who said that the ruins had once been the palace, *gemb*, of King Germā Asfārē, also called Meskur *Abba* Orit and we learned that his wife was named Gomut. This is the King Newāya-Māryām whose royal name was Wedem-Asfārē who in some sources is referred to as Germā Asfārē. Apparently he ruled for ten years, from 1371 till 1379/80 A.D. (Schneider 1983: 107), but otherwise the royal chronicles are significantly silent about him (Basset 1881: 94) except for a possible suggestion that there was a civil war (Conti Rossini 1949: 283-284). Recent research, however, reveals that his brother and successor Dāwit, took the throne by an act of violence in the course of which Newāya-Māryām was eliminated. Some religious groups strongly resented Dāwit's action and an important centre of this opposition was situated in Dāwnt – precisely the region in which we had made our discovery (Tedeschi 1974: 573-579). While there were no immediate answers to our investigations, another discovery made during the same 1997 trip provided some new elements for solving the puzzle.

On April 7, as we were on our way from Lālibalā towards Waldyā, at the suggestion of Mulugēta Haile Māryām, we stopped at the 52 km mark to inspect some ruins he had learned about from the local people. He was informed that the Ministry of Culture had apparently posted an order prohibiting digging at the site. Whether this edict was strictly observed is not known, but according to Mulugēta's informants no one had visited the place before our arrival there. The area is known as Gidān and the ruins were currently being used as a church bearing the name of Enṣo Gabre'ēl. They are situated to the right of the road some 50 m from it. The ruins, however, are not visible from the road because the slope rises steeply from the road level.

The ruins are partly hidden by bushes and one big Wild Olive tree, *Olea africana*, growing on their northern side (Fig. 15), while an old and huge African Pencil Cedar,

Juniperus procera, growing nearby is an indication of the age of the ruins. The best preserved portions are the northern and eastern walls, which are almost complete to the top and their average height is 4 m including the 30 cm base.

The ground plan of the ruins shows that the original structure consisted of two buildings extending from west to east and the passage between them was about two metres wide. The dimensions of the rectangular-shaped main building were 8.80 m wide on eastern side by 6.50 m long on northern side. The eastern wall has one narrow opening which appears to be original. At present the second square opening is filled with four blocks of stone, but it seems that originally it was part of the wall consisting of two large blocks (Fig. 16). The northern wall is extended approximately 13 m and includes the length of the main building, measuring 6.50 m (Fig. 17), the 2 m wide passage and a small additional structure 4.20 m wide (Fig. 18).

On the western side there were two rooms divided by a narrow corridor. A part of the outside western wall is still 2.60 m high and the last surviving top-slab of the ancient roofing is still in place. The main entrance to the building was probably in the middle of this wall (Fig. 19). One chamber has not yet been excavated and is fairly complete. It had a door to the corridor but no opening to the outside. According to certain people in the area, this could be a possible indication that there is a room underneath (Fig. 20). The walls in the second room have mostly collapsed but there is still an arched exit to the corridor (Fig. 21). It also appears that the above buildings were not the only stone structures in the compound. Close to it there are remnants of another small structure and there are cut stone blocks scattered in the immediate vicinity.

When the ruins were incorporated into a newly built church, a very crude southern wall was constructed, because it had been missing in the old building according to local reports. A similarly crude roof was constructed and adorned with a simple cross (Fig. 22). The form of this improvised church is necessarily rectangular, and consists of the sanctuary, *maqdās*, and cantors place.

The building was constructed with large blocks of stone shaped with the same accomplished skill as those in Dabr Takla Hāymānot, however, here they appear more uniform and their average measurements are 42 to 48 cm high (Fig. 23) and 1.25 m to 1.46 m wide (Fig. 24). No mortar was used and the blocks fit perfectly together. The regularity of the manner of laying the blocks and joining them at the corners reveals the presence in the area of similarly able and well-trained craftsmen as those who created Dabr Takla Hāymānot. We presume that this occurred in the 14th century or perhaps earlier.

In contrast to the people in Dabr Takla Hāymānot, the Enṣo people appear to have no recollection or oral history relating to the origin of the building. They produced, however, a large iron lectern with arms extending to a length of 1.20 m which they recently found by digging the ground. This unusually large lectern obviously belonged to the original furniture of an old church. We did not, on this occasion, see either old crosses or books.

Although the Enṣo Gabre'ēl ruins are situated a short distance from Lālibalā, the original buildings were constructed differently and cut blocks of stone were used. It is possible, however, that the vanished royal palace above Bēta Gabre'ēl in Lālibalā was also constructed of similarly-fashioned stone blocks – some of which were still in place in the early 1970s. The discovery of the ruins at Dabr Takla Hāymānot would suggest the presence of foreign craftsmen in late 14th century Ethiopia, while the discovery of those at Enṣo Gabre'ēl might indicate an even earlier vigorous construction programme of either royal residences or churches built with neatly shaped blocks of stone. This recent discovery thus reveals cultural aspects of a little-known period in Ethiopia's history.

Bibliography

Basset, R.
1881   Études sur l' histoire d' Éthiopie. *Journal Asiatique, série VII, t. XVIII:* 93-183.

Buxton, D. R.
1970   *The Abyssinians.* London.

Beckingham, C. F. and Huntingford, G.W.B. (eds.)
1961   The *tābot.* Appendix III to *The Prester John of the Indies. A true relation of the Lands of the Prester John being the narrative of the Portuguese Embassy to Ethiopia in 1520 written by Father Francisco Alvares.* Cambridge: 543-548.

Conti Rossini, C.
1949   Su due frasi dalla Cronaca Abbreviata dei re d'Etiopia. Istituto Universitario Orientale, *Annali vol. III.* Napoli: 283-284.

Crummey, D.
1999   *Land and Society in the Christian Kingdom of Ethiopia.* Urbana - Chicago.

Schneider, R.
1983   Notes éthiopiennes. *Journal of Ethiopian Studies XVI:* 105-113.

Tedeschi, R.
1974   Les fils du Négus Sayfa-Ar'ād d'après un document arabo-chrétien. *Africa XXXIX, 4:* 573-587.

Wright, S.
1957   Notes on Some Cave Churches in the Province of Wallo. *Annales d'Éthiopie II:* 7-13.

Stanislaw Chojnacki

Acknowledgement

The autor is indebted to Mrs Carolyn M. Gossage for the final editing of the text.

Photographic Acknowledgements

Paul B. Henze: Figs. 1, 2, 4, 6, 7, 12, 14-24;
Kafeyālew Tolosā: Figs. 3, 5, 8, 9, 10, 11, 13

Fig. 1   View of western edges of Dāwnt high-plateau.

Fig. 2   Church of Dabr Takla Hāymānot.

Fig. 3   Dabr Takla Hāymānot. Chest for
          keeping the *tābot*.

Fig. 4   Dabr Takla Hāymānot. Northern
          wall of the maqdās.

Fig. 5   Dabr Takla Hāymānot. Recently
          constructed door in ancient wall.

Fig. 6   Dabr Takla Hāymānot. Wall of
          the maqdās.

Fig. 7   Dabr Takla Hāymānot. South wall
with defensive window.

Fig. 8   Dabr Takla Hāymānot. Pilaster,
southern wall.

Fig. 9   Dabr Takla Hāymānot. Niche, western wall.

Fig. 10   Dabr Takla Hāymānot. Adjustment of blocks in the wall.

Fig. 11   Dabr Takle Hāymānot. South end of a ruined structure in front of the church.

Fig. 12   Dabr Takla Hāymānot. North end of the same structure.

Fig. 13   Dabr Takla Hāymānot. Gate in the wall surrounding the church.

Fig 14   Dabr Takla Hāymānot. North pillar of the gate.

Fig. 15   North view of Enṣo Gabre'ēl partly hidden by Wild Olive tree.

Fig. 16   Enṣo Gabre'ēl seen from the east.

Fig. 17   Enṣo Gabre'ēl. Northern view, right, on the main structure.

Fig. 18   Enṣo Gabre'ēl. Northern view, left, on the additional structure.

Fig. 19   Enṣo Gabre'əl. Additional structure seen from the west.

Fig. 20   Enṣo Gabre'əl. Additional structure
seen from the south.

Fig. 21   Enṣo Gabre'ēl. View of two rooms in additional structure with the arched exid.

Fig. 22   Enṣo Gabre'ēl. South view of church and additional strukture.

Fig. 23   Enṣo Gabre'ēl, detail of the wall constrction.

Fig. 24   Enṣo Gabre'ēl, detail of the wall construction.

Zur Geschichte der Materialerfassung in der aksumitischen Münzkunde

Wolfgang Hahn

Bei der Aufarbeitung der historischen Zeugnisse zur Geschichte Aksums im 1. Band der DAE hat Enno Littmann auch die ihm aus der Literatur zugänglichen Münzen sowie solche aus Museumssammlungen zusammengestellt und kommentiert. Damals waren nicht viel mehr als 70 Jahre vergangen, seit der Frankfurter Forschungsreisende Eduard Rüppell (1794-1884) erstmals aksumitische Münzen mitgebracht und publiziert hatte – das war 1840 gewesen. Damit fällt deren Debüt in der Numismatik relativ spät, denn die gleichzeitige griechische-römische Münzprägung war um die Mitte des 19. Jahrhunderts bereits weithin beforscht. Das Bekanntwerden von mehr Material und seine Vorstellung in den numismatischen Fachzeitschriften Englands, Frankreichs und Deutschlands war zunächst ein langsamer Prozeß, dessen Stationen im 1. Kapitel von Munro-Hay's Buch *Coinage of Aksum* nachgezeichnet werden.[1] Die folgenden Ausführungen sind dazu als eine Art statistischer Ergänzung gedacht, um einen Eindruck davon zu geben, in welchem Ausmaß unsere Materialkenntnis im Laufe der 160 Jahre seit Rüppell sukzessive angewachsen ist und daß wir trotzdem das Stadium der Grundlagenforschung noch nicht hinter uns gebracht haben, wenn es um die mengenstatistische Auswertung geht, die zum methodischen Rüstzeug des Numismatikers gehört.

Littmann steht in der Geschichte der aksumitischen Münzforschung am Ende der ersten Halbzeit. Er konnte 1913 insgesamt 84 aksumitische Münzen versammeln, und zwar 24 in Gold, 9 in Silber und 51 in Kupfer. Er fand sie großteils in Aufsätzen oder Miszellen publiziert. Ihre Standorte waren vornehmlich die Sammlungen der renommierten Museen Europas wie London, Paris, Wien, Berlin und St. Petersburg. Die Provenienz dieser Münzen und ihr Besitzerstammbaum ist ein Stück Forschungsgeschichte: Auch nach Rüppell, dessen Münzen im Museum seiner Heimatstadt Frankfurt gelandet sind, haben Forschungsreisende solche Kuriosa mitgebracht, so 1861 aus Massaua Theodor von Heuglin (1824-76) für die Universitätssammlung von Tübingen; 1868 aus Adulis Richard Holmes, der als Archäologe der britischen Magdala-Expedition beigegeben war, für das Britische Museum. Aus dem Jemen, der immer reich an goldenen Fundmünzen aksumitischer Prägung war, haben zu Beginn des 20. Jahrhunderts die beiden bekannten Südarabienforscher Eduard Glaser (1855-1908)

---

1 Munro-Hay - Juel-Jensen: 1995; Rezensionen: Luegmeyer 1998: 250-259; West 1999: 5-6. Aus der bei Munro-Hay S. 53-69 gebrachten Bibliographie wird hier auf die Zitate verwiesen (ausgenommen neuere Literatur).

und David Heinrich Müller (1846-1912) die Sammlungen in Wien und München bedient. Schließlich hat auch Littmann einige Münzen erworben und mitgenommen; sie liegen heute in der Berliner Staatsbibliothek.

Andere Materialaufkäufer waren altertumskundlich interessierte Diplomaten, die in den Gegenden tätig waren, wo ihnen aksumitische Münzen vorgelegt wurden. Da ist vor allem der englische Offizier und Kolonialbeamte William Francis Prideaux (1840-1914) zu nennen. Er war in den 1860er und 1870er Jahren in Südarabien, Ostafrika und schließlich Indien im Einsatz und befand sich unter den Gefangenen des Kaisers Theodor II. Die von ihm gesammelten und beschriebenen aksumitischen Münzen landeten dann im Britischen Museum.

Schließlich erbrachten die ersten größeren Ausgrabungen, die offiziellerseits durch die Italiener 1906/07 in Adulis durchgeführt wurden, Hunderte von Fundmünzen. Littmann waren sie freilich nur aus der kursorischen Grabungspublikation von Paribeni bekannt. Darin finden sich bloß die Goldmünzen identifiziert, während für die Massen an mehr oder weniger schlecht erhaltenen Kupfermünzen eine spätere Bearbeitung angekündigt wurde. Dazu ist es freilich nie gekommen. Das Kupfer blieb in Asmara, das Gold kam nach Rom ins Museo Coloniale (Africano), wurde dort in den frühen 1980er Jahren gestohlen und im internationalen Münzhandel zerstreut.

Als die Bände der DAE publiziert wurden, waren erst wenige aksumitische Münzen in den professionellen Münzhandel geraten; das erste Auktionsvorkommen ist für 1905, in Amsterdam, zu vermerken, gefolgt 1913 in Paris. Es handelte sich dabei um Goldmünzen jemenitischer Provenienz, ähnlich der von Glaser, Müller und anderer Museumseinlieferern, wie etwa Nuri Bey, einem Antiquitätenhändler in Konstantinopel, der vor dem 1. Weltkrieg die Eremitage in St. Petersburg mit aksumitischen Goldmünzen versorgte. Littmann hatte als Nichtnumismatiker von diesen Quellen noch keine Kenntnis.

Deren Erfassung begann jedoch bald danach, als ein italienischer Sammler aus Mailand auf den Plan trat, dessen Namen, Arturo Anzani, in der Geschichte der aksumitischen Münzforschung nicht gebührend genug hervorgehoben werden kann. Geboren 1879, begann er zunächst mit dem Sammeln römischer und griechischer Münzen, bis die Adulis-Funde sein Augenmerk auf die Aksumiten lenkten, zumal er 1913-18 bei der Kolonialverwaltung in Eritrea bedienstet war. Von Beruf Buchhalter, war er exaktes Arbeiten gewohnt. Im Jahre 1926 legte er ein neues Stückcorpus-Verzeichnis vor, kombiniert mit einem Kommentarteil, der alle bis dahin erschienene einschlägige Literatur einbezieht. Dieser 90seitige Beitrag erschien mit 12 Phototafeln in der RIN und sollte für lange Zeit das Referenzwerk der aksumitischen Numismatik bilden. In den 13 Jahren seit der Littmann'schen Zusammenstellung war das Material durch Publikationen von Sammlungsakquisitionen stark angewachsen. Dazu konnte Anzani im Korrespondenzwege auch unpublizierte Sammlungen erfassen, sowohl öffentliche als auch private. Insgesamt sind es 6mal mehr Münzen als bei Littmann, nämlich 513, davon 163 Gold, aber nur 18 der damals noch wenig bekannten Silbermünzen; was ihm an Abbildungen greifbar war, hat Anzani reproduziert, so gut es ging, und damit den Grund für die weitere Dokumentation gelegt. Natürlich sammelte er auch selbst, wie es fast alle getan haben, die sich je mit aksumitischen Münzen befaßt haben; es ist dies ein allgemeines Phänomen in der Numismatik, erklärbar durch die Faszination, die von diesen geschichtsträchtigen und in größerer Zahl verfügbaren Originalen ausgeht. Im Jahre 1926 besaß Anzani insgesamt 93 Münzen, ein Fünftel davon in Gold. Er beobachtete den Markt und pflegte die Verbindung zu anderen Privatsammlern.

Ein solcher war auch der berühmte Äthiopist Carlo Conti-Rossini (1872-1949), der seine Sammlung – nicht ganz zutreffend – für die größte hielt; sie bestand zwar aus 141 Münzen, darunter aber bloß 6 in Silber und kein Gold. Conti-Rossini publizierte sie im Rahmen einer Studie über das aksumitische Münzwesen 1927, zur gleichen Zeit, als die Arbeit von Anzani erschien, die er im Folgejahr nicht gerade freundlich rezensierte. Daraufhin sah sich Anzani zu weiteren, durchaus seriösen Ausführungen veranlaßt, die im folgenden Band der *RIN* gedruckt wurden, allerdings mit einiger Verspätung. Darin konnte er zusätzliche Abbildungen zur Erstpublikation nachtragen und eine Reihe von neuaufgetauchten Stücken einarbeiten, insbesondere aus Privatsammlungen.

In den Folgejahren war Anzani bestrebt, Münzen und Informationen für die weitere Materialdokumentation zusammenzutragen, worüber seine Korrespondenz mit dem Lyonneser Sammler Claudius Cote Aufschluß gibt, die zusammen mit dessen Münzen zu guter Letzt im Pariser Münzkabinett gelandet ist (1960). Schließlich begann Anzani in der *RIN* 1941 eine als Artikelfolge geplante Reihe, die er *studi supplementari* nannte. Es ist sehr schade, daß davon nur 2 Teile erschienen sind, die über die heidnische Zeit nicht hinausgehen. Der 2. Weltkrieg ließ das Erscheinen der Zeitschrift ins Stocken geraten und Anzani verlor, krankheitsbedingt, die notwendige Arbeitsenergie. Als seine Sammlung 1955 von den Erben über den Schweizer Handel an Kaiser Haile Selassie verkauft wurde, zählte sie 207 Münzen, davon 23 in Gold und 30 in Silber. Die weiteren Schicksale dieser Sammlung sind obskur: da sie der Kaiser als Privatbesitz betrachtete, verschenkte er einige Stücke als Mitbringsel an den münzensammelnden König von Schweden, Gustav VI., der sie dem Stockholmer Museum überließ. Was noch vorhanden ist, sollte sich in dem kaum zugänglichen Palastmuseum von Addis Abeba befinden, doch ist dies kein allzu großer Schaden für die Forschung, denn die wichtigsten Teile der Sammlung Anzani sind in seinen Publikationen greifbar, die den Namen dieses sonst wenig beachteten und keines Nachrufs gewürdigten Münzliebhabers weiterleben lassen. Die eher unbedeutende Sammlung seines Widersachers Conti-Rossini ist in den Besitz der römischen Akademie der Luchse übergegangen.

Nach dem 2. Weltkrieg nahm das Materialaufkommen im Münzhandel sprunghaft zu. Dabei hatte der ursprünglich in Asmara ansässige Münz- und Briefmarkenhändler Francesco Vaccaro seine Hand im Spiel, sozusagen als Erstverteiler. Er belieferte Spezialsammler wie den schon erwähnten Claudius Cote mit seinen Angeboten direkt, anderes ließ er nach Italien in den Handel einfließen, wo es sich zunehmend in den gedruckten Verkaufslisten und Auktionskatalogen niederschlug. Italienische Rückwanderer aus Eritrea wie Giuseppe Tringalli haben weiteres Material mitgebracht und verkauft. Vaccaro hat einen kleinen Typenkatalog verfaßt und 1967 in Mantua zum Druck gebracht. Leider besteht der Verdacht, daß er auch mit den ab ca.1960 auftretenden modernen Münzfälschungen etwas zu tun gehabt hat, die nur z. T. mit den Anfängen des Kulturtourismus in der späten Haile-Selassie-Zeit zusammenhängen.

Daß in Italien noch immer kleinere und auch größere, aber aus diversen Gründen ungenannt bleibende Privatsammlungen existieren, wird aus gelegentlichen Veröffentlichungen deutlich: so konnte erst kürzlich eine recht umfangreiche Sammlung durch Luigi Pedroni in aufwendiger Weise publiziert werden (Pedroni 1997/98-2000: 7-147): sie umfaßt immerhin 408 Münzen, worunter nebst 11 Goldmünzen das Silber mit 156 Exemplaren ungewöhnlich stark vertreten ist. Auch im Zeitalter des Internets hat der Druck von Sammlungspublikationen in der antiken und in der mittelalterlichen Numismatik überall dort seine Berechtigung, wo die Materialerfassung noch keinen ausreichenden Sättigungsgrad erreicht hat, um eine verläßliche, alle zu erwartenden Typen und Varianten enthaltende, Monographie von längerfristigem Wert zu schreiben. Daher hat es auch schon vor Pedroni gedruckte Kataloge aksumitischer Münzsammlungen gegeben, wie den der Sammlung des bekannten Althistorikers Franz Altheim (1898-1976) mit 283 Münzen, davon 5 in Gold und 17 in Silber, bearbeitet von Reinhold Walburg, und dann die des Archäologen und Aksum-Spezialisten Stuart Munro-Hay mit 517 Münzen, davon 51 in Gold und 67 in Silber, natürlich von ihm selbst bearbeitet. Der allergrößte Teil dieser Sammlung (nach Abzweigung von Spitzenstücken) ist übrigens an die äthiopische Regierung verkauft worden und soll jetzt in der Nationalbank in Addis Abeba aufbewahrt werden, ist daher so gut wie unzugänglich und ein neuerliches Beispiel dafür, wie wichtig detaillierte Sammlungspublikationen sind.

Von den öffentlichen, d. h. großen Museumssammlungen liegt nur im Falle des Britischen Museums eine solche vor, und zwar ebenfalls aus der Hand von Munro-Hay;[2] hier ist zwar kein Verlust für die Forschung zu befürchten, aber dieser Katalog reiht sich in eine lange Publikationstradition des Hauses ein. Leider enthält der Band keine sammlungsgeschichtlichen Ausführungen, aber diese wurden in einem Artikel von Vincent West nachgeholt (West 2001: 28-32). Das Britische Museum hat derzeit die numerisch größte öffentliche Sammlung aksumitischer Münzen außerhalb Äthiopiens mit 620 Exemplaren, davon 107 in Silber, aber nur 28 in Gold. Mit Abstand folgen: das Museum der American Numismatic Society in New York mit 226 Exemplaren, davon nur 13 in Gold sowie 25 in Silber und die Bibliotheque Nationale in Paris, mit 34 Gold- und 27 Silbermünzen von insgesamt 123 Exemplaren relativ goldreich. In diese drei Museen sind – außer dem gelegentlichen Erwerb von Einzelstücken und Münzgruppen aus dem Handel – auch Komplexe von Privatsammlungen eingegangen. Eine solche Endlagerung wäre eigentlich für alle Privatsammlungen im Sinne der Forschung zu begrüßen, denn so wird die Zerstreuung der Schätze von ambitionierten und kenntnisreichen Spezialsammlern vermieden, die oft mehr Gelegenheiten zum Erwerb wahrnehmen konnten als die großen Museen, für die Aksum nur ein kleines Mosaiksteinchen ist. Die Existenz mehrerer namhafter privater Sammlungen

2   Munro-Hay 1999; Rezensionen: Juel-Jensen 1999: 182; Ricci 1999: 243-244; West 1999: 8; Hahn 2000: 215-217.

in England, Frankreich, Italien, Deutschland und den USA ist bekannt; wieviel davon apokryph bleibt, läßt sich freilich nicht wirklich abschätzen.

Nun noch zur wenig befriedigenden Situation in Äthiopien selbst. Außer an den beiden erwähnten Stellen werden aksumitische Münzen an zwei weiteren Institutionen in Addis Abeba gehortet. Das archäologische Nationalmuseum bewahrt die über 1500 Münzen der französischen Grabungen aus den 1950er und 1960er Jahren; ihre detaillierte Publikation ist überfällig und durch Eric Godet versprochen und, dem Vernehmen nach, demnächst auch endlich zu erwarten. Zu guter Letzt hat auch das Institut für Äthiopische Studien an der Universität Addis Abeba begonnen, aksumitische Münzen von dem in der Hauptstadt zusammenströmenden Antiquitätenmarkt zu erwerben. Das dort im Zunehmen begriffene Verständnis für die Bedeutung dieses kleinen Zweiges am Baum des historischen Kulturerbes ist immerhin positiv zu vermerken. Die Grabungsmünzen der jüngeren Kampagnen sind im kleinen Lokalmuseum von Aksum verblieben. Die Briten haben ihr Fundmaterial vorbildlich publiziert (Phillipson 2000); auch von den neuesten deutschen Ausgrabungen (Ziegert), ist dies zu erwarten.

Die offiziell, d. h. auf Grabungen gefundenen Münzen bilden freilich nur einen Bruchteil dessen, was aus dem Boden Aksums kommt und von der dortigen Bevölkerung aufgelesen wird. Das immer und überall festzustellende Phänomen, daß Goldmünzen nur selten auf Grabungen zum Vorschein kommen, schlägt auch hier, wo überhaupt nur eine Goldmünze jemals registriert wurde, zu Buche. Hortfunde von Goldmünzen kommen zumeist zerstreut in den Handel und lassen sich bei dessen Beobachtung am vermehrten Auftreten von Gruppen gleichartiger Münzen erahnen.[3] Auch der große Al Madhariba Fund aus dem Südjemen war ein Zufallsfund und dürfte mit seinen ins Museum von Aden gekommenen 868 aksumitischen Goldmünzen nicht vollständig erhalten sein, denn das Handelsvorkommen gleichartiger Exemplare ließ in den Folgejahren eine auffällige Belebung erkennen. Dieser Schatzfund ist jedenfalls ein Musterbeispiel für eine zufallsbedingte, starke Verzerrung der Zahlenstatistik. Er hat die Menge der damals bekannten aksumitischen Goldmünzen fast verdreifacht und das erklärt das Mißverhältnis zwischen den Zahlen der Gold- und Silbermünzen.

Wie umfangreich ist nun das aus der ca. 350 jährigen Münzprägung auf uns gekommene Material? Wenn man sich die Mühe macht, die Stückverzeichnisse in Munro-Hay's Buch von 1995 als Steinbruch auszuschlachten, kommt man zwar auf diverse Zahlen, aber sie sind mit Vorsicht zu genießen, denn die Autoren geben viele Nachweise, die sich auf Mehrfachbelege stückidentischer Exemplare zurückführen lassen, bedingt durch das Wandern des Materials im Handel. Am Institut für Numismatik und Geldgeschichte der Universität Wien, wo sehr viele Handelskataloge zusammenströmen, ist man seit über 25 Jahren bemüht, die numismatische Hinterlas-

---

3 Ein offenbar 1963/64 in Aksum entdeckter Schatzfund mit jedenfalls über 40 Goldmünzen der ältesten Prägeschicht (Endubis) ist ein derartiger Fall von Zerstreuung im Handel, vgl. Bourlier 1968: 67-70.

senschaft von Aksum zu dokumentieren. Kritisch gesichtet, beläuft sich die Anzahl der registrierten Goldmünzen zur Zeit auf etwa 1500, die der Silbermünzen auf etwa 1000. Die Zählung der Kupfermünzen ist vor allem wegen der unübersehbaren Masse der anonymen Münzen fast illusorisch. Sollte die von St. Wenig begonnene Prospektierung in Eritrea jeweils zu einer systematischen Grabungstätigkeit führen, ist mit einem Explodieren dieser Zahlen zu rechnen. Bei diesen Größenordnungen dürfen wir jedoch den Blick für die Relationen nicht verlieren: verglichen mit den Mengen der gleichzeitigen Münzproduktion des römischen Reiches war Aksum ein Leichtgewicht.

Abkürzungen

RSE   Rassegna di Studi Etiopici
Num.Circ.   Spink's Numismatic Circular
BIEA   British Institute in Eastern Africa
RIN   Rivista Italiana di Numismatica

Bibliographie

Bourlier, P.
1968   Numismatique axoumite. *Collectioneurs et collections numismatiques (Catalogue d'exposition, Hotel de la monnaie)*. Paris: 67-70.

Hahn, W.
2000   Rezension von S. Munro-Hay: Catalogue of the Aksumite Coins in the British Museum. *Aethiopica 3:* 215-217.

Juel-Jensen, B.
1999   Rezension von S. Munro-Hay: Catalogue of the Aksumite Coins in the British Museum. *Num.Circ. 107:* 182.

Luegmeyer, A.
1998   Rezension von S. Munro-Hay und B. Juel-Jensen: Aksumite Coinage. *Aethiopica 1:* 250-259.

Munro-Hay, S.
1999   *Catalogue of the Aksumite Coins in the British Museum*. London.

Munro-Hay, S. und Juel-Jensen, B.
1995   *Aksumite Coinage.* London.

Pedroni, L.
1997/98 Una collezione di monete aksumite. *Boll. di Numismatica 28/29:* 7-147.
-2000

Phillipson, D. W.
2000   Archeology at Aksum 1993-97. *BIEA Memoir 17,* London.

Ricci, L.
1999   Rezension von S. Munro-Hay: Catalogue of the Aksumite Coins in the British
        Museum. *RSE 93:* 243-244.

West, V.
1999a   Rezension von S. Munro-Hay: Catalogue of the Aksumite Coins in the British
        Museum. *Orient. Num. Soc. Newsletter 160:* 8.
1999b   Rezension von S. Munro-Hay und B. Juel-Jensen: Aksumite Coinage. *Orient.
        Num. Soc. Newsletter 159:* 5-6.
2001   The early history of the British Museum collection of Aksumite coins. *Orient.
        Num. Soc. Newsletter 167:* 28-32.

Unexplored Aksumite Sites in Tigray[1]

Paul B. Henze

Tigray is rich in evidence of Aksumite occupation and activity. The purpose of this essay is to provide a description of several kinds of sites I have visited which appear to merit serious archaeological investigation. It is no more than a modest contribution to the process of cataloguing Aksumite remains in northern Ethiopia, for this is a very broad subject. Work on Aksumite civilization began in earnest with the discoveries of the great German archaeologist Enno Littmann in the first years of the 20th century. It has been under way for almost of a century, but has been intermittently interrupted by periods of political uncertainty and military activity. Prospects for systematic surveys which will identify more sites seem good at the present time. Ethiopia has barely reached the level of elementary exploration that major Middle Eastern areas already enjoyed by the mid-19th century. Concentration on the important sites in and around Aksum itself has tended, unavoidably, to draw attention away from other archaeologically rewarding areas.

In visiting large churches in Tigray in recent years my attention has often been called to crypts and tombs of apparent Aksumite origin by the priests. The fact that churches have been built over such sites shows how a sense of holiness has persisted since very ancient times, possibly the pre-Aksumite period. Other sites, where tombs appear to be absent, reveal beautifully cut and laid foundations of a type that are first found in Ethiopia at Yeha (7th century BC) (Fig. 1), which seem to have continued to be laid during the entire Aksumite period and perhaps during later times. One of the most striking examples is the Church of *Maryam Tehot*[2] in southern Agame (Fig. 2).

Though I have visited the site at least four times since 1991, I found priests on only one occasion to let me inside. They did not call attention to a crypt under the main section of the church, but one may exist. Several cut blocks that display Aksumite affinities lie around the churchyard. At the NE corner of the church a large rectangular cut slab is standing (Fig. 3). On a visit in the early 1990s I observed large pot fragments that had been dug from graves in an extensive cemetery area east of the

---

1 Note: This essay is a condensation of a presentation made in Munich in early May 2002 at a conference dedicated to Ethiopian archaeology and history. It was dedicated to the memory of Enno Littmann and attended by approximately 175 scholars, historians and friends of Ethiopia at the Munich Ethnographic Museum.
2 This church is located in a euphorbia grove on the right side of the main highway between Senkata and Edaga Hamus. The modern church was probably built, or rebuilt, within the last century or two, but the whole site, not only the foundations, is rich in evidence of Aksumite remains.

church. The area was too overgrown with weeds and brush on my most recent visit to examine it carefully again.

At a number of other Tigrayan churches I have been shown crypts/tombs cut deep into the rock below. The quality of the rock-cutting is high. These include *Kerneseber Mikael*, a few miles north of Adigrat (Fig. 4), *Arbatu Insesa* in Aksum itself, *Hauzien Tekle Haymanot* and *Degum Selassie* at the east end of the Geralta massif.

The last-named is particularly interesting because it was newly built only in the early 1990s over the most southerly of a group of three carefully cut Aksumite tombs. Its *maqdas* extends into an upstanding rock behind the church. A crypt beneath the floor of the *maqdas* extends deep downward. The whole region appears to have been an area of Aksumite activity. Three Aksumite stelae stand in the center of Hauzien's marketplace (Fig. 5). Hauzien was the site of an unprovoked Derg bomb attack on a busy market day in the 1980s in which hundreds of people were killed. For many years a large unexploded bomb lay beside the stelae in the market place but has recently been removed and the stelae surrounded by a low wall. A tall stela has recently been constructed as a memorial at the north end of the town.

Rising to an average height of more than 2,500 m well to the east side of the main north-south highway is the plateau of Atsbi with the town of Atsbi situated somewhat to the north of the center. This gently rolling plateau is punctuated by rock outcroppings ideal for cutting churches or building forts (Fig. 6). It averages perhaps 25 km in width and extends at least 40 km in a north-south direction and continues northward into a region called Atsbidera. Evidence is good, I believe, that the Atsbi plateau must have been a major area of Aksumite settlement. At several locations relatively small stelae (up to 2 m) remain standing.

The entire plateau is laced with old tracks, some of which lead downward to the coastal desert region of Arho from where salt has been brought up to the plateau since very ancient times. The landscape shows signs of long cultivation. Most naturally occurring trees were cut long ago but have been in part replaced during the past century by eucalyptus. At many of the highest parts of the region, however, often in the neighborhood of churches, cedars continue to grow, many quite luxuriantly. Churches carved into the rock are frequent throughout the region. They include well-known hilltop sanctuaries: *Mikael Amba* and *Mikael Barka*, beautiful cliff sites such as *Debre Selam Mikael* and *Cherqos Agobo*, as well as very old stone-built churches crowning gently rising hills such as *Zarema Giyorgis*.

Determining the age of rock churches is one of the most challenging tasks in Ethiopian archaeology. To judge by the elaborateness and quality of the rock carving, *Mikael Amba* and *Mikael Barka* appear to be of the 14th century, carved probably at the same time as the major churches of Tsada Amba and the Tembien. *Debre Selam Mikael* may be earlier, though it has also been judged rather late – 14th century – by David Buxton (1947: 76-77). It nevertheless displays a great many distinctively Aksumite features (Fig. 9). To me the most interesting church I have come across in this region is *Cherqos Agobo*. It is a small church built primarily of flat rocks, carefully laid and reinforced with wooden beams. It is located on a ledge on a steep cliff and nestles under an overhang that protects it from all but the most inclement weather. It has features which link it to the oldest Aksumite building in Ethiopia: the church on Debre Damo (Figs. 7 and 8).

It must have been built at a time when wood was plentiful. The inner structure is entirely of wood with the same features that are duplicated in cut stone in later churches.[3] To me this church displays most of the features one would imagine a very early Aksumite church to have. Are there other Aksumite remains in the vicinity? I cannot say. Two visits during the same day last November brought no evidence of habitations or foundations in the area, but there was no time to examine the surroundings of the church in detail. Careful examination of the area might well bring noteworthy features to light.

Though after long palaver with clergy and elders we were refused entry into *Zarema Giyorgis*, the site is intriguing and merits further study. Here a very early church with Aksumite features has been encompassed within a new stone church built only three years ago.

Mrs. Ruth Plant visited this church in the 1970s and Ato Kebede Amare, Cultural and Tourism Commissioner of Tigray, examined it in 1999 when the new church which now surrounds it was being constructed. The main features of the original church were described by Mrs. Plant:

> This is a freestanding built church, the only one known at the present time... The original entrance is placed centrally through an Aksumite door leading ... to a semi-circular space ... with a band of Aksumite detail at head height, built in wood. The roof is of displaced wooden trusses resting on wooden decorated capitals. Flat beams run west-east, supported by chamfered stone Aksumite columns and an Aksumite frieze. There is also Aksumite detail in wood around the ... apse of the sanctuary. There is a wooden screen before the Sanctuary arch. The roofs, mainly flat over the side aisles, are constructed so that they form patterns, whilst that to the room to the left of the Sanctuary is a wooden lantern roof ... – Here is seen for the very first time a complete church, including the roof trusses, which one also comes across in rare occasions in rock work ... This church [dates] some time between Debre Damo and many of the rock-cut examples (Plant 1985: 120-122).

One of the most curious features of this churchyard is an area of exposed rock to the northwest of the inner yard where great numbers of large round holes have been drilled into surface rock to a depth of half a meter (Fig. 10). I have never come across another example of this kind of cutting anywhere in Ethiopia. No one there could explain the purpose of the holes. They were obviously cut long ago.

Two other sites I have visited in the last two years appear to me to merit attention: *Menebeiti/Chimara* and *Mai Adrasha* (Figs. 11, 12 and 13). My attention was drawn to

---

3 The inner sections of Debre Selam, for example, duplicate most of the features of *Cherqos Agobo* in stone cut from the living rock.

the first of these when I was returning in December 2000 from a visit to Zalambessa, accompanied by Ato Kebede Amare. He led us about 3 km east of the main highway into a valley on the north side of Emba Fasi. We arrived at an immense pile of cut stones not far from a country church, a Tekle Haymanot. The stones, of well cut hard granite, appeared to have belonged to a large building which had collapsed long ago. Brush and vines were growing among them. Many had distinct Aksumite designs. Villagers told us that they had originally hoped to build their new church of the old ones, but had been unable to do so.

Another kilometer or two farther up a gentle slope brought us to a still used rectangular church standing under sparse trees where our attention was directed to more Aksumite stones lying on and in the ground around the church. The site was called *Chimara*. Local people told us there was a tomb inside the simply built rectangular church but no priest could be found to let us in. The entire area appears worth examining carefully.

Mai Adrasha is the most exciting site of all I have seen in recent years (Fig. 14). It is an enormous area of heaps of rocks in fields a few hundred meters south of the main highway to Aksum about 4 km east of Enda Selassie, the capital of Shire. At the Shire branch of the Tigray Cultural office I was introduced to two young archaeologists engaged in a surface survey of western Tigray, Niall Finneran from SOAS in London and Chester Cain, an American now at the University of Witwatersrand in South Africa. With the help of two recent history graduates from Addis Ababa University, they had just surveyed the Mai Adrasha site and drawn a map of it to scale.[4] They urged my party, on return from the Monastery of Debre Abbay, to stop at May Adrasha on the way back to Aksum, which we did. The site is as extensive as a large Middle Eastern mound. It was recently discovered to be the scene of digging by local peasants seeking gold and other coins for sale in Aksum. They also find pottery. During the rainy season, when they cannot work in their fields, as many as 200 people have been observed there digging. A stream flows past the foot of the site. Local people take earth there for panning.

We examined the site in some detail. In many places the peasants had dug holes to a depth of 3-4 meters. Some of these have exposed well built walls, flat slabs, many kinds of cut stones. These, of course, do not interest the local diggers.

The Tigray Cultural and Information Bureau has had the site declared off-limits to local diggers and was attempting to arrange a guard. When I returned to Addis Ababa a few days later I found that the discovery of Mai Adrasha was being publicized in newspapers. Finneran told me that he was hoping to get permission and funds to excavate there systematically, for finds already exposed by illicit digging have included pottery that appears to date from very early pre-Aksumite times as well as quantities of mostly pre-Christian coins. He believes the site may be a significant satellite settlement of Aksum itself.

---

4   Both had worked with David Phillipson's group at Aksum a few years before.

Evidence of Aksumite activity is scattered everywhere in Tigray. Local people seem to have a particular regard for inscribed stones. They are often kept in church treasuries. I have been shown good examples in the treasury of the church beside the great temple at Yeha and in the treasury of the church of Abba Pantelewon on the eastern edge of Aksum.

We are likely to be only at the beginning of a period of discovery of a great number of new Aksumite sites not only in Tigray but farther south as well. Kebede Amare has recently reported a site south of Lake Ashangi in southern Tigray:

A preliminary test excavation took place between 8 and 15 June 2001. The research was conducted by a team of Ethiopian archaeologists from ARCCH and a sociologist from the Department of Culture, Tourism and Information of the Southern Zone [of Tigray]. The site is called Mifisas Bahri. Test excavations were made at three different locations. An area of 1x7 m. was excavated on the north side. At the depth of 80 cm. three cemeteries were noted. On the southern side another area was excavated and buildings of two periods were exposed. One is a church built of red limestone with huge, well-carved pillars and crosses. 2.5 m. beneath this structure an older building was identified. Burnt remnants of crops – apparently *dagusa* – were found. Cattle bones and well-decorated Aksumite pottery, charcoal and bricks were found. The topography of the area indicates that other buildings may be found.

In the last few years French excavations in Manz in the process of publication have proved rich in Aksumite material. I would not be surprised if Aksumite finds are made in future years in Gojjam and Wollega.

Bibliography

Buxton, D. R.
1947   The Rock-hewn and other Medieval Churches of Tigre Province, Ethiopia. *Archaeologia CIII: 76-77*, Oxford.

Plant, R.
1985   *Architecture of the Tigre, Ethiopia.* Ravens Educational and Development Services. Worcester (UK).

Fig. 1   Foundations of Yeha Temple.

Fig. 2   Aksumite Foundations at Maryam Tehot.

Fig. 3   Aksumite Slab at Maryam Tehot.

Fig. 4   Kerneseber Mikael is built over Aksumite tombs.

Fig. 5   Stelae in Hauzien Marketplace.

Fig. 6   Landscape in Atsbi.

Fig. 7   Agobo Cherqos, North face.

Fig. 8   Agobo Cherqos, Aksumite construction.

Fig. 9   Debre Selam, Aksumite building structure.

Fig. 10   Round holes in rocks at Zarema.

Fig. 11   Aksumite ruin at Menebeiti, Agame.

Fig. 12   Broken Aksumite pillars at Menebeiti.

Fig. 13   Aksumite carred stone at Menebeiti, Agame.

Fig. 14   Mai Adrasha, illicit digging in the rocky mound.

"Go West, Young Man, Go West!"

Jacke Phillips

Enno Littman and his team ventured far inland of the Red Sea coast in their 1906 exploration of northern Ethiopia. They stopped occasionally on their way to record a number of smaller sites, before arriving at Aksum to conduct the majority of their multi-facetted archaeological and ethnographic fieldwork. They went no farther westwards than the immediate vicinity of the town. Much fieldwork has since been conducted in the area of Eritrea and northern Ethiopia, chiefly at sites investigated and first published in any detail by the *Deutsche Aksum-Expedition*. The DAE remains a fundamentally important reference for subsequent Ethiopian studies. However, surprisingly little fieldwork has been attempted farther west of Aksum, and the archaeology of this region remains very little known.

The city of Aksum itself has long been known as the capital of an extensive empire that, in its heyday during the 3rd through 6th c. AD, controlled both sides of the southern Red Sea and therefore the entire East-West sea trade. Our earliest record of its existence is the *Periplus of the Erythraean Sea*, the c. 40 AD mercantile handbook that mentions 'την μητροπολιν τον 'Αξωμιτην' ('the metropolis of the Axomites'). The *Periplus* goes on to comment that 'into it is brought all the ivory from beyond the Nile through what is called Kyeneion (Κυηνειον, west of the Blue Nile south of Khartoum), and from there down to Adulis' (4:2: 8-10).

Indeed, a rich quantity of exotic resources is found west of Askum, and these too would have been brought through here to the Red Sea coast. The recent BIEA excavations at Aksum itself (Phillipson et al. 2000; see also Phillips 1998) have highlighted the extensive quantity of ivory, both raw and elaborately carved by Aksumite artisans, as well as the imported and locally-produced glassware, and pottery imported from all directions that was found there, as well as clear evidence for impressive and permanent habitation at Aksum as early as perhaps even the 8th c. BC. Aksum, the city, was the heart of the Aksumite empire that extended as far as Yemen across the Red Sea and at least to the Bab el-Mandab, that subdued the various nomadic peoples of the desert and highlands east of the Nile river, and apparently provided the final blow to the dying Meroitic civilisation. One Aksumite king 'had a road constructed from the lands of my empire to Egypt' in order to maintain access through his lands to those of his neighbours west and north (Munro-Hay 1991: 222-223; Eide et al. 1998: #234).

Aksum itself appears on maps as virtually *the* westernmost site of Aksumite influence. The modern district of Shire in north-west Ethiopia, west of Aksum, and some 140 by 200 km in extent, remains very little investigated archaeologically and very little known (Godet 1977: 35, 45, 55; Tekle 1997: 25, 27-28). As the *Periplus* quotation, the road leading to Egypt made some 300 years later and the recent BIEA excavations all make clear, however, it was of considerable importance in ancient times for the transmission of exotic goods from inner Africa to the Red Sea coast.

This importance can be shown for all millennia from Neolithic times, as I have described elsewhere (Phillips 1997; 2003). And that physically the most logical and logistically simplest route immediately west of Askum is directly through the middle of the Shire district – an east-west land corridor like the well-studied north-south water-based corridors of the Nile and the Red Sea.

A short pilot season to test the feasibility of a proposed survey was conducted in November 2001, in order to assess the archaeological potential of the Shire district (Fig. 1). The Shire District Survey Project was supported financially by the British Institute in Eastern Africa and the Society of Antiquaries of London, as a joint project with the Authority for Research and Conservation of the Cultural Heritage in Ethiopia, and under its permit as the 'Shire District Survey Project.' Fieldwork combined both ethnographic and archaeological elements within its remit, to see which of the proposed study avenues were suited to the region and were likely to produce workable data. Its results have confirmed the importance of the Shire district and already have begun to shed light on the relationship of Shire both east to Aksum and beyond to the Red Sea, and west towards the Nile Valley.

The survey ran for a period of only three weeks, in collaboration with Ethiopian ARCCH archaeologists Tekle Hagos and Asamerew Dessie. It had several interrelated agendas. Niall Finneran concentrated on the identification and recording of new prehistoric and historic sites, in order to develop a Sites and Monuments Record for the area, a region where only six archaeological sites had previously been recorded (Finneran 2003). Chet Cain and Michael Harlow began to document the crop and land use patterns and agricultural practices of the region, with a view to comparing these with evidence both for earlier practices as they are recognised in future seasons, and for practices farther west as the highlands descend to the eastern lowlands of the Sudan. And my interest in the area centres on Shire's relationships with its neighbours, especially to the east and west. Initial analyses by all team members form the basis of this very preliminary report.

The survey was based in the region's administrative town of Endasellassie, about 50 miles and two hour's drive west of Aksum. The immediately surrounding region is the beginning of the descent to the lowlands of the eastern desert of the Sudan and already is some 1000 m lower in altitude than Aksum. The large flat plain southwards is cut by the steep gorge of the Tekezze River, whilst immediately to the north are steep escarpments with smaller plains beyond, cut by other gorges that feed into the Gash River. The Aksum-Gondar tarmac road turns southwards at the town.

The team concentrated in the areas immediately surrounding the few already known sites, most importantly the Aksumite sites of Mai Adrasha and Semema/Heritay and the MSA site of Mai Mesanu. These sites all are unpublished as yet, and were shown to us in 1995 and 1997 by our late friend and colleague Ato Gebre Kidan Wolde Hawariat of the Tigray Bureau of Culture, Tourism and Information regional office at Endasellasie. Ato Gebre Kidan was instrumental in the development of our survey project but sadly he died in 2001, before actual fieldwork could begin. A further site concentration was investigated at Mai Hine, where Ato Asamerew had noted an MSA site near the roadside. The survey developed outwards as further sites were located. Each site, its identifiable surface remains and its immediate landscape were described, recorded and, when possible, dated. Global Positioning System (GPS) readings, accurate to an 8-meter radius, were taken to locate sites accurately on the detailed 1:50,000 maps supplied by the Ethiopian Mapping Authority.

The ultimate goal of this aspect of the survey, planned from the beginning, is to develop a Sites and Monuments Register (SMR) for the use of the Ethiopian authorities. Our model is the SMR developed for the UK, where individual numbered sites are located on large-scale maps and are cross-referenced with detailed data sheets giving an outline of site description and risk assessment. The register – which will ultimately reside at the district Bureau office – is designed to be easily used, simple to consult and self-sustaining in terms of adding new information. Specially translated forms for the SMR in Tigrinya are now being constructed to serve this purpose for the Shire authorities. Apart from providing the most complete possible dossier of archaeological sites in the region – a useful tool for scholars – the register may also be consulted by building developers before commencing work, and judgements may then be made on the potential archaeological sensitivity of a given area before construction or enlargement of future buildings or alternate land use begins.

The team identified some 25 new sites in the short field time available. For those interested in statistics these are 1 ESA, 3 MSA, 14 LSA, 2 MSA/LSA, 4 Aksumite, and 1 Mediaeval/Recent, in addition to the 1 MSA, 1 MSA/LSA and 4 Aksumite sites already known. The comparative lack of Mediaeval and recent sites reported is due to the fact that many are still occupied and in use today. Many churches, for example, have been in the same location for centuries. Ato Tekle and Ato Asamerew also had noted a number of sites during a war-damage survey; these are not included in the statistics just quoted.

Potentially the most important site so far recorded is Mai Adrasha, a large settlement and cemetery site first identified by Ato Gebre Kidan on either side of the main road, dating from late Pre-Aksumite to Post-Aksumite times, at least a millennium, according to its surface ceramics.[1] Unfortunately, the site recently has been the focus of considerable illicit excavation – not for antiquities or artefacts but for gold, the natural kind. Local families have been potholing the area for the past few years, and panning the soil for gold in the nearby stream. In doing so, they have destroyed or contaminated at least 40 percent of the site, as they exposed and tossed aside artefacts in order to collect the soil for panning (Fig. 2). The local authorities and the survey team together have managed to suspend this practice, simply by passing on by word

---

1　Readers should be aware that Paul Henze's conference paper, 'Unexplored Aksumite Sites in Tigray,' includes several significant factual errors in his discussion of the Mai Adrasha site, based on his visit to the region during the pilot season in November 2001. Unfortunately, hard copies of this paper were distributed at the Littmann conference itself, and thus are in circulation. Reference to the Mai Adrasha site in this paper should not be cited.

of mouth that this is an archaeological site now under the protection of the authorities and that it should not be interfered with. Those caught 'in the act' were informed, although no one was arrested, but the word now has gone out in the region and so far seems to have had the desired effect. Eventually, however, the site will need monitoring and physical protection. Finds from this site, now held by the Endasellasie authorities, include clay vessels, figurines and seals (some of the last inscribed in Ge'ez), stone, bronze and iron tools, bronze jewellery, silver and bronze Aksumite coins (one gilded), glass vessel fragments and beads in several colours, even a small silver nail and some imported goods.

In tandem with the site survey, the beginnings of an ethno-archaeological study and of modern agricultural practices were conducted in the region. Elderly inhabitants of two quite separated villages utilising different quality soils were interviewed to ascertain their present and past agricultural practices, and the reasons for these changes. In both cases, the pastureland is of good quality but insufficient for the number of sheep, goat and cattle raised by the village, and for part of the year they are moved farther away to hotter lowlands near the Tekezze River. The quality of available cropland differs between the two villages, one being of noticeably poorer lithosolic soil than the other. Nonetheless, in both cases a variety of mostly indigenous crops are grown, but the Near Eastern grains (barley and emmer wheat) are conspicuously lacking or uncommon (Fig. 3).

One landowner also keeps bees for honey, to be sold in the local market, and his wife produces specialised *injera* stove lids, also for sale. Pottery production is strictly limited to women. The market supplies 'urban' products for the villagers, such as clothes, cookers and metal goods, as well as spices and staple foods not locally grown. Much of this has not changed substantially in living memory, with the exception of available 'urban' products and the changes and collectivisation instituted under the Derg.

Land ownership was redefined after the Derg, and now is controlled by the local government and a local committee, but broadly speaking along similar pre-Derg lines. The crops themselves appear still to be chiefly older non-hybridised varieties, although the government at all levels is encouraging farmers to use modern types.

Similar interviews were conducted with elderly monks at several churches in the region, who filled in details of the rise and fall in circumstances of their institution. As a result, a history of the immediate region has begun to emerge in relation to the wider history of Ethiopia and its rulers.

These preliminary data are still being studied for further insights and publication elsewhere, and I shall concentrate on the period and area of my interest for this paper. The extent of the Aksumite culture and its empire has never been drawn on any map, but certainly extends west into our survey area from as early as the Proto-Aksumite period, in the last centuries BC and the first AD, in other words for the few centuries before until roughly the time of the *Periplus*. The region's importance during Aksumite times, and strong evidence for the continuity of sanctified places in the region, is indicated by the church of Weybla Mariam. It is built directly upon a stepped probably Aksumite podium. It is much smaller in scale but otherwise related to the Aksumite podium upon which the cathedral of Mariam Tsion (the Ethiopian parallel for the Vatican to Catholics) was constructed sometime before the 9th century. The monks here have found numerous Aksumite coins within the church compound, and the large Aksumite cemetery site of Heritay excavated by Gebre Kidan in 1994 is just nearby.

They also have and still use a number of church antiquities, some of which also are related to Aksumite material. The Askumite use of stelae as grave markers also extends into Shire, for such stelae have been found at six of our recorded Aksumite sites. Some are displaced or in re-use in church compounds, but others are associated with Aksumite graves. These were excavated by a bulldozer widening the main road east of Endasellasie.

A total of 25 surface collections were made, mostly of lithics but the Aksumite and Mediaeval sites are dated ceramically. These collections, and the sites from which they came, clearly indicate that the Aksumite cultural sphere extended farther west than Aksum for some distance and in some quantity. Some new elements are included in the ceramic design and shape repertoire, that possibly are a regional distinction, but further data is required before this can be demonstrated. As an example, the majority of shapes and surface decoration are comparable between material from the Shire region and those from Aksum and farther east. Nonetheless, Early Aksumite closed vessels from the cemetery at Heritay, north-east of Endasellassie, recovered by Gebre Kidan, display a depressed body distinctly lacking in those of similar date from Aksum and elsewhere. Evidence for relations in other directions is not as clear, especially since the material remains of the regions north, west and south of Shire are little documented. Sites farther west must be located and their characteristics need to be recorded to trace the westward decrease of the Aksumite tradition, and the corresponding increase in traditions from other directions.

This simply is due to a lack of survey and excavation in these regions, not to mention publication of the little work that *has* been done – virtually nothing is known about the areas immediately north, west and south of Shire, as well as of Shire itself. With luck, the situation will change in the next few years.

Bibliography

Eide, T., Hägg, T., Pierce, R. H. and L. Török (eds.)
1998 *Fontes Historiae Nubiorum III.* Bergen.

Finneran, N.
2003 Defining the Shire archaeological landscape, Ethiopia: towards a practicable Sites and Monuments Register. In: *Mitchell, P. J., Haour, A. and Hobart, J. H. (eds.): Researching Africa's Past: New contributions for British archaeologists.* Oxford School of Archaeology. Oxford: 140-146.

Godet, E.
1977 Répertoire de sites pré-Axoumites et Axoumites du Tigré (Éthiopie). *Documents pour servir a l'Histoire des Civilisations Ethiopiennes (=Abbay)* 8: 19-58.

Munro-Hay, S. C.
1991 *Aksum: An African Civilization of Late Antiquity.* Edinburgh.

Phillips, J. S.
1997 Punt and Aksum: Egypt and the Horn of Africa. *Journal of African History 38:* 423-457.
1998 Aksum and the Ivory Trade: New Evidence. In: *Äthiopien und seine Nachbarn/ Ethiopia and its Neighbours. 3. Wissenschaftliche Tagung des Orbis Aethiopicus, Gniew 25-27 September 1997,* Orbis Aethiopicus. Frankfurt: 75-84.
2003 Egypt, Nubia and Ethiopia. In: *Z. Hawas (ed): Egypt at the Dawn of the Twenty-First Century: Proceedings of the Eighth International Congress of Egyptology, Cairo, 2000 II History and Religion.* American University in Cairo Press. Cairo: 434-442.

Phillipson, D. W. et al.
2000 *Archaeology at Aksum, Ethiopia, 1993-7.* British Institute in Eastern Africa Memoir 17/Society of Antiquaries of London Report 65. London.

Tekle Hagos
1997 *Aksumite Sites in Tigray (Ethiopia): The Significance of their Distribution.* M.Phil. diss., University of Cambridge.

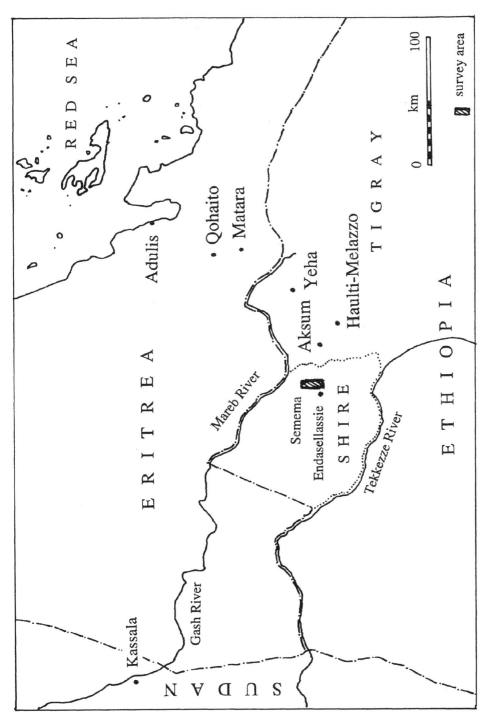

Fig. 1   Map indicating the location of the Shire District.

Fig. 2   Mai Adrasha, hole dug out by local
inhabitants between ancient walls.

Fig. 3   Compound at ethno-archaeological interview site.

The Archaeological Sites of Adulis and Metara

Rezene Russom

Eritrea as a small East African Nation is the last country to gain its independence from a successive colonial domination. Rich as it is in ancient history and archaeology no significant scientific research has ever been made to unveil the mystery of the ancient civilization of the people and the land. The purpose of my paper at this juncture is therefore, to point out some interesting facts on the archaeological sites of Adulis and Metara. Adulis as a major trading centre and gateway to the external world was a famous port in the whole Red Sea region. This port played a major role in the commercial activities with the ancient Romans, Greeks and Sassanian Persia and hence extremely precious items were exchanged between the partners. Test excavations had been conducted by the British some time in the 1870's and later by the Italians.

Metara

Metara as huge urban site on the main line to the ancient kingdom of Axum was largely the bread basket to the growth and expansion of the economic and political power of the city state. The unscientific excavations conducted by the joint French and Ethiopian archaeological mission in the late 1960's has greatly damaged the site, and yet we know nothing of the whereabouts of the most objects recovered from there. The epigraphic inscriptions that we see on the stela in Metara tell us a significant story about the political life of the people with their neighbours. Littmann's interpretation on the writings is highly important in regard to it. However, the recent destruction of this precious and irreplaceable artifact by irresponsible invaders is something by mere disappearance of which we can loudly announce the demolition of of a part of human history.

II. The History of the Horn of Africa

Philology and the Reconstruction of the Ethiopian Past[1]

Gianfrancesco Lusini

The article by Carlo Conti Rossini, *Appunti ed osservazioni sui re Zāguē e Takla Hāymānot*, published more than one hundred years ago (Conti Rossini 1895), can be rightly regarded as the first example of a systematic application of the philological method to the reconstruction of the Ethiopian past. In that essay the comparative presentation of the sources, accompanied by their scrupulous criticism, allowed the Italian scholar to determine some crucial dates of the medieval Ethiopian history. The analysis of the literary traditions had a twofold result: on the one hand, the reconstruction of the events which brought about the consolidation of the Zāg\ʷē dynasty (1137); on the other, the refutation of the narrative about the so-called Solomonic "reestablishment" (1270), for centuries imposed as the "true story" by the ecclesiastic milieu of Dabra Libānos of Šawā. In the first case, he clearly showed that the exploitation of the literary sources in Ge'ez could balance the deficiencies of the Arabic chronicles, by offering to the scholarly attention previously underestimated Ethiopic documents. Borrowing an expression from the text criticism one could apply here the motto *recentiores, non deteriores*, or, in other words: a later source is not inevitably less valid. In the second case, the contents of these traditions proved to be acceptable as a basis for further research only after a preliminary examination and comparison of the sources, in order to separate the documentary core from the later narrative inventions. This positivistic methodology presented in the 1895 essay was later improved by the same Conti Rossini,[2] chiefly thanks to the experience of his stay in Eritrea (1899-1903).[3] Yet, the premises were given, namely the necessity to regard Ethiopic literary traditions always as texts for political and religious propaganda, though sometimes built up by using sources and pieces of information useful to the modern historiographical purposes. Other components of this scientific work – namely, comparative linguistics, epigraphy or paleography – were involved in the general definition of philology as the historical science aimed at the criticism of the sources.

---

1 This paper was written during a semester spent at the University of Hamburg (October 2001 - March 2002), funded by the "Alexander von Humboldt-Stiftung", under the direction of Prof. Siegbert Uhlig, to whom I like to express my gratitude.
2 See, for instance, the second essay on the fall of the Zāg\ʷē dynasty: Conti Rossini 1922.
3 Scanty material for the intellectual biography of the Italian scholar can be found in a few articles by Lanfranco Ricci (1971-72; 1982; 1987; cp. 1986: 160-162). See also the documented commemorations by Enrico Cerulli (1949) and Martino Moreno (1950).

After more than a century of research, the methodological sensitiveness of the scholars in the field of Ethiopian studies is augmented. Today, the XIXth century meaning of philology necessarily includes text criticism: the importance of this exercise for the scientific reconstruction of the literary texts in Ge'ez, rather underestimated in the years of Conti Rossini, is now obvious.[4] Progressively, "young" disciplines like codicology and diplomatics (Lusini 1998: 5-16) are contributing to the knowledge of the ways how the written learning was passed over in Ethiopia since the Antiquity till nowadays. In the sphere of these developments the exploitation of the Ethiopic texts for the historiographical research never failed. Rather, today the need to take into account all the chances given by the constellation of disciplines composing the philology *lato sensu* – namely the criticism of the sources starting from their material consistency up to the analysis of their ideological construction – has become stronger than ever. Today, I want to present one more example of application of this approach to a highly meaningful episode of the Ethiopian history: the foundation of the cathedral in Aksum, taken in its relationships with the contemporary political frame. Particularly, I will examine the sources in order to verify the hypothesis that in these events a role was played by the king Kālēb/Ella Aṣbeḥā and to determine which consequences this initiative had in the formation of the ideology and the symbolics of the Ethiopian kingship.

* * *

The Ge'ez hagiographic traditions commemorating the first steps of the Christian mission into the Kingdom of Aksum still present a serious dilemma to the scholars. For a long period the value of the medieval lucubrations around Libānos, the *Ṣādqān* and the "Nine Saints" as historical sources has been substantially admitted. Recently, a considerable scepticism has made its way (Marrassini 1981: 197 and 203; 1999a: 159), due to the big chronological distance between the years when such homiletic-hagiographic texts were written (XIVth-XVth c.) and the age they assume to refer to (V[th]-VIIth c.): the matter, which – to tell the truth – has been known to the scholars since the very beginning (Conti Rossini 1928: 161). Moreover, the fact that the first generation of interpreters falsely reconstructed unlikely "Syriac" influences upon the first phase of the history of Ethiopian Christianity, relying mostly upon these Ge'ez traditions, contributed to the reappraisal of their value (Marrassini 1990; 1999b), as if the sources were partially responsible for the misinterpretation. That things are not exactly so can be easily proved. One can not leave out, for instance, the existence of archaeological confirmations to certain traditions, as a clear sign that such narratives must have a historical ground. Let's take, for instance, the *Gadla Libānos*, in which it is told that king Gabra Masqal's wife founded a church in Faqādā (Conti Rossini 1903:

---

4   Except a few isolated resistances of cultural and personal character, like those exhibited in
     Ricci 1997. For a survey see Marrassini 1987.

32): near the actual Foqādā, in Dahānē ('Agāmē)[5] among ruins of important buildings, the remnants of an Aksumite church stand out.[6] Sometimes the possibility has been alleged that certain traditions were invented to justify the presence of archaeological ruins appearing mysteriously to the eyes of the local people, as the result of the impression they made on the "naïve" Ethiopian minds. This kind of explanations treats the written sources like the oral traditions, which different communities elaborated in order to interpret the presence on their territory of ancient ruins of undetermined past ages.[7] Though this can sometimes be true, yet in our case other elements should be also taken into account.

First, the supposed *a posteriori* attribution of certain ruins to the age of the Aksumite saints requires in any case the existence of the traditions related to the missionaries coming from *Rom*, i.e. the Byzantine Empire. In other words, the problem is simply postponed, and the origins of the legend, recorded by many sources dating back to different times, would continue to ask for an explanation. Second, in Ethiopia there exists an unbroken tradition of recording historical memories, gathered and written down inside churches and monasteries (Lusini 2001a). It is on this cultural chain that the perception of the past – and of its distance – relies, and the Aksumite "origins" are often present in the XIVth-XVth c. Ethiopian literature, particularly in the chronographical texts.[8] The royal lists (Conti Rossini 1909), for instance, and the monastic genealogies,[9] in spite of their obvious deficiencies, express the need of filling up the documentary gaps, which the learned men were forced to remedy time after time by silence or by invention. Third, the Aksumite literary heritage transmitted to the medieval times is in no way negligible[10] and the radical scepticism toward the reliability of the hagiografic traditions doesn't take into account the possibility, in some cases already proved, that certain texts could have been written again or updated several centuries after their first draft.[11] Likewise, the iconological study of the

---

5   On the site see Godet 1977: 37 and 47 (without registration of the Christian ruins).
6   Described in Conti Rossini 1925: 484-489 (29. Le rovine di Dahané); Bausi 1999: 18 (note 25) and 24.
7   As in the case, for instance, of the Arātu ruins, Māy Awālid valley, in the 'Ansabā basin (Karan, Eritrea). One can see there a monumental podium with stairs, called by the local people "the angāreb of Samaraččon", with reference to the traditional genealogies; Piva 1907; Dainelli - Marinelli 1912: 525-527; Godet 1980-82: 81-82.
8   On this special literature see particularly the works of Otto Neugebauer: 1979; 1979a; 1981; 1982; 1983; 1988; 1989. For a recent edition of one of the most important texts see Getatchew Haile 2000.
9   Getatchew Haile 1982-83; 1992; Lusini, forthcoming.
10   Among the more recent studies see Bausi 1998, and Voicu 1998: 19-23.
11   Starting from the meaningful case of the Old Testament: see now Knibb 1999. The *Acts of Mark*: Getatchew Haile 1981. The *Ancoratus* of Epiphanius: Proverbio 1997. In the same sense one can interpret the text coincidences between the dedicatory inscription engraved by order of king Lālibalā (about 1186-1225) on the *manbara tābot* of the Golgotā church, in

(continued...)

illustrated cycles of the medieval Ethiopian manuscripts, with their proved connection to the early Byzantine patterns, not unknown in the Vth-VIIth c. Aksum, is another sign of the capability of the Ethiopian tradition to transmit ancient elements for centuries.[12]

In one case at least the evidences lead to contradict the more radical manifestations of scepticism. This is the case with a monastic centre and the related documents, both considered ancient by the ecclesiastical tradition and actually tracing back to a period preceding the XIVth-XVth c. Among the land charters gathered in the *Golden Gospel* of Dabra Libānos, no. 7[13] contains the text of a land grant, donated *(wahabku)* by king Lālibalā (about 1186-1225) to the Eritrean monastery *(laMaṭā' za'Ahām)*. The text is dated 1225 and there is little doubt about its authenticity. The title *ḥaḍāni Lālibalā*, imitating that of the Aksumite inscription of Dān'ēl (VIIIth/IXth c.), the royal formula *be'esi 'āzāl za'iyetmawwā 'laḍar*, reproducing the one used by the kings of Aksum, the technical verb *aksamku* describing the deed's promulgation (cp. the words *zentu kesum* below in the same text), with a possible etymological reference to the name of the city of Aksum itself[14] – all these elements let one believe the document and its datation true. Consequently, it testifies not only that Dabra Libānos already existed in the XIIth/XIIIth c., but also that the high prestige of the convent was acknowledged by the king. Thanks to these elements, one can admit that the Ge'ez texts related to the appearance of Christianity in Ethiopia were drawn up using oral or written sources which, among the inventions of the literary genre, had preserved the memory of ancient facts. The identification of those facts remains the responsibility of the researchers.

If manuscripts of hagiographic texts older than XIVth c. are not known this is owed to the simple fact that the final composition of the *gadlāt* is recent. In fact, thanks also to the recovery of the traditions pivoting on the Aksumite saints, an official version of the events related to the Christianization of Ethiopia was imposed in the XIVth-XVth c., serving the political and religious ambitions of the kings. The result was, in a way, an attempt of philological reconstruction, based on the *Kebra nagaśt* and having as a

---

11 (...continued)
   the capital of the Zāg{w}ē kingdom (Gigar Tesfaye 1984), and the homily *Ba'enta sanbatāt*, written by the Ethiopian metropolite or by another authoritative clergyman in the first half of XIV c. (Lusini 1993: 130-175). The list of the corresponding passages is the following: Lusini 1993: 132, ll. 13-15 = Gigar Tesfaye 1984: 115 (side 1, ll. 1-2); Lusini 1993: 144, ll. 19-20 = Gigar Tesfaye 1984: 115 (side 2, ll. 3-4); Lusini 1993: 154, li. 14 - 156, li. 6 = Gigar Tesfaye 1984: 115 (side 2, li. 12) - 116 (side 2, li. 16). Since the two texts cannot be interdependent, one must admit that they separately exploited an ancient source, like a canonical collection similar to the Sēnodos, apparently already existing in the Aksumite age; see Lusini 2001: 556-557.

12 For some case studies see Fiaccadori 1993 and 1995, and the analysis in Balicka-Witakowska 1997.

13 Conti Rossini 1901: 189-192; see also Bausi 1997: 13-23.

14 Ricci 1994: 188-190; for a different hypothesis see Müller 1998.

target the establishment of a fundamental thesis: the political alliance and the common eschatological destiny of the Byzantine emperor and the Aksumite king. The origins of these political and religious beliefs are ancient, but it was in the years between the 1270 turning point and the reign of Zar'a Yā'qob (1434-1468) that they provoked the composition of such texts as the *Fekkārē Iyasus* and the *Rā'eya Šenutē*, describing the decisive role to be played by the Ethiopian king at the end of times (Conti Rossini 1899: 216; Fiaccadori 1992: 80-81).

* * *

An emblematic case is the story of Abrehā and Aṣbeḥā, the mythical couple of brothers whom the tradition – refreshing the memory of the IVth c. Kings 'Ēzānā and Sā'ezānā – claims credit for having promoted the introduction of Christianity into the Kingdom of Aksum. The origins of the legend, starting from the association of two personalities of the same age, have been reconstructed since long time. Aṣbeḥā is Kālēb/Ella Aṣbeḥā, son and successor of Tāzēnā at the end of Vth c., the king who, about 525, imposed the political authority of Aksum on both sides of the Red Sea (Brakmann 1994: 81-96). Abrehā is the name of the Christian leader, of Ethiopian origin, ruling over South Arabia a few years after Kālēb's victory on the king of Ḥimyar, Yūsuf As'ar Yaṯ'ar, called Ḏu Nuwās, and the temporary unification of the two kingdoms (Conti Rossini 1928: 259). In this case, too, the myth seems to contain the re-elaboration of ancient facts transmitted in some way up to XIVth-XVth c.

A passage in the *Maṣḥafa Aksum* ascribes the foundation of the Māryām Ṣeyon church[15] to Abrehā and Aṣbeḥā, an element which deserves our attention. As a well-known tradition claims, Aksum is the "mother of the Ethiopian towns" (*'emmon la'ahgura 'ityoṗyā*) – both because of its antiquity and because of the presence of the main sanctuary of the Ethiopian Christianity in it, the *gabaza 'aksum* (Littmann - Krencker 1906: 3; Lensi 1937). The archaeological evidence confirms that the cathedral traces back to an old date,[16] probably to the years of Kālēb, as one can suppose on the basis of different indications. First, the historical situation of the first half of the VIth c. has to be considered. It was dominated by the economic and political conflict between the pro-Byzantine Ethiopia and the pro-Sassanian Yemen for the control of the trade routes along and around the Red Sea (Harmatta 1974; Loundine 1974), and by the ideological and religious confrontation between the two monotheistic communities, both claiming to be the *Verus Israël*. The annexation of Ḥimyar completes the picture, and provides a valid context for the construction of a big Christian Temple in Aksum. Its foundation would then be tied to the military victory of the Ethiopian

---

15 Conti Rossini 1909-10: 3 (text) and 3 (transl.)
16 Krencker 1913: 136-140; Monneret de Villard 1938: 21-31; Contenson 1963: 3-14; Munro-Hay 1991: 209; Phillipson 1997: 114-116; Munro-Hay 2002: 308-315 (History of the Cathedral of Maryam Ṣeyon).

Christianity, that is to the historical defeat of the Yemenite Judaism. A piece of evidence in support of this idea is the inscription Kālēb wrote in order to commemorate an expedition against the Ag^wēzāt, namely the passage reading (ll. 36-38): WGBZH / ḤNṢK WQDSK BḤYL 'GZ' BHR W'R'YN 'GZ' B/ḤR QDSH WNBRK DB Z MNBR, "I build its *gabaz* and I consecrated it by the Lord's strength. Lord revealed me its holiness and I sat down on this throne". The temptation is strong to recognize in this passage a reference to the *gabaza 'aksum*, i.e. to the cathedral: this would be a contemporary evidence of its construction, tracing back straight to the first half of the VIth c.[17] The emphasis the text gives to the motif of the holiness descending from God and investing the building through the king appears symbolic of a religious belief in which an essential role is played by the Temple. As a confirmation, it can also be considered that, from this time on, the word *gabaz* appears as an element in royal names such as Ella gabaz,[18] or Zagabaz[a Aksum], successor of Kālēb, and Terdāʿ gabaz,[19] the mythical princess whom the tradition ascribes a political role in the times preceding the consolidation of the Zāg^wē dynasty. Though the occasion for the writing of the Kālēb's text is provided by an expedition against the Ag^wēzāt, the inscription contains an explicit reference to the victory on Ḥimyar in the passage immediately preceding the celebration of the new cathedral (ll. 34-35): W'T WHBN SM 'BY KM 'ḌB' ḤMR WFNWK Ḥ / YN SLBN ZSMR MSL 'ḤZBY WTKLK MQDS BḤMR, "He gave me a big name in order I fought against ḤMR. I sent ḤYN SLBN ZSMR with my army and I founded a sanctuary in ḤMR" (Drewes 1978: 27-32; Munro-Hay 1991: 230). It is a little surprise that there is no reference to the name of Māryām Ṣeyon or to the medieval image of the church, tied to the later myth of the transfer of the Ark. In fact, in the course of the centuries the symbolism of the cathedral certainly underwent remarkable changes, not less than its external appearance, even if in both eras – the Aksumite and the medieval – its role as sanctuary of the *Verus Israël* appears central.

As far as the onomastics is concerned, it has been observed that the names of the Christian Aksumite kings can provide useful data for the historical reconstruction, confirming the picture already drawn. After ʿĒzānā and up to Kālēb, names like Ouazebas, Eon,[20] MHDYS,[21] Ebana, Nezool (Nezana), Ousas (Ousana, Ousanas) and Tāzēnā don't exhibit meaningful changes in comparison with the pre-Christian tradition. Starting from Kālēb (about 510-530), instead, a model inspired by the Old Testa-

17 Schneider 1974: 770-777 = Bernand et al. 1991: no. 191.
18 Munro-Hay 1991: 89, 93 187 and 194, who suggests the identification of Ella Gabaz with W'ZB; yet, see Lusini 2001a: 553, who assumes the sequence: Kālēb (about 510-530), Ella Gabaz (about 530-534), W'ZB/Gabra Masqal, son of Kālēb (about 534-548).
19 Conti Rossini 1921-23: 374-375 (8. Sul nome proprio di donna Terdāʿ gabaz).
20 The reading Nōe is in contrast with the direction of the writing; the suggestion traces back to Littmann 1913a: 55, followed by Hahn 2001: 125.
21 The interpretation of this name as Matthia is in contrast with the documentary evidence; the suggestion is in Hahn 2001: 127.

ment appears,[22] reflected in the names of Israēl (550 ca.), Gersem (580 ca.) Ḥataz (590 ca.) and Iōēl (600 ca.), whose relationship with episodes of the history of Israel is certain.[23] Apparently, the establishment of the Christian faith, rooted in the Old Testament and at the same time strongly anti-Judaic, arose from the anti-Ḥimyarite political and military strategy. In other words, the dissolution of the economic and religious rival and the unification of the two kingdoms supported the elaboration of an ideological display based upon the transfer of the holiness and symbolically expressed by the foundation of the new Temple of the *Verus Israël*, i.e. the cathedral of Aksum. In this sense another evidence is instructive, namely a passage from the *Book of the Ḥimyarites*, ch. 48 (= fragm. xxvii'), in which Kālēb, after his victory on Ḏu Nuwās, is said to have brought many prisoners and fifty princes of the South-Arabian royal house[24] with him. The chance that this transfer of members of the Yemenite Jewish aristocracy actually took place should not be ruled out, and in any case the Syriac text seems to contain a reference to a strategy of political and religious integration brought forward by the Aksumite king. The *Kebra nagaśt*, too, after all, talking about the transfer of the Ark, makes use of a similar literary device, when it narrates of Bayna Leḥekem's arrival in Ethiopia – together with the first-borns of the main Israelite families.

As a part of the same process, in the years following the military conflict with Ḥimyar the Ethiopian religious culture, though keeping a constant "Christian" polemics against the people guilty of deicide, acquired an ever stronger Judaic mark, noticed by external observers at least from the XIth c. (Taddesse Tamrat 1972: 209; Lusini 1993: 27). These "Judaic" features of the Ethiopian Christianity have been often attributed to old and obscure religious contacts with Jewish communities or missions.[25] More likely, we are dealing with a phenomenon described in sociology: an external conflict can give rise to new manifestations of ethnicity inside a community,[26] in our case in the form of a conscious *imitatio Veteris Testamenti*.[27] In this context, the founding myth of the Ethiopian kingship, related in its official form by the *Kebra nagaśt*,[28] receives an explanation more plausible than the commonly accepted theories, according to which the story would express unlikely collective memories of

---

22 Marrassini 1994: 206; 1995: 8; Hahn 2001: 124-128; Hahn - Kropp 2000.

23 See Joshua 15,13-19 (Kālēb), Genesis 35,10 (Israēl), Exodus 2,22 (Gersem), 1Chronicles 4,13 (Ḥataz), Nehemia 11,9 (Iōēl).

24 Moberg 1924: 56a, ll. 17-18 (text), p. cxlii (translation); Shahîd 1963.

25 Ullendorff 1956; 1968: 73-115; Hammerschmidt 1965; Pawlikowski 1971-72; Isaac 1972; 1973.

26 Smith 1981; 1992: 95-101. An application of these principles to the state building process in Ethiopia and Eriythrea is in Clapham 2000.

27 According to the principles effectively applied in the articles by Maxime Rodinson: 1963; 1964; 1964 a; 1965; 1972. See also Marrassini 1987b, and Lusini 1993: 27-31.

28 In fact, the oral tradition transmitted ancient and important versions of the legend, different from the one exploited in the *Kebra nagaśt*; see Littmann 1904: 13-40.

Ethiopian past dominated by indefinite Jewish (Solomon) and South-Arabian (the Queen of Sheba) presences. Accordingly, the capital city of the Ethiopian State received the religious attributes of a "New Jerusalem", among which the central place was occupied by the foundation of the cathedral, intentionally imitating the church of the Holy Sepulchre, or inspired by the plan of a Constantinian basilica (Heldman 1993; 1992: 227). Probably the model lying under the simultaneous celebration of both the capital and its king derives from the contacts between Aksum and Byzantium, as the same is characteristic for a complex of traditions connected to the Roman emperors (Cerulli 1974; Marrassini 1983). In fact, the VIth-VIIth conflicts with Persians and Arabs about the defence and the consolidation of the eastern borders of the Empire provided an occasion for the development of two interrelated images: Constantinople as the "New Zion" and the emperor as an earthly figure of the heavenly βασιλεὺς, both destined to last for several centuries (Patlagean 1994: 459-461; 1998). The "Byzantine" model allowed the Ethiopian king to face the more severe criticism pronounced against his earthly functions (Lusini 2001a), as those exhibited in the *Shepherd* of Hermas[29] or in the *Antichrist* of Hyppolitus[30], so that he could begin to claim for himself the immanent role of defender of the faith (Marrassini 1993: 22-39) and the eschatological function of guide of all the Christians till the end of times (Lusini 1999b). Apparently, the *terminus ante quem* of this sacralization of the highest Ethiopian authority seems to be provided by the two inscriptions of the *ḥaḍāni* Dān'ēl, the lord of Aksum who, in the VIIIth or IXth c., defined himself as a member of a monastery near the capital *(walda dabra ferēm)*.[31] The most ancient evidence of the fulfilled process is in Abū Ṣāliḥ, the Arab writer of Armenian origin who, reporting the information obtained by travellers between the end of the XIIth c. and the beginning of the XIIIth c., retold the legend of Solomon and the Queen of Sheba and celebrated Ethiopia not only as the land pretending to own the Ark of the Covenant, but also because this Country was ruled by kings devoted to religious life (Evetts 1969: 284-288; Marrassini 1994: 206).

---

29 Abbadie 1860; Dillmann 1861; Beylot 1988; Raineri 1993; Piovanelli 1994: 329-330; 1993: 197-199; Lusini 1999a; 2001c. Greek Text: Körtner - Leutzsch 1998: 105-497.
30 Greek Text: Norelli 1987. Ethiopic version: Caquot 1965; Beylot 1991.
31 Littmann 1913b: nos. 12 and 13 = Bernand et al. 1991: nos. 193 I-II; Fiaccadori 1996: 327-328 (II. Dabra Ferēm).

Bibliography

Abbadie, A. d'
1860   Hermae Pastor. *Abhandlungen für die Kunde des Morgenlandes* 2: 1-110
       (text) and 113-182 (transl.).

Balicka-Witakowska, E.
1997   *La Crucifixion sans Crucifié dans l'art éthiopien. Recherches sur la survie de
       l'iconographie chrétienne de l'Antiquité tardive.* Bibliotheca nubica et
       aethiopica 4. Warszawa.

Bausi, A.
1997   Su alcuni manoscritti presso comunità monastiche dell'Eritrea, III. *Rassegna
       di studi etiopici 41:* 13-55.
1998   L'Epistola 70 di Cipriano di Cartagine. *Aethiopica 1:* 101-130.
1999   Appunti sul Gadla Libānos. *Warszawskie Studia Teologiczne 12* (Miscellanea
       Aethiopica S. Kur oblata): 11-30.

Bernand, E., Drewes, A. J. and Schneider, R.
1991   *Recueil des inscriptions de l'Éthiopie des périodes pré-axoumite et axoumite,
       introd. de Francis Anfray, I. Les documents.* Paris.

Beylot, R.
1988   Hermas: le Pasteur. Quelques variantes inédites de la version éthiopienne. In:
       Mélanges A. Guillaumont. Cahiers d'Orientalisme 20. Genève: 155-162.
1991   Hippolyte de Rome, Traité de l'Antéchrist, traduit de l'éthiopien. *Semitica 40:*
       107-139.

Brakmann, H.
1994   ΤΟ ΠΑΡΑ ΤΟΙϹ ΒΑΡΒΑΡΟΙϹ ΕΡΓΟΝ ΘΕΙΟΝ. *Die Einwurzelung der Kirche
       im spätantiken Reich von Aksum.* Bonn.

Caquot, A.
1965   Une version ge'ez du traité d'Hippolyte de Rome sur l'Antichrist. *Annales
       d'Éthiopie 6:* 165-214.

Cerulli, E.
1949   Carlo Conti Rossini. *Oriente Moderno 29:* 93-102.
1974   Gli imperatori Onorio ed Arcadio nella tradizione etiopica. In: *IV Congresso
       Internazionale di Studi Etiopici.* Roma: 15-54.

Clapham, C.
2000   Guerra e fomazione dello stato in Etiopia e Eritrea. *Afriche e Orienti II, 3/4:*
        110-118.

Contenson, H. de
1963   Les fouilles à Axoum en 1958. Rapport préliminaire. *Annales d'Éthiopie 5:* 3-
        16.

Conti Rossini, C.
1895   Appunti ed osservazioni sui re Zāguē e Takla Hāymānot. *Reale Accademia*
        dei Lincei. Rendiconti, ser. V, IV: 341-359 and 444-468.
1899   Note per la storia letteraria abissina. *Reale Accademia dei Lincei. Rendiconti,*
        ser. V, VIII: 197-220.
1901   L'Evangelo d'oro di Dabra Libānos. *Reale Accademia dei Lincei. Rendiconti,*
        ser. V, X: 177-219.
1903   *Ricordi di un soggiorno in Eritrea.* Asmara: 25-41.
1909   Les listes des Rois d'Axoum. *Journal Asiatique, ser. X, XIV:* 263-320.
1909-10 *Documenta ad illustrandam historiam I. Liber Axumae,* CSCO 54. Aeth 24,
        CSCO 58. Aeth 27.
1921-23 Aethiopica. *Rivista di studi orientali 9:* 365-381 and 449-468.
1922   La caduta della dinastia Zagué e la versione amarica del Be'ela Nagast. *Reale*
        Accademia dei Lincei. Rendiconti, ser. V, XXXI: 279-314.
1925   Aethiopica (IIª serie). *Rivista di studi orientali 10:* 469-520.
1928   *Storia d'Etiopia, I. Dalle origini all'avvento della dinastia salomonide.*
        Bergamo.

Dainelli, G. and Marinelli, O.
1912   *Risultati scientifici di un viaggio nella Colonia Eritrea.* Firenze.

Dillmann, A.
1861   Bemerkungen zu dem äthiopischen Pastor Hermae. *Zeitschrift der Deutschen*
        Morgenländischen Gesellschaft 15: 111-125.

Drewes, A. J.
1978   Kaleb and Himyar: another reference to HYWN? *Raydan 1:* 27-32.

Evetts, B. T. A.
1969   *The churches & monasteries of Egypt and some neighbouring countries attrib-*
        uted to Abû Sâlih, the Armenian. 2nd ed., Oxford.

Fiaccadori, G.
1992   *Teofilo Indiano.* Ravenna.

1993 Bisanzio e il regno di 'Aksum. Sul manoscritto Martini etiop. 5 della Biblioteca Forteguerriana di Pistoia, in Quaecumque recepit Apollo. *Scritti in onore di Angelo Ciavarella, a c. di Andrea Gatti, Bollettino del Museo Bodoniano di Parma 7:* 161-199.

1994 Prototipi miniati dell'Ottateuco etiopico. *Bollettino del Museo Bodoniano di Parma 8:* 69-102.

1996 Epigraphica Aethiopica. *Quaderni Utinensi 8:* 325-333.

Getatchew Haile

1981 A new Ethiopic version of the Acts of St. Mark (EMML 1763, ff. 224ʳ-227ʳ). *Analecta Bollandiana 99:* 117-134.

1982-83 The Monastic genealogy of the line of Täklä Haymanot of Shoa. *Rassegna di studi ethiopici 29:* 7-38.

1992 A fragment of the Monastic Fathers of the Ethiopian Church. In: *P.O. Scholz, R. Pankhurst and W. Witakowski (eds.), Orbis Aethiopicus. Studia in honorem Stanislaus Chojnacki natali septuagesimo quinto dicata, septuagesimo septimo oblata, I.* Bibliotheca Nubica, 3. Albstadt: 231-237.

2000 *Bāhra Hassāb.* Collegeville, Minnesota.

Gigar Tesfaye

1984 Inscriptions sur bois de trois églises de Lalibela. *Journal of Ethiopian Studies 17:* 107-126.

Godet, E.

1977 Répertoire de sites pre-axoumites et axoumites du Tigré (Ethiopie). *Abbay 8:* 19-58.

1980-82 Répertoire des sites pré-axoumites et axoumites de l'Ethiopie du Nord II. Erythrée. *Abbay 11:* 73-113.

Hahn, W.

2001 Noe, Israel und andere Könige mit biblischen Namen auf axumitischen Münzen. Der Gottesbund als Legitimation der christlichen Königsherrschaft im alten Äthiopien. *Money Trend XII, 12:* 123-128.

Hahn, W. and Kropp, M.

2000 The biblical names of Axumite kings as attested on their coins as indication for a political program based on the AT. Paper presented at the XIVth International Conference of Ethiopian Studies. (Addis Ababa, 2000)

Hammerschmidt, E.

1965 Jewish elements in the cult of Ethiopian Church. *Journal of Ethiopian Studies 3:* 1-12.

102   Gianfrancesco Lusini

Harmatta, J.
1974   The struggle for the possession of South Arabia between Aksūm and the
         Sāsānians. In: *IV Congresso Internazionale di Studi Etiopici*. Roma: 95-106.

Heldman, M.E.
1992   Architectural symbolism, sacred geography and the Ethiopian Church. *Jour-
         nal of the Religions in Africa 22*: 222-241.
1993   Maryam Seyon: Mary of Zion. In: *R. Grierson (ed.), African Sion. The sacred
         art of Ethiopia*, New Haven - London: 71-75.

Isaac, E.
1972   An obscure component in Ethiopian Church history. An examination of vari-
         ous theories pertaining to the problem of the origin and nature of Ethiopian
         christianity. *Le Muséon 85*: 225-258.
1973   *A new text-critical introduction to Maṣḥafa Berhān, with a translation of book
         I.* Leiden.

Knibb, M.A.
1999   *Translating the Bible, The Ethiopic version of the Old Testament.* Oxford.

Körtner, U.H.J. and Leutzsch, M. (eds.)
1989   *Papiasfragmente. Hirt des Hermas.* Darmstadt.

Krencker, D.
1913   *Deutsche Axum Expedition II. Ältere Denkmäler aus Abessiniens.* Berlin.

Lensi, G.C.
1937   Acsum, città santa. In: *Atti del Terzo Congresso di Studi Coloniali, IV (III
         Sezione: storica archeologica).* Firenze: 151-161.

Littmann, E.
1904   *The legend of the Queen of Sheba in the tradition of Axum.* Leyden - Prince-
         ton, New Jersey.
1913a   *Deutsche Axum Expedition I. Reisebericht der Expedition. Topographie und
         Geschichte Aksums.* Berlin.
1913b   *Deutsche Axum-Expedition IV. Sabäische, Griechische und Altabessinische
         Inschriften.* Berlin.

Littmann, E. and Krencker, D.
1906   *Vorbericht der Deutschen Aksumexpedition.* Berlin.

Loundine, A. G.
1974   Sur les rapports entre l'Éthiopie et le Himyar du VIᵉ siècle. In: *IV Congresso Internazionale di Studi Etiopici*. Roma: 313-320.

Lusini, G.
1993   *Studi sul monachesimo eustaziano*. Napoli.
1998   Scritture documentarie etiopiche (Dabra Deḫuḫān e Dabra Ṣegē, Sarā'ē, Eritrea). *Rassegna di studi etiopici 42*: 5-55.
1999a   Per una nuova edizione del Pastore di Erma etiopico. In: *M. Bandini and G. Lusini, Nuove acquisizioni intorno alla tradizione testuale del Pastore di Erma in greco e in etiopico, Studi classici e orientali 46*: 625-635.
1999b   Escatologia e Scrittura nelle più antiche tradizioni etiopiche. *Annali di storia dell'esegesi 16*: 235-240.
2001a   L'Église axoumite et ses traditions historiographiques. In: *B. Pouderon and Y.-M. Duval (eds.), L'historiographie de l'Église des premiers siècles*. Théologie historique, 114. Paris: 541-557.
2001b   Elementi romani nella tradizione letteraria aksumita. *Aethiopica 4*: 42-54.
2001c   Nouvelles recherches sur le texte du Pasteur d'Hermas. *Apocrypha 12*: 79-97.
forthcoming   Per una storia delle tradizioni monastiche eritree: le genealogie spirituali dell'ordine di Ēwosṭātēwos di Dabra Ṣarābi. In: *Mémorial Paul Devos*, Cahiers d'Orientalisme 25. Genève.

Marrassini, P.
1981   Una Chiesa africana: l'Etiopia fra Antiochia e Alessandria. In: *XXVIII corso di cultura sull'arte ravennate e bizantina*. Ravenna: 193-203.
1983   Giustiniano e gli imperatori di Bisanzio nella letteratura etiopica. In: *XXX corso di cultura sull'arte ravennate e bizantina*. Ravenna: 383-389.
1987a   L'edizione critica dei testi etiopici. Problemi di metodo e reperti linguistici. In: *Linguistica e filologia. Atti del VII Convegno Internazionale di linguisti (Milano, 12-14 settembre 1984). Brescia*: 347-356.
1987b   Sul problema del giudaismo in Etiopia. In: *Atti del Congresso AISG. Roma*: 175-183.
1990   Some considerations on the problem of the 'Syriac Influences' on Aksumite Ethiopia. *Journal of Ethiopian Studies 23*: 35-46.
1993   *Lo scettro e la croce. La campagna di 'Amda Seyon I contro l'Ifāt (1332)*. Napoli.
1994   Un caso africano: la dinastia zague in Etiopia. In: *Bertelli, S. and Clemente, P. (eds.), Tracce dei vinti*. Firenze: 200-229.
1995   *Il Gadla Yemreḥanna Krestos*. Introd., testo critico, trad. Napoli.

1999a   Il Gadla Abreha waAṣbeḥa. Indicazioni preliminari. *Warszawskie Studia Teologiczne 12* (Miscellanea Aethiopica S. Kur oblata): 159-179.
1999b   Ancora sul problema degli influssi siriaci in età aksumita. In: *L. Cagni (ed.), Biblica et Semitica. Studi in memoria di Francesco Vattioni*. Napoli: 325-337.

Moberg, A.
1924   *The Book of the Ḥimyarites. Fragments of a Hitherto Unknown Syriac Work.* Lund.

Monneret de Villard, U.
1938   *Aksum. Ricerche di topografia generale.* Roma.

Moreno, M. M.
1950   Carlo Conti Rossini. *Rivista di Antropologia 38:* 3-15.

Müller, W. W.
1998   Südarabisches zum Namen Aksum. *Aethiopica 1:* 217-220.

Munro-Hay, S.
1991   *Aksum. An African civilization of Late Antiquity.* Edinburgh.
2002   *Ethiopia: The Unknown Land.* London.

Neugebauer, O.
1979a   *Ethiopic Astronomy and Computus.* Sitzungsberichte der ÖAW, philos-hist. Kl. 347. Wien.
1979b   Ethiopic Easter computus. *Oriens Christianus 63:* 87-102.
1981   *The 'Astronomical' Chapters of the Ethiopic Book of Enoch (72 to 82).* Kobenhavn.
1982   'Halving' and 'doubling' in Ethiopic computus treatises. *Orientalia 51:* 409-410.
1983   Abū Shāker and the Ethiopic Hasāb. *Journal of Near Eastern Studies 42:* 55-58.
1988   *Abu Shaker's "Chronography".* Sitzungsberichte der ÖAW, philos.-hist. Kl. 498. Wien.
1989   *Chronography in Ethiopic sources.* Sitzungsberichte der ÖAW, philos.-hist. Kl. 512. Wien.

Norelli, E. (ed.)
1987   *Ippolito. L'Anticristo.* Firenze.

Patlagean, E.
1994   La double Terre Sainte de Byzance. Autour du XIIe siècle. *Annales. Histoire, sciences sociales 49:* 459-469.
1998   Byzantium's Dual Holy Land. In: *B.Z. Kedar and R.J. Zwi Werblowsky (eds.), Sacred Space, Shrine, City, Land.* London - Jerusalem: 112-126.

Pawlikowski, J. T.
1971-72 Judaic spirit of the Ethiopian Orthodox Church. A case study in religious acculturation. *Journal of the Religions in Africa 4:* 178-199.

Phillipson, D. W.
1997   *The Monuments of Aksum.* Addis Ababa.

Piovanelli, P.
1993   Les aventures des apocryphes en Éthiopie. *Apocrypha 4:* 197-224.
1994   Nouvelles perspectives dans l'étude des "apocryphes" éthiopiens traduits du grec. In: *C. Lepage (ed.), Études Éthiopiennes, Actes de la Xe Conférence Internationale des Études Éthiopiennes (1988), I.* Paris: 323-330.

Piva, A.
1907   Una civiltà scomparsa dell'Eritrea e gli scavi archeologici nella regione di Cheren. *Nuova Antologia, ser. III, 16:* 325-335.

Proverbio, D. V.
1997   Introduzione alle versioni orientali dell'Ancoratus di Epifanio. La recensione etiopica. *Miscellanea Marciana 12:* 67-91.

Raineri, O.
1993   Il Pastore di Erma nel secondo testimone etiopico. *Orientalia Christiana Periodica 59:* 427-464.

Ricci, L.
1971-72 Presenza di un maestro. Carlo Conti Rossini. *Rassegna di studi etiopici 25:* 5-13.
1982   Conti Rossini, Carlo. In: *Dizionario Biografico degli Italiani XXVI:* 527-529.
1986   Studi di etiopistica. In: *Gli studi africanistici in Italia dagli anni '60 ad oggi. Atti del convegno (Roma, 25-27 giugno 1985).* Roma: 150-166.
1987   Leo Reinisch e Carlo Conti Rossini. In: *H.G. Mukarovsky (ed.), Leo Reinisch. Werk und Erbe,* Sitzungsberichte der ÖAW., philos.-hist. Kl. 492. Wien: 279-287.
1994   Post scriptum to Roger Schneider, Remarques sur le nom Aksum. *Rassegna di studi etiopici 38:* 183-190.
1997   Tra alHiğra e banalità. *Rassegna di studi etiopici 41:* 107-108.

Rodinson, M.
1963   L'Éthiopie a-t-elle été juive? *Revue des Études Juives 2*: 399-403.
1964a   Sur la question des "influences juives" en Éthiopie. *Journal of Semitic Studies 9:* 11-19.
1964b   Review of Edward Ullendorff, The Ethiopians, Oxford, U.P., 1960. *Bibliotheca Orientalis 21:* 238-245.
1965   Le problème du christianisme éthiopien: substrat juif ou christanisme judaisant? *Revue d'Histoire des Religions 167:* 113-117.
1972   Review of Edward Ullendorff, Ethiopia and the Bible, Oxford, U.P., 1968. *Journal of Semitic Studies 17:* 166-170.

Schneider, R.
1974   Trois nouvelles inscriptions royales d'Axoum. In: *IV Congresso Internazionale di Studi Etiopici.* Roma: 767-786.

Shahîd, I.
1963   The Book of the Himyarites. Authorship and Authenticity. *Le Muséon 76:* 349-362.

Smith, A. D.
1981   War and ethnicity: the role of the warfare in the formation of self-images and cohesion of ethnic communities. *Ethnic and Racial Studies 4:* 375-397.
1992   *Le origini etniche delle nazioni.* Bologna.

Taddesse Tamrat
1972   *Church and State in Ethiopia 1270-1527.* Oxford.

Ullendorff, E.
1956   Hebraic-jewish elements in Ethiopian (Monophysite) christianity. *Journal of Semitic Studies 1:* 216-256.
1968   *Ethiopia and the Bible.* Oxford.

Voicu, S. J.
1998   Verso il testo primitivo dei Παιδικὰ τοῦ κυρίου Ἰησοῦ "Racconti dell'infanzia del Signore Gesù". *Apocrypha 9:* 7-85.

A "Missing" Letter from Emperor Téwodros II to the Queen Victoria's Special Envoy Hormuzd Rassam

Richard Pankhurst

Emperor Téwodros of Ethiopia, in the course of his protracted dispute with the British Government, despatched well over thirty letters to Queen Victoria's special envoy Hormuzd Rassam. The latter indicates, in his *Narrative of the British Mission to Theodore* (London, 1869), that he received no less than thirty-seven such letters. Thirty-four of them were in Amharic, and three of them in Arabic. All but three of the Amharic letters are preserved in the British Library's India Office and Records department, and are included in Sven Rubenson's impressive *Acta Aethiopica volume II, Tewodros and His Contemporaries, 1855-1868* (Rubenson 1994). Each of the three "missing" letters deserve some comment.

The first of these letters (Rubenson 1994: 167) exists only in the English translation preserved in the India Office and Records (EUR F 103, fol. 86). Written by Téwodros, apparently on 4 February 1866, it bears a note by Rassam, stating that the original letter had been "sent to him with a request that it should be returned to him [Tewodros] after it had been translated into English". This, as Rubenson notes, was "obviously done", as the original is missing from the Emperor's other letters, and "has not surfaced in the years that have passed" (Rubenson 1994: 272). It was probably lost in the British looting of Maqdala, in which the soldiers, intent on seizing more valuable articles, appear to have paid but scant attention to letters.[1]

The second letter missing from the India Office and Records collection (Rubenson 1994: 186) was written two months later, on 4 April 1866. Its whereabouts are at first sight something of a mystery in that it is preserved not in London, but in the Ethiopian National Library in Addis Ababa. Rubenson thus writes: "How this letter came to be separated from the King's other letters to Rassam and ended up in the National Library in Addis Ababa was not known to the library staff when they were consulted in 1990" (Rubenson 1994: 292).

How this letter became separated from Téwodros's other correspondence remains a matter of conjecture, though light may be provided by the history of the third letter discussed below.

The question as to how the letter now in Ethiopia reached the Ethiopian National Library can, however, be answered definitively. The epistle in question was purchased in London in 1956 by Basil Robinson, Keeper of Metalwork in the Victoria and

---

1   On the looting of Maqdala, see R. Pankhurst 1973: 15-42.

Albert Museum, and given by him to Rita Eldon, later Rita Pankhurst, my wife. She it was who presented it to the National Library, where she was then employed.

The third letter, with which we are mainly concerned, was received by Rassam five months or so later, on 15 or 16 September 1866, but is undated. He mentions this epistle in his memoirs, where he describes it as a "polite note", and also publishes a rough English translation of it (Rassam 1869: II, 228). An incomplete Amharic text of this letter (Rubenson 1994: 199) exists in the India Office and Records, but only in an incomplete copy which lacks the opening lines of greeting (Rubenson 1994: 305). This omission was not insignificant, for the deleted passage is interesting in that it refers, in friendly terms, to the Téwodros's European captives. The importance of the missing words is implicitly recognised by Rassam, where he states that he was "glad to find" that Téwodros had "for the first time deigned to notice" the European captives the British envoy had been sent to liberate (Rassam 1869: II, 227-228).

The letter is of interest also in that it refers to – and helps to date – the completion, by the Emperor's European craftsmen, of a "large mortar". This was in all probability the famous weapon Sevastapol, called after the then recent battle in the Crimean War.

This "missing letter", and a contemporary English translation, have recently been traced by the present writer. They are currently in Britain, in the possession of a private collector on Africa and the Middle East, who wishes to remain anonymous. Attached to this letter is a Note which indicates how it became separated from the rest of Téwodros's correspondence. This note states: "The above Original letter from King Theodore to Dr Rassam was presented to Captain Anderson by him in June 1868". The captain, about whom we have been unable to trace any information, was doubtless a member of the Napier Expedition engaged in Rassam's liberation. It was this gift to Captain Anderson that excluded the letter in question from the Rassam collection, and hence the absence of the letter's complete text in Rubenson's *Acta Aethiopica.*

The above Note leads us to suppose that Rassam, who gave the letter and translation to Captain Anderson, was not above disposing of a letter. He may similarly have parted with Téwodros's earlier epistle, of 4 April 1964, which Basil Robinson subsequently purchased in London, and which Rita presented to the National Library in Ethiopia.

The Letter

The letter, which deserves to be included in any new edition of the *Acta,* begins with the opening lines missing from the India Office and Records version. They may be translated as follows:

In the name of the Father, and of the Son and of the Holy Ghost, King of Kings Téwodros. May [this letter] reach Ato [i.e. Mister] Hormuzd Rassam. How are you?

Thank God, I am well. Greetings to Hakim [i.e. Doctor] Blogn [i.e. Blanc 1868], Ato Prido [i.e. Prideaux][2] and your brothers.

The remainder of the letter, which is identical to the copy in the India Office and Records, and hence to Rubenson's text, continues:

Because I despatched Leyeh[3] and his companions in a hurry, I did not send you a message. How have you and your brothers spent the rainy season?[4] By the power of God, I am coming; fear not, we will meet.

Since we separated, by the power of God, a large cannon[5] has been made for me; when it is finished I shall inform you.

By the power of God, do not be afraid, I shall not forsake you. Say to Ato Kémeron [i.e. Cameron],[6] Ato Kokob [i.e. Mr. Stern],[7] and his companions, on my behalf, "How have you passed the rainy season?"

2   Lieut. W.F. Prideaux, formerly third Assistant Resident in Aden, had earlier been Rassam's colleague in the British administration. He was by this time one of Téwodros's European captives. Rassam 1869: I, 66.
3   Leyeh, who held the military title of Shōlōqa, i.e. Commander of a Thousand Men, was one of Téwodros's officials, entrusted with carrying messages for the Emperor. Rassam 1869: II, 273. Blanc, who distrusted him, described him as "a great spy, and confident of the Emperor". Blanc 1868: 195.
4   A reference to the rains of 1868, which were by then drawing to a close.
5   Possibly the great mortar called Sevastapol after the famous battle in the Crimean War. Rassam 1869: II, 303-304. See also, Blanc 1868: 332-333; Markham 1869: 367; Mondon-Vidailhet 1905: 56, 58; Weld Blundell1906-7: VI, 26-27, 33; Waldmeier 1886: 93-94.
6   Consul Duncan Cameron, one of Téwodros's principal European captives, on whom see Arnold 1992: 332 (index).
7   The Protestant missionary Henry Aaron Stern. Because the name Stern in his native German meant "star" he had come to be known in Ethiopia as *kokob*, the Amharic translation of that word. On his life and activities in Ethiopia see his two semi-autobiographical works: *Wanderings among the Falashas in Abyssinia* (London, 1862) and *The Captive Missionary* (London, 1868).

Bibliography

Arnold, P.
1992   *Prelude to Magdala*. London: 332 (index).

Blanc, H.
1868   *A Narrative of Captivity in Abyssinia*. London.

Markham, C. R.
1869   *A History of the Abyssinian Expedition*. London.

Mondon-Vidailhet, F. M. C.
1905   *Chronique de Théodorus II roi des rois d'Ethiopie (1853-1868)*. Paris: 56, 58.

Pankhurst, Rita
1973   The library of Emperor Tewodros II at Mõqdõla (Magdala). *Bulletin of the School of Oriental and African Studies (1973), XXXVI, 1:* 15-42.

Rassam, H.
1869   *Narrative of the British Mission to Theodore* (I and II). London.

Rubenson, S.
1994   *Tewodros and His Contemporaries*. Addis Ababa and Lund.

Waldmeier, T.
1886   *The Autobiography of Theophilus Waldmeier*. Leominster.

Weld Blundell, H.
1906-07 History of King Theodore. *The Journal of the African Society VI:* 26-27, 33.

In the name of Father the Son & the Holy Ghost one God, King of Kings Theodorus may this reach Mr. Hormuzd Rassam, How have you spent the rainy season? I am well God be praised. Dr. Blanc, Mr. Priaeaux your brethren, how have they spent the rainy season? ask them for me, Seh I have sent in a great hurry, therefore it happened that I did send you no compliments through him. How have you with your Brethren passed the rainy season? By the power of God I am coming, Dont fear we shall meet again. Since we have separated by the power of God a big gun has been made after it is finished I shall send you word again, By the power of God be of good cheer, I have no enmity against you, Ask for me Messrs Cameron & Stern how they have passed the rainy season—

The above Original letter from King Theodore II to Dr. Rassam. was presented to Captain Anderson by him in June 1868.

The Struggle for Power in Ethiopia in the Beginning of the 20th Cent. and the Role of European Powers

Hanna Rubinkowska

At the end of the 19th and the beginning of the 20th cent. three colonial powers, Great Britain, Italy and France, were seriously interested in the area ruled by the Ethiopian Emperor. Germany joined the group just before the outbreak of the First World War. Whilst the European powers were in the process of subordinating Africa, Ethiopia was faced with the urge to defend its independence. Yet, at the same time the Ethiopian nobles were able to take advantage of the European politics to achieve their own aims, namely the struggle for power within the country. Such development compelled the Ethiopians to conduct active foreign policy.

In the beginning of the 20th cent. all these European countries had their legations established at the emperor's court. Germany was the last to do so after signing the commercial treaty with Mənilək II in 1905 (Bairu Tafla 1981: 106). Both European diplomats in Ethiopia and Ethiopians had some basic knowledge of mutual cultures. But they still were observing each other's different and obscure worlds with curiosity. It seemed obvious for the Ethiopians that the Europeans came to their land to exploit its resources and conquer their homeland. The Europeans, on the other hand, were unable to understand either Ethiopians' behaviour or their political aims. The Europeans' belief of that time in their superiority over the Africans, if it can be discussed as belonging to the past, made them unable to find any sense in the way Ethiopian politicians acted, whether in their domestic or foreign policy. The classification of cultures as civilised or barbaric[1] did not help. The Ethiopians who appreciated the enemy apparently managed to understand cultural differences much better. They could use their advantage in their policy towards the European powers, what may have constituted one of the reasons that helped them to protect their independence during the colonial era.

European activity in the region had much impact on Ethiopia's fate, and the problem seems worth to be considered from the Ethiopian point of view. I will try to explore how the Ethiopians managed to achieve their aims, especially in the domestic affairs, using Europeans' engagement. Taking the example of German's and Great Britain's activity, I would like to discuss the period of intense struggle for power under the rule of *ləǧ* Iyasu (1910-1916) and during the initial period of Empress

---

1   See Archer's report (March 27, 1917, FO: 371/2854). In the report Zäwditu's coronation is described as a "gorgeous and barbaric spectacle".

Zäwditu's (1916-1930) reign up to 1919. The period discussed is even more interesting from the European point of view, as it is the time just prior to and during the First World War.

In the process of preparing the paper I went through the documents of the Foreign Office in London which raised some questions about the role of the British policy in Ethiopia in the period discussed. These include the existence of Secret Service or other diplomatic reports that are not in the main collection of the Foreign Office files for Ethiopia. These documents may fill the gap that is going to be discussed in the paper.

I find that the events in Ethiopia were caused by the domestic situation in the first place. I also believe that those who joined the struggle for power in the country were not influenced by Europeans but instead tried to take advantage of the Europeans' interest.

In the period discussed Ethiopia had its Council of Ministers with a Minister for Foreign Affairs.[2] In practice, it was not him who dealt with the foreign policy (Marcus 1987: 28). During the reign of *ləǧ* Iyasu he himself controlled foreign relations. When Zäwditu was enthroned, the Heir to the Throne, Täfäri Mäkʷännən managed the foreign policy and contacts with representations of the European countries. But in this matter, like in any other the last decision was to be taken by the Empress.[3]

The threat for the British interests

In the period discussed Ethiopian nobles were leading a fierce struggle to rule the country. The available sources do not give an explicit answer as to who ruled Ethiopia at the time and how big the group of leaders was. It is most probable that, after Empress Taytu[4] had lost her power in 1910, the uncrowned ruler *ləǧ* Iyasu[5] took power with his father *ras* Mika'el[6] acting in the background.[7] Iyasu stayed in power until 1916. When he was overthrown, the triumvirate consisting of Empress Zäwditu,

---

2 Mulugeta Yəggäzu – *däǧǧazmač*, Minister of Finance since 1907, later Minister for Foreign Affairs and then Minister of War.
3 This matter as well as other dealing with Zäwditu's significance are discussed in my Ph.D. thesis on which I am currently working.
4 Ṭaytu Bəṭul (ca.1850-1918) – *ətete*, crowned spouse of Mənilək II.
5 In May 1909 Mənilək II declared Iyasu the Heir to the Throne (Bahru Zewde 1991: 116), in 1911 the edict was decreed naming Iyasu the Emperor (Reishies 1937).
6 Mika'el (ca.1850-1918) – *ras*, governor of Wällo and Təgre provinces, *nəguś* since 1914.
7 See Smidt 2001 on the importance of *ras* Mika'el's activity during Iyasu's reign.

Minister of War Habtä Giyorgis[8] and the Heir to the Throne *ras* Täfäri Mäk^wännən ruled the country. Frictions among the triumvirs and struggle with representatives of other groups did not end. For obvious reasons, this kind of situation in an independent African country before and during the First World War was of great interest for the European governments. It was apparently a considerable threat for Great Britain's interests. As for the Germans, the situation allowed them to try to fulfil their aims in the First World War.

Contrary to most Ethiopian emperors, Iyasu searched for support among the followers of Islam and other non-Christian religions in Ethiopia. They constituted a significant force in Ethiopia. Iyasu also established contacts with the world of Islam outside Ethiopia: the Ottoman Empire and Somali movements under *sayyid* Muhammad Abdalläh Hassan known by the British as "Mad Mullah"[9]. The contacts between Iyasu and the Ottoman Empire in the German area of influence, together with the activities of Mad Mullah and Mahdist movements in Sudan were highly alarming for the British. Financed by the Germans and fanned by their propaganda, Iyasu and his allies were a real threat for the British territories in the region and for the result of the World War I. Germany's offer to Ethiopia included the enlargement of her territory to its "ancient size" in the north and in the west in return for supporting Germany in the war. They proposed territories which were at that time under the British and Italian rule. The same offer contented British Somali area for Mad Mullah's country in the case of co-operating in defeating the Allies (Scholler 1980: 312f.). In 1915 Germans were informed that *ləǧ* Iyasu and his father *ras* Mika'el supported German plans towards Ethiopia and that the preparation for the war was taking place in Wällo province ruled by *ras* Mika'el. The negotiations with Mad Mullah, hindered by the enemy's agents took place. They ended with delivery of arms from Iyasu to Mad Mullah (Scholler 1980: 312f.). The British must have been aware of the situation. Their fears were expressed in the correspondence between the office of the Ministry for the Foreign Affairs in London and Great Britain's representatives in Ethiopia. This threat did not end when Iyasu was dethroned (see: Thesiger to Balfour, June 6 1917, FO: 371/2854). The British tried to resolve the situation. These attempts were reflected in the plan of the British and to send Coptic priests to Ethiopia for propaganda against Iyasu. The plan was not executed as the Allies were afraid of the reaction of the local clergy to Egypt's intervention (Memo of the Italian Embassy, June 13, 1916, FO: 371/2593). From the reports one may judge that the British wanted to give the matter a careful consideration. Wilfred Thesiger, the British Minister, suggested participation in dethroning Iyasu, but only in case they could be sure of the common sympathy towards Iyasu's enemies (Thesiger to Bart, June 1, 1916, FO: 371/2594). He wrote that Iyasu's activities were not against European interests but only for the strengthening of

---

8   Habtä Giyorgis (?-1927) – *fitawrari*, politician and army commander, Minister of War during Mənilək II's, Iyasu's and Zäwditu's reigns.
9   Sayyid Muhammad Abdalläh Hassan, "Mad Mullah" (ca. 1864-1920) – Somali political and religious leader.

his position by the followers of Islam in Ethiopia. Thesiger suggested to stay quiet and be patient waiting for the events without acting (Thesiger to Sperling, n.d., FO: 371/2594).

Although from the contemporary point of view this evaluation of the situation may seem to be correct, in the situation of that time it was curious. It seemed to be more unjustly optimistic than a proper analysis of the events. The research shows that, in spite of Iyasu's intentions, his activities were a big threat for Great Britain and her Allies (Scholler passim; Marcus 1987: 14).

It seems obvious that in the international situation of the period Great Britain should have got engaged in the removal of Iyasu from power. At the same time the opposition against Iyasu, lead by the Christian nobility from the southern province of Šäwa grew stronger. In 1916 the *coup d'état* took place that finally removed Iyasu from power. Avoiding capture he still was a serious threat for the government in Addis Abäba and the British policy in the region.

Contrary to what one can expect, the British documents seem to prove the absence of British participation in constructing the *coup*, in spite of successive reports that should have made the British aware that this kind of action was necessary. Existence of sources presenting different information makes this lack of proofs even more interesting. One can guess that the activity of the British representatives in Ethiopia was not fully reflected in the reports sent to the Ministry for the Foreign Affairs in London which now are collected in the files for Ethiopia.[10]

The British Mission

Wilfred Thesiger was the British Minister in Addis Abäba in 1909-1919. Gerald Campbell was a Consul General since 1916. He also substituted for Thesiger during the latter's visits to Europe. The post of Consul to Harär was held by Hugh Dodds at that time. The reports of Thesiger as well as other diplomats were concentrated on the domestic situation in Ethiopia and the issues that were of greatest importance to the British, namely, the project of concession of the Ţana lake dam and activity of the other European powers in the region. The excerpts describing the political situation in Ethiopia allow best to judge the attitude of diplomats to the Ethiopian power elite as well as the policy they concluded. The analysis of this attitude suggests that the British were not aware of the actual state of play at the Ethiopian court in the times of

---

10 Wilfred Thesiger's son writes about his father's and Täfäri's cooperation in the period discussed (Thesiger 1992: 23, 93). Berhanou Abebe in his last article proves T.E. Lawrence's presence in Ethiopia during Iyasu's reign and his engagement in the fight with the Muslim threat for the British. These pieces of information are even more interesting when one remembers Richard Greenfield's opinion that it is not possible to prove gossips about presence of Lawrence in Ethiopia (Greenfield 1969: 138).

both *ləǧ* Iyasu and Empress Zäwditu. From the distance of eighty years and equipped with the increased knowledge on the Ethiopian culture we have the perspective that the British diplomats of that time lacked and hence our view of the Ethiopians' activities is now different. One should also remember that the attitude towards the Ethiopians reflected in the correspondence should be described as the "official" one. In such reports there was surely no subjective views presenting either positive or negative emotions towards people among whom the diplomats lived. It is impossible, however, not to notice the tendency in the reports to describe Ethiopians as "children" and treat them with "little respect" as some reports say.

Gerald Campbell in one of his reports described the state of affairs at the court. He found the relations between Habtä Giyorgis and Täfäri to be more friendly after their previous quarrel. From this example he drew the conclusion that the Ethiopians were like children, who temporarily forgot an argument they had just had (Campbell to Curzon, July 3 1919, FO: 371/3497). Another report gives an account of events after which the British seemed to loose "what little respect" they had for the Abyssinian government (Campbell to Sperling, December 2, 1918, FO: 371/3494). This concerned the influenza epidemic in 1918 which caused death of 10 thousand people in Addis Abäba alone (Thesiger 1992: 63). The way the Ethiopian rulers acted was different from what was expected from people representing power in Europe in similar circumstances. Campbell described the situation when all the members of the triumvir, church dignitaries and the most powerful landlords locked themselves in their households. Täfäri was one of the victims almost killed by the epidemic. He expected one of the few physicians in Addis Abäba to cure only him and "God would take care of all the rest". Even when he recovered he did not pay much attention to the state matters. When the Italian Minister, Count Colli, called the palace to arrange a meeting with the Heir to the Throne he was not allowed to talk to Täfäri. Moreover, Colli was only asked about two ponies that Italians had promised to Täfäri (Campbell to Sperling, December 2, 1918, FO: 371/3494; Marcus 1987: 36f.).

The British perception of Zäwditu was not different from their perception towards other Ethiopian politicians. Moreover it shows the lack of understanding of the situation at the court. Zäwditu was seen as a tool in the hands of landlords opposing Täfäri and tied to German influences at the court (see: Thesiger to Balfour, September 6, 1917, FO: 371/2854; September 21, 1917, FO: 371/2854; Campbell to Curzon, August 23, 1919, FO: 371/3497). Thesiger mentioned her "vanity" and "ignorance" (Thesiger to Balfour, April 5, 1918, FO: 371/3126). The reports prepared by Campbell gave information that presented the situation at the court more realistically. First, he seemed to appreciate the true significance of Zäwditu and especially her official position in the state much higher then Thesiger did. In Campbell's reports, which differ from those by Thesiger, Zäwditu was presented as a person making the final decisions on many state matters. But even for Campbell Zäwditu's decision of 1919 to support Täfäri and terminate the court dispute was completely surprising and incomprehensible. The decision that was undertaken against British expectations seems to have been of grave importance to the Ethiopian history. The Empress decided to strengthen the position of the Heir to the Throne and to pass the power to him. She summoned the landlords to the palace and read a letter declaring that she had no son and *ras* Täfäri had no parents, consequently they were as mother and son, and she gave him power to govern the country. Then Zäwditu addressed Täfäri Mäk^wännən's adversary Habtä Maryam and pointing at Täfäri said: "There is your master" (Campbell to Curzon, September 13, 1919, FO: 371/3497). This event, so surprising for the British, decided the fate of the triumvir and the transfer of power on to Täfäri Mäk^wännən. The event can be seen both as a result of Täfäri and Zäwditu's cooperation, that British were not aware of, as well as of the pressure executed by Täfäri upon the Ethiopian Ministers with the help of his troops (Marcus 1987: 33f.).

Perception of Täfäri Mäk^wännən's significance

The British perception of the Ethiopian politicians generally does not seem to be difficult to describe. Their perception of Täfäri Mäk^wännən, however, is very complicated. At the same time the answer for the question of British perception of the Heir to the Throne may help to understand the British engagement in the Ethiopian politics in the period discussed.

British reports on the situation in Ethiopia describe a country in chaos and lacking a powerful ruler. After 1916 it was reported that the only person that could rule Ethiopia in accordance with the British interest would be *ras* Täfäri Mäk^wännən. He was perceived as willing to rule Ethiopia according to London's recommendations (see: Thesiger to Balfour, June 19, 1917, FO: 371/2855). The only obstacle for him in ruling the country, as reports say, was his lack of possibilities to fulfil his plans due to his weak position. One may suspect that the British aim would have been to strengthen Täfäri's position which in turn could allow them to control Ethiopia. Meeting the British expectations Täfäri managed to strengthen his position in 1919 after Zäwditu's decision referred to above. The correspondence between London Office and the representation in Addis Abäba shows that the change of situation in favour of Great Britain was only due to the internal situation in Ethiopia and not to the intervention of any European power. The question if this is true remains open. The analysis of the documents on arms and munitions supply for Täfäri may be the best example. In the period discussed the embargo on the arms sales to Ethiopia was in force. After 1916, when the new government was trying to strengthen its position, the shortage of arms and ammunition was one of the main problems that Täfäri faced. Therefore he tried to persuade the European powers to support him in his struggle with Iyasu residing in Mäqdäla by delivering arms and planes which would be used to conquer Iyasu. This action would strengthen Täfäri who was perceived by the British as their ally. The issue of arms supply was discussed with the French and Italians (see: Campbell to Balfour, February 8, 1918, FO: 371/3127). According to the reports, in their strengthening of the Heir to the Throne's position they saw the strengthening of their own influence in Ethiopia. This kind of help was promised to Täfäri many times, however, the delay was so long that the outcome of the World War I was decided and the threat of Iyasu's power was not so important any more. The delay was probably caused by the fear of uncontrolled use of the arms, for example, of delivery of the old arms to the anti-British movement in the British controlled areas and supporting their enemies this way (Marcus 1987: 29). Such line of conduct was apparently risky in the situation when possible victory of the Iyasu party could have decided on the British future, and that not only in the area. One should also bear in mind that Iyasu was not seen as the only threat to the British interests. The British also saw Täfäri's enemies at Zäwditu's court and the Empress herself as dangerous for them. They believed Zäwditu was under a certain influence of the anti-British party and in close contact with the Germans. Täfäri appeared to them their only ally at the court. Here the question arises if in this situation British had decided to wait for the events to happen without interfering, or if they had acted without leaving any information in the Foreign Office reports. The British desire to exert influence on Ethiopia's policy towards British enemies i.e. Germany and Turkey, as well as to control Ethiopia's domestic policy is obvious. It is evident from the reports that the British believed in Täfäri's assurances of his will to lead his policy in compliance with their wishes. They described Täfäri as "our friend", who if would fail "there is no one to fill his place". Then, as major Dodds anticipates, there would be chaos and "the power of influence of legation will be nil" (memorandum, Dodds, August 19, 1919, FO: 371/3497). It seems that Täfäri was seen as a possible tool to secure British goals, but still too weak to be able to push for British ideas at the Ethiopian court. Both Thesiger and Campbell flared up with every next event which they saw as a chance for Täfäri to take over the full power in the country. They blamed him for using his chances and deserving his unstable position.[11]

The problem, however, looks different from the Ethiopian perspective. In the period of 1916-1919 Täfäri tried to accommodate himself at the Ethiopian court. The British were right noticing his rather weak position.[12] Still they did not see other aspects of the complex situation. Täfäri was not very keen on gaining power through force mostly because he was sure it would not last. Täfäri had a much greater chance to succeed by winning the trust and building up a good relation with the Empress. His patience in waiting for the right moment and thus strengthening his position turned out to be a success. Täfäri's passiveness and patience, which allowed him to take over in Ethiopia, was misinterpreted by Thesiger as Täfäri's weakness or even stupidity. In the early period of the triumvirate, Thesiger tried to radically influence Täfäri's actions. He advised him to create his own Council instead of co-operating with the existing Council of Ministers. According to Thesiger's suggestions he himself

---

11 Campbell cabled to London that, according to his secret but not confirmed information, Täfäri was intriguing against Minister of War again. "If he does it and fails again, he will deserve to suffer" (Campbell, July 26, 1919, FO: 371/3497).

12 Haylä Səllase cared for the next generations to believe that he had acted as the only ruler of Ethiopia since 1916 already. I am sure this picture is not quite true. Harold Marcus described Täfäri as a very weak politician during the period discussed. Täfäri's real position is very hard to define and needs additional research.

would be designated to create the Council for Täfäri (Thesiger to Grey, November 22, 1916, FO: 371/2854). Numerous times he urged Täfäri to strengthen his power. The British believed that it would help them to get rid of the Germans and the Turks in Ethiopia as well as break the remaining ties between Ethiopia and the Central Powers. The aim was to turn Ethiopia into an unmistakable supporter of the Allies while keeping her in their sphere of influence (Thesiger to Grey, December 8, 1916, FO: 371/2594). Täfäri responded to all these pressures by declaring his will to co-operate with the British, but also underlining his weak position which served as a reason not to follow their instructions. It seems that this political weakness that Täfäri underlined did not fully reflected his real position at the court. It served primarily as a good argument allowing him to make the British believe in his intentions of co-operating without being subordinated at the same time. Täfäri did not want to get involved in any activity which could lead to the threat for the government in Addis Abäba.

An attempt to remove the Germans and the Turks from Ethiopia which was suggested by the British could lead to the growth of pro-Muslim movements and activate the forces of *laǧ* Iyasu, still potentially very dangerous. Moreover, Täfäri probably did not wish to antagonise the Germans who had been respected in Ethiopia for many years and perceived as a balance for the Italian, French and British influences. Germany was accepted as a lesser danger for Ethiopia's independence. On the other hand, Täfäri, who wanted to strengthen his own position, could not have too close relations with any foreign power. But still he wanted to make Thesiger trust him. That was the reason why Täfäri tried to inspire Thesiger's confidence about being loyal to Great Britain as well as about his will to reform the country.

Campbell's remarks concerning Täfäri seem to be more accurate than those of Thesiger. In 1919, in his report of June 12, Campbell wrote that Täfäri played a European towards Europeans, and an Abissinian towards Abissynians. This remark seems to be very accurate to appreciate Täfäri's behaviour. In the same report Campbell wrote that Täfäri did not want to introduce any reforms even if he had the power to enforce them (Campbell to Curzon, July 12, 1919, FO: 371/3497). One may agree with this assumption only if introducing reforms lead to a process of conforming the Ethiopian politics to the demands of Great Britain or other European countries. In any other case, the modernisation of Ethiopia definitely was the aim of Täfäri Mäkʷännən.

According to the reports sent by Thesiger he seemed to fully believe in how the situation was presented to him by Täfäri. One may judge that the British saw the situation at the court according to how it was presented to them by Täfäri. They apparently under-evaluated the role of Empress Zäwditu, and were unaware of the possible co-operation between the Empress and the Heir to the Throne.[13] They treated impor

---

13 It is hard to judge on Zäwditu and Täfäri's mutual relation. They hardly knew each other before 1916 and probably in the first period of Zäwditu's reign they had to work on their relation. Still Zäwditu's decision of 1919, so surprising for the British, to give the executive power in the country to Täfäri, means that by that moment the Empress and the Heir to the

(continued...)

tant landlords as a group of people whose activity is impossible or hard to anticipate, but by all means associated with the threat for the British interest in the country. I believe, that the fact that Täfäri was able to speak European languages was quite important for Täfäri and Thesiger's mutual relation. *Ras* Täfäri Mäk^wännən was the first Ethiopian ruler who spoke fluent French and possibly spoke or understood other European languages. This efficiency was of great importance for the history of the Ethiopian foreign relations as well as for the creation of the image of the Heir to the Throne outside of his country. British diplomats did not speak Amharic and had to communicate with the Ethiopian politicians, except *ras* Täfäri, with the help of the translators. Since 1916 Täfäri as the representative of his country was the least difficult for the diplomats to communicate with. The services of the translator were, as one can imagine, very difficult for the Europeans and when they could do without them they probably had the impression of a more effective exchange of ideas. This was one of the reasons why Täfäri could take control over the foreign affairs. Another important consequence of Täfäri's command of a European language was the fact, that the European comprehension of the Ethiopian court and politics was mostly modelled by *ras* Täfäri Mäk^wännən.

Täfäri's relation with Thesiger

With all these circumstances in mind the relation between Täfäri and Thesiger seems to be puzzling. The literature does not only tell us about Täfäri's sympathy towards the British but also describes close and private relations between Täfäri and Thesiger (Marcus 1987 passim). In Thesiger's reports sent to the London Office one can not find a trace of such close relations between them. The impression one gets after reading the documents is quite different. It seems that the Ethiopian Heir to the Throne and the British Minister were two distant personalities concentrated on their own aims. There seems to be no place in their relations for the liking or acquaintance beyond the frame of diplomatic relations, especially bearing in mind the attitude of the British towards the Ethiopians described above. This attitude referred to Täfäri as well. Different conclusion can be drawn on the base of Thesiger's son memories. As an adult he had several occasions to meet Emperor Ḥaylä Śəllase I. The Emperor treated him in a very special way and emphasised ties between him and young Thesiger's father. Apart from mutual sympathy Emperor remembered the help the British diplomat once offered him (Thesiger 1992: 23, 93).

Another argument for the existence of a good relationship between Thesiger and Täfäri that cannot be traced in the British archive is the fact that in 1916 Täfäri left his newly-born son Asfa Wässän with the British diplomat's family. Täfäri at that time was

---

13 (...continued)
    Throne had worked out their cooperation.

preparing for the war with Iyasu and it was Thesiger to take care of the Heir's son (Thesiger 1992: 51). It seems to prove Täfäri's trust in Thesiger. The doubts described above may prove that important events in the Ethiopian-British relations were not mentioned in the British reports.

Recapitulation

The trust of the British in Täfäri's will to support them described in the documents were only partially consistent with Täfäri's true plans. He definitely wanted to introduce changes into the country and wanted to use European participation. But in fact he only wanted to introduce the kind of reforms he thought necessary for the country. Täfäri Mäkʷännən was concerned with the interests of his own country in the first place and did not wish to accept any foreign policy towards Ethiopia that he would not see as good from the Ethiopian point of view. One of Täfäri's features that were often described was his patience and ability to wait for the best moment, sometimes very long, to fulfil his aims. That is why it seems that he deliberately made the British believe that he was ready to follow policy recommended by them. It allowed him to control British activities and possibly use their engagement for his own purposes, that is for strengthening his own position in the country and justification of the state's efficiency. It seems impossible that the events in Ethiopia in the period of intense struggle for power and with a considerable German involvement could run according to the British will without their intervention. The analysis of the Public Record Office documents does not lead to the conclusion that representatives of Great Britain were carrying out activities to strengthen Täfäri's power. But at the same time the knowledge of the situation in Ethiopia and other sources suggest different opinion. The existence of different documents that are not in the main Foreign Office collection seems to be the answer for the unexpected content of the reports. If the British had undertaken actions that were not noted in the reports delivered by the diplomats to the office in London, what seems to be very likely, it shows Täfäri's ability to use British involvement in the internal struggle for power and their wish to subordinate Ethiopia for his own purposes. Täfäri's success was that the British did not realise what the situation at the court and in the country was; likewise they did not understand the role of the Empress and the landlords in the country. Without thinking much they saw them as German allies and British enemies. It helped Täfäri to lead his own policy. There is no proof of money support for Täfäri even though such kind of support seems to be the most probable one. Most of his activities were successful thanks to his wealthy position. I think that in spite of a possible involvement of British representatives in the Ethiopian events, the growth of Täfäri Mäkʷännən's power was most of all the result of internal situation. It was, however, profitable both for Täfäri Mäkʷännən and for Great Britain. Still, the question of the specific role of Great Britain and other European Powers in the internal struggle for power remains open.

Bibliography

Anonymous
1997   *The Encyclopaedia of Islam*. Vol. 9. Leiden 2.

Bahru Zewde
1991   *A History of Modern Ethiopia 1855-1974*. London - Athens - Addis Ababa.

Bairu Tafla
1981   Ethiopia and Germany, Cultural, Political and Economic Relations, 1871-1936.
        Äthiopistische Forschungen 5. Wiesbaden.

Bartnicki, A. and Mantel-Niećko, J.
1978   *Geschichte Äthiopiens*. Berlin.

Berhanou Abebe
2001   Le coup d État du 26 Septembre 1916 ou le dénouement d une décennie de
        crise. *Annales d Éthiopie 17*: 307-357.

Greenfield, R.
1969   Ethiopia, A New Political History. London.

Marcus, H. G.
1987   *Haile Sellassie I, The Formative Years, 1892-1936*. Berkeley - Los Angeles -
        London.

Reishies, S.
1937   *Abessinien als Kampfobjekt der großen Mächte von 1880-1916 auf Grund der
        diplomatischen Akten*. Bleicherode.

Scholler, H.
1980   German World War I aims in Ethiopia, – the Frobenius-Hall-Mission. In: *Jo-
        seph Tubiana (ed.), Modern Ethiopia, From the Accession of Menelik II To the
        Present*. Proceedings of the Fifth International Conference of Ethiopian Stud-
        ies. Rotterdam: 303-326.

Smidt, W. G. C.
2001   The Coronation of nägus Mikael in Desse in May 1914: A Photograph From
        the Nachlass Jensen and Its Historical Background. *Annales d'Éthiopie 17*:
        359-371.

Thesiger, W.
1992   *The Life of my Choice*. London.

Public Record Office Documents

FO: 371/2593; 371/2594; 371/2595 (1916)
FO: 371/2853; 371/2854; 371/2855 (1917)
FO: 371/3125; 371/3126; 371/3127 (1918)
FO: 371/ 3494; 371/3495; 371/3497; 371/3498 (1919)

Glossary

(based on: Andrzej Bartnicki – Joanna Mantel-Niećko: 621-647 and Encyclopaedia of Islam, vol. 9: 115)

däǧǧazmač	lit. "the one to command at the door (of an emperor's tent)"; one of traditional, high army titles
fitawrari	lit. "atacking at the head"; traditional army titel, commander of the vanguard or the main commander of the emperor's or provincional governors' army
ləǧ	lit. "child"; the meaning is close to this of "infant"
nəguś	lit. "king"; independend ruler, his only sovereign, and only formally is the emperor
(nəguśä nägäśi)	
ras	lit. "head"; one of the highest military and court titles in Ethiopia
sayyid	honory title for Muḥammad's Abdalläh Ḥassan heirs

An 8th Century Chinese Fragment on the Nubian and Abyssinian Kingdoms – Some Remarks

Wolbert Smidt

Due to the general lack of sources from late antiquity on the Aksumite kingdom and the surrounding areas, the appearance of even minor new sources on this dark period will be of some interest. With this paper I shall present small pieces of an 8th century text, mainly preserved in a 9th century Chinese encyclopaedia. This ancient text certainly refers to an African country – scholars has been agreeing on this since about 120 years. Since some time the idea has been discussed that the fragment should refer to the East African coast, especially the Eritrean region. I will demonstrate, that the identification of the regions mentioned with the Nubian and Aksumite kingdoms is possible. This document has never been discussed in Ethiopian Studies so far, but deserves to be mentioned at least in footnotes, as it contributes to our knowledge of the Aksumite kingdom in a situation of decline, as I believe to be able to show.[1]

The fragments we have are mainly preserved in the huge encyclopaedical work of Du You, the *Tong Dian* ('Source Material on Political and Social History') of the early 9th century. In an overview over countries in the far West he briefly tells the story of his relative Du Huan, who has lived in the mid-8th century and quotes passages from his travel report called *Jing Xing Ji* ('Record of My Travels'), which, however, has been lost. Du You quotes him seven times. Some other pieces of it has been quoted by other ancient Chinese authors. All these texts had been produced during the Tang dynasty, one of the few Chinese dynasties, which were characterized by a strong interest for the countries outside the reach of the Chinese Empire; it was even a fashion at the court to be clothed in the "Turkish" way. The Chinese in that period were also involved in a number of military conflicts with expanding Arabs.

It was such a military expedition, during which Du Huan left his homeland. A Chinese army met an Arab army (the "Dashi") in Uzbekistan in the year 751, but the Chinese were dramatically defeated near Tashkent. Several thousand Chinese soldiers and officers, among them Du Huan, were brought to the Abbasid Caliphate. It is known, that many of them then settled there permanently as artisans, introducing the technical knowledge of the Chinese – like paper-making[2] – into the Caliphate, as Du Huan reports (in the capital Kufâ; shortly later, in 762 A.D., Baghdad was founded).

---

1 One of Littmann's main interests being the reconstruction of the ancient past, a discussion of these fragments might be appropriate on this conference.
2 Some of those Chinese captives were employed when the paper mill of Samarkand was set up, cf. Zhang Jun-yan 1983: 97.

Du Huan, however, started to travel in and outside the Caliphate and finally took a ship in "Molin guo" ('the country of Molin'), as he calls it, and returned from there to Guangzhou (Kanton).

The first general passage on his travels in *Tong Dian* reads as follows:
"The relative Huan was fighting in the West under General Gao Xianzhi; in the 10th year of the government device Tianbao [751] he arrived at the Western Sea;[3] in the first year of the government device Baoying [762] he returned to Guangzhou on board of a trade ship and wrote the *Jing Xing Ji*."[4]

Du Huan during his travels went far "southwest" of the East Roman Empire, and from there reached the country Molin, "respectively Laobosa". The mid-11th century author Ouyang Xiu tells us in the *Xin Tangshu*[5], based on Du Huan's travel account:

"Coming from Fulin one reaches, after having crossed the desert in a southwestern direction and having travelled for 2,000 Li, a country called Molin, respectively Laobosa."

This passage is of crucial importance, as it provides us with some basic information on the geographic location of Molin. The term "Fulin" is well documented in ancient Chinese texts; it is the Tang dynasty term for the East Roman Empire (derived from Soghdian "From", Persian "Hrom")[6]. Du Huan himself describes the geographic location of Fulin: "The empire of Fulin lies in the west of the country of Shan [Syria, Arab. 'Sham']. It is separated from it by mountains and several thousand Li, and is also called Daqin[7]." Syria had been lost by the East Roman Empire to the Caliphate not long before. – Du Huan's account implies that he has himself been at the Southern borders of the East Roman Empire, when he started his journey to Molin. His full account (i.e. the fragment) of his journey to Molin reads as follows:

"We also went to Molin, southwest of Yangsaluo. One reaches this country after having travelled 2,000 Li. The people there are black, their customs rough. There is little rice and cereals and there is no grass and trees. The horses are fed with dry fish,

---

3 This term is known from ancient Chinese geography, meaning the Mediterranean Sea (the Chinese envoy Gan Ying is the first to reach the "West Sea" at the boundaries of the Roman Empire, according to Chinese historiography, in 97 A.D.; cf. Zhang Jun-yan 1983: 92).

4 I am particularly indebted to Matthias Anton for his readiness to translate these passages from ancient Chinese into German. He has also translated a paper of the Chinese historian Shen Fuwei (1980) for me. All text fragments are quoted after Shen Fuwei; if diverging versions appear in other texts, I quote them in footnotes. – I equally thank Prof. Dr. Ruth Cremerius, Department of Sinology, University of Hamburg, for translating the entry on Du Huan from the Chinese Great Encyclopaedia (1995). – Tang Songgen of the Chinese Embassy in Asmara, Eritrea, historian by formation, had the infinite kindness to provide me with a number of relevant Chinese publications related to the topic.

5 Chapter 221, on the "Dashi" (*Dashi-zuan*). The Tang dynasty term for Arabs, "Dashi", is derived from Tajik, cp. Zhang Jun-yan 1983: 93.

6 See Tubach 1999: 65; Smidt 2002: 21.

7 This term, often used to designate the (East) Roman Empire, underlines the identification of Fulin with the East Roman Empire.

the people eat XX [word not identified] and also Persian dates. Subtropical diseases [malaria] are widespread.

After crossing the inland there is a mountainous country, there are a lot of confessions. The followers of the confession of the Dashi [i.e. Islam] have a means to denote the degrees of family relations, but it is degenerated and they do not bother about it.[8] They do not eat the meat of pigs, dogs, donkeys and horses. They do not respect neither the king of the country, nor their parents. They do not believe in supernatural powers [or: deities and ghosts], they perform sacrifice to heaven and to no one else. According to their custom every seventh day is a holiday, on which there is no trade [or: no bargain] and no cash transactions, whereas when they drink alcohol, they are behaving in a ridiculous and undisciplined way during the whole day.

Within the East Roman confession [i.e. the Christian religion] the medical doctors know diarrhoea – or they recognize it already before the outbreak of the disease, or they open the brain and insects come out."

The fragment cuts short here. Even if quite brief and partially curious it contains a number of most interesting details, which deserve a closer analysis.

1. The geographical location of Molin:
   Molin is situated southwest of Yangsaluo; the context suggests that Du Huan's journey took 2,000 Li.
2. The climate and the population of Molin:
   Molin has an arid climate; the population is black.
3. There is still another country or land:
   This land is mountainous and lying further inland. NB: Another version of this fragment, which otherwise is almost identical, has "mountains and lakes one after the other" (Shen 1980).
4. The population of the mountainous country:
   There is a number of different religions.

Together with the fragment quoted first it seems clear that the journey then must have started somewhere southwest of the East Roman Empire. The identification of Yangsaluo, however, is unclear at first sight. It is used as a point of reference for Molin and should lie near the southern borders of the East Roman Empire. Additionally it should be a major area or city and caravan post on a journey from the centre of the Caliphate further west and then southwest to the countries of the "blacks", i.e. Africa. Therefore it seems not improbable that Jerusalem is meant; in fact Chinese historiography has already come to this conclusion, as the toponym

8   Zhang Jun-yan 1983: 96f., translates this phrase quite differently: "According to (...) [Islam], they would be judged by their students and kindreds, even if they had committed some small faults, wouldn't worry to be punished." The rest of the passage on Islam is rendered very similarily, however.

"Yangsaluo" also appears in another ancient text, the *Weilue*, in a context, which allows its identification with Jerusalem.[9]

The distance given should of course be regarded as approximative. However, ancient Chinese travellers or officers, trained also in geography, were not unaware of distances. Their figures are thus more than only imaginative. The distance of 2000 Li roughly corresponds to 1300 km. This would lead us to an area somewhere in the Sudan. Du Huan also mentions that one needs to cross a desert and describes an arid country. From the context it is clear that there should be enough water to allow fishing, and it should not be far from the Sea, as Du Huan travelled back starting from Molin (!) by ship to arrive finally at Kanton. This was possible from the Sudanese and Aksumite ports, 'Aydhâb, Badhi` (today's Massawa)[10] or Adulis (today's Zula). South-Arabian ports can be excluded, as South Arabia, even if partially fitting into the description, was not lying "southwest" of Fulin.

Since the first discussion of the fragment by sinologists in 1871 (Bretschneider) there have been quite a number of theories on the exact location of Molin, the first serious ones published by Friedrich Hirth (1885, 1909). As I have already discussed most of them (Smidt 2002), I should not repeat all the discussion here. The most important ones are the identification with "an East African State" (Hirth 1885, 1909; in 1885 he identifies it with the Nubian kingdom of 'Alwa, which, however, lies a bit too much southwest in the Sudan at the Blue Nile to correspond to Du Huan's description), others identify it with Malindi (*Malin* in Ming dynasty Chinese, which, however, does not correspond to the description of the route between Fulin and Molin and not to the distance given; Laufer 1919[11]), and with Ethiopia – due to the name of the Aksumite god "Mahrem", allegedly used for the country (which is historiographical imagination, as Mahrem was a pre-Christian god known in Aksum in

---

9 Cf. Shen Fuwei 1980: 47. I thank Ambassador Werner Daum for his critical remark on this identification. He found it problematic, as Jerusalem as a term was not in use any more, but rather al-Quds, which, however, would sound too different from "Yangsaluo". The use of "Yangsaluo", however, does not seem surprising to me, as Du Huan was not travelling in areas completely unknown to Chinese geography and historiography – a number of Chinese designations of areas and cities therefore should be dependent on older Chinese sources (as the use of the term "Fulin" also shows). Nestorian Christianity was quite present in Tang dynasty China (cf. Tubach 1999), and the biblical term "Jerusalem" should thus have been more present in Chinese geography than a more recent designation. – The question on the identification with Jerusalem might need further inquiry; but even if put into doubt, this would not change much in the identification of the approximate route of Du Huan, as we do know that it should have started somewhere south of the East Roman Empire and have ended in the country of the blacks in a southwestern direction.

10 Cp. Lusini 2003; Badhi` is still today the term how local nomads call Massawa.

11 Also Filesi 1962:37 identifies "Mo Lin" with Malindi, following irrelevant secondary literature (Oliver - Fage 1962:97); he does not seem to know Du Huan's text, but only the later notes on that country in *Xin Tangshu* and does not undertake any analysis. In a later note (Filesi 1962:39) he even misspells it "Ma-lin", the old Chinese word for Malindi, and translates the "2000 Li" inappropriately with "duemila miglia".

the 4th century and before, but certainly not anymore in the 8th century; Shen Fuwei 1980; Snow 1988 follows this hypothesis, slightly changing the area identified into "Eritrea", cp. also Böckelmann 1998).

In my first publication on the subject I, however, have not said everything necessary on the identification of Molin and Laobosa. Du Huan's fragment is precise enough to allow a quite reliable identification of those areas. It should especially be noted, that the text implicitly speaks of *two* countries, which has largely been overlooked until now. The location of Molin has often been discussed, while Laobosa had often been ignored. The "mountainous land" has often been identified with Molin, even if the text itself does not suggest this. Molin is described by Du Huan as an arid area lying south of a desert (in a plain!), and only if travelling further "inland" one reaches a mountainous land. The version quoted by us seems to have omitted the detail, that in that mountainous land there were lakes, which are appearing in another version of the same fragment.

One should first have a closer look on the arid country, which can be reached after crossing a desert. In late antiquity the following Nubian kingdoms existed south of Egypt, nourished by the Nile, but surrounded by deserts: the Christian kingdoms of Napata (the successor state of Meroe) and of Mekuria, which, however, merged into one before ca. 700 A.D. due to pressure by Arab armies.[12] The emerging kingdom was now called Mekuria (Greek; Arab. al-Maqurra, al-Muqurra); only later it became also known as the kingdom of Dongola (Dunqulah), as Dongola was her capital. This Christian kingdom was linked by trade routes with the Christian Abyssinian kingdom, lying in the mountains further south, and with the Red Sea ports. When Du Huan arrived in the Sudan in 762 A.D. or slightly before, he can only have arrived in that kingdom.

The term "Molin" would also fit into the kingdom's name. The reduction and modification of both consonants and vowels by Chinese speakers makes it often difficult to recognize the original word or name behind its Chinese version. To start with – the "l" would certainly correspond to an "r" or "l", and the original word would probably start with an "m". Both would correspond to the kingdom's name. Here it is interesting to note that the syllable "Mo" is pronounced with a rising and falling tone; this makes it possible that it is the reduction of a longer syllable or two syllables; "Muqu-", unpronouncable in Chinese, can in fact appear as "Mu" or "Mo". The ending syllable "lin" would have preserved the "r" and the occasionally appearing "i".

Shen Fuwei (1980: 51) points to an interesting historical coincidence: After several military conflicts with Egypt, the kingdom of Mekuria had to send a high rank hostage to the Abbasid Caliph in 758, the king's son.[13] This was followed by an exchange of embassies. Snow (1988: 4) rightly underlines that this would make it explainable, how the Chinese officer Du Huan might have left the centre of the Caliphate, where he was staying with the other Chinese captives: "The inclusion of a Chinese in the party

12 Egypt had been conquered in 640 A.D.
13 *Journal of Egyptian Archaeology* 61, 1975: 241-245.

may have been intended to awe them by exhibiting the vast range of peoples who were subject to Arab rule". Additionally such an expedition could provide him with a chance to travel back to China by sea, which would explain his personal motivation.

The term "Laobosa" remains to be explained. It does not appear in the main fragment of Du Huan, but in a secondary ancient text referring to his travel report. The passage "a country called Molin, respectively Laobosa" in Chinese is ambiguous. The term "respectively" is expressed with the ancient character for "say", which can also be read as "and" or, in this context, "and [another country called...]"[14]. In this case it should be read as "countries called Molin and Laobosa". Shen Fuwei (1980: 46), however, suggests that the same region is meant (as he identifies the term "Molin" with Ethiopia!), but he also points to the possibility, that two different countries may be meant. I should prefer the second possibility, as the fragment itself suggests the existence of two different countries,[15] even if not naming the second, the mountainous country further inland. If one takes the distances into account, one should come to the conclusion, that the 2000 Li would be enough to reach the Nubian kingdom of Mekuria – but there are no mountains within this area, and no lakes. The only area possible to be identified with this description is Abyssinia (the European term for the ancient Arabic term al-Habasha), which is lying further south, above all characterised by her mountains and by the lakes nourishing the Nile and other rivers. It was well connected with Nubia by ancient trade routes. NB: Du Huan's travel account makes it clear that he has visited Molin (Mekuria), but he does not speak of having been in the mountainous land himself. This is important, if we analyse the ethnographic details he gives on that area.

The original word behind the Chinese term "Laobosa" is easily identifiable – it can only be Arabic "al-Habash", i.e. the Ethiopian highlands. This ancient territorial designation for the Aksumite kingdom (in contrast to the ethnonym al-Habash, 'Abyssinian') is well-known from classical Arabic (cp. al-Tabarî's *Annals* of the 9th/10th century or ibn al Wadhîh al Ya'qûbî's 9th century *History*). It might be interesting to note here, that ancient Arabic geography had a quite fixed pattern in listing the

---

14 I thank Xi Yiyang, student at Shanghai University, for his remarks on this.

15 This is supported by the secondary mid-11th century Chinese text, which I have mentioned above, which clearly depends on Du Huan's travel account, even if interpreting it. The *Xin Tangshu*, ch. 221, speaks of two countries: "Crossing the desert in the south-west of Fu-lin, at a distance of 2,000 li there are two countries called Mo-lin ('Alwa, or Upper Kush) and Lao-p'o-sa (Maqurra, or Lower Kush). Their inhabitants are black and of a violent disposition. The country is malarious and has no vegetation. They feed their horses on dried fish, and live themselves on *hu-mang* (the Persian date – *Phoenix dactylifera*). They are not ashamed to have most frequent illicit intercourse with savages; they call this 'establishing the relation between lord and subject.' On one of seven days they refrain from doing business, and carouse all night." (Quoted after Hirth 1885; note his identification with the Nubian kingdoms of al-Maqurra and Alwa). Filesi 1962: 39; also translates this passage, but misspells "Ma-lin", which in his translation is identical with "il vecchio P'o-sa" (= 'old Bosa', i.e. "Laobosa").

countries from the Red Sea to the Indian Ocean: These are al-Misr (Egypt) – al-Muqurra (or other designations for Nubian kingdoms) – al-Habasha (Abyssinia) – Barbara (Berber, i.e. the Somali coast) – Zanj (Azania, i.e. the country of the "blacks"). Correspondingly almost all these terms (or as I believe: all of them!) also appear in ancient and medieval Chinese geography,[16] which generally depends on Arabic sources for areas in the far West. It is sometimes assumed that Chinese knowledge of Africa was almost non-existant before the famous 15th century expeditions of the Ming dynasty admiral Zheng He, whose fleet "discovered" the East African coast between the mouth of the Red Sea and Malindi (Kenya) from 1417 to 1433. However, the Somali coast is already described[17] in a 10th century Chinese Tang dynasty text (Duan Chengshi, *Yuyang za zu*, 'Assorted Dishes from Yuyang'), with details, which show that only the Horn of Africa can be meant;[18] and Oman in Southern Arabia has even been mentioned already at the end of the 1st century A.D. (Zhang Jun-yan 1983:92). The oldest map, which shows the whole of Africa in an approximately realistic shape, is a Chinese world map of 1389 A.D. (s. Cao Wanru 1990-97). On it also the Horn of Africa can very roughly be identified.

The ethnographic details reported by Du Huan can be discussed briefly here, as I have already made an analysis of it (Smidt 2002: 25-26). Interesting is certainly the Chinese perspective on the countries visited. He does not describe them as hospitable places, he seems rather surprised about quite a number of habits – they (even) do not eat dogs! In the arid lands of Molin (Mekuria) dried fish is fed to horses. This is a topos, which is reproduced in another medieval source, which may well be based on Chinese traditions: Marco Polo, who resided in China in the 13th century, in his travel account also spoke about the country of the "Abasce" (Abyssinians) and the ports of the Red Sea in some detail. In the Arab port of "Escier" (i.e. Shir/South-Yemen, the

---

16 More on this s. Smidt 2002: 23, esp. footnote 47, 24; see also below. The list would be: *Mushili* (Misr) – *Molin* (Mekuria) – *Laobosa* (al-Habash) – *Bobali* or *Bibaluo* (Berbera) – *Zhongli* (Zanj). The terms *Mushili* for Egypt and *Bibaluo* for Berbera appear in the *Zhu Fan Zhi* ('Records of Foreign People' or 'Gazetteer of Foreigners') of Zhao Rugua of 1225 A.D., cp. Zhang Jun-yan 1983: 101, and Cerulli – Freeman-Grenville 1960: 715. The term *Bobali* for Berbera is recorded in a text of the Chinese scholar Duan Chengshi, who died in 863 A.D., the *Yuyang za zu* ('Assorted dishes from Yuyang'), cf. Cerulli - Freeman-Grenville 1960: 715

17 and perhaps mentioned even in the 8th century already : The Tang dynasty geographer Jia Dan (730-805 A.D.) has written *The Route to the Foreign Countries Across the Sea from Canton*, mainly based on Arabic sources. His note "In the west of the maritime route from Canton to the Arab country by the south end there is the San-lan country" has been understood as a reference to Zayla' at the Somali coast, cf. Zhang Jun-yan 1983: 93.

18 They "do not eat the Five Grains, but only meat. They are given to sticking a needle into the veins of their cattle and drawing out the blood, which they mix with milk and consume raw. They wear no clothes, but merely use goatskins to cover the parts below their waists." (After Snow 1988: 13 and Duyvendak 1949: 13.) Still today Cushitic peoples in the Horn of Africa are known for drinking milk mixed with blood, which is regularly taken from the living cow.

second area described after Abyssinia) the horses are fed with dried fish (Polo 1983: 378, 489). One shall add, that the lack of cereals, as described by Du Huan, was certainly true especially for the coastal areas.

The description of the mountainous country – Laobosa – goes into more detail; especially his understanding of Islam and the Christian religion is quite interesting. The formula "they pray to the Heaven only"[19] perfectly corresponds to other notes on the monotheistic religions of the West in later Chinese texts: The 'Gazetteer of Foreigners' of 1225 A.D. (mentioned above) notes on the Somali people: "They serve heaven and do not serve the Buddha".

The contexts suggests, that the Muslims of Laobosa are especially traders. They appear as strict followers of their religion (they stop any trade on the seventh day), but they do not obey the king. This might refer to the situation of decline of the Aksumite kingdom, which had lost control over the trade to the (Muslim!) Arabs on the Red Sea. It is interesting, that the lack of respect for the king is connected with the Muslim traders of this country. The sharp remark of Du Huan on drunk people appears as a contrast to the disciplined observation of the religious holidays; in fact alcoholic beverages are really traditionally known also among Muslims in the Horn of Africa.

Du Huan's short remarks on the Christians of that country seem a bit surprising. However, taken into account, that he might have heard that story from traders coming from Laobosa without possibly having seen it himself, the explanation seems quite simple: It is true, that traditional medicine is deeply enrooted in ancient Abyssinian Christianity, the clergy itself being its most important preserver still today; diarrhoea is really a most widespread phenomenon and well-known within traditional medical practise; and "opening the brain" is not as surprising as it seems: a very ancient medical practise is the cutting of the skin of the forehead, the eyebrow or the cheek. It is often said, that this should help the "bad blood" to pour out, followed by the bad spirits ("insects"), which caused the disease.[20]

The colourful text of Du Huan is the first ancient account on the visit of a Chinese in African countries. He has first visited the Nubian kingdom of Mekuria and has then reached the coast, from where he left Africa with a trader's ship. If he left it from Badhi' (probably not Adulis, as this Aksumite port was in decline) in today's Eritrea or from the Sudanese coast (Aydhâb, north of Sawakin), cannot be said with any sufficient degree of certainty any more. An Eritrean port seems probable, as Indian traders were reported there already in ancient times; this would also easily explain Du Huan's notes on Laobosa – which he might not have visited himself, but to which

---

19 This is the translation of Zhang Jun-yan 1983: 97, of the relevant passage in Du Huan's travel account.
20 Most interestingly there is still today in Tigray an old tradition of magic healing, which corresponds well to the practice described by Du Huan. E.g., when a person is suffering from a tinitus or other ear diseases, magical plants and liquids are applied to the ear, having an immediate effect, and living insects are subsequently coming out of the ear (according to interviews with elders in Endärta, carried out during field research in June 2004).

then he would have come very close at least. The greatest importance of this fragment certainly lies in the fact, that it is one of the very few sources, which give an impression of the late Aksumite kingdom and its multitude of religions, co-existing with each other.

Bibliography

Anonymous
1999ff. Du Huan. In: *Zhong guo da bai ke quan shu (Chinese Great Encyclopaedia)*, *Vol. 2*. Beijing: 1118.

Böckelmann, F.
1998 *Die Gelben, die Schwarzen, die Weißen*. Frankfurt am Main.

Bretschneider, E.
1871 *On the Knowledge Possessed by the Ancient Chinese of the Arabs and Arabian Colonies, and other Western countries, mentioned in Chinese books*. London.

Cao Wanru:
1990-97 *Zhongguo gu dai di tu ji* (An Atlas of ancient maps in China). 3 Vols. Beijing.

Cerulli, E. and Freeman-Grenville, G. S. P.
1960 Somali, history. In: *The Encyclopaedia of Islam, New Edition, Vol. IX*. Leiden - London: 715-716.

Duyvendak, J. J. L.
1949 China's Discovery of Africa. London.

Filesi, T.
1962 *Le Relazioni della Cina con l'Africa nel Medio-Evo*. Milano.

Hirth, F.
1885 *China and the Roman Orient. Researches into their Ancient and Mediaeval Relations as Represented in Old Chinese Records*. Leipzig - München (Shanghai - Hong Kong ²1939, Chicago ³1975).
1909 Early Chinese Notices of East African Territories. In: *Journal of African and Oriental Studies* 30: 46-57.

Laufer, B.
1919 *Sino-Iranica. Chinese contributions to the history of civilization in ancient Iran*. Chicago.

Leslie, D. D. and Gardiner, K. H. J.
1996   *The Roman Empire in Chinese Sources*. Roma.

Lusini, G.
2003   Badhi`. In: *Siegbert Uhlig (ed.), Encyclopaedia Aethiopica, Vol. 1*. Wiesbaden:
        430-431.

Munro-Hay, S.
2003   China. In: *Siegbert Uhlig (ed.), Encyclopaedia Aethiopica, Vol. I*. Wiesbaden:
        714-715.

Oliver, R. and Fage, J. D.
1962   *A Short History of Africa*. Harmondsworth.

Polo, M.
1983   *Il Milione. Die Wunder der Welt*. Zürich.

Sergew Hable Sellassie
1972   *Ancient and Medieval Ethiopian History to 1270*. Addis Ababa.

Shen Fuwei
1980   Tang dai du huan de mo lin zhi xing (Du Huan's Journey to Molin in the Tang
        Period). In: *Shijie lishi ('World History')*. No. 6. Beijing (in Chinese).

Smidt, W.
2002   A Chinese in the Nubian and Abyssinian Kingdoms (8th Century). The visit of
        Du Huan to Molin-guo and Laobosa. In: *Chroniques yéménites 2001, 9*: 17-
        28.

Snow, P.
1988   *The Star Raft. China's Encounter with Africa*, London.

Tubach, J.
1999   Die nestorianische Kirche in China. In: *Nubica et Aethiopica*, Internationales
        Jahrbuch für koptische, meroitisch-nubische, äthiopische und verwandte
        Studien, IV/V, 1999/1994-95: 61-193.

Zhang Jun-yan
1983   Relations between China and the Arabs in Early Times. In: *The Journal of
        Oman Studies 61*: 91-109.

III. The Ethiopian Church

Saintly Shadows[1]

Stuart Munro-Hay †

1. The Nine Saints of Ethiopia

The centuries of obscurity, the 'dark ages', of Aksumite history are illumined for us only at brief moments, in the reigns of King Ezana and King Kaleb, for example, when we have enough documentation to be able to make some sort of commentary. Thanks to the coinage we know the names of a sequence of kings from Endubis to Armah or Gersem, but for most of the Aksumite period, apart from a few inscriptions, and the anonymous evidence of archaeology that furnishes us with so much information about Aksum's culture in general, that is nearly the entire sum of our information.

Yet the Ge`ez hagiographers fill in quite lavishly one section of the Aksumite 'dark age', in the late fifth and early sixth centuries, with the rich tapestry of the lives of the so-called 'Nine Saints'. We have the kings of Aksum, Sa`aldoba or Sal'adoba, Ella Amida or Alameda, Tazena, Kaleb with his two sons Gabra Masqal and Israel, Ella Gabaz or Za-Gabaza Aksum and King Sahel; we have the metropolitan bishop Eleyas; we have serpents and archangels, and a surfeit of miracles and monastery building. Above all, central to this setting, we have the life stories of the nine (or more, because there are variants in the lists) pre-eminent holy men of the first phase of Ethiopian monasticism.

These monks, the Ge`ez stories inform us, were all foreigners, several of royal or near-royal Roman birth. They sowed Christianity and the monastic life in the countryside in the heartlands of the kingdom of Aksum, mostly, that is, in Tigray or just over the Mareb river in what became Eritrea. Modern historians have searched for the likely reasons why these persons, from Syria, Anatolia or other regions of the Byzantine (Roman) empire, might have come to Aksum at this period of its history. Some have fallen on the happy explanation that they were exiles fleeing from persecution against the monophysite belief (in the one nature of Christ), by Byzantine duophysite (two natures) or melkite (royal/imperial) authorities, after the division of eastern Christianity confirmed by the failure to agree at the council of Chalcedon in 451 AD. Ethiopia, following the tenets favoured by the patriarchate of Alexandria,

---

1   This section, in an earlier version, was presented as one of the four Main Papers in the First Littmann Conference, Munich, 2002. The comments of my colleagues there have much enriched the theme.

from which came Ethiopia's bishops, would have been a haven for these exiles, the only independent monophysite monarchy in the world.

To sum up the purported origins and monastic foundations of the Nine Saints, the following list summarises the information offered by the different Ge`ez *gadlat* (life stories, sing. *gadl*, a literary genre invented perhaps at the end of the fourteenth century) and homilies:

Afse of Esya (Asia, Edessa?). Afse met Yeshaq (Garima, see below), who had just abdicated the throne, at Rome (Constantinople). After a retreat at a monastery in Egypt, he accompanied Yeshaq and the other saints to Ethiopia in the reign of King Ella Amida. After some time together they separated. After various travels with Yeshaq, Afse founded his monastery at Yeha. King Kaleb visited him there, and Afse built a church in which he installed a *tabot* (the characteristic altar-tablet of Ethiopian churches) of Maryam that he had with him. The saint having expelled a serpent from the womb of the queen (who later gave birth to Prince Gabra Masqal), King Kaleb granted revenues to the community. Afse was succeeded by Qozmos. He is remembered in the *Synaxarium* with Guba 'of the ninety (sic.) saints of 'Engelga...'

Alef, of Caesarea, founded monastery in Bi'isa or Behesa near the Mareb river. His name is replaced by that of `**Os** in *Gadla Abba Garima*; Pero Pais, however, believed that 'Abba Oz' was a later name given to Guba. The *Synaxarium* for 4 Tahsas notes that 'on this day we commemorate Abba `Ôs and the virgins...'. It also provides a brief mention for Alef on 11 Magabit (which does not appear in all versions).

Garima (or Yeshaq), son of Masfeyanos (Maximianus?[2]), king of Rome, and Queen Sefengeya. Ruled Rome for seven years. (Maximianus was emperor of Rome 286-305, and his son Maxentius succeeded 306-312, when he was drowned after the battle with Constantine at the Milvian Bridge). Garima was summoned by Pantalewon, reaching Aksum by air with the aid of the archangel Gabriel. He received the monastic habit from Pantalewon. They were joined later by Liqanos, Yemata, Sehma, Guba, Afse, Mata`a, and `Os. Garima built a monastery at Madara east of Adwa. Gabra Masqal built him a church there. He is commemorated in the *Synaxarium* on 17 Megabit with a salutation, and on 17 Sane with an abbreviated version of his *Life*.

Guba, from Cilicia. Stayed with Pantalewon for a while then disappeared into the Baraka desert. His commemoration in the *Synaxarium* is with Afse on 29 Genbot.

Liqanos, of Qwestentenya (Constantinople). Established himself at Dabra Qwanasel, Aksum. He is not mentioned in the *Synaxarium*.

Pantalewon, of a noble Roman family. Built his cell at Beta Qatin, Aksum. Kaleb visited him before his Himyarite war against Finhas, king of Saba. He died in the reign of Kaleb's successor, King 'Sahel', in 246, era of Diocletian (530AD) according to his *gadl*. He is remembered in the *Synaxarium* with Garima (17 Sane), with the Martyrs of Najran (26 Hedar), with Kaleb (20 Genbot), and also on 6 Teqemt.

2   Rossini 1897: 173.

Sahma (Sehma), of Antioch. Settled at Sadenya or Sadya about twenty-five miles north-east of Adwa. In the *Synaxarium* his brief commemoration is on 16 Ter.

Yemata (Yem'ata), of Qusyat, possibly a place in Egypt, established a monastery in the mountainous region of Garalta. A brief salutation to Yemata 'whose body was buried in a rock at the top of a mountain' occurs in the *Synaxarium* for 28 Teqemt.

Za Mikael Aregawi, son of Yeshaq and Edna of the royal family of Rome. He became a monk with Pachomius (d. 348), attracting seven of the other saints there also. Visited Rome and Aksum, which he found already converted. Returned to Rome, and brought the other saints back to Aksum with him in the fifth year of King Ella Amida son of Sa`aldoba. Yeshaq (Garima), his relative, king of Rome, abdicated and joined them. In the sixth year of King Tazena the saints separated, and Za Mikael departed to found Dabra Damo or Dabra Halleluya. King Kaleb sent to him to tell him he was about to attack the infidel Finhas, king of Saba, who had killed many people of Najran. Kaleb, victorious, later informed Za Mikael that he had become a monk with Pantalewon. From the birth of Christ, the *gadl* states, to Abreha and Asbeha, was 244 years; from Abreha and Asbeha to Gabra Masqal, 124 years; total 368 years. In the *Life of Abba Garima*, Mata`a or Libanos replaces Za Mikael Aregawi. He is commemorated in the *Synaxarium* on 14 Teqemt with a brief outline of his life.

Libanos or **Mata`a**, a tenth saint, replaces Za Mikael in *Life of Abba Garima*. From the royal family of Rome, son of Abreham and Negest, engaged to the daughter of the 'king of Qwestentenya', but became a monk with St. Pachomius (d. 348) in Egypt, then came to Ethiopia/Eritrea. Stayed in Baqla in northern Eritrea translating the gospel of Matthew into Ge`ez, and in Serawe and Shimezana. Summoned to Aksum, he found himself in conflict with Metropolitan Eleyas and King Za-Gabaza Aksum or Ella Gabaz. A monk called Adhanani reconciles them. Later King Gabra Masqal built him a church at Guna Guna in Bur`, and he or his queen built others elsewhere. Some versions of his *Life* state that he lived for 567 years. Libanos is generally not included among the Nine Saints but as a separate and isolated holy man, sometimes called the 'Apostle of Eritrea'. 'Libanos who is Mata`a' is mentioned in the *Synaxarium* with Pachomius on 3 Ter, and a brief *Life* is provided on 2 Hedar. His *gadl* exists in the form of a homily on his life purportedly written by Bishop Eleyas of Aksum, with whom he had eventually made peace through the intervention of Adhan(ann)i. Mata`a is said (in one only of the four different recensions of his *gadl*, apparently fifteenth century in date) to have written (translated) the gospel of Matthew into Ge`ez. Other names exist for Libanos: Yesrin, or even an identification as Yasay king of Egypt.[3]

---

3 Haile 1990: 29-47; Bausi 2000 (unpublished paper). Bausi traces the development of the story through the younger and fuller recensions of the bishop's homily. Only some of these include his royal descent, for example, not mentioned in the earliest copies. Bausi 1999: 21 and n. 33.

2. The *Lives* of the Saints

This is the story of the Nine Saints as the Ge`ez documents outline it, and as modern ethiopianists have interpreted it.[4] But what happens when one applies ordinary historical criticism to the tales of these late fifth and early sixth century missionaries? The result is startling, and interesting in terms of the study of mythmaking in Ethiopia. It illustrates how strongly late legends have permeated our view of Ethiopian history. The Nine Saints vanish. Not one of these figures, supposedly deeply rooted in the soil of Ethiopia from the late fifth or early sixth century, seems to possess any real identity before the late fourteenth or fifteenth century compilation of their *Lives*, and the even later augmentation or alteration of these tales as events demanded it. Libanos or Mata`a alone, the 'tenth saint', is an exception, with acceptable evidence for an earlier appearance.

Long ago, Carlo Conti Rossini began a process of analysis of Ethiopian historical documents, in his case dealing with the legends of the Zagwé. Since then, historians have entered profoundly into such text criticism, scholars such as Manfred Kropp, Alessandro Bausi, Gianfrancesco Lusini and others offering new perspectives on the royal chronicles, hagiographies and other literature. Paolo Marassini, too, applied the same methods to the stories about the Nine Saints, but although for a long time scholars, including Conti Rossini himself, have been aware of the problems, the Nine Saints still tend to appear with rather more solid backgrounds than they really seem to deserve.

The *Lives* of a few of the Nine Saints (most do not even have an extant history of any kind, and are known solely by a name and a supposed place of origin) are preserved only in versions of this fourteenth-fifteenth century period and later. It was then that the literary genre of the *gadl* was invented. These tales, the chief – indeed the only – authority for these supposedly central figures in early Ethiopian monastic life, were almost certainly compiled nine hundred or more years after the Nine Saints' supposed achievements in Aksumite Ethiopia, and until now we have no proof of the existence of any older documentation concerning them except in the case of Libanos-Mata`a. According to Ignazio Guidi, the legendary, or panegyric, *Life* of Lalibela, written in the time of Emperor Dawit (1380-1412) or a little later, was the first of the *gadlat* of the native saints of Ethiopia: 'con la vita di Lalibela s'iniziava un'agiografia nazionale…'[5] Soon followed the *Life* of another Zagwé king, Na'akuto-La'ab, then the *Life* of the 'Apostle of Eritrea', Libanos or Mata`a, with the *Ta'amra Libanos* or Miracles of Libanos appearing under Emperor Yeshaq (1414-29).[6] We know that the *Life* of Pantalewon had already appeared by 1425, or at least we may assume that it is

---

4   See for example Tamrat, 1972: 23-25; Kaplan 1984: 16-17; Munro-Hay 1997: 75-77.
5   Guidi 1932: 39-40.
6   Of nine mss. known to A. Bausi, one is mid-fourteenth century, one late fourteenth-early fifteenth century, the rest later: Bausi 2000 (unpublished paper).

Pantelewon of Ethiopia who is concerned, and not Pantaleon of Nicomedia, the 'great martyr and wonderworker' and imperial physician so revered in the eastern churches after his martyrdom under Diocletian.[7]

The sparse notes about the Nine Saints in the Ethiopian *Synaxarium*, a compilation of readings for each day of the liturgical year, were added to 'Ethiopianise' the work at some time after the original Ge`ez translation. This was apparently prepared by a certain Abba Sem`on in the fourteenth century. In some cases these additions are based on the fifteenth century *gadlat* of the saints, but by the time they were included in the *Synaxarium*, probably in its later sixteenth century recension, one can be sure that there were already well-developed stories about the saints circulating in monkish and popular milieux in Ethiopia. One must not forget, too, that these *gadlat* were 'perpetually renewed' texts,[8] like the *Kebra Nagast*, and, as we have just seen, the *Synaxarium*. Recopying as old manuscripts wore out was a constant process, and rivalry between monasteries, for example, could lead to certain aspects of a *gadl* being suppressed and others being added. Mere copying could become substantial revision and editing, resulting in a new version with significant 'improvements'. Variants in the stories are therefore only to be expected.

Naturally enough, the Nine Saints eventually became well integrated into the liturgy of the church. In the books of chants or antiphonaries there are hymns addressed to Garima and Libanos Mata`a, and others in the *Zemmare* or hymnal to Pantalewon, Aregawi, and Yemata, as well as to Yared and Abba Salama. These would have been composed, copied and assimilated as the stories about the ancient heroes of the church developed.

The content of the saints' *Lives* is hagiographical in nature, designed to inspire and to emphasise Christian aspects. They are filled with miracles and extremely short on historical information. What there is, is often contradictory, as when Za Mikael Aregawi is said to have become a monk with the great Egyptian monastic leader, Pachomius (who died in 348), but also to have consulted with Kaleb and Gabra Masqal some two hundred years later. Identification with Pachomian succession was extremely important. Much later Ethiopian monastic genealogies still endeavour to trace a direct succession through the great Egyptian ascetic St. Anthony of the Desert, via Makarios, and Pachomius, to the saint who is the subject of the genealogy, a monastic succession usually impossibly short in terms of generations over the span of centuries.[9] Yet as was noted long ago, in the prolix *Life* of Pachomius there is no hint of a Za Mikael Aregawi, or of any of the others among the Nine Saints supposedly his

---

7   Rossini 1923-25: 508.
8   Kaplan 1981: 107-123 and 1984.
9   Haile 1992: 236 – Anthony, Macarius, Bamoy/Bamoda = Palemon, Pachomius, Theodore, Za Mikael Aregawi etc.

disciples.[10] Retired Roman emperors and other royal persons who have taken up the religious life do not usually remain so anonymous.

Paolo Marrassini, while accepting that 'their historical value was nil for individual facts related' nevertheless considered the ensemble of the *gadlat* 'notable as a general testimony.' The *gadlat* were, he considered, all inspired, in the last analysis, by writings translated in the preceding decades.[11] This certainly appears to be true. With such examples in mind, the ecclesiastic compilers created a monasticism of the past in the image of that of the present, with noble, even royal, abbots installed with their followers in relatively remote areas, whose activity supposedly had a powerful impact on the local people and even on the rulers.

The *Gadla Afse*, in one version summarised by Roger Schneider, contains obvious anachronisms.[12] Afse received baptism from Patriarch Timothy – the possibilities are: Timothy I of Alexandria, 380-385: Timothy II of Alexandria, 458-477. Timothy I of Constantinople, 511-518, a contemporary of King Kaleb of Aksum, seems out of the running. Afse spent seven years at Scetis in the Egyptian desert as a monk under the revered ascetic Makarios, who dwelt there from about 330-390, followed by three years with Patriarch Athanasius of Alexandria (326-373). When Afse announced that he had to go to Ethiopia, he was consecrated bishop of the country by Athanasius. (This part of the tale seems to have been taken from the life of Frumentius, first bishop of Aksum, and in fact consecrated by Athanasius). After that he was conveyed on a cloud, a frequent method of transport in Ethiopian hagiographies, to Aksum, where Minas was bishop. Afse met Aregawi, who was brought to Aksum by St. Michael, and the two saints went to 'Rome' to see the patriarch there, Alexander (not a pope of Rome, but patriarch of Constantinople, 328-340). All nine of the saints then assembled to receive the monastic habit from Pachomius (d. 348), except Afse, who already had received it from Makarios. These dates can just about seem credible. But later – more than a century later – the saints all went, with their *tabotat* and other cult

10 Guidi 1894, 1896: 55. It is often stated that the monastic rules of Pachomius, together with a number of other works, was translated in Aksumite times, offering evidence for Aksumite interest in monastic life. But although this could have been the case, no manuscripts from so early a period in fact survive, and it is difficult to be sure of the exact date of translation. The attribution depends on 'tradition'. To cite Stoffregen-Pedersen 1990: 13 and 54: La tradition attribue également aux Neuf saints la *Règle monastique* de saint Pacôme (dont la troisième partie est une addition aksumite), la *Vie de saint Antoine* par saint Athanase et le *Qerlos* (Cyrille), un recueil d'écrits patristiques comprenant notamment de *De recta fide* de Cyrille d'Alexandrie. All these works were popular, and, with the *Physiologus* or *Fisalgos*, and the Bible, are stated to be the earliest translations in almost all works on Ethiopian literature. Only of the biblical translation can we be absolutely certain, and even that only in the sixth century. Haile1982-83: 23ff., where the descent is shown as: Anthony, Macarius, Pachomius, Theodore, Aregawi, and then in Ethiopia Krestos Bezana, Masqal Mo'a, Yohanni, Iyasus Mo'a and Takla Haymanot.
11 Marrassini 1981: 197, 203.
12 Schneider 1985: 105-118.

objects, to Aksum, where they were received by Alameda, son of Sal'adoba, a (legendary) late fifth century king of Aksum. They remained there through the reigns of his successors Tazena and Kaleb, whom they assisted with their prayers in his war against Finhas (Jewish king of the Yemen in the early 520s). Kaleb retired to become a monk with Abba Pantalewon, Gabra Masqal succeeding him on the throne. All but Tazena and Kaleb among these kings are quite unknown from Aksumite evidence, such as coins and inscriptions. They occur only in the late hagiographies and king lists.

To conclude this tale of Afse, a hermit came to the Nine Saints to tell them that (despite these carefully listed kings' reigns), a serpent, Agabos or Galabos, had been reigning over Ethiopia for twenty-five years. By the intercession of their prayers, the serpent was killed by Christ. (In the story of Abba Garima, the huge serpent is reported to the saints by the governor of Aksum, and eventually destroyed by God through the power of prayer: Pantalewon, `Os and Yeshaq (Garima) are named).[13] Soon, the saints separated to go to their own monasteries, and at Adwa Afse raised a rich and good Muslim, Sa'id, from the dead, and converted many other Muslims... At Dabra Hamalmal (Yeha), Afse installed three *tabotat* in the tower there, Our Lady in the centre, with Gabriel and Mikael on each side. After other miracles, Afse built a church next to the old tower, and King Gabra Masqal came to the consecration, offering many fiefs for its maintenance. The colophon of this version of *Gadla Afse*, with its many oddities and anachronisms, states that it was copied for *ras* Seyum in 1952 from a manuscript found at the important monastery of Gunda Gunde in Agame. The creation and augmentation of *gadlat* was far from dead even in the twentieth century.

Much material is shared between several *gadlat*, while other elements emphasise a particular saint's achievements. It has been pointed out that *Gadla Afse* does not mention that King Gabra Masqal built the church at Dabra Damo, stating instead that the king constructed the church of Maryam at Yeha (using, incidentally, Greek artisans, a claim similar to that which later Ethiopians were to make about the churches of Lalibela, even though they are patently creations of the Ethiopians themselves, in the distinctive Aksumite architectural style).[14] The *Lives* owe their royal chronology to the late king lists, citing, as we have noted, kings quite unknown from the coinage of the Aksumite rulers of the period (except for Kaleb, and his father Tazena who is named on Kaleb's coins). Other aspects in the *Lives* derive from stories such as the tale of the martyrs of Najran. In some cases, the lists of the saints vary, excluding certain names and adding others.

The *Lives* of Za Mikael Aregawi and Pantalewon reflect the prejudices of Dabra Damo, the famous monastery situated on an *amba* in northern Tigray, not too far from Aksum, while the *Life of Abba Garima* is written from the viewpoint of Enda

---

13 Littmann 1904: 21-24.
14 Sellassie 1964: 202.

Garima, also in Tigray. Taddesse Tamrat,[15] examining the traditions about new monastic communities established since the mid-thirteenth century, mentions that at this
time 'references to monastic communities are limited to some of the ancient establish-
ments of the Nine Saints'. There appear in fact to be no such references (except for
Libanos-Mata`a) in documents dating before the fifteenth century. In the (later copies
of) land grants that survive, there seems to be no trace of these saints' names in the
form of churches or monasteries dedicated to them. Even the name of a *nebura'ed* of
Dammo (Dabra Damo) in the circle of influence of Ya'ibika Egzi, an important local
governor in Tigray, around 1318 (see below), suggests only that there was a church or
monastery on the *amba* then. It would not be surprising to find the monastery flourishing there by this time. It was well after the foundation of the great southern monasteries (Dabra Hayq in 1248, Dabra Asbo, c. 1284, renamed Dabra Libanos in honour
of Abba Libanos in Zara Yaqob's reign), and other Tigray monasteries of this later
period, like that of Dane'el or Dabra Maryam of Garalta, where the monastic reformer
Ewostatewos (1273-1352) attended as a young man, are also attested.[16] However,
although Abba Aregawi *may* already by that time have been regarded as the founder
of Dabra Damo, we cannot prove it. The *Gadla Aregawi* and other works cite the
succession of abbots after the founder: Matyas, Yosef, Masqal Bezana, Madhanina
Egzi, Masqal Mawa'i. The seventh is Abba Yohanni 'of the Desert', who is said to have
taught, among others, two famous Ethiopian monastic leaders, Iyasus Mo'a of Dabra
Hayq and Takla Haymanot of Dabra Asbo, in the thirteenth century. This is an impossibly short succession for a period from the late fifth century (to say nothing of
Aregawi's putative pupillage under Pachomius in the first half of the fourth century)
to the mid-thirteenth century.[17] The *Gadla Takla Haymanot* presents the matter in an
even more improbable way, placing Abba Yohanni in fourth place after Aregawi.[18]

Conti Rossini cites a manuscript of the *gadl* of Garima from the d'Abbadie collection, which he considered to date shortly after the work's completion, in the fifteenth
century. Unlike subsequent manuscripts, it lacks details about the concession of fiefs,
and also lacks a section that describes certain difficulties that would come to the convent. These, Conti Rossini suggests, were the ravages the Catholics would subject it to
in the 1600s (as described by the Jesuit Manoel Barradas, one of the perpetrators).[19]

In the case of Garima, the land grants that name Abba Garima are just those that
arouse the deepest suspicion, as in similar grants in favour of Aksum church attrib-

---

15 Tamrat 1972: 109, n. 1.
16 This Dane'el, monastic 'father' of Ewostatewos, is said to have been the spiritual son of
    Bishop Yeshaq of Tawakita, himself the spiritual son of Athanasius, bishop of Armenia:
    Haile 1992: p. 232. If Tawakita is the name of a bishopric, it is not an Ethiopian see, there
    being only the one bishop or metropolitan in the country.
17 Haile 1992: 231-232.
18 Rossini 1895: 455. A typical list of this sort, of c. 18th century date, is noted by Strelcyn 1978:
    ms. 32, p. 45; Anthony, Maqarios, Pachomius, Aregawi za Damo, Masqal Mo'a, Krestos
    Bezan, Yohanni, Iyasus Mo'a, Abuna Takla Haymanot.
19 Rossini 1913: Part IV, p. 49, ms. 177.

uted to the kings Abreha and Asbeha or Anbasa Wudem. Grants by King Gabra Masqal to Garima,[20] and the attribution by Zotenberg of a thirteenth century date to a manuscript written at Madera, the monastery supposedly founded by Garima, are far from supplying convincing evidence of Aksumite date for the foundation. A note in the manuscript from Madera mentions that at the order of Simeon, the *nebura'ed* of the convent, 'this book of *Gadla Sam`at* [Acts of the Martyrs] was written at Madera in the house of Abba Garima...',[21] but Zotenberg's date for the manuscript's production is more than questionable. Ignazio Guidi includes *Gadla Sama'etat* among works translated into Ge`ez at the time of Abba Salama, metropolitan bishop of Ethiopia from the middle of the fourteenth century (1344-1388). It is mentioned in a list of works held by the Ethiopian convent in Jerusalem in 1425.[22]

Strelcyn uncertainly attributes a manuscript containing a collection of homilies to the fourteenth (?) century.[23] The manuscript, which includes homilies attributed to several bishops of Aksum, including Theophilus, Minas, and Elyas on the Holy Fathers, 'for the festival of Abba Garima' (the 17th of the month) was commissioned by a *nebura'ed* Joseph for the church of Beta Masqal of Gwenagwena. Elyas is the metropolitan who is supposed in other stories to have been accused of simony by Abba Libanos, who was accordingly exiled by King Za-Gabaza Aksum.

An early and more precisely dated reference to Garima's monastery appears in a document dated to the year of Creation 6934, EC 1434, or 1441-2AD, in which the *liqa kahenat* of Garima and Dabra Mikael, Takla Mikael, is cited with other distinguished churchmen such as Gabra Mikael, *nebura'ed* of Aksum.[24] This is all a very long way from the sixth century.

3. The Monks and the Monasteries

The literary evidence for these saints' lives in Ethiopia thus derives solely from extremely late records, dating well into the reigns of the so-called Solomonid dynasty kings (1270 onwards). What else is there?

The church at Dabra Damo is generally judged to be very old, following the story (in the late *gadlat*) that King Gabra Masqal built the church there, but again the evidence is very uncertain. David Buxton suggested that 'Debra Damo had survived from as early as the tenth or eleventh century'.[25] In other words, it is a post-Aksumite structure. As in many parts of Tigray, there is a snake legend about Dabra Damo, relating that when Abba Aregawi came here God commanded a large snake to assist him to

20 Rossini 1901: 184-186, nos. 1-5; Rossini 1909: 21-22, nos.3-4.
21 Zotenberg 1877: 198; Collection de vies de saints et de martyrs, ms. no. 131; 'Ecriture sur deux colonnes, du XIIIe siècle'.
22 Guidi 1932: 31.
23 Strelcyn 1978: ms. 56; p. 89-92.
24 Cerulli 1943: 118.
25 Buxton 1964: 241.

climb the precipitous rock face, under the protection of the archangel Gabriel. This could perhaps hint at the memory of some pagan installation there previously, and a church, as was so often the case, might have succeeded it at some time after the kingdom of Aksum had become generally Christian. However, whatever the age of the original church, it does not necessarily have any relation to the tale of the Nine Saints.

The attribution to the monastery of a very ancient foundation date has more to do with mediaeval realities that with the fifth or sixth century. In mediaeval Solomonid times, after the first few reigns of the dynasty, the abbots or monks of Dabra Damo saw their foundation flourishing, with accruing power and influence in the kingdom, and royal patronage. They also saw powerful rival monasteries, with a different, southern, regional bias, arising to threaten this pre-eminence. It seems likely that, spurred by this challenge, they sought to establish for their monastery a rather splendid past with a royal 'Roman' founder for the monastery, and a royal Aksumite builder, the indispensable Gabra Masqal, for their church. In a further step, they made sure that it was spread about that the highly revered founders of rival southern monasteries actually once sat at the feet of an abbot of Dabra Damo spiritually descended from the great Egyptian cenobites. Given the current prestige of the monastery, such an attribution shed great lustre on the pupils as well. It seems to have been eagerly enough accepted by their hagiographers, since by this means such southern monastic leaders as Iyasus Mo`a and Takla Haymanot could to be viewed as successors to a monastic line stretching back to the glorious days of King Gabra Masqal in Ethiopia, and then to Pachomius in Egypt. Without the intervention of a Tigray monastery of putative Aksumite origin, the Amhara hagiographers could not make this vital connection for their heroes.

It is more than a little suspicious that the other Tigray monasteries of the Nine Saints, which never attained the same rank as Dabra Damo in the Solomonid period, are never mentioned as the source of leaders for southern monasteries, nor are lesser figures than the greatest southern monastic leaders (Iyasus Mo`a, Takla Haymanot and Basalota Mikael) said to have derived from the monastery of Dabra Damo. The entire process was carefully selective. It may also be significant that very early in the period of the evangelisation of the south, prominent monks like Anorewos or Basalota Mikael are said to have spent time in Tigray. Perhaps they played a greater part than has been generally realised in inspiring or re-inspiring monasticism there? Northern (Tigray-Eritrean) monasticism need not all have been inherited from ancient times, or even from such Zagwé period monasteries that existed in the north, like Dabra Libanos of Ham in Shimezana. Nevertheless, it does seem that Dabra Damo and a few other places in Tigray were already sufficiently well established by the early fourteenth century for them to be claimed as schools of ecclesiastical learning for monks who were to teach later in the south.

It is enough to observe, in the work of a modern Ethiopian scholar, the critique of numerous *gadlat* of these monks who spread Christianity in the south. Taddesse Tamrat cites the stories of many of these fourteenth and fifteenth century characters in his important book *Church and State in Ethiopia 1270-1527*. He is compelled continually to point out how distortions and anachronisms have crept in – what he calls the 'vital process of the transformation of hagiographical traditions'. These include changes to conform with later religious politics, the desire I have just mentioned to trace monastic ancestry from St Anthony, 'chronologically untenable' attempts to include a dead but attractively eminent saint in a particular life, efforts to emphasise the seniority of one monk over another, assertions of foundation in the Aksumite period, and sometimes the desire to have the subject journey to some highly revered spot.[26] If there could be such tampering even with the *Lives* of these late figures, how much more potential was there with those of the supposed saints of eight hundred years or so before?

This does not mean to say that there were not monks in Aksumite times, nor that they did not take part in disseminating Christianity in the Aksumite region, nor that monasteries and churches were not built by kings of Aksum. We cannot completely dismiss the general setting of such figures as the Nine Saints and others simply because there is no contemporary documentation. Many historians of Ethiopia have expressed the hope, at least, that there is a real core to some of the lush 'narrative inventions' that the Ethiopian clerics produced.[27] This seems likely. We infer from their coinage and inscriptions, and the whole general tenor of the evidence, that Aksumite kings were profoundly Christian, and that they constructed churches. Monasticism might be reasonably supposed to have entered Ethiopia at this time as well. It is hard to imagine that, as a child of the Egyptian church, no echoes of the profoundly influential monasticism of the Egypt of the fourth and later centuries did not penetrate. It may have spread in the hinterland of Aksum in much the same way as hinted at by the *gadlat* of the Nine Saints and the other holy men known generally as the *sadqan*. There may well have been something of a 'second conversion' among the people, spreading in the fifth and sixth centuries the influence of the Christianity introduced at the court and in the capital city by Frumentius in the mid-fourth century. The monasteries of the Nine Saints were all situated in the Aksumite region, in Tigray, with that of Libanos in Eritrea. All are plausible therefore as Aksumite foundations. Incidental mention of other monasteries in the later thirteenth century, like that of Dabra Maryam in the Garalta where Ewostatewos' uncle was abbot, attest that monasticism was by that time at least well rooted in different parts of the Tigray region.

---

26 Tamrat 1972: 116, n. 1; 156-157; 162, n. 1; 166, 183, n. 1; 194, n. 6; 195, n. 2, 202, n. 5 etc. (This book is one of the fundamental studies of modern times for the religious and political history of Ethiopia, based on chronicles, unpublished Ge`ez texts of different types, older historical works and other materials). Takla Haymanot's great-grandfather is said to have travelled to Aksum and Dabra Garima. Taddesse Tamrat considers this to be 'almost certainly an attempt to increase the importance of the saint's family', while observing that 'the essential part of the story, that some of the distant Christian settlers [in Shewa] used the educational facilities of Tigré, is not inconceivable as a general pattern.' It is worth noting that the 'earliest monastic school' at Hayq (p. 203) was founded c. 1284, so there would not necessarily have been an impulsion for new candidates to go much further north to Tigray to acquire monastic learning.

27 Cf. Lusini in this volume.

Even so, it is of little value to adduce the existence of early monasticism on the strength of late documents. One scholar remarks: 'the hagiography of a certain Abba Matta states that the anchorite came to Ethiopia on the recommendation of Abba Pachomius... In Ethiopia, Matta is said to have befriended a local monk, an indication that he came to Ethiopia not to introduce monasticism but to strengthen it'.[28] But should we take such hagiographical statements seriously? That tale comes from no Aksumite document, no Zagwé document, but from the *gadl* of Libanos-Mata`a, a much later and therefore much more suspect source – and one, moreover, that we know to have been revised at times.

The recent *gadl* of Abba Salama, Frumentius, first bishop of Ethiopia, copied in 1936, illustrates the ingenious shifts the writers of the *gadlat* might need to make to meet the demands of their readers. Forced to cope with triple claims that (1) it was Frumentius who converted Ethiopia, (2) that the Levite priesthood had long been installed in Ethiopia, and (3) that Candace queen of Ethiopia, whose eunuch was converted by the apostle Philip on his way back from Jerusalem, was actually queen of today's Ethiopia, rather than queen of Meroë in modern Sudan, the author came up with some unusual solutions. Ethiopia was in fact Christian since Philip's time. The people practised circumcision after the Levite fashion, but lacked both baptism and the eucharist. The country had a bishop, Minas, who explained all this to Abba Salama. Salama went to Alexandria to receive consecration from Athanasius, and it was thus he who completed Ethiopia's conversion to the true and complete practice of the faith.[29]

Whatever suppositions we might make about the 'long tradition of monasticism prior to the fourteenth century' in Tigray,[30] we have no reliable evidence before late Zagwé times even for the existence of the Eritrean foundation of Abba Libanos, nor is there the least trace of any factual evidence until the early fifteenth century that allows us to think of Tigray monasteries dedicated to any of the Nine Saints. There is no evidence until even later than that for most of the names of the purported founders of these monasteries as they are attributed in the *gadlat*. In crediting the historicity of the Nine Saints we accept patently fanciful hagiographic tales, with manifest factual errors on a major scale, told in the mode of a literary genre flourishing about a thousand years after the subjects' deaths. On the face of it the lives of the Nine Saints as presented in the Ge`ez stories seem no more likely than the story literary imagination has embroidered in the *Alexander Book* about the great king of Macedonia, or the development of the character of King Solomon of Israel to a lord of magic, master of demons and *jinn*. Yet we know Alexander lived, and a good deal about what he did,

28 Haile 1993: 48.
29 Schneider 1987: 153-165. I thank Getatchew Haile for calling my attention to a much earlier copy of Salama's *gadl*: EMML 1763, ff. 84v-86r, copied between 1336 and 1340, published in *Analecta Bollandiana*, vol. 97, 1979: 309-318. This, evidently, does not include some of the later accretions, mention of Gondar etc, found in the more recent edition.
30 Kaplan 1992: 71.

and we have, at least, the Bible story about Solomon, though in this case not yet backed up by any other sound historical or archaeological source.

The *gadlat* also may not have been the pure imaginings of court clerics or scholar-monks. They perhaps had some basis in local memories and/or legends that had developed in the Tigray region. Church buildings, some quite old, existed at certain locations, nothing astonishing in a land converted as early as Ethiopia had been. Did these gradually become associated – or were they even legitimately associated in some way or another in some cases – with names eventually attributed to individual holy men of ancient times who became included in the group known from the fifteenth century (?) as the Nine Saints? It seems reasonable to presume that such local stories developed, or were newly coined, over a period preceding the writing of the *gadlat*, which would have been based partly on them, and partly on the general style of the current hagiographical genre. At any rate, the *gadlat* agree well enough with local legends as they were recorded some half a century to a century after the *gadlat* were compiled. We can affirm this because from about 1516 we do at last have confirmatory evidence, from Ethiopian sources but recorded by foreigners, for the Nine Saints, and for their firm identification with certain monastic foundations.

A fortunate chance has preserved an early European record of the Nine Saints, as provided by an Ethiopian in Italy. The Ethiopian Thomas, claiming to be a Dominican, arrived at the convent of Sta. Caterina at Pisa in 1516. He related various tales that were taken down by the prior Silvestre de Marradi, and which eventually saw publication by Serafino Razzi.[31] Thomas admittedly describes the saints as Dominicans (with Takla Haymanot as well), presents Mata`a in the guise of a nun called Imata, and dates their departure from Rome to 1316 – but together Arghai, Grima, Leuanos, Panthaleon, Sama, Aleph, Asse and Aguloa are easily recognisable, with Imata, as the Nine Saints. They have been neatly transposed into another setting designed to augment Thomas' fraudulent claim in Italy.

A foreigner in Ethiopia at almost the same time, Francisco Alvares, backs up this evidence. He recorded the names of five of the monasteries of the Nine Saints as he travelled across Tigray in the 1520s.[32] The monasteries seem to have been well known and mostly flourishing by this time. Abafaçem (Abba Afse) is described as a town, evidently indicating Yeha, as Alvares describes the 'tower' or temple there. The nearby church, the priests said, was one of the first seven to be built in the country when Christianity arrived there. The church of Abbalicanos (Abba Liqanos) at Aksum, 'like an annexe of the great church of Aquaxumo, and... served by its canons', is noted, with the comment 'this saint lies here, and they say that he was confessor of Queen Candace' – a new and extravagant addition to his *Life*, let alone to his already confused chronology. Abbapantalian (Abba Pantalewon) church, also at Aksum, with its three hundred steps, is also described. The saint is described as 'a very holy man'. The body of the saint himself was kept in this place, which, Alvares records,

---

31 Razzi 1588.
32 Beckingham and Huntingford (eds.) 1961: 240, 161, 163-164, 165-166, 170.

possessed large revenues, fifty canons or *dabtara*, and an official holding the office of *nebura'ed* like that of Aksum. Next, Alvares mentions the monastery of Abba Garima, five leagues from Aksum: 'they say that this Abbagarima was King of Greece, and that he left his kingdom, and came to do penance, and there ended his life in sanctity'. Despite the many who came on pilgrimage to seek cures there, it was 'a small monastery of few monks and small revenues'. The Arabic chronicle called *Futuh al-Habasha*, too, describing events just after this in the 1530s, confirms the name. The author comments that *imam* Ahmad Grañ, leader of the invading Muslim army, learned while in Tembien that the Ethiopian emperor, Lebna Dengel, was at Aksum. He set out in pursuit, reaching 'the land called Aba Qarima two parasangs distant from Aksum' where some of the 'idolaters' (Christians) were holding out in three forts.[33]

Alvares also mentions the monastery of Abbamata (Abba Mata`a) at Garalta, which he was not able to visit. His route having passed from Adwa to Aksum, and then back via Adwa to Amba Sanayt and on eastwards to 'Maluche', perhaps Alequa, passed within sight of the monastery, but sight and attainment in this mountainous part of Ethiopia are very different things. Alvares was told that it could be reached only by 'clinging on with the hands'. He described it as 'a monastery of Our Lady, named Abbamata'.

Oddly, despite the Portuguese visit there in 1541 to rescue Empress Sabla Wangel, described by Castanhoso,[34] Dabra Damo does not figure in any of the other Portuguese accounts except that of Barradas much later, in the seventeenth century. We have, therefore, little information on the development of Aragawi's legend at this time beyond Barradas' simple phrase: 'on the crest of the mountain there is a church named after Abba Aragavy, who was one of the Nine Priests who came from Rome to Ethiopia to spread the faith, and they hold and venerate him as a saint'.

In a note published in 1612 by Luis dos Anjos, nearly a century after Alvares' visit to Ethiopia, we have a European account of all the Nine Saints taken from an Ethiopian book, including Aregawi, though he is recorded, strangely, under the name João.[35] Dos Anjos states that hermits reached Ethiopia 'during the time of the Council of Chalcedon'. He had found, in the church of St. Stefano dei Mori in Rome, 'where the Indian and Ethiopian Christians live', the following record:

... to Africa came nine monks wearing black habits and leather belts. And it is written that their names were as follows; João, who was old and acted as their prior (this can only be Za Mikael Aregawi),[36] Licanos, Pantalião, Garime, Saamâ, Affe, On (Os), Gublâ, Lampta (Yemata): these are the men who founded monasteries in Ethiopia and whose bodies are venerated as though they were saints.

---

33 d'Abbadie, Paulitschke 1898: 355.
34 de Castanhoso 1902.
35 Barradas 1996: 188-189, cites dos Anjos 1612: Ch. XX, p. 109.
36 Haile suggests to me that the name refers to Abba Yohanni. He might here be conflated with his predecessor?

Barradas confirmed that these saints were known in Ethiopia, but denied that there was any connection, as claimed by dos Anjos, between Ethiopia and the Augustinians. Dos Anjos cited the Venetian historian Sabbelico, or Marcantonio Leto, for the statement that some Ethiopian monks who came to Italy in 1490 claimed that there were uncountable Augustinian monks in Ethiopia. There were doubtless uncountable monks of the orders of Takla Haymanot and Ewostatewos in Ethiopia at this time: but… Augustinians? The attribution may be similar to Zorzi's (and others') interpretation of other Ethiopian monks as Franciscans, and Razzi's crediting of Thomas as a Dominican. They might have judged the Ethiopians simply by the appearance of the habits, or because of some misinterpreted remark. Or, more cynically, perhaps the monks claimed these associations both to disguise their possibly dangerous heretical affiliation (orthodox Alexandria), and to benefit from free lodgings. It is not difficult to imagine monks from one place being compared, and even identified, with those from another, particularly given the difficulties of interpreting.

In the case of Abba Mata`a (also called Libanos) of Eritrea – not usually classed as one of the Nine Saints – there does seem to be reliable evidence of rather earlier date. Near the site of the monastery of Dabra Libanos of Ham, in Shimezana, southwest of Senafe, Conti Rossini wrote, there are traces of Aksumite ruins, and indications of a populous centre. He considered the attribution of an early date for the convent 'not without foundation'[37] It may be so. Lusini mentions that in the *Gadla Libanos* king Gabra Masqal's wife founded a church at Faqada, and at today's Foqada in Dahane, Agame, the ruins of an Aksumite church are visible.[38] Yet there are hundreds of such Aksumite sites in Ethiopia and Eritrea, with or without relationship to local saints. Several of the sites of the monasteries of the Nine Saints have very old antecedents, none more impressive than pre-Aksumite Yeha. Mere propinquity with Aksumite ruins does not prove any Aksumite connection for the monasteries, though the ruins – if they really are churches – would announce the spread of Christianity in the hinterland of Aksum. All we can say for the moment is that a church and monastery of Abba Mata`a at Ham or Aham in Shimezana, even if not in the surviving buildings of today, did exist by King Lalibela's time, around 1200.

A famous church of Libanos exists at Lalibela. Libanos is the only predominantly Ethiopian (by adoption) saint commemorated there, all the other churches being dedicated to Jesus, Mary, the Cross, archangels, virgin martyrs, or international saints like Mercurios and George. It is usually assumed that this dedication was first applied in the time of King Lalibela, reigning in the late twelfth and early thirteenth century. Even if there is no real evidence to support this, mention of Libanos under his other name, Mata`a, is apparently confirmed from mid-late Zagwé times by the land charters (in late copies) found in the Golden Gospel of Dabra Libanos[39] or Enda Abba Mata`a. The charters are attributed to thirteenth century figures, Lalibela, Delanda, a

---

37 Rossini 1901: 178.
38 Cf. Lusini in this volume.
39 Ibid.: 186-192.

shadowy ruler of the late pre-Solomonid period (1268), and Yekuno Amlak among others.

The land grants of Lalibela mention *Mata`a za-Aham* with the names of what seem to be two (or three?) churches, presumably associated with the church of Abba Mata`a of Ham: Beta Masqal and Beta Maryam and the Virgins: nuns, or a church of the Virgin Martyrs?) A document of Yekuno Amlak also mentions these three names. The dedications are similar to three of those (at least today) at Lalibela. Further Dabra Libanos charters purportedly emanate from some of the abbots or `*aqabe sa`at* (abba) Mata`a, such as Tasfa Haywot and Yerdana Krestos in Lalibela's time, and from Yekuno Amlak when the head of the monastery was the *nebura'ed of Aksum and `aqabe sa`at za-beta Mata`a* Tekeste Berhan. A grant by one Sanbat Mahara dates to Wedem Arad's reign, and this, and another from the same reign, with a third from 1319 by Ya'ibika Egzi, governor of Intarta in Tigray in Amda Seyon's reign, mention Sanbat Mahara's son Asfeha, `*aqabe sa`at (za)-Mata`a*. Others grants to (*abba* or *abuna*) *Mata`a za-Aham* and to the *beta krestiyan za-Mata`a* emanate from Emperor Amda Seyon and his family or officials in the fourteenth century. The last in this reign is dated 1328, when the `*aqabe sa`at Mata`a* was Gabra Krestos son of Barnabas. Even later is a disciplinary ordinance issued for *makana Mata`a* while Gabra Krestos was still in office, dating from Sayfa Arad's time (1344-72). Another of Tasfa Iyasus, *seyum* of Gelo Makeda, dates from the reign of Zara Yaqob, in 1459.

Can we on the strength of these documents say that Libanos, Abba Mata`a, was a known and revered figure by mid-Zagwé times at least – a mere seven hundred or so years after his supposed activities under Gabra Masqal, or nearly nine hundred years after his supposed monkhood under Pachomius? Not quite. Every one of these documents mentions only the name Mata`a. Only an undateable document copied in the eighteenth century, no. 31, of two *wayzaro*, Qeddista Kesos and Eleni, enlarges to *Mata Libanos*, with another eighteenth century list of spiritual succession, document no. 34, which names Anthony, Macarius, Pachomius, and *Libanos Mata`a*.[40] We do not know if the names Libanos and Mata`a were identified in early times, only that Abba Mata`a was a revered figure in southern Eritrea in mid-late Zagwé and early Solomonic times. The *Life* of Libanos, which was or became *abba* Mata`a's other name, is an early example of the *gadlat* genre. A *Gadla Libanos* manuscript, EMML 1763, dating between 1336 and 1340, seems to be the first document to clearly testify to the use of the dual names Mata`a and Libanos.[41] The *Ta'amra Libanos* (*Miracles of*

---

40 Followed by Madhanina Egzi, Tasfa Masqal, Bahayla Masqal, Tasfa Maharat, Zena Yohannes, Saga Mata`a, Sanay Manfas, Efrem, Krestos Abuhu, Yerdana Egzi, Fitsum Amlak, Yemherana Egzi, Tensa Krestos, Berhan Masqal, Yafqerana Egzi, and Mahare Egzi. Rossini 1901: 219 attempts to identify them with the other (secular) names in the grants.
41 Pers. comm. A. Bausi.

Libanos) was written at more or less the same time as the other saints' *Lives*, in the reign of Yeshaq in the fifteenth century.[42]

Some other Dabra Libanos charters, it should be added, are attributed to that shadowy figure so popular in all the tales of the Nine Saints, as well as in the *Kebra Nagast* – the legendary son of Kaleb, Gabra Masqal. In the *Gadla Pantalewon*, exceptionally, a King Sahel is mentioned instead as the successor of Kaleb. Conti Rossini bluntly described these supposed early charters as 'atti indubbiamente apocrifo, che trae origine del *Gadla Libanos*'.[43] Monks were quite capable, after inventing a scenario in the *gadl* of a saint dead – if he ever actually existed – a millennium before, of forging supporting texts that not only justified the *gadl* but legitimised certain territorial claims of the monastery. However, Conti Rossini correctly remarks that to have forged the later grants (from Zagwé times onwards) would have involved infinitely more complex inventions including a system of political geography, partition of feudal holdings, regal protocols, dates, feudatories, courtiers, and successive holders of certain offices of state. In the Zagwé and later grants from Dabra Libanos, all of these details are presented in a manner that more or less guarantees their basic reliability as historical documents (though not necessarily guaranteeing the sometimes variable lists of territories supposedly granted). Such supporting features are only too obviously absent from the 'earlier' grants.

Aksumite monasteries might have existed. There might have been legends about their founders, some perhaps containing a kernel of truth that survived over a millennium to be included in the *gadl* of the local saint concerned. It may be, as Lusini says, that 'in Ethiopia there exists an unbroken tradition of recording historical memories...', a 'cultural chain' on which a certain perception of the past relies. There may have even been old texts that were being rewritten or updated. If so, we lack any clear knowledge of such matters until the fourteenth century when, we might presume, what information that existed began to be woven into the framework of the new history that was being created. If old texts existed and were being used, they must have been exceptionally poor in credible historical material. As Lusini himself adds, the royal lists and monastic genealogies express the Ethiopians' need at that time for 'filling up the documentary gaps, which the learned men were forced to remedy time after time by silence or invention'.[44] It seems to have been only under the inspiration of the florescence of the newer southern monasticism in Shewa and Amhara under such figures as Iyasus Mo'a or Takla Haymanot, and the appearance of the *gadlat* of the ecclesiastics of late Zagwé and Solomonic dynasty times, that the Tigray *gadlat* of the Nine Saints first appear as written documents, and that their names enter history. Perhaps any northern monasteries of Aksumite date that might have survived the fall of Aksum, and lasted on into Zagwé times, suffered further neglect with the concentration of power in Lasta. Does the (re)generation of their

---

42 Ibid.: 177-178.
43 Ibid.: 184-186.
44 Cf. Lusini in this volume.

history indicate genuine use of old material – Lusini writes of 'recovery of traditions pivoting on the Aksumite saints' – or does it rather indicate invention from silence?

We do seem to have good indications that the monastery of Mata`a (Libanos) was flourishing, or began to flourish, in late Zagwé times, but there is no such evidence for any of the others. Nor indeed is there much information about Aksum itself, once the seat of the primate of the church in Ethiopia. In Zagwé times, even the metropolitan, the *History of the Patriarchs* informs us c. 1210, was consecrated for Arafa (Adefa, the Zagwé capital that is now called Lalibela), the royal city. It was there that King Lalibela assigned him a residence.

The next phase, a new and vigorous southern monasticism soon associated with the Solomonic court in Amhara, may have emphasised a certain continuing marginalization of the northern church, particularly if, until the reign of Amda Seyon, the Amhara monarchy could exercise relatively little control there. The *gadlat* of Iyasus Mo'a and Takla Haymanot claim that it was at Dabra Damo that the monks who went south were trained, but these claims seem to date from the time Dabra Damo had become something distinguished, a power to be reckoned with. It was these supposed disciples of the abbots of Dabra Damo who founded other monasteries that were to become Dabra Damo's great rivals, indeed to completely eclipse it with time. In Solomonid Ethiopia, ruled more or less firmly from Amda Seyon's time from a centre in Amhara, north-south based regional religious differences began to develop, perhaps not unnaturally given the north's ancient and prestigious past, and its centrifugal tendencies. The dissident monastic movements of Ewostatewos in the fourteenth century, and of the Estifanosites in the mid-fifteenth century, were northern manifestations, both of which found themselves in dispute with the church and the state. They sprang up in old Christian regions, in contrast to the almost frontier lands where Christian monks laboured in the pagan or partly Muslim south, in Shewa and other regions. One manifestation of these monastic reforming movements was the foundation of many new northern monasteries. It was under such circumstances that the Tigray monasteries, whether of ancient foundation or not, began to see their own founders' stories presented as literature.

There is enough of magic and miracle and distorted history in the tales of the Nine Saints to render them doubtful from the start as faithful historical documents. This is natural enough given their spiritual *raison d'être*, to edify and praise. Carlo Conti Rossini long ago illustrated what other forces might be at work in the composition and redaction of these works. Observing how the *gadl* of Abba Garima or Yeshaq differs from those of Aregawi and Pantalewon, suppressing the name of Aregawi (who is replaced in this instance by Mata`a or Libanos), he noted that this constituted an 'undoubted sign of unfriendly relations between the clergy of Madara and those of Debra Damo'. He cited similar matters in relation to *Gadla Afse*.[45] Others, too, have remarked this confusion manifest in the *gadlat* about events in the lives of the saints –

---

45 Rossini 1939: 152, 154-155. See also his *Storia d'Etiopia*: 160.

or perhaps rather not confusion but careful manipulation to a specific end.[46] Local Tigrayan monastic politics played their part in amending certain facets of the stories about the Nine Saints – as they certainly did in the stories about Iyasus Mo'a and Takla Haymanot.[47] Doubtless similar considerations, perhaps on a more national scale, had influenced their creation in the first place.

The Dabra Damo tradition expressed in *Gadla Aregawi* stresses that the two great Ethiopian saints Iyasus Mo'a and Takla Haymanot derived their monastic origin from Aregawi's own monastery. This both gave them greater credit, and presented Dabra Damo as a major and old monastic centre, motherhouse of the greatest southern monasteries. Another famous monk, Basalota Mikael (early 1300s), is also said in his late fourteenth or early fifteenth century *gadl* to have been a pupil at Dabra Damo. According to the *gadl* of Iyasus Mo'a, who died in 1291-1292, Basalota Mikael was also a pupil of this revered abbot of St. Stephen's monastery, situated on an island in Lake Hayq. Dabra Damo monastery was regarded, at least at the time of the composition of these *gadlat*, as the centre *par excellence* for aspiring monks to undergo their religious training.

For by the time *Gadla Aregawi* and the *gadlat* of Iyasus Mo'a and Takla Haymanot were written, Dabra Damo was indeed flourishing. The monastery was destined, late in its life if we believe that it was a sixth century foundation, to become, for a limited time, very powerful and influential in religious and court life in Ethiopia. In the *Life of Abba Iyasus Mo'a*, the holy man is said to have become a monk at Dabra Damo under Abbot Yohanni from c.1241-1248, that is, in late Zagwé times. Iyasus Mo'a lived from c.1211 to 1292, but his *gadl* was composed only in the late fifteenth century with sometimes contradictory borrowings from the rather earlier *Gadla Aregawi*. Dabra Damo's rising status was reflected by the claim that Iyasus Mo'a entered into the monkhood there. More solid confirmation of the possibility that the monastery was indeed prospering not long after the lifetime of Iyasus Mo'a appears to come from a land grant of 1318/19, of Ya'ibika Egzi (though we possess only a copy of the sixteenth century). It mentions Yeshaq, *nebura'ed* of Aksum, the presumed 'translator' of the *Kebra Nagast*, together with other distinguished ecclesiastics such the *aqabe sa`at Mata`a* Asfeha, the *aqabe sa`at* of Dabra Zayt Tesfa Seyon, and *nebura'ed* Yafqeranna Egzi of Dammo, presumably the same as Dabra Damo. Perhaps in the case of Dabra Damo we can suggest that a certain prominence had been gained even some time before this, if we consider the (supposed) age of the church, or, dating even earlier, some of the objects that have been found there (such as Kushana coins from north India, the occasional Aksumite coin, old textiles and so on).[48] Yet even these indications suggesting early occupation, whether as monastery or, perhaps, fortress and refuge, do not confirm that Dabra Damo was a monastic centre founded by Za Mikael Aregawi in the sixth century. Aregawi's name is never mentioned in any

---

46 Tamrat 1972: 165-166.
47 Kur 1965: iv ff.
48 Buxton 1947: 1-42; D. Mathews and A. Mordini 1959: 1-58.

early document.

The claim that a pupil of Iyasus Mo'a, Takla Haymanot, dwelt for twelve years at Dabra Damo, which he left to found a monastic house at Dabra Asbo (Dabra Libanos) in Shewa – soon destined to outshine both Dabra Damo and Hayq as a force in Ethiopian politics and religious life – may derive from a desire to make him equal to his master by ensuring him the same prestigious Dabra Damo education. To this saint, in his *gadl*, was later attributed the pivotal position of Iyasus Mo'a in assisting the establishment of the Solomonic monarchy under Yekuno Amlak, a literary take-over directly reflecting the accruing political and religious power of Dabra Libanos of Shewa, Takla Haymanot's monastery, and the concomitant decline of Hayq.

Dabra Damo's influence spread far and wide from the time of Amda Seyon (1314-1344), who destroyed the local power of the family of Ya'ibika Egzi in Tigray. In King Dawit's reign (1382-1411) the prominent monk Abba Giyorgis of Gasacha (also called Giyorgis of Sagla), son of Hizba Seyon, a royal chaplain, was *nebura'ed* of Dabra Damo. The monastery seems to have retained its importance under Emperor Zara Yaqob, if the Abba Nob who was consulted in 1450 during the course of the quarrels about sabbath observance between the king and the northern monks, followers of Ewostatewos, was indeed the *nebura'ed* of Damo of that name. Nob was later, however, included among rebels against the king.[49] In 1468 Emperor Baeda Maryam summoned Abba Mattewos of Dabra Damo among others to pray for the late Emperor Zara Yaqob. The emperor offered silks and five hundred ounces of gold to the monastery. This fourteenth and fifteenth century prominence must have been endangered by increasing rivalry for royal favour from the rising power and influence of other monastic houses nearer the imperial centre. In turn, the rise of rivals fuelled the desire of northern monasteries to assert ancient and eminent prestige as religious conflict escalated, a desire that could perhaps explain the composition of the *gadlat* of several of the Nine Saints, and the development of some of the stories about them.

4. The Syrian Question

It is often simply stated that the Nine Saints were Syrians. We read, for example: 'that they were Syrian monks has been generally assumed...', and in other passages they are referred to as 'these Syrians', 'the Syrian missionaries', etc. In addition, they 'are generally credited with the translation of the Scriptures into Ge'ez'.[50]

This 'general' opinion is, in its way, a breathtaking leap given the quality of the evidence. The 'Syrian-ness' of the Nine Saints comes down to the purported place of origin of two or at most three of them, as recorded in the fourteenth and fifteenth century Ge'ez hagiographical texts, while the only one actually reported to have

---

49 Tamrat 1972: 241.
50 Ullendorff 1968: 52-53, citing Guidi 1922: 126.

made a translation into Ge`ez is Libanos, not usually subsumed among the Nine Saints. According to the profoundly unreliable attributions of origin, one saint, Afse, came from Esya, perhaps Asia (Asia Minor, Turkey today), or perhaps Edessa in north Syria. Another, Alef, derived from Caesarea – perhaps the Caesarea now in Israel, on the Mediterranean, in the greater Syrian province. A third saint, Sahma, hailed from Antioch. Of the rest, five (counting Libanos as well) are firmly seated on or near the throne in Constantinople (Byzantium), or come from 'Rome', or Constantinople, and two others come from Cilicia (now southeastern Turkey) and perhaps Egypt. We can therefore say that they are all supposed to originate from the Roman empire – but to subsume them *in toto* as Syrians is grossly exaggerating.

If, for a moment, we did accept the possibility of the Syrian elements evoked by modern studies of the information in the *gadlat*, while rejecting the fifth-sixth century attributions, how might the legends of the Nine Saints have begun their development? One might conceivably look to the time of the influx of Syrian ecclesiastical influence in Ethiopia between about 1230 and 1294. At the beginning of this period a native Ethiopian metropolitan, Thomas, was consecrated for Ethiopia by Patriarch Ignatius II of Antioch in Syria. Although nothing further is known of this metropolitan, royal letters sent by Yigba Seyon (1285-1294) and his courtiers to Egypt mention 'Syrian metropolitans' of Ethiopia in his reign and in the reign of his father Yekuno Amlak (1270-1285).[51]

During this period of relatively strong Syrian ecclesiastical influence, Tigray churches and monasteries might have suffered relative neglect from the Lasta-centred Zagwé monarchy. The Zagwé were doubtless more interested in promoting Adefa, their capital in Warawar district (later called Roha and Lalibela). From the evidence we have, they seem to have attempted to strengthen their support in the north by grants of land to Abba Mata`a's monastery at Ham in Shimezana, or in nearby Bihat, whence the queen, Masqal Kebra, bore the title *ba`alta Bihat*, Lady of Bihat.[52] We have nothing that might indicate that they supported the pretensions of the ancient capital of Aksum and its satellites, far from it indeed, when we consider that the bishop of Ethiopia, once metropolitan of Aksum, was then consecrated for Zagwé Adefa. After the Zagwé there followed Tigray's virtual independence in the early Solomonid reigns under the rulers of Intarta of the family of Ya'ibika Egzi. Meanwhile, an upsurge of monastic activity at Hayq and other places in the south was creating

---

51 Rossini 1939: 71-98; p. 74, and *Acta Marqorewos*, p. 21 (trad.). Rossini suggests that the Syrian metropolitan mentioned in a 1290 letter of Yigba Seyon might be identified with the Petros al-Qabqalis of *Gadla Marqorewos*. Because Patriarch Ignatius was (supposedly – this was not true) converted to Catholicism by Fra Fillipo, the Dominican provincial, confirming this in a letter to Pope Innocent IV in 1247, Coulbeaux suggested that Dominican influence reached Ethiopia with this metropolitan, an idea now generally abandoned.

52 Rossini 187, no. 6; 190, no. 7. Belen Saba, Amda Seyon's queen, inherited this title later, see no. 20, p. 204. The superior of Debra Libanos in the last reigns of the Zagwé dynasty, the *aqabe sa`ata Mata`a*, Yerde'ana Krestos, was a man of Bugna; one supposes, though he seems to have been greatly revered, originally a political appointment.

new contenders for ecclesiastic influence nearer to the heartland of the recently-in-stalled Amhara monarchy. These elements, in the manner already explained above, could have stimulated the desire of Tigray monasteries, whayever their real foundation date was, to claim saintly foreign founders back in Aksumite times. Possibly, too, the presence of the Syrians at the head of the church in Ethiopia, with an influence that must have penetrated into every part of Ethiopia whether controlled directly from Amhara or not, could account for any apparently Syriac influences observed in the onomastics.

An alternative, perhaps, for some elements in the *gadlat*, including the Syrian attribution of two or three of the Nine Saints, might have been an inspiration from the Georgian church, which attributes the arrival of monasticism and the foundation of monasteries to the same period, and to Syrians. There are thirteen Syrian saints recognised by the Georgian church, and a cycle of their biographies, *The Lives of the Syrian Fathers*, was written by Catholicos Arsenius II (c. 955-980).[53] The Syrian saints were, it has been suggested, monophysite monks expelled from Syria. Exactly the same suggestion has often been made for the reason behind the arrival of the Nine Saints in Ethiopia. Even if these Georgian saints' *Lives* were not available in Ethiopia, monks and other visitors of Ethiopian and Georgian nationality would certainly have met in Jerusalem, where Copts, Armenians, Syrians and others also congregated.

Texts of the *Lives* and other works of Syrian ecclesiastics were translated into Ethiopic during the different phases of literary flowering of the fourteenth until the sixteenth centuries, many from Arabic versions. These could also have influenced the redaction of the Ethiopic *gadlat*, and perhaps encouraged the presentation of Syrian elements.[54] Yet despite this Syrian element in the Ethiopian ecclesiastical make-up,

---

53 Lang 1956: 82.
54 I thank Dr. R. Grierson for informing me that among the ecclesiastics whose works were translated were: Aphraat, 'the Persian Sage', who died c. 345; Aron of Serug, a monastic leader, died c. 337, whose *Life* was translated into Ethiopic in the fifteenth century; Barsumas, a Jacobite archimandrite, who died c. 457, whose *Life* appears to have been translated into Ethiopic at the end of the fourteenth century; Dionysius Bar Salibi (a Jacobite bishop who died in 1171, and whose biblical commentaries were translated into Ethiopic in the reign of Sarsa Dengel; Ephrem 'the Syrian', or 'of Nisibis', who died in 373, the greatest of Syriac poet-theologians, some of whose works were translated into Ethiopic under Zara Yaqob; Evagrius of Pontus, who died in 398, and who like Afse was a disciple of Makarios in Scetis. His mystical treatises, preserved in Syriac, were also translated into Ethiopic around the sixteenth century; Isaac of Nineveh, or 'the Syrian', the most famous of Syrian mystical writers, briefly bishop of Nineveh in the late seventh century, whose works were translated into Ethiopic in the fifteenth century; Jacob of Serug, a poet and theologian, probably Jacobite, who died in 521, and who was known as 'the Flute of the Holy Spirit'. Some of his work was translated into Ethiopic, for example in the homilies for Holy Week in the *Gebra Hemamat*, by Abba Salama (c. 1350-90), and more in Zara Yaqob's time; John Saba, 'of Dalyatha', a sixth century mystical writer, whose book on the monastic life, called *Aregawi Manfasawi* in Ethiopic, was translated from Arabic at Lebna Dengel's command; Philoxe-
(continued...)

from Frumentius of Tyre, via the intense Syrian literary interest in the war between Kaleb and Himyar, to the thirteenth century Syrian metropolitans and on to the translations of Syriac works via Arabic in the fourteenth and later centuries,[55] another inter

54 (...continued)
nos, bishop of Mabbug, a monophysite theologian who died in c. 523, and to whom is attributed the Ethiopic *Filkesyus*, a work concerning monastic life translated by Abba Salama or under his influence; and Severus, bishop of Antioch, a prominent monophysite theologian who died in 538. His *Life* was also translated into Ethiopic.

55 When this section was distributed as the main paper in the session on the church at the first Littmann Conference at Munich (2002), Veronika Six kindly sent me a note about another possible source of Syrian influences, over time. Some aspects might have emanated from Egypt, where Syrians and Ethiopians met together in monasteries. The source she recommended to me, Meinardus 1962, did indeed offer some challenging evidence, which I reproduce here in note form: Most of the Ethiopan metropolitans came from the monasteries of Egypt. One or two, like John in the mid-ninth century (from Baramus) and Michael (c. 1210, former bishop of Fuwa) returned there. Baramus is said to have been the home of Abyssinian monks longer than any other Wadi Natrun monastery (Meinardus 1962: 153). Lord Curzon 1837 reported an Abyssinian 'college' at Dayr al-Suryan, with a 'rather substantial library of Ethiopian books kept in their leather cases'. Meinardus illustrates this from Curzon 1837 (Meinardus 1962: 257). Von Suchem 1895: 80, mentions that in the Egyptian desert there were cells and hermitages, many of them occupied by Indians (i.e. Ethiopians), Nubians and Syrians living under the rule of St. Anthony and St. Macarius. Jean Thénaud, visiting St. Catharine's monastery in 1512, heard that the monastery of St. Anthony was occupied by Syrian monks. Schefer 1884: 81. Wansleben, in 1672, visited St. Anthony's and recorded that there had been an Ethiopian monastery in the enclosure there too, but was now completely ruined (Wansleben 1677: 302, cited by Meinardus, 1962: 51). Alvares (in Ethiopia in the 1520s) mentions the pilgrimages via Debarwa and Hamasen to Sawakin, and on to Egypt to St. Anthony's monastery, and there was apparently an Ethiopian community there at certain times (Meinardus 1962: 45). One of them wrote a penitential tract there in 1561 (Cerulli 1943: 419). In 1634-35 Agathange de Vendôme was at Dayr Abu Maqar, where he acquired the famous polyglot Bible, the Codex Barberianus Orientalis, written in Ethiopic, Syriac, Coptic, Arabic and Armenian. It was lost for a while, but bought for Cardinal Barberini in 1637 (Meinardus 1962: 186). Prince Umar Tusun's study of the Natrun monasteries divided them into periods when the different monasteries flourished. His fifth period, c. 1347-1440, is the only one to include the Abyssinians. Toussoun 1931: 51-58, cited by Meinardus 1962: 203. Maqrizi, c. 1419-1441 (Wustenfeld 1845: 111) wrote that the monastery of St. Elias, that belonged to the Ethiopians, had, like the monastery of Anba Yuhannis Kame, suffered from the depredations of (wood)worms, and collapsed. The monks had gone to live at the monastery of the Virgin of St. John the Short (Meinardus 1962: 258 from Wustenfeld 1845: 111). Maqrizi reported that the former Jacobite monastery of Bu Bishai had been in Syrian hands for three hundred years. In the second half of the fifteenth century, the monastery was to become something of a literary centre, several Syrian writers working there on homilies and the like. In later times, a very large collection of Syriac manuscripts was purchased here for the British Museum. From the ninth century, Syrians seem to have been at the monastery named for them, Dayr al-Suryan (Meinardus 1962:
(continued...)

pretation is possible.

It may be that the whole 'Syrian' scenario, like the very existence of the Nine Saints themselves, belongs in the realm of myth. In this case, it would belong to a rather newer phase of Ethiopian mythmaking, created by such ethiopianists as Ignazio Guidi and Carlo Conti Rossini at an earlier stage in the study of Ethiopian religious history, and since enshrined, because of their great eminence, in the literature. In recent times Paolo Marrassini – though apparently not questioning the actual existence of the saints – casts doubt on the 'Syriac' elements in, for example, the etymology of their names.[56] He also notes that the two place names associated with Syria in the hagiographies, Caesarea and Antioch, are both met with so often in the literature that their citation as the place of origin of two of the saints is more or less meaningless. This is certainly true. With Jerusalem and a few other places these famous towns occupy a dominant position in such works as the *Synaxarium*. Marrassini accordingly wonders 'whether their citation in connection with the Nine Saints was not a matter of mere religious and literary fiction'.

Turning to the linguistic evidence, Marrassini finds in the toponyms, the personal names of the saints, and the speculations about certain Aramaic or Syriac loanwords or transcriptions of biblical names – the ultimate defence of the entire 'Syrian' theory – nothing at all really convincing for Syrian influences in the country in the sixth century. The linguistic evidence for Syrian influences comes down, he suggests, to 'a total of *five* or *six* words surely connected with religious activity'. This, he finds 'very scarce evidence indeed'. He concludes that 'the people who translated the Bible into their own language must have been the *Ethiopians themselves!*' This seems to remove the whole base of the theory of Syriac missionaries, leaving to be explained only the problem of the few Jewish Aramaic words in the Ge`ez Bible, supposed by some scholars to indicate a strong Jewish substratum in early Christian Aksum.

There is of course no need to deny all Syrian influence in Aksumite Ethiopia. A good deal of evidence indicates that there was a Syrian presence at times. A strange account of early Syrian influence is preserved by Philostorgius in his epitome of Photius. In detailing the itinerary of Theophilus, sent to look into church matters in the region, Photius recorded:

From greater Arabia Theophilus proceeded to the Ethiopians who are called Auksoumitas, living near the entrance of the Red Sea, 'quod Oceanus illic sese

---

55 (...continued)
  246ff.). Manuscripts and inscriptions in Syriac confirm this. By 1413 plague had decimated the monasteries, and a note by a visiting monk, Mar Simeon of Kartamin, records that only Rabban Moses of Husn Kifa was living there. Dayr al-Muharraq at Qusqam, or a church nearby, was occupied by Ethiopian monks from the fourteenth to the sixteenth century (Meinardus 1962: 291). See Cerulli 1943: 353; Crawford 1958: 129. d'Orleans 1668, mentions Meherrak, which was inhabited by Abyssinians. Wansleb also mentions al-Muharraq and the monastery of the Ethiopians in 1673: 361 (Meinardus 1962: 292). This association with Ethiopians has declined in modern times (Meinardus 1962: 300).

56 Marrassini 1990: 35-46.

insinuans efficit' [which they try to make out is the Ocean in that place??]. At one end the Red Sea divides into two branches leading to Clysma and Aila. In its outer gulf, on the left, live the Auksoumitai, thus called after the metropolis. For the metropolis is called Auksoumis. Next to these Auxumites, but to the East, dwell the Syrians, who stretch to the other ocean. [or, Before these Auksoumitwn, towards the east, at the outer extent of Ocean, dwell Syrians; Adulitae??]. For Alexander the Great of Macedonia placed them there after he had removed them from Syria; indeed they still use the language of the land of the Syrians even until now. They are all quite black because of the rays of the sun. Xylokassia is native, and kassia, and kassamon and kinnamwmon (cassia, cinnamon). There are many elephants. Theophilus penetrated little among them (Syrians); but when he came to the Auksoumitais, and put everything into order, he returned to the Roman dominion. He received many honours from the emperor, but no particular city as his bishopric.[57]

Who were these Syrians? Is this just a worthless tale, employing as so often a fabled historical character like Alexander for verisimilitude? Or is it a genuine memory of some sort of old Syrian colony, for some reason settled in the region of Adulis, and still sufficiently Syrianised in the fourth century to have retained their language, although doubtless intermarriage (rather than the sun) had changed their colour? If so, we have another possible explanation – bizarre but perhaps neither more nor less credible than the Nine Syrian Saints – for the presence of some Syriac words in the Ge`ez language in the mid-fourth century AD.

More important, Bishop Frumentius had come from Tyre in Phoenician Syria, and there were vigorous Syrian ecclesiastical contacts maintained with Ethiopia at the period of the Himyar war c. 520, as such works as the Syriac *Book of the Himyarites* prove. It has been pointed out that Syrian architectural elements are visible in Aksumite churches,[58] and given these fourth to sixth century associations, this would not be surprising. However, one might also recall that much of this basic style, of apsidal buildings with two rooms flanking the apse, a columned hall formed of nave and two aisles, and sometimes a narthex, were also common to Coptic Egypt, let alone the larger Roman world in the much used basilical form.

The Syrian influences were renewed in an unexpectedly immediate way with the presence of Syrian ecclesiastics in Ethiopia in late Zagwé times and throughout the first two reigns of the Solomonid period. However, these reiterated Syrian influences, important though they might have been in other ways, have no reference to any supposed 'Syrian-ness' of the Nine Saints. It might also be as well to remember that Ethio-

---

57 Translation of Photius' Epitome of Philostorgius, Migne *PG* 65, 1864, *Philostorgii Ecclesiasticae Historiae* (ex Ecclesiasticis Historiis, epitome, confecta a Photio Patriarchia), Book III, Para 6.

58 Campbell (cf. in this volume) recalls 'David Buxton's work on the origin of Ethiopian churches published in *Archaeologia* in 1947 and 1971. Buxton shows that the floor plans of early Ethiopian churches – including Adulis – follow 4th-6th century Syrian models, despite being contained within an 'Aksumite' exterior form. Surely these findings deserve mention in any analysis of a possible Syrian connection'.

pia neither has nor had, by and large, any reserves about attributing elements of its culture to foreigners. In fact, they seem to have preferred to do so, even when the elements concerned were thoroughly Ethiopian. Ethiopia's monarchy, it was claimed, derived from Israel, its great official and ecclesiastical families likewise. Its church was based on the work of a Syrian or Syrian Greek and his Egyptian successors. Greeks and Egyptians are often claimed as builders of the chief monuments of the country. In such a climate, when writing about the missionaries of the north, their attribution as 'Romans', usually noble or even royal in status, one of whom translated one of the Gospels into Ge`ez, is hardly surprising. Possibly the efforts of Metropolitan Salama, nicknamed 'the translator', Coptic bishop of Ethiopia c. 1348-1388, may have encouraged the view that it required a foreigner to organise such work.

5. Conclusion

Whatever influences might have engendered them, the tales about the Nine Saints as we have them give the impression of being cobbled together from what was available at the time of their composition and later augmentation, the fifteenth century and after. Some are supposed to have been finally written down by fifteenth century clerics. The bishops of Aksum Yohannes (*Gadla Abba Garima*) and Yeshaq (*Gadla Pantalewon*), are supposed to have recorded two of the most famous *Lives* in the fifteenth century – a rather curious attribution, given that as metropolitans they should have been foreigners, Coptic Egyptians, not perhaps the most likely authors of the *Lives* of sixth-century Ethiopian monks. The attribution may be imaginary, part of the programme to bestow more prestige on the monasteries concerned. On the other hand, there was an *episqopos* Yohannes who arrived in Ethiopia around 1439. A metropolitan Yeshaq arrived in 1482, but as far as the *Gadla Pantalewon* is concerned, a date before 1425 seems firmly established for its composition.[59] Perhaps in the case of *Gadla Aregawi* a monk of Dabra Damo was the author.[60]

The 'historical' sources for these works are not far to seek. King lists, very likely compilations especially prepared to justify the Solomonic succession claimed by the Amhara dynasty, and to remove legitimacy from the Zagwé whom they displaced, supplied the succession of monarchs. These 'Aksumite' monarchs were, however, never more than mere names in a list except for a very few characters around whom tales were spun. There are several phases. Abreha and Asbeha replace the historically attested King Ezana for the conversion to Christianity. Ella Amida, Sa`aldoba, Kaleb and his sons Gabra Masqal and Israel, are cited for the stories of the Nine Saints, the

---

59 Haile 1981: 113-114 for *Gadla Pantalewon*. The name of course, and his noble Roman blood, could derive from the other famous Pantaleon of Nicomedia, an important town just to the east of the capital, Byzantium.
60 Rossini 1939: 152.

Himyar war, and the *Kebra Nagast* apocalypse. Dagnajan, Anbasa Wudem and Dil Naod are the kings who are supposed to represent the end of old Aksum, ushering in the period of Queen Gudit and the arrival of the Zagwé. Current ecclesiastical practise was evoked in describing ecclesiastical activities like the installation of *tabotat* in churches attributed to the sixth century, or monks or priests carrying *tabotat*. Well-known places in the eastern Christian world were selected for the saints' origins, and to the most important of the saints were attributed prestigious imperial Roman (Byzantine) birth. Inspiration could also be drawn from the many *gadlat* of other monks, Ethiopian and foreign, written or translated at the time. Miracles and wonders fill the rest of the *Lives*. There is nothing, except the reiteration of a few royal names and the well-known episode of the Himyar war, which really evokes ancient Aksum. Even in the case of the Himyar war, the story as the *gadlat* relate it derives not from older more reliable records, but seemingly, considering the use of the name Finhas, from the same source as used by the author of the *Kebra Nagast*.

Finally, we should consider the iconography of the nine holy men in Ethiopia. Nowadays in Aksum or in churches of Tigray and other regions, the Nine Saints are frequently the theme of paintings. A particular favourite is Abba Aregawi and his snake at Dabra Damo. Like the comic-strip painting of the story of the queen of Sheba, they are often assumed to be typical examples of the old Ethiopian religious repertoire. Yet these themes do not appear in the older manuscript books that have been preserved, nor are there any traces of ancient church paintings that include them. 'Old' paintings of Liqanos and Pantalewon are found in a psalter dating – apparently – to the last quarter of the fifteenth century, and Pantalewon, Aragawi, and Yemata are pictured at Cherqos Wuqro church in Tigray in a context apparently (following palaeographic criteria) of 'the fifteenth century at the latest'.[61] It has been suggested that the Nine Saints appear in the seven now surviving carved representations of holy figures in the church of Golgotha at Lalibela, plus two others that would have been destroyed. If once they were known as the Nine Saints, would such a fact have been forgotten, and the attributions altered? When Alvares saw these, he noted only two, and they were supposed to be St. Peter and St. John. Nowadays inscriptions above four of them name them as Yohannes, Giyorgis, Qirqos and Estifanos. Another modern attribution adds the three other images in the Sellassie chapel opening off this church to the putative nine, and suggests the twelve apostles.[62]

---

61 Balicka-Witakowska 1984-86: 17-48, fig. 31.

62 Munro-Hay 2002: 213. These were also noted in a comment by Ian Campbell in his 'Remarks on Aspects of the Ethiopian Church in the Fifth and Sixth Centuries', who notes their turbans, which also appear in the Guh paintings. Campbell also notes another example of reattribution, usefully for my theme here: 'Perhaps some mention should be made of the 'Abba Garima' gospels, if only for the absence of any tangible evidence to link them to a Syrian Abba Garima. These manuscripts are not yet dated, but even if they date from the 6th century (which, I understand, is possible, based on recent cabon-dating), the portrait supposed by priests at the church to be that of Abba Garima is actually one of a set of four

(continued...)

The Nine Saints all appear on the famous dome painting of the church of Enda Abuna Yemata of Guh[63] – the church of Abbamata on its rocky pillar, seen at a distance by Alvares on his travels – dating to the sixteenth or seventeenth century, and in many later works. There is apparently no evidence from anything older, and there is no surprise in finding representations of the saints concerned at these dates. It seems that, as with the literature, so with the art – nothing can be traced that confirms the reputed age of Ethiopia's Nine Saints.

Bibliography

Balicka-Witakowska, E.
1984-86 Un psautier éthiopien illustré inconnu. *Orientalia Suecana* 33-35, 17-48.

Barradas, M.
1996   *Tractatus Tres Historico-Geographici (1634). A Seventeenth Century Historical and Geographical Account of Tigray, Ethiopia.* Ed. by R. Pankhurst, Wiesbaden.

Bausi, A.
1999   Appunti sul Gadla Libanos. *Warszawskie Studia Teologiczne,* 10/2, 'Miscellanea Aethiopica': 11-33.
2000   Some Observations on the Gadla Libanos. Unpublished. *16. Conference of Ethiopian Studies, 6-11 November 2000, Addis Ababa.*

Beckingham, C. F. and Huntingford, G. W. B. (eds.)
1961   The Prester John of the Indies. A True Relation of the Lands of the Prester John, being the narrative of the Portuguese Embassy to Ethiopia in 1520 written by Father Francisco Alvares. The translation of Lord Stanley of Alderley (1881) revised and edited with additional material. 2 vols. Cambrigde.

Buxton, D.
1947   The Christian Antiquities of Northern Ethiopia. *Archaeologia,* 92: 1-42.
1964   Ethiopian Medieval Architecture – the Present State of Studies. *Journal of Semitic Studies,* 9, 1: 241.

---

62 (...continued)
   evangelists, and the painting is almost certainly Coptic'.
63 Gerster 1970: 135, and fig. 188. Liqanos, Garima, Pantalewon, Sehma, Guba, Aragawi and Afse are named, while Alef is left without a label. Yemata himself shown in a separate picture, on horseback. The saints all wear massive *temtem,* ecclesiastical turbans, except for Liqanos who wears the monastic hood.

Cerulli, E.
1943a *Il Libro Etiopico dei Miracoli di Maria...* Rome.
1943b *Ethiopi in Palestina: II.* Rome.
1965 Corpus Scriptorum Christianorum Orientalium. *Actes de Iyasus Mo'a, abbé du couvent de St-Etienne de Hayq,* vol. 260, Scriptores Aethiopici, T. 50, Luvain: iv ff.

Crawford, O. G. S.
1958 *Ethiopian Itineraries 1400-1524.* Cambridge.

Curzon, Lord Robert
1837 *Monasteries of the Levant.* London.

d'Abbadie, A. and Paulitschke P.
1898 *Futûh el-Hábacha,* des conquêtes faites en Abyssinie au XVIe siècle par l'Imam Muhammad Ahmad dit Gragne, version française de la chronique Arabe du Chahâb ad-Dîn Ahmad; publication begun by Antoine d'Abbadie, completed by Phillipe Paulitschke. Paris.

de Castanhoso, M.
1902 *The Portuguese Expedition to Abyssinia, 1541-1543,* translated and edited by R. S. Whiteway, London.

d'Orleans, Ch.-F.
1668 *Relation du Voyage du Sayd, ou de la Thébiade.* Paris.

dos Anjos, L.
1612 *De vita et laudibus... Aur. Augustini Hipponensis episcopi... libri sex,* Coimbra.

Gerster, G.
1970 *Churches in Rock.* London.

Guidi, I.
1896 Il "Gadla 'Aragâwî". *Atti della R. Accademia dei Lincei, ser. 5, vol. 2.* Rome.
1922 La chiesa abissina. *Oriente Moderno, II.*
1932 *Storia della Letteratura Etiopica.* Rome

Haile, G.
1981 Religious Controversies and the Growth of Ethiopic Literature in the Fourteenth and Fifteenth Centuries. *Oriens Christianus 65:* 113-114.
1982-83 The Monastic Genealogy of the Line of Täklä Haymanot of Shoa. *Rassegna di Studi Etiopici 29:* 7-38.
1990 The Homily of Abba Eleyas, Bishop of Aksum, on Mätta`. *Analecta Bollandiana 108:* 29-47.

1992   A Fragment on the Monastic Fathers of the Ethiopian Church. In: *P. Scholz et al. (ed.) Studia in honorem Stanislaus Chojnacki...*, Orbis Aethiopicus, Albstadt: 231-237.
1993   Ethiopic Literature. In: *R. Grierson (ed.) African Zion. The Sacred Art of Ethiopia.* New Haven and London: 47-56.

Kaplan, S.
1981   Hagiographies and the History of Medieval Ethiopia. *History in Africa 8*:107-123.
1984   *The Monastic Holy Man and the Christianization of Early Solomonic Ethiopia,* Wiesbaden: 16-17.
1992   *The Beta Israel (Falasha) in Ethiopia.* New York and London.

Kur, S.
1965   *Actes de Iyasus Mo'a abbé du couvent de St-Etienne de Hayq,* trad. par S. Kur, avec une introduction par E. Cerulli, Corpus Scriptorum Christianorum Orientalium, Script. Aeth. 49.

Lang, D. M.
1956   *Lives and Legends of the Georgian Saints.* London.

Littmann, E.
1904   *The Legend of the Queen of Sheba in the Tradition of Aksum.* Bibliotheca Abessinica, I. Leyden, Princeton.

Lusini, G.
2004   Philology and the Reconstruction of the Ethiopian Past [s. Beitrag in vorliegendem Band].

Marrassini, P.
1981   Una Chiesa Africana: L'Etiopia fra Antiochia e Alessandria. *Corsi di Cultura sull'Arte Ravennate e Bizantina 28:* 193-203.
1990   Some Considerations on the Problem of the 'Syriac Influences' on Aksumite Ethiopia. *Journal of Ethiopian Studies 23:* 35-46.

Mathews, D. and Mordini, A.
1959   The Monastery of Debra Damo. *Archaeologia 97:* 1-58.

Meinardus, O.
1962   *Monks and Monasteries of the Egyptian Deserts.* Cairo.

Munro-Hay, S.
1997   *Ethiopia and Alexandria.* Warsaw - Wiesbaden.
2002   *Ethiopia, the Unknown Land.* London - New York.

Razzi, S.
1588   *Vite dei Santi et Beati del Sacro Ordine de' frati predicatori.* Lucca.

Rossini, C. C.
1895   Appunti ed osservazioni sui re Zague e Takla Haymanot. *Rendiconti della Reale Accademia dei Lincei, serie 5, vol. 4.* Rome: 341-359, 444-468.
1897   L'Omilia di Yohannes, vescovo d'Aksum, in onore di Garima. *Actes du Xie Congrès Int. des Orient.* Paris: 139-177.
1901   Conti Rossini, L'Evangelo d'Oro di Dabra Libanos. *Rendiconti della Reale Accademie dei Lincei, Classe di Scienze Morali, Storiche e Filologiche, ser. 5, vol. 10:* 177-219.
1904   Gadla Marqorewos seu Acto Sancti Mercurii. In: *Carlo Conti Rossini (ed.), Corpus Scriptorum Christianorum Orientalium, Scriptores aethiopici, versio, Series altera, T. XXII.* Leipzig.
1909-10 Liber Axumae. Corpus Scriptorum Christianorum Orientalium, *Scriptores aethiopici, series alters, T. VIII.* Paris: testo, 1909; versio, 1910.
1913   Notice sur les manuscripts éthiopiens de la collection d'Abbadie', *Journal Asiatique, juillet-août: Part IV:* 5-64.
1925   Aethiopica (II Serie), *Rivista degli Studi Orientali, X:* 480-520.
1928   *Storia d' Ethiopia.* Bergamo.
1939a   La leggenda di Abba Afse in Etiopia. *Mélanges Syriens offerts a M. René Dussaud, I.* Paris: 151-156.
1939b   Sulle Missioni domenicane in Etiopia nel secolo XIV. *Rendiconti della Reale Accademia dei Lincei, Classe di Scienze Morali, Storiche e Filologiche, ser. 7, I:* 71-98.

Schefer, C.
1884   *Le voyage d'outremer de Jean Thénaud et la relation de l' ambassade de Dominico Trevisan auprès Soudan d'Egypte.* Paris.

Schneider, R.
1985   Les Actes d'Abba Afsé de Yeha. *Annales d'Ethiopie 13:* 105-118.
1987   Les Actes d'Abuna Salama. *Annales d'Ethiopie 14:* 153-165.

Sellassie, S. H.
1964   New Historical Elements in the "Gedle Aftse". *Journal of Semitic Studies 9:* 200-203.

Stoffregen-Pedersen, K.
1990   *Les Ethiopiens.* Eds. Brepols, Belgium.

Strelcyn, S.
1978   *Catalogue of Ethiopian Manuscripts in the British Library acquired since the Year 1877.* London.

Suchem, v. L.
1895   Ludolph von Suchem's Description of the Holy Land, and of the Way Thither. Written in the Year 1350. In: *A. Stewart (trans.) Palestine Pilgrims' Text Society, XII*. London.

Tamrat, T.
1972   *Church and State in Ethiopia, 1270-1540*. Oxford.

Toussoun, O.
1931   *Etude sur le Wadi Natrun, ses moines et ses souvents*. Alexandria.

Ullendorff, E.
1968   *Ethiopia and the Bible*. London.

Wansleben, J. M.
1677   *Nouvelle Relation en forme de Journal, d'un voyage fait en Egypte en 1672, et 1673*. Paris.

Wustenfeld, F.
1845   *Maqrizi's Geschichte der Copten*. Göttingen.

Zotenberg, H.
1877   *Catalogue des mss éthiopiens dans la Bibliothèque Nationale*. Paris.

What Happened to the Original Church Unity in Ethiopia?

Petros Berga

1. Introduction

A fundamental aspect of twentieth century Church life is the ecumenical movement "justifiably called the great fact of twentieth century church history" (Hoedemaker et al. 1995: 1). Shortly after gaining autocephalous status the Ethiopian Orthodox Church became a full member of the World Council of Churches (1955) playing an important role in the African branch (ACC) and being represented by observers at the Second Vatican Council. The "*unum sint'* unum" (Napier 1962: 382) of Pope John XXIII became an important theme at the Council, resulting in a paradigmatic shift in ecumenical relations. This entailed the momentous step of "recognising other churches as separated brothers and sisters" (Ratzinger - Bertone 2001: 4), and "encouraging the faithful to participate wholeheartedly in the ecumenical movement" (Pope John XXIII 1965: 4). At the beginning of the document "Ecclesia in Africa" Pope John Paul II spoke warmly of St. Frumentius the apostle of Ethiopia and "expressed profound respect for the Church of Ethiopia which shares with the Catholic Church a common origin and the doctrinal and spiritual heritage of the early church" (Pope John Paul II 1999: 32). This paper is orientated towards the relations between the Tewahedo Orthodox Church of Ethiopia and the Catholic Church and, since they are close enough in doctrine to comprise an area of ecumenical activity with hope of achieving concrete results.

The ecumenical movement in Ethiopia is progressing at a slow pace; the purpose of this paper is to show why, and to see what can be done to encourage the dynamic for unity. My emphasis is on activating the process by which Orthodox and Catholics in Ethiopia can rediscover the original unity of the early church. This is conceived of as a hermeneutic process, describing a circular movement. The phenomenality of church existence is marked by a history of division and denominational rivalry, my concern is not the lived experiences of these encounters, but rather the emancipatory possibilities inscribed in them. The process of ecumenical engagement could be described in terms of a cosmic drama, consisting of an emanation out of the state of unity and a future return to it with an intervening period of division.

The paper consequently describes three stages; firstly understanding how the two churches gradually grew apart from their common origin. Secondly explaining how the Christology and teaching of the two churches crystallised in specific dogmatic forms (texts) and how they interrelate. Thirdly analysing the way in which matters of faith and denominational differences are experienced in the cosmology of Ethiopian Christians, illuminating the importance of cultural, political and social factors. The aftermath of communism resulted in nationalist fundamentalism within Orthodoxy (worldwide), while Vatican II style ecumenism was hesitantly and partially received in Ethiopian Catholic circles. Tradition bridges the present and past, providing the interpreter with cognative potential, a reservoir from which emancipatory action can draw. Nurturing dialogue and co-operation facilitate achieving a fused horizon. Unity implies a long process of gradual mutual transformation, learning to listen and appreciate each other. As Eastern and western churches sharing one source, we are gradually learning that we can compliment each other. The final achievement will mean the fulfilment of the high-priestly prayer of Christ for unity (John 17:21).

2.   The Genesis of Christianity in Ethiopia

Church historians of different persuasions tended towards a polemic approach, reading back into the historical events support for claims that their communities were the oldest and most original. However, it can be argued that the original situation in Ethiopia was unity in diversity (Isaac 1972: 225-258), constituting a model for the future. Following the introduction of Christianity under King Ezana documented by coins and inscriptions, Ethiopian Christianity retained a heterogenous nature, gradually changing with the isolation of Ethiopia through Muslim conquest of surrounding areas and subsequent retreat into the mountainous interior. Even after Ethiopia was caught up in the anti-Chalcedonian movement emanating from Syria and Persia a wide spectrum of different groups existed (Grillemeir 1975: 305-323).

Old Testament elements were influential in encouraging the creation of a specific Christian cultural matrix, interweaving aspects of culture and religion. A unique traditional education system nurtured a local devotional literature and spirituality attaching great importance to religious poetry – *queney*, and the study of the classical language Geéz. A foreign observer stated: "The school is the recruiting ground for the church service, it is the mortar in the building of the Christian life of the country, and in outlying areas is the main missionary factor."[1] There were early links with Egypt the nearest patriarchal centre, but proof of an unbroken Egyptian Episcopal succession came much later (Isaac 1972: 225-258). A gap of several hundred years in the documentation of early Ethiopian Christianity encourages conjecture. An unbiased reading of the sources reveals contradictory evidence indicating a wide spectrum of movements including features associated with Catholic orientation. A gradual movement

---

1   Rev. D. O'Hanlon in: R. Pankhurst *"History of Education, Printing and Literrture in Ethiopia.- 1. The Old Time Ethiopian Church Education."* In: Addis Tribune [Newspaper] (Addis Ababa 7.8.1989) p. 13.

towards the consolidation of a uniform non-Chalcedonian State Church culminated in the 15th century (under King Zeraye Ya'akob). The *Meshafa Berhan* is one of the traditional sources documenting the struggle with variant movements including an earlier Jewish Christian tradition at this period.[2]

Ethiopian Orthodoxy tended towards a 'sapiential tradition' expressing truths through symbolism and vivid phrases rather than dialectics or logic, thus indicating a life of faith determined by custom and social convention rather than doctrine. The Ethiopian Orthodox rite had special features including a mystical contemplative character, with a rich variety of forms, preserving ancient heritage in a living way.[3]

Rumours of the mysterious Prester John,[4] kindled European interest in Ethiopia, bringing Portuguese explorers. They saved the Christian empire from extinction at the hands of Muslim invaders under Ahmed Gran,[5] equipped with Ottoman firearms. However, they also provoked a brutal civil war through attempts to impose western style Roman Catholicism,[6] while also stimulating the development of Ethiopian architecture and aspects of cultural life.

Attempts at establishing a Catholic missionary presence in Ethiopia continued intermittently, reaching a climax in the nineteenth century. St Justin de Jacobis and Cardinal Massaja succeeded in establishing Missionary movements in the North and South respectively.[7] The former advocated the use of the Ge'ez rite and valued central highland cultural heritage, while the latter encouraged the growth of a Latin rite. Catholic missions were caught up in the movement for modernisation, playing a notable role in the introduction of Western secular education. The distinction between this and westernisation became controversial during the consolidation of the Ethiopian Catholic Church in the 20th century.[8] Catholic and Orthodox respected tradition,

---

2   The excellent translations of original documents by Getachew Haile give much insight into the importance of Zar'a Yaáqob's reign in consolidating the faith, such as Haile 1992.
3   A special feature of the Ethiopian Church is the regular use of all 14 ancient anaphoras The Coptic Church only regularly uses three, see Summer 1963.
4   Prester John was associated with the Emperor of Ethiopia who came to be the object of European interest, see Ramos 1998: 44-54.
5   Between 1531 and 1543 Ethiopia was dominated by the Muslims and Christian culture destroyed. It was only with Portuguese aid that King Galawdewos (Claudius 1540-59) was able to defeat the Muslims and restore the Christian Kingdom.
6   In 1636 Mendez was expelled, the union was dissolved, and many Catholic missionaries were put to death. The country was closed to Catholic missionary activity for two hundred years (Hyatt 1928: 32-24).
7   In 1846 the vast territory of the prefecture was divided into two circumscriptions: Eritrea, Tigray and Amhara under the name of 'Apostolic Vicariate of Abyssinia' entrusted to the Lazarists with bishop de Jacobis as head, and the rest of Ethiopia as the 'Apolstolic Vicariate of the Galla' committed to the Capuchin Friars, with Bishop G. Massaja as head.
8   There are in Ethiopia today eight Catholic jurisdictions – five apostolic Vicariates, two Eparchies or Dioceses and one Prefecture – they are still grouped in two distinct zones or cultural areas.

but in different ways: the former tempering it with adaptation to modernity, in contrast to the conservatism of the latter.

3.   Doctrine and Other Issues Dividing the Catholic and Tewahedo Orthodox Churches

The first great division of early Christendom occurred at the Council of Chalcedon, venerated by Catholics (and Byzantine Orthodox). Ethiopians and other oriental Orthodox regard it as manifesting an inter-Patriarchal power-struggle with strong political elements and complain of the injustices done to their champion Dioscorus. The ensuing propaganda war apparently affected Ethiopia through Syrian influence at a fairly early date, according to internal evidence in traditional sources (*Querollos* and *Didascalia*). Mistrusting any suggestion of duality in Christ Ethiopians were drawn into the negative Oriental Orthodox reaction to the teaching of the Tome of Leo, considering it lacking in clarity. In the aftermath of the council political and cultural factors were influential including a submerged 'oriental' 'native' popular Christianity, both sides claimed to correctly interpret Cyril of Alexandria.

The formal distinction between nature and hypostasis constituted the essential innovation of the Chalcedonian definition, while its ambiguity has led to continued misinterpretation in Ethiopia. On analysis the main differences between pro and anti Chalcedonian positions appear to be semantic and philosophic,[9] motivated by an exaggerated fear of Nestorianism and Eutychian heresy.[10] However, a lack of attempts at mutual understanding[11] institutionalised differences, which became part of the communities' sense of identity.

Pope Shenouda III of Alexandria stated clearly that rewriting a satisfactory wording of common faith acceptable to all could transcend these misunderstandings."[12] A

---

9   "Modern theologians agree that the difference was mainly one of terminology. The basic problem was that the Council of Chalcedon spoke in the abstract terms of Greek philosophy" (Baur 1994: 25).

10 "At this distance in time and history it is easy to see that the tension between the oriental Orthodox and Byzantine views perhaps kept both from the pitfalls of Nestorian and Eutychean positions of which each suspected the other. It is difficult to see today any substantial divergence in the teachings of the oriental and orthodox churches regarding the person and nature of Christ"(Abraham 1956: 25).

11 "Whatever the creed of Chalcedon's true interpretation may be, Leo is constantly attacked in *Heymanote Abaw* as having taught that the incarnate Christ was (in) two *billawe,* and his teaching is thus open to at least some of the objections levelled at Nestorius" (Cowley 1970: 36).

12 Patriarch Shenouda (1997: 15): "The problem of the two natures and two wills has its roots here (i.e. at Chalcedon) and thus began disruption and conflict within the church. Now we

(continued...)

series of recent agreements on formulation of christological doctrine between Catholics and specific Oriental Orthodox Churches excluded the Ethiopians, who nevertheless participated in the pro-oriente discussions in Vienna. Ethiopian Orthodox scarcely saw Christological differences as an obstacle to relations with the Russian and Greek Orthodox Churches sharing the same Christology as Roman Catholics. Ethiopian Orthodox and Catholics are united in veneration to Mary and the intercession to the saints, whereas papal primacy, the *filioque* clause, the concept of the two wills and purgatory remain divisive issues. Movement towards unity is impeded by non-doctrinal factors playing an important role in the lives of ordinary believers.

4.   Ecumenical Perspectives for Full Reconciliation and Full Communion

A plausible search for unity needs to be grounded in the reality of the present sombre situation, whose negative factors can be seen to be transient. Mutual movements for forgiveness and reconciliation should be initiated to heal past wounds, gradually altering negative stereotypes. The Portuguese period recalls Orthodox grievances while Orthodox overlords oppressed Catholics of minority ethnic groups.

The experiential world of ordinary believers indicates a considerable gap between the pragmatics of denominational differences and official attitudes. Rural Orthodox often feel closer to Muslims than other Christians, reflecting ingrained attitudes and communist official policy recognising only Orthodoxy and Islam as official Ethiopian faiths. The ordinary people scarcely discern official differences in teaching, but rather emphasise unquestioningly following the faith of the fathers.[13] Orthodox are more tolerant than Catholics of elements from traditional indigenous religions.[14]

The matrix of interwoven religion and culture in Ethiopia makes Orthodoxy a way of life associated with a national cultural tradition. 'Natural identity' is placed beyond rational questioning, those who step outside their 'natural group' being regarded as traitors (Mertus - Frost 1998: 65). Catholics are frequently accused of not being completely Ethiopian. The posts communist influx of well-financed foreign Protestant

---

12 (...continued)
   are trying to settle this question by attempting to rewrite a satisfactory wording of our faith, which would be acceptable to all."

13 Such tendencies confirm the words of the Ethiopian philosopher Zar'a Ya'aquob (sixteenth century Ethiopian philosopher): "Man aspires to know truth, but this endeavour is difficult. Hence people hastily accept what they have heard from their fathers and shy away from critical examination." Quoted from: Serequeberhan 1994: 117.

14 These include beliefs in positive and negative spiritual hierarchies and different methods used to influence them, as expressed in the use of amulets with sacred representations: "The figurative image, is promoted to a medicinal or even talismanic status" (Mercier 1997: 87).

missions increased animosity, feeling threatened many Orthodox reacted negatively against anything perceived of as foreign.

The Catholic Church's high profile involvement in modern education and development work contribute significantly to public life, but is suspiciously regarded as a secret means of proselytising. Internal tensions within the Ethiopian Orthodoxy make it impossible for the present Patriarch to make any conciliatory gestures towards ecumenical relations.

Despite serious material problems and persecution the communist period was a time of growth for Christianity in Ethiopia.[15] The Ethiopian Orthodox Church transformed herself into a grassroots people's movement through the activities of parish councils, Sunday school,[16] youth organisations and charismatic preaching hermits. Highly differentiated forms of religion appear in the face of serious socio-political threats, when old certainties are undermined.[17] Such fundamentalist[18] tendencies defend a culture favouring survival, but are detrimental for inter-church relations. However, an inherent tendency in Orthodoxy seeks consensus above sectarian tendencies, so stabilisation and more openness can be expected.

The ancient Ethiopian Geéz rite long used in the Catholic Church of Northern Ethiopia, gradually came in to more widespread use. However, the assumption that sharing one rite is beneficial for ecumenism proved not to be necessarily correct. Many Orthodox resented the chopping and shortening of the liturgy thought to bring a curse rather than blessing. The adoption of local Ethiopian traditions was often seen as subterfuge to blur distinctions and gain converts. Local Catholic tendency to interpret rite as liturgy and ritual separated from theological and spiritual context created complications, contradicting the regard for 'authenticity' advocated by the Vatican documents.

"In the wake of Vatican II the assertion of an exclusive identity between the one Church of Christ and the Roman Catholic Church" (Sullivan 1989: 10-12), ceased, facilitating rediscovery of aspects of the ancient church including the concept of the church as communion. A massive shift in theological self-understanding contributed to unity in diversity being seen positively. However, the transition from Vatican I to Vatican II theology implied a shift from the stability and security of classified defined systems, to a more post-modern open-ended dialogue type-approach, constituting a challenge which many preferred to ignore. On the Catholic side the ecumenical spirit of Vatican II was impeded by the emergence of 'tribal mentalities' emanating from the

---

15 On the eve of the revolution the apparently strong and powerful Church had become a state subsidiary. The confiscation of church lands and feudal privileges, caused terrible suffering but effectively made her more popular with the intelligentsia and youth. See Millard 2001: 123 and Leenco 1999: 198.

16 In 1988 there were 5,985 active Sunday Schools according to: Berhanu 1989: 62.

17 See Bruce 1996: 96 and Hunter 1999: 150.

18 Fundamentalism can be defined as: "great religious passion, a defiance of the *Zeitgeist*, and a return to traditional sources of religious authority". Kelly 1978: 170-171, see also Woodhead-Heelas 2000: 461.

strong ethnic element in current politics, following the implementation of the federal system. Meanwhile instability or even oppression made many cling more fanatically to Orthodoxy as the symbol of national unity.

Desire for unity is inherent in the Christian faith, but Catholics emphasise its organisational form, while Orthodox see rather a concept of spiritual unity with an eschatological fulfilment. The final goal is the unity of faith; but unity is oppressive if achieved with haste. It should be a continuous living process, rather than a diplomatic compromise. It is connected with the paradoxical and apophatic fullness of the mystery of salvation, which is more genuinely suggested by symbols than by intellectual definitions.[19]

Despite the problematic impeding unity, there are positive factors encouraging it. These consist both of internal and external elements. There is a dynamic for unity, which expressed itself in joint projects, ecumenical cooperation by the Bible Society during the period of communist oppression and the writings of intellectuals such as Alemayu Moges. Meanwhile increasing integration in Christian Africa, encourages positive interaction in the ecumenical context, Ethiopia is no longer an isolated island of Christianity. The changing situation in Ethiopia concerning ethnicity and the Ethiopian Orthodox Missionary presence in the Caribean oblige a reformulation of the traditional relationship between religion and culture. The situation in the Diaspora necessitates some ecumenical contact. The increased politicisation of militant Islam in the Horn of Africa in contrast to the tolerant synchretistic Islam of the past,[20] is a powerful element obliging Christian solidarity, as well as the creeping influence of secularism and consumerism.

5.   Conclusion

An inclusive ecclesiology is required to express the broad vision of Vatican II, and counteract the tensions within Orthodoxy following the fall of the iron curtain. Increased Orthodox-Catholic tension resulted in the important joint statement issued at

---

19 Dumitri Satanlioe quoted in: Metropolitan Emilianos of Calabria 'Neglected Factors Influencing Unity'. In: Eastern Churches Review 1 (London 1968) p. 412.

20 However, there is a transformation of local Islam, which has lost its previous African nature as a tribal religion is becoming a strong political philosophy. This is part of an ongoing attempt to politically annex the Horn of Africa to the Muslim Middle East. At least three important Muslim separatist movements constitute a serious threat to the Ethiopian regime. Islamic propaganda leaflets describe the 'Ethiopian empire-state' as 'a predominantly Muslim land in turmoil, where 'awakened Muslims call for *Jihad*. See Erlich 1980: 405 and al-Hashimi 1987: 49, 56.

Balamand (Lebanon 1993)[21] entitled "Uniatism, Method of Union of the Past and the Present Search for Full Communion". Basic models for a more open ecclesiology are provided by the concepts of *Koinonia* or communion, the African concept of the church as family, and Mary as the icon of the Church.[22] The basic principles in these models assist us to formulate a series of steps for the progress of the ecumenical movement. The universal framework for representing essential truths of systematic philosophy has to give ground to modes of 'edifying philosophy', calling for 'open-ended conversation.' The post-modern way of thinking constituted a challenge, which many preferred to ignore, clinging rather to the securities of nineteenth century thought, this was certainly the case in Ethiopia.[23]

The first important step in on the way to unity is establishing an atmosphere of fraternal love. This requires mutual trust, something that is sadly lacking at the moment. It is important for the different sides to really know each other and appreciate each other's traditions. This will gradually encourage a sense of complementing each other rather than competing with each other. The next important stage is a new kind of dialogue a postmodern emphasis on lived metaphors reaching beyond dialogue and discursive reality to 'participation and transference'. Postmodern approaches facilitate appreciating and reconciling different ways of conceptualising the truth. The most controversial aspect of doctrine concerns the nature of the Petrine ministry, which will take much time to resolve. The path to unity will be a long one and will involve many stages. In the initial period much patience is required, various unfavourable circumstances will only be altered in the course of time, but the dynamic for unity exists and is slowly becoming more compelling. The contemporary ecumenical movement could become the cacophony of a second tower of Babel if the partners do not really listen to each other (Genesis 11:7). On the contrary it could become a second symphony of Jerusalem as at Pentecost, where each family announced in its own tongue the wonders of God (Acts 2:11) (Birmelé 2002: 3).

21 Which advocates to "strive for a common reading of the history of the two churches and their relations" (Roberson 1995: 19).
22 The words of Patriarch Demetrios are as appropriate for the Ethiopian Orthodox Church as for the Byzantine Church: "The common dogmatic and theological heritage developed about the venerable person of the all-holy mother of God can once again construct an axis of unity and reunion of the separate parts." Quoted in: McPartlan 1998: 16 and Patriarch Demetrios 1988: 255.
23 It implies a shift from standing outside or above to situating oneself elsewhere within the field of enquiry, an emphasis on lived metaphors, facilitating reaching beyond 'dialogue and discursive reality' into participation and transference (Jackson 1996: 5).

Bibliography

Abraham, C. A.
1956   Chalcedonian and non-Chalcedonian Churches. *Sobernost 3,19:* 372-374.
        London.

Al-Hashimi, A. A.
1987   *The oppressed Muslims in Ethiopia.* Washington.

Baur, J.
1994   *2000 Years of Christianity in Africa. An African History 62-1992.* Nairobi.

Berhanu, L.
1989   *The Role of the Ethiopian Orthodox church in Pre and Post Revolution in Rela-
        tion to the Universal Church.* Senior Essay – Sociology and Social Administra-
        tion. Addis Ababa.

Birmelé, A.
2002   Un choix fondamental dans le dialogue oecuménique moderne. La différence
        comme partie intégrante du concensus. *Nouvelle Revue Théologique 124/1:*
        24-44. Brussels.

Bruce, S.
1996   *Religion in the Modern World. From Cathedral to Cults.* Oxford - New York.

Cowley, R. W.
1970   The Ethiopian Church and the Council of Chalcedon. {The Ethiopian Church
        and the Heretics}. *Sobernost 6/1:* 33-38, London.

Erlich, H.
1980   The Horn of Africa and the Middle East: Politicization of Islam in the Horn
        and Depoliticization of Ethiopian Christianity.' In: *J. Tubiana (ed.), Proceed-
        ings of the Fifth International Conference of Ethiopian Studies. Nice 1977,*
        Rotterdam: 405-410.

Grillemeir, A.
1975   Christ in Christian Tradition. Volume II, Part IV. In: *J. Bowden (trans.), The
        Church of Alexandria with Nubia and Ethiopia after 451.* First Published
        1965. London - Oxford.

Haile, G.
1992   *The Mariology of the Emperor Zar'a Ya'eqob of Ethiopia.* Texts and Transla-
        tions. Orientalia Christiana Analecta 242. Rome.

Hoedemaker, B., Houtepan, A. and Witvliet, T.
1993   *Oecumene als leerproces. Inleiding in de Oecumenica.* First edition 1993.
        Utrecht.

Hunter, J. D.
1999   Fundamentalism and Social Science. In: *D. G.Bromley (ed.), Religion and the
        Social Order. New Developments in Theory and Research,* vol. I. Greenwich
        Cn. - London.

Hyatt, H. M.
1928   *The Church of Ethiopia.* London.

Isaac, E.
1972   An Obscure Component in Ethiopian Church History. An Examination of
        Various Theories Pertaining to the Problem of the Origin of Nature of Ethio-
        pian Christianity. *Le Museon 85.* Louvain: 225-258.

Jackson, M.
1996   *'Things as They Are. New Directions in Phenomenological Anthropology'.*
        Bloomington.

Kelley, D.M.
1978   Why the Conservative Churches are still Growing. *Journal for the Scientific
        Study of Religion 17,2:* 165-172. Chicago.

Leenco, L.
1999   *The Ethiopian State at the Crossroads. Decolonization and Democratization
        or Disintegration?* Lauwrenceville.

McPartlan, P.
1998   Mary and the Catholic-Orthodox Dialogue. *One in Christ XXXIV,1:* 3-17. Bed-
        ford.

Mercier, J.
1997   *Art that Heals, the Image as Medicine in Ethiopia.* New York.

Mertus, J. and Frost, K. M.
1998   Faith and Tolerance of Minority Religions: A Comparative Analysis of Roma-
        nia, Ukraine and Poland. *Journal of Ecumenical Studies XXXVI,1:* 65-80.
        Philadelphia.

Millard, C. S.
2001   The Living Legacy of Aksum. *National Geographic*. 2001 (July): 110-125.
        Washington.

Napier, C.
1962   The Orthodox Church and the Second Vatican Council. *Sobornost 4, 7*: 382-
        398. London.

Patriarch Shenouda
1997   *The One Nature of Christ* (third print). Cairo.

Patriarch Demetrios
1988   The Visits of the Ecumenical Patriarch Dimitrios I to Rome, 1987. *One in
        Christ XXIV, 3*: 252-265. Bedford.

Pope John XXIII.
1965   *Decree Unitatis Redintegratio Concerning the Catholic Participation in the
        Ecumenical movement Chapter 1*. Rome.

Pope John Paul II.
1999   *Post-Synodal Apostolic Exhortion. Ecclessia in Africa*. Rome.

Ramos, M.J.
1998   Ethiopia in the Geographical Representations of Medieval and Renaissance
        Europe. In: *R. De Silva (ed.), Cultures of the Indian Ocean*. Lisbon: 44-54.

Ratzinger, J. and Bertone, T.
2001   The Full Text of the Note on the Sister Churches. *Vatican Web site Protocol
        Number 121/99-10995*.

Roberson, R.G.
1995   Balamand and Beyond: The State of Catholic-Orthodox Relations. *Catholic
        Near East 21, 4:* 16-21. New York.

Serequeberhan, T.
1994   *The Hermeneutics of African Philosophy, Horizon and Discourse*. New York -
        London.

Sullivan, F.A.
1989   The Decrees on Ecumenism: Presuppositions and Consequences. *One in
        Christ XXVI, 1:* 10-12. Bedford.

Summer, C.
1963   The Ethiopian Liturgy, an Analysis. *Journal of Ethiopian Studies 1,1*: 40-46.
        Addis Ababa.

Woodhead, L. and Heelas, P.
2000   *Religion in Modern Times. An Interpretive Anthology*. Malden Ms. - Oxford.

Union – Unterwerfung – Erweckung
Anmerkungen zu den ersten Missionsversuchen in Äthiopien

Walter Buder

Vorbemerkung

Wie aus dem Thema schon ersichtlich, handelt es sich nicht um Mission im engeren Sinn, sondern um versuchte Einflußnahme auf eine bestehende, die äthiopisch-orthodoxe Kirche.

1. Die Jesuiten in Äthiopien (1557 bis 1632)

Nach dem Konzil von Chalkedon i.J. 451 und nach dem Schisma von 1054 war Rom immer bestrebt, die „Union" mit der griechisch-orthodoxen und mit den morgenländischen Kirchen wiederherzustellen. Zu den letztgenannten gehörte auch die äthiopische Kirche. Union bedeutete freilich in den Augen Roms nicht Wiedervereinigung gleichberechtigter Kirchen, sondern Anerkennung des päpstlichen Primats und des katholischen Dogmas.

In Äthiopien fanden diese Bemühungen ihren Höhepunkt und zugleich ihr vorläufiges Ende, als nach dem verheerenden Krieg mit Achmed Ibn Ibrahim, bekannt als Mohamed Grañ, portugiesische und spanische Missionare des Jesuitenordens 1557 ins Land kamen. Sie konnten predigen und lehren, sofern sie die Eigenständigkeit der äthiopischen Kirche beachteten. Beliebt beim Adel und beim Klerus war Pedro Pais. Seinem Einfluß ist es wohl zu verdanken, daß Kaiser Susneyos i.J. 1622 den katholischen Glauben annahm und sechs Jahre später diesen dem Reich verordnete. Darüber hinaus forderte der Nachfolger von Pais, der vom Papst ernannte Patriarch von Äthiopien, Afonso Mendes, die Wiederholung der Taufe, die Einführung der lateinischen Liturgie und des römischen Heiligenkalenders und außerdem den bis dahin in Äthiopien unbekannten Kniefall vor dem Patriarchen.

Das Volk und die große Mehrheit des Klerus und des Adels rebellierten, nach einem gewissen Zögern auch sein Sohn Fasilides. Susneyos mußte die alte Ordnung wiederherstellen und 1632 abdanken, die Jesuiten wurden des Landes verwiesen.

Anhänger des katholischen Glaubens mußten fliehen; darunter auch Abba Gregorius, der Freund und Berater von Hiob Ludolf.

Die Folge der Auseinandersetzung war, daß sich Äthiopien für mehr als hundert Jahre europäischem Einfluß gegenüber verschloß, von wenigen Ausnahmen abgesehen.

2. Die ersten protestantischen Missionare in Äthiopien (1634 bis 1843)

Die protestantische Mission ging nicht von den Staats- und Landeskirchen aus. Es waren einzelne, die den Kontakt mit anderen Kirchen suchten. Zu ihnen gehörte Peter Heyling, der als Begleiter des neu ernannten Abuna 1634 in Äthiopien eintraf (zwei Jahre nach Vertreibung der Jesuiten!) und sich dort bis 1652 aufhielt. Hochbegabt, bescheiden und geschickt im Umgang mit hoch und niedrig, missionierte er nicht, sondern suchte das Gespräch. Er unterrichtete die Söhne des Adels, übersetzte das Johannesevangelium aus dem Ge'ez in Amarinia und soll auch Berater des Kaisers gewesen sein. Auf der Rückreise nach Europa sei er vom Sultan von Suakin getötet worden, weil er sich weigerte, Muslim zu werden, berichtet Abba Gregorius.

Herzog Ernst der Fromme von Sachsen-Gotha (gest. 1675) unterstützte in jeder Hinsicht die äthiopischen Studien seines Hofrates Hiob Ludolf (1624-1704). Beide bemühten sich um einen direkten Kontakt zu Äthiopien und seiner Kirche und ebenso um eine Allianz christlicher Nationen einschließlich Äthiopiens, um der Türken Herr zu werden, die bereits wieder tief nach Ungarn eingedrungen waren und 1683 zum zweiten Mal vor Wien standen.

Diese Bemühungen blieben erfolglos, aber sie zeigen doch, daß es neben den verfaßten, stark binnenorientierten Staats- und Landeskirchen eine ökumenisch gesinnte Minderheit gab, zu der auch schon Peter Heyling gehörte.

Herausragender Vertreter dieser ökumenischen Gesinnung war Nikolaus Graf von Zinzendorf (1700-1760). Wie für Luther war für Zinzendorf Kirche Gemeinschaft der Geheiligten, die sich, so Zinzendorf, in allen Kirchen findet. Das entscheidende Glaubenskriterium ist die Hingabe an den Gekreuzigten, alles andere ist zweitrangig. Keine Kirche kann ein Supremat beanspruchen, jede Kirche hat ihre besonderen Gaben von Gott empfangen. Diese Überzeugung Zinzendorfs findet ihren Niederschlag in seiner Liedersammlung von 1753. In ihr sind Lieder und Hymnen vieler Kirchen enthalten, u. a. auch vierzehn Hymnen der äthiopischen Kirche.

Diese offene Gesinnung findet sich ansatzweise auch im Pietismus und in der Erweckungsbewegung, die in der Mitte des 18. Jahrhunderts in England entstand und dem Pietismus neuen Auftrieb gab. Kernstück der Verkündigung waren das „reine Evangelium" und die „Erweckung" der Menschen, die zur „Wiedergeburt" und zur Gnadengewißheit führen sollte. Durch die Erweckung einzelner Christen aber sollten alle Kirchen, vor allem die Kirchen des Ostens, von innen heraus reformiert werden, da ihnen die Frohe Botschaft verschüttet sei durch Marien- und Heiligenverehrung, durch Werkgerechtigkeit und äußeren Prunk und, auf Äthiopien bezogen, durch die

Übernahme jüdischen Brauchtums wie Sabbatheiligung und Beschneidung, an der schon die Jesuiten Anstoß genommen hatten.

So wurde die Frohe Botschaft zum Dogma, das alles verwarf, was sich mit christlicher Tradition verband, aus der Menschen Kraft und Trost für den Alltag schöpfen.

Die Prediger der Erweckungsbewegung übersahen dabei, daß sie selbst ja auch in einer Tradition standen und daß in der Bibel, von Menschenhand geschrieben, die Frohe Botschaft auch nur gebrochen überliefert ist.

Erweckt und geprägt von der Theologie der Erweckungsbewegung wirkten die Missionare Samuel Gobat, Carl W. Isenberg und J. Ludwig Krapf von 1830 bis 1843 in Äthiopien. Sie wurden zunächst freundlich aufgenommen, Kleriker und Laien waren aufgeschlossen für ihre Botschaft und beeindruckt von ihrer Bibelfestigkeit, aber auch von ihrem selbstlosen Einsatz. Aber das Blatt wendete sich, als die Missionare nicht nur alles in Frage stellten, was die Eigentümlichkeit der äthiopischen Kirche ausmacht, sondern dieser sogar das Recht absprachen, sich als Kirche zu bezeichnen. Vor allem deshalb blieben sie weitgehend erfolglos und mußten 1843 das Land wieder verlassen, ungeachtet der Tatsache, daß viele Äthiopier sie in guter Erinnerung behielten.

Die Jesuiten scheiterten, weil sie die äthiopische Kirche Rom unterordnen wollten, die protestantischen Missionare aber, weil sie als Fremde ihre Theologie der äthiopischen Kirche gewissermaßen aufdrängen wollten.[1]

Ausblick

Die beiden Irrwege sind Geschichte. Sind sie es wirklich? Sicher, in der katholischen Kirche wie in den protestantischen Kirchen bemüht man sich heute um mehr Verständnis für die andere Konfession und auch um Verständnis für die orthodoxen Kirchen. Der christologische Streit von Chalkedon kann als überwunden gelten. Es gibt nicht nur den Ökumenischen Rat der Kirchen in Genf, sondern auch ökumenisch ausgerichtete Partnerschaften zwischen Gemeinden. Erwähnt sei die Tabor Society, in der Christen aus Äthiopien und Deutschland sich um den Erhalt der Kirchenschulen und ihrer Tradition in Äthiopien bemühen.

Aber der Weg ist noch weit zu einer Ökumene im Sinne Zinzendorfs, zu einer Ökumene des gegenseitigen Gebens und Nehmens, die die Vielfalt christlichen Le-

---

1 Auf die Tätigkeit katholischer und protestantischer Missionare in den folgenden Jahrzehnten wird an dieser Stelle nicht näher eingegangen. Sie führte auf katholischer Seite zur Gründung der Unierten Kirchen in Eritrea (1930) und in Äthiopien (1951). Die protestantische Mission konzentrierte sich auf die unter Menelik II eroberten Gebiete, vor allem auf die Bekehrung der Oromo. Aus den Missionsgemeinden entstand 1959 die Mekane Jesu Kirche.

bens bejaht und sich daran freut. Diese Ökumene ist dann auch fähig, fruchtbar den notwendigen Dialog mit anderen Religionen zu führen.

Bibliographie

Baum, W.
2001   *Äthiopien und der Westen im Mittelalter*. Klagenfurt.

Beck, A.
1865   *Herzog Ernst der Fromme*. Weimar.

Crummey, D.
1972   *Priests and Politicans. Protestant and Catholic Mission in Orthodox Ethiopia 1830-1868*. Oxford.

Hammerschmidt, E.
1967   *Äthiopien. Christliches Reich zwischen Gestern und Morgen*. Wiesbaden.

Heyer, F.
1971   *Die Kirche Äthiopiens*. Berlin und New York.

Jones, A. H.-M. und Monroe, E.
1968[2]   *A History of Ethiopia*. Oxford.

Kirchschläger, R. und Stirnemann, A. (Hrsg.)
1992   *Chalzedon und die Folgen*. Innsbruck und Wien.

Jobi Ludolfi
1686   *De bello Turgico feliciter conficiendo*. Frankfurt a.M.

Michaelis, J.-H.
1724   *Sonderbarer Lebenslauf Herrn Peter Heylings...* Halle.

Motel, H.
1949   *Zinzendorfs Beitrag zur Ökumenischen Frage*. Ev. Missionsmagazin N.F. 93.

Rubenson, S.
1976   *The Survival of the Ethiopian Independence*. London.

Tsadua, A. P.
1973   The Catholic Church in Ethiopia. *Zeitschrift für Kulturaustausch. Sonderausgabe "Äthiopien"*. Stuttgart.

Wohlgemut, J. (Hrsg.)
2000   *Dekrete der ökumenischen Konzilien*. Bd. 1 und Bd. 2. Paderborn.

Zeitschriften:
Der Evangelische Heidenbote. Jg. 1828-1846, Basel.
Das Ausland. Jg. 1830-1846, München, später Stuttgart.

Remarks on 'Aspects of the Ethiopian Church in the Fifth and Sixth Centuries'

Ian Campbell

I regret that at the last moment, commitments in Washington have made it impossible for me to attend this large and important meeting of Ethiopianists. Instead of the paper on the church of Yemrähannä Krestos which I had planned to present, I have compiled some brief remarks on Dr Munro-Hay's main paper on the theme of the Ethiopian Church. I hope that my remarks may contribute to the debate which is bound to be stimulated by this excellent paper.

Dr Munro-Hay is to be congratulated on a most comprehensive review of the evidence for the existence of Ethiopia's 'Nine Saints'. In summary, it does seem that there is very little real evidence indeed; it comes as something of a shock to watch these legendary figures vanish like the morning mist when subjected to the author's incisive analysis.

I mention below some additional aspects which might be worthwhile considering both 'for' and 'against' the existence of the Nine Saints, and go on to suggest some approaches to addressing the lacunae in our knowledge of the Christian Aksumite era, the 'dark ages' which followed, and the shadowy Zagwe period itself.

1. Earliest Evidence of the Nine Saints

The Bas-Reliefs at Beit Golgotha

Seeking early evidence of the existence of the Nine Saints, the author considers Lalibela, where the church of Abba Libanos suggests that Mata'a may have become a known and revered figure at least by mid-Zagwe times, ie by the 12th century. This represents one of the earliest – perhaps the earliest reference to one of the Nine Saints. However, while at Lalibela, we should mention the bas-reliefs at Beit Golgotha. Although most writers have noticed only one or two figures, there are, in fact, seven, plus the possibility of a further two which may have been destroyed when doorways were installed in two of the niches. Monti della Corte and George Gerster have pointed this out, and have suggested that they may represent the Nine Saints. Most scholars consider that the inscriptions at Golgotha are likely to date from modern times, and the fact that the (later) paintings of the Nine Saints at Guh also depict the saints in turbans suggests that we should not dismiss Monti della Corte's theory out of hand.

Paintings at Genetta Maryam

While on the subject of iconography, George Gerster also mentions the depiction of Anna Pantalewon at Genetta Maryam; I believe the paintings at this church are generally attributed to the 13th-14th century.

The 'Abba Garima' Gospels

Perhaps some mention should be made of the 'Abba Garima' gospels, if only for the absence of any tangible evidence to link them to a Syrian Abba Garima. These manuscripts are not yet dated, but even if they date from the 6th century (which, I understand, is possible, based on recent carbon-dating), the portrait supposed by priests at the church to be that of Abba Garima is actually one of a set of four evangelists, and the painting is almost certainly Coptic. The canon tables, on the other hand, suggest strong Armenian associations.

The Syrian Connection: Early Ethiopian Church Architecture

Perhaps the most interesting revelation in the author's Main Paper is the quotation from the Epitome of Photius, reporting the existence of a Syrian community in the region of Adulis. This reminds us of David Buxton's work on the origin of Ethiopian churches published in *Archaeologia* in 1947 and 1971. Buxton shows that the floor plans of early Ethiopian churches – including Adulis – follow 4th-6th century Syrian models, despite being contained within an 'Aksumite' exterior form. Surely these findings deserve mention in any analysis of a possible Syrian connection.

2. Clarifications and Other Suggestions

Claims and Rivalries Among the Monasteries

I am confused by the arguments that northern monasteries claimed association with southern monastic figures and monasteries, and that hagiographers of southern monastic figures claimed northern monastic associations, both to enhance their own prestige. It seems difficult to reconcile these two statements. The answer is probably in the chronology, but it could do with some clarification, if one or other of the claims is to be held up as evidence for doubting the tales of the Nine Saints.

The Conclusion Section

The section of text entitled 'Conclusion' actually contains new material and debate, which is all pertinent to the argument. The question of attribution, historical sources and iconography justify major sections of text in their own right. The true conclusions, on the other hand, begin only with the last sentence, and could be usefully developed.

3. Avenues for Further Research

Parallel Legends in Other Orthodox Churches

I find the author's comments on parallel legends in the Georgian church very interesting, and unusual in a paper on Ethiopian cultural history, which is often studied as though the Christianisation of Ethiopia took place in isolation, whereas in reality it was but one thread in a rich tapestry of influences and counter-influences affecting the Mediterranean, parts of Europe as far-flung as Ireland, Asia Minor and north-east Africa. It should thus come as no surprise that, for example, the Lives of Ethiopian, Anglo-Saxon and Celtic saints are in many cases very similar, and that the legend of St Yared is paralleled by an almost identical legend in the Armenian Orthodox Church. This latter discovery, documented recently by Richard Pankhurst, has, astonishingly, taken a long time to come to light. I therefore suggest that in our efforts to separate the 'history' from the 'legend' in Ethiopian Christian literature, we must become equally familiar with the legends and literature of the other Orthodox churches.

Byzantine Orders in Church Building and Iconography

While there is a dearth of literature from either the Aksumite period, the 'dark ages' or the Zagwe dynasty, there are many churches (or, rather, remains of churches), and a few paintings and other forms of iconography. I suggest that we focus more of our attention on this available evidence, and subject it to new forms of scrutiny. One such aspect is the use throughout various parts of Christendom, at various times, of Byzantine orders in architecture and iconography. Geometric canons and methods for surveying and laying out important buildings by the Ancient Egyptians and the Ancient Greeks are known and documented, as are the revival of some of these orders by Christian builders and iconographers, especially after iconoclasm. What is less well covered is the use of these systems in architecture and iconography outside Byzantium (the exception is Russian iconography and Syrian and Anatolian church building, which have been studied in this respect to some extent).

In recent years I have verified the use of Byzantine geometric orders in 12th century Zagwe church of Yemrähannä Krestos, the 13th century (?) bas-reliefs at Beit Golgotha, early 14th century Ethiopian manuscript paintings in Tigray and the Lake Tana region, wall paintings at Qorqor Maryam, and the moon-face style icons of the mid-15th century. Use of the geometric orders is not difficult to establish; what is more difficult is to determine the source and the nature of the influences which may have led to their use. In the case of Yemrähannä Krestos, the findings are that the ground plan follows the ancient modular system employed in 4th-6th century Syrian churches, but that the elevations follow a more complex, Byzantine order which enabled masons to determine elevations from the ground plan without measuring instruments such as yardsticks. These Byzantine orders are thought to have been employed in Syria at the time of the crusades, and were certainly used there after the crusades, but they were used to build elaborate, domed, cruciform churches, not those of ancient 'basilica' design. This suggests that the Syrian influence arrived in Ethiopia in the 4th-6th centuries, but the Byzantine orders could have arrived from almost anywhere in Byzantium, including, possibly, Egypt.

Similar studies of Ethiopia's Aksumite church ground plans, especially Dabra Damo, could yield valuable information. Initial indications are that the ancient modular system used in Syria is common to many of Ethiopia's earliest churches, adapted to the 'rebated' and 'recessed' Aksumite form.

Another, related, aspect is the question of building units. Byzantine churches were often built using the unit of a 'cubit' (Greek or Royal Babylonian), or, after the 6th century, a 'foot'. Where design influences in Ethiopia were direct, (ie, involving foreign masons in Ethiopia), the use of imported yardsticks would have been possible. However, indirect influences (ie, Ethiopian masons being trained in Constantinople or in other Orthodox centers), would be less likely to result in the use of standardized measurements. In the case of Yemrähannä Krestos, there is an indication that a 5-cubit yardstick was used, with windows and wall thicknesses set at two cubits, but this finding is only tentative. It will be necessary to examine a number of churches before any definite conclusions in this regard can be reached.

These are a few examples of the sort of analysis which can be conducted on the evidence we already have, in order to learn more about the pattern of influences in Ethiopian art and architecture, and, in turn, to shed more light on the shadowy periods of the empire's history.

The Tradition and Transmission of the Ethiopic Testaments of the Three Patriarchs

Martin Heide

Besides the well-known "Testament of Abraham" (TestAbr) there are two additional testaments among the so-called "Testaments of the Three Patriarchs" (TestIII). They are known as the "Testament of Isaac" (TestIsa) and the "Testament of Jacob" (Test-Jac). These testaments call for the celebration of the 28th day of the Ethiopic month Nähase.

All three testaments introduce us to those events that immediately precede the death of the patriarchs. God sends his archangel Michael to inform them to prepare for death and to make their will.

In the TestAbr, this famous patriarch does not want to go with Michael. He wants to see the inhabited world before his death. After consulting with God, Michael takes Abraham along on a world tour. First, Abraham can have a look on this world, seeing many people committing sins and engaged in crime. He immediately in his wrath calls death upon these sinners. Nevertheless God is more compassionate than Abraham, and he wants to give to each sinner time for repentance, and therefore tells Michael to instantly stop his world tour. Michael then leads Abraham to the place of judgement. There Abraham realizes the terrible fate of all those sinners after their departure from their bodies. Abraham repents of his former wrath; he even now pleads on behalf of those whom he wanted to punish with death. Finally, Abraham is taken back home to die. As Abraham still refuses to die, Death is ordered in a beautiful disguise to trick Abraham. Abraham then, after having seen Death's normal resemblance, dies. His soul ascends to heaven on a celestial chariot, escorted by angles, while his body, in correspondence with the biblical tradition, is buried in the sepulchre he had already bought for his wife Sarah.

Although the TestAbr is called a testament, it exhibits only few traits of the genre "testament". For instance, Abraham neither instructs his descendants, nor imparts ethical advice to those who have gathered around his deathbed. Some scholars have argued, therefore, that this testament should rather be classified as a romance.

After an introductory homily, focussing on the belief in God and in the message of the saints, the TestIsa pictures again the archangel Michael on his mission. After having told Isaac to make his will and to set his house in order, the archangel departs, and Isaac informs Jacob of his near death. Jacob wants to accompany his father. Nevertheless, Isaac tenderly encourages him to stay and tells Jacob of his ancestry from Adam on and leading ultimately to Jesus, the Messiah. Following that comes an important part of the TestIsa, Isaac's speech on the strict obligations on all priests. After that, Isaac is raptured to the eternal world. First, an angel takes him on a tour through hell, where he sees the tortures inflicted on sinners. This vision is modeled after similar tours of hell (e.g., in the Apocalypse of Peter). Afterwards, he is taken to heaven, where he sees his father Abraham among the 'pure ones', and all saints gathered together to welcome him. A conversation starts between God and Abraham, wherein God ensures compassion and forgiveness for every believer who is doing good works, especially for those believers who keep the memorial day of Isaac, the 28th of Nähase. Isaac finally returns to his bed where he dies. His soul is taken up to heaven on a holy chariot, cherubim and seraphim singing before it.

The TestIsa inclines more to the genre "testament", since it does show Isaac instructing his son Jacob and those gathered around his deathbed.

In the TestJac, Michael likewise informs Jacob of his near death. Jacob is ready to die, because he has seen his son Joseph again after he came down to Egypt (cf. Gen 46: 30f). After that, another angel closely resembling Isaac appears to him. He tells him that he is his guardian angel and that he had already saved him from Laban and from his brother Esau. After Jacob's guardian angel departs, Jacob calls for his son Joseph and instructs him about his burial (Gen 47: 29f). The narrator continues with Ephraim's and Manasseh's blessing, followed by a shortened version of Jacob blessing his twelve sons (Gen 49). After that, like Isaac, Jacob is raptured to the eternal world. First, an angel takes him on a tour through hell, then he is taken to heaven with all its bliss. Finally Jacob returns to his bed where he dies. The Lord comes down and takes his soul to heaven on a holy chariot, and Jacob is borne upwards while cherubim and seraphim go before it. After relating Gen 50: 1-14, the narrator encourages the reader to keep the memorial day of Jacob, which is the same for all three Patriarchs, the 28th of Nähase. Finally, the TestJac ends with an invocation for those who wrote it, read it and explained it.

The TestJac follows more closely the biblical account than the former two testaments. Only one Ethiopic version (Täklä Mika'el: 1986) pictures Jacob instructing his sons. This instruction, however, is modeled closely after Gen 49.

The TestIII may have come into being somewhere between the 2nd century B.C. (TestAbr) and the 3rd century A.D. (TestIsa, TestJac). Only the testament of Abraham, however, is known in Greek. It is generally accepted that the TestAbr has a Jewish origin, although no Hebrew or Aramaic version is known. Even in Qumran, no traits of an alleged Hebrew or Aramaic origin of the TestAbr could be unearthed.

The TestIsa and the TestJac are neither known in Hebrew nor in Greek. All three testaments, however, are known to have Bohairic, Arabic and Gə'əz versions.

Now, it is a well-known fact, that Gə'əz literature is based mainly on Arabic sources, and these Arabic mss (manuscript(s)) again are usually based on Coptic mss. Coptic sources of the TestIII are not known before the 9th century A.D., and the earliest Arabic ms dates to the 16th century (Heide 2000: 7,8). The earliest known Gə'əz ms was copied in the 15th century. Therefore, it is allowed to assume that the Gə'əz version of the Three Patriarchs was translated from the Arabic during the "Second Period" of Ethiopic Literature, after the Zâgwe-Dynasty, according to the division favoured by scholars like Enno Littmann (1964). This is also generally confirmed by Heinzgerd Brakmann in his monograph on the Ethiopic Church (1994: 144f.).

The Gəʿəz version can be divided into three sub-types. This fact already shows us that the Gəʿəz version should be valued as an important textual witness to the TestIII.

First, we have a literal translation from the Arabic, extant in three mss and in a bilingual popular edition in Gəʿəz and Amharic from Addis Abäba.

Secondly, we have the Falasha version, evidently based on the type of text resembled by the mss mentioned above.

Thirdly, we have a free translation from the Arabic, preserved in full for the TestIsa and the TestJac; for the TestAbr, however, in a fragmentary form only.

The first and second type of translation should be philologically classified as one recension (Recension I), which will be proved hereafter. The third type of translation is a different one and should be classified as a different recension (Recension II).

Now, in the *Clavis Apocryphorum Veteris Testamenti*, the subject "Abraham – Isaac – Jacob" (Haelewyck 1998: 56-61) informs us, that the Ethiopic version (*Versio aethiopica*) of the TestIII has two recensions: "Exstant duae recensiones (recensio Falachaeorum, recensio christiana)." The *Clavis Apocryphorum Veteris Testamenti* may be right in classifying these recensions according to theological criteria (similarly Delcor 1973: 18f), but viewed from the perspective of philology, these types of translation must be classified differently.

First of all, we have the literal translation from the Arabic.

We may take it as a working hypothesis that this verbal translation from the Arabic is what I would call the "Ethiopian Standard Text" of the TestIII. This becomes obvious, if we realize some very simple facts:

1. The textual evidence for this literal translation stretches from the 15th to the 20th century. We have one ms from the 15th century, and a second manuscript that is obviously a copy from this ms, dating to the 18th century, both extant in the Gunda-Gunde collection of the late Roger Schneider. This text is – with some minor variations – also the text of a bilingual popular edition in Gəʿəz and Amharic from Addis Abäba, published by Täklä Mika'el in 1986.
2. This text served evidently also as a *Vorlage* for the Falasha version, since the Falasha version shows all typical features of our literal translation, with, of course, some mainly theological motivated alterations.

If we take a more close look at this literal translation, we encounter very often a word-by-word translation of the Arabic *Vorlage* into Gəʿəz in lexemes and syntactical constructions (cf. Kropp 1986: 328):

	Arabic	Gə'əz: Lit. Translat.	Notes
A 8:13	النفوس الخارجة من اجسادها	ነፍሳት ፡ እንተ ፡ ተወጽአ ፡ እምሥጋሃ ፡	Syntax rendered 1:1
I 2:30	اعطانيه الرب اعطيك اياه	ዘወሀበኒዮ ፡ እግዚአብ ሔር ፡ አሁብከ ፡ ኪያሁ ፡	A verbal form that takes two suffixes
J 4:8	هؤلاء اولادى الذي اعطانيهم الله	እሉ ፡ ውሉድየ ፡ ዘወሀበ ንዮሙ ፡ እግዚአብሔር ፡	
I 4:47	لدخولى اليك باوقار	በበአትየ ፡ ኀቤከ ፡ በጾርየ ፡	Two infinitives closely following
I 5:21	فرايته يضرب امواجه	ወርኢክዎ ፡ እንዘ ፡ ይዘብጥ ፡ መዋግዲሁ ፡	A descriptive verbal form translated accurately

Table 1: Ethiopic Method of Translation

For example, a verbal form that takes more than one suffix is quite rare. But here (rows 3 and 4) we find it in Arabic, and word by word reproduced again in Gə'əz.

The second type of translation that belongs still in the realm of the "Ethiopian Standard Text" is the Falasha version. The Falasha version is based on the literal translation and has those features well-known from the literature of the Beta ∃sra'el:

1. The introductory formula of the Falasha version is in all three testaments ይትባረክ ፡ እግዚአብሔር ፡ አምላክ ፡ እስራኤል ።

2. The Falasha version is *not* a newly created translation from the Arabic. When Maurice Gaguine delivered in 1965 his thesis on "The Falasha Version" of the TestIII, he chose ms Or 1878 of the Cambridge University library as his leading manuscript. Edward Ullendorff (1961: 64) characterized this ms as follows: "Despite the fact that this Falasha version leaves out all Christian formulae [...], there remain quite a few unexpurgated Christian allusions, including a reference to Athanasius' authorship of the work (which was translated from Coptic into Arabic and thence into Ethiopic)". Gaguine agrees with him, but adds that "Christian elements are omitted only when glaringly overt" (Gaguine 1965: 12). Only some Falasha mss show a tendency of, for instance, substituting consistently እግዚአብሔር for እግዚእ. The samples of the literal translation listed in table 1, e.g., exist verbatim in nearly all Falasha mss as well.

We have, of course, also to take into account that some Christian readings that we would judge to be "typical Christian" have been embraced by the Beta ∃sra'el, too. In the TestIsa, we have the context of Isaac entering heaven, where he is welcomed by these words: "Holy, holy, holy is the God of Hosts, the perfect" etc. Now in all Ethiopic recensions, this verse (TestIsa 6:5, ed. Heide 2000) reads:

ቅዱስ ፡ ቅዱስ ፡ ቅዱስ ፡ እግዚአብሔር ፡ ፀባ ኦት ፡ መልአ ፡ ሰማየ ፡ ወምድረ ፡ ቅድሳተ ፡ ስብሐቲከ ። We can see here that the wording of Isaiah's vision (Is 6:3) was shaped to the benediction known from the Coptic and Ethiopian mss, because God's glory is said to fill not only the heaven, but also the earth, and it explicitly says "the glory of *thy* praise", which is not known from Isaiah. Nevertheless, this Christian benediction is also commonly used in Falasha prayers (Leslau 1951: 121f.) and therefore entered the Falasha version unchanged.

The third type of translation, to be classified philologically as a different type of recension, is extant in only one manuscript of the Bibliothèque Nationale in Paris. It is a free translation from the Arabic. Table 2 displays some typical differences between this recension and the "Ethiopian Standard Text". Recension I – and that is equally valid for the Ethiopian Standard text in its Christian shape and in its Falasha shape – prefers essentially Arabic syntax disguised in Ethiopic letters, lexemes and morphemes. Recension II, on the other side, takes more liberty in rendering its *Vorlage* (these examples are from the latter two testaments, since the TestAbr is fragmental only):

	Arabic Version	Gəʿəz Recension I	Gəʿəz Recension II
I 2:6	وهو ياتى اليك	ወውእቱ ፡ ይመጽእ ፡ ኀቤከ ፡	ወይመጽእ ፡ ኀቤከ ፡
I 3:2	وهو ينظر اليه	እንዘ ፡ ውእቱ ፡ ይኔጽር ፡ ኀቤሁ ፡	እንዘ ፡ ይኔጽር ፡
I 4:2	وهو يصعد بقرابينه	እንዘ ፡ ውእቱ ፡ የዐርግ ፡ ቍርባናቲሁ ፡	የዐርግ ፡ ቍርባነ ፡
J 2:2	وهو حافظا	እንዘ ፡ ውእቱ ፡ የዐቅብ ፡	እንዘ ፡ የዐቅብ ፡
J 3:2	وهو يشكر	እንዘ ፡ ውእቱ ፡ ያአኩቶ ፡	እንዘ ፡ ይሴብሕ ፡
J 7:6	وهم في اجسادهم	እንዘ ፡ ውእቶሙ ፡ በሥጋሆሙ ፡	እንዘ ፡ ሀሎ ፡ በሥጋ ፡

Table 2: Rendering of circumstantial clauses in Ethiopic

As we can see in table 2, Recension I hyper-correctly – perhaps it is even more appropriate to classify it as "pseudo-correctly" – resembles its Arabic *Vorlage*. Recension II, on the other hand, tries to move away from the Arabic *Vorlage*, creating a syntax that sounds more Ethiopic than Arabic. Recension II does not follow the Arabic as close as does Recension I; it does not, e.g., feature the verbal form with two suffixes (compare table 1, rows 3 and 4) and similar constructions.

Recension II has another unique feature. At various points, the writer apparently felt that the text of the TestIII should be adapted to phrases known from the Ethiopian Bible. So, in Recension I of the TestIsa 5:28 the name of the chief officer in hell is given as አብድልማኮስ (which has led to some speculation about its etymology). Now, this Ethiopic name is more or less modeled after the Arabic, and it is safe to argue that አብድልማኮስ should be read as a Semitic name, meaning "the servant of the God Malik", and not, as was done before, as the Greek name Τεμελουχος (Heide 2000: 45f). In Recension II, however, we get a totally different name, that is ማልኮስ ። Those who know their Ethiopic bible well realize, of course, hat this name apparently was taken from the gospel of John (18:10): Malkos was the name of the high priest's servant, of whom Peter in an effort to save his master cut off the right ear.

Table 3 lists further examples (quite a number could be added) that can be found in the TestIsa and TestJac. The biblical references are given in addition to the references of the testaments:

	Rec. I, close to the Arabic	Recension II	Biblical phrase
I 1:8 2Cor 1:3	እስመ ፡ እግዚአብሔር ፡ መኃሪ ፡ ወመስተሣህል ፤	ወውእቱ ፡ እግዚአብ ሔር ፡ አብ ፡ ምሕረት ፤	አብ ፡ ምሕረት ፡
I 2:2 1Joh 1:9	ወኣረጋዊስ ፡ ምእመን ፡ አቡነ ፡ ይስሐቅ ፡	ኦኣረጋዊ ፡ መእመን ፡ ወጻድቅ ፡ አቡነ ፡ ይስሐቅ ፤	መእመን ፡ ውእት ፡ ወጻድቅ
I 2:13 Mt 25:46	ተሐውር ፡ ጎበ ፡ ፍግዓ ፡ ወዕሪፍት ፡ እስከ ፡ ለዓለም ፤	ተሐውር ፡ ውስተ ፡ ዕረፍ ት ፡ ወሕይወት ፡ ዘለዓለም ፤	ወየሐውሩ ፡ …ውስተ ፡ ሕይወት ፡ ዘለዓለም ።
I 2:25 Mt 5:8	ብፁዓን ፡ እሙንቱ ፡ ሶበ ፡ በጊዜ ፡ ይሬእይዎ ፡ ለእግዚአብሔር ፤	ብፁዐን ፡ ኮሎሙ ፡ እለ ፡ ይሬእይዎ ፡ ለእግዚአብሔር ፤	ብፁዓን ፡ … እስመ ፡ እሙንቱ ፡ ይሬእይዎ ፡ ለ እግዚአብሔር ።
I 4:41 Eph 4:17	ኢይምላእ ፡ ከርሡ ፡ በስታየ ፡ ወይን ፤	ወኢይስከሩ ፡ ወይን ፤	ወኢይስከሩ ፡ ወይን ፤
J 2:21 1Pet 3:13	ትትቀነዉ ፡ ላዕለ ፡ ንጽሕናከ ፡ ወትሬኢ ፡ ምግባራቲከ ፡ ሕሪት ፤	ቀንእት ፡ ላዕለ ፡ ንጽሕናከ ፡ ወምግባርከ ፡ ሠናይ ፤	ትቀንኡ ፡ ለገቢረ ፡ ሠናይ ፤
J 5:12 Hbr 13:22	ሀገሩ ፡ ለፍቁር ፤	ሀገሩ ፡ ለእግዚአብሔር ፤	ሀገረ ፡ እግዚአብሔር ፤
J 7:20 ICor 6:9	ኢይወርሱ ፡ መንግሥተ ፡ እግዚአብሔር ፤	ኢይሬእያ ፡ ለመንግሥተ ፡ እግዚአብሔር ፤	ኢይሬእዋ ፡ ለመንግሥ ት ፡ እግዚአብሔር ፤

Table 3: Word-by-word vs. Bible-phrased translation

In the first column, we again find Recension I, closely resembling its Arabic and Coptic *Vorlage* respectively. These readings can be traced in all subversions of Recension I, that is in the mss from the Roger Schneider collection, in the modern edition of Täkla Mikael and in the Falasha version. In the second column, we suddenly discover a more "biblical" rendering of the Arabic *Vorlage*.

In row 2, for example, we find the expression "now the believing old man, Isaac our father", whereas this is changed in Recension II to "oh, believing and righteous old man, Isaac our father", which can be also translated as "oh, *faithful and just* old man, Isaac our father" in accordance with 1John 1:9.

Row 5, Recension I says "he should not fill his belly by the drinking of wine", while Recension II adapts this to Eph 4:17 "and be *not drunk* with wine". Row 7, Recension I has the "the city of the beloved", changed to "the city of *God*" in accordance with Hebr 13:22 in Recension II. Finally, row 8 reads a verse often repeated in the testaments: "they will not inherit the kingdom of God", changed in Recension II to the more biblical "they will not *see* the kingdom of God" (I Cor 6:9).

Conclusion

The Testaments of the Three Patriarchs call for the celebration of the 28th of the month Nähase. They picture the Patriarchs as ready to leave this earth more or less willingly. Before their final fate is sealed, they are allowed to view the destiny of the sinners and the saints.

Only the TestAbr is known in Greek, but all three Testaments are preserved in Coptic, Arabic, and Ethiopic. The Ethiopic or Gə'əz version is extant in two Recensions. Recension I is based on an Arabic *Vorlage* and looks like a word-by-word translation. Recension I can be subdivided in a Christian and a Falasha version. Both versions stick closely to their original. The few different readings of the Falasha version are theologically motivated. This observation also confirms the theory generally accepted by scholars, that the Falasha-literature was generally based on available Christian literature and not created from other sources; the Falasha version of the TestIII can be labeled therefore as a "soft de-Christianized" version.

Recension II is based on the Arabic, too, but uses a rather free stile of translation. Recension II is, by the way, not a reworking of Recension I. This becomes obvious at some places where Recension II has a totally different rendering of the Arabic *Vorlage* than all mss belonging to Recension I. Some patriarchal names of TestIsa 3:15,16 (from a list following Gen 5 and 11), namely 0ርጎ ፡ ዘፈው፦ጎ ፡ ዓኮር – corresponding to the Bohairic and Arabic *Vorlage* respectively - were changed in ms 134 alone to the names ሴርጎ ፡ የጌC ፡ ዓሖም (Heide 2000: 45, 48). In TestIsa 2:12, ms 134 alone has changed the Arabic passive form توخذ "thou shalt be taken" into the corresponding active form اخذا "I shall take you", whereas Recension I mis-perceived the Arabic form as توجد "you shall find". Half of the verse TestJak 3:5 "... and with your seed, which comes after you. And this land in which you are: I shall give it to you and to your seed forever", preserved in the Bohairic and Arabic version, is found only in Recension II (Ms 134).

Additionally, the writer of Recension II has adapted his text at various occasions to those words of the New Testament that were familiar to him. This phenomenon is also known from other Gə'əz literature. Apparently some of those who copied manuscripts tended to unconsciously reproduce not the exact wording of the *Vorlage*, but a similar phrase they were more familiar with, due to their profound knowledge of the Gə'əz bible.

Bibliography

Aeščoly, A. Z.
1951   *Recueil de textes falachas: introduction, textes éthiopiens (édition critique et traduction), Index*. Paris.

Brakmann, H.
1994   *Die Einwurzelung der Kirche im spätantiken Reich von Aksum*. Bonn.

Delcor, M.
1973   *Le Testament d'Abraham: Introduction, traduction du texte grec et commentaire de la recension grecque longue, suivie de la traduction des Testaments d'Abraham, d'Isaac et de Jacob d'après les versions orientales*. Studia in Veteris Testamenti Pseudepigrapha 2, Leiden.

Gaguine, M.
1965   *The Falasha Version of the Testaments of Abraham, Isaac and Jacob*. A critical study of five unpublished Ethiopic manuscripts with introduction, translation and notes (unpublished Ph.D. thesis), Manchester.

Haelewyck, J. C. (ed.)
1998   *Clavis Apocryphorum Veteris Testamenti*. Brepols.

Heide, M.
2000   *Die Testamente Isaaks und Jakobs: Edition und Übersetzung der arabischen und äthiopischen Versionen*. Aethiopistische Forschungen 56. Wiesbaden.

Kropp, M.
1986   Arabisch-äthiopische Übersetzungstechnik am Beispiel der Zena Ayhud (Yosippon) und des Tarikä Wäldä-'Amid. *ZDMG 136:* 314-46.

Leslau, W.
1951   *Falasha Anthology – The Black Jews of Ethiopia*. Yale Judaica Series, vol. VI. New Haven.

Littmann, E.
1954   Äthiopisch. Die äthiopische Sprache. In: *B. Spuler, Bertold (Ed.), Handbuch der Orientalistik, 1. Abteilung, 3. Band: Semitistik*. Leiden: 350-375.

Täklä Mika'el
1986   የአብርሃም ገድል ፡ የይስሐቅ ገድል ፤ የያዕቆብ ገድል ፤ የሣራ ገድል (ድርሳነ ኤፍሬም) በ፩
        ህታዊ ፤ አ፩ ተክለ ሚካኤል ተዘጋጀ 'The Life of Abraham, The Life of Isaac, The
        Life of Jacob, The Life of Sarah (Homily on Ephraim), edited by the monk
        abba Täklä Mika'el'), Addis Abäba. (Mr. Girma Fisseha of the
        Völkerkundemuseum in Munich very kindly gave me this booklet for
        research).

Rossini, C. C.
1922   Nuovi appunti sui Giudei d'Abissinia. *Accademia dei Lincei, Rendiconti 31.*
        Roma: 221-240.

Sanders, E. P.
1983   Testament of Abraham. In: *Charlesworth, J. H., The Old Testament
        Pseudepigrapha, vol I.* New York: 871-902.

Stinespring, W. F.
1983   Testament of Isaac und Testament of Jacob. In: *Charlesworth, J. H., The Old
        Testament Pseudepigrapha Vol I,* New York: 903-918.

Ullendorff, E. and Wright, S. G.
1961   *Catalogue of Ethiopian Manuscripts in the Cambridge University Library.*
        Cambridge.

Der Asboberg des Heiligen Pantalewon und der Qanazel des Heiligen Liqanos in den 1970er Jahren

Friedrich Heyer

Die Ankunft der Neun Heiligen in Äthiopien in der Herrschaftszeit des Königs Ella Amida II. etwa um das Jahr 480 bedeutete geradezu eine "zweite Evangelisation" im Lande. Die frommen Äthiopier sehen in diesen aus allen Landschaften des Römischen Reiches kommenden Asketen gleichsam die Repräsentanten der ganzen christlichen Ökumene, von Rom, Byzanz, Antiochien, Kilikien. Die Neun Heiligen waren Träger griechischer und aramäisch-syrischer Namen, antichalcedonensische Bekenner, die die Religionspolitik der byzantinischen Kaiser aus ihrem Machtbereich vertrieb. Das Volk von Aksum nahm die Byzanzflüchtlinge liebevoll auf. Ein Jahr und neun Monate hausten sie in der Königsresidenz bei einem schattenspendenden Baum in einem Quartier, das Beta Qätin hieß. Dann zerstreuten sie sich im Land, um an verschiedensten Orten ihrer Askese zu leben und den Glauben der umwohnenden Bevölkerung zu festigen. Weil das Volk sie nicht alle davonziehen lassen wollte, zogen der heilige Liqanos und der heilige Pantalewon auf zwei Gipfelspitzen nicht fern von Aksum, auf die Berge Asbo und Qanasel.

Von den Neun Heiligen erzählt das Gädl des Pantalewon: "In einem Glauben geeint lebten die Heiligen mit König und Metropolit in der Stadt Aksum, den Glauben an Christus bestätigend. Da der König gern bei ihnen verweilte, weil er sie sehr liebte und gern ihren Lehren lauschte, sich auch über ihre Taten erstaunte, blieben sie 9 Jahre in Aksum. Als der König starb, begruben sie ihn ehrenvoll unter Tränen im Königsgrab. Darauf wurde Tazena, Vater des später so berühmten Kaleb, König von Aksum. auch er war ganz willig, den Willen der Heiligen zu erfüllen. Bald aber erklärten diese: "Es ziemt uns nicht, hier in irdischem Müßiggang zu verweilen. Wir sollten statt dessen besser in Ängsten schweben und zwischen Bergen, Höhlen und Erdlöchern heimatlos herumirren."[1] Sie grüßten sich mit dem Friedenskuß und gingen auseinander, ein jeglicher mit seinen Jüngern.

Da ging auch der heilige Pantalewon aus der Zelle. Er hatte ja von Kindheit an wie Samuel im Haus des Herrn seinen Platz. Sein Vater war ein hochgeachteter Mann gewesen, der dritte in der Rangfolge unter den Personen, die zur Rechten des Kaisers der Römer sitzen durften. Von der Zeit an, da er von der Mutterbrust abgesetzt worden war, hat er in Mönchskoinobien gelebt. Solange Pantalewon zusammen mit seinen Mitbrüdern in den Königsgemächern von Aksum weilte, hatte man ihn während

---

1 CSCO series aethiopica 9 (1961); Amharic Church Dictionary, Edition Heidelberg 1989, III. 169.

der ganzen Nacht in der Kirche aufrecht wie eine Säule stehen sehen. Nie hatte er eine Hore versäumt, sei es bei Tag oder Nacht. Als diese Knechte Gottes auf die verschiedenen Berggipfel auseinandergingen, bat das Volk, daß doch nicht alle allzu fern von ihnen wegzögen. Der König, die Priester, Mann und Frau weinten. In der Stadt selbst wollten die Heiligen zwar nicht bleiben. Aber Pantalewon und Liqanos zogen nur eine geringe Entfernung weg, wegen des Geschreies des Volkes. Der heilige Abba Liqanos stieg auf den Qanasel-Berg, Pantalewon auf seine Bergspitze.[2]

Anfang Oktober ist der jährliche Festtag Abba Pantalewons. Im Senkessar des Tages liest man: "Dieser heilige Mann war der Sohn adliger Leute unter den Großen Roms zur rechten Hand des Kaisers. Als die Mutter ihn entwöhnt hatte, tat sie ihn in ein Kloster." Sein späteres Eremitenleben wird so beschrieben: "Abba Pantalewon ging auf die Spitze eines kleinen Berges und machte sich selbst eine Zelle, welche fünf Ellen lang, zwei weit und drei tief war. Deren Dach war ein einziger Stein und sie hatte keine Tür, sondern nur eine schmale Öffnung. Und er stand auf seinen Füßen eine Zeitdauer von 45 Jahren, ohne sich niederzusetzen oder sich zum Schlaf zu legen. Er aß und trank so wenig, daß seine Haut an seinen Gebeinen klebte, und seine Augenbrauen waren durch seine Tränen weggewaschen."[3]

Wo die Felswand, die die Straße von Aksum nach Adua anfänglich säumt, Raum gibt für ein Quertal, zieht sich der Weg nach Abba Pantalewon hin, bald steiler aufsteigend. Hunderte von Frauen und Männern, in frische weiße Shamma gehüllt, steigen im erwachenden Tag hinauf, eine weiße Zick-Zack-Linie durch die grüne Landschaft. Wo der Weg den Grat erreicht, steht, wie von einer Faust emporgestemmt, ein steiler Felsen. Dort droben lebte und betete Abba Pantalewon.

Die Deutsche Aksum-Expedition hat die alte Klosteranlage, die auf dem Berg entstanden war, 1906 freigelegt.[4] Eine aus behauenen Blöcken gefügte Treppe führt zum Gipfel. In den Außenmauern der Kirche fand die Expedition sabäische und griechische Inschriften. Priester zeigen die Zelle, in der Pantalewon 45 Jahre ohne Speise und Trank stehend gebetet hat. Der heilige Yared soll bei einem Baum am Fuß der Felssäule seine Hymnen gedichtet und mit Melodien versehen haben. Von König Kaleb erzählt man, er sei am Ende seines Lebens Einsiedler in Abba Pantalewon geworden und habe hier sein Grab gefunden.

Gouverneur Ras Managasha, vorbildlich mit der Orthodoxie verbunden, hat eine neue Kirche auf der Felsbekrönung errichtet. Nur Männer dürfen hier beten. Für die heranpilgernden Frauen befindet sich unterhalb eine eigene Kirche. Zu ihr trägt die Prozession den Tabot und umkreist mit Gesang und Tanz der Däbtära dies Gotteshaus.

---

2   Conti Rossini 1904. Eine neu entdeckte Quelle über Abba Liqanos oder Matta'e stellt Ms
    EMML 8509 aus Tana Qirqos dar. Vergl. Sergew Hable Selassie 1993.
3   Senkessar I 116; CSCO XVII 41.
4   Littmann 1913 I, XIV und I Absch. III 2c; Doresse 1956: 113 sieht in Abba Pantalewon ein
    vorchristliches Heiligtum.

Die beiden Asketen Pantalewon und Liqanos hatten zwei benachbarte wie von der Natur dafür vorbereitete Felssäulen vorgefunden, durch eine etwa zwei Meilen breite Senke getrennt, aber doch auch nahe genug, um beim Gebet hinübergrüßen zu können. Das Kirchlein auf dem Däbrä Quanasel, das die Tradition des Abba Liqanos wachhält, ist halb verfallen. Steine mit eingemeißelten Kreuzzeichen sind ins Mauerwerk eingelassen.

Das Gädl schreibt über den Berg des Pantalewon: "Dieser Berg, von Blitzen umloht, war ein schreckenerregender Berg wegen der Stimme Gottes des Vaters, die zum hl. Pantalewon herabdrang ... Dieser Berg wurde Wohnstatt des Tag und Nacht Wachenden.

Berg, Prediger der Heiligen!
Berg, Reiniger der Sünden!
Berg, Stärker der Gerechten!
Berg, Tröster der Angefochtenen!
Berg, Licht der Blinden,
Der Stimme Gottes wegen, die zu Dir herabstieg!
Dieser Berg ist kleiner als die Berge von West und Ost, Süd und Nord.
Aber wegen des Herrn Stimme, die auf ihn herabstieg,
Ist er größer als alle Berge Äthiopiens."[5]

Wird am Festtag des Heiligen das Gädl des Pantalewon verlesen, dann bekommt die Gemeinde folgendes zu hören: "Hört her, meine Lieben, damit ich mit Euch reden kann! Wenn jemand fragt, warum eigentlich stand der Heilige 45 Jahre lang hier auf diesem Berg? Etwa wegen seiner eigenen Sünden? – dann antworte ich ihm: Oh Du, der Du solches Lügenzeug redest! So steht es nicht! Sondern deswegen verhielt sich jener Heilige so, damit er vermöge der Schönheit seines Handelns dem Herrn wohlgefällig werde und für alle Barmherzigkeit erflehe, vor allem für dieses Land Äthiopien. Für den König, nämlich für seinen Sieg über die Feinde, die Ruhe im Land und den Frieden mit den Regionalherrschern. Für die Bischöfe, Priester und Diakone, nämlich für einen Priesterdienst in Schönheit. Für die Mönche, Jungfrauen und Witwen, daß sie in Beständigkeit ausharren. Für die Christen, die in der Ehe leben, nämlich für die ihre unbefleckte Lebensart. Für die Kinder, ja selbst für die Unfrommen, für die Kranken, daß ihnen geholfen werde, für die Handelsleute, daß sie einen Hafen finden, für die Gefangenen, da sie freigelassen werden ... Für die Bäume und Blumen, daß die Quellgründe ihnen Wasser spenden. Für der Stiere Kraft und für der Kühe Milch. Das alles erflehte Pantalewon für uns. Seht, meine Brüder, wie mächtig in seinem Herzen das Mitgefühl war mit aller Kreatur."[6]

Um das Weihrauchwunder des Hl. Pantalewon zu verstehen, muß man wissen: Wenn der Priester Weihrauch entzündet, benutzt er eine Holzkohle (Kasal), die aus dem Holz geheiligter Bäume (Ölbaum und Set) gewonnen wird. Auf dieser Holzkohle wird der Weihrauch (Etan) zum Glühen gebracht. Kasal wird im Betlehem-Haus

---

5 CSCO XVII 43 f.
6 CSCO series aethiopica 9 (1961) Amharic Church Dictionary, Edition Heidelberg 1989 III.

zubereitet und aufbewahrt. Profaner Gebrauch ist verboten, obwohl jede Familie zum Kaffeekochen ihrerseits Holzkohle benutzt.

Von Abba Pantalewon wird berichtet, daß er einmal die für den Kirchengebrauch nötige Holzkohle auf wundersame Weise herstellte. Sein Schüler pflanzte am frühen Morgen ein kleines Bäumchen in ein Loch nahe bei der Cella und hatte es auf Befehl des Heiligen dreimal mit Wasser zu begießen. Bis zum Abend war ein großer Baum herangewachsen und zur Holzkohle verbrannt. In der Nachthore diente diese schon zum Räuchern.

Abkürzungen

CSCO   Corpus scriptorum christianorum orientalium. Paris - Rom - Leipzig - Louvain.

Senkessar   Hugo Duensing, Liefert das äthiopische Synaxar Materialien zur Geschichte Abessiniens? Göttingen 1900.

Bibliographie

Anonymus
1989   Amharic Church Dictionary, Edition Heidelberg III.

Conti Rossini, C. (Übersetzer)
1904   Gadla Pantalewon seu Acta Sancti Pantaleonis. In: *CSCO Scrip. aeth. XVII.* Rom: 40 f.

Sergew Hable Selassie
1993   Identität. In: *Journal of Archives of Ethiopia 1:* 11-15.

Doresse, J.
1956   Les premiers monuments. *Novum Testamentum* X, no. 3: 113.

Littmann, E. et al.
1913   Deutsche Aksum-Expedition. 4 Bände Berlin.

Ethiopian Monasticism Between Tradition and Modernity

Joachim Persoon

Introduction

The aim of this presentation is to describe the practice of modern Ethiopian monasticism its 'life force' in terms of spirituality and social interaction. Monasticism is a ritualised[1] life style with specific social functions, which adapts tradition to the modern context. Insight is gained from a phenomenological approach promoting transcultural understanding. Merleau-Ponty contrasted the dominating Western approach (the *Kosmotheoros*, a dominating and all compassing look) (Merleau-Ponty 1964: 113, 187) with phenomenology's attempt to look at the object "by plunging oneself into it, seeing an object in so far as it forms a system or world" (Merleau-Ponty 1962: 67, 68). Ethiopian Orthodoxy is propagated by its own culturally orientated indigenous systems; consequently 'intellectual colonisation' should be avoided. Edward Said warned of the nexus between power and knowledge (Wallia 2001: 54), reminding of history's emancipatory potential (Wallia 2001: 12), and advocating an emphasis on the iconography of signs, symbols and language.

Varying in outward forms Ethiopian monasticism has a unifying core of monastic spirituality, a 'technology' for personal transformation and spiritual advancement, constituting an organic body perpetuating and propagating the faith. An "ensemble of processes it organizes the invention of a mystic body," (de Certeau 1992: 14) endowed by nervous energy with transformative power.[2] My intention is to describe the movement of this mystical body through concentric areas of interaction (after the paradigm of the 'sacred dance event') reflecting the sociological meaning of the Ethiopian interpretation of space. The pattern of a charged centre surrounded by concentric circles of significance.[3]

---

1   "By ritual we mean a system of symbolically pregnant, rule governed, and formalized activity and speech that people repeat as required by social prescription and the meanings of which are established by social convention." Laughlin and Throop 2001: 717.

2   See: Merleau Ponty 1962: 52, 73 and Langer 1976: xv, 15, 56, 131.

3   Thus reflecting the sociological meaning in the Ethiopian interpretation of space, the pattern of a charged centre surrounded by concentric circles of significance (Kebede 1999: 218, f.n. 94). "The dominant configuration in the Amhara's experience of space is that of concen-

(continued...)

Inspiration can be gained from traditional concepts such as sacred dance, which heightens the emotion of the onlookers, and holy water a symbol of immediate contact with inexplicable divine power. They exemplify the aspirations of the monastic life, a more intense experience of the vocation of all Christians to a transformed sacred life and personal regeneration. After mentioning some of the characteristics of the phenomenological body of Ethiopian monasticism, I shall trace its passage through concentric circles of social encounter.

Distinguishing Characteristics of Ethiopian monasticism

Ethiopian Monasticism is understood as an uncompromising imitation of Christ, and also finding complete unity of heart by uniting with the one, the absolute (Guillaumont 1978: 41). A "creative process forging a sacred self as a cultural creation" (Csordas 1997: 42). Religion, theology and spirituality as strategies, shape, control and dictate patterns of human experience, rewriting the binary opposition between spirit and matter in terms of the "dynamic of power-knowledge and embodiment" (Carrette 1999: 6). The Eastern Fathers remained faithful to the Biblical understanding of the human being as a unity that God radically transcends and can entirely transfigure (Clement 2000), expressed in the process of deification. Ethiopia preserved the "monistic conception of Semitic and Old Testament influence" (Yohannes 1997: 211–218) reflected in the *tewahedo* united nature Christology of the Ethiopian Orthodox Church. "God became man in order to deify us, is a well known verse by Ethiopian scholars."[4]

In post-reformation Europe mysticism's relation with the body fell victim to gnosis and alienation from tactile forms (de Certeau 1988: ix). In contrast Ethiopian spiritual writings preserve a sense of embodiment, reflected in the popular genre of *Melke'e* devotional literature, praising the physical features of Christ, Mary and the Saints.[5] Concepts of sacred time determine monastic practice, under communism public time became the arena of domination and habitual practice the site of resistance. In Ethiopian thought "Time is the exclusive weapon of God, epitomizing the fleeting nature

---

3   (...continued)
    tric circles. ... The pattern of a charged centre surrounded by concentric circles of decreasing significance recurs in the main areas of Amhara life. ... this spatial pattern is found in the traditional organization of the military camp of a negus or ras and in spontaneous arrangements during festivals." Levine 1965: 74-75.
4   From E. Mail correspondance with Fisseha Tadesse, Ethiopian Scholar studying in Germany 14.3.2002.
5   *Melke'e* in Geéz form physiognomy, a poetic literary genre with verses honouring specific parts of the body. Melk'e Yesus 52 verses, that of Mary 57, of Mika'el 53, verses etc... Abba Gabré Yesus Haylu 1982: 126-134.

of things" (Kebede 1999: 216-217) corresponding to the 'chimeric nature of human meaning and forms of life' in post-modernism (Gosden 1994: 5).

Ethiopian monks are guardians of the *tabot,*[6] symbolising the unaproachable God, totally giving himself yet veiled by the brilliance of his light, representing the "central 'still point' in the circle of worldly action where understanding and being coincide" (Klostermaier 1997: 159-160). Ethiopian tradition likens monks to angels, messengers of word and flesh images of transformation, who turn toward each other above the arc, guarding and calling the divine presence between them. In Heidegger's words creating the clearing where Being can become manifest (Jantzen 2002: 233-235).

Ethiopian monastic traditions share traditional arts approach to the universalistic features of primitivism, opposing the inauthentic fragmented world of industrial modernity. As reservoirs of the non-alienated (Hiller 1991: 64-65), they indicate a return to the primordial being, rudimentary and essential. Ethiopian monks "sought out places where heaven met earth, drawing out their spiritual aura" (Bittel 1990: 43) integrating their abodes into the natural milieu. They share postmodernists view of wilderness as 'sacred space' counterforce to the momentum of totalising power', antidote to the 'hyperreality' and 'simulation' of urban culture. Monasticism constitutes a "ritual flight to the desert, creating the 'sacred' as liminal space," (Antonnen 2000: 204) where a heightened awareness of the "stimulus provided by 'numinous' (Prattis 2001: 38) symbols, bridges the gap between society and separated areas of reality."[7]

Ethiopian monasteries inhabit a stark world, reminiscent of Celtic Ireland's bleak landscape of round monastic enclosures.[8] Monasticism is a struggle *tegadelo,* yet warrior and performer[9] combine in ascetic discipline and self-cultivation. The monk died to the world during his induction rite, yet like Christ, dancing on a shaft of light (in traditional paintings) he is called to proclaim the good news of the resurrection to those in Hades.

The Classic Ascetic form of Monasticism: The monk and God

The classic ascetic form of monasticism is considered the most charcteristic in Ethiopia. Asceticism comes from the Greek root *askeo, askesis,* physical exercise, striving and piety, designating techniques designed to weaken the flesh but strengthen the soul expounded in the Ethiopian "book of the monks". A second nature is created grounded in the sacred dicta. Philiksios stated a monk should "arouse spiritual envy

---

6 The original ark is believed to be kept in a chapel in Axum guarded by a specially appointed monk.
7 Macrae, C. Review article: 2000: 250 refers to Celtic scholar Nagy 1981-82.
8 As described in Bittel 1990: 57-84.
9 A striking example is the Chinese martial arts tradition of *Kung Fu* (holding fast), developed in a Buddhist monastery and now associated with theatrical performance.

by the virtue, depth and attractiveness of his devotions, overcoming Satan and challenging others to imitate him."[10] Like "postmodern theology ascetic spirituality retrieves language and imagery from previous especially biblical sources to enable personal and social formation by a bricolage activity combining ancient source-materials and contemporary realities" (Wallace 2002: 203-204) in a model of ascetic-mystical transformation. A steady "re-enactment of basic psychological inner spiritual dramas" (Snyder 1992: 85, 87) like Quantum theory and non-dualistic experience involves puzzles and paradoxes, disclosing levels of reality more inclusive than matter-energy.

Ethiopian asceticism creates a sacred self, shaped and controlled by the soul as a mechanism of power. The body not negated, but transformed, is transcended and divinised, reaching the extreme limit "the ascetic grows angelic wings or gains heavenly crowns" (Haile 1991: 993-994). Rather than intellectual depth he is "characterised by prayer, supplication and repentance" (Kebede 1999: 195) after years of service he devotes himself to prostrate, supplicate, fast and pray. Interviews with *bahitawian* indicate beliefs and practices associated with "altered states of consciousness (ASC's) regulation of body temperature, minimization or prevention of injury, and enhancement of immune systems (longevity)" (Bushell - Bademariam 1998: 47, 48, 50).

Tradition enumerates a scale of ten spiritual levels *Ma'arege Monokosat*, referring to purity of the flesh, spirit and heart.[11] A universal system of progression by degrees associated with Evagrius of Pontus and Platonic thought, constituting a "ladder of ascent adepts climb to recover their true nature, ultimately in the direct vision of God."[12] Spiritual corporality appears most dramatically in attainment of the level of the *soweran*. Invisible they are indicated by the smell of incense, the sound of bells and chanting.[13] In 1979 newspapers documented Abba Walda Belaiy Michael's disappearance before a group in Asebot.[14] The *Soweran* resemble the living dead (African

---

10 "Filiksios" Chapter 39: 67, Ch. 48: 83, Ch. 58: 94, Ch. 85: 119…cf. Tesfa Gebre Selasse 1988.

11 This corresponds to the original tripartite division: the physical *pagranutha* purifcation of the passions, the psychological *naphshanuta*, passivity of the intellect, and the spiritual level: *ruhanuta.*

12 See: Linge 2000: 541-543. Evagrius of Pontus' teaching was associated with that of Origen and Didymus the Blind and with them was formally condemned at the Fifth Ecumenical Council in 553. However, his writings in Greek and Syriac survived and continued to be influential because they were attributed to more Orthodox monastic writers.

13 Every now and then one of these lost or hidden monasteries is supernaturally revealed and becomes a cultic centre, a striking example being Boreda Dinq Washa in Goma Gofa. Forty four tabots were found here, by a Protestant man named Hata Chilalo (member of one of the ethnic minorities). He related that the Holy Virgin appeared and revealed the cave to him, she told him to repent and be baptized, it became an important church centre, where many miracles occurr.

14 He was born in Wollo and had a good job in a hotel till 1960. After seeing visions of the Virgin he became a monk and later entered Asebot monastery. This whole section is based on the article: Anonymous "The monks who have gained the spiritual level of bilocation

(continued...)

ancestors), in postmodern terms "authentic human existence transforms temporality into an experience of eternity-within-finitude, no longer an atomistic ego, unrestricted by everyday categories" (Zimmerman 1992: 245-270).

The important monasteries Mahbere Sellassie and Waldibba exemplify the traditions of the *cenobium* and *laura,* community orientated or loosely grouped settlements. In Mahbere Selassie[15] (Chilga Sudanese border) a pristine rule and an uncompromising life-style disallowing personal property was preserved. The revolution swept away feudal pride and arrogance diminishing prestige and wealth, but the monks turned need into virtue strengthened their resolve,[16] becoming an important point in the monastic circuit for younger monks.

Waldibba, a lowland desert adjoining the Simien mountains, straddles the Tigray/Gondar border. It has 86 water sources, takes four days to cross by foot, and is renowned for its hard conditions of life. A wilderness sanctuary reputedly protected by divine wrath it preserves a unique monastic culture, a special way of interacting with nature, architecture and life style. Jacques Mercier and Girma Elias in December 1976,[17] describe a thriving community. During the communist period numbers increased probably now exceeding 1,500. Mahbere Selassie and Waldibba function as a spiritual dynamo a 'Mount Athos' of Ethiopia, testifying to the vitality of the contemplative ascetic spirituality at the heart of the church.

Traditional Community Orientated Form of Monasticism: The monk and the believer i.e. Christian Society

There was also a tradition of socially orientated semi-urban monasteries such as Merthula Maryam, Debre Werk and Dima Giorgis in East Gojjam. They exemplify the tradition of "the church as embodiment of Ethiopian culture" (Isaac 1971: 254) like the Buddhist "*Sangha monks* acted as both the traditional intelligentsia and the traditional educators" (Gombrich - Obeyesekere 1988: 207) Monasteries housed ascetics, constituting centres of sacredness for the community. However, also accruing "economic and social functions administration of lands, provisions for travellers and social welfare" (Miller - Wertz 1996: 175).

---

14 (...continued)
    have reached over 2,000." Ma'adot {Month of Tirr} 1993: 6.
15 For detailed exposition of the rule see: Persoon 1997: 496-519.
16 The Afe-Memher quoted the example of honey. Formerly this had been brought to the monastery by the peasants from the surrounding area, now it was sold across the border in Sudan. Consequently a proposal had been put forward to allow the purchase of sugar for the sick brethren. However, this was firmly rejected as an unnecessary compromise.
17 The latter wrote a detailed and valuable description of the visit including an account of the history of the monastery: Elias 1977: 93-117.

Traditional Amhara culture made land ownership the source of both wealth and prestige. Monastic feudal fiefs embodied spiritual influence in worldly power as spheres of spiritual influence expressed in the literary formulae of the *kidan* (Tamrat 1984: 196-197), and organised to supply the requirements of the cult. Monasteries furnished the major elements of social and economic infrastructure, from banking and marketing facilities to education, law and aid to the needy. The customary law of the Amhara was based on the '*Tatayeq-Muget*' mode of litigation (Jambere 1984: 245), monks, served as judges and arbitrators. At Debre Worq, the shade of a huge tree served as court of litigation and place of local assembly.

Monasteries' assistance to the poor and needy was eventually institutionalised in charitable trusts, and later facilitated by co-operation with international agencies (Abba Gorgorios 1984: 391-396), including cooperation between the Orthodox Development Commission and World Vision especially in the period 1977-1989. During the famine of the mid 1980's a government minister Atto Shimelis Adunya developed a policy of using monasteries and churches as aid distribution centres.

Traditional education, training for church and public service was largely oral and based on memorization, monks being patrons and occasionally important teachers. Even in 1982, there were as many as 400 students studying in the "*Zema Beyt*" at Wusha Gedel, Debre Libanos. The quadrupling of government schools places (1974-1984) and a national literacy campaign (1979 illiteracy from 93% to 25%) (Haile Selassie 1997: 222-224) challenged the church monopoly of education. However, the major factors discouraging the traditional system appear to have been government policies preventing wandering and begging and forced military conscription.

The revolution caused impoverishment through nationalisation of rural land (March 1975).[18] Consequently three distinct phases, initial harsh repression, cautious conciliation and finally attempts to utilise the church for party interests ended in Marxist power structures deferring to Christianity (Pankhurst 1992: 149, 171). The church and the monasteries were said to anticipate communism, through social life, and social concerns (Gutierrez 1983: xi). The strict *quebat* monastery of Koga (Hulat Edju Enesay-Gundewayne) received special praise.

Joint interests encouraged preservation of cultural heritage and a museum was establishment at Merthula Maryam. The villageisation policy met with violent opposition in Gojjam, prompting the intervention of the (abbot) *Re'isä Re'usan* – Abba Mikael Tadesse to mediate a peaceful solution. Monasteries position at the apex of a close – knit homogenous Orthodox society was undermined by the removal of feudal privileges. Yet they cooperated in the process of the church recreating itself as a popular institution, new institutions tapped potential energies dormant in the population. Power was not imposed from above, but depended on consent from below according to the Gramscian concept of hegemony, via civil society. Monks came out of their isolation, being more engaged in activities of benefit to the wider community. The culturally orientated network of relationships maintaining a dynamic orthodox society

---

18 Interview Abba Berhane Meskel Tadele, Addis Ababa 26.8.99.

was replaced by one, which was spiritually orientated. The proliferation of monks and nuns in novels and plays shows their important role in the public sphere.

Monasteries as Points of Encounter with Other Religions and Dissemination of the Faith. Monks and Non-Believers

Monks and monasteries were traditionally at the cutting edge of the encounter with peoples of other religions and evangelism this took different forms. The Christianisation of Southern Ethiopia in the late 14th Century and 15th centuries depended on the impetus of the monastic clergy Mt. Zuqwala and lake Zwey playing an important role (Balisky 1997: 107). On lake Zwey a modern monastery on the shores of the lake has replaced the ancient monastery on Tolu Godu Island. Established with aid from the WCC it was used for retraining hermits and eventually turned by Abune Gorgorios into an orphanage and training centre for young people. Following the establishment of the church of the Arch-angel Gabriel it was recognised as a monastery. Abune Gorgorios realised the importance of effective organisation and a pragmatic attitude to festival and Sabbath observance and welcomed even the families of non-Christian students. Long-term programmes for boarders and shorter courses were combined. He effectively produced the intellectual framework required for the propagation and defence of the Orthodox faith. Recently a similar centre for evangelistic activities has been established at the ancient monastery of Mehur Yesus in the Guragey area.

Zuqwala Abo atop a lofty volcano in South Showa exemplified a different mode of inter-religious interaction and evangelism, illustrates the common difficulties (Derg period) of land dispute with former labourers, the struggle to maintain respect for the sanctity of the site and its fragile ecology. The general despair of the communist period made it very important to escape from the 'unreality of time' and to join the rhythms of 'cosmic great time' associated pilgrimage festivals. Better access roads encouraged streams of visitors, frequenting the festivals celebrated there, bringing the faithful into contact with the source of their faith and generating a mass dynamism and energy release, which was very important in the preservation of religious influence. A unique feature is the peaceful coexistence of Christian and Oromo pilgrimage rites sometimes performed concurrently (Pankhurst 1992: 23-24). The monastery was also influential in spreading Christianity among the surrounding Oromo tribes. Relations between the church and ethnic minorities changed significantly after the revolution. During the last ten years the Orthodox Church has consciously begun to project the image of being multi-ethnic.

Monasteries in the Urban Setting. The Monk and the City

A major feature of life in Africa during the twentieth century has been the rapid growth of cities, and the leadership of urban elite's. Christianity and cities have a dialectic relationship of attraction and repulsion exemplified by Babylon antithesis of all that is holy,[19] and the heavenly Jerusalem (Revelations 21: 11-21).[20] It is striking that Western churches are being desacralised, while in Ethiopia new churches are being built.[21] Large-scale permanent monastic settlement in urban centres, a phenomenon of the twentieth century, resulted from the Ethiopanisation of the Orthodox Church hierarchy, the reforms of Haile Sellassie and the events of the Derg period. The aftermath of the Red Terror and general social crisis created a need for spiritual solace attracting monks to come to the cities to preach and teach.

Ethiopians associate monasticism with the wilderness, urban monasticism being considered a contradiction in terms. Yet the fathers said that the desert animals sometimes entered the cities, and city environment gives special opportunities, for teaching, and modern education.[22] Institutions such as the Sunday schools, youth movements (imported from Egypt), evening preaching programmes and teaching of charismatic hermits, in which monks played an important role facilitated Church renewal.

The Monastery of Noh Kidaney Meheret is situated in the forested North-Eastern outskirts of the city gaining prominence due to miraculous healings, pastoral care expressed particularly in rituals of immersion and exorcism. It was said that "the healing miracles of Christ were duplicated there."[23] New facilities were built and the monks acted as mentors to the local deacons. Consequently the monastery became a focus of spiritual power, hope and aspirations.

Medhaney Alem, Miskaney Hizunan was carefully planned and organised by the royal initiative as a place of experimentation and innovation. Its *tabot* accompanied the emperor into exile becoming connected with the restoration of Ethiopian independence. Established to serve high school students, it pioneered the introduction of the vernacular liturgy and the first Sunday School (1956). Even after the revolution good advisors and a tradition of inspiration for effective and even imaginative administration made it successful, an impressive modern school was built with modern aid. This was the base of Abba Ma'aza, pioneer of the popular *mastawquot* or vesper ser-

---

19 "The town was regarded as the City of Sin, in which 'our children' got lost, and from where all evil influences came." Baur 1994: 337.

20 Its significance is well described in Fava 1995: 173-179.

21 This is apparently true of other African countries: "The African City of the 1990's is still much more religious than other cities in the world. In Nairobi 80% Christians and 800 churches". Baur 1994: 335

22 Interview Abba Walda-Giorgis Gebrre-Christos Addis Ababa 5.6.1998.

23 Anonymous "*Yey Hamere Noh Kidane Mehret Yey Lemat Iqued*' – the Ark of Noah Kidane Mehret Development Plan" (undated recent special church magazine from Addis Ababa) p. 3.

vices movement. Imaginative projects included a clinic, pastry shop and special services for the deaf and dumb in sign language.

During the twentieth century the churches' impact on urban society came to determine whether or not she would continue to exercise a dynamic role in national life. A
large monastic urban presence was instrumental in stemming the atheistic tide, diminishing the gap between the monks and laity, promoting church solidarity and the
diffusion of a monastic spirituality. However, city life eroded an essential aspect of
monasticism its ability to be different and transcendent.

Conclusion

Ethiopian monasticism is in the process of reinventing itself in response to the enormous changes the country has gone through. My intention was not to 'give a timeless
snapshot of it' but rather to designate the axis of transformation around which the
object is reconstructing itself (Platvoet - Molendijk 1999: 84). The unifying core of
monastic spirituality constitutes "a body, shaped and controlled by the idea of the
soul as a mechanism of power" (Carrette 1999: 116). It manifesting itself in different
ways reacting intuitively so as to perpetuate its essential functions. The drift to the
cities should be seen in this light. The mystic body of Ethiopian monasticism does not
cease to find new ways of projecting itself. Like the sacred dance bringing intensity of
experience and like holy water contact with inexplicable divine power regenerating
the church of Ethiopia. The horror of civil war and constant crisis in late twentieth
century Ethiopia produced a: "rootlessness and dispair born of a profound distrust
towards reason. The holy folly or crazy wisdom (of the ascetics became) an alternative route to kindle the love of wisdom in the hearts of contemporary men and
women."[24]

---

24 The Wisdom of the Holy Fools in Postmodernity Phan 2001: 731.

Bibliography

Abba Gabré Yesus Haylu
1982   Considérations théologiques sur le Melke'a-Sellasie de Abba Sebhat Le'ab. In:
        *S. Rubenson (ed.) Proceedings of the Seventh International Conference of
        Ethiopian Studies*. Lund: 126-134.

Abba Gorgorios
1984   Social Ministry of the Ethiopian Orthodox Church in the past and the Present.
        In: *T. Beyene (ed.), Proceedings of the Eighth International Conference of
        Ethiopian Studies*. Addis Ababa: 391-396.

Anonymous
1993   *The monks who have gained the spiritual level of bilocation have reached
        over 2,000*. Ma'adot (Month of Tirr). Addis Ababa: 6.
o.J.   *Yey Hamere Noh Kidane Mehret Yey Lemat Iqued – the Ark of Noah Kidane
        Mehret Development Plan*. Undated recent special church magazine from
        Addis Ababa: 3.

Antonnen, V.
2000   What is it we call 'Religion?' Analysing the Epistomological Status of the Sa-
        cred as a Scholarly Category in Comparative Religion. Method and Theory in
        the Study of Religion. *Journal of the North American Association for the Study
        of Religion. 12-1/2*. Springfield: 193-205.

Balisky, P.
1997   *Wolaita Evangelists: A Study of Religious Innovation in Southern Ethiopia,
        1937-1975*. Doctoral Thesis University of Aberdeen.

Baur, J.
1994   *200 Years of Christianity in Africa: an African History, 62-1992*. Nairobi.

Bittel, L. M.
1990   *Island of the Saints: Monastic settlement and Christian Community in Early
        Ireland*. Cornell University Press. Especially Chapters II, The Monastic enclo-
        sure. Ithaca (N.Y.) London: 57-84.

Bushell, W. and Bademariam, B. D.
1998   From Hagiography to Ethnography: Towards a Better Understanding of Ad-
        vanced Ethiopian Christian Ascetics. In: *T. Beyen, R. Pankhurst and B. Zewde
        (eds.): Proceedings of the Eleventh International Conference of Ethiopian
        Studies, vol. II*. Addis Ababa University Press. Addis Ababa: 41-60.

Carrette, J. R.
1999   *Foucault on Religion. Spiritual Corporality and Biblical Spirituality*. London -
         New York.

Clement, O.
2000   *On Human Being; a Spiritual Anthropology*. Translated by J. Hummerstone.
         New York.

Csordas, T. J.
1997   *Language, Charisma, and Creativity. The Religious Life of a Religious Move-
         ment*. Berkeley - Los Angeles - London.

de Certeau, M.
1988   *The Writing of History*. Translated by T. Conley. New York.
1992   *The Mystic Fable Vol. I. The Sixteenth and Seventeenth Centuries*. Translated
         by M. B. Smith. Chicago - London.

Elias, G.
1977   The Monastery of Abrentant in Waldibba. In: *Abbay: Documents pour servir a
         l'histoire de la Civilisation Ethiopienne*. Paris: 93-117.

Fava, F.
1995   La Jérusalem nouvelle, une Symphonie architechturale. In: *Christus 166*.
         Paris: 173-179.

Gombrich, R. and Obeyesekere, G.
1988   *Buddhism Transformed. Religious Change in Sri Lanka*. Princeton.

Gosden, C.
1994   *Social Being and Time*. Oxford.

Guillaumont, A.
1978   Esquisse d'une Phénoménologie du monachisme. In: *Numen, XXV/1*. Leiden:
         41.

Gutierrez, G.
1983   *The Power of the Poor in History*. Translated R. R. Barr. New York - Lima.

Haile, G.
1991   Ethiopian Monasticism. In: *A. S. Atiya (ed.), Coptic Encyclopedia*. New York:
         993-994.

Haile Selassie, T.
1997   *The Ethiopian Revolution 1974-1991. From a Monarchial Autocracy to a Military Oligarchy*. London - New York.

Hiller, S.
1991   *The Myth of Primitivism. Perspectives on Art*. (Reprint 1992, 1993, 1996) London - New York.

Isaac, E.
1971   Social Structure of the Ethiopian Church. In: *Ethiopian Observer XIV/4*. Addis Ababa: 254.

Jambere, A.
1984   Tatayaq Muget: The traditional Ethiopian Mode of Litigation. In: *T. Beyene (ed.), Proceedings of the Eighth International Conference of Ethiopian Studies*. Addis Ababa: 245.

Jantzen, G. M.
2002   Barely by a Breath …: Irigaray on Rethinking Religion. In: *The Religious. Blackwell Readings in Continental Philosophy*. Malden - Oxford: 233-235.

Kebede, M.
1999   *Survival and Modernisation. Ethiopia's Enigmatic Present: A philosophical Discourse*. Lawrenceville - Asmara.

Klostermaier, K. K.
1997   The Hermeneutic Centre. In: *Journal of Ecumenical Studies 34:2*: 159-160.

Langer, M. M.
1976   *Merleau-Ponty's Phenomenology of Perception. A Guide and Commentary*. London.

Laughlin, G. and Throop, C. J.
2001   Imagination and Reality: On the Relations Between Myth, Consciousness, and the Quantum Sea. In: *Zygon "Journal of Religion and Science"*, Vol. 34/4 Chicago: 717.

Levine, D.
1965   *Wax and Gold. Tradition and Innovation in Ethiopian Culture*. Chicago - London.

Linge, D. E.
2000   Leading the Life of the Angels: Ascetic Practice and Reflection in the writings of Evagarius of Pontus. In: *The American Academy of Religion 68: 43*. Philadelphia: 541-543.

Macrae, C.
2000   Myth Liminality and a Rational Universe. In: *Studies in World Christianity 6/2*. Edinburgh: 254-259.

Merleau-Ponty, M.
1962   *The Phenomenology of Perception*. Translated by C. Smith. London - New York.
1964   *The Visible and the Invisible*. Translated by A. Linguis. Evanston.

Miller, D. M. and Wertz, D. C.
1996   *Hindu Monastic Life. The Monks and Monasteries of Bhubaneswar*. Manohar.

Nagy, J. F.
1989   Liminality and Knowledge in Irish Tradition. *Studia Celtica 10:3*. Dublin: 271-283.

Pankhurst, A.
1992   Pilgrimage to Mount Zuqwala: A Model for Peaceful Coexistence? In: *Ethiopian Review*. Addis Ababa: 23-24.

Pankhurst, H.
1992   *Gender Development and Identity*. London - New Jersey.

Persoon, J.
1997   Le Monastère de Mahbêrê Selassié. In: *Irenikon. Revue des Moines de Chevtogne 4*. Chevtogne: 496-519.

Phan, P. C.
2001   The Wisdom of the Holy Fools in Postmodernity. In: *Theological Studies 62/4*. Milwaukee: 731.

Platvoet, J. G. and Molendijk, A. L. (eds.)
1999   *The Pragmatics of Defining Religion. Contexts, Concepts and Contexts*. Series: Studies in the History of Religions 84. Leiden - New York - Köln: 84.

Prattis, I.
2001   Understanding Symbolic Process – Metaphor, Vibration, Form. *Journal of Ritual Studies. 15/1*. Pittsburgh: 38-54.

Snyder, G.
1992   The Real Work: Interviews and Talks 1964-1979. In: *W. Scott (ed.), Post-modern Approaches to Spirituality*. NewYork: 85-90.

Tamrat, T.
1984   Feudalism On Heaven and Earth. In: *S. Rubenson (ed.), Proceedings of the Seventh International Conference of Ethiopian Studies*. Upssala Michigan: 196-197.

Tesfa Gebre Selasse (ed. and trans.)
1988   *Filiksiyos*. The Second Part of the Ethiopian Book of Monks. Ethiopian Calendar (i. e. approx 1995 A.D.). Addis Ababa.

Wallace, M. I.
2002   God is Underfoot Pneumatology After Derrida. In: *J. D. Caputo (ed.), The Religious, Blackwell Readings in Continental Philosophy*. Maldon Oxford, Blackwell Publishers: 203-204.

Wallia, S.
2001   *Edward Said and the Writing of History*. Cambridge - Lanham - Toronto.

Yohannes, S. B.
1997   On Gadl as Basis for Constructing the Notion of the Human Person in Ethiopian Philosophy. In: *Ethiopia in Broader Perspective Vol. III*. Kyoto: 211-218.

Zimmerman, M.
1992   The Blessing of Otherness: Wilderness and the Human Condition. In: *M. Oelschlaeger (ed.), The Wilderness Condition. Essays on Environment and Civilization*. New York: 245-270.

Some Aspects of the Religious Policies of Emperors Zär'a Yae'qob (1434-1468) and Yohannes IV (1872-1889) and the Development of the Ethiopian Orthodox Tewahdo Church

Zewde Gabre-Sellassie

Opening remarks in memory of Professor Enno Littmann

At the outset, I wish to express my sincere thanks and appreciation for the organizers of this conference for their kind invitation and for giving me the opportunity to honour Professor Enno Littmann whose *magnum opus* on Aksum was accomplished in 1906 when my father was the governor of Western Tigray and the Nibure Id of Aksum. Subsequently, he published four volumes which described the work of the Deutsche Aksum Expedition.

I grew up hearing about the miraculous man who came from Germany and spoke fluent Ge'ez, the classical language of Ethiopia. Those who met him spoke insatiably of his amiable personality, of his graceful manner, of the close tie of friendship which developed between him and my father during his short stay from January to April 1906, as well as with his team comprising of Theodor von Lüpke, Daniel Krencker and Erich Kaschke, who carried out the archaeological excavation and the epigraphical work.

The undertaking of the German team under the leadership of Professor Littmann laid the foundation for the subsequent archaeological and epigraphical work at Aksum.

Almost forty years later, when I was a student in England, I got in touch with Professor Littmann and subsequently I cherished the memorable privilege of visiting him twice at Tübingen. We corresponded in Ge'ez at frequent intervals. The intense curiosity, which he still possessed on everything pertaining to Ethiopia even at an advanced age in the twilight of his remarkable life, was amazing.

It is my singular pleasure to share some of the correspondence in my possession with you, which I have attached as an Appendix to the paper I am delivering at this conference.[1]

---

1 [For technical reasons this appendix cannot be published in this volume. The editors.]

As described in Professor Edward Ullendorff's obituary, written a few months after his death, in 1958, Professor Enno Littmann was: "the last great representative of that school of Semitic studies, which was still able to embrace the field of Semitic scholarship". He was indeed, "among the greatest *ethiopisants*" of the Twentieth century (Ullendorff 1958: 364). Ethiopia, in particular, owes Enno Littmann a great deal.

―――――――

The paper covers the religious policies pursued by two Emperors: Zär'a Yae'qob and Yohannes IV. The former reigned in the late medieval period (1434 to 1468) and the latter in the modern period (1872 to 1889). It aims to provide a bird's eye view of the problems the Ethiopian Church and state encountered and the solutions adopted during these two different periods. Both can be considered as important landmarks in the development of the Ethiopian Church.

– Both Zär'a Yae'qob and Yohannes IV did not grow up groomed to be an Emperor.
– Both succeeded to the throne at a mature age of Thirty-Five.
– Both were crowned at the Holy church of Ṣiyon at Aksum.
– Both were devoted Christians, followers of the mainstream Orthodox Tewahdo Alexandrian doctrine.
– Both were married to daughters of Muslim chiefs after they had them converted to Christianity. Zär'a Yae'qob married Elleni, daughter of the chief of Hadiya, and Yohannes married Halima who was named Mistre Sellassie, daughter of a chief of northern Afar.
– Both were confronted by Islamic threat.
– Both relied on uniformity of religion as a rallying force.
– Both endeavoured to strengthen the monasteries and the churches by generous grants of land and endowments.
– Both succeeded in getting more than one bishop from Egypt.
– Both attempted to Christianise those who adhered to traditional religions (pagans) and, to a lesser degree, Muslims and followers of unreformed Judaism (the Fallashas).

I. The Expansion of Monastic Establishment in Ethiopia

The advent of the Nine Saints, followed by the Tsadqans, who came from different locations in the Byzantine Empire, established the monastic institution in Ethiopia. At first in the northern provinces in Tigray and Shimezana (in present day Eritrea), and subsequently expanding southwards deep into the interior. During the Aksumite period, the adjacent territory of the Agäw, Wag and Lasta were absorbed by the

Aksumite culture and religion. The churches were built in settlements along the caravan routes to the goldmines located in the region of Fazogli across the present border with the Sudan. The importance of these monastic communities lay in serving as permanent centres of Christian learning.

During the thirteenth century, the expansion of the Empire intensified a number of indigenous Ethiopian evangelists who had their training and had acquired the pursuit of monastic habitation in the old established monasteries like Däbrä Damo in Tigray an Däbrä Libanos in Shimezana. They set up monasteries in strategic areas in the periphery for the propagation of the Christian faith and they trained younger disciples.

The pioneer for the evangelization of the Amhara and Shoa region in the south was Iyasu Mo'a (d. 1292) of the island monastery of Däbrä Hayq, who began his career around 1248. Among his disciples was the Shoan apostle St. Takla Haymanot who in turn founded Däbrä Asbo, which later came to be known as Däbrä Libanos.

In the north, Abba Daniel of Däbrä Maryam in Gär'alta (Tigray) similarly developed his own community. Among his disciples Ewosṭatewos moved to Seraye (Eritrea) and established his own community. The House of Takla Haymanot and the House of Ewosṭatewos became the two religious organizations, which militantly propagated Christianity in the peripheral regions of the Empire, inhabited predominantly by pagans. They also endeavoured to proselytise Muslims and the Agäw adherent of pre-Talmud Judaism, known commonly as the Fallasha, who prefer to be called "Bétä Israel".

The relationship between the sovereigns and monastic communities had not been always cordial. Individual monks had been flogged and lost their lives for admonishing and excommunicating the sovereigns. The militant leaders of the new monastic movements came into open conflict with Emperor Amdä Ṣiyon and his son Säyfä Ar'id who succeeded him. Başalotä Mikael of the House of Täklä Haymanot denounced Amdä Ṣiyon for his non-Christian matrimonial habits of having more than one wife and a number of concubines. Başalotä Mikael was beaten and was sent in exile to Tigray, where he remained the rest of his life. Similarly, Etchege Filipos and Abba Anorewos excommunicated Amdä Ṣiyon for his marital relation with his father's wife. Anorewos was flogged to death at Däbrä Birhan while Filipos and the other monks were exiled to Tigray.

After the death of Amdä Ṣiyon, bishop Yae'qob succeeded to obtain from the new Emperor Säyfä Ar'id a solemn promise to abide by having only one wife and allow the monks who were exiled by his father to return. Soon, however, Säyfä Ar'id broke his promise and married three wives. The Egyptian bishop Yae'qob and some monks excommunicated him. Säyfä Ar'id retaliated by expelling Ya'eqob to Egypt and sending the monks who excommunicated him into exile.

In the northern region, Abba Ewosṭatewos, the founder of the House of Ewosṭatewos in Seraye (Eritrea), is reported in the same period to have demanded similar moral reforms from the local rulers.[2] Thus several native Ethiopian saints came into being during and after the thirteenth century who established famous monasteries in the different parts of Ethiopia. To mention only few examples: from the House of Täklä Haymanot following the founder Bäṣalotä Mikael, Filipos, Anorewos, the Elder, Samuel of Däbrä Wägäg (Asebot) Qewstos, Märha Kristos, Zena Marqos and Anorewos the younger in Shewa and the South. Mädhanine Egzi'e of Däbrä Mänkol, Samuel of Däbrä Abby and Waldiba, Samuel of Qoyeṣa, in Tigray, and Aron in Amhara. From the House of Ewosṭatewos following Absadi the founder of Enda Maryam Qohayin in Seraye, Filipos the founder of Däbrä Bizän, Märqorewos founder of the monastery of Däbrä Dimah in Dembellas, Bakimos, and Gäbrä Yesus who established the monastery of Däbrä San in Emfraz, among the followers of Judaism.

The Emperors generously granted land and other endowments to these monasteries and the church in general. They in turn were the most effective stimulus in rallying public support for the sovereigns especially in times of war.

II. The Religious Policy of Emperor Zär'a Yae'qob (1434-1468)

When Zär'a Yae'qob acceded to the throne and during his reign of thirty-for years, the serious challenge which he faced was the threat from Muslim sultanates who were tributaries to the Emperor of Ethiopia. They came under effective control by the series of victories scored against them by his earlier predecessors, during the reigns of Amdä Ṣiyon (1314-1326), Säyfä Ar'id (1344-1372), Dawit (1382-1411) and Yisehaq (1414-1429) (Trimingham 1952: 66-76). In the intervening period after the death of Yisehaq and the accession of Zär'a Yae'qob, the empire had fallen intó turmoil due to ineffective successive reigns. This enabled the Muslim sultanates under the leadership of Badlay, son and successor of Sa'ad ad-Din, to seize the opportune moment to shake the foundation of the Christian empire. Zär'a Yae'qob bravely faced the challenge, defeated and killed Badlay in 1445 (Perruchon 1893: 88).

Zär'a Yae'qob, however, realised the danger to his empire due to the endemic attacks from Adal because of its links with the wider Islamic world. To counteract this danger Zär'a Yae'qob's major preoccupation became to expand the Ethiopian Church by stamping out paganism.

To this end, he adopted a drastic policy against pagan ritual and practises, which resulted in exterminating a large number of his subjects including members of his own family. Strengthening the Church necessitated avoiding the interruption of ordination due to the frequent absence of bishops. Zär'a Yae'qob, as Harbe before him in the eleventh century during the Zagwe period, demanded that more than one bishop to be sent from Egypt. While Harbe failed, Zär'a Yae'qob succeeded in getting two bishops, Abba Mikael and Abba Gabriel who were sent to Ethiopia 1438.

---

2   Taddesse Tamrat 1972: 116-117, citing Gadla *Ewosṭatewos*.

The schism due to the defiance of the House of Ewosṭatewos

Zär'a Yae'qob endeavoured to close the rift, which was raging in the Ethiopian Church due to the controversy between the House of Takla Haymanot supported by successive Egyptian bishops and the House of Ewosṭatewos over the celebration of the Sabbath. the latter considered the celebration of the Sabbath as a cardinal tenet in accordance with the Ten Commandments and the Apostolic Canons.[3] As a result of the difference that arose, a schism came into being. Members of the House of Ewosṭatewos were denied ordination and their founder with some of his followers left for exile around 1337, through Egypt, the Holy Land, Cyprus to Armenia, where he remained until he died in 1352. His followers returned after the death of Ewosṭatewos to join those who had remained in Ethiopia under the guidance of Absadi, founder of Däbrä Maryam at Qohayin in Saraye. the returnees were enlightened by the exposure received during their sojourn of fourteen years in Armenia. They were armed with zeal and inspiration.

The Religious Council of Däbrä Miṭmaq

Zär'a Yae'qob, who undoubtedly was the most profound theologian among the Ethiopian sovereigns of all time as proven by his own writings such as *Mäshafä Milad, Mäsafä Birhan* among others. He was determined to end the schism, which hampered his scheme of unifying and strengthening the Ethiopian Church.

He presided at the Religious Council of Däbrä Miṭmaq in 1450. There, he convinced, with a certain degree of coercion, the recalcitrant bishops and clerics to reconcile with members of the House of Ewosṭatewos. He proclaimed a decree, which declared that both the Sabbath and Sunday must be respected as the day of rest by the Ethiopian Church.[4] Thus the schism terminated, the rift was closed, and the House of Ewosṭatewos was reunited with the mainstream of the Ethiopian Church.

The Stephanite Movement 1428-1508

Esṭifanos, the founder of this movement came from his birthplace in Agame to the monastery of Abba Samuel of Qoyeṣa, in Shire, where he was ordained and had the monastic training. During his stay at the monastery for twelve years he was inclined to follow the hermetic life. He became disenchanted by the change, which was taking place in the monastic life. He disapproved vehemently the involvement in worldly affairs and the acquisition of wealth, which he considered against the vow which they

---

3   Taddesse Tamrat 1972: 207, citing Gadla *Ewosṭatewos* : 90-91.
4   Taddesse Tamrat op. cit. p. 230.

had taken and contrary to the teaching of the Founding Fathers of Monasticism.[5] When his ideas came to be known, his refusal to abrogate led to his isolation and eventual expulsion from the monastery.

Estifanos was then accused by his enemies of being a heretic, who disseminated evil ideas to his disciples, that the excessive veneration of Mary and the intercession of angels and saints are contrary to the true tenet of Christian doctrine. He was detained in prison by the order of the local governor in Shire. Subsequently he was taken to the Imperial Court. He defended himself and he was cleared from crime. He succeeded to return to Shire after seven months with a royal order that anyone who wishes to follow his teaching my freely do so.

After the accession of Zär'a Yae'qob Estifanos got himself into serious trouble, when he was summoned to the Imperial Court for the second time. At his first encounter with Zär'a Yae'qob, he provoked the emperor's anger by expounding his belief of the separation of Church and State, which was a diametrically opposite view to that of Zär'a Ya'eqob. He was allowed to return to shire, however, after he was flogged.

Subsequently, Estifanos was ordered to attend a religious council in Aksum, which he declined to accept. Finally, an order was issued to bring him by force to the Imperial Court for the third time. When he appeared before Zär'a Yae'qob, he refused to prostrate on the ground that he only prostates to God.

His unequivocal stand exacerbated the fury of the emperor. His manner was regarded as disdainful to the anointed sovereign, which was a capital crime. Estifanos was beaten, his hands were cut off and he was thrown in a dungeon for the remainder of his life, which only lasted for another seven months.[6]

The suffering he had sustained made him a martyr in the eyes of his followers, who continued the movement switching their centre of activities from Shire to his homeland in Agame in accordance to their founder's last will. Yisehaq, one of the prominent disciples of Estifanos, founded the famous monastery of Gunda Gundi, on the edge of the escarpment bordering Agame and the Afar territory adjacent to the Red Sea, an area inhabited almost exclusively by Muslims.

Zär'a Yae'qob passed a decree in 1454 ordering the extermination of the followers of the Stephanite Movement. As a result, a mass persecution occurred, supervised by Aqabe Saat Ameha in which, according to some estimate, no less than 30,000 persons have perished.[7]

Among those who escaped from falling victim, some managed to go into exile to different countries. The movement, however, far from coming to an end, was revived again by the returnees.

---

5 Interview with Märgeta Girmay Elias, an authority of the Monastic History in the Ethiopian Orthodox Patriarcate in Addis Ababa.
6 Interview with Girmay Elias.
7 Interview with Margeta Girmay Elias.

Gäbrä Yesus, one of the returnees moved to Bagēmdir and founded the monastery of Däbrä San in Emfraz. There, he started his activities and succeeded in proselytising a large number of Fallasha, or Bétä Israel, followers of an archaic form of Judaism.

Ezra, another of the returnees, who had been exiled in Egypt came back equipped with technical knowledge of building a water mill as well as being ordained by the Syrian Patriarch in Jerusalem. Ezra actually was sent to Egypt with some of his colleagues by Abekerezun precisely to remedy the shortage of ordained priests among the followers of the movement after most of them perished in the mass persecution, which the movement sustained.

There was a substantial difference of attitude between the pro Däbrä Mitmaq followers of the House of Ewostatewos and the followers of Estifanos. The former had refused to receive Holy orders from the Coptic bishop even after Emperor Dawit granted them a complete freedom of movement, and despite the excommunication imposed on them they were allowed to observe the Sabbath. The Stephanites, on the other hand, did not break away from the mainstream of the Ethiopian Church and even after the excommunication was imposed on them, their followers were receiving Holy Orders from the Coptic bishops in disguise. So, in a way, it was easier for the Stephanites to be absorbed into the mainstream of the Ethiopian Church.

This is borne out by the fact related by Taddesse Tamrat, citing Gadle Ezra, who states: Ezra's technical knowledge got him summoned to the court of Emperor Naod (1494-1508) to demonstrate his skill. He stayed there from 1499 to 1508. During this period, he openly declared, that "neither Estifanos nor his followers had ever refused to revere St. Mary of the Cross ... He demanded the excommunication against Estifanos and his followers be annulled".[8] His request was granted, the Stephanites, thus were reunited with the mainstream of the Ethiopian Orthodox Tewahdo Church.

After the death of Naod, apparently the anti-Stephanites persecution was revived and did not cease until a common shock submerged the differences among the Christians, when the Muslim invasion led by the Imam Ahmad Ibrahim al Gahzi occurred from 1527 to 1542.[9]

In conclusion, Zär'a Yae'qob was certainly one of the greatest Emperors of Ethiopia, despite the harsh measures he imposed on his subjects in implementing his policy and his matrimonial habits. He remained polygamous throughout his life contrary to Christian precepts.

During his reign, Art and Literature flourished under his patronage. Zär'a Yae'qob presided at the Religious council of Däbrä Mitmaq, imitating Constantine the Great, his regal name's sake, the unification of the Houses of Takla Haymanot and Ewostatewos was accomplished by subtle diplomacy and mild coercion. He succeeded in containing the Islamic threat from the endemic incursions led by Badley, the Sultan of Adal, whom he defeated and killed. He consolidated the conquest of his predecessors. Some of his successes were, however, ephemeral. The procurement of

8   Taddesse Tamrat 1966: 115.
9   Interview with Girma Elias and Taddesse Tamrat, Rassegena Di Studi Ethiopici XXII, p. 115.

the two bishops withered during his own lifetime, since no replacement was sent from Egypt who could ordain priests and deacons for the last ten years of his reign and the following thirteen years after he passed away.

III. The Religious Policy of Yohannes IV (1872-1889)

There is no doubt that Yohannes was an ardent follower of the *Ethiopian Orthodox Tewahdo Church* or the Alexandrine doctrine of the Two Births. He strongly desired to enhance the propagation of his faith by unifying the different Christian sects and by activating the process of evangelization among the non-Christians subjects of his empire. The use of religion as a rallying force was also common practice in those days, in the absence of secular ideology, especially when the country was facing an external threat. Last but not least, the pressure exerted through the Holy See of St. Mark, in Egypt, on whom the Ethiopian Church depended for its bishops from the Fourth century until mid Twentieth century, was a strong factor in formulating the religious policies, which were adopted during the reign of Yohannes.

The priorities of Yohannes' religious policies were: first to establish doctrinal unity within the Orthodox Church and elevate the morality of the clergy. Second, to prevent political intrigues of foreign missionaries by expelling them or keeping them out of the Christianized areas of Ethiopia. Third, to encourage evangelization and proselytization of Muslim and the followers of the traditional religions (pagans).

As early as 1868, Yohannes, when he was only a ruler of Tigray and was known as Dejazmatch Kassa, sent a mission to Egypt to procure a bishop from the Holy See of St. Mark in replacement of Abuna Selama who had died in October 1867. One of the preliminary conditions insisted upon by the Coptic Patriarch was to obtain assurance that the Catholic missionaries would be expelled.

Subsequently, after sending a second mission complying with all the demands in June 1869, Abuna Atnatewos was consecrated and sent to Ethiopia. To assist the new bishop and serve as his closest counsellors on religious matters, Kassa (Yohannes) appointed the best clergies renowned for their piety and learning. Mamhir Walda Kidan, a native of Wogera, in the province of Gondär, who had earned great fame while teaching theology an Moṭṭa Giyorgis, in Gojjam, was renamed Tewoflos and was given the highest ecclesiastical post of Etchege, while Qésē Gäbez Hailu who was brought from the Convent of Däbrä Damo and renamed Iyasu was appointed as Nibure Id of Aksum.

Unifying the Different Orthodox Sects

Since the coming of the Jesuits during the sixteenth and seventeenth centuries, various interpretations on the nature of Christ had began to develop. They were mainly three main branches with subdivisions in each of them.

The *Tewahdo* claimed to adhere to the true Alexandrine doctrine of the Holy See of St. Mark as testified by a letter dated 1808 from the Patriarch of Alexandria in which he expounded the doctrine of the church that attributes only Two births to Christ, namely from the father and from the Virgin Mary – and anathematized the views expressed by the other two sects.

The *Qibat* (Unction) sect followers, found mainly in Gojjam and a few places in Tigray, had develop about three varieties of the interpretations, but all agree that through unction and union in the womb of the Virgin, the flesh had become divine.

The *Ṣega* (Grace) or Sost Lidet (Three Births) sect attributed the unction only to the Word at the time of Baptism when, according to their doctrine Christ attained a Third Birth, by adoption. The Ṣega sect flourished in Shoa and to some extent in Gondär.

Both Tewodros and Täklä Giyorgis (Giorgis) who reigned before Yohannes attempted to unify the three Christian sects in the country proclaiming that they all must adhere to the doctrine of the Holy See of St. Mark. *Atse* (Emperor) Täklä Giorgis (1868-1872) issued a proclamation in 1868, which stated:

"All those who do not profess the doctrine of abba Selama (the creed of Alexandria) must go to a territory, which I do not rule." (Rossini 1925: 464)

Aleqa Zanab, the trusted chief of scribes of Tewodros states:

"When Tewodros went to Shoa by flogging the clergy who had expelled Abune Selama, he made them embrace Tewahdo. There were even some who were mutilated." (Zanab 1902: 4.)

However, Menelik encouraged the Sost Lidet sect, although he never expressed support for their doctrine openly. Menelik had sent Mekbib to bring Massaja who was detained by Sultan Abu Baker, the ruler of Zeyla. Massaja was received by Menelik at Litche on March 6, 1868.

The arrival of bishop Massaja in Shoa in March 1868 was interpreted by some of the Sost Lidet adherents as expressing Menelik's intention to strengthen their faith by bringing in Catholic bishops (Massaja 1929: ix).

Massaja and Mekbib brought letters from the British who were at war with Tewodros. Originally, Massaja had actually intended to go to the Oromos, as his appointment was that of an Apostolic Bishop of Kaffa and the Oromos. Menelik, however, wanted his aid and insisted that he should stay with him in Shoa.

Menelik gave land grants to the Catholic churches in Tegulet, Galan, Aman, Birbirsa (the area around Addis Ababa's Qidus Giorgis (St. George) Church, Finfine, Daro, and Kataba, according to Pere Ferdinand's Journal.[10]

In January 1878, Yohannes came to Shoa. On Yohannes's insistence, Massaja and most of the Catholic missionaries were expelled. The renowned theologian Täklä Sion, who belonged to the "Three Births" or *Sega sect*, exiled himself to Jerusalem.

The Religious Council of Boru Meda

The religious Council at Boru Meda was held in May 1878. Emperor Yohannes presided and most renowned clerics headed by Etchege Tewoflos and the highest dignitaries of the realm including King Menelik of Shoa were present. There the doctrinal dispute between the Three Births – the *Sega sect* and the Two Births – the Tewohdo (Alexandrian) was settled in favor of the latter. While some renounced their creed and agreed to embrace the official confession of the faith, others, notably Waldibé Engida and Zurambé Engida refused and denounced the verdict of the council.

Yohannes was enraged and subjected them to corporal punishment by having their tongues cut off. This act certainly was a blatant cruelty, regardless of the motive to bring unity to the church and nation.

The Religious council of Däbrä Tabor

Another religious Council was held at Däbrä Tabor, in 1881, which settled the dispute between the *Qibat* (Unction) sects and the *Tewahdo*. Orthodox which is the principal creed supported by the Alexandrian Church. Again, it was decided in favour of the Tewahdo or Two Births·creed.

Yohannes was not only interested in maintaining the unity of the Church, but he also wanted to improve the moral life of the clergy. In a letter to Nibure Id Iyasu dated 7 Tiqimt 1872 (October 17, 1879) he stated that the *Debteras* (cantors) should not be allowed to serve in the church without adhering to the moral commandments dictated by the Church (Zewde Gabre Sellassie 1975: 108-109).

A setback occurred in the religious activities due to the lack of a bishop after the Ethio-Egyptian wars. Atnatewos, the Metropolitan died on June 28, 1876 and Ethiopia was left without a bishop until 1881, when Yohannes finally succeeded in obtaining four bishops from Egypt consecrated by the Holy See of St. Mark.

One of the four bishops, namely Abune Marqos, who was intended for Gondär, died immediately after arrival at Samera near Däbrä Tabor in Begemdir and was buried at Hiruy Giorgis, a church built by Yohannes. Petros remained as Metropolitan

---

10 Pere Ferdinand's Journal 1866-1878, 1879-1885, MSS. 334 and 342, respectively. Institute of Ethiopian Studies, Addis Ababa University.

with the Emperor in Tigray, Mattewos was given to Menelik for Shoa and the territories under him, while Luqas was given to Tekle Haymanot for Gojjam and the territories under his command. The presence of three bishops instead of one, as had been the case almost all the time since the fourth century, was a novelty. The exception was a brief period during the reign of Zär'a Ya'eqob in the fifteenth century when two bishops had come simultaneously. It was, therefore, a novelty, which considerably enhanced the activities of the Church throughout the Empire.

Strengthening the Orthodox Tewahdo Church

Fortifying the Orthodox Tewahdo Church was top in Yohannes's agenda form the early days of his career when he was Dejazmach Kassa, ruler of Tigray, and subsequently throughout his reign. In order to stimulate the evangelization process and facilitate the spread of church education, he built several churches in Tigray, Begemdir, Wollo, Shoa and Gojjam. Yohannes also endowed many prosperous villages in Tigray to the holy sanctuary of St. Mary of Zion at Aksum; to the ancient monasteries of Tembien, such as Enda Abba Hadera, Tchekh, Qeqema, Tegoga, and Enda Abba Selama. He lavishly endowed Dimma Giorgis in Gojjam. He constructed the cathedral of Däbrä Birhan Sellassie, dedicated to the Holy Trinity at Adwa. He rebuilt Däbrä Libanos in Shoa, the Holy See of St. Täklä Haymanot, with twelve domes in the ancient site of the church, which was demolished by Ahmed ibn Ibrahim el-Ghazi, nicknamed Gragn, in the sixteenth century. He built the church of the Holy Trinity at Boru Meda in Wollo, as well as the church of Hiruy Giorgis near Däbrä Tabor, in Begemdir. He also found the famous centre of learning, Däbrä Elias and built the church of Qidus Mikael (St. Michael) at Dess in the district of Gozamen and of Qidus Yohannes (St. John) at Daligew, in Eastern Gojjam. Although, this is by no means an exhaustive list, it is intended to serve as a sample.

Outside Ethiopia, Yohannes followed the example of the ancient emperors such as Kaleb, Lalibela, and Zär'a Yae'qob in taking keen interest in the Ethiopian community in the Holy Land. Since the early period of Christendom, Ethiopian monks, priests, laymen trickled across the deserts of Sudan, Nubia, and Egypt to Jerusalem for pilgrimage. Some monks settled there and had acquired holy places. During the sixteenth century, when Ethiopia was ravaged by the Islamic invasion and subsequently during the eighteenth century and first half of the nineteenth century, known as the "Era of the Judges", the number of pilgrims dwindled and due to lack of provisions, the monks became utterly destitute. During those periods, Armenians and Copts after providing them modest assistance took many of their possessions. Yohannes considered the presence of the Ethiopian community in the Holy Land and their welfare of paramount importance, both on historical and spiritual grounds. He corresponded with King George I of the Hellenes[11] and Sultan Abdel Hamid of Turkey appealing for their assistance to protect the Ethiopian community, as he referred in his letter addressed to the Abbot and member of the Ethiopian monastery in Jerusalem[12].

Yohannes sent to Jerusalem gold coins, captured from the Egyptian forces after their defeat at the Battles of Gundet and Gurae in November 1875 and March 1876, respectively. In addition on 28 Megabit 1873 (April 5, 1881) he sent a total sum of 85,000 Thalers 35,000 of which were earmarked for the construction of the new church.[13] On 18 Megabit 1879 (March 26, 1887), he sent additional 11,500 Thalers for the construction of the church through Monsieur Francois Soumagne, the French Vice-Consul at Massawa,[14] and another 40,000 Thalers on December 27, 1887. Thus, specially for the construction of the church and purchase of land, a total of 86,500 Maria Theresa Thalers[15] plus four boxes of gold coins, the amount of which remains unspecified, and a large quantity of elephant tusk and civet, to be sold in Jerusalem, in compliance with the request of the Abbot, were sent by Yohannes. The proceeds were to be used for the construction of the church.[16] He also sent a sum of 108,300 Thalers for provisions during the period 1869 to 1887.

Mämhir Wäldä Säma'et, a Shoan monk of high moral standing, intelligent and exceedingly industrious, also invested a large portion of the funds, which he received for provisions, in real estate by purchasing large tracts of land outside the city wall, near the residence of the British Consul.

The church was constructed on part of the purchased land, which already had

---

11 Archive of the Ethiopian Monastery in Jerusalem (AEMJ). Referred to in a letter from Yohannes addressed to Abba Wäldä Säma'et and the members of the monastery of Jerusalem dated Zebul 1 Pagume 1873 (September 6, 1880) in which King George I is referred to as Negus Giorgis. In another letter addressed to "Abune Wäldä Säma'et, Abbot of the Ethiopian monastery in Jerusalem, written from the camp at Säma Negus, dated Tiqimt 27, 1877 (November 5, 1884) King George I of Greece is also referred to as "King of Rome", which is Arabic usage of "Rumi" for Greece based on the Byzantium reference to Constantiople as the "New Rome".

12 AEMJ: Referred to in a letter from Yohannes to Abba Wäldä Säma'et and members of the Ethiopian Monastery in Jerusalem, dated Adwa, Yekatit 14, 1874. (February 21, 1882) and 19 Tahsas 1879 (December 27, 1886).

13 AEMJ: Yohannes to Mämhir Wäldä Säma'et and members of the Ethiopian Monastery in Jerusalem written from the camp of Baba 28 Megabit 1873 (April 5, 1881).

14 AEMJ: Yohannes to Mämhir Wäldä Säma'et and members of the Ethiopian Monastery in Jerusalem, Meqele, 18 Megabit 1879 (March 26, 1887).

15 The value of the Maria Theresa Thalers during most of the nineteenth century was approximate £ 0.30.

16 Abune Mattewos, former Ethiopian Archbishop in Jerusalem asserts that the number of boxes containing gold coins sent by Yohannes were actually six. Abune Mattewos, *Debre Siltan be Yeruselem* (1996), p. 89. The additional two must have been sent after Yohannes's letter dated December 27, 1887 – in which he stated that he had sent four boxes of gold; or else they were acquired from the sale of the elephant tusk and civet, which Yohannes sent to Jerusalem.

some buildings, used for the residence of the monks and nuns. The services of the architects Conrad Shieq and later Pasqual Seraphim were used to build the magnificent church, which is known as Däbrä Guenet (The Mount of Paradise), dedicated to St. Mary, which is referred to as Kidane Mehret (The Covenant of Mercy), located adjacent to what is now named Ethiopian street. "The compound of Däbrä Guenet", says Jean-Baptist Coulbeaux, "will immortalize the king John [Yohannes] more than his palaces at Maqalle and all the other buildings he had built in Ethiopia" (Coulbeaux 1929: II, 479).

When Yohannes died in the battle of Metemma, in March 1889, the construction of the church was almost complete with the exception of the dome. At this juncture, Mämhir Wäldä Säma'et, the abbot of the monastery, sold a piece of land, which fetched 9000 gold coins, 2000 of which were used to complete the church and the remaining 7000 for the purchase of another property within the ancient wall of the city of Jerusalem, which once belonged to Jean Charles Gellad, commonly known by the name of Hanna Carlo, who formerly had been a dragoman of the (Catholic) Custody of the Holy Land and subsequently the dragoman of the French consulate when it was established in 1843. After the death of Hanna Carlo in 1875, his family sold the land and the house on it, between the 7th and 8th stations of the Cross near the Via Dolorosa. This new acquisition eventually became the residence of the Abbots of the Ethiopian Monasteries in the Holy Land and is now the residence of the Ethiopian Archbishop.

The Relations with Foreign Missionaries

When Yohannes assumed power over Tigray in 1867 as Dejazmatch Kassa, Catholic and Protestant missionaries were operating in northern Ethiopia. Catholic missionaries had been already planted in Agame, Akälä Guzai, and Bogos. The acute dilemma which he had to face, as Rubenson points out, was "how to maintain friendship with the Christian countries in Europe and keep the doors open to desirable influence, without permitting the growth of the religious community hostile to the national Church and weak in its loyalties to the Ethiopian state".[17]

The Catholic Lazarist and Protestant missionaries who were operating in northern Ethiopia were led by their excessive zeal to become political agents of foreign governments in order to propagate their faith freely and protect their converts.

The presence at Massawa of Werner Munzinger from 1865 to 1875 and the missionaries close association with him turned out to be one of the most detrimental factors in moulding their hostile relation with Yohannes. Munzinger was a native of Switzerland, with insatiable political ambition. Catholic by faith and friendly with both the Catholic and the Protestants missionaries and an oriental scholar, he was married

17 Bairu Tafla (ed. trans.), Chronicle of Yohannes IV, 1872-1889 (Wiesbaden 1977), text, fol. 151ra and trans. Rubenson 1976: 275.

to a native lady from Bogos (present day Eritrea). He had served as Vice-consul of France at Massawa from 1865 to 1871. Similarly, he also served as a British agent just prior to and during the British expedition to Magdala 1867-1868. Then, when he became disappointed by the lack of colonial ambition in this part of the world by both the British and the French, Munzinger switched his allegiance to Egypt and was appointed as governor of Massawa in 1871 with the Ottoman title of Bey. Subsequently, he occupied Bogos in 1872 and was elevated to the rank of Pasha and Governor-General of Eastern Sudan and the Red Sea Littoral, from 1873 to 1875.

Munzinger was leading a contingent of 400 men to open a southern front with the assistance of Menelik against Yohannes; simultaneously while the main Egyptian forces attacked from the north in November 1875, when he was ambushed and killed with his followers by the men of Mohammed Hanfari, the Sultan of Aussa, while traversing the Afar desert.

The Catholic missionaries earned the jealousy and hatred of the Orthodox clerics mainly due to the fact that the former were proselytising exclusively Christians of the Orthodox denomination. The pressure from the Coptic Patriarchate to expel the missionaries was also considerable, to the extent that it was one of the principal preconditions demanded by the Patriarchate in order to comply with the request of sending a bishop to Ethiopia in 1868.

Mgr. C. Delmonte had travelled to Adwa to complain to Dejazmatch Kassa about the persecution of the Catholics in Akälä Guzai on December 15, 1868. Reporting to M. Étienne, his superior on his audience with Kassa, he stated that Kassa said to him:

> *"In Ethiopia there are beside Christians, Jews, Muslims and even Pagans; he tolerated these, why should he now persecute Catholics? Kassa advised me to refer the matter to the Viceroy of Egypt who could easily and promptly settle this affair ... by demanding the Coptic bishop to leave you free as you are in Egypt."*[18]

Wherever the Catholic Mission was established in northern Ethiopia, some of the priests, whether on their own initiative or under instruction, were encouraging the chiefs of the localities in which they were operating and their converts to seek French and even Egyptian protection. Earlier in 1860, Shum Agame Aregawi, in 1864, the Christian chiefs of Anseba, Bogos, Mensa, Bijuk and Addi Gayan had written to Napoleon III seeking French protection (Rubenson 1976: nos. 79, 145). Prior to his accession to the throne, Yohannes as Dejazmatch Kassa, assumed power over Tigray and Marab Melash (beyond the Marab river) in 1867, Dejazmatch Hailu Täwälde Mädhin, the governor of Hamasen, with the help and encouragement of members of the Catholic mission wrote to Ismail Pasha, seeking Egyptian protection. Abba Emnetu, a native Catholic priest, who had served earlier as secretary to the delegation of Agew Negusse to Rome in 1859 during the reign of Tewodros – Served as an envoy of Dejazmach Hailu to Egypt (Rubenson 1976: nos. 223, 224).

18 Lazarist, Annales de la Congregation de la Mission, Delmonte to M. Etienne, Massawa Dec. 15, 1868, XXXIV, 252-253.

Hailu was replaced by Dejazmatch Wäldä Mikael Solomon, head of the rival House of Hazzega, which contested for power against the House of Tseazzega, of which Dejazmatch Hailu was the head. Two years later, due to the combined influence of Munzinger and the Catholic Mission, Wäldä Mikael wrote to Napoleon III, expressing his desire to become more independent and secure the protection of France. This letter was sent with Munzinger's suggestion that France should seize this opportunity for securing his friendship.[19] Some villages inhabited by Catholic converts in Akälä Guzai refused to pay taxes on the pretext that it would be supporting the heretical Ethiopian Orthodox Tewahdo Church and as Catholics they regarded themselves French subjects. Although there is not tangible evidence that they were advised by the missionaries not to pay taxes, it appeared quite probable at the time.

Dejazmatch Kassa (Yohannes) wrote an appeal in March 1870 to Napolean III stating that:

"I am not saying that Catholic religion is bad. But, my lot is the faith of [the Holy See of St.] Mark of Alexandria ... And now I shall count it as a great favor if you stop these priests for me ... Other explorers and merchants are welcome".[20]

The death of Mgr. Delmonte in May 1869, the arrival of Abune Atnatewos, the Coptic metropolitan, in July, and the close connection with Munzinger of Mg. J. M. Touvier, who had become in charge not only of Bogos but of northern Ethiopia mission as a whole, led to further deterioration of the fragile relations that had existed between Kassa (Yohannes) and the Catholics.

When Kassa (Yohannes) ordered the Catholic priests to leave their station at Halay in Akälä Guzai, Munzinger, the Vice-Consul of France at Massawa, wrote a threatening letter on March 3, 1871 as follows;

"You should not be ignorant [of the fact] that all those rulers who have dared to oppose the Catholic priests have all fallen. You shall also fall like them ... And I, as I knew how to conduct and lead the English into Abyssinia I shall know how to lead the French against you".[21]

Such a threat could only aggravate the situation. The fact that France, at the time, was preoccupied with her own problems after the disastrous defeat she sustained in the Franco-Prussian war and that Munzinger's threat was a mere bluff did not detract from the anger it caused Yohannes.

The Catholic missionaries plotted against Kassa (Yohannes) in 1871, Mgr. J. M. Touvier wrote a letter to Täklä Giorgis:

"Now skilled men have come from our country to do something useful for the ruler of Tigre. But I have told them the ruler of Amhara is our friend but that of Tigre is not. Therefore, you should transfer your services to the ruler of Amhara."

19 AECP, Massouah 3 fol. 280. Welde Mikael to Napoleon III, August 22, 1869.
20 AEMD, afrique 62, fol. 105, Kassa to Napoleon III, March 10, 1870.
21 AECP, Massouah 3, fol. 328 V.

They advised Täklä Giorgis to cross over to Tigre as soon as possible. If he did not come to Tigre by May 1871, his kingdom would be destroyed. Kassa found the letter in the tent of Täklä Giorgis after the Battle of Assam, on July 11, 1871.

Blatta Gäbre Mädhin, Kantiba Wäldä Ananiya, and Dejazmach Täsfay were sent in the same month to Akälä Guzai where they looted the Catholics and burnt their churches, including a church in Agame built by Mgr. De Jacobis.[22]

After Munzinger transferred his service to Egypt and was appointed governor of Massawa in April 1871, his successor and appointee as acting Vice-Consul of France, the Austrian Franz Hassen, tried to persuade the French government to send a military expedition to depose Kassa (Yohannes). Subsequently, in the name of the Catholic population of Akälä Guzai, a formal request was made seeking the protection from Egypt in August 1871, instigated by Munzinger and Touvier (Rubenson 1976: 293).

During a four-hour audience granted to the newly appointed Vice-Consul of France, Ernest de Sarzec, on December 2, 1872, Yohannes recounted his grievances at the activities of his predecessor Werner Munzinger, Franz Hassen and the Catholic bishop Mgr. Touvier, Yohannes showed him the letter of Touvier written to his rival Emperor Täklä Giorgis, and the arrogant letter of Munzinger dated March 3, 1871. He responded, however, to the request of the consul during the audience given on December 16, 1872 and accorded a compensation of 4,000 Thalers, a sum which Mgr. Touvier estimated to be the amount of damages sustained by the mission during the raids incurred in 1871.[23] Relations improved considerably between Yohannes and the Catholic Mission during the tenure of de Serzec. Mgr. Touvier and his associate Pere Duflos, however, continued their ties much more with Munzinger and actively supported the Egyptian cause during the ensuing conflict.

Protestant missionaries such as Reverends Flad and Krapf also expressed antagonistic sentiments toward Yohannes personally and the Ethiopians in general. Flad, in a letter dated July 1875 to Robert Fleming, the British diplomat in Egypt stated:

"I am convinced that Abyssinia by herself will never be good for anything. In all Abyssinia there is not one person capable of governing this country and improving the conditions of its people ... Only foreign rule could save this miserable country ruined by internal wars, by robbers, assassins and bad subjects."[24]

Again, a few weeks later, referring to the forthcoming conflict between Egypt and Ethiopia, he stated:

"As for me, I hope that the affair will be completely and definitively settled in a very short time, so that the vanity of this man (Yohannes) will be brought down and he will be humiliated as he deserves, and Abyssinia once conquered by Egypt will be

---

22 Bibliotheque Nationale, Paris – Collection Mondon Vidailhet – Ms Ethiop. 259. Chronicle of Yohannes by Lemlem, ff. 15-19.

23 AECP, Massouah, 3 fols. 311-328 Serzec to Remusat, January 17, 1873, and in J. de Coursac (1926, pp. 156-166). The same report of de Serzec to Comte de Remusat of January 17, 1873 is given with some commentary.

24 National Archive of Egypt, Abyssinia 9/1, fols. 127-128, cited in Rubenson 1996: 8.

delivered from all its bad subjects ... and enjoy the good fortune of a good government and open its door to civilization and evangelization.[25]

After the defeat of the Egyptian forces at the battle of Gunda Gundi, in the district of Gundet, in November 1875, Krapf, who was disturbed by the rumor that the Egyptians did not intend to annex Ethiopia or any part of it, wrote as follows:

"The Egyptian army ... will be forced to occupy ... the province of Hamasen in Tigray and Chilga on the west side ... if I were the sovereign of Egypt, I would occupy these above-mentioned provinces even if all Europe were against me ... To make peace without humiliation serves no purpose as far as I am concerned."[26]

The opposition to the missionaries was based mainly on their divisive activities and their involvement in advancing the interest of foreign powers, not only in the northern provinces, but all over Ethiopia.[27]

The Catholic Capuchin missionaries in Shoa, including Mgr. Massaja were expelled by the order of Yohannes in 1878, not only in compliance with the order given earlier by the Coptic bishop Atnatewos in his letter to Menelik (1873), but also due to their political involvement in advancing Italian interests to the detriment of Ethiopian unity. Both from the political and the religious points of view, by boosting the Tsega sect, who adhered to the "Three Births" doctrine, which was opposed to the official Alexandrian doctrine of "Two Births", they used them as a divisive factor.

Mgr. Massja returned to Italy and became a Cardinal while his assistant, Mgr. Taurin de Cahagne, moved to Harar with the other missionaries. When Ethiopia occupied Harar in 1887, the Catholic missionaries were allowed to remain there. But even after the death of Yohannes, the opposition of the Coptic bishop and the Ethiopian Orthodox clergies was such that during the reigns of Menelik, Iyasu, Zewditu, and Haile Sellassie up to the Italian invasion of 1935-1936, a Catholic bishop was not allowed to cross the Awash River and reside in the capital, while the Catholic Missionaries were allowed to operate in non-Christian areas.

Neither the Protestant nor the Catholic missionaries refrained from sowing seeds of disintegration, be it intentional or unintentional. The Oromo were regarded by Krapf as the "Germans of Africa" potential client and allies of Germany (Rubenson 1996: 7). It was also Krapf who first suggested that the Oromo should adopt the Latin alphabet, which recently has come into effect. The French missionary Martial de Salviac, on the other hand, in his book Les Gallas, *Le Grand Peuple Africain* (de Salviac: 1902) claimed that the "Gallas" (Oromo) were originally "Gauloise", which

---

25 National Archive of Egypt, Abyssinia 9/10 fol. 124.
26 National Archive of Egypt, Abyssinia 9/10 fols. 186-187; Rubenson 1996: 9.
27 de Coursac 1926: 163-164 and AECP Massouah 3 fol. 311-328 Serzec to Remusat, January 17, 1873. As recounted by Yohannes to E. de Serzec during his audience on December 2, 1872, given in his report to the French Ministry of Foreign Affairs, dated January 17, 1873.

was repeated without hesitation by one of the Ethiopian Catholic scholars Ato Atsme, in his *Ye Galla Tarik* (History of the Galla).[28]

Ernest de Sarzec concluded in his report dated January 17, 1873, to Comte de Remusat, which we already have cited earlier, with the remark regarding the Emperor Yohannes as follows:

> *"[Yohannes] far from being a sectarian fanatic as his enemies represent him ... He does not ignore that to emancipate the country he must have it admitted to the concert of nations ... But to reach this goal, he needs the assistance and concurrence of Europe, without which he knows, nothing can be achieved."* (de Coursac 1926: 170)

Relations with Muslims

The religious policy of Yohannes towards the Muslims is varied and complex. One can discern three phases in this policy: the first phase lasted from 1872 to 1878, the second from 1878 to 1882, and the third from 1882 to 1889. During the first phase, his campaigns against the Raya Azebo Muslims and the Kunama pagans should be seen in the light of consolidation of his rule by suppressing rebellions rather than as religiously motivated campaigns. During the second phase, the Egyptian invasion and the propaganda, instigated by Egyptian *fakhirs*, in Wollo and other Muslim areas in favour of the invaders forced Yohannes to vigorously call for conversion of Ethiopian Muslims to Christianity. During the third phase, Yohannes softened his policy to avoid the repercussion in Egypt of Coptic Christians.

After he defeated Täklä Giorgis in July 1871, prior to his coronation, he had intended to bring two of the non-Christian rebellious regions in Tigray under his rule. He marched towards Azebo in October 1871, but returned from the border to prepare for his coronation, which was due in January 1872. He sent a punitive expedition under the command of Dejazmatch Hagos against the Kunama in Adiabo because they refused to pay tribute, interfered with the trade between Tigray and Wolqayit, killed Mr. Thomas Powell, a Protestant missionary, and raided and gunned the famous monastery of Waldeba, located on the other side of the Takaze river in Wolqayit.

After his coronation, form April to August 1872, the campaign against the Oromo of Azebo took place. The Oromo sanctuaries were destroyed but no churches replaced them. It was simply to force their submission and eliminate their threat to the Christians. After the submission, they were left alone to carry on normal life. Abdallah, the chief opponent among the Raya Azebo, submitted to Yohannes after

---

28 Atsme Giorgis (Atme) Ye Galla Tarik (Historiy of the Gallas) originally produced as a manuscript toward the beginning of the twentieth century. Recently published, ed. and translated by Bairu Tafla under the title: Atsme Giorgis and his Works: History of the Gallas and the Kingdom of Shoa, Stuttgart, 1987.

killing the famous rebel *Dejatch* Wäldä Yesus of Wojjirat and Enda Mehoni. He was rewarded by being appointed as governor of Azebo despite the fact that the campaign looked like a Christian crusade against the Muslims.

While Yohannes was campaigning in Azebo, Egypt occupied Bogos. The attention of Yohannes was diverted to the new menace. In the meantime, northern Oromo resistance to the authority of the Emperor and their threat against the Christians were annihilated. Not only Abdallah in Raya Azebo but also Abba Qubin in Qobo was appointed as governor over the northern Oromo tribes.

Between the years 1873 and 1878, Yohannes was preoccupied in consolidating and defending his Empire against successive invasions by a Muslim power. The religious factor of his policy did not surface until after this period.

After the Council of Borumeda in 1878, which was designed to unify different Christian Orthodox sects, Yohannes issued a proclamation stating the rationale for conversion of Muslims throughout the greater Wollo area, specifically addressing the leaders:

"All this used to be Christian land until Gragn [Ahmad ibn Ibrahim el Ghazi (1542-1543)] ruined it and compelled the people to abandon their religion. Now, let all, whether Muslim or Galla [adherent of traditional religions] believe in the name of Jesus Christ. Be baptized, if you wish to live in peace, preserving your belonging, become Christian ... Thereby, you will govern in this world and inherit the one to come." (Guebre Sellassie 1930-31: II, 156)

The policy of Yohannes towards Muslims, between 1878 and 1882, was greatly influenced by the successive Egyptian invasion in 1875 and 1876 and the fact that a state of hostility persisted between Egypt and Ethiopia until the Hewett Treaty of 1884. It was basically motivated by strategic and political considerations focusing on Wollo. On the eve, during and in the aftermath of the Egyptian campaigns, Wollo was the centre for propagating the concept that there is no division between the spiritual and the temporal in Islam. the loyalty of all Muslims must be to their coreligionists (the Egyptian invaders), not to the country in which they lived (Ethiopia). Sheikh Tolha bin Gia'efär, a native of Argobba, with other *fakhirs* had established centres of dissent in the districts of Gerfa, Riqe and Wara Qalu up to 1885 to incite revolts.

Mestewat, the widow of Imam Liban Amädé, who died in 1857, and the mother of Abba Waṭṭew, one of the rival claimants to the lordship of Wollo, had sent as early as 1870 an emissary, named Mohammed bin Yusuf, a native of Adwa, to the Khedive of Egypt seeking assistance against Christian encroachment of her territories. Although there is no tangible evidence that the Khedive complied with her request, arms and cannon allegedly supplied by Egypt were seized when the revolt of Hassan Wodajo of Derra was suppressed in 1878.

As a result, Yohannes used a combination of force and coercion, especially manipulation of land-use rights and office holding privileges, in order to convert the Muslims of Wollo. The head of the rival ruling houses of Wollo, Imam Mohammed Ali and Imam Amädé Liben, agreed to be baptized in order to retain their command over their respective territory. Yohannes himself became the godfather of Mohammad Ali who was renamed Mikael and was granted the title of Ras. Menelik who joined in the campaign became the godfather of Amädé Liben who was renamed Haile Mariam with the title of Dejazmatch, at the request of Yohannes.

The conversion of the two Imams, who claimed direct descent from the Prophet Mohammed and commanded the strategically important regions, was a great achievement for unifying the nation. Wollo, which had ceased to be autonomous after Menelik incorporated it around 1867, gradually regained its autonomous status by 1885 under Yohannes.

Eminent theologians were appointed to serve as apostles among the Muslims and followers of traditional religions. *Mämhir* Akale Wold of Wollo, *Getaye* Girmay for Werehimano, *Aqabe* Seat Gäbru for Gondär, and *Abba* Wäldä Giorgis for Gojjam.

In November 1878, Raya Azebo rebelled. It was sacked and churches were built, although most of the inhabitants remained Muslims. Ras Gäbrä Kidan Zemo was appointed over the regions as governor of Zabul. Yohannes spent the dry season of 1880 in Warababo, pursuing the Christianization mission. In the same year, Yohannes and Menelik campaigned between Argobba and Nätch Sar. Although it was primarily intended to suppress a revolt, according to oral tradition, the population was forced to convert to Christianity. While some Muslims fled from their homes, the rest who feared harassment and wished to preserve their patrimony complied with the order to be baptized.

The mechanism by which the Christianization policy was executed followed a similar pattern. Initially, the chiefs were offered the choice of retaining their official position only if they were converted to Christianity or else they would be obliged to forfeit their command. Most of the chiefs preferred to retain their command by accepting conversion. They were then instructed to build churches and encourage their followers to be baptized. At this juncture, those who were vehemently opposed to this policy retaliated by burning the newly built churches, driving away the clergy and harassing the converts. This, in turn, would lead to governmental raids, pillaging, and killing in suppressing the revolts, which arose in different localities.

Thus, simply sword and fire did not execute the conversion as some chroniclers lead us to believe and as stated by critics. One must not overlook Yohannes's instruction to Menelik and Ras Adal (later King Takla Haymanot) of Gojjam: "Not to treat Muslims too harshly, lest the Copts in Egypt suffer reprisal."[29]

Almost in every city throughout the empire the traders were mostly Muslims, since they had better access to the surrounding territories, which were inhabited by their coreligionists. Yohannes appointed a number of prominent Muslim merchants as *"Negadrases"* – superintendents of commerce – in different localities.

Yohannes's relations with the Afars generally were most cordial, since the time he was a rebel during the final years of Tewodros' reign, when he lived among the Afars

---

29 Yohannes to Menelik, 9 Miazia 1871 (April 6, 1879). The letter, which contained this instruction, is reproduced in Heruy Walda Sellassie's printed, but unpublished History of Ethiopia: Addis Ababa (Circa 1935): 68. Heruy states that a similar letter was written to Ras Adal.

in the eastern escarpment of Tigray. Indeed, he married a daughter of an Afar chief of Damohoita. Neither the Tigrean Afars nor those of Aussa were in any way affected by the religious policy, which coerced other Muslims in adjacent territories of Wollo.

The cause of the 1885 Wollo rebellion was alleged to be the death of Dejazmatch Mohammed Sadiq, chief of Täkulä Däré, who refused to pay taxes and was shot while fleeing to Awsa by soldiers of Ras Araya Sellassie Yohannes, who was given the command over Wollo. The underlying cause, however, was opposition to exorbitant taxation, which was imposed on the population. Resentment at the conversion policy, which was imposed on them undoubtedly, was a factor, as well, instigated by Sheikh Tolha bin Gia'efär. There was also an element of rivalry between the two contestant Ruling Houses to the lordship of Wollo. Abba Djebel, son of Abba Waṭṭew, joined the rebellion as he was displeased with the favour bestowed on the head of the rival Ruling House, Ras Mikael, who was given the command of Wärähimeno with the title of Ras in 1878 and the whole of Wollo in 1885, when Ras Araya Sellassie, the Emperor's son, was shifted to Gondär. Once Mikael acquired the whole of Wollo, he shared the government of Wärähimeno with his cousin Abba Djebel and peace was restored in the province. One must beware not to confuse repression of revolt with actions taken to coerce the people to adopt Christianity, which is often overlooked.

A large number of Muslims had adopted Christianity in order to preserve their office or to improve their status in land holding. Richard Caulk cites an anonymous chronicler from Gondär who has given an account of the reaction of the Mahdist commander when he arrived in Gondär in January 1888 and was welcomed by the former Muslims who claimed that they were forced to be baptized. According to this chronicle, the Mahdist commander reproached them recalling that:

> *"Yohannes told you if you were willing to be baptized; if not, do not be. So be gone lest my people see your bad example for you have been baptized when you were given the freedom to refuse."*[30]

Some Muslim zealots fled to neighbouring Muslim countries and appealed for their intervention. Christian critics of the religious policy of Yohannes allege that the conversion was so superficial that most of the new converts remained faithful to their traditional religion. The Muslims continued to practise Islam by night and Christianity in daylight.

It cannot be denied, however, that a serious attempt was made by placing the most outstanding clerics in Wollo so that they could disseminate the teaching of Christianity. There may, however, be some truth in what the critics say, since it would be unrealistic to expect instant transition from one religion and way of life to another.

Nevertheless, the religious policy combined with the farsighted administrative method adopted by Yohannes had attained the desired objective. Whatever might be said, the fact still remains that when Yohannes marched to fight against the Mahdists at Metemma in 1889, Wollo, to a large degree remained faithful to the end while some traditional Christian subjects were recalcitrant in joining the emperor.

---

30 Wylde 1888: 5; Caulk 1972: 28.

Relations with Fallashas

The religious policy of Yohannes towards the Fallashas is described by James Quirin who, in his book *The Evolution of Ethiopian Jews* quotes a written document of the Fallasha community, which states that when attempts were made by local chiefs to force the Fallashas to be converted to Christianity, "a group of prominent Bétä Israel priests from Wolqayt, Dembia and Simien, led by *Abba* Mahari, went to Yohannes where he was living at Däbrä Tabor and appealed to him:" The Emperor then said:

> *"They should not be compelled to adopt our religion. However, when the missionary Flad brought four Ethiopians after they studied in Europe in 1874, Yohannes allowed them to preach the Gospel among the Falashas as long as European missionaries are excluded."* (Quirin 1992: 176-177)

Regarding his attitude towards Fallasha (Bétä Israel), Qes Asres Yayehe, who for decades served the Fallasha community as a teacher, spiritual, and community leader since early part of the twentieth century, testifies that his own relative Ergoboie was favoured by King Yohannes who exempted her from all government taxes for seven generations. This made her and her offspring popular for marriage and relationships. As a result, they have multiplied more than any other generation of the Ethiopian Jews (Qes Asres Yayehe 1995: 137).

It does not appear, therefore, that Yohannes had opposed the Fallashas (Bétä Israel) indiscriminately; although he would have preferred to see them embrace Christianity without the involvement of foreign missionaries.

Thus, Yohannes was far from being the fanatic, the European missionaries and their Ethiopian disciples like judged him to be. His own chroniclers, who almost invariably were clerics, also misportray him as a heroic champion of Christianity who eliminated indiscriminately all those subjects who resisted to adopt his religion. He, nevertheless, did pursue policies which were motivated by religious and political objectives, stimulated by a desire for an internal political unity based on religion.

Concluding Remarks

The Ethiopian Church, as stated by so many scholars, has been for centuries the custodian of the cultural, political and social life of the people. Among the main obstacles which hampered the development of the Ethiopian Church it would be appropriate to mention the crucial ones.

The absence of bishops in the country who could ordain priests and deacons in order for the Church to function effectively throughout the country. From the fourth century when the first bishop, Selama *Käsaté Birhan* (the Illuminatior), who was consecrated by Athanasius, the Patriarch of Alexandria, at the request of the Ethiopian sovereign, up to Kyrillos, the last Egyptian bishop, who died in October 1950, there have been 113 Egyptian bishops who came to Ethiopia in succession.[31]

During this period which extends for more than sixteen centuries vacancies had occurred many times which lasted often for a long period. At times, the Egyptian rulers interfered or the Coptic Church was unwilling to send the replacement promptly. For centuries the Coptic Church refused to consecrate more than one bishop for the Ethiopian Diocese, and it decreed that no Ethiopian could be consecrated as a bishop. It was quite an achievement, therefore, that Zär'a Yae'qob succeeded to obtain two and Yohannes four bishops simultaneously. It is regrettable, however, that it did not last long in both cases. During the reign of Zär'a Yae'qob, there was no replacement after the two bishops died, so that there was no bishop in Ethiopia during the last ten years of his reign and for the following thirteen years after his death. Of the four bishops who came to Ethiopia during the reign of Yohannes, one died immediately on his arrival and after the death of two of them during the reign of Menelik, no replacement was requested. Indeed, after the death of Abuna Luqas, bishop of Gojjam, a replacement was sent, but he was sent back immediately. Only Abuna Mattewos, remained until he died, in December 1926 and was replaced by Kyrillos, the last Coptic bishop to Ethiopia. Generally, it appears that Ethiopian sovereigns with a few exceptions were reluctant to have more than one bishop. The underlying reason being the fear of a bishop falling on the hand of a rival since legitimacy is obtained by anointment performed by a bishop during a coronation ceremony. It was only during the reign of the Empress Zewditu (1916-1930), and the Regency period of Ras Taferi that by patient negotiation and subtle diplomacy four Ethiopian clerics were consecrated in Egypt in 1929 and a fifth one in Addis Ababa during the visit of the Coptic Patriarch to Ethiopia in 1930, to serve under the Egyptian Metropolitan.

Finally, after the liberation of Ethiopia during the Second World War, a series of negotiations again took place with the Coptic Church, which resulted gradually in the Ethiopian Church in attaining autocephalous status (Erlich 2000: 23-46).

On 25 July 1948 five Ethiopian clerics were consecrated as Archbishops by the Coptic Patriarch and it was agreed on the death of Anba Kyrillos that he would be replaced by an Ethiopian Metropolitan. Based on this agreement after the death of Anba Kyrillos in October 1950, Patriarch Yusab II consecrated Abuna Basilios in Cairo, the most senior Ethiopian bishop, who had held the post of Etchege in 14 July 1951 in Cairo, as the first Ethiopian Metropolitan.

Subsequently, the Coptic synod agreed in 1958 that Ethiopia would have its own Patriarch, while some form of affiliation will be maintained with the Coptic Church. In June 1959, during the visit of Emperor Haile Sellassie to Egypt, the consecration of Abuna Basilios as head of an autocephalous Church was accomplished.

After the death of Abuna Basilios, in 1970, the last vestige of the tie of the Ethiopian Church with the Coptic Church terminated, when the enthronement of the second Ethiopian Patriarch Abune Tewoflos was celebrated in Ethiopia without the

---

31 Heruy Walda Sellassie 1928-29.

blessing of the Holy See of St. Mark. Today, I believe, there are no less than 40 bishops in Ethiopia now.

The other obstacle to the development of the Ethiopian Church has been the lack of prayer books and the Gospel in sufficient quantity to serve the churches throughout the country. With the advent of the printing press in the twentieth century, this problem is not as severe as it had been in the past, but even now the problems still persist.

The language barrier in the country with no less than seventy vernacular languages has been also adversely affecting the development of the Church. Even today, to a lesser extent it remains to be an obstacle. This is the challenge, which the Church must solve in order to get a full participation of the people especially in the peripheral areas of Ethiopia.

Let me conclude with a few remarks on the resolution of the Schism that had faced the Ethiopian church during the two reigns of Za'ra Ya'eqob and Yohannes IV.

At different periods in its long history the Ethiopian church had been afflicted by division among its members on various issues.

Zär'a Yae'qob succeeded in closing the rift between the Houses of Täklä Haymanot and Ewosṭatewos, the two principal monastic organisations, at the council of Däbrä Miṭmaq by decreeing that the Sabbath should be honoured and observed as well as Sunday. Zär'a Yae'qob's failed to contain the Stephanites movement; instead he resorted to mass persecution which resulted only in strengthening the movement. The Stephanites were eventually reunited with the mainstream of the Ethiopian Tewahdo Church during the reign of his grandson Emperor Naod (1494-1508).

It is regrettable, therefore, that so many lives perished and so much suffering was inflicted on loyal subjects mainly due to the insatiable crave for authority, which did not tolerate any slight deviation from the dictate of the sovereign.

Some four centuries later, Yohannes succeeded in the Councils of Boru Meda and Däbrä Tabor to put an end to the blatant division within the church by making the *Ṣega Lijoch*, the adherents of the Three Births doctrine and the followers of the *Qibat* (Unction) sect respectively, to renounce their creed and embrace the Tewahdo, Alexandrian doctrine, which attributes Two Births to Christ (Archbishop Gorgorios: 77-83).

The punishment inflicted on those who refused to renounce their belief was cruel. In any case, even those who agreed to adopt the official version on the Nature of Christ could still remain faithful to their former belief paying lip service to the newly adopted version. But gradually the division within the Church undoubtedly subsided and it is not conspicuous any more.

The same can be said of Zär'a Yae'qob's policy towards paganism, which he forcefully attempted to stamp out; and for a Limited period, of Yohannes's attempt to force conversion on the Muslims. With the laps of time and thank to the efforts of highly learned clerics who were placed in Wollo, the centre for the propagation of Islam, substantial success was scored, however, in securing a large number of converts.

The Church needs to improve a great deal in order to win over the people by conviction rather than coercion. Further, it has to wake up from its slumber and revitalise itself as the pioneers had done in the thirteenth and the fourteenth centuries.

Abbreviations

AECP   Affaires Etrangeres, Correspondence Politique des Consuls
AEMD   Archive du Minister des Affaires Etrangers, Memoires et Documents
AEMJ   Archive of the Ethiopian Monastery in Jerusalem
OUP   Oxford University Press

Bibliography

Archbishop Gorgoryos
?   *Yä-Ityopya Ortodoks Täwahedo Betä Krestiyan Tarik*. Addis Ababa: 77-83.

Bairu Tafla
1977   (ed. trans.), *Chronicle of Yohannes IV, 1872-1889*. Wiesbaden.
1987   *Atsme Giorgis and his Works: History of the Gallas and the Kingdom of Shoa*. Stuttgart.

Caulk, R.
1972   Religion and State in the Nineteenth century Ethiopia. *Journal of Ethiopian Studies 10/1*: 28.

Coulbeaux, J.-B.
1929   *Histoire Politique et Religieuse de l'Abyssinie*. Paris: II, 479.

de Coursac, J.
1926   *Le Regne de Yohannes*. Paris.

de Salviac, M.
1902   *Le Gallas: Le Grand Peuple Africain*. Paris.

Erlich, H.
2000   Identity and Church: Ethiopian – Egyptian dialogue 1924-59. *Int. J. Middle East Studies 32*: 23-46.

Guebre Sellassie
1930-31 *Chronique de Regne de Menelik*. 2 Volumes, Paris: II, 156.

Heruy Walda Sellassie
1928-29 *Wazema*. Addis Ababa.
ca. 1935 *History of Ethiopia*. Addis Ababa: 68. Printed, but unpublished.

Massaja, G.
1929   *I miei tretacinque anni di missione nell'alta Ethiopia*. Tivoli: ix.

Perruchon, J.
1893   *Les Chroniques de Zär'a Yae'qob et de Bä'edä Maryam*. Paris: 88.

Qes Asres Yayehe
1995   *Traditions of the Ethiopian Jews*.: 137.

Quirin, J. A.
1992   The Evolution of Ethiopian Jews. University of Pennsylvania: 176-177.

Rossini, C. C.
1925   Epistolario del Debtera Aseggachegn di uadla. *Rendiconti della Reale
         Accadamia die Lincei, xxv:* 464.

Rubenson, S.
1976   *The Survival of Ethiopian Independence*. London.
1994   Tewodros and his contemporaries, 1855-1868. *Acta Aethiopica, 2*. Addis
         Ababa, Lund.
1996   *The Missionary Factor in Ethiopia: Consequences of a colonial context*. Lund.

Taddesse Tamrat
1966   Some Notes on the Fifteenth Century Stephanite Heresy. *Rassegena Di Studi
         Etiopici 22:* 115.
1972   Church and State in Ethiopia 1270-1527. *OUP:* 116-117, 207, 230.

Trimingham J. S.
1952   *Islam inEthiopia*. OUP: 66-76.

Ullendorff, E.
1958   Professor Enno Littmann. *Africa*, vol. 28: 364.

Wylde, A. B.
1888   *,83 to 87' in the Soudan, with an account of Sir William Hewett's Mission to
         King John of Abyssinia*. 2nd ed. London.

Zanab, D.
1902   *The Chronicle of King Theodore of Abyssinia.* Ed. from the Berlin Manuscript
        with translation and notes by Enno Littmann. New York - Leipzig: 4.

Zewde Gabre Sellassie
1975   *Yohannes IV, Political Biography.* OUP: 108-109.

IV. Enno Littmann und die Deutsche Aksum-Expedition

Enno Littmann: Leben und Werk

Rainer Voigt

1. Quellen

Enno Littmann gehört zu den Orientalisten, die ihr Fach in einer ungewöhnlichen Breite und Tiefe vertreten haben, wie man den 550 Titeln seiner Bibliographie[1] (in *Ein Jahrhundert Orientalistik*, 1955)[2] entnehmen kann. Littmann hat unsere Kenntnis in vielen Bereichen, namentlich in denen der Arabistik, der semitischen Epigraphik und der Äthiopistik, entscheidend geprägt.[3] Darüber hinaus schlug Littmann eine für damalige und heutige Verhältnisse ungewöhnliche Laufbahn ein, die ihn von der Feldarbeit in orientalischen Ländern direkt auf die Professur an einer deutschen

---

1 Mit Nachträgen in Schall 1959. Die Sachgebiete umfassen vor allem: den Orient allgemein, die allgemeine Sprachwissenschaft und Schriftkunde, die Semiten im allgemeinen, das Aramäische, das Hebräische (mit dem Alten Testament), das Arabische (mit dem Islam), abessinische Sprachen, Türkisch, Zigeunerisch und die deutsche Sprache (Littmann 1955: ix-x). Dabei stehen sprachwissenschaftliche neben volkskundlichen, literaturwissenschaftlichen und historischen Untersuchungen.

2 In diesem Band haben Rudi Paret und Anton Schall – außer seiner Bibliographie – 16 Nachrufe Littmanns auf berühmte Orientalisten zusammengestellt (vgl. die Liste sämtlicher Lebensbilder und Nachrufe Littmanns in *Ein Jahrhundert Orientalistik* (1955: 146-149). Die so geehrten Äthiopisten, Arabisten und Semitisten, mit denen Littmann auch persönlichen Umgang pflegte, sind: C. Bezold, A. Dillmann, I. Guidi, Chr. Snouck Hurgronje, G. Jacob, M. Lidzbarski, M. Meyerhof, E. Mittwoch, C. A. Nallino, Th. Nöldeke, Fr. Prätorius, H. Reckendorf und J. G. Wetzstein. Hinzu kommen – in Verbindung mit seinen äthiopischen Jahren – Naffaʻ wad ʻEtmān (sein wichtigster Tigre-Gewährsmann), Fr. Rosen (Legationsrat in Addis Abeba) und R. Sundström (Missionar in Eritrea). Ein weiterer Nachruf – auf J. Wellhausen – erschien 1956. Mit Sundström arbeitete Littmann auch wissenschaftlich zusammen, s.u.

3 Im folgenden werden, so weit als möglich, die Monographien erfaßt. Auf Artikel wird nur gelegentlich verwiesen. Dies wird im Einzelfall der Bedeutung der Beiträge nicht gerecht. So möchte ich insbesondere auf den wichtigen Artikel verweisen, in dem Littmann den südarabischen bzw. frühnordarabischen Ursprung der libyschen Schrift nachgewiesen hat (Littmann 1904: 423-440). Diese auch von mir vertretene Sicht hat sich noch nicht allgemein durchgesetzt, s. aber den Beitrag „Berberisch" in *Der Neue Pauly – Enzyklopädie der Antike: Altertum*, 2, 1997: 564. In einem anderen, kurzen Artikel hat Littmann in kufischen Schriftzügen eines Gemäldes in Quṣayr ʻAmrah den ägyptischen Statthalter des Byzantinischen Herrschers *Muqauqis* erkannt, der 640/41 von den Arabern besiegt wurde (Littmann 1955a).

Universität, zuerst nach Straßburg und schließlich für den größten Teil seines Lebens nach Tübingen führte.

Bei meinem Abriß stütze ich mich für die frühe Zeit auf Littmanns Autobiographie, die er, im 70. Lebensjahr stehend, seiner Frau zu ihrem 50. Geburtstag (am 20.12.) 1944 widmete. Das handschriftliche (mit Bleistift geschriebene) Manuskript aus Littmanns Nachlaß, welcher in der Staatsbibliothek Berlin verwahrt wird, habe ich persönlich eingesehen; eine gedruckte Fassung liegt vor (1986). Eine kurzgefaßte Autobiographie „am Grabe zu verlesen" wurde „bei einer intimen Trauerfeier" von Rudi Paret vorgetragen (Paret 1959: 14). Der Text erschien ein Jahr nach seinem Tod in *The Library of Enno Littmann* (1959: xiii-xx mit Abb.). Außerdem standen mir Kopien der Personalakte aus Tübingen zur Verfügung.[4]

2.   1875-1894: Jugendzeit in Oldenburg i.O.

Richard Ludwig Enno Littmann wurde am 16. September 1875 in Oldenburg i.O. (oder Oldenburg i. Gr., d.i. im Großherzogtum), Hauptstadt des Großherzogtums Oldenburg, als Sohn eines dort ansässigen Buchdruckereibesitzers geboren. Sein Vater (1829-1893) stammt aus einem Ort nicht weit vom sächsischen Lützen und trug den Vornamen Gustav Adolphe – wegen des dort 1632 gefallenen Schwedenkönigs.

Seine Mutter (Sophie, geb. Jacoby, 1843-1924) stammte aus einem niederdeutsch-friesischen Geschlecht. Sie wurde (*1843) in „einem einsamen Bauernhof 15 Kilometer nördlich von Oldenburg" (*AB*, S. 4) geboren. Ihr Vater kam „aus dem Lande Butjadingen, war also friesischer Herkunft" (*AB*, S. 5). Littmanns Interesse für das Friesische rührt wohl daher.

Enno Littmann, „das neunte von zwölf Kindern" (*AB*, S. 8), verbrachte seine Kindheit und Jugend in Oldenburg, das damals weniger als 20.000 Einwohner zählte (1888 waren es 21.438, s. *Meyer* 1885-91).[5] „Einmal in jedem Sommer wurde an einem Sonntag eine Fahrt nach dem großelterlichen Hause [mütterlicherseits, R.V.] unternommen" (*AB*, S. 9). Dort „wurde natürlich Niederdeutsch gesprochen, und ich eignete mir diese Sprache bald an" (*AB*, 10) – wie es in der Autobiographie heißt.

Ostern 1885 kam er in die Sexta. Damals erhielt er, weil ein älterer Bruder „auf See ging" „einen Sitzplatz bei Tische im Eßzimmer, während ich vorher beim Essen hatte stehen müssen" (*AB*, S. 11).

Das Interesse an Sprachen zeigte sich bei Littmann schon früh. Auf der Schule zog ihn das Lateinische und später das Französische und Griechische an, und aus Grammatiken in der Bibliothek seines Vaters, der Dolmetscher im Napoleonischen Heere gewesen war, erlernte er die Grundzüge des Englischen, Italienischen und Spani-

---

4   Universitätsarchiv Tübingen, 126/387.
5   1824 verzeichnete Oldenburg lediglich „750 Häuser und 5200 Einwohner" (*Brockhaus Conversationslexicon* 1824).

schen. In der Untersekunda (d.i. der 6. Gymnasialklasse) begann er mit dem Hebräischen. Zum 15. Geburtstag bekam er eine arabische Grammatik[6] geschenkt, die er in einer Buchhandlung gesehen und sich gewünscht hatte. Sein Vater schenkte ihm in der Folgezeit Lehrbücher anderer „morgenländischer" Sprachen. So konnte sich Littmann neben dem Arabischen[7] noch auf der Schule die Grundlagen bzw. gewisse Kenntnisse des Hebräischen, Syrischen und Neupersischen aneignen. Durch Privatunterricht verdiente er sich das erste Geld. Der Tod des Vaters 1893 bedeutete einen Einschnitt, der dadurch gemildert wurde, daß er gerade dabei war, seine Heimatstadt zu verlassen.

3. 1894-1899: Studium in Berlin, Greifswald, Halle und Straßburg

Nach dem Abitur (1894) ging Littmann im April 1894 nach Berlin, um dort orientalische Sprachen zu studieren. Wie damals üblich, stellte er sich den einschlägigen Professoren vor, wie Eduard Sachau, Eberhard Schrader und August Dillmann. Dillmann[8] empfahl ihm eine „gründliche philologische Durchbildung" (*AB*, S. 32). Bedenken wegen späterer Berufssorgen versuchte er mit der Bemerkung zu zerstreuen: „Seien Sie nur ruhig! Wenn Sie was leisten – tüchtige Leute bringen wir immer noch durch" (*AB*, S. 32). Dies war kurz vor Dillmanns Tode (1894).

Da das Studium der Orientalistik auch damals keine gesicherten Berufsaussichten bot und er in den Genuß eines Stipendiums gelangen wollte, wählte Littmann als Fach die Theologie mit dem Schwergewicht auf dem Alten Testament. In Greifswald studierte er neben der Theologie bei dem Arabisten Georg Jacob.[9] Zu einer Arbeit von Jacob über *Das Leben der vorislâmischen Beduinen* (Berlin 1895) konnte er einen Index beisteuern. Daß er wenig später nach Halle wechselte, wo er insgesamt sechs Semester studierte (1895-1898), mag auch an Jacob gelegen haben, der 1896 als Privatdozent nach Halle ging. Den Ausschlag für den Studienwechsel gab jedoch der Äthiopist Franz Praetorius, der 1893 nach Halle berufen worden war.[10] Damit liegen zwei der drei Schwerpunkte von Littmanns Forschertätigkeit schon früh fest, nämlich die Äthiopistik und die Arabistik (später kam die semitische Epigraphik oder Inschriftenkunde hinzu). Littmann studierte in Halle sechs Semester „Theologie und Philologie" (*AB*, S. 459). Durch eine Übung angeregt, nahm er (für den Germanisten und

---

6   S. B. Manassewitsch (1880).

7   Jetzt nach der vorzüglichen Grammatik von Albert Socin, die später (1904) von Brockelmann bearbeitet und herausgegeben wurde. Diese Ausgabe hat viele weitere (teilweise neubearbeitete) Auflagen erlebt, z.B. 13. Aufl. Leipzig 1953.

8   S. Littmanns Nachruf auf A. Dillmann in *Ein Jahrhundert Orientalistik* (1955:1-10).

9   S. Littmanns Nachruf auf G. Jacob in *Ein Jahrhundert Orientalistik* (1955: 96-109).

10 S. Littmanns Nachruf auf Fr. Praetorius in *Ein Jahrhundert Orientalistik* (1955: 37-45). Praetorius kehrte 1909 nach Breslau zurück, wo er 1880-1893 Ordinarius gewesen war.

Dialektologen Otto Bremer)[11] in den Sommerferien 1897 die ostfriesische Sprache der zu Oldenburg gehörigen Insel Wangerooge auf. Die grammatischen Materialien sind nicht erschienen; lediglich die Texte (*Friesische Erzählungen aus Alt-Wangerooge*, Oldenburg i.O.) mit hochdeutscher Übersetzung kamen 1922 heraus (= Nr. 508).[12] „Auf abessinischem Gebiet begann ich in Halle selbständig zu arbeiten" (*AB*, S. 54). Er bearbeitete einen äthiopischen Text[13] und wandte sich dann entschieden dem Tigre zu, einer im nördlichen und westlichen erythräischen Tiefland gesprochenen äthiosemitischen Sprache. Auf eine Behandlung der Pronomina[14] folgte – im Alter von 23 Jahren – die Doktorarbeit über *Das Verbum der Tigresprache in Abessinien*, Halle 1898.[15] Das Material wurde vorwiegend aus Tigre-Publikationen zusammengetragen; eigene Aufnahmen des Tigre sollten später folgen. Im selben Jahr (1898) bestand er auch das „Staatsexamen für das Lehramt an höheren Schulen" (*AB*, S. 56) mit Religion und Hebräisch als Hauptfächern und Deutsch, Lateinisch und Englisch als Nebenfächern (*AB*, S. vvii). Bei Friedrich Blass[16] mußte er einen griechischen Text ins Lateinische übersetzen.

Im Wintersemester 1898/99 studierte Littmann in Straßburg im Elsaß vor allem bei dem großen Theodor Nöldeke,[17] dessen damals vierjährige Enkeltochter Elsa (*1894) er 22 Jahre später (1921) heiraten sollte. Er hörte in Straßburg aber auch bei Julius Euting und H. Hübschmann. 1899 erschien seine zweite Monographie: *Über die Abfassungszeit des Tritojesaja*, Freiburg (u.a.).[18] Ostern 1899 war Littmann wieder in Oldenburg und „dachte nun daran, in das höhere Lehramt einzutreten. Da nahm mein Geschick plötzlich eine andere Wendung" (*AB*, S. 62).

---

11 Zu Bremer s. den Beitrag von O. Basler in der *Neuen Deutschen Bibliographie*, 2 (1955: 581-582). O. Bremer hat insbes. über die Phonetik, das „Plattdeutsche" und deutsche Dialekte (wie den von Nürnberg) gearbeitet.

12 Die *Nachrichten für Stadt und Land – Zeitschrift für Oldenburgische Gemeinde- und Landes-Interessen*, 56 (1922), = Nr. 195 (21. Juli) sprechen von einem kleinen Heft, das „die Erzählungen eines alten Insulaners wiedergiebt" – „Die Oldenburger werden besondere Aufmerksamkeit für die letzten Reste einer Sprache haben, die ihnen so nah und doch so fern ist."

13 Zu A. W. Schleicher's „Geschichte der Galla" *ZA 11* (1896: 389-400) (= Nr. 340).

14 Pronomina im Tigrē, *ZA 12* (1897: 188-230, 291-316) (= Nr. 341).

15 = Nr. 342, auch in *ZA 13* (1898) und *14* (1899) als Artikel erschienen.

16 Bekannt geworden vor allem durch seine *Grammatik des neutestamentlichen Griechisch* (Göttingen 1896), die viele Neuauflagen erlebt hat; die 11. bearb. Auflage (1961) wurde von Albert Debrunner und die 14. neu bearb. u. erw. Auflage (1976) von Friedrich Rehkopf betreut.

17 S. Littmanns Nachruf auf Th. Nöldeke in *Ein Jahrhundert Orientalistik* (1955: 52-62).

18 In das Alte Testament wurde er von Emil Kautzsch eingeführt. Zu Littmanns alttestamentlichen Arbeiten s. in aller Kürze Eißfeldt (1958: 13-15).

4.   1899-1906: Reisejahre (in Syrien-Palästina und Abessinien) und
      Tätigkeit in Amerika

Durch die Bekanntschaft mit einem amerikanischen Studenten, der in Halle promoviert hatte (William K. Prentice), wurde Littmann eingeladen, an einer Expedition
nach Syrien teilzunehmen. An der Expedition nahmen außerdem Howard C. Butler[19]
und Robert Garret teil, beide von der Princetoner Universität. Die „American Archaeological Expedition to Syria" Oktober 1899 – Juli 1900 führte von Beirut aus zuerst zu
den „Ruinenstätten zwischen Antiochien und Aleppo" (AB, S. 90) und dann durch den
gesamten nordsyrischen Raum bis nach Transjordanien und Jerusalem. Littmann
nahm die syrischen, palmyrenischen, nabatäischen, hebräischen, safaïtischen und
arabischen Inschriften auf, machte arabische und türkische Sprachaufnahmen und
sammelte Volkstexte und Lieder. Den einen Monat in Jerusalem nutzte er zur Arbeit
mit Äthiopiern, darunter dem bekannten Gelehrten Kefla Giyorgis, mit dem er *Die
altamharischen Kaiserlieder* (erschienen Straßburg 1914, = Nr. 381) durchgehen
konnte. Er nahm auch die dortigen äthiopischen Handschriften auf.[20]
    Die Ernte dieser Expedition war reich. Littmann steuerte zu den „Publications of
an American Archaeological Expedition to Syria in 1899-1900" den 4. Band (*Semitic
Inscriptions*, New York 1904, = Nr. 88) bei. Zahlreiche Publikationen (außer den genannten) basieren auf dem in Syrien gesammelten Material, wie Arbeiten zum Kara-
göz[21] und eine Liste der Beduinen-Stämme des Ostjordanlandes,[22] sowie folgende
Monographien: *Arabische Schattenspiele* (Berlin 1901, = Nr. 179), Zur Entzifferung der
Ṣafâ-Inschriften (Leipzig 1901, = Nr. 180), *Neuarabische Volkspoesie*, Berlin 1902, =
Nr. 183), *Modern Arabic Tales, vol. 1. Arabic Texts* (Leiden 1905, = Nr. 191). Daneben
erschien aber auch eine Übersetzung des äthiopischen Jubiläenbuches (1900).[23]
    Die Freundschaft mit den amerikanischen Expeditionsmitgliedern führte zu einer
Einladung nach Princeton, auch damals schon eine angesehene Universität, wo er
1901 eine Stelle als Custodian of Manuscripts and Instructor in Semitic Languages
antrat. Damals zählte Princeton 5000 Einwohner. Die deutsche Wissenschaft stand in
hohem Ansehen. „Damals galt es in Princeton beinahe als notwendig, deutscher Dr.
zu sein, wenn man Professor werden wollte" (AB, S. 186). Littmanns Auswanderung

---

19 Zu Howard Crosby Butler (1872-1922) s. *Who is Who in America*, vol. 1. 1897-1942, Chicago
    (1943) (1962: 177).
20 Die äthiopischen Handschriften im griechischen Kloster zu Jerusalem. *ZA 15* (1900: 133-
    151) (= Nr. 346).
21 Ein arabisches Karagöz-Spiel, *ZDMG 54* (1900: 661-680) (= Nr. 175), *Arabische Schatten-
    spiele*, mit Anhängen von G. Jacob, Berlin 1901 (= Nr. 179).
22 Eine amtliche Liste der Beduinenstämme des Ostjordanlandes. *ZDPV 24* (1901: 26-31) (= Nr.
    178).
23 Das Buch der Jubiläen, *Die Apokryphen und Pseudepigraphen des Alten Testaments*, übers.
    u. hrsg. von E. Kautzsch, 2 Bde., Tübingen: 31-119 (= Nr. 345).

nach Amerika im Alter von 26 Jahren wurde von seiner Mutter – sein Vater war schon acht Jahre tot – und manchen seiner Lehrer, die er befragte, befürwortet, von Th. Nöldeke aber nicht gut geheißen (s. *AB*, S. 175). In Princeton hatte er die Sammlung Garrett zu katalogisieren (erschienen 1904: *A List of Arabic Manuscripts in Princeton University Library*, = Nr. 190). Auch in Princeton und Leipzig erschien 1902 *The Chronicle of King Theodore of Abyssinia* (= Nr. 351). Ganz heimisch scheint Littmann in Amerika nicht geworden zu sein; in seiner Autobiographie äußert er sich nicht dazu. 1904 kehrte er auf jeden Fall nach Deutschland zurück. Auf der Rückfahrt arbeitete er an den beiden Schriften (*Ḥatäta* ‚Untersuchungen') von Zer'a Ja'qob und Walda Heywat, den beiden – angeblichen[24] – *Philosophi Abessini*, die im „Corpus Scriptorum Christianorum Orientalium" (CSCO) 1904 mit lateinischer Übersetzung erschienen (= Nr. 355), deutsch 1916 (*Zar'a-Jacob – Ein einsamer Denker in Abessinien*, Berlin, = Nr. 384). 1904 erschien auch *The legend of the Queen of Sheba in the tradition of Axum* (Leiden - Princeton, = Nr. 357).

Die engen Beziehungen zu Princeton dauerten an. Noch 1904 nahm er an einer kürzeren Expedition nach Syrien teil. Wohl auf Littmanns Anregung geht eine andere Princetoner Expedition zurück, die ihn nach Abessinien führte. Die „Princeton (University) Expedition to Abyssinia" 1905-1906 verschaffte ihm nun endlich die Möglichkeit, sich den Sprachen und Literaturen der abessinischen Völker zu widmen. Von seiner Doktorarbeit her bestens mit dem Tigre vertraut, nahm er sich dieser zweitgrößten Volksgruppe in der *Colonia Eritrea* an.

Nach einer Vorbereitung der Reise in Rom, wo er die Hilfe der beiden führenden italienischen Äthiopisten Ignazio Guidi (1844-1935)[25] und Carlo Conti Rossini (1872-1949)[26] erfuhr, kam Littmann im Oktober 1905 in Massaua in der *Colonia Eritrea* an. Von Asmara aus reiste er im Oktober 1905 mit sechs Maultieren über Kärän (ital. Cheren) nach Gäläb (Gheleb),[27] dem Hauptort der tigresprachigen Mänsa' (Mensa). Dort befand sich eine schwedische Mission, wo er ideale Bedingungen für seine Arbeit

---

24 Wie Littmann damals nicht erkannte. Daß die beiden Schriften den guten Ge'ez-Kenntnissen des freigeistigen „italienischen Paters Justus von Urbino" (*AB*, S. 213) (= Giusto da Urbino) zu danken sind, erkannten später C. Conti Rossini (Lo Ḥatatä Zar'a Yá'qób e il Padre Giusto da Urbino, *Rendiconti dell Reale Accademia dei Lincei*, 5, 29 (1920: 213-223) und E. Mittwoch (*Die amharische Version der Soirées de Carthage, mit einer Einleitung: Die angeblichen abessinischen Philosophien des 17. Jahrhunderts*, Berlin - Leipzig 1934). Mittwoch wies besonders auf die Ähnlichkeit des Stils der beiden altäthiopisch verfaßten *Ḥatäta* mit dem der *Soirées de Carthage* (*Mäṣḥafä täkahǝdo bä-haymanot*) hin, einer Missionsschrift, die von G. da Urbino aus dem Französischen ins Amharische übersetzt wurden. Littmann hat dies neidlos anerkannt, s. seine Besprechung von Mittwochs Arbeit in *OLZ 38* (1935), Sp. 448-451.

25 S. den Nachruf von Littmann in *Ein Jahrhundert Orientalistik* (1955: 63-73).

26 S. L. Ricci: Carlo Conti Rossini, *Dizionario biografico degli Italiani*, vol. 28, Roma 1983: 527-529.

27 Der Ort ist auf der offiziellen Karte *Eritrea: National map 1:1,000,000*, (Asmara) 1995, verzeichnet.

fand.[28] Er arbeitete dort mit dem schwedischen Missionar R. Sundström zusammen, der ein Kenner des Tigre war. Littmann hatte mit ihm bereits 1904 zwei Tigre-Texte veröffentlicht (Sundström - Littmann: *En sång på Tigrē-språket*).

Im Januar 1906 unternahm R. Sundström im Auftrag der Princeton University Expedition eine Exkursion nach Adulis, um die Ruinenstätten des alten aksumitischen Hafens in Augenschein zu nehmen. Darüber liegt ein Bericht vor (Sundström 1907).

Durch die Hilfe von R. Sundström konnte sich Littmann auch der Mitarbeit von Naffa' wad 'Etmân,[29] eines besonders befähigten Tigre, versichern. Naffa' hat Littmann nicht nur während seines Aufenthaltes in Eritrea, sondern auch später als Gewährsmann in Straßburg 1907-1909 „unschätzbare Dienste" geleistet (Littmann: *Ein Jahrhundert Orientalistik*, S. 14).

In den knapp zwei Monaten, die Littmann in Eritrea verbrachte, sammelte er eine große Anzahl von Fabeln, Geschichten, Legenden, Liedern und volkskundlichen Texten aller Art. Ergebnis seiner Forschungen waren die fünf Bände der *Publications* dieser Expedition, die in Leiden 1910-1915 erschienen. Die ersten beiden Bände enthalten die *Tales, Customs, Names and Dirges of the Tigrē tribes* in Tigre mit englischer Übersetzung, die restlichen drei Bände die *Lieder der Tigrē-Stämme* in Tigre mit deutscher Übersetzung (= Nr. 374). Auf das Tigre sollte er später in mehreren Publikationen zurückkommen und seine Beschäftigung mit dieser drittgrößten äthiosemitischen Sprache durch ein umfassendes Wörterbuch krönen, das in Zusammenarbeit mit Maria Höfner größtenteils nach seinem Tod erschienen ist (s.u.).

Neben dem Tigre befaßte sich Littmann auch – wenn auch nicht mit demselben Gewicht – mit der tigrinischen Sprache und Literatur.[30] Das Tigrinische wird im erythräischen und äthiopischen Hochland gesprochen und ist die wichtigste äthiosemitische Sprache nach dem Amharischen. Es ist zudem die drittgrößte lebende semitische Sprache – nach dem Arabischen und Amharischen. Auch zu anderen in Äthiopien gesprochenen Sprachen, wie dem Amharischen und dem Galla, heute meist Oromo genannt, liegen Arbeiten aus seiner Feder vor (z.B. *Galla-Verskunst*, Tübingen 1925, = Nr. 397).

Neben diesen sprachlichen, volkskundlichen und literaturwissenschaftlichen Studien war es das erklärte Ziel der Princeton University Expedition, die Ruinen von Aksum aufzunehmen und nach Inschriften abzusuchen. Außerdem sollten altäthiopische und amharische Manuskripte gesammelt werden. Diese Aufgaben konnten nicht in dem ursprünglich geplanten Rahmen durchgeführt werden. Denn Littmann wurde bei seiner Ankunft in der *Colonia Eritrea* 1905 als Leiter einer deutschen Aksum-Expedition angeworben (s.u.). Das größte Verdienst bei der Realisierung dieses Projek-

---

28 Einen Überblick seiner Beschäftigung mit dem Tigre gibt er in Littmann: Preliminary report, S. 155-165.

29 Das zweite Element *wad* (< *wald*) bedeutet ‚Sohn von'. S. den Nachruf auf Naffa', der 1909 unter ungeklärten Umständen auf der Schiffahrt von Neapel nach Catania umkam, in *Ein Jahrhundert Orientalistik* (1955: 14-25).

30 S. seinen Bericht in Littmann: Preliminary report, S. 165-167.

tes gebührt wohl dem Orientalisten und Diplomaten[31] Friedrich Rosen (1856-1935), der 1905 nach der Aufnahme diplomatischer Beziehungen in außerordentlicher Mission in Addis Ababa war.[32] Über diese Reise berichtet anschaulich und mit vielen Informationen über Land und Sitten (und 160 Abbildungen)[33] sein Bruder Felix Rosen (*Eine deutsche Gesandtschaft in Abessinien*, Leipzig 1907).

In einer Unterredung mit dem Kaiser Menilek II. von Äthiopien berichtete Fr. Rosen diesem von dem großen Interesse des Deutschen Kaisers an den Ausgrabungen antiker Stätten und von den erfolgreichen deutschen Ausgrabungen in Babylon, worauf der äthiopische Kaiser „ein lebhaftes Interesse" an den Tag legte und „den Deutschen Kaiser bat, Fachleute zur Untersuchung der Ruinen von Aksum zu entsenden" (*DAE* I, S. v).[34] Daraufhin befahl der Deutsche Kaiser im Herbst 1905 die Entsendung einer deutschen Expedition und deren Finanzierung „aus dem allerhöchsten Dispositionsfond". Damit war die Expedition beschlossen, und als Leiter wurde E. Littmann vorgesehen, der wie kein anderer für diese Aufgabe geschaffen war. Daß Littmann auch tatsächlich mit dieser Aufgabe betraut wurde, lag an Fr. Rosen, den er bei seinem Aufenthalt in Jerusalem (wohl 1900) kennengelernt hatte. Im Sommer 1905 kam es auf Norderney zu einem damals geheim gehaltenen Treffen zwischen Littmann und Rosen, auf dem die schwierigen Probleme des Wechsels von der amerikanischen zur deutschen Expedition besprochen wurden. Über dieses Treffen berichtete Littmann später (1935) im Nachruf auf Rosen (*Ein Jahrhundert Orientalistik* (1955), S. 77f.).

Littmann kam im Oktober 1905 in Massaua (in der *Colonia Eritrea*) an, wie oben schon dargelegt wurde. Wie er in seinem Preliminary Report (1907) schreibt, wurde er kurz nach seiner Ankunft „asked to lead this expedition to Aksum". Robert Garrett erklärte sich daraufhin damit einverstanden, daß Littmann „under his patronage" und durch seine Munifizenz „and as a member of Princeton University" von den vereinbarten Aufgaben der Expedition nur die Studien zum Tigre und Tigrinischen abschließen und möglichst viele Handschriften sammeln, die vereinbarte Erforschung Aksums aber der Deutschen Aksum-Expedition (DAE) überlassen sollte. So ist es in der Folge auch gemacht worden. Vor allem die fünf umfangreichen Bände mit den Tigre-Texten sind in der Reihe *Publications of the Princeton Expedition to Abyssinia*, Leiden 1910-1915, erschienen. Von den Handschriften, die Littmann in Aksum sammeln konnte, insgesamt 316, davon 167 Zauberrollen, wurde „ein Teil" von der Königlichen Bibliothek zu Berlin erworben, während „der Rest in den Besitz von Mr. Robert Garrett" überging (*DAE* I, S. v). In seinem Preliminary Report (1907: 169) spricht Littmann von

---

31 Genauer „Geheimer Legationsrat und Vortragender Rat im Auswärtigen Amt", s. Rosen *Eine deutsche Gesandtschaft* (1907: vi).

32 S. *Deutsche Biographische Enzyklopädie*, Bd. 8 (1998: 389).

33 Darunter auch solche von Friedrich Rosen.

34 S. Littmann - Krencker: *Vorbericht* (1906: 3f.) und den Bericht von F. Rosen in *Eine deutsche Gesandtschaft* (1907: 265f.).

68 Handschriften, die nach Berlin kamen. Daß die Mehrzahl nach Princeton ging, entsprach der erwähnten Vereinbarung.

Als wissenschaftlicher Leiter der Expedition war also Littmann bestimmt worden, der füglich zu dem deutschen Team wechselte.[35] Regierungsbaumeister Daniel Krencker war technischer Leiter, Regierungsbaumeister Theodor von Lüpke war Assistent des technischen Leiters und Fotograf (er hatte vorher in Baalbek gearbeitet), Stabsarzt Erich Kaschke (schon 1910 verstorben) war ärztlicher Berater der Expedition. Der bekannteste dieser Mitarbeiter Littmanns war Daniel Krencker (1874-1941), der 1900-1904 an der deutschen Expedition zur Erforschung der Bauten von Baalbek, Palmyra und anderen Stätten in Syrien und Jordanien teilgenommen hatte.[36]

Die Arbeitsteilung war folgendermaßen geregelt: „Littmann führte die Verhandlungen mit den italienischen Behörden und den Abessiniern, nahm die Inschriften auf und machte sprachliche Studien; Krencker leitete die Ausgrabungen und die Aufnahme der Monumente und Gebäude; v. Lüpke machte in erster Linie sämtliche photographische Aufnahmen, bearbeitete aber auch eine Reihe von Monumenten und Gebäuden, so namentlich die große Kirche von Aksum, ferner eine Übersichtskarte von Aksum; Kaschke leistete der Expedition und den Abessiniern ärztliche Hilfe, machte ethnologische und zoologische Sammlungen und phonographische Aufnahmen von Gesängen in tigrinischer, amharischer und arabischer Sprache sowie Proben von abessinischer Musik" (*DAE* I, S. v).

Der Verlauf der Expedition wird in *DAE* I, S. 1-25 geschildert:

29. Dezember 1905-13. Januar 1906: Die Reise von Massaua bis Aksum,

13. Januar-6. April: Der Aufenthalt in Aksum,

6.-29. April: Die Rückkehr von Aksum nach Massaua.

Die Rückkehr zog sich so lange hin, weil die Expedition die Gelegenheit nutzte, verschiedene Orte und Ruinenfelder auf dem Wege (s.u.) zu besuchen und soweit als möglich aufzunehmen.

In der knappen Zeit von nicht einmal drei Monaten Aufenthalt ist es dem Expeditionsteam gelungen, eine außergewöhnlich reiche Ernte einzufahren. Eine der Hauptaufgaben war die Dokumentation der altäthiopischen Inschriften, Graffiti und Symbole vor allem in Aksum, aber auch an anderen besuchten Orten. Als weitere Hauptaufgabe wurden nicht nur die berühmten aksumitischen Stelen und die Ruinen von Kult- und Palastbauten, sondern auch alle Kirchen sowie einige Wohnhäuser in Aksum dokumentiert. Obwohl der Schwerpunkt der Erforschung in Aksum lag, wurden auch auf der Reiseroute liegende historische Orte beschrieben, wie die Ruinen und Kirchen in ʿAdua, Jeha (Yāḥa), Däbrä-Damo, Mäṭära, Toḵonda', Qoḥaito u.v.a. Dane-

---

35 In *AB* schreibt Littmann, daß er erst mit der Annahme des Rufes nach Straßburg „aus amerikanischen Diensten" ausschied.

36 Später führte Krencker Ausgrabungen u.a. in Trier (der sog. „Kaiserpalast", der sich als Thermenanlage herausstellte), Ankara und Qal'at Sim'an durch, vgl. seine *Römische Tempel in Syrien* (mit W. Zschietschmann, Berlin - Leipzig 1938) und *Die Wallfahrtskirche des Simeon Stylites in Kal'at Sim'an* (Berlin 1939), s. Schwingenstein (1982).

ben wurden auch Kultgegenstände, Geräte und alles volkskundlich Verwertbare aufgezeichnet. Es wurden die Feste der äthiopisch-orthodoxen Kirche beschrieben und über die Arbeitsmethoden der Einheimischen beim Hausbau berichtet.

Zu den Materialien, die nach Deutschland mitgenommen wurden, gehörten neben den Handschriften auch Kleinfunde, Münzen und Hunderte von Fotografien von Inschriften, Gebäuden und Landschaften, die sich als unschätzbare Hilfe bei der Rekonstruktion der ursprünglichen Verhältnisse vor hundert Jahren erwiesen haben und noch erweisen werden, da nur ein Teil dieser Aufnahmen bisher veröffentlicht wurde.[37]

Nach der Rückkehr[38] erschien gleich ein *Vorbericht der Deutschen Aksumexpedition* (von E. Littmann und D. Krencker, Berlin 1906) und im Jahre 1913 das vierbändige großformatige[39] Werk *Deutsche Aksum-Expedition*, hrsg. von der Generalverwaltung der Königlichen Museen zu Berlin (Berlin 1913, = Nr. 379),[40] an dem Littmann einen wesentlichen Anteil hat. Die Bände gliedern sich folgendermaßen:

Band 1. Enno Littmann, unter Mitwirkung von Theodor von Lüpke: *Reisebericht der Expedition, Topographie und Geschichte Aksums*, vi, 64 S., 3 Tafeln und 44 Textabb. [Abschnitt I. Reisebericht und Abschnitt III. Zur Geschichte Aksums von E. Littmann, Abschnitt II. Zur Topographie Aksums von Th. v. Lüpke.].

Band 2 [in zwei Teilen]. Daniel Krencker, mit Beiträgen von Theodor von Lüpke und einem Anhang von Robert Zahn: *Ältere Denkmäler Nordabessiniens*, [A] *Text*, viii, 242 S., 439 Textabbildungen [Der Anhang von R. Zahn (S. 199-231) behandelt die Kleinfunde; sie wurden dem Antiquarium der Königlichen Museen zu Berlin übergeben.].

[B] *Tafeln*, xxxi Tafeln.

Band 3. Theodor von Lüpke, unter Mitwirkung von Enno Littmann und Daniel Krencker: *Profan- und Kultbauten Nordabessiniens aus älterer und neuerer Zeit*, 112 S., xi Tafeln, 281 Textabb.

Band 4. Enno Littmann: *Sabäische, griechische und altabessinische Inschriften*, ix, 96 S., 1 Karte, 109 Textabb.

Durch die Expedition und die nachfolgende ausführliche Publikation wurde die interessierte Öffentlichkeit zum ersten Mal gründlich und umfassend über die aksumitische Kultur informiert, die – an der Nahtstelle von Vorderem Orient und Afrika liegend – ägyptische, afrikanische und vorderorientalische Elemente aufgreifend den südlichsten Ausläufer der hellenistischen Welt darstellt, die im 4. Jahrhundert das Christentum annahm und zu einer ostafrikanischen Großmacht mit städtischer Kultur

---

37 Zusätzlich zu den in *DAE* enthaltenen Aufnahmen sind einige Fotografien zu beachten, die in Phillipson: *The Monuments of Aksum* (1997) publiziert wurden.

38 Mit dem italienischen Dampfer Amerigo Vespucci über Assab nach Aden und „von dort kehrten wir mit frohem und dankbarem Sinne über Ägypten in unsere Heimat zurück" (*DAE* I: 25).

39 Mit den Maßen 38 x 27 cm.

40 Eine Auswahl der Texte, ins Englische übersetzt, mit Abbildungen enthält Phillipson 1997.

und Münzwesen aufstieg. Seit dem Ende des ersten Jahrtausends versank die städtische Kultur und Aksum wurde, obwohl es Krönungsort der äthiopischen Kaiser blieb, zu einem Dorf, das die Deutsche Aksum-Expedition noch vor den Veränderungen durch die italienische Kolonialmacht und die moderne Zeit aufnehmen und dokumentieren konnte.

5.   1906-1914: Straßburg und Kairo

Noch in Äthiopien erhielt Littmann – den Ruf nach Princeton ablehnend – 1906 den Ruf auf das orientalische Ordinariat an der Universität Straßburg als Nachfolger von Theodor Nöldeke,[41] ohne vorher in Deutschland eine Stelle an einer Universität innegehabt zu haben. Damit war Littmann mit 31 Jahren schon auf dem Höhepunkt seiner Karriere. Als Teilnehmer mehrerer Orientreisen besaß er eine reiche Materialsammlung und hatte schon auf verschiedenen Gebieten Bedeutendes veröffentlicht. Ein Vergleich mit seinem Vorgänger bietet sich an. Theodor Nöldeke, einer der größten Orientalisten, war – wie Littmann in seinem Nachruf[42] auf ihn schrieb – „der deutsche Gelehrte alten Stils in seiner höchsten Vollendung". Von Natur aus von wenig robuster Konstitution, gelangte er nie in den Vorderen Orient. Doch kannte er „die Völker des nahen Orients besser als manch einer, der dort Jahre lang gelebt hat. Auch in den Sprachen fehlte ihm die Praxis" (S. 53), wenn er auch Bedeutenderes zu orientalischen Sprachen beigetragen hat, als viele polyglotte Orientreisende. Demgegenüber drängte es Littmann schon früh in den Orient, und er übte sich gerne in den orientalischen Sprachen. „Analytische Kleinarbeit lag ihm mehr als umfassende Synthese", bemerkt Rudi Paret (1985) – und gerade dies, die umfassende Synthese war die Stärke von Theodor Nöldeke.

Von 1906 bis 1914 lehrte Littmann in Straßburg, nur unterbrochen durch die Lehrtätigkeit an der neugegründeten Kairiner Universität und durch Teilnahme an einer Forschungsreise nach Kleinasien zur Aufnahme lydischer Inschriften (*Lydian Inscriptions*, Leiden 1916, = Nr. 79).

41 S. C. Snouck Hurgronje: Theodor Nöldeke 1836-1930. *ZDMG 85* (1931: 239-281).
42 S. Littmanns Nachruf auf Th. Nöldeke in *Ein Jahrhundert Orientalistik* (1955: 52–62), S. 62.

6.   1914-1918: Göttingen und Berlin; 1918-1921: Bonn; 1921-1958:
      Tübingen, Baltimore und Kairo[43]

1914 ging er als Nachfolger von Julius Wellhausen[44] nach Göttingen. Anfang 1916 bis
Ende 1918 wurde er eingezogen; er diente als Mitarbeiter an der kartographischen
Abteilung des „Stellvertretenden Generalstabs der Armee" in Berlin (Littmann: Sketch
1959: xviii). Zu Littmanns Aufgaben gehörte die Erstellung von Namenslisten für os-
manische Karten (s. Nr. 486-487). 1918 ging er als Nachfolger von Carl Heinrich Becker nach Bonn, wo er seine spätere Frau, Nöldekes Enkelin, kennenlernte, und
schließlich 1921 als Nachfolger von Christian Friedrich Seyboldt[45] nach Tübingen,
dabei einen gleichzeitigen Ruf nach Berlin ablehnend. In Tübingen hatte nun Littmann endlich seinen Platz gefunden; spätere Rufe (nach Heidelberg, München, Balti-
more und Göttingen) lehnte er alle ab. In Tübingen lebte er von 1921 bis 1958 (1949
emeritiert), also länger als in jeder anderen Stadt – nur unterbrochen durch verschiedene Reisen nach Kairo bzw. Alexandrien (siebenmal) zu Vorträgen an der von Prinz
Fuad gegründeten Universität und zur Teilnahme an Sitzungen der ägyptischen Akademie.
        Die Aufarbeitung der Materialien seiner Expeditionen nach Syrien und Abessinien
förderte noch zahllose weitere Bücher zu Tage: *Semitic inscriptions* in vier Bänden,
Leiden 1914-1949 (= Nr. 94); (mit D. Magie und D. R. Stuart) *Greek and Latin inscriptions* in sieben Faszikeln, Leiden (1907-)1921 (= Nr. 124); *Zur Entzifferung der tha-
mudischen Inschriften*, 1904 (= Nr. 188); *Tschakydschy – ein türkischer Räuberhaupt-
mann der Gegenwart*, Berlin 1915 (= Nr. 485); *Abessinische Klagelieder*, Tübingen
1949 (= Nr. 422).
        Nach der Abessinienreise gewann das Arabische und die arabische Volksliteratur
im Laufe der Zeit immer mehr das Übergewicht über das Äthiopische und die
Inschriftenkunde (s. aber *Thamūd* und *Ṣafā – Studien zur altnordarabischen
Inschriftenkunde*, Leipzig 1940, = Nr. 247). Dies belegen folgende Bücher, die zwischen 1908 und 1955 erschienen sind:
        Arabische Beduinenerzählungen in zwei Bänden, Straßburg 1908 (= Nr. 195);
        Arabic proverbs, collected by A. P. Singer, Kairo 1913 (= Nr. 199);
        *Das Malerspiel – ein Schattenspiel aus Aleppo nach einer armenisch-türkischen
        Handschrift*, Heidelberg 1918 (= Nr. 488);
        Zigeuner-Arabisch, Bonn-Leipzig 1920 (= Nr. 498);
        Jäger und Prinzessin – ein neuarabisches Märchen aus Jerusalem, Bonn 1922 (=
        Nr. 217);

---

43 Dies sind die Überschriften, die er für die unausgearbeitet gebliebenenen Kapitel seiner
    Autobiographie vorgesehen hatte.
44 S. Littmanns „Erinnerungen an Julius Wellhausen" (1956).
45 Zum Leben und Werk dieses weniger bekannten Orientalisten s. R. Hartmann (1922) und
    W. Riethmüller (1970).

Tausendundeine Nacht in der arabischen Literatur, Tübingen 1923 (= Nr. 220);
Finianus – Die Abenteuer eines amerikanischen Syrers, Tübingen 1932 (= Nr. 232);
Arabische Märchen, Leipzig 1935 (= Nr. 234);
Kairiner Sprichwörter und Rätsel, Leipzig 1937 (= Nr. 240);
Morgenländische Spruchweisheit – Arabische Sprichwörter und Rätsel, Leipzig 1937 (= Nr. 241);
Ägyptische Nationallieder und Königslieder der Gegenwart, Leipzig 1938 (= Nr. 243);
Kairiner Volksleben – Arabische Texte, Berlin-Leipzig 1941 (= Nr. 251);
Arabische Beduinenerzählungen, 1949 (= Nr. 257);
Mohammed im Volksepos – Ein neuarabisches Heiligenlied, Kopenhagen 1950 (= Nr. 259);
Arabische Geisterbeschwörungen aus Ägypten, Leipzig 1950 (= Nr. 260);
Aḥmed il-Bedawī – Ein Lied auf den ägyptischen Nationalheiligen, Mainz-Wiesbaden 1950 (= Nr. 262);
Islamisch-arabische Heiligenlieder, Mainz-Wiesbaden 1951 (= Nr. 264);
Arabische Märchen, Leipzig 1954 (= Nr.527);
Arabische Märchen und Schwänke aus Ägypten, Mainz-Wiesbaden 1955 (= Nr. 272);
Die schönsten Liebesgeschichten aus Tausendundeiner Nacht, 2 Bde, Zürich 1955 (= Nr. 274);
Die schönsten Geschichten aus 1001 Nacht, Wiesbaden 1955 (= Nr. 275);
Die schönsten Geschichten aus 1001 Nacht, Berlin 1957 (Ausgabe für die Jugend, = Nr. 534);
Arabische Märchen, Leipzig 1957 (= Nr. 538);
Arabische und abessinische Dichtungen, Zürich 1958 (= Nr. 100).

Über den Kreis der Fachgelehrten hinaus wurde Littmann durch seine monumentale Übersetzung von den *Erzählungen aus den Tausendundein Nächten* (nach der Calcuttaer Ausgabe) bekannt, die nicht nur philologisch genau, sondern auch künstlerisch anspruchsvoll ist. Sie erschien zuerst in sechs Bänden in Leipzig 1921-1928 (= Nr. 216) und wurde verschiedentlich (³1954), auch in Auswahl, nachgedruckt.

Rudi Paret, ein Schüler Littmanns, hielt in einem biographischen Beitrag (1985) fest, daß Littmann „keine Vorlesungen und selten einen öffentlichen Vortrag" hielt. Dies verwundert, hatte er doch – abgesehen von seinen zahlreichen Märchenbänden – noch einige andere für einen weiten Leserkreis bestimmte Arbeiten verfaßt, wie *Ruinenstätten und Schriftdenkmäler Syriens* (Leipzig 1916, = Nr. 121), *Morgenländische Wörter im Deutschen* (Tübingen 1920, ²1924, = Nr. 3, 7), *Vom morgenländischen Floh* (Leipzig 1925, = Nr. 9) und *Abessinien* (Hamburg 1935, = Nr. 404).

Eines seiner wichtigsten Werke, zusammen mit Maria Höfner verfaßt, ist (größtenteils) posthum[46] erschienen: das *Wörterbuch der Tigrē-Sprache* (Mainz 1962). Das Erscheinen der ersten drei Lieferungen (= Nr. 541) durfte Littmann noch erleben. Mit der Verzettelung der Texte allerdings hatte bei diesem Werk Maria Höfner die Hauptarbeit unternommen.

Enno Littmann verstarb im Jahre 1958. Seine Witwe Elsa Littmann, geb. Nöldeke, überlebte ihn um 25 Jahre (gest. 1983). Als ich in den 60er (1964-1967) und dann wieder in den späten 70er und frühen 80er Jahren (1976-1988) in Tübingen studierte und als Assistent (des Nachfolgers seines Nachfolgers) auch lehrte, wehte dort noch der genius loci von Littmann. So hörte ich von seiner Wohnung in der Mörikestraße 8, wo Littmann bis zuletzt seine Seminare zwischen Bücherstapeln abzuhalten pflegte (s. die Fotos in *Library* 1959). Zum Schluß möchte ich meines Tübinger Lehrers Rudi Paret (1901-1983) gedenken, der bei Littmann studiert hat und 1952 sein Nachfolger wurde. Ihm verdanken wir die bislang ausführlichste Würdigung von Enno Littmann (1959).

Von den zahlreichen Ehrungen, die ihm zuteil wurden, ist er in seiner kurzgefaßten Autobiographie (*AB*) besonders auf das Jubiläum der Universität Kairo eingegangen, an der er so oft gelehrt und auch einmal (1910-1912) als Dekan gewirkt hatte. Die arabische Rede als Ehrendoktor 1950 war für ihn „ein Höhepunkt meiner Tätigkeit als Erforscher und Förderer des Morgenlandes" (Littmann Sketch, S. xix). Als einer von den drei Ordensmitgliedern, die den Krieg und den Nationalsozialismus überlebt hatten, empfand er es als große Ehre, im Auftrag von Präsident Heuß den erloschenen Orden *Pour le mérite* für Wissenschaft und Künste zu neuem Leben zu erwecken, den Orden, in den er 1931 aufgenommen wurde und dessen Kanzler er 1952-1955 gewesen war.

Abkürzungen

AB   (Autobiographie) Leben und Arbeit von Enno Littmann. Handschriftliches Manuskript aus dem Nachlaß Enno Littmann (245/90), 1944 [gedruckt 1986, Biesterfeldt, H. H. (Hrsg.)]

DAE   Deutsche Aksum-Expedition, Band 1-4, Berlin 1913

Sketch   Autobiographical sketch - An meinem Grabe zu verlesen. *The library of Enno Littmann 1875-1958* [...], Leiden 1959: xiii-xx

WZKM Wiener Zeitschrift für die Kundes des Morgenlandes

ZA   Zeitschrift für Assyriologie

ZDMG Zeitschrift der Deutschen Morgenländischen Gesellschaft

ZDPV   Zeitschrift des Deutschen Palästina Vereins

---

46 Die erste Lieferung erschien 1956, die zweite 1957 und die dritte 1958, s. die Besprechungen in *WZKM* 54 (1957: 264-267), 55 (1959: 168-170), 58 (1962: 214-216) durch V. Christian.

Bibliographie

Basler, O.
1955   Otto Bremer. *Neue Deutsche Bibliographie, Bd. 2:* 581-582.

Biesterfeldt, H. H. (Hrsg.):
1986   E. Littmann – Leben und Arbeit: Ein autobiographisches Fragment (1875-1904). *Oriens, 29/30:* 1-101. (s. *AB*)

Blass, F.
1896   *Grammatik des neutestamentlichen Griechisch.* Göttingen.
1961   *Grammatik des neutestamentlichen Griechisch.* Bearbeitet von Albert Debrunner. 11. Aufl. Göttingen.

Brockelmann, C.
1904   *A. Socins Arabische Gramatik, Paradigmen, Literatur, Übungsstücke und Glossar.* 5. verb. Aufl. Berlin.

Conti Rossini, C.
1920   Lo Ḥatatä Zar'a Yá'qób e il Padre Giusto da Urbino. *Rendiconti dell Reale Accademia dei Lincei 5, 29:* 213-223.

Christian, V.
1957   Besprechung von E. Littmann und M. Höfner: Wörterbuch der Tigrē-Sprache. *WZKM 54:* 264-267.
1959   Besprechung von E. Littmann und M. Höfner: Wörterbuch der Tigrē-Sprache. *WZKM 55:* 168-170.
1962   Besprechung von E. Littmann und M. Höfner: Wörterbuch der Tigrē-Sprache. *WZKM 58:* 214-216.

Eißfeldt, O.
1958   *Enno Littmann † am 4. Mai 1958 – Gedenkrede.* Tübinger Universitätsreden 4. Tübingen.

Fischer, T.
1983   *Bericht über die vorläufige Sichtung des wiss. Nachlasses von Enno Littmann im Hause seiner am 6. Juni 1983 zu Tübingen verstorbenen Gemahlin Elsa Littmann, geb. Nöldeke.* Bochum - Tübingen (Unveröffentlichtes Manuskript).

Gätje, H.
1960   Lehre und Forschung in den vorderorientalischen Sprachen an der Universität Tübingen. *Attempto 8:* 20-26.

Hartmann, R.
1922   Christian Friedrich Seybold 1859–1921. *Der Islam 12*: 202-206.

Höfner, M.
1955   *Jahrhundert, Ein, Orientalistik:* s. Littmann 1955b.

Kautzsch, E. (Übers. u. Hrsg.)
1900   Das Buch der Jubiläen. *Die Aprokryphen und Pseudepigraphen des Alten Testaments*. 2 Bde. Tübingen: 31-119.

Krencker, D.
1939   *Die Wallfahrtskirche des Seimeon Stylites in Kal'at Sim'an*. Berlin.

Krencker, D. und Zschietschmann, W.
1938   *Römische Tempel in Syrien*.

Littmann, E.
1897   Pronomina im *Tigrē*. *ZA 12:* 188-230, 291-316.
1898   *Das Verbum der Tigresprache in Abessinien*. Halle.
1900a   Die äthiopischen Handschriften im griechischen Kloster zu Jerusalem. *ZA 15:* 133-151.
1900b   Ein arabisches Karagöz-Spiel. *ZDMG 54:* 661-680.
1901a   *Arabische Schattenspiele*. Mit Anhängen von G. Jacob. Berlin.
1901b   Eine amtliche Liste der Beduinenstämme des Ostjordanlandes. *ZDPV 24:* 26-31.
1904   L'origine de l'alphabet libyen. *Journal Asiatique 10, 4:* 423-440.
1907   Preliminary report of the Princeton University Expedition to Abyssinia, with contributions by Richard Sundström. *ZA 20:* 151-182.
1935   Rez. zu Mittwoch 1934. *OLZ 38:* Sp. 448-451.
1955a   Muḳauḳis im Gemälde von Ḳuṣair 'Amra. *ZDMG 105:* 287-288 mit Tafeln.
1955b   *Ein Jahrhundert Orientalistik: Lebensbilder aus der Feder von Enno Littmann und Verzeichnis seiner Schriften*. Zum 80. Geburtstag am 16. September 1955 zusammengestellt von Rudi Paret und Anton Schall. Wiesbaden.
1956   Erinnerung an Julius Wellhausen. *ZDMG 106:* 18-22 (Leicht veränderter Nachdruck des 1918 in Oldenburg erschienenen Originals, s. Ein Jahrhundert Orientalistik 1955: 146).
1959a   *The library of Enno Littmann 1875-1958* […], Leiden (Catalogue No. 307).
1959b   Autobiographical sketch - An meinem Grabe zu verlesen. *The library of Enno Littmann 1875-1958* […], Leiden 1959, S. xiii-xx. [= Sketch]

Littmann, E. und Höfner, M.
1962   *Wörterbuch der Tigrē-Sprache*. Wiesbaden.

Littmann, E. und Krencker, D.
1906   *Vorbericht der Deutschen Aksumexpedition.* Berlin.

Manassewitsch, B.
1880   *Die Kunst die arabische Sprache durch Selbstunterricht schnell und leicht zu erlernen.* Leipzig.

Mittwoch, E.
1934   *Die amharische Version der Soirées de Carthage, mit einer Einleitung: Die angeblichen abessinischen Philosophien des 17. Jahrhunderts.* Berlin - Leipzig.

Oldenburg, H. F.
1997   Enno Littmann. *Deutsche Biographische Enzyklopädie 6:* 428.

Paret, R. und Schall, A. (Hrsg.)
1955   *Ein Jahrhundert Orientalistik: Lebensbilder aus der Feder von Enno Littmann und Verzeichnis seiner Schriften.* Zum 80. Geburtstag am 16. September 1955. Wiesbaden.

Paret, R. (Hrsg.)
1935   *Orientalistische Studien: Enno Littmann zu seinem 60. Geburtstag [...].* Leiden.
1959   Enno Littmann (1875-1958). *ZDMG 109:* 9-15.
1985   Enno Littmann. *Neue Deutsche Biographie 14:* 710-711.

Phillipson, D. W.
1997   *The Monuments of Aksum, an illustrated account* based on the work in A.D. 1906 of the Deutsche Aksum-Expedition [...] (Berlin, 1913) translated by Rosalind Bedlow and including previously unpublished photographs from the Staatsbibliothek zu Berlin. Addis Ababa - London 1997.

Ricci, L.
1983   Carlo Conti Rossini. *Dizionario biografico degli Italiani, vol. 28.* Rom: 527-529.

Riethmüller, W.
1970   Kaiserfreund[47] und Korankenner: Zum Gedenken an den Orientalisten Christian Friedrich Seybold (1859-1921) aus Waiblingen. *Remstal 26:* 64-68.

---

47   Gemeint ist Kaiser Don Pedro II. von Brasilien.

Rosen, F.
1907   *Eine deutsche Gesandtschaft in Abessinien.* Leipzig.

Schall, A.
1959a   Supplement to the Bibliography of Enno Littmann. *The library of Enno Litt-mann 1875-1958* [...], Leiden 1959, S. xxi-xxii. [Fast identisch mit dem fol-genden Artikel.]
1959b   Ergänzung zum Verzeichnis der Schriften von Enno Littmann. *ZDMG 109:* 14-15.
1975   Aksum – der Geist des alten Abessinien: Vor hundert Jahren wurde Tübin-gens berühmtester Orientalist Enno Littmann geboren. *Tübinger Tagblatt,* Dienstag, 16, September 1975.

Schleicher, A. W.
1896   Geschichte der Galla. *ZA 11:* 389-400.

Schwingenstein, Chr.
1982   Daniel Krencker. *Neue Deutsche Biographie 13:* 8-9.

Snouck Hurgronje, S. C.
1931   Theodor Nöldeke 1836-1930. *ZDMG 85:* 239-281.

Sundström, R.
1907   Report of an expedition to Adulis. In: *E. Littmann, Preliminary report of the Princeton University Expedition to Abyssinia. ZA 20:* 172-182.

Sundström, R. und Littmann, E.
1904   *En sång på Tigrē-språket,* upptecknad, öfversatt och förklarad af R. Sund-ström, utgiven och översatt till tyska af E. Littmann.Uppsala - Leipzig 1904.

Voigt, R.
1997   Berberisch. *Der Neue Pauly– Enzyklopädie der Antike: Altertum 2:* 564.

Gelehrter und Diplomat
Friedrich Rosen und die Begründung der diplomatischen Beziehungen zwischen Deutschland und Äthiopien: Der Mann, ohne den es die Axum-Expedition nicht gegeben hätte

Werner Daum

„Gelehrter und Diplomat" – mit diesen überaus treffenden Worten würdigte die Vossische Zeitung am 29. August 1931 das Lebenswerk Friedrich Rosens zu dessen 75. Geburtstag. Um Friedrich Rosen geht es in diesem Aufsatz. Um einen deutschen Diplomaten, der zu den faszinierendsten und unbekanntesten Gestalten zugleich dieser an ungewöhnlichen Figuren – neben Intriganten und Sesselpoppern – nicht armen Behörde gehörte, dessen klares, vorausschauendes und unerwünschtes Urteil in der Marokkokrise und zum Verhältnis mit England eine durchaus glanzvolle Karriere im *Dienst* nicht hinderte, dem die neue Republik den Posten des Reichsaußenministers anvertrauen konnte. Doch als solcher hinterließ er nur eine bescheidene Spur in den Fußnoten der Geschichte. Sein wirkliches Vermächtnis, fortdauernd bis heute, liegt anderswo:

Friedrich Rosen hatte den Beruf ergriffen, der am besten seinen Neigungen entsprach, und für den er das richtige Gepäck mitbrachte: Kenntnis und Liebe zu den *mirabilia* des Orients, seinen Sprachen, Dichtern und Menschen, und einen klaren Blick für die *realia*: Politik, Wirtschaft, Geschichte und das Abwägen von Einflußmöglichkeiten und Interessen. Sein Blick war in einer für seine Zeit ganz ungewöhnlichen Weise offen für das Fremde, zugleich wußte er um die Bedeutung von Verwaltungen, um die unersetzbare Funktion von Institutionen, und wie man kunstvoll damit umgeht. Dank seines vorausschauenden Charakters und planender List vermochte es Rosen, seine größte und bis heute fortwirkende Leistung zu erbringen, indem er einen bedeutenden amtlichen Auftrag in der vollkommensten Weise zum Erfolg führte, und ihn zugleich so umbog, daß er wie selbstverständlich in etwas Größeres und Bleibendes mündete: die deutsche Axum-Expedition, welche Äthiopien seinen Platz auf der Landkarte der großen alten Zivilisationen der Menschheit zuwies, und, so darf man sagen, der Identität dieser großen Nation stolzen und symbolkräftigen Ausdruck verlieh. Ja, richtig: Friedrich Rosen begründete auch die diplomatischen Beziehungen zwischen Deutschland und Äthiopien. Das ist jetzt bald 100 Jahre her.

Friedrich Rosen, 1856-1935

Dem Helden dieser Geschichte war der Orient in die Wiege gelegt. Sein Vater, Georg
Rosen, war über die orientalischen Sprachen und die Dolmetscher-Laufbahn in den
auswärtigen Dienst gekommen, war von 1852 bis 1867 preußischer Konsul in Jerusalem, und danach bis 1875 Generalkonsul in Belgrad: zuerst für Preußen, dann des
Norddeutschen Bundes, und schließlich des Deutschen Reichs. Verheiratet war er seit
1854 mit der Engländerin Serena Moscheles: wir werden darauf zurückkommen ...
müssen.
   Der Onkel, Friedrich August Rosen, 1805-1837, hatte die orientalistische Tradition
der Familie begründet. Von Wilhelm von Humboldt freundschaftlich gefördert, studierte er bei Franz Bopp – dem Begründer der indoeuropäischen Sprachwissenschaft
– Sanskrit. 1828, im Alter von 23 Jahren, erhielt Rosen einen Ruf als Professor der
orientalischen Sprachen an die neugegründete Londoner Universität. Die Vollendung
seiner Arbeiten zur Herausgabe des Rigveda und arabischer mathematischer Handschriften vereitelte sein früher Tod.

Friedrich Ballhorn-Rosen, 1774-1855

Begonnen hatte diese Reihe ungewöhnlicher Begabungen mit Friedrich-Ernst
Ballhorn-Rosen. Ein Geheimnis webt sich um diesen Mann, das sich heute aus den
Akten und dem Gedruckten nicht mehr entschlüsseln läßt:
   Friedrich Ballhorn war Professor der Rechte an der Universität Göttingen, wo ihm
die dort studierenden Söhne der lippischen Fürstenfamilie zur Aufsicht anvertraut
waren. Zuvor, in den Jahren 1801 und 1802, war Ballhorn als Hauslehrer im Haag, bei
einem Grafen Hogendorp, tätig, wo auch ein Baron Roozen verkehrte. Und dieser
soll, so heißt es in der Familienchronik, in seinem Testament dem Freunde Ballhorn
den Namen Roozen/Rosen vermacht haben, als „Dank für einen Liebesdienst". In
einem Brief schrieb Ballhorn später seinem Sohn dazu: „Ein alternder Vater mag seinem Sohn nicht gern confessions à la Rousseau machen, sonst würde es mir leicht
werden mit Dir darüber zu reden". Was mag da geschehen sein? Jedenfalls hat auch
mitgespielt, daß Ballhorn durch die Namensänderung den ewigen Scherz mit der
Verballhornung los wurde (der Ballhorn, der der Verballhornung den Namen gab,
Lübecker Drucker des 16. Jh., ist mit unserem Ballhorn nicht verwandt). Die Namensänderung (zuerst in Ballhorn-Rosen) erfolgte offiziell mit seiner Berufung zum Vize-
Kanzleidirektor (1817) und späteren Kanzler des Fürstentums Lippe: „Kanzler" – das
war der Justizminister des kleinen Landes. Die Berufung war über die Bekanntschaft
des Tutors mit den jungen Prinzen zustande gekommen.

Georg Rosen, 1820-1891

Etwas mehr verweilen müssen wir bei Georg Friedrich Wilhelm Rosen, dessen letzter Dienstposten im Auswärtigen Amt der *Generalkonsul* in Belgrad war. Man vergißt leicht, daß das türkische Reich noch Anfang des 20. Jahrhunderts bis an die Adria reichte. Auch Serbien gewann seine volle Unabhängigkeit erst durch den Berliner Kongreß 1878 – und erst von da an durfte der deutsche Vertreter in Belgrad den Titel „Gesandter" führen.

Auch Georg Rosen darf man als Diplomat und Gelehrten bezeichnen, vielleicht in dieser Reihenfolge. In Leipzig und Berlin studierte er Persisch, Armenisch und Arabisch, als 23jähriger veröffentlichte er seine „Elementa Persica". Doch hielt es ihn nicht an der deutschen Universität: er wollte den lebendigen Orient kennen, zu dessen Erforschung damals ein großes Maß an Mut und Abenteuerlust gehörte. Die erste Reise führte 1843/44 im Auftrag der Berliner Akademie in den Kaukasus: Früchte wurden zwei Werke über kaukasische Sprachen, darunter eine Sprachlehre des Ossetischen. Später widmete er sich vor allem der persischen, aber auch der türkischen Literatur; einige ihrer schönsten Texte übersetzte er ins Deutsche: den Rumi 1849, und das Tuti Nameh 1857. Sein Hauptwerk, vom Auswärtigen Amt gefördert – das gibt es in dieser intellektuellsten deutschen Behörde auch heute noch –, entstand in der Belgrader Zeit, eine zweibändige Geschichte der Türkei im 19. Jahrhundert (Leipzig 1866–67). Erst jüngst wurden Georg Rosens Verdienste um die bulgarische Literatur wiederentdeckt: hier sind insbesondere Rosens „Bulgarische Volksdichtungen" von 1879 zu nennen.

Durchaus farbiger als Rosens philologisches und historisches Lebenswerk aber erscheint mir der Weg seines Berufes, den man aus der Personalakte des Auswärtigen Amts einschließlich mancher Klippen (vom Schiffbruch bis zur Ungnade Bismarcks) rekonstruieren kann:

Am 14. Oktober 1844 ergeht der Erlaß an „Herrn Dr. Georg Rosen Wohlgeboren in Constantinopel", womit er „der dortigen Kgl. Gesandtschaft behufs Ausbildung und demnächstiger Anstellung als Dragoman überwiesen wird". Am 19. Januar 1845 erhält er „zur Entschädigung für Verluste gelegentlich erlittenen Schiffbruchs eine außerordtl. Beihülfe von 500 Talern", am 21. August 1847 wird ihm der Rothe Adler Orden IV. Klasse verliehen, am 14.Oktober 1858 (Rosen ist seit 13. März 1852 *Consul* in Jerusalem) erhält er „für seine Verdienste um das Evang. Bisthum und die Evang. Stiftungen daselbst den Adler der Ritter des Hohenzollerschen Hausordens", 1859 das Ritterkreuz Erster Klasse des Königlich Baierischen Verdienstordens vom heiligen Michael.

Dann erfolgt am 9. Dezember 1867 die Versetzung von Jerusalem nach Belgrad, als Konsul, mit dem „Titel" General-Consul, und 700 Talern (jährlichem) Salär, aus denen vom 14. Dezember 1869 an („Ernennung" zum General-Consul) stolze 3000 Taler Gehalt und weitere 3000 Taler Auslandszulage werden.

Doch plötzlich ist das alles zu Ende: Am 15. Mai 1875 wird Rosen in den einstweiligen Ruhestand versetzt. Grund war Rosens kritische Berichterstattung über die russischen Aktivitäten auf dem Balkan, und insbesondere in Serbien. Solche Warnung

vor dem, wie man seit Sarajevo 1914 weiß, durchaus auch politischen Panslawismus
wollte Bismarck nicht hören, der vielleicht zu sehr an die dynastischen Bindungen zu
den Romanoffs glaubte. Doch machte wohl Rosen auch in Belgrad aus seiner Einschätzung der Dinge kein Hehl – so daß schließlich sogar der Zar selber gegenüber
unserem Botschafter in Petersburg die Rede darauf brachte. Jeder Diplomat, über den
sich einmal ein russischer Außenminister beim eigenen Außenminister über Men-
schenrechtsaktivitäten eines fernen deutschen Botschaftsrates 1. Klasse beschwert
hat, kann nachvollziehen, welch unangenehmen Rechtfertigungsdruck solch aller-
höchste Ungeneigtheit zur Folge hat, in meinem Fall glücklicherweise ohne negative
Folgen. Georg Rosen starb am 29. Oktober 1891.

Friedrich Rosen

Zurück zu Friedrich Rosen. Geboren am 30. August 1856 in Leipzig. Ein – aus heuti-
ger Sicht – kurioser Eintrag in seiner Personalakte: Fürstlich lippische Staatsangehö-
rigkeit. Nach dem Abitur in Detmold studierte er neuere und orientalische Sprachen
in Berlin, Leipzig, Göttingen (Staatsexamen), und zwei Semester in Paris an der Ecole
des hautes études. Nach Schuldienst in Deutschland Privatlehrer der Söhne des Prinzen Albrecht von Preußen, dann im Hause des Vizekönigs von Indien, Lord Dufferin.
Als im Jahre 1887 in Berlin das Seminar für Orientalische Sprachen gegründet wurde
(weil auch Deutschland eine *praktische* Schule wie die *Langues O.* für seinen
Diplomaten- und Orientnachwuchs brauchte) wurde Rosen als Dozent für Persisch
und Hindustani eingestellt. 1888 Heirat mit Nina Roche, 1853 in London geboren. Wir
werden auch darauf zurückkommen ... müssen.
  1890 trat Rosen ins Auswärtige Amt ein. Sein erster Posten: Dolmetscher-Aspirant
in Beirut (29. April 1890). 1891 dann Verwalter der Dragomanatsstelle bei der Gesandtschaft in Teheran; 1892 erhielt er die „etatsmäßige Stelle des Dragomans in Teheran". Nach einem Jahr in der Zentrale vertretungsweise als Leiter des Konsulats
Bagdad abgeordnet (5. Januar 1898), wenig später (4. Oktober) wieder nach Teheran
versetzt. Am 4. April 1899 nach Jerusalem berufen, wo ein paar Jahrzehnte früher sein
Vater 15 Jahre lang die gleiche Stelle innegehabt hatte. Als Kind in Jerusalem hatte
Rosen – neben dem zu Hause gesprochenen Deutsch und Englisch – sich das
Umgangs-Arabisch der Levante angeeignet. Jetzt fand er dort gewiß nicht nur Auf-
frischung der Sprache, sondern muß auch die äthiopischen Klöster Jerusalems als
selbstverständlichen Teil der religiösen Landkarte des Orients in sein Bild der Welt
aufgenommen haben.
  Kurz vor seiner Ausreise wurde er am 30. Mai 1899 vom Kaiser empfangen. Wir
wissen nicht, was bei dieser Audienz gesagt wurde – der Kaiser kam aber gewiß auf
seine gerade ein halbes Jahr zurückliegende Orientreise nach Jerusalem (29. Oktober
bis 4. November 1898), Damaskus und Baalbek, zu sprechen. Die Reise hatte ihn tief
beeindruckt. Wilhelm II. besaß, wie sich gerade aus der Dokumentation der Orientreise ergibt, ein gewissermaßen doppeltes Geschichtsverständnis: einer dynastischen

Sendung, zu der seine Einordnung in den mächtigen Ablauf großer Ereignisse gehörte, und zum andern eine gewisse Ehrfurcht und Bewunderung geschichtsmächtiger Ereignisse und ihrer noch sichtbaren archäologischen Monumente. Man darf auf dieses Geschichtsbewußtsein Wilhelms II. gern und treffend Schillers Wort von den dreitausend Jahren anwenden. So kam es, daß Wilhelm II. historischen Forschungen – gerade auch auf die großen alten Kulturen des Orients bezogen – in besonderem Maße aufgeschlossen war, einschließlich der Bereitschaft, sich für solche Projekte bei der Regierung und ganz unmittelbar mit seinem eigenen Dispositionsfonds zu engagieren. Deutschland verdankt, wir haben Tendenz es zu vergessen, Wilhelm II. nicht nur die Saalburg, sondern auch zahllose von ihm beförderte oder ganz oder teilweise finanzierte Ankäufe in unseren Museen, und Förderung und Sympathie der großen deutschen archäologischen Expeditionen.

Das alles war Rosen natürlich bekannt. Bei seiner Äthiopienmission, 5 Jahre später, waren der Kaiser und sein ungewöhnliches Interesse an Geschichte und Archäologie Teil von Rosens „Plan". Doch blieb dies nicht die einzige Begegnung mit dem Kaiser: vom 11. bis 27. März 1904 nahm Rosen (seit 24. Dezember 1900 im Auswärtigen Amt, Leiter des Orientdezernats, seit dem 31. März 1901 mit dem Titel Wirklicher Legationsrat und Vortragender Rat) an der Mittelmeerreise des Kaisers teil. Hier hat Rosen gewiß die Gelegenheit genutzt, den Kaiser in seiner Abneigung gegen die forsche Bülow'sche Marokkopolitik zu bestärken. Es ist bezeichnend, daß Wilhelm II. noch unmittelbar vor der Landung in Tanger (31. März 1905), die die Marokkokrise heraufbeschwor, diesen Schritt vermeiden wollte, und ihn schließlich nur auf Drängen Bülows und Holsteins unternahm. Die deutsche Politik hatte die Festigkeit der Bindung zwischen Frankreich und England falsch einge- und die eigenen politischen und wirtschaftlichen Druckmittel überschätzt. So wurde aus der Landung in Tanger statt des erhofften Fanfarenklangs nur eine nutzlose und schädliche Provokation – Rosen spricht von einer „Posse"! Rosens (deutsche) Memoiren schildern diese Ereignisse, an denen Rosen sehr intensiv Anteil nahm, überaus plastisch.

Von Dezember 1904 bis Mai 1905 dann die *Kaiserlich Deutsche außerordentliche Gesandtschaft nach Abessinien*". Noch in Äthiopien erfuhr Rosen von seiner Ernennung zum Gesandten in Tanger. Man kann sich dies gar nicht anders erklären (auch wenn die Akten darüber schweigen), als daß dem Kaiser bewußt geworden war, wieviel Porzellan zerschlagen worden war, und wie sehr es geboten schien, jetzt den Mann der Vernunft, der vergeblich gewarnt hatte, gerade dorthin zur Verhinderung weiteren Unheils zu entsenden. Der Kaiser zu Rosen am 6. Juni 1905: „Wir haben inzwischen in Marokko eine kleine Nebenaktion gemacht, und ich habe Sie zum Gesandten in Tanger ernannt, da werden Sie viel zu tun bekommen!".

Weitere Karriere-Stationen: Gesandter in Bukarest (1910), Gesandter in Lissabon (1912), Gesandter im Haag (1916). Am 23. Mai 1921 zum Reichsminister des Auswärtigen ernannt, am 26. Oktober 1921 Entlassung auf eigenen Antrag. Sein erfolgreichstes Buch, die Ruba'iyat des Omar Khaiyam („Die Sinnsprüche Omars des Zeltmachers"), erschien zuerst 1909, und seit vielen Jahrzehnten – bis heute – bei Insel.

Aus der kurzen Zeit als Außenminister sind wohl nur zwei Dinge berichtenswert: Der Friedensvertrag zwischen Deutschland und den USA (25. August 1921) und die

Koordinierung der deutschen Rußlandhilfe (Schwerpunkt medizinische Hilfe), die
Rosen persönlich leitete. Die Initiative, in der schrecklichen Hungersnot, die den
Sowjetstaat heimsuchte, zu helfen, das Eingehen auf den Hilferuf Maxim Gorkis, kam
von Walther Rathenau; Rosen nahm sie auf. Mit Rat, Tat und ihrem Namen engagier-
ten sich nicht nur Gerhart Hauptmann, Albert Einstein und Max Reinhardt, sondern
auch Borsig, Bosch, Duisberg, Hugenberg, Thyssen, Stinnes, Siemens. Doch war die
deutsche Hilfe, war das unermüdliche Tätigwerden Fridtjof Nansens nur ein Tropfen
in der schrecklichen Not. In der Sowjetunion verhungerten 1921/22 rund fünf Millionen Menschen.

Im Herbst 1935 besuchte Rosen seinen Sohn Georg, auch er, in jetzt dritter Generation, im diplomatischen Dienst, in Peking. Hier starb Friedrich Rosen am 26. November an den Folgen eines Beinbruches.

Georg Rosen, 1895-1961, *Mischling 1. Grades*

Auch Georg Rosen, der Sohn, war deutscher Diplomat. Auf Umwegen brachte er es
schließlich zum deutschen Botschafter, auf Umwegen und Irrwegen, die die Umwege
und Irrwege der deutschen Geschichte sind.

Georg Friedrich Murad Rosen wurde am 14. September 1895 im Teheraner Vorort
Schimran geboren. Studium der Rechte in München, Oxford, Leiden, Münster (dort
1921 promoviert). Seit 18. März 1917 Soldat, an der Westfront verwundet, EK II, 1924
Heirat.

1921 – sein Vater war jetzt Minister – Eintritt in den auswärtigen Dienst; 1923 Ende
der Attachézeit, Laufbahnprüfung bestanden. Posten in Kopenhagen, Chicago, New
York, in der Zentrale, dann Reval, ab Ende 1933 in Beijing (damals noch Peping),
1935 Tientsin, dann Mukden, Nanking.

Dann taucht ganz unerwartet in den Akten ein Schriftstück auf, für das es keinen
erkennbaren Vorgang gibt: Mit Telegramm vom 3. Dezember 1937 interveniert Botschafter Dr. Trautmann (Nanking) beim Auswärtigen Amt wegen „beabsichtigter Versetzung in den Wartestand": „Rosen hält hier aus in schweren Zeiten. Sein Vater und
sein Großvater sind im auswärtigen Dienst gewesen. Könnte nicht für ihn eine Aus-
nahme von den Arierbestimmungen gemacht werden?" Mit einem Privatdienstschrei-
ben hat Trautmann sich noch einmal nachdrücklich für Rosen eingesetzt – selbst dazu
gehörte damals schon einiger Mut.

Dann mußte Rosen eine Aufzeichnung über seine Vorfahren vorlegen (15. September 1938). In dem Aktenvermerk vom 19. September 1938 heißt es dazu:

„Nach dem von LS Rosen auf Grund der Bestimmungen des DBG und der ergan-
genen Runderlasse am 12.2.1934 vorgelegten Abstammungsfragebogen und den von
ihm dazu abgegebenen weiteren Erklärungen sind seine beiden Großväter General-
consul Georg Rosen und Schulleiter Antonin de la Beaume deutschen bzw. artver-
wandten (französischen) Blutes gewesen. Seine beiden Großmütter dagegen seien
zwar selbst evangelischen Glaubens, aber als Töchter des Pianisten und Komponisten

Ignaz Moscheles (sie waren Schwestern) jüdischer Abstammung gewesen. Rosen ist danach Mischling 1. Grades."

Am 21. Dezember 1938 war es dann soweit:

„Im Namen des Deutschen Volkes versetze ich den Legationssekretär Dr. Georg Rosen gemäß § 44 des Deutschen Beamtengesetzes in den Wartestand.

Berlin, den 21. Dezember 1938

Der Führer und Reichskanzler

Adolf Hitler"

– der Erlaß ist von Ribbentrop mitgezeichnet.

Ende November 1938 war Rosen nach England gegangen, bat dann darum, seinen Aufenthalt dort zu genehmigen (was immerhin geschah), wurde bei Kriegsausbruch interniert, ging dann in die USA, wo er an verschiedenen Universitäten Sprachen unterrichtete.

Ende April 1944 wurde er in den Ruhestand versetzt, es muß alles seine Ordnung haben: „Legationssekretär Dr. Georg Rosen ist durch Urkunde des Führers vom 21. Dezember 1938 in den Wartestand versetzt worden. Dr. Rosen ist Mischling. Seine Wiederverwendung kommt daher nicht in Betracht.

Er muß aus diesem Grunde nach § 77 (2) DBG, nachdem nunmehr die fünfjährige Wartestandszeit abgelaufen ist, in den Ruhestand versetzt werden."

Rosens in Berlin zurückgebliebene Frau war bei einem Fliegerangriff im März 1944 ums Leben gekommen ...

In den Akten findet sich auch ein Brief Rosens an seinen zuständigen Personalreferenten, LS Adolf Freudenberg, vom 12. November 1933, wo er sich in fast trotziger Weise zu seinen Vorfahren bekennt:

„Meine beiden Großväter heirateten Töchter des in seiner Zeit berühmten Pianisten und Komponisten Ignaz Moscheles. Wenn ich auch infolge des heutigen Beamtenrechts diesen Teil meiner Abstammung durch meine Frontkämpferzeit zu kompensieren genötigt bin, so möchte ich mit Nachdruck und Stolz betonen, daß mich dieser Vorfahr mindestens ebenso stark wie meine unmittelbaren Ahnen von väterlicher Seite mit einem großen Abschnitt deutscher Kultur- und Geistesgeschichte verbindet. Er war in früheren Jahren in Wien Schüler Beethovens und später in Freundschaft mit ihm verbunden. Der letzte Brief Beethovens ist an Ignaz Moscheles gerichtet, ebenso die Briefe derjenigen Personen, die bis zuletzt am Sterbebett Beethovens weilten. Alles, was die Nachwelt über die letzten Stunden Beethovens weiß, stammt aus einem Briefe, der an meinen damals in London lebenden Urgroßvater gerichtet ist. Ebenso, wie er sich als junger Mensch in den Dienst des großen Meisters stellte, der ihm die Abfassung des Klavierauszugs seines ‚Fidelio' übertrug, hat er nach dessen Tode für sein Werk gearbeitet, so z. B., indem er die 9. Symphonie in England gegen die Lauheit des Publikums durchsetzte."

Zurückgekehrt nach Deutschland (1949), arbeitete Rosen kurze Zeit bei der Bizonen-Verwaltung in Frankfurt, 1950 wurde er wieder in den auswärtigen Dienst übernommen und als einer der drei Neubegründer unserer diplomatischen Vertretung nach London geschickt. Während Schlange-Schöningen in Brown's Hotel residieren durfte (wo meine Frau und ich uns im ungefähren Zweijahresrhythmus einen

Tee leisten), war Rosen im Regent Palace Hotel untergebracht, auch recht standesgemäß. Von 1956 bis 1960 war Rosen Botschafter in Montevideo; am 22. Juli 1961 starb er in Detmold.

Felix Rosen, 1863-1925

Das ist der letzte Rosen, von dem wir hier zu handeln haben, *sub specie* der Expedition nach Äthiopien. Er war mit dabei, hat fleißig Pflanzen gesammelt und ein schönes Reisebuch veröffentlicht, aber doch, wenn man's recht betrachtet, trotz seines wirklichen Dabeiseins dazu wohl weniger beigetragen als jene Vorfahren, die seinem Bruder die Lust am Orient in die Gene gelegt hatten.

Die Äthiopien-Expedition sollte in Friedrich Rosens Vorstellung neben dem dienstlichen Zweck auch der Wissenschaft Nutzen bringen. Darum gehörten ihr Johannes Flemming, als Kenner des Ge'ez an, der sich vor allem um alte Manuskripte bemühen sollte, und eben Felix R., Friedrichs Bruder. Felix Rosen, Professor der Botanik, davon die letzten 20 Jahre seines Lebens in Breslau, war für naturwissenschaftliche Beobachtungen zuständig, sollte in erster Linie die äthiopische Pflanzenwelt erforschen und Specimina sammeln.

Felix Rosens Buch „Eine deutsche Gesandtschaft in Abessinien" bietet durchaus eine Ergänzung zu den Akten (sein Bruder Friedrich hat die Äthiopien-Expedition, ja wohl die Krönung seines Lebens, in den eigenen Memoiren seltsamerweise nur ganz kursorisch gestreift), vor allem aber eine höchst lebendige und warme Schilderung des exotischen Abenteuers. Einer jener klassischen Reiseberichte, die Wissensvermittlung, Forschung, Beobachtung von Sitten und Treiben mit der *petite histoire* verbinden, und – eher bewußt als unbewußt – das fremde Leben in sehr anrührender Weise zum Erfahrungshorizont der geliebten eigenen Kleinstadt kontrastieren.

In dem Buch, das man mit viel Vergnügen liest, findet man auch 100 Jahre später die Wirklichkeit Ostafrikas wieder: nicht bloß, weil Städte, „Straßen", Teestuben und Obrigkeit ähnlich geblieben sind, sondern weil die Menschen, ihr Tun und Handeln, ihre Wünsche und Fragen die gleichen sind wie damals.

Bei Felix Rosen lesen wir deshalb manches, wo die Akten nur knapp berichten: zum Beispiel, daß auch durchaus ein bißchen Luxus dabei war bei dieser Expedition: die erste Strecke, von Dschibuti bis Dire Dawa, legte die Gesandtschaft mit der Eisenbahn zurück. Und in dem Wagen macht sie nach ein paar Stunden „eine angenehme Entdeckung: unser Wagen enthielt einen Eisschrank, und dieser einen kalten Imbiß samt dem nötigen Getränk. So konnten wir mit den französischen Herren, die so vortrefflich für unser leibliches Wohl gesorgt hatten, auf gute Freundschaft anstoßen."

Das „Anstoßen" soll uns Anlaß sein, zu einem anderen, höchst praktischen Aspekt der Expedition abzuschweifen: auch Diplomaten müssen essen, Botaniker und Gardesoldaten (die militärische Begleitung der Mission bestand aus neun Angehörigen der Gardes du Corps) ohnehin. Man hatte vorgesorgt. Die Reiseverpflegung war in Berlin dort zusammengestellt worden, wo man auch heute wieder gut sitzt, bei Borchardt in der Französischen Straße. Dort hatte Holstein seinen festen Platz, wo er täglich beim Mittagessen mit mißmutigem Gesicht Ränke und Intrigen plante, um Deutschlands Außenpolitik ohne Rücksicht auf Lage und Stimmung der Welt zu steuern, Personalentscheidungen so zu lenken, daß an Berichten von den Botschaftern nur das kam (oder oben vorgelegt wurde) was ihm in den Kram paßte, und wo er, so möchte man vermuten, die gute Küche des Borchardt weder schmeckte und schon gar nicht schätzte – doch insoweit irrt man. Holsteins Briefe sind kleine Meisterwerke des Stils und oftmals Zeugnisse schöner Menschlichkeit, und auch als Feinschmecker darf man ihn durchaus bezeichnen.

Borchardt hatte also die Verpflegung der Expedition geliefert: den Bedarf für je 24 Stunden in einer Tageskiste, je eine für die Herren (mit der Aufschrift O.M. – Offiziersmenage –) und eine für die Mannschaften (M.M. – Mannschaftsmenage) und einer laufenden Nummer. Je zwei Kisten entsprachen der Traglast eines Maultiers. Drin war keine Erbsensuppe, und wenn wir auch nicht mehr die genauen Packlisten besitzen, so lesen wir doch (bei Vollbrecht) von „Sardellenleberwurst auf Pumpernickel gestrichen, einem Lieblingsgericht Doktor Flemmings,“ von Cervelatwurst, Sardinen in Öl und in Tomatensoße, von Huhn, Rebhuhn, Perlhuhn, von Rotwein und Fachinger Wasser, gekochter Zunge, kalten Bouletten, Roastbeef und einer Konserve mit Beefsteak, welche auf festem Spiritus heiß gemacht wurde, aber auch von Sekt und Havannas.

Viele Stellen in Felix Rosens Reisebuch sind lesenswert, doch möchte ich hier nur Rosens feine und einfühlende Charakterisierung Meneliks II. erwähnen und von dem schönen und ausführlichen Porträt einen einzigen Satz herausgreifen: „Wie er uns empfing, voll Ruhe und Würde, und zugleich mit einer gewissen Liebenswürdigkeit, die nichts von verletzender Herablassung in sich barg, hatten wir den Eindruck, vor einem wirklichen König zu stehen ...“ (Seite 179).

Felix Rosen, geboren am 15. März 1863, verbrachte wie sein Bruder die ersten Lebensjahre im väterlichen Haus in Jerusalem. Welche Bedeutung Rosens Arbeiten zur Variabilität von *Erophila verna* oder seine Beschreibung von *Chytridium Zygnematis* oder sein Aufsatz über die systematische Stellung der Spalt- und Schleimpilze für die Geschichte der Menschheit haben, vermag ich als Nichtbotaniker nur schwer zu beurteilen. Aber zwei Dinge hat Rosen hinterlassen, die es wert sind, erinnert zu werden: Ein Buch „Die Natur in der Kunst“, in dem er das Sehen des Kunstliebhabers auf Pflanzen und Natur lenkte, und so einen neuen Weg zum Verständnis des gebildeten und des geschaffenen Schönen wies, sowie die Anlage des ersten historischen Gartens 1913 in Breslau, mit Nachpflanzung des St. Gallener Gartens, eines Paradiesgärtleins, eines Renaissancegartens, und so fort. Am 8. August 1925 starb Felix Rosen durch Mörderhand, die ihn im Schlafe traf.

Die „Kaiserlich Deutsche außerordentliche Gesandtschaft nach Abessinien", 1904/1905

Diese Gesandtschaft ist der wichtigste Angelpunkt in der deutsch-äthiopischen Geschichte: sie bildet nicht nur den Beginn der diplomatischen Beziehungen zwischen den beiden Staaten, vielmehr war es Friedrich Rosen – und zwar Rosen ganz allein – der in Addis Abeba die Axum-Expedition plante, das Projekt dann in die richtigen administrativen Wege leitete, später die Finanzierung sicherte und schließlich Littmann als ihren Leiter plazierte. Wir wollen uns in diesem Aufsatz auf die großen Züge konzentrieren, im einzelnen soll die Geschichte der Gesandtschaft und der Axum-Expedition in einem späteren Beitrag zur 100-Jahr-Feier der Axum-Expedition ausgeführt werden.

Begonnen hatte alles ein paar Jahre vorher: im April 1899 wurde Friedrich Rosen von Teheran – über Berlin – nach Jerusalem versetzt. Wilhelm II. hatte die Stadt auf seiner Orientreise ein halbes Jahr vorher besucht, war tief beeindruckt und von der Fülle des Gesehenen im wahrsten Sinne überwältigt nach Deutschland zurückgekehrt. Das Ende des Kulturkampfes lag gerade ein Dutzend Jahre zurück, und Wilhelm beschloß – vielleicht nicht aus Sympathie so doch jedenfalls aus Staatsklugheit – auch für seine katholischen Untertanen in Jerusalem einen symbolkräftigen Ort zu fördern. Auf Wilhelms Bitte stellte der Sultan in Konstantinopel ein Stück Land auf dem Berg Zion zur Verfügung, dort, wo der Überlieferung nach Maria gestorben war, *Dormitio Sanctae Virginis*. Aus Rosens (englischen) Memoiren erfährt man, daß das Auswärtige Amt (einmal eine richtige Entscheidung Holsteins, der Rosen sogar persönlich informierte) angesichts der durch dieses hohe Interesse sehr viel größeren Bedeutung des Jerusalemer Postens schon im Januar 1899 Rosen als neuen Konsul vorschlug. Er war natürlich der richtige Mann, in der heiligen Stadt aufgewachsen und arabisch sprechend. Und für einen solchen Ort brauchte man einen Diplomaten, der auch etwas von Marmor verstand, wie Wilhelm von Humboldt es einmal formuliert hatte.

Wie sehr der Kaiser – später – Rosen mit Jerusalem verband, zeigt sich an der hübschen Anekdote, die Rosen in seinen Memoiren berichtet: der Kaiser war ganz überzeugt, Rosen habe ihn 1898 in Jerusalem geführt, und ihm Geschichte und Bauwerke verständlich gemacht. Rosen traf jedoch erst im April 1899, kurz vor seiner Versetzungsreise, zweimal mit dem Kaiser zusammen, der mit ihm ganz detailliert über die neue Aufgabe sprach. Rosen war überrascht und beeindruckt von Wilhelm II. – das hatte er nicht erwartet: *My first impression was that of a particularly kind and amiable gentleman whose lively way of talking and whose keen interest in the subject of conversation were striking* ... (Memories, Seite 261 f.).

Rosen ist nach Ausweis der Akten in den Folgejahren noch mehrfach mit dem Kaiser zusammengetroffen. Für unser Thema muß die Mittelmeerfahrt Wilhelms II. mit der Hohenzollern (Abfahrt am 11. März 1904 in Bremerhaven) am folgenreichsten gewesen sein: Rosen war bis Neapel (24. März) dabei. Im kleinen Kreis eines solchen Schiffes ließen sich natürlich viele Fragen mit der gebotenen Ausführlichkeit erörtern.

„Äthiopien", damals noch Abessinien, war zu jener Zeit in den Blick der großen Politik geraten. Dafür gab es zwei Gründe: den spektakulären Sieg Meneliks bei Adwa (1896) und zum anderen Faschoda (1898). Als Marchand am 10. Juli 1898 im südlichen Sudan, in Faschoda am Weißen Nil eintraf, hatte er quer durch Afrika nicht nur ein Dampfschiff (in Einzelteilen), sondern auch einen Vorrat Champagner geschleppt. Kitchener, der soeben den Sudan vom Mahdi zurückerobert hatte, wollte ein französisches Festsetzen im Süden nicht dulden. Auch durch die gerne akzeptierte Einladung zum Champagner ließ er sich nicht umstimmen und hielt die französische Mission fest. London stellte sich hinter ihn, beinahe wäre es zu einem Krieg mit Frankreich gekommen - und nur dessen innenpolitische Lähmung durch die Dreyfus-Affäre führte zum schließlichen Nachgeben Frankreichs. Damit mußte Frankreich die Idee einer Landverbindung zwischen Senegal und Dschibuti aufgeben, strebte aber gleichwohl auch jetzt noch nach einer *„prépondérence économique et politique de l'Océan Indien jusqu'au Nil Bleu"*, wie Rosen in einer Aufzeichnung vom 11. Juli 1905 zitiert. England hatte sich mit *Kap bis Kairo* durchgesetzt. Zu Äthiopien, das seine Unabhängigkeit behauptet hatte, mußten die Mächte jetzt ganz normale Beziehungen aufnehmen. Frankreich, Italien, Rußland und die USA waren schon vertreten, Deutschland konnte nicht zurückstehen, im März 1905 folgte Österreich-Ungarn.

Deutschland hatte ein Interesse an der Erhaltung der Selbständigkeit Abessiniens, da bei einer Aufteilung nur England, Frankreich und Italien profitieren konnten. Das war also der Grund für die Aufnahme diplomatischer Beziehungen und den Abschluß des Handelsvertrages.

Am 14. Dezember 1904 reiste die Gesandtschaft mit den Lloyddampfer *Friedrich der Große* aus. Vor der Abreise, am 9. Dezember, war sie noch von Wilhelm II. zur Audienz empfangen worden. Am 6. Januar 1905 in Dschibuti, von dort, man war ja schon im 20. Jahrhundert, mit der Eisenbahn nach Dire Dawa, weiter mit Pferden und Mauleseln nach Addis Abeba, damals noch Adis Abeba geschrieben.

Die Aufnahme der diplomatischen Beziehungen

Nirgendwo in den Akten gibt es einen Vorgang mit dieser Überschrift. Das hat in der Vergangenheit zu einiger Verwirrung geführt, und weil es natürlich, *sub specie aeternitatis*, wichtig ist, wann genau das hundertjährige Jubiläum zu feiern ist (wie entsetzlich, wenn es ein paar Wochen zu spät wäre!) wollen wir der Frage einen Absatz widmen.

Der Tag ist der 12. Februar 1905, Rosens erste Audienz bei Menelik II.: „Kaiserliche Gesandtschaft heute feierlich in Hauptstadt eingezogen. Ras-Tassamma und Minister Ilg waren mit zahllosem Gefolge entgegengekommen und ritten zu meinen beiden Seiten zur großen Audienzhalle wo Negus auf Thronsitz mit Krone geschmückt uns mit größten Ehren empfing. Ich überreichte Allerhöchstes Handschreiben wobei Gardes du Korps präsentierten und Salut schossen", schreibt Rosen in seinem Telegramm Nr. 9 vom 12. Februar 1905, abgegangen 6.45 Uhr p.m., in Berlin eingegangen am 13. Februar um 1.10 Uhr p.m.

Also, das ist das Beglaubigungsschreiben (Vollbrecht, Seite 72, gebraucht sogar den richtigen Ausdruck). Rosen erwähnt den *terminus technicus* nicht einmal, weil alle Beteiligten wußten, worum es geht. Damals wie heute ist es das Handschreiben des Souveräns – oder des Bundespräsidenten – gerichtet an den Souverän oder Präsidenten des fremden Staates, das aus einem realen Kontakt diplomatische Beziehungen werden läßt. Sie sind also nicht erst mit dem Abschluß des Freundschafts- und Handelsvertrages am 7. März 1905 zu datieren, wie dies bisher wohl allgemein angenommen wurde. Der Vertrag hatte für unsere Wirtschaft andere erfreuliche Folgen: immerhin hat das Deutsche Reich schon 1911 nach Äthiopien u. a. 19.794 kg Bier und 12.385 kg Glasperlen exportiert.

„Gelehrte lieber noch nicht informieren, die plaudern wie die alten Weiber"

So schrieb Wilhelm an den Rand von Rosens Telegramm Nr. 18 vom 10. März 1905. Dieses Telegramm verdient hier im vollen Wortlaut zitiert zu werden:

„Habe Kaiser Menelik vorgestellt, daß Deutschland Möglichkeit der Beteiligung an allen *internationalen* Unternehmungen offen gehalten werden müsse. Negus hat mir darauf deutsche Beteiligung an äthiopischer Staatsbank, ferner Option der Beteiligung an Eisenbahnbau, wenn international, unter gleicher Bedingung wie bisher interessierten Mächten schriftlich zugesagt. Außerdem hat Negus auf meinen Vortrag über Wichtigkeit Axum'er Altertümer und hohes Interesse für deutsche Wissenschaft, Seiner Majestät dem Kaiser Recht zu Ausgrabung im ganzen Bezirk Axum eingeräumt. Axum, 2000jähriger Sitz verschiedener Kulturepochen, nur oberflächlich erforscht, weil bisher gegen Europäer streng abgeschlossen. Ausführlicher Bericht folgt. Negus erhofft telegraphischen Dank seiner Majestät des Kaisers und Königs. Geheimhaltung einstweilen noch notwendig, bitte daher, Gelehrtenkreise nur vertraulich informieren, evtl. Drahtantwort chiffrieren. Abreise Anfang nächster Woche. Rosen".

Wilhelm II. hat auf Eisenbahn und Staatsbank gar nicht reagiert, sondern nur auf Axum. Die Marginalie lautet vollständig:

„Bravo Rosen! Hat seine Sache ganz vortrefflich gemacht! Soll hohe Dekoration erhalten!
Telegramm an Negus vorlegen. Gelehrte lieber noch nicht informieren, die plaudern ebenso wie die alten Weiber."

Zwei Drittel von Rosens Telegramm sind Axum, ein Drittel ist Eisenbahn. Auch Wilhelm hat richtig reagiert: Sein Danktelegramm (25. März 1905) lautet wie folgt:

„Mein Spezialgesandter Rosen hat mir gemeldet, daß Euere Majestät mir das Recht zur Ausgrabung der Alterthümer im ganzen Bezirk von Axum ertheilt haben. Ich habe von dieser Meldung mit lebhafter Genugtuung Kenntniß genommen und spreche Euerer Majestät für die im Interesse der Wissenschaft hocherfreuliche Maßnahme meinen warmen Dank aus.
Wilhelm I.R."

Ich will hier nicht im einzelnen Rosens Vorgehen aus den Akten rekonstruieren. Aber sie sprechen, wenn man gewohnt ist, sie zu lesen, und wenn man auch selber solche

Akten produziert hat, eine deutliche Sprache. Rosen hatte den Auftrag, diplomatische Beziehungen aufzunehmen und einen Handelsvertrag zu schließen. Beides hat er erledigt. Aber verstanden hat er seinen Auftrag in erster Linie als kulturelle Mission. Er berichtete dem Negus immer wieder von der Geschichte Mesopotamiens und Vorderasiens, von den deutschen Ausgrabungen dort, von Hammurabi und Babylon, und wie deutsche Archäologen neues Licht auf die Ereignisse der Bibel lenkten. In diesen illustren Kreis könne auch Abessinien treten. Wie sehr mußten diese Worte eine Saite anrühren bei einem Herrscher, der seine Abstammung auf Salomon und die Königin von Saba zurückführte!

Der Herrscher Äthiopiens zeigte durchaus Interesse an diesen Fragen – „noch von keinem fremden Vertreter habe er etwas über derartige Dinge gehört" (Schriftbericht Nr. 16 vom 13. März 1905). Auch das wird man gerne glauben, wenn man in seinem Leben so viele Diplomaten getroffen hat. Andererseits ist auch deutlich (aus den Akten, und wenn man den Orient kennt), daß Menelik den Wunsch oder auch nur die ausdrückliche Genehmigung einer Ausgrabung in Axum *nicht* geäußert hat. Meneliks Sympathie hat Rosen in eine Zusage umformuliert:

Rosen wäre nicht der kluge Verwaltungsbeamte gewesen, wenn er nicht das, was er dem Negus in den Mund gelegt hatte, gleich schriftlich fixiert hätte: „Um unser Recht auf Ausgrabungen in Axum auch für die Zukunft festzulegen, habe ich dasselbe in meinem Schreiben an Kaiser Menelik, das mir höchstdieser zu bestätigen geruhte" (wer den Orient kennt, weiß, daß Rosen auch dieses Bestätigungsschreiben in der Kanzlei des Negus selber angeregt und wohl auch diktiert hat) „ausdrücklich erwähnt":

„... Ein weiteres Zeichen des Wohlwollens Eurer Majestät erblicke ich darin, daß Eure Majestät auf meinen Vortrag über die Wichtigkeit der axumitischen Alterthümer und über das hohe Interesse, das die deutsche Wissenschaft – in erster Linie Seine Majestät Kaiser Wilhelm II. – an der Erforschung der frühesten Perioden unserer Religion und Kultur nehmen, gestattet haben, daß der Bezirk von Axum von deutschen Gelehrten durch Ausgrabungen erforscht wird.
Ich glaube Eurer Majestät versichern zu dürfen, daß mein allergnädigster Herr durch die hiermit von Eurer Majestät bewiesene Gemeinschaft des wissenschaftlichen Interesses ganz besonders angenehm berührt sein wird."
(Auszug aus Rosens Schreiben an Menelik, vom 7. März 1905)

Das Antwortschreiben des Negus an Rosen ist in seiner Allgemeinheit kaum zu überbieten. Offensichtlich wurden hier diplomatische Beziehungen, Handelsvertrag und Axum in einem Topf zusammengekocht:

„Der Löwe hat gesiegt aus dem Stamme Juda.
Menelik II., eingesetzt von Gott, König der Könige von Äthiopien, an Dr. Rosen, den Kaiserlich deutschen Gesandten, dessen Vollmacht richtig befunden ist.
Friede sei mit Dir!
Deinen Brief, datiert vom 28. Februar (= 7. März) habe ich erhalten. Ich freue mich darauf, daß Du die zwischen uns vereinbarten Angelegenheiten Unserem erhabenen Freunde Wilhelm II., König der Könige Deutschlands, bei Deiner Zusammenkunft mit Ihm bekannt machen wirst, und hoffe, daß Du Seine Absichten

Mir zur Kenntniß bringen wirst.
Den 30. Yekatit 1897 im Jahre des Heils, Adis Abeba geschrieben
(= 9. März 1905)."

Mit diesen beiden Schreiben und dem von ihm ganz präzise angeregten *Danktele-gramm* des Kaisers hatte Rosen aus seiner eigenen Idee und der allgemeinen Sympathie Meneliks II. eine völkerrechtliche Zusage des Negus, deren Annahme durch Wilhelm II. und ihre Überführung in die deutsche politische Wirklichkeit zustande gebracht. Und das alles ohne „Weisung", aber doch sehr im Interesse Deutschlands, im Interesse Äthiopiens, und, so darf man durchaus sagen, im Interesse der Menschheit. Für solche Initiativen ist die Gestimmtheit im Auswärtigen Amt heute enger geworden.

Zurückgekehrt nach Deutschland widmet Rosen sich, obwohl längst zum Gesandten in Tanger ernannt, der Aufarbeitung seines Axum-Planes. Einmal mußte die Expedition bewilligt und finanziert werden, und zum anderen wollte Rosen als ihren Leiter Enno Littmann. Natürlich konnte er die Axum-Expedition als einen Wunsch Meneliks nur deshalb erscheinen lassen, weil er wußte, wie positiv Wilhelm II. darauf reagieren würde. Mit dem Kaiser traf er am 6. Juni 1905, dann am 13. Juni zum Essen im Neuen Palais in Potsdam („Mittags hier um 1 Uhr im Königlichen Schloss zur Frühstückstafel") sowie erneut am 18. Oktober im Neuen Palais an der „Allerhöchsten Frühstückstafel" zusammen. Auf seinen Vortrag im November 1905 wurden die Mittel für die Littmann-Expedition vom Kaiser aus seinem Dispositionsfonds bewilligt. Übrigens stammten auch die insgesamt 21.000,- Mark, die Johannes Flemming, der Äthiopist in Rosens Gesandtschaft, für den Ankauf alter Handschriften erhalten hatte, aus dem kaiserlichen Dispositionsfonds.

Eben jenen Littmann hatte sich Rosen von Anfang an als Leiter der Axum-Expedition vorgestellt. Die Akten sprechen auch hier für den, der sie zu lesen versteht, eine beredte Sprache, obwohl und gerade weil sich alles, wenn man nur den Wortlaut ansieht, wie selbstverständlich zu entwickeln scheint. Der „Vorgang" muß in die richtigen – fachlichen – Hände, aber alleine lassen darf man diese Hände nicht. Im Bericht des General-Direktors der Königlichen Museen, Schöne, vom 6. November 1905, wird das Drängen Rosens auf schnellste Entsendung der Axum-Expedition deutlich, da sonst „bei dem Kaiser Menelik die ungemein günstigen Dispositionen für ein solches ... Unternehmen sich in unvorteilhafter Weise abschwächen möchten"). Natürlich – solch eine Gelegenheit, für die es außer allgemeiner Sympathie eben *keine* klare Zusage Meneliks gegeben hatte, mußte *sofort* ergriffen werden.

Und ferner (im gleichen Bericht): „Für die erstere Stellung (Orientalist) und gleichzeitig Leitung des Ganzen brachte Herr Minister (= Gesandter) Rosen einen jüngeren Semitisten Dr. Enno Littmann in Vorschlag ...". Er kannte ihn schon seit einigen Jahren, hatte ihn um die Jahrhundertwende in Jerusalem getroffen, und war überzeugt, hier den richtigen Mann zu haben. Littmann hatte (1898) über das Verbum der Tigresprache promoviert, und war jetzt mit der Princeton-Mission in Abessinien und Eritrea. Es galt, einen Weg zu finden, ihn dort „abzuwerben", ohne es zum Bruch mit den Amerikanern kommen zu lassen. Das besprachen die beiden Männer im Sommer 1905 in Norderney. Littmanns Abschluß-Bericht hat der Kaiser im Oktober 1906 eingehend gelesen.

Jetzt mußte noch die Finanzierung gefunden werden. Die Akten sind voll von Vorgängen, wie sich die Reichsregierung, die preußische Regierung und die Museumsverwaltung die Frage zu- und wegschieben. Bezahlt hat (und auch hier darf man Rosens Wirken vermuten) schließlich der Kaiser:

> *„An die Minister der auswärtigen (= Reichs) und*
> *der geistlichen p. Angelegenheiten*
> *und den Finanzminister (die beiden letzteren Preußen)*
> *Auf Ihren gemeinschaftlichen Bericht vom 17. November d. Js. will Ich hierdurch*
> *genehmigen, daß zur Erforschung der axumitischen Altertümer nach dem von*
> *Ihnen dargelegten Programm sofort eine Expedition nach Abessinien entsandt*
> *werde und daß die Kosten derselben bis zur Höhe von „Neunzigtausend Mark" aus*
> *Meinem Dispositionsfonds bei der Generalstaatskasse bestritten werden.*
> *An Bord M.S. Kaiser Wilhelm II.,*
> *Kiel, den 19. November 1905.*
> *Wilhelm R. "*

Das war der Mann, von dem man uns erzählt, daß er sich nur für Pomp und Pickelhauben interessiert habe.

Jetzt bleibt nur noch eine Frage offen: Das alles wußte Littmann ja ganz genau. Ohne Rosen hätte es eine deutsche Axum-Expedition nie gegeben. Ohne Rosen hätte sich auch nie dafür die Finanzierung gefunden. Und ohne Rosen wäre niemals Littmann zu ihrem Chef ernannt worden. Warum verschweigt Littmann das alles in seinem Nachruf auf Friedrich Rosen?

Paralipomena

Die Rosen-Gesandtschaft in Addis Abeba, ihre politischen Hintergründe, das Aussäen des Axum-Gedankens, der Abschluß des Handels-Vertrages, aber auch die Bemühungen Rosens, nach seiner Rückkehr die Axum-Expedition zustande zu bekommen und Littmann zu beauftragen, was ich hier doch recht summarisch dargestellt habe, wird in einem zweiten Aufsatz zur Hundertjahrfeier der Axum-Expedition mit der gebührenden Ausführlichkeit dargestellt. Dort möchte ich auch zu einer weniger bekannten Frucht von Littmanns Forschungen in Äthiopien schreiben, nämlich der volkstümlichen axumitischen Form der *Legende von der Königin von Saba*: von Etiye Azeb, von dem Drachen, dem die Menschen eine Jungfrau opfern mußten, von den sieben Heiligen und vom Eselshuf der Königin.

Literatur

Die zahlreichen orientalistischen Veröffentlichungen der Rosen-Dynastie sind hier nicht im einzelnen aufgeführt. Für Friedrich Rosen findet sich ein Schriftenverzeichnis bei Littmann. Meine umfassendste Quelle waren die Akten des Auswärtigen Amts im AA und im Bundesarchiv. Das Finden und Interpretieren hat mir Herr Dr. Grupp vom Politischen Archiv des Auswärtigen Amtes sehr erleichtert. Für seine Hilfe gilt ihm mein herzlicher Dank.

Bibliographie

Eckstein, K.
2001   Der Blick auf das Fremde (Sammlung Friedrich Rosen im Lippischen Landes-museum Detmold). In: *G. Bernhardt und J. Scheffler (Hrsg.), Reisen, Entde-cken, Sammeln.* Bielefeld.

Keipert, H.
1983   Neues über Georg Rosen als Übersetzer slavischer Volksdichtung. In: *H.-B. Harder und H. Rothe (Hrsg.), Studien zu Literatur und Kultur in Osteuropa.* Köln: 81-138.

Krencker, D.
1906   Tägliche Rundschau vom 1. und 2. August 1906.

Littmann, E.
1935/55 (Nachruf auf) Friedrich Rosen. *ZDMG 89:* 391-400 und in *Ein Jahrhundert Orientalistik.* Wiesbaden: 74-82.

Rosen, F.
1907   *Eine deutsche Gesandtschaft in Abessinien.* Leipzig.

Rosen, Fr.
1930   *Oriental Memories of a German Diplomatist.* London.
1931-59 *Aus einem diplomatischen Wanderleben.* 4 Bände, Berlin.

Rosen, G. und Klingemann, K.
1917   *Die Familie Ballhorn-Rosen. Ein Beitrag zu deutscher Sippen- und Bürger-kunde.* Coblenz.

Schaede, R.
1926   Nachruf auf Felix Rosen. In: *Beiträge zur Biologie der Pflanzen, XIV*: 261-282.

Stache-Weiske, A. (Hrsg.)
1999   *Welch tolle Zeiten erleben wir! Die Briefe des lippischen Kanzlers Friedrich Ernst Ballhorn-Rosen an seinen Sohn Georg in Konstantinopel*. Detmold.

Vollbrecht, H.
1906   *Im Reiche des Negus Negesti Menelik II*. Stuttgart - Berlin - Leipzig.

Individualität und Bindung:
Die Geschichte des Äthiopischen (Gəˁəz) im Spiegel von Wolf Leslaus *Comparative Dictionary*

Manfred Kropp

Erklärende Vorrede

Der nachfolgende Artikel hat einige Besonderheiten. Er bewahrt im wesentlichen Form und Stil des mündlich vorgetragenen Manuskripts anläßlich der Bewerbung auf die Professur „Afrikanische Sprachen und Kulturen, Schwerpunkt Äthiopistik" an der Universität Hamburg, 2. 5. 1990, wenn man so will, der Versuch eines Enkelschülers von Enno Littmann, die Nachfolge des Mannes anzutreten, der dem – wohl einzigen deutschen – äthiopistischen Schülers Littmanns in herzlicher Feindschaft verbunden war.

Weiterhin steht er an der Stelle eines von mir gehaltenen Vortrags auf der ersten Littmann-Konferenz *Archaeology and History of the Horn of Africa* (München 2002): 'The two shores of the Red Sea: An essay on the History of Ethiopia and the Horn of Africa'. Es war der Versuch, ausgehend von den Forschungen Enno Littmanns, ein heutiges Bild der Forschung zur Geschichte des historischen Raums auf beiden Seiten des Roten Meeres nachzuzeichnen. Schon während der Erstellung der Vortragsfassung wurde mir, als Enkelschüler Littmanns, im direkten, dann aber auch einem sehr verschlungenen, von der direkten „akademischen" Abstammung sehr verschiedenen Sinn, klar, daß dies auch eine Auseinandersetzung mit Littmann als Historiker werden würde; nebenbei bemerkt nicht das erste Mal: ein noch unveröffentlichter Vortrag und Aufsatz ‚Des Kaisers Claudius kurze energische Kampagne. Eine kritische Betrachtung zur Unbrauchbarkeit – wenn auch unbewußter – preußisch-militärischer Denkweise in der historischen Quellenkritik' wurde freilich als Ersatz für den vorliegenden erwogen. Er ist aus den gleichen hier noch vorzutragenden Gründen zurückgestellt worden. Da er auf einem Colloquium Africanum am Frobenius-Institut der Universität Frankfurt am Main auf Anregung eines Bewunderers, wenn auch nicht direkten Schülers von E. Littmann, Eike Haberland, entstand, hoffe ich, diese Arbeit, ihm gewidmet, doch in Bälde publizieren zu können.

Freilich, es waren nicht nur die vielfältigen Verpflichtungen der Direktorenstelle am Orient-Institut, vormals der DMG, nun der Stiftung D.G.I.A., in Beirut, die eine druckreife Fertigstellung meines damaligen Vortrags verhinderten. Schon in der Diskussion danach ergab sich, daß man dem *tābiˁat-tābiˁīn* „Nachfolger der Nachfolger" (in der islamischen Überlieferungshierarchie, also wohl Enkelschüler auf die akademische Abstammung übertragen) auch hier wieder die notorische Unzuverlässigkeit und Verzerrung vorzuwerfen hatte: in der Darstellung der wissenschaftlichen Auffassung und Leistung des „Meisters". Um auf diese Einwände, besser Vorwürfe eingehen, fundiert eingehen zu können, ist eine nochmalige gründliche Überarbeitung und ebensolches Überdenken erforderlich; abzusehenderweise wird sich mein Bild in Details, nicht in den Grundzügen ändern. Gleichwohl, diese Überarbeitung steht noch aus.

So habe ich denn ein anderes Gebiet ausgesucht, auf dem Littmann Hervorragendes geleistet hat, und wo die Frage einer zeitgebundenen historischen Einstellung nicht derart von Belang ist und zu Auseinandersetzungen führen kann. Der Gegenstand steht gleichwohl, wenn man sprachhistorische Forschung als Teil der Geschichte, und nicht nur der Sprach- und Kulturgeschichte begreift, in engem Bezug zum Thema der ersten Littmann-Konferenz. Nimmt auch den Ansatz wieder auf, von Littmanns Forschungen ausgehend den heutigen Stand und die zukünftigen Aufgaben der Forschung zu betrachten. 1962 erschien das *Wörterbuch der Tigre-Sprache* (Littmann - Höfner 1962). Das zugrundeliegende sprachliche Material hatte Littmann knapp 50 Jahre zuvor schon veröffentlicht (Littmann 1910-1915.). Damals verfügte er – will man für das Folgende dem *tābiʿat-tābiʿīn* und der mündlichen Überlieferung glauben – infolge der langen engen Zusammenarbeit mit seinem Gewährsmann Naffaʿ Wadd Etman eine quasi-muttersprachliche Beherrschung des Tigre, und hätte das Wörterbuch – auch nach eigener Aussage – gleich folgen lassen sollen. Ohne auf die Auswirkungen der langen Verzögerung einzugehen, kann man doch sagen, daß in den zahlreichen etymologischen und vergleichenden Angaben des Werks eine, wenn auch aufs Tigre bezogene Vorstufe von Wolf Leslaus *Comparative Dictionary of Gǝʿǝz (Classical Ethiopic)* (im folgenden *LCD*) zu sehen ist.

Die etymologischen Wörterbücher zum Hamito-Semitischen aus der russischen Schule verfolgen andere Ziele als die beiden eben genannten Werke. Sie sind etymologische Wörterbücher im Sinne der sprachhistorischen, speziell phonologischen Rekonstruktion hamito-semitischer Wurzeln in Bereiche der Vergangenheit, für die keinerlei textliche Überlieferung existiert, etwa Orel - Stolbova (Leiden 1995); man vergleiche die wichtigen Addenda et Corrigenda to Hamito Semitic Etymological Dictionary (Diakonoff - Kogan 1996 oder Militarev - Kogan 2000). Das LCD, und sein kleiner Vorgänger, Littmanns *Wörterbuch der Tigre-Sprache*, hat eine andere Anlage: Es arbeitet mit dem Material von Texten und versucht die – schriftlich und z.T. auch mündlich überlieferte – Geschichte der Schlüsselwörter aufzuzeigen, wobei, aufgrund der Natur menschlicher Geschichte, insbesondere Fremd- und Lehnwörter, *calques linguistiques* und Lehnübersetzungen eine Rolle spielen. Wenn den oben genannten Wörterbüchern ein indogermanisches Wurzelwörterbuch gleichzusetzen war, so sind – dem Stand der Forschung und der Disziplin entsprechend – Littmanns Wörterbuch und LCD zwei-, dreisprachige Übersetzungs-Wörterbücher mit zaghaften Ansätzen in einigen Lemmata zu dem, was einmal für diese altsemitischen Kultursprachen ein etwa Friedrich Kluges *Etymologischem Wörterbuch der deutschen Sprache* vergleichbare Werke sein sollten. Am ehesten ist dieses Ziel für das Akkadische (soweit dies für eine Sprache mit begrenzter lebendiger Tradition möglich ist) mit Wolfram von Sodens *Akkadischem Handwörterbuch* und für das Hebräische, z.T. auch Aramäische, soweit im Bereich jüdischer Kultur angesiedelt, erreicht worden. Für das Syrische liegen mit dem *Thesaurus syriacus* und Brockelmanns *Lexicon syriacum* Vorarbeiten vor; allerdings ist hier, angefangen von der Erforschung der nicht bearbeiteten handschriftlichen Überlieferung, noch vieles zu leisten. Für das Arabische ist, trotz insgesamt hoher Forschungsleistung, die Situation unter dem Gesichtspunkt des Zieles eines „Kluge für die arabische Sprache" ganz unbefriedigend. Für das Altäthiopische ist die Situation ähnlich wie für das Syrische. Mit dem LCD ist in der Aufarbeitung und Zusammenfassung der historisch-philologischen Arbeit seit August Dillmanns *Lexicon linguae aethiopicae,* also rund 150 Jahre, ein wichtiger Schritt getan.

Einleitung

Wie es schon im Titel anklingt, so wird es meine Einleitung zur Gewißheit machen: ich sehe das Äthiopische in einem anthropomorphistischen Vergleich und hoffe, daß die hier anwesenden Islamkundler mich deswegen nicht gleich in einen „*miḥna*-Prozeß" hineinzerren werden. Freilich, der Anthropomorphismus ist mir aufgezwungen worden, er ist Frucht eines „letzten Drittels der Nacht", das die islamischen Mystiker als Zeit intensiver Gedankenarbeit und Erleuchtung rühmen; ein anderer Teil der Menschheit kennt es – in mehr prosaischer, aber nicht desto weniger intensiv empfundener Weise – als die Anlaufzeit des Migräneanfalls – so etwa ab vier Uhr morgens; unbearbeitete intellektuelle Probleme verknäueln sich in oft bildhafter Weise mit dem anbrandenden Kopfschmerz und erzeugen bizarre Gedankenfolgen, die freilich, und das verbindet diese Menschen doch mit den Mystikern, im Kern Lösungen der anstehenden Arbeiten enthalten mögen.

Launische Parabel

So wurde mir, in jenem besagten Drittel der Nacht, ein seltsames Paris-Urteil aufgezwungen: Die Wahl des Herzens und des Verstandes für lange zukünftige Jahre der Erforschung zwischen drei semitischen Sprachen, die sich in eigenartig verschlungener Repräsentation Auge und Ohr zeigten.

Das Hebräische des Alten Testaments, von einem Rabbi bald in ashkenasischer, bald in – echt semitischer – jemenitischer Weise rezitiert; dem Texte entsprach zu Häupten des Rabbi ein Trugbild, bald eine hübsche Hebräerin Europas, wie sie wohl Heine besungen haben könnte, bald eine Levantinerin, die ihre Verwandtschaft zur Phönizierin nicht verleugnen konnte.

Diese Erscheinungen machten Platz einem arabischen *Šayḫ* und Rezitator – ich kann mich hier nicht auf Rifʿat oder al-Ḥuṣarī festlegen – der unter teilnehmenden und mit Ausrufen folgendem Publikum Koranverse aus seinem Buche auf dem Betpult vor ihm rezitierte; – über ihm in scharfem Lichte und Konturen eine herb-arabische Schönheit, die in ihren Bewegungen der Rezitation folgte, sie augenfällig machte.

Schließlich ein äthiopischer Mönch, der auf einem Baumstumpf vor einer Kirche seinem halbwüchsigen Schüler bald halblaut, bald mit erhobener Stimme Psalmen vortrug. Immer aber hatte der Vortrag den unverwechselbaren, weichen und doch vollen – ich wage zu sagen afrikanischen – Klang, dem – ebenfalls zu Häupten der beiden – als flüchtiges Luftbild über dem Wipfel einer Sykomore eine anmutig dahinschreitende äthiopische Schönheit entsprach.

Freilich eine schwierige und bedrückende Entscheidung – so recht die Ausgeburt eines anstehenden Vortrags – wie Sie jetzt wohl vorschnell urteilen mögen. Ich werde Ihnen meine Wahl vorenthalten, die – um der Mystik eine Grenze zu setzen – eher von elementareren Faktoren im praktischen Leben bestimmt wird.

Der Anlaß, le fait du LCD

Nein! – mein Alptraum war durch etwas anderes hervorgerufen: die zu schreibende Rezension eines Wörterbuchs, in diesem Falle des *Comparative Dictionary of Gǝʿǝz (Classical Ethiopic)* von Wolf Leslau. Schwieriger als eine solche Rezension kann eigentlich nur sein, ein solches Wörterbuch selbst zu schreiben. Dies lag nicht an mangelnder Vertrautheit oder Aversion gegen Werk und Autor, im Gegenteil; doch fällt es paradoxerweise nicht leicht über ein Buch zu referieren, das seit seinem Erwerb mehrmals täglich in die Hand genommen und zu Rate gezogen wird, mit dem somit eine Fülle von Erfahrungen verbunden sind, auf das sich schon Ergebnisse der eigenen Arbeit stützen. Leslaus Buch – LCD als Abkürzung schlage ich vor, hoffentlich im Einklang mit den Regeln der Abbreviologie – wird seinen festen Platz neben Dillmanns nunmehr über hundertjährigem *Lexicon linguae aethiopicae* haben. Sein Wert und seine Bedeutung sollte man einfach in den kommenden Jahren nach der Zitierhäufigkeit (in der Art eines *Social Science Citations Index*) messen, und eine Rezension könnte sich erübrigen. Denn was könnte sie sinnvollerweise anderes sein als der Beginn von – lassen Sie es mich für die Zukunft der Äthiopistik hoffen – Hunderten von Einzelstudien, die dieses Buch auslösen sollte.

Etymologische Wörterbücher zum Äthiopischen

Nein, für eine Würdigung dieses Werks mußte über dem atomistisch in die Tausende von Lemmata verteilten Einzelinformationen eine Erhöhung und Abstraktion zum Begriff gefunden werden, die der Leistung Leslaus den angemessenen Platz in der Wissenschaftsgeschichte anwies, zugleich die genaue Etappe dieser Geschichte definierte. Und dieser Begriff wurde mir durch die Trugbilder in Migränekonvulsionen suggeriert: Es galt die Individualität dieser schönen Dame Gǝˁǝz, bei aller Familienähnlichkeit zu den anderen semitischen Schönheiten, herauszustellen, etwaige andere Verwandtschaften zu berücksichtigen, und aus der bewegten Biographie, d.h. Geschichte, ihre besonderen Charakterzüge zu erklären. Im Grunde legt Leslau, ohne es ausdrücklich zu sagen, in seinem LCD Charakterisierung und Grundzüge der Sprachgeschichte der Gǝˁǝz vor, für den, der dieses Buch strukturierend und ordnend benutzt und liest. Um diesen Gedanken einzuführen zunächst einige Bemerkungen zu verwandten Büchern und etwas Anekdotisches zur Entstehung des LCD.

Neben Brockelmanns *Lexicon syriacum* (2. Aufl. 1928), dem jetzt bis zu den ersten Buchstaben des Alphabets gediehenen *Dictionnaire des racines sémitiques* (jetzt fortgeführt von David Cohen) und dem ebenfalls nicht abgeschlossenen, schwer zugänglichen, und in seiner jetzigen Form ebenfalls nicht mehr fortgeführten Werk von Diakonoff für das Hamito-Semitische, das in seiner sehr eigentümlichen Form von verschiedenen Schülern einerseits veröffentlicht wurde, andererseits von anderen, wie Militarev nach neuen, besonders phonologischen Studien und Prinzipien überarbeitet erscheint, steht nun Leslaus *Comparative Dictionary* – also weit mehr als sein Titel verrät – als das umfangreichste, modernste und zuverlässigste etymologische Nachschlagewerk nicht nur für den Äthiopisten, sondern auch für den Semitisten allgemein und auch für den Kuschitisten, d.h. in höherer Einheit Hamito-Semitisten.

Der eher bescheidene, aber mit Bedacht gewählte, wenn nicht erzwungene Titel läßt sich aus der Entstehungsgeschichte und dem Lebenswerk Leslaus erklären. Als logische Folge seines *Etymological Dictionary of Harari* (1963) – eine äthio-semitische Stadtsprache Äthiopiens in islamischem Milieu – und seines schon monumental beeindruckenden *Etymological Dictionary of Gurage "Ethiopic"* hatte er ein *Etymological lexicon of Gǝˁǝz* geplant und angekündigt. Gurage, ein südäthiopisch semitisches Dialektbündel illiterater Sprachen, ist bruchstückhaft seit etwa zweihundert Jahren bekannt, erschlossen durch Wortlisten und kleinere Textsammlungen und Grammatiken – darunter einige von Leslau selbst – somit ohne erkennbare historische Tiefe, ohne die vielfältige Funktion und den Reichtum einer Jahrtausende alten Schrift- und Kultursprache. Es ließ sich, vom komplizierten Bereich der Verwandtschaft und Entlehnung und deren exakter Belegung in Lautentsprechungen zum Kuschitischen einmal abgesehen, der auch für das Gǝˁǝz noch anzusprechen sein wird – in vollständiger Ausschöpfung des Materials in einem etymologischen Werk darstellen. Für das Gǝˁǝz, das Lateinische und Mittellateinische der äthiopischen Kultur und Geschichte, mußte dieser Anspruch aufgegeben werden. Dies nicht wegen der begrenzten Leistung Leslaus – das vorliegende Werk, d.h. LCD – gehört in eine Kategorie mit Dillmanns *Lexicon*, „des ouvrages qui font peur et qui découragent par leur monumentalité", nach dem Urteil eines meiner verehrten Pariser Lehrer. Nein, es war die realistische Konsequenz aus der Natur des Objekts – ich entschuldige mich für das Neutrum – gegenüber der ausgeprägten Individualität der Dame Gəʿəz: Sprache ist etwas Weibliches, gehört dem weiblichen Prinzip an, und gegenüber einem Realitätssinn und einer Weltsicht, die sich im Neutrum dafür ausdrückt, wie etwa im Schwedischen *språket*, habe ich doch ein profundes Mißtrauen. Ein solches Lexikon müßte eigentlich erwachsen aus dem Stande der Vorarbeiten in den verschiedenen Zuliefererdisziplinen, Äthiopistik und anderen semitistischer Einzelphilologien bzw. Sprachwissenschaften, der Kuschitistik, aber auch der Erforschung des Spät- und Provinzialgriechischen, des Koptischen, ganz zu schweigen von der historischen Erforschung des Raumes in der eigenen Überlieferung und Ergebnissen der Archäologie. Daß diese (noch) nicht vorliegen, erzwang den nüchternen Titel *Vergleichendes Wörterbuch,* dem lange Forschung erst noch folgen muß, um einmal ein etymologisches Lexikon schreiben zu können.

Sprachzeugnisse zum Gəʿəz, vom Altertum bis zur Neuzeit

Damit wären wir bei einer ersten Betrachtung der Eigenart und Geschichte des Gəʿəz angekommen, die ich kurz zusammengefaßt skizziert habe. Romanisten wissen nicht genau, wie das Schriftlatein sich zu der gesprochenen Sprache der Zeit verhielt; als Resultat einer theoretischen, aber nach allen Regeln der Kunst erstellten Rekonstruktion der Ausgangssprache aus den romanischen Sprachen, ergibt sich etwas recht vom Klassischen Latein Verschiedenes. Die Interpretation dieses Tatbestands hat innerhalb der Pilotwissenschaft Romanistik zu einer lebhaften Diskussion geführt: Verzerrung durch die noch nicht endgültig verfeinerten Rekonstruktionsmethoden – lückenhafte Dokumentation – oder ein dialektal differenziertes Vulgärlatein als Ausgangspunkt? Zumindest Punkt zwei der Argumentation „lückenhafte Dokumentation" kann einem Äthiopisten, der die zur Verfügung stehenden Dokumente im Romanischen anschaut, nur ein Lächeln abringen – sei es nun eines des Mitleids oder der Verzweiflung. Denn von authentischem Gəʿəz haben wir nur wenige Inschriften, insgesamt nur einige hundert Wörter, und wir wissen nicht, wie sich diese Kultursprache zu gesprochenen Sprachen der Zeit verhielt, ob die stattliche Dame somit Mutter, Großmutter oder etwa nur Großtante der heutigen schönen Äthiopierinnen ist.

Diese Dokumentation entspricht der ersten Periode des belegten Gəʿəz, die eben durch weiße Flächen glänzt: Authentische Dokumente des Gəʿəz aus einer Zeit, in der die späteren typischen lautlichen Zersetzungen der äthio-semitischen Sprachen noch nicht, oder nur in ganz wenigen, nicht unumstrittenen Fällen zu beobachten sind. Interessanterweise ist dieses kleine Korpus bei Leslau nicht vollständig verzeichnet.

Ich vermisse Wörter wie *mstᶜzl*, das wohl einen religiösen Ritus bezeichnet; *mzlt* auf einem Bronze-Gegenstand – eines der ältesten Zeugnisse eines Königs von Aksum – und *ṣwt/bdḥ* (Opferformen) in aksumitischen Inschriften. Die fehlende Deutung kann nicht der Grund für den Ausschluß sein, gibt es doch solches Wortgut in einer noch anzusprechenden Schicht des Lexikons in reicher Fülle; und gerade aus methodischen Gründen sollten natürlich die frühesten und echten Sprachzeugnisse des Gəᶜəz in einem solchen Lexikon – ich gebrauche den Begriff in doppelten Sinne – einen Ehrenplatz haben. Damit kommen wir zu einem zweiten Problem des dargelegten Forschungsstandes: Wohl aus Platz- somit ökonomischen Gründen verzichtet Leslau auf Belege, bis auf ganz wenige Fälle; er verzeichnet genau lediglich die Forschungs- und Sekundärliteratur, auf die man zur Überprüfung und Weiterarbeit verwiesen ist. Dies macht den Dillmann weiterhin unentbehrlich, solange keine Bibelkonkordanzen oder etwa komplette Textkorpora, und sei es auch nur der gedruckten Texte, bestehen. Hier freilich sollte der Äthiopist nicht nur mit Neid auf den besser ausgestatteten Theologen oder Patristiker schauen – die griechischen Kirchenväter liegen gänzlich auf Computerfiles vor – sondern sich schleunigst unter Ausnutzung der nunmehr zur Verfügung stehenden elektronischen Hilfsmittel um Abhilfe bemühen und die entsprechenden Arbeitsinstrumente schaffen.

Immerhin kann schon aus den wenigen Texten etwas gesagt werden: die kulturelle Symbiose mit dem Griechischen und dem Altsüdarabischen ist aus Bilinguen und Lehnwörtern zu erkennen; läßt also auch den legitimierten Schluss zu, in erst später bezeugten Texten des Gəᶜəz solchen Einfluß anzunehmen und in gegebenem Falle anzuerkennen; dabei erscheint die Begrenzung auf rein literarischen Einfluß in Form von Übersetzungen und schriftlicher Bildung unzutreffend; gerade bei griechischen Wörtern kann man nach Inhalt und Form z. B. durchaus Eingang in die lebendige, gesprochene Sprache annehmen, in mündlicher Vermittlung, u. U. über Vulgärformen der griechischen Koiné oder schon das Koptische.

Die ganze weitere materielle Belegung des Gəᶜəz stammt aus einer Zeit, in der es lediglich Kultur- und Bildungssprache war, was immer es zuvor war, und ist materiell, durch das Alter der Textzeugen, durch runde 600 Jahre von der Zeit der Inschriften getrennt. Wir haben praktisch keine Handschriften aus der Zeit vor 1300 n. Chr.; nur wenige Objekt- und andere Inschriften, die sicher vor 1300 n. Chr. zu datieren wären. Auf diesen materiellen Überlieferungsbefund muß immer wieder hingewiesen werden, wenn man im einzelnen um Etymologien, Bedeutungen, Formen streitet.

Das soll nicht heißen, daß wir mit aller gebotenen Vorsicht, keine Zeugnisse authentischen Gəᶜəz aus der Zeit zuvor anerkennen können. Aus der Eigenart der Sprache, Stil und Inhalt sind einige Teile der Bibel, Teile des theologischen Schrifttums und wenige Reste einer weltlichen Literatur in ihrer Entstehung einer ersten Akkulturationsphase durch Übersetzungen nach der Christianisierung, somit ab dem 4. Jh. n. Chr. bis etwa 7. Jh. zuzuschreiben; chronologische Aussagen sind allerdings gerade über das Ende dieser Periode sehr theoretisch. In diesen Texten finden sich griechische, z. T. auch semitische Fremdwörter, deren Affiliierung zum Aramäischen in Einzelheiten noch nicht festlegt, aber natürlich Auskunft über Herkunft und Verbindungen der Übersetzer zum Rest des christlichen Orients geben könnte. Die sprachliche

Form der Handschriften, nicht immer authentisch, zeigt lautlichen und sonstigen Einfluß der nunmehr (um 1300 n. Chr.) schon anzusetzenden Semitensprachen wie Amharisch und Tigrinya; darüber hinaus wird der Textbefund durch die in der nächsten Periode einsetzende Revision besonders der Bibeltexte anhand christlich-arabischer Vorlagen weiter kompliziert; zum anderen beweist die Notwendigkeit einer Revision die wachsende Verderbnis der Texte auf dem Traditionswege.

Ab dem 13. Jh. bis im Grunde ins 20. Jh., bis in die Gegenwart hinein also, ist die Geschichte die belegte Geschichte des Gəʿəz als Schriftsprache des christlichen Äthiopien, z. T. auch des jüdischen Äthiopien, anzusetzen. Es entstehen zu verschiedenen Perioden Übersetzungen theologischen, aber auch historischen Schrifttums aus dem Arabischen in reicher Zahl, mit deutlich sichtbaren Folgen in der Sprache. In geringerem Maße folgen ab den 16. Jh. Beeinflussungen aus europäischen Texten.

Einflüsse auf das mittelalterliche Gəʿəz

Dieser Akkulturationsprozeß mit Importen von außen wird aber überlagert durch eine Anreicherung der Schriftsprache mit Elementen aus den lebenden Sprachen, den Muttersprachen der Schreiber, der natürlich auch in den Übersetzungen festzustellen ist, sich aber reiner in den Originalschriften vom 14. bis zum 20. Jh. zeigt, insbesondere der Hagiographie, dann aber auch der Historiographie. Zu den komplizierten Problemen der Abschichtung des betreffenden Wortgutes noch einiges später, wichtig schon jetzt, daß formal oft in keiner Weise Gəʿəz von gəʿəzisiertem Amharisch oder Tigrinya abzusetzen ist; obwohl heilige Sprache, war es doch auch, um bei Heine zu bleiben, „eine Sprache, der jeder ans Mieder greifen durfte". Ich hoffe, mit diesen knappen Worten die Stellung des Gəʿəz umrissen zu haben. Die Parallelen zum Mittellatein sind zweifellos auch strukturell am fruchtbarsten. Die Parallelen zum Klassisch-Arabischen schon wesentlich problematischer: keine grammatische Pflege, wie man das ausdrückt; man kann aber auch sagen, die Schriftsprache wurde nicht totgepflegt, sondern zeigt eine lebendige Geschichte, war Ausdruck ihrer Zeit und deren Kultur, regional differenziert – und, wer weiß, ist vielleicht noch einmal in der Lage, eine wichtige Rolle für die kulturelle Einheit des in der Gegenwart so leidvoll zerrissenen Äthiopien zu spielen; als Steinbruch für Neologismen und zum Ausbau neuer nationaler Sprachen dient es ohnehin.

Als eine der letzten Anreicherungen aus der Spätzeit der Schriftsprache will ich das allerdings nicht ganz unumstrittene *bällämä* zitieren, das von frz. *plume* abgeleitet wird; leider fehlt die Stellenangabe im LCD für weitere Nachforschung; es ist wohl doch dem 19. Jh. zuzuordnen. Überrascht das Fehlen des P-Lautes, den das Gəʿəz ja durchaus in doppelter Form zur Wiedergabe eines nicht aspirierten p also hier angebracht für Fremdwörter hat; aspiriert u. U. ein archaisches Überbleibsel gemeinsemitischen Erbes; oder etwa eine kuschitische Beeinflussung: man merkt schon, wo an den Rändern des phonologischen Systems der gesicherte Grund abbröckelt. Doch retten wir uns zunächst auf die Wortebene: sicherlich hat diese Bildung, da nicht im Amharischen belegt, nie eine sprachliche, im strengen Sinne des Wortes, also ausgesprochene, angewandte Realität besessen.

Methode des Vergleichs

Bevor wir in diesem Zusammenhang mit einer ganz besonderen Quelle, die ich in der Belegung des Gəˁəz mit Fragezeichen als mündliche Tradition bezeichnet habe, und damit zum wohl eigenartigsten und kuriosesten Teil des Lexikons kommen, noch einige Worte zum Methodischen: Leslau bietet natürlich die erarbeiteten Entsprechungen der Konsonanten des Gəˁəz zu den anderen semitischen Sprachen. Für viele und recht eigenartige, durch die Bedeutung gesicherte Entsprechungen im Gəˁəz, fehlen allerdings wohl Regeln für den kombinatorischen Lautwandel, die im einzelnen noch herauszuarbeiten und zu erforschen wären.

Dies alles sind Zeichen einer starken, allerdings im semitischen Rahmen ausgeprägten Originalität, die noch größer wird, wenn man auch noch die nur zweifelhaften semitischen Etymologien heranzieht.

Es fehlt eine Tabelle der Lautentsprechungen zu den kuschitischen Sprachen, dies sowohl im Hinblick auf die genetische Verwandtschaft, wie auch im Hinblick auf die Gesetzmäßigkeiten der Entlehnung, die freilich in beiderlei Richtung zu spezifizieren wäre; gleichzeitig auch chronologische und einzelsprachliche Abschichtungen erfahren müßte. Hier ist auf seiten der Kuschitistik über den von Dolgopolsky gemachten Versuch einer historischen Phonologie der kuschitischen Sprachen noch viel zu leisten, bevor dieses wichtige und für die Kultur- und Begegnungsgeschichte der Völker im Horn von Afrika so wichtige Gebiet klarer übersehen werden kann – wenn man sich nicht der skeptischen Ansicht von K. H. Schmidt anschließen will, „daß die genealogische Rekonstruktion von Sprachen ohne Tradition – von der Rekonstruktion vorhistorischer Sprachfamilien ganz zu schweigen – ein kaum durchführbares Unterfangen" sei (*ZDMG 116*, 1966: 17). Gerade auf diesem Gebiet aber ist es möglich, über die genetische Verwandtschaft hinaus die Eigenheiten des äthiopischen Sprachbundes aufzuzeigen, wie wir noch sehen werden.

Mit diesem Instrumentarium versehen führt Leslau in LCD seine Vergleichungen durch; entschließt sich aufgrund der Lückenhaftigkeit der lautgesetzlich gesicherten Entsprechungen zu einem pragmatischen, den Bereich der Entlehnung in beiden Richtungen abdeckenden Verfahren, für das Kuschitische, teilweise auch bei unsicheren Verhältnissen in vorsichtigen Termini für das Semitische: *common*, soweit eine verwandtschaftliche Beziehung zu etablieren ist, *borrowed (from Cushitic)* bei einem erkennbaren Lehnwort aus dem Kuschitischen im Gəˁəz und *passed (into Cushitic)* beim umgekehrten Fall; also in allen anderen, in denen vage Anklänge zu verzeichnen sind.

Fremd- und Lehnwörter

Der Begriff des Lehnworts ist weit gefaßt: Gəˁəz war für Jahrhunderte eine „tote" Sprache – auf den Sinn und Unsinn dieses Anthropomorphismus oder Biologismus, geprägt von Sperone Speroni in der Renaissance – will ich polemisch nicht eingehen, da ich mich in anderer Hinsicht schon zu sehr eines ähnlichen Vergehens schuldig gemacht habe.

Tote Sprache, aber schriftlicher Ausdruck einer lebendig sich entwickelnden Kultur; durch Übersetzungen bereicherte es sich um Hunderte, Tausende von Wörtern aus dem Arabischen; z. T. dort schon Fremdwörter, Bestandteil einer Schicht gemeinsemitischer Fremdwörter; eine nicht übertriebene Ansetzung, wenn man die Produktivität von sekundär daraus entwickelten, äußerlich gut semitischen Wurzeln in den einzelnen Sprachen bedenkt. Solche Fremdwörter waren z. T. auch reine Transkriptionen, in der Mehrzahl der Fälle nie Teil einer gesprochenen Sprache, wenn auch eine reiche Zahl von Fremdwörtern wiederum mit den lebenden semitischen Sprachen gemeinsam ist; dann allerdings auf einen anderen Übermittlungskanal, die gesprochene Sprache hinweist, und oft inhaltlich an die Dinge anknüpft, die ebenfalls wanderten: Handelsgüter; Waffen; Stoffe, usw. Gleiches gilt für Lehnwörter aus den Semitensprachen Äthiopiens, die, gegen eine alte Ansicht Nöldekes, Teil des Gəˁəz-Lexikons sind. Zu beachten ist, daß uns nur Fälle, in denen Lautgestalt und Morphologie die betreffenden Wörter sicher als Intarsien im Gəˁəz ausweisen, überhaupt greifbar werden. Sehr viel schwieriger ist der Fall einer lediglich semantischen Übertragung, dies auch bei Entlehnungen aus dem Arabischen, zu fassen, bei dem die äußere Gestalt keinen Anhaltspunkt gibt, ganz abgesehen davon, daß uns authentisches Gəˁəz nur in einem begrenzten Korpus bekannt ist.

Aufbau der Lexikonartikel

Ich muß noch einmal, die Rezension nachzeichnend, auf den Aufbau der Artikel in Leslaus Lexikon angeben, dessen Lektüre zum Anregendsten gehört, was mir in den letzten Jahren auf den Schreibtisch gekommen ist, auch wenn ich nicht mehr ganz der naiven Ansicht eines Hammer-Purgstall bin und die Lektüre von Wörterbüchern angehenden Orientalisten schlichtweg empfehle. Doch in dem die weit verstreuten wissenschaftlichen Ergebnisse der Erforschung des Gəˁəz aus über 300 Jahren zusammentragenden Werk liegt im Grunde eine äthiopische Geschichte und Kulturgeschichte im Spiegel und in Form eines Lexikons vor.

Das Lemma ist fett gedruckt in Umschrift und in Originalschrift angegeben. Es folgen grammatische Erläuterungen in Klammern; selten Quellenangaben. Die englische Bedeutung geht an Klarheit und Präzision über Dillmanns lateinische hinaus; nicht nur wegen des Zwangs der Latinität – über das Gelehrtenlatein Dillmanns wäre ein eigener Aufsatz zu schreiben – sondern wegen der Belesenheit Leslaus, hinter dessen lapidarer Angabe *LT Literature* sich eine jahrzehntelange arbeitsreiche Auswertung der veröffentlichten Texte verbirgt. Allerdings wäre gerade hier die Stellenangabe hilfreich.

Hier ist auch der Bereich, in dem in der Zukunft am meisten zu ergänzen sein wird. Meine Sammlungen zu den Gebrauchstexten wie Hofordnungen, Landurkunden und sonstige Schriftstücke bietet schon im embryonalen Stadium reiches Material:

Für die Wortuntersuchungen sind die Angaben, wie das Beispiel von *mäläsay* zeigt, von entscheidender Bedeutung, weil ein Wort nur in seinem spezifischen Kontext und Gebrauch deutbar wird; allein die Wurzeletymologie etc. ist kein Wegweiser zum Sinn in der aktuellen Sprache.

In kleinerem Kursivdruck folgt nun als Unterbau und eigentliches *pièce de résistance* die Vergleichung mit Angabe der einschlägigen Forschungsliteratur. Dieser ist in seinem Aufbau – in statistischer Weise – an die Quellenangabe, zumindest in einem bestimmten Fall geknüpft; er zeigt zugleich den seltsamsten und problematischsten Teil des verarbeiteten Sprachmaterials an: Fehlt er nämlich, bzw. steht an seiner statt *an enigmatic form, a strange form* o. ä., so ist die Quellenangabe in der Mehrzahl der Fälle ein einheimisches *säwaséw*. Über diese Art von äthiopischem Wörterverzeichnis, Realglossar und Helfer bei der Erklärung schwieriger Bibelwörter und seine Entstehung unterrichtet ein gesonderter Beitrag von Getatchew Haile in der Einleitung. Dabei spielt der mündliche Traditionsweg von Lehrer zu Schüler eine große Rolle; die Handschriften sind oft nur Mit- und Nachschriften, die freilich nicht nur das Material eines Lehrers, einer Schule enthalten, sondern im Laufe eines wandernden Gelehrtenlebens nach und nach ergänzt und erweitert wurden. Kein Wunder also, daß sich Wörter der seltsamsten Bildungen und Bedeutungen finden, von denen oft nur schwer zu entscheiden ist, ob sie überhaupt irgendeine sprachliche Realität haben oder hatten:

seydemu 522 a Mond; *muryansu* 362 b "water for the gabata bowl" (türk. *su* "water" wäre abenteuerlich); *marzan* "compilation, abridgement of a book". Vieles hat Leslau mit seiner umfassenden Kenntnis als Verschreibungen oder Verballhornungen bekannter Wörter entlarven können, damit zeitraubende und mühselige Irrwege für andere erspart. Anderes zeigt eigentlich eher Züge eines willkürlichen Kleriker - und Vagantenjargons, der auch sonst in Äthiopien für andere soziale oder Berufsgruppen belegt ist, etwa die vielfältigen und phantasiereichen Bezeichnungen für „Kirchentüren und Teile der Kirche": *Appalippe, hepelope, qufabi, taduhi, tufahi, gabroduhi, salembi;* „Mönch werden": *bäyämä* "Presbyter/Diakon": *dera,* „wo ein Mönch lebt" *yera.* Man könnte weiteres anfügen bei Bezeichnungen, für die ich über 100 Termini fand – was nicht heißen soll, dass der äthiopische Klerus den Stein der Weisen gefunden habe – von Edelsteinen, Pflanzen usw.

Abgesehen von solchen Fällen bleibt die methodische Frage: Sind Wörter, die sich nur in solchen Quellen finden, dem Gəʿəz zuzurechnen? Denn dies hieße, abgesehen von der vagen Möglichkeit, sie eines Tages in unveröffentlichten Handschriften und Texten zu finden, daß sich authentisches Gəʿəz in mündlicher Gelehrtenüberlieferung durch die Jahrhunderte erhalten habe? Ein ähnlich gelagertes Problem stellt sich ja auch für die traditionelle Aussprache des Gəʿəz: Inwieweit hat sie noch Elemente oder Spuren einer historischen Aussprache bewahrt; inwieweit ist sie nur willkürliche, von den lebenden Semitensprachen beeinflußte Schulkonvention.

Ohne auf diese Frage eine kategorische Antwort geben zu können oder zu wollen, gebe ich noch weitere Beispiele für die Art des Materials, das sich in den genannten Quellen findet:

Zwei Beispiele

aṣfar, aṣfur (DL 1397 aus einem *säwasəw*): "crudely made hockey ball" (45 b); nach einem Vorschlag von A. Ambros vom griechischen *sphaira* "ball". Träfe dies zu, so wäre ein sonst nicht belegtes griechisches Fremdwort (mündlich) überliefert und schließlich für einen Gegenstand des Alltags verwandt worden. Läßt hier allerdings schon die Lautgestalt zweifeln, so wird man das arabische *uṣfūra* „Zapfen, Pflock am Sattel; spitzes Holz- oder Metallstück (auch Schiffsnagel)" vorziehen. Ich habe im Moment keinen Beleg, ob die Metapher im Arabischen „Vogel, Spatz" – auch für das Äthiopische gilt: als Synonyme werden amharische Wörter *fadät* oder *gwemay* „Schakal, oder anderes Tier" angegeben (Guidi, *Vocabolario* 718; 892) neben *erur* „Ball"). Ob es im Arabischen dann für etwas wie einen Hockeyball gebraucht wurde? Doch ist im historischen Kontakt und der Vermittlung von Spielen usw. speziell zur Mamlukenzeit ein Wandern eines solchen Begriffes wahrscheinlich. Somit hätte sich ein sonst nicht belegtes arabisches Lehnwort in den *säwasəw* erhalten.

Ein anders gelagertes Beispiel: LCD 220-22L. *hedä* "to rob, take by force" mit allen Abschattierungen wird ein *hayada* "to glitter, shine", nach den *säwasəw* zur Seite gestellt; *hayadi* "that glitters, shines". Dies ist ohne Zweifel der abgekürzte Gebrauch der Wendung *heda ʿayna/aʿyəntä*; (2 Sam 6,14 usw.) „das Auge rauben, blenden= strahlen, glänzen", die auch in den Chroniken sehr beliebt ist.

Fremdwörter als Zeugnisse der (Sprach-)geschichte

Die weiteren, nun echten Möglichkeiten der Kommentierung des Wortgutes durch den Vergleich ergeben, strukturell gelesen, eine Abschichtung des Gəʿəz-Wortschatzes, stellen, wie schon gesagt, zugleich eine Geschichte der Herkunft dieser Sprache und ihres Schicksals in geographischer, ethnischer und sprachlicher Hinsicht und in afrikanischer Umgebung von der Zeit des Hellenismus und der Spätantike bis in die Gegenwart dar. Erinnern wir uns, daß noch 1964 a.m. = 1971/72 Veröffentlichungen unter dem Titel *Tənsaʾe Gəʿəz* „Renaissance des Gəʿəz" erschienen, die für eine weitere Verwendung dieser Sprache in der Gegenwart plädierten. Nicht nur der

Fall des Ivrit macht hier eine sofortige, harte Ablehnung unmöglich: da die politische Zukunft des Landes gänzlich unvorhersehbar ist – sollte es gänzlich unmöglich sein, daß das Gəʿəz bei der Identitätsfindung eines neuen Äthiopien eine wichtige Rolle spielen wird?

Diese Fremdwörter kommen aus der Übersetzungsliteratur der ersten Zeit, sowie den theologischen Schriften wie Qerellos und weltlichen Werken wie Physiologus; sie datieren, wenn auch erst in den späteren Handschriften belegt, aus der aksumitischen Zeit und der ersten Periode der äthiopischen Literatur. Ihrer Natur nach in der Mehrzahl literarische Übernahmen, die aber durch den Gebrauch in Predigt und Verkündigung des neuen Gedankenguts der Religion sicherlich auch Eingang in die Volkssprache fanden, wie die Bezeugung verschiedener solcher Termini in den modernen Volkssprachen beweist; natürlich ist hier die Problematik der zeitlichen Ansetzung solcher Einschmelzungen nicht zu unterschätzen; sie ist zugleich an das Problem effektiver und tiefgreifender Mission und Christianisierung gebunden; also auch hier immer wieder der Rückverweis sprachlicher Probleme auf historisch zu klärende Zusammenhänge.

Daneben gab es aber in der Welt der Spätantike auch engen Kontakt in Handelsbeziehungen, und die Häfen waren nicht nur Stellen des materiellen, sondern auch des sprachlichen Austauschs von Seeleuten, Handwerkern, Kaufleuten. So ist anzunehmen, daß auch griechische Wörter der Volkssprache, evtl. auch in koptischer Form, auch durch Arabien vermittelt, in das Gəʿəz kamen, worauf verschiedentlich hingewiesen wurde. Inhaltlich sollten solche Wörter bestimmten materiellen Sphären zuzuordnen sein; lautlich ist z. T. koptischen Einfluß auszumachen: *kʷarapita* aus *graphida* 293 b "pencil tablet ink". In der lebendigen Sprache scheint es zu einer Pseudo-Wurzel *kʷrp* „schreiben, arbeiten" gekommen zu sein. Die andere Wurzel *krp* "wash, cleanse" wohl nicht als semitisch anzusetzen. Auch kein Beweis für Grimmes semitische P-Laute; die vorgeschlagene Verbindung zu Altsüdarabisch *mkrb* „Reiniger, Gereinigter, Priesterfürst" fällt auch inhaltlich aus, da *mkrb* heute als „Bundesschließer, Oberhaupt der Föderation" erklärt wird.

Der gleichen Sphäre der Vermittlung und Tradition gehören die wenigen indischen Wörter an, *nage* „Elefant" (ind. *nāga*); *sokar* „Zucker" (*sarkarā*), *banian* „Kaufmann"; *berälle* (Beryll). Des weiteren Wörter für Gewürze, Parfüms (Ingwer, Moschus, Narde) u.ä. Zu erwähnen ist, daß die Idee der äthiopischen (Pseudo-)Silbenschrift mit für die verschiedenen Vokale gleichartigen Abwandlungen einer Grundform, die ursprünglich lediglich den Konsonanten meinte, aber jetzt auf inhärierendes kurzes ‚a' eingeschränkt ist, von ähnlichen Prinzipien der Devanagari-Schrift abgeleitet wird. Einige wenige persische Lehnwörter bezeugen die Verbindungen zu Persien; die Spärlichkeit der Zeugnisse ist allerdings genauso erstaunlich wie im Jemen, wo ebenfalls trotz großer politischer Einflußnahme schon vor dem Islam Persien wenig Spuren hinterlassen hat.

Schließlich gibt es die große Zahl - literarischer und volkssprachlicher – arabischer Lehnwörter – die durch Übersetzungen, aber auch durch den lebendigen Kontakt mit arabischsprechenden Glaubensgenossen aus Ägypten usw. in vielfältiger Art und bis in unsere Zeit in die Schriftsprache Gəʿəz gewandert sind. Beispiele erübrigen sich.

Der gemeinsemitische Fremdwortbestand in Theologie, Philosophie, Naturwissenschaften und Medizin, mit dem Syrischen zumeist geteilt, ist in Grundzügen bekannt. Für die Übersetzungen ins Äthiopische gilt es noch eine weitere, schwierige Sphäre zu erforschen: die der Lehnwurzel, d.h. lediglich der semantischen Übertragung ohne äußere Kennzeichnung der Fremdheit – Lehnwurzeln, produktiv; ich habe Beispiele in meinem Aufsatz ‚Arabisch-äthiopische Übersetzungstechnik am Beispiel der Zena Ayhud (Yosippon) und des Tarikä Wäldä-ᶜAmid‘ (Kropp 1986: 314-346) gesammelt. Das Problem ist in anderer Richtung als das der falschen Freunde zwischen genetisch eng verwandten Sprachen (Spanisch und Italienisch (*burro*), Deutsch und Englisch (*become/bekommen*)) bekannt; was hier als komisches Mißverständnis vorliegt, z. T. auch in den Übersetzungen als Fehler vorkommt, wird produktiv in der Zielsprache zur semantischen Erweiterung genutzt; mit anderen Worten engl. *become* könnte nun, in der Schriftsprache, wirklich „erhalten" heißen.

Ich will Sie nicht mit Schwedischem ermüden, darf aber an das schöne Beispiel des *snäll-taget* „Schnellzug" erinnern, der mit Schwedisch *snäll* = „freundlich, nett" nichts zu tun hat, aber natürlich von lexikalischen Einzelfall ausgehend ein neues, produktives Lexem schaffen kann, das dann eifrige Philologen kommender Jahrhunderte unbeirrt zu einer Grundbedeutung der Wurzel zusammenbinden werden.

Es gibt einige weitere, seltene und auch seltsame Fremdwörter aus europäischen Sprachen; besonders die Lektüre des Buchstaben Aleph und Ain zu Beginn bieten im LCD Beispiele, dies weil solche aus dem Lateinischen o.a. herzuleitenden Beispiele eigentümlicherweise öfters den arabischen Artikel *el-* aufweisen: Beispiel *El-Korep* (neben *karap* und *korep*); auch hier ist zu fragen, wie diese Wörter, wenn sie je von *corpus* abzuleiten seien, ins Gǝᶜǝz gekommen sind; ob etwa der arabische Artikel spätere gelehrte Zutat in der inner-äthiopischen Überlieferung sein kann, also nichts über eine arabische Vermittlung aussagt; oder sollte *īl-* Gott gemeint sein (Hokuspokus-Wörter)?

Lexikalische Anbindung nur im ‚Äthiopischen‘

Es folgt der ganze große Bestand von Lehn- und Fremdwörtern aus afrikanischen Sprachen – allerdings beschränkt sich Leslau auf Angaben über das Kuschitische wird mit unter der Angabe *Ethiopic* subsumiert, die also über die genetische semitische Verwandtschaft, die die hamito-semitische umfaßt, und weiterhin, ohne diesen Begriff *expressis verbis* zu verwenden, den äthiopischen Sprachbund, der abgesehen von der genannten genetischen Verwandtschaft seit mindestens 3000 Jahren auf dem äthiopischen Hochland besteht, und dessen sprachliche Phänomene sich des öfteren besser mit den Methoden der Balkonologie als mit denen der historisch-vergleichenden, rekonstruierenden Methode erklären lassen. Vergleiche Ansätze zu solchen Area-Studies etwa bei Appleyard und dessen Beitrag zum gebrochenen Satz cleft sentence im äthiopischen Raum bei den verschiedensten Sprache. Hier ist die Sprachtypologie – wie schon von dem zitierten K.H. Schmidt vertreten – eine Hilfsdisziplin der historischen Sprachwissenschaft.

Ist also nur *Ethiopic* als Vergleich möglich, so handelt es sich bei dem betreffenden Wort um einen Bestandteil dieses Sprachbundes; falls in der Unterrubrik auch *Cushitic* fehlt, so handelt es sich – immer den gegebenen Stand unserer Kenntnis absolut gesetzt – um Sondergut der äthio-semitischen Sprachen, gegenüber den asiatisch-semitischen. Hier überrascht die relativ hohe Eigenständigkeit, die sich in einer doch recht großen Zahl solcher Wörter ausdrückt. Zu bedenken bleibt freilich immer die recht bruchstückhafte Kenntnis vieler semitischer Einzelsprachen, die das hier als äthiopisch-semitisches Sondergut auftauchende Material einmal aufgewiesen haben mögen. Freilich gibt es manche Sonderbestandteile in der Wurzelstruktur, die gerade solches Sondergut begründen.

Auch inhaltlich ist dieses Sondergut einer Untersuchung wert. Es handelt sich um die Begriffe der natürlichen Umwelt, die freilich vom Vorderen Orient abweicht: Jahreszeiten: *Hagay, kerämt*; Gebirgs- und Oberflächenformationen: *Däga, čoqē*, Tiere: *Hobäy* – Affe, Pflanzen (eine große Zahl nicht identifizierter Termini, die in manchem noch Aufklärung in der Untersuchung lebender Begriffe finden kann: *ensete*. Aber auch Ausdrücke für Produkte der menschlichen Tätigkeit sind zu finden: *dabbo* Brot, aus der Landwirtschaft, für Musikinstrumente, Bezeichnungen für Dämonen, etc.

So deutet manches darauf hin, daß die kuschitischen Völker auf vielen Gebieten die Gebenden waren: Untersuchungen der Anthropologie und der Prähistorie, speziell zum Problem der frühen Nahrungsmittelproduktion und des Getreideanbaus und seiner Herkunft, untermauern den sprachlichen Befund.

Neuerdings orientiert sich auch die Forschergruppe um Militarev und Shnirelman in der Frage des Afro-Asiatischen an diesen Ergebnissen; versucht mit einer verfeinerten Methode der Glottochronologie Fragen der Rekonstruktion des Afro-Asiatischen und der „Urheimat" der Afro-Asiaten zu lösen. Doch abgesehen von dieser sehr weiten Perspektive bleibt, wie eigentlich nach der geographischen und natürlichen Umgebung und der Abgrenzung dieser Umgebung gegen andere Länder, in denen Semitensprachen gesprochen werden, zu erwarten war, der Befund der Sonderstellung des äthiopischen Sprachbundes bestehen; über das Lexikon hinaus sind hier natürlich auch in der Sprachentwicklung Fragen der Morphologie und der Syntax mit einzubeziehen; wobei im methodischen Ansatz die einfache Erklärung des Substrats überwunden werden muß. Für das Lexikon bildet LCD eine gute Arbeitsgrundlage; das Hauptproblem bleibt die Erstellung, bzw. der Nachweis der Unmöglichkeit von lautregelrechten Entsprechungen.

Der umfangreichste Block bildet freilich, und das bestätigt ja nun Gəˁəz als semitische Sprache, derjenige im Lexikon, der mit Semitic und Ethiopic zu untermauern ist; er bildet den semitischen Kern des Gəˁəz, „das auf die semitischen Sprachen genauso viel Licht wirft, wie es von ihnen empfängt". Wenn auch dieses gut bezeugte semitische Erbe in vielem schon bekannt ist, so wären doch, wie schon gesagt, manche Gesetzmäßigkeiten des eigenäthiopischen Lautwandels und der Wurzelstruktur (kombinatorischer Lautwandel, Metathesen, Reimwortbildungen, um nur einige anzusprechen) noch in Einzelheiten zu untersuchen.

Dieser semitische Kernbestand bildet die Folie, den Hintergrund, gegen den erst die Sonderstellung des Gəᶜəz zu erkennen möglich war, ähnlich wie in der Dialektgeographie, die für das Äthiopische sicherlich eine größere Bedeutung gewinnen wird – nicht: "each word has its own history", sondern im Gəᶜəz: "many words have a history of their own" – erst die allgemeinen und gültigen Lautgesetze das Sonder- und Einzelschicksal bestimmter Wörter erhellen.

Um auf die Wurzeln zu kommen: nach meiner Schätzung ist etwa die Hälfte der bekannten semitischen Verbwurzeln im Gəᶜəz belegt. Arabisch nach Leslau: 240/320.

So bleibt die schöne Äthiopierin geheimnisvoll – die Familienähnlichkeit mit der herben Beduinin auf der asiatischen Seite des Roten Meeres, mit der eher fülligen Levantinerin am Ufer der Mittelmeeres, ist nicht zu leugnen –, doch die Individualität afrikanischen Kolorits und afrikanischen Blutes, verbunden mit einem Hauch des Okzidents und des fernen Indiens machen ihre Anziehungskraft aus, deren einzelne Züge und biographischen Geschehnisse man wohl zu ergründen versuchen mag; so ist es ein von ihr gehauchter Kuß, wenn man einzelne Wörter deuten kann, eine Etymologie erhellt, einer ihrer Züge bekannt und vertraut wird. Es bleibt auf das Ganze gesehen das unentwirrbare und nicht zu enträtselnde Geheimnis ihres Ursprungs und ihrer Lebenskraft, das uns immer in ihren Bann schlägt und uns dazu bringt, in hingebungsvoller Liebe wieder ein Detail zu erklären, wohl wissend, daß wir damit den Reiz des Unerklärlichen, der fühl- und erlebbaren Schönheit im ganzen nur vermehren.

Schlußbetrachtung

Fassen wir zusammen: Gəᶜəz hat eine reiche, belegte Geschichte. Freilich, die nicht belegte existiert für uns nicht mehr, vielleicht war sie noch reicher als die uns bekannte. Von des Tagen des Hellenismus weitergetragen durch die Schrift, aber auch in einem, für uns erstaunlichen, merkwürdigen Teil weitergetragen in mündlicher Tradition, den wir Schriftgläubige die Tendenz haben, nicht wahrzunehmen, nicht wahrnehmen zu wollen, ungläubig zu belächeln. Dabei sind gerade die Mechanismen der mündlichen Überlieferung wichtig, nicht nur für die Geschichte eines semitischen Nachbaridioms, des Arabischen. Gerade in dieser Frage ergeben sich die Berührungspunkte in der Methode und im Stoffe zu der Afrikanistik allgemein, die ja vorzüglich mit mündlichen Quellen arbeiten muß.

Auf der anderen Seite ist zu sagen, daß die Dame Gəᶜəz eine Sonderstellung in ihrem geographischen Raume einnimmt, wenn man einmal Nordafrika mit seiner arabisch-islamischen und lateinischen Vergangenheit ausschließen will. Aber unsere Erdaufteilung in Kontinente ist ja so selbstverständlich nicht, daß man nicht sagen könnte, Gəᶜəz hat die Sonderstellung in Afrika.

„Last der Vergangenheit und Fesseln des Sprachbaus" nannte ich einmal, sicherlich polemisch überspitzt, einen Vortrag in Bochum, der in überarbeiteter Form noch

der Veröffentlichung harrt. Er galt dem Klassischen Arabisch. Vieles reizte mich zum
Vergleich mit dem Gəˁəz: die genetische Verwandtschaft, eine Schriftsprache, nur
noch als Kultursprache weitergetragen, eine heilige Sprache, wenn auch das Inspira-
tionsverständnis bei Christen und durch die Bibelübersetzung zwangsläufig anders
sein muß. Ich will den ohnedies hinkenden Vergleich nicht ausführen. Aber mir will
scheinen, das Gəˁəz ist luftiger, individueller – vielleicht weil es nie die erdrückende
Pflege von Grammatikern und Sprachwächtern erfahren hat, zugleich aber doch dem
lebendigen Ausdruck von Sprechern anderer Muttersprachen zur Verfügung stand. Es
hat somit das Glück gehabt, das dem Schriftarabischen versagt blieb. Aus einem Stadium relativ lebendiger Entwicklung, etwa zu Beginn des 19. Jhs., mit den Schriftstel-
lern des sogenannten sprachlichen Niedergangs, wurde das Schriftarabische, ironi-
scherweise durch christliche Autoren und Sprachpfleger, wieder in den erstickenden
Zwang einer nicht vollkommenen oder nur mit größter Mühe zu erlernenden
grammatischen Norm zurückgepresst, in der die Form den Ausdruck überwuchert,
zugleich ihre Anwender der wichtigsten Quelle möglicher Entwicklung, ich meine
den lebendigen Ausdruck einer gefühlten Muttersprache, beraubt. Dies hat nun das
Gəˁəz so nicht erfahren: Jede originale Gəˁəz-Schrift, aber auch die Übersetzungen,
tragen einen eigenen Stempel, sind Landschaften und Zeiten zuzuordnen, somit Teile
eines langen, ereignisreichen Weges.

Was nutzt nun diese Archivtätigkeit für eine Sprache, die bald verschwinden
könnte? – Freilich, wenn man sich auf den utilitaristischen Standpunkt stellt, wenig:
auch wenn man anführen könnte, daß das Verständnis des Amharischen und anderer
Semitensprachen Äthiopiens unvollkommen bleibt ohne das Gəˁəz. Doch hilft hier
ein Gedanke von Rilke weiter, der in neuerer Zeit zumindest teilweise eine Bestäti-
gung findet: Was unser Geist der Wirrnis abgewinnt, kommt irgendwann Lebendigem
zugute: Wenn es auch manchmal nur Gedanken sind, sie lösen sich in jenem Blute,
das weiterrinnt.

Mögen sich die Wörter und Geschichte des Gəˁəz in jenem Blute lösen, das le-
bensspendend für Äthiopien weiterrinnt.

Bibliographie

Diakonoff, I. M. and Kogan, L. E.
1996   Addenda et Corrigenda to Hamito Semitic Etymological Dictionary by Orel, V. E. and O. V. Stolbova. *ZDMG* 146: 25-38.

Kropp, M.
1986   Arabisch-äthiopische Übersetzungstechnik am Beispiel der Zena Ayhud (Yosippon) und des Tarikä Wäldä-ʿAmid. *ZDMG.* 136,2 = Festgabe der DMG an die ausländischen Teilnehmer des 32. International Congress of Asian and North African Studies: 314-346.

Littmann, E.
1910-15 *Tales, Customs, Names and Dirges of the Tigre Tribes.* Leiden.

Littmann E. und Höfner, M.
1962   *Wörterbuch der Tigre-Sprache. Tigre-Deutsch-Englisch.* Akademie der Wissenschaften und der Literatur Mainz. Veröffentlichungen der Orientalischen Kommission 11. Wiesbaden.

Militarev, A. and Kogan, L. E.
2000   *Semitic Etymological Dictionary.* Vol.1: Anatanomy of Man and Animals. (*Alter Orient und Altes Testament.* 278,1). Münster.

Orel, V. E. and Stolbova, O. V.
1995   *Hamito Semitic Etymological Dictionary.* Leiden.

Fotografien als historisch-geographische Quellen für Eritrea am Beispiel von Aufnahmen der Deutschen Aksum-Expedition

Alfons Ritler[1]

Eritrea und Nordäthiopien in den Fotografien der Deutschen Aksum-Expedition

Nur wenige Jahrzehnte nach der Erfindung der Fotografie um 1839[2] gehörten portable fotografische Apparate und Entwicklungsverfahren bereits zur Standardausrüstung von Afrikareisenden. Gegen Ende des 19. Jahrhunderts stieg nicht nur die Zahl der Reisenden nach dem Horn von Afrika, sondern auch die Menge der Fotografien zu dieser Region massiv an (vgl. Pankhurst, Gérard 1996: 23). Diese frühen Fotografien sind heute erstklassige, unersetzliche, aber auch notwendigerweise diskutable Quellen für historisch-geographische Analysen zu Eritrea und Äthiopien. Im Rahmen der Deutschen Aksum-Expedition (DAE) von 1906 wurden rund neunhundert Fotografien zu verschiedenen, vorwiegend archäologischen Themen hergestellt. Die Eigenschaften des Mediums Fotografie ermöglichen es, daß viele der archäologischen Fotografien gewissermaßen „automatisch" auch Informationen zu räumlichen Strukturen mitliefern. Im folgenden soll die Bedeutung dieser Fotografien für die historische Geographie bzw. Umweltgeschichte andiskutiert und anhand von zwei Fallbeispielen exemplifiziert werden.

---

1 Geograph und Historiker, Dr. phil.-nat., assoziiertes Mitglied des Centre for Development and Environment (CDE), Geographisches Institut der Universität Bern (Schweiz).
2 Diese Jahreszahl bezieht sich auf die Vorstellung der sog. ‚Daguerreotypie' in Paris, unterschlägt aber die dazu notwendigen Vorarbeiten und älteren Fototechniken wie z.B. die Camera obscura (vgl. Baatz 1997: 10-20).

Die historische Situation am Horn um 1906 und die Umstände des Reisens

Als die Deutsche Aksum-Expedition Ende 1905 Eritrea erreichte, hatten sich die zeitweilig unsicheren politisch-geographischen Strukturen der Region vergleichsweise nur wenig stabilisiert (vgl. Volker-Saad 2004). Italien hatte mit den Käufen von Assab um 1882 und Mitsiwa (Massaua) um 1884/85 (Lill 1987: 216) die Basis für eine koloniale Expansion in Ostafrika gelegt. Nach der berühmten Schlacht von Adwa um 1896, wo die räumliche Expansion der italienischen Kolonialisierung durch das äthiopische Heer gestoppt wurden, waren die Grenzen zwischen der italienischen Kolonie Eritrea und Äthiopien fixiert und wurden bis 1935 nicht mehr angetastet (u.a. Brogini Künzi 2001, Lill 1987: 231, 236, 337ff.). Die eritreische Kolonialverwaltung begann sich nach schwierigen Anfangsjahren administrativ und wirtschaftlich in ihrer relativen kleinen Kolonie nur langsam zu konsolidieren. Verschiedene Verträge mit Äthiopien und anderen Kolonialmächten sicherten die politisch-geographische Situation ab. Nach einer kurzen, wenig erfolgreichen Ausrichtung als Kolonie für italienische Siedlerinnen und Siedler von 1890 bis 1895 wurde die Kolonialpolitik bis in die 1930er Jahre auf Rohstoffexporte konzentriert (Tekeste Negash 1987: 33-37, Bahru Zewde 1991: 85, Volker-Saad 2004). Bis Anfang des 20. Jahrhunderts war die Handelsbilanz Eritreas trotz stark gesteigerten Exporten negativ. Ob Eritrea für die italienische Volkswirtschaft insgesamt überhaupt profitabel war, wird in der Fachwelt kontrovers diskutiert (Tekeste Negash 1987: 39, Yemane Mesghenna 1988: 114, 201ff., vgl. Taddia 1986: 329ff.).

In Äthiopien begann Italien schon kurz nach der Schlacht von Adwa wieder, diesmal auf friedlichem Wege, ein Netz von wirtschaftlichen und politischen Kontaktpunkten aufzubauen (Bahru Zewde 1991: 96-97). Äthiopien seinerseits hatte seit den 1870er Jahren seine feudale Herrschaftsstruktur unter den Kaisern Yohannes IV. (1872-1889) und Menelik II. (1889-1913) immer mehr verfestigt und zentralisiert. Menelik rüstete Äthiopien massiv auf und hatte bereits unter Yohannes IV. begonnen, das Staatsgebiet weit nach Süden zu vergrößern. Äthiopien wurde so zur starken, quasi innerafrikanischen Kolonialmacht, die sich erfolgreich und mit Geschick auch gegen die anderen Kolonisatoren England und Frankreich behauptete (Ibid.: 42-85). Die Beziehungen zwischen Äthiopien und Eritrea bzw. Italien blieben bis 1935 relativ stabil (Ibid.: 150-55).

Die Reise der Deutschen Aksum-Expedition von Mitsiwa (Eritrea) bis nach Aksum in Nordäthiopien 1906 konnte also unter politisch nicht optimalen, im Alltag dennoch recht unproblematischen Rahmenbedingungen stattfinden. Dafür sorgte auf eritreischer Seite der Gouverneur Martini, obwohl der Kolonialverwaltung die rein wissenschaftlichen Ziele der DAE eher suspekt erschienen (Volker-Saad 2004). Auf äthiopischer Seite unterstützte Dajjazmach Gabra-Sellase Barya-Gabr, ein hoher politisch-militärischer Führer in Tigray, auf Geheiß von Menelik die Deutschen (Deutsche Aksum-Expedition 1913: I, v). Dank der Vorarbeit der deutschen Expedition unter

Friedrich Rosen 1904-1905 in Äthiopien (Ibid.: vgl. Rosen 1907, Ritler 2001: 108-109) konnte das Interesse des Kaisers Menelik II. für die äthiopische Geschichte und Kultur geweckt und so gleichzeitig die Unterstützung von höchster Stelle gewonnen werden (Bairu Tafla 1981: 57-60).

Wie bei den meisten Reisen jener Zeit wurden für diese Expedition die trockenen Monate zwischen Oktober und März gewählt, was das Vorhaben sehr erleichterte und viel berechenbarer machte. Gefahren und Verzögerungen durch unpassierbare Flüsse, rutschige Wege und Wasserschäden beim Material konnten so weitgehend ausgeschlossen werden (vgl. Ritler 2001: 78, McCann 1994: 851). Auf der Rückreise Mitte April 1906 machte sich jedoch bereits die Regenzeit mit ersten starken Regenfällen und Gewittern bemerkbar (Deutsche Aksum-Expedition 1913: I, 24).

Der Naturraum und dessen Nutzung

Für das bessere Verständnis der unten folgenden Bildbesprechungen bedarf es einiger Hinweise zu den natürlichen Grundlagen, insbesondere für die Gegend, worauf sich die beiden Fallbeispiele beziehen (südliches Hochland von Eritrea).

Das Hochland von Eritrea und Nordäthiopien bildet der nördliche Ausläufer der plattentektonisch bedingten Dehnungszone in Ostafrika. Die Geologie des Hochlandes ist vorwiegend präkambrisch, um Adi Keyh teilweise auch vulkanisch geprägt. Nur vereinzelt finden sich mesozoische Sedimente aufgeschlossen, so etwa bei Senafe. Quartäre Sedimente sind weitgehend auf die großen Flußtäler begrenzt (Eritrea 1995, Liebi: 1993: 23-24). Die Topographie wird durch eine starke tektonische Stufung im Osten des Hochlands zum Tiefland und Roten Meer hin charakterisiert. Gegen Westen und Nordwesten sind die Übergänge zum Tiefland uneinheitlicher. Das Hochland besteht im Zentrum und Süden aus weitläufigen Ebenen und Beckenlandschaften zwischen rund 1500 bis 3000 Metern über NN, die westlichen und nördlichen Ränder zerfallen teilweise in Tafelberge.

Für das Klima sind die Wechsel von Regen- und Trockenzeit charakteristisch. Die Tiefländer sind semi- bis vollaride Zonen. Die Regen beschränken sich weitgehend auf das Hochland, übersteigen aber auch hier nur gerade im Süden des Hochlandes und um Asmara Niederschlagswerte von 500 oder gar 700 Millimeter pro Jahr (Eritrea 1995). Die Regen fallen, bedingt durch die innertropische Konvergenz sowie Steigungseffekten, weitgehend in der nur kurzen Regenzeit von zwei bis drei Monaten im Sommer und zwar meistens zwischen Juni und September (Eritrea 1995, Hurni 1982: 46-47). Die Niederschläge weisen häufig eine hohe Intensität auf, fallen also in kurzer Zeit in großer Menge. Mit zunehmender Höhe wird die Verdunstung kleiner, bedingt durch die tieferen Temperaturen. Dennoch weist auch das Hochland ein vorwiegend semiarides Klima mit gleichzeitig hoher Niederschlagsvariabilität auf (Eritrea 1995, FAO 1994, zit. in Murtaza 1998: 31, Liebi 1993: 24-25). Die Monatsmittel der Temperaturen differieren im Jahresgang um rund 5 bis 10 °C und liegen allesamt über 10 °C. Die Werte von Asmara (2349 m) schwanken beispielsweise zwischen ca. 14 (Januar) und 18 °C (Mai), jene von Mitsiwa (5 m) zwischen ca. 24 (Dezember) und 34 °C (Juli) (Eritrea 1995).

Durch die differierenden klimatischen und geologischen Bedingungen ergeben sich eine Vielzahl von Bodentypen. Die Böden des vergleichsweise feuchten Hochlandes, welche intensiv genutzt wurden und werden, sind vorwiegend braune Böden, tendieren bei abnehmender Niederschlagsmenge zu sandigen gelben Böden (vgl. Hurni 1986: 9, 26, Liebi 1993: 24). Bereits im 19. Jahrhundert waren diese Böden stark erodiert, insbesondere in Hanglagen. Größere Bodentiefen beschränkten sich bereits im 19. Jahrhundert aufgrund der hohen Erosivität der Niederschläge und der frühen Entwaldung auf flache Gebiete und Tallagen (Liebi 1993: 56-57). Terrassen verschiedener Bauart sind heute als Boden- und Wasserkonservierungsmaßnahmen relativ weit verbreitet und findet man bereits bei geringen Hangneigungen (vgl. Hurni 1986: 26, 30, FAO 1994, zit. in Murtaza 1998: 31). Ob im Hochland Terrassen an der Schwelle zum 20. Jahrhundert tatsächlich inexistent waren (vgl. Taddia 1986: 96), bedürfte einer eingehenderen Überprüfung und wird weiter unten diskutiert (vgl. Fallbeispiel Toconda, Abb. 1). Liebi (1993: 56-58, Anhang III, 29-63) fand keine diesbezüglichen Aussagen in den von ihr ausgewerteten historischen Reiseberichten. Immerhin wird die Existenz vieler Steine in Feldern belegt, welche von den Reisenden des 19. Jahrhunderts jedoch vorwiegend als Einschränkung des Anbaus wahrgenommen wurden. Nur wenige erkannten deren Bedeutung und bewußte Nutzung für die – allerdings beschränkte – Reduktion der Wassererosion (vgl. Yohannes Gebre Michael 1999: 108, Murtaza 1998: 37).

Wie bei den Böden wurde auch die Vegetation durch die Nutzung im Laufe des wohl fünftausend Jahre alten Ackerbaus in diesem Raum vielfältig modifiziert (Murtaza 1998: 45-46) und entsprach bereits im 19. Jahrhundert und vor allem im Hochland längst nicht mehr der von Natur aus möglichen Vegetationsdecke. Im Tiefland sind Halbwüste und Dornsavanne die vorherrschende Vegetation. Dank des besseren Wasserangebotes im Hochland (mehr Niederschlag, geringere Verdunstung) sind ab einer gewissen Höhe über NN auch bzgl. Wasser anspruchsvollere Bäume und Trockenwälder möglich. Spezielle Formationen sind außerdem dank des Feuchteangebotes in Flußniederungen zu beobachten (Liebi 1993: 26).

Das Hochland mit seiner intensiven und ausgedehnten landwirtschaftlichen Nutzung war bereits im 19. Jahrhundert stark entwaldet und wies am ehesten noch in peripheren Lagen Resten von Wald auf, außerdem Buschareale im Stadium der Degradation oder Regeneration und die typischen Haine bei christlichen Kirchen (Liebi 1993: 28-29, 55-56, 69-70). Die – wie im Falle von Äthiopien (vgl. Ritler 1997, 2001, McCann 1997) – herumgereichten hohen Prozentzahlen der Waldfläche um ca. 1900 (angeblich 30 %) und die behauptete katastrophale Entwaldung im 20. Jahrhundert (z.B. Eritrean Agency for Environment 1995, zit. in Murtaza 1998: 31) widersprechen fundamental den Resultaten von Boerma (1999) und Liebi (Ibid.: 62-63, 66). Die vielen Fotografien der DAE lassen diese Zahlen ebenfalls in zweifelhaftem Lichte erscheinen.

Die Landnutzung in Eritrea und Nordäthiopien weist eine naturraumbedingte Streuung von intensivem Ackerbau kombiniert mit Viehwirtschaft im Hochland bis zu extensiver Weidewirtschaft mit teils nomadischer Lebensweise im Tiefland auf. Bewässerungsmaßnahmen können heute in geeigneten Arealen relativ häufig beobachtet werden, scheinen im Hochland jedoch erst im 20. Jahrhundert markant ausgedehnt worden zu sein, was mit der gleichzeitigen starken Bevölkerungszunahme eng verknüpft sein dürfte. Die Bevölkerungszahl soll 1893, am Ende der katastrophalen Rinderpest-Epidemie, rund 191 000 Menschen betragen haben,[3] um 1905 wieder 275 000, um 1952 betrug sie rund 1,031 Millionen und um 2000 rund 4,1 Millionen Menschen (Killion 1998: 343-344, www.worldbank.com). Zu den häufigsten aktuellen Bewässerungsmaßnahmen gehören Ableitungen von Bächen und Flüssen, von denen die meisten jedoch nicht ganzjährig fließen, sowie kleine Staubecken, in denen Wasser aus der Regenzeit noch für einige Wochen in der Trockenzeit aufgehoben werden kann. Wegen der kurzen Regenzeit, den unsicheren und eher geringen Regenfällen werden heute auch in jenen Hochlandregionen Wasserkonservierungsmaßnahmen getroffen, wo die Niederschlagsmenge statistisch für Regenfeldbau ausreicht (Eritrea 1995, Liebi 1993: 54-70, 85, Murtaza 1998: 33-42).

Im Hochland herrscht wie im benachbarten Äthiopien das rund zwei Jahrtausende alte subsistenzorientierte „Ox-Plow-System" vor (McCann 1995, Liebi 1993: 29-32, Murtaza 1998: 34-38, 45-47). Trotz systemischen Unterschieden, die mit den historischen Wanderungen und ethnischen Eigenheiten erklärbar sind, weist dieses Anbausystem einige typische und allen Spielarten gemeinsame Eigenschaften auf: Eine diversifizierte Anbaustruktur mit Getreidearten, Hülsenfrüchten und Gemüse streut die vielfältigen Anbaurisiken.

Der im Vergleich zur Hacke Zeit sparende Pflugbau ist ein zentrales technologisches Charakteristikum. Er bedingt idealerweise zwei ziehende Ochsen und damit eine Rinderzucht, was wiederum Konsequenzen für die Nutzung der Landwirtschaftsflächen nach sich zieht. Nebst bebauten Flächen müssen permanent Weiden, Brachen und nach der Ernte oft auch Ackerflächen dem Vieh zur Nahrungsbeschaffung bereit gestellt werden. Dieses liefert im Gegenzug vielfältige und für den ländlichen Alltag wichtige Produkte wie Milch, Fleisch, Leder etc., außerdem Mist für die Düngung und als Brennholzersatz. Da die Trockenzeit eine starke Einschränkung des Regenfeldbaus bedeutet, die Bodenregeneration in den semiariden Zonen außerdem Brachen nahe legt, ist die Viehwirtschaft ein integrierender Teil eines ausgeklügelten Systems. Nicht zuletzt dank der Mobilität des Viehs half und hilft der viehwirtschaftliche Teil des Systems Umweltkrisen (Dürren, Heuschreckenplagen etc.) abzudämpfen.

Von den in den verschiedenen Gebieten herrschenden komplexen politisch-ökonomischen und sozialen Strukturen sei nur kurz das für die folgenden Ausführungen relevante System der Tigrinerinnen und Tigriner (Tigrinya) im Hochland skizziert:

---

3   Killion (1998: 343-344) bezeichnet diese erste von Italien vorgenommene Schätzung von 1893 als sicherlich zu tief veranschlagt: Es seien nicht alle Gebiete im Westen und Norden erfaßt worden, außerdem sei es sehr wahrscheinlich, daß es wegen der Rinderpest 1888-1892 zu einer vorübergehenden Auswanderung mit nachmaliger Rückkehr vieler Emigrierten gekommen sei. Auch die Zahl von 1905 sei wahrscheinlich zu tief geschätzt.

Das in der Vorkolonialzeit prinzipiell feudalistische System beinhaltete vielfältige Landrechtsformen. Damit waren verschiedene Abgaben und Leistungen für die jeweiligen Herrscher verbunden, welche im „abstrakten Sinne" (Liebi) die eigentlichen Eigentümer des Landes waren. Auf lokaler Ebene hatten die Gemeinden in der Regel jedoch einen hohen Grad an Selbstbestimmung, wie sie mit ihren Ressourcen umgehen wollten. Vererbbare Rechte der Landnutzung in der Herkunftsgemeinde ermöglichten es den betreffenden Familien, das Land dieser Gemeinde im gebührenden Umfang und auch nach längerer Unterbrechung wieder mitzubenutzen. Ein erheblicher Teil des Landes innerhalb einer Gemeinde wurde periodisch, meist gemäß der demographischen Entwicklung neu aufgeteilt, um einen wachsende ungleiche Landverteilung abzumindern. Ein Landeigentum im kapitalistischen Sinne war inexistent. Die periodische Landneuverteilung motivierte kaum, aufwändige anbauverbessernde Maßnahmen einzuführen. Nebst naturbedingten Krisen setzten Kriege, marodierende Heere und invadierende Nachbarvölker eine immer wiederkehrende Herausforderung und Bedrohung des Systems dar (Murtaza 1998: 50-54, Liebi 1993: 42-48, Pankhurst 1966a, 1966b).

Dieses vorkoloniale Anbausystem blieb trotz einer kurzen Phase der kolonialen Enteignungen (wegen den erwarteten italienischen Siedlerinnen und Siedler von 1890 bis 1896) weitgehend intakt. Der größte Teil des enteigneten Landes wurde bis 1907 zurückgegeben, der Alltag und die Organisation der ländlichen Gebiete blieb danach von der Kolonialpolitik wenig beeinflußt (Liebi 1993: 87-88, 95-101, Volker-Saad 2004).

Fotografien als historisch-geographische Quellen

Für das bessere Verständnis umwelthistorischer Strukturen und Prozesse in Eritrea (und anderswo) benötigen wir aussagekräftige historische Quellen. Um gut gesicherte Erkenntnisse zu erhalten, sind wegen der Verschiedenartigkeit der Quellen und Analysemethoden Schwierigkeiten zu überwinden, die manchmal erst disziplinenübergreifend gemeistert werden können. Da wir uns hier auf Fotografien als Quellenart beschränken, sind einige grundsätzliche, quellenkritische Fragen gegenüber alten Fotografien zu stellen.

Fotografien werden bewußt oder zumindest routinemäßig hergestellt. Reisefotografien sollen in jener Zeit meist die Reise, die erreichten Ziele und die vorgefundenen Gegenstände dokumentieren und diese häufig auch einer bestimmten Öffentlichkeit bekannt machen. Diese Fotografien gehören damit in den meisten Fällen zur Kategorie der Überlieferungen (Tradition). Als Überrest kann sie dann betrachtet werden, wenn sie ungewollt der Nachwelt erhalten blieb (z.B. als unabsichtlich nicht entsorgter Abfall).

Jede Fotografie bildet einen bestimmten Gegenstand, eine Situation oder eine Landschaft ab. Der gewählte Bildausschnitt entspricht im Idealfall den Absichten des oder der Fotografierenden. Für die uns speziell interessierenden Landschaftsfotografien existieren jedoch technisch und physikalisch bedingte Grenzen (Bildschärfe, Körnigkeit, Kontrast, Lichtverhältnisse), welche die Auswertungsmöglichkeiten generell und insbesondere ab einer gewissen Distanz deutlich einschränken. Diese kritische Distanz liegt für eine seriöse Auswertung von Bildelementen bei Aufnahmen mit Normalbrennweiten je nach Vorlage bei vielleicht zweihundert bis maximal etwa zweitausend Metern.

Was dargestellt werden soll, wird von gerätetechnischen Kenntnissen und der konkreten Situation (vgl. Tyrrell 1985), von wahrnehmungspsychologischen und ästhetischen und damit soziokulturell bedingten Kriterien wie Normen und Konventionen beschränkt bzw. beeinflußt (Fritzsche 1996: 15, Theye 1985: 25). Außerdem können Fotografien für verschiedene, insbesondere politische Zwecke hergestellt und verwendet respektive instrumentalisiert werden, ob vom Fotografen oder der Fotografin gewollt oder nicht (vgl. Ryan 1995). Die vermeintlich ‚objektive Darstellung der Wirklichkeit' (Fritzsche) ist somit bezüglich ‚Objektivität' als auch bezüglich ‚Wirklichkeit' nicht gegeben, obwohl das Medium Fotografie dies nahelegt und Fotografien (immer noch zu) oft als ‚wahr', ‚wirklichkeitstreu' und ‚objektiv' fehlinterpretiert werden (Ryan 1995: 55, Theye 1985: 5, 24-25).

Der Entscheid, was, wie, wann, warum, wenn überhaupt fotografiert werden soll, kann bei Beherrschung der Technik in der Regel wie beabsichtigt umgesetzt werden. Im Unterschied beispielsweise zu einem Text erfaßt aber eine Fotografie auch meist unvermeidliche oder unbeabsichtigt einfließende Einzelheiten, da die Kamera ohne Selektion alle vorhandenen Lichtreflexe des Bildausschnittes einfängt (Häfeli 1997: 70), soweit die technischen Bedingungen (optische Qualität des Objektivs, Schärfe des Films oder der Filmplatte) dies zulassen. Beim Fotografieren kann mit der Wahl des Ausschnittes, des Bildaufbaus (Vorder-/Hintergrund) und technischer Manipulation (Tiefenschärfe, Belichtungsdauer) die Bildinformation zwar bis zu einem gewissen Grade beeinflußt werden. Aber was einmal auf einem Positiv oder Negativ belichtet ist, konnte vor dem digitalen Zeitalter höchstens noch mittels nachträglicher Bearbeitung bei der Reproduktion im Labor (Helligkeit, Kontraste) oder mittels Retouchieren des Originals oder der Reproduktion manipuliert werden. Die insgesamt wenig beeinflußbare Detailfülle einer Fotografie kommt nun aber der Landschaftsanalyse zugute, da oft geographisch relevante Elemente abgebildet werden, die bei einer schriftlichen Beschreibung derselben Situation mit großer Wahrscheinlichkeit fehlen würden (vgl. Fritzsche 1996: 20). Das Foto von Toconda (Abb. 1) ist ein Beispiel einer solchen Konstellation.

Um die Bildelemente einer Fotografie identifizieren und adäquat einschätzen zu können, müssen die historischen, geographischen und kulturellen Eigenheiten des dokumentierten Ortes sowie die Situation und die Absichten des oder der Fotografierenden möglichst weitgehend bekannt sein, sonst können Bildelemente oft nur phänomenologisch bewältigt werden (vgl. Fritzsche 1996: 16-18, 23-24, Geary 1990, 1995, Steiger 1997: 45-49).

Weiter schränkt der Bildausschnitt die Aussagekraft der Fotografie ein: Was sich außerhalb dieses Bildausschnittes im Moment der Aufnahme befindet, bleibt vollständig ausgeschlossen. Immerhin wurden auf Reisen hie und da mehrere Fotografien in der betreffenden Umgebung oder sogar Panoramaaufnahmen (zwei oder mehrere bewußt aneinander gereihte Bilder) gemacht, was späteren Betrachterinnen und Betrachtern die geographische Einordnung erleichtert und die Aussagemöglichkeiten verbessert. Im Falle der DAE gibt es in der Regel immerhin zwei bis vier Varianten von einem Standort, Panoramaaufnahmen jedoch kaum. Aber auch so können wichtige Einzelheiten unsichtbar bleiben, z. B. Landschaftselemente, die durch die Topographie, Siedlung, Vegetation oder abgebildete Personen verdeckt werden. Schließlich ergibt sich aus der ‚Übersetzung‘, der Beschreibung, Analyse und Interpretation des Bildes in sprachlicher Form (Häfeli 1997: 69), wie sie hier als Methode zur Anwendung kommt, eine Problematik, die mittels einer sorgfältigen Quellenkritik und möglichst eindeutiger, sachlicher und transparenter Sprache (Nippa 1996: 19) angegangen werden muß.

Die Bedeutung historischer Fotografien für die historische Geographie außereuropäischer Räume

Verschiedene Historikerinnen und Historiker haben in jüngerer Zeit darauf hingewiesen, daß Fotografien in der Geschichtswissenschaft bislang kaum als spezifische und ernstzunehmende Quelle wahrgenommen und folglich nur selten eingehend analysiert wurden. Fotografien würden als „suspekt, oder doch ... unseriös" betrachtet und seien bisher nur, wenn überhaupt, zu kommerziellen und illustrativen Zwecken in historischen Werken verwendet worden (Fritzsche 1996: 11-13). Diese Einschätzung gilt prinzipiell auch für die historische Geographie und die Umweltgeschichte. Zwar etablierte sich die wissenschaftliche Verwendung der Fotografie in der Geographie schon vor Jahrzehnten, aber weniger als Quelle im historischen Sinne als vielmehr als möglichst aktuelles Arbeitsmittel (vgl. Hornberger 1973).

Dies alles erstaunt insofern, als mit der geradezu explodierenden Zahl von Fotografien seit Ende des 19. Jahrhunderts heute eine unvorstellbare Menge an Primärquellen existiert, die der historischen Analyse harrt. Zu Eritrea und Äthiopien existieren für die Zeit vor ca. 1930 nach einer konservativen Schätzung weltweit Zehntausende von Fotografien (Ritler 2001: 88). Allein die DAE produzierte rund neunhundert „brauchbare" Negative (Littmann, Krencker 1906: 36). Es ist daran zu erinnern, daß bereits zu Beginn des 20. Jahrhunderts die Fotografie in Europa und USA weit verbreitet war: Hier gab es mehrere hundert fotografische Gesellschaften und Klubs, einige zehntausend Berufsfotografen, und bereits Millionen Amateurfotografinnen und Amateurfotografen, davon allein in Großbritannien um 1905 ungefähr 4 Millionen (Gernsheim 1983: 558-559).

Ethnologinnen und Ethnologen, Anthropologinnen und Anthropologen sowie einige Historikerinnen und Historiker mit außereuropäischen Forschungsschwerpunkten haben in den 1980er Jahren begonnen, die Fotografie als eigenständige Quellengattung zu betrachten und zu benutzen (Theye 1990: 377-378). Sie sichteten und analysierten fotografische Bestände, oft fanden und retteten sie gleichzeitig weitere unbekannte und vermeintlich wertlose Schätze. Zwei grundverschiedene analytische Ansätze wurden und werden dabei praktiziert: „Bilder als Dokumentationen zur Geschichte und Erscheinungsformen fremder Kulturen oder als Materialien zur Geschichte der europäischen Auseinandersetzung mit dem anderen", wobei der erste Ansatz seriöserweise nicht ohne die Auseinandersetzung mit dem zweiten Ansatz auskommt (Geary 1990: 426).

Für die historische Geographie lassen sich aus historischen Fotos von außereuropäischen Regionen viele neue und höchst wünschenswerte Erkenntnisse gewinnen. Denn im Unterschied zu Europa und Nordamerika, wo eine vergleichsweise große Zahl hervorragender und verschiedenartiger Quellen für die historische Geographie existiert, muß im Falle von Eritrea und anderen Ländern der so genannten „Dritten Welt" weitgehend auf Reiseberichte und frühe Fotografien zurückgegriffen werden, weil andere Quellen wie z.B. Karten fehlen, schweigen oder für unsere Fragestellungen keine oder nur wenig brauchbare Aussagen machen.

Die fototechnischen Bedingungen auf Reisen an der Schwelle zum 20. Jahrhundert

Die ältesten heute noch existierenden Fotografien zu Eritrea (und Äthiopien) sind jene, die anläßlich der englischen Expedition unter Napier 1867 und 1868 gemacht wurden (Pankhurst, Gérard 1996: 19-20). Die frühesten Fotografien zu Äthiopien stammen vom britischen Missionar Henry A. Stern, der 1859 das Hochland erreichte. Diese sind verschollen;[4] einige daraus entstandene Gravuren finden sich jedoch unter anderem in Sterns "Wanderings among the Falashas in Abyssinia" (1862). Noch ältere fotografische Dokumente stammen von James Bruce (1769-1773 in Abessinien), der mit einer Camera obscura Vorlagen für diverse Gravuren herstellte (Pankhurst, Gérard 1996: 19). Von Beginn an wurde die Fototechnik jedoch immer weiterentwickelt, verbessert und vereinfacht. Für die Quellenkritik spielen deshalb Kenntnisse über die verwendeten Geräte und Systeme häufig eine wesentliche Rolle. So können die Umstände der Quellenentstehung und deren Eigenschaften besser verstanden werden.

Jegliche Reisefotografie war mit vielfältigen technischen und situativen Problemen konfrontiert, die es zu meistern galt. Auf einer mehrmonatigen oder gar mehrjährigen Reise in ein Land, das keinerlei Infrastrukturen für eine fotografische Verarbeitung aufwies, stellte sich für die Fotografinnen und Fotografen das Problem der rechtzeitigen und technisch einwandfreien Verarbeitung des belichteten Filmmaterials. Setzten Verfahren aus der Mitte des 19. Jahrhunderts eine mobile Dunkelkammerausrüstung voraus, die alles in allem nicht selten über hundert Kilogramm wog (Baatz 1997: 29,

---

4 Donald Crummey vermutet, daß diese Fotografien im 2. Weltkrieg bei einem deutschen Bombenangriff auf London zerstört wurden (mdl. Mitteilung 14.4.1997).

Gernsheim 1983: 199-211, 330-334), befreite „das Trockenplattenverfahren [ab 1880] die Fotografen von der Dunkelkammer vor Ort und die Kamera vom Stativ" (Baatz 1997: 58). Sprichwörtlich erleichtert wurde das Fotografieren dann mit dem Ersatz von Glasplatten durch Rollfilm aus Zelluloid, der 1887 entwickelt und ab 1891 in der revolutionär einfachen Kodak-Kamera verwendet wurde (Baatz 1997: 59, 65-66, Gautrand 1998: 237-239). „Parallel zu den neuen Fotomaterialien konstruierte man bessere Kameratypen, Verschlüsse und Objektive: Insbesondere leichter zu handhabende Kameras, mit denen mehrere Aufnahmen hintereinander gemacht werden konnten, wurden gebaut. Handkameras, bei denen der Fotograf nicht mehr mit Stativ und schwarzem Tuch hantieren mußte, waren jetzt verfügbar. Aber auch die Balgenkameras erfuhren um die Zeit um 1880 Verbesserungen durch erweiterte Verstellmöglichkeiten und eine genauere Justierung der Schärfeeinstellung" (Baatz 1997: 60-61).

Trotz der vielen neuen und handlicheren Fotoapparate konnte man noch lange nach 1900 nicht auf relativ umständliche Kamerasysteme verzichten, sofern man hohe Ansprüche bezüglich Bildqualität und Einsatzmöglichkeiten stellte. Die fotografische Situation setzte einen sorgfältigen Aufbau, die Einrichtung des zu belichtenden Materials, manchmal das Abwarten eines günstigen Augenblickes und eines geeigneten Lichteinfalls voraus. Damit ist angedeutet, daß eine Fotografie einen bewußten Entscheidungsprozeß voraussetzte, der mit dem heutigen ‚Knipsen' wenig zu tun hat.

In den Fotografien der DAE steht bei etwa der Hälfte der Fotografien das archäologische Interesse im Vordergrund. Inwiefern der jeweilige Hintergrund bzw. nichtarchäologische Anteil des Bildausschnittes in die Bildaussage bewußt einfloß, ist nur unvollständig zu beantworten. Sicherlich spielte die räumliche Situation des archäologischen Gegenstandes eine erhebliche Rolle, um diesen in seinem Umfeld zeigen zu können, was Teil der archäologischen Dokumentation darstellt. Aufgrund der Zielsetzung der Expedition dürfte jedoch einer optimalen Abbildung des archäologischen Gegenstandes Priorität eingeräumt worden sein.

Nur in wenigen Reiseberichten und Fotosammlungen finden sich Angaben zur verwendeten Technik und müssen indirekt z.B. über Negativformate und die damals marktgängigen Modelle zu eruieren versucht werden. Der Vorbericht der DAE von 1906 führt nun aber erfreulicherweise die vom mitgereisten Fotografen von Lüpke benutzten Apparate akkurat auf (Littmann, Krencker 1906: 36) und beweist damit, daß sich die Expedition auf die damals modernsten professionellen Geräte stützen konnte (vgl. Baatz 1997: 61-62):

„1)1 Meßbildinstrument mit Pantoskop von 19,5 cm Brennweite und 20x20 cm Plattengröße.
2)1 Balgkamera mit Zeissschem Anastigmat und Plattengröße 13x18 cm.
3)1 Görz-Anschütz-Klappkamera mit ‚Dagor'-Objektiv für 9/12 Platten und Films."

In einer Fußnote wird außerdem vermerkt, daß die verwendeten Platten „fast sämtlich orthochromatische Isolierplatten der Aktiengesellschaft für Anilin-Fabrikation" waren (Littmann, Krencker ibid.).

Methodik der fotografischen Auswertung

In der Ethnologie, Anthropologie, Volkskunde und Kunstgeschichte wurden Verfahren entwickelt, wie aus historischen Fotografien bestimmte Aussagen herausdestilliert werden können. Die methodische Bewältigung von Fotografien zu außereuropäischen Kulturen bleibt aber in mancher Hinsicht noch ungeklärt (u.a. Theye 1990: 378) bzw. eurozentrisch (sinngemäß Nippa [1996]: 18).

Gute Beispiele von geographischen Auswertungen historischer Fotografien sind an einer Hand abzuzählen, wenn wir von diversen Arbeiten mit Fotovergleichen (‚Fotomonitoring' oder ‚Fotorekonstruktionen') absehen, die sich im übrigen erstaunlich selten bei einer ausführlichen Beschreibung und Analyse des Bildinhaltes aufhalten. Eingedenk dieser unbefriedigenden Situation hat Scheidegger (1999) anhand von äthiopischen Landschaften die bislang methodisch und inhaltlich beste mir bekannte Fotorekonstruktion vorgelegt.

Für die hier verwendete Fotoanalyse stammen die wichtigsten methodischen Hilfen und Anregungen von Nippa ([1996]: 10-21), Hofer (1996: 115-117), Hornberger (1973: 25-27) und Scheidegger (1999).

Nippa ([1996]: 22) verweist auf die Detailfülle jeder Fotografie, fordert uns deshalb auf, die Fotografien mit der Lupe nach Details abzusuchen und deren Bedeutung zu befragen, wobei „Nebenüberlieferungen", damit sind alle möglichen Quellen gemeint, welche ein bestimmtes Detail erklären helfen können, zu Rate zu ziehen seien. Dieses „Lesen" in den Fotografien soll möglichst unvoreingenommen geschehen, das Fassen von Bildinformationen in Begriffe „muß die Zuverlässigkeit haben, die ein Lexikon oder ein Wörterbuch besitzt" (Ibid.: 19). Sie warnt gleichzeitig davor, Bildunterschriften als bare Münze zu nehmen, sie „scheinen etwas zu beweisen und erleichtern das Hinsehen" (Ibid.: 18), verleiten aber auch, wichtiges zu übersehen, das uns zu anderen Erkenntnissen führen könnte.

Hofer (1996: 114-117) hat eine ausführliche, systematische „Bildquellenkritik" vorgelegt, die sich an den Standards der Quellenkritik von historischen Texten anlehnt (vgl. Opgenoorth 1997). Diese Systematik wird in den Fallbeispielen zu Eritrea abgekürzt angewendet.

Die Fotografien der DAE

Mit einem eigens mitgereisten Fotografen, Theodor von Lüpke, der mit drei Fotoapparaten über neunhundert Negative herstellte (s.o., Littmann, Krencker 1906: 36) wird klar, daß die Fotografie auf dieser Expedition eine wichtige Rolle für die Dokumentation der verschiedenen Ergebnisse spielte. So gesehen gehorcht diese Expedition den üblichen Standards von ambitionierten Reisen um 1900. Anders als die meisten Reisenden jener Zeit verzichteten die Autoren jedoch auf einen ausführlichen

Reisebericht und konzentrierten sich auf die Darstellung der wissenschaftlichen Ergebnisse (Littmann 1913: I, v, vgl. Bairu Tafla 1981: 57-60). Im Band I (Littmann 1913: I, v) ist auf wenigen Seiten ein lediglich kurzer, aber sehr präziser chronologischer Überblick über die Reise und die Tätigkeiten zu finden. Zu den begangenen Routen gebe es bereits ausreichend gute und detaillierte Reiseberichte, begründen die Autoren dieses Procedere (Ibid.).

Obwohl Abbildungen überwiegend archäologische Stätten und Einzelheiten festhalten, beinhalten oberflächlich geschätzt die Hälfte der Aufnahmen andere Themen: Es finden sich Fotografien zu Siedlungen und Landschaften wie Aden, Mitsiwa, Adwa, Aksum, zu verschiedenen Dörfern und dem eritreischen und nordäthiopischen Hochland, zur Ethnologie, nämlich Personen bei ihren alltäglichen Verrichtungen, ihre Häuser und Geräte. Verschiedene Aufnahmen zeigen kirchliche Personen, Riten und Gegenstände und schließlich auch immer wieder Ansichten vom Reisealltag der Gruppe wie Camps, Zelt-Einrichtungen oder Mitglieder und Helfer der Expedition. Diese Aufnahmen eignen sich nebst der Archäologie selbstredend auch für Auswertungen in den anderen erwähnten oder angedeuteten Disziplinen, wie Ethnologie, Kirchengeschichte, Wirtschafts-, Technik- und Tourismusgeschichte.

Von Lüpke hat beim Fotografieren verschiedene, für die Auswertungen verwendbare Hilfestellungen benutzt. Häufig plazierte er irgendwo im Bild eine Person, meist einen Einheimischen in der typischen ‚Shema‘, einem weißen Baumwollgewand, um die Größenordnung der abgebildeten Elemente zu zeigen. In mehreren Fällen wurden zwei oder drei Fotografien des selben Ortes aus verschiedenen Blickwinkeln gemacht. Dies diente wohl nicht nur dazu, zur Sicherheit eine oder mehrere Varianten des betreffenden Ortes bzw. Gegenstandes zu haben, sondern vielmehr, um die Aussagekraft der fotografischen Dokumentation zu verbessern.

Ansichten von zwei Landschaften des eritreischen Hochlandes

Anhand von zwei aussagekräftigen Fotografien aus dem Bestand der DAE folgen nun exemplarische Bildbesprechungen, welche die Möglichkeiten – und Grenzen – dieser Quellenart skizzieren. Beide stammen aus der Gegend von Adi Keyh, rund sechzig km südöstlich im Hochland auf Höhen von rund 2500 Metern über dem Meer (Übergang der Höhenstufen Weyna Dega und Dega). Die Wahl ergab sich aus dem technisch und historisch-geographisch bedingten Auswertungspotential. Die räumliche Nähe der beiden Fotografien ist für die vorwiegend methodisch orientierte Darstellung irrelevant. Außerdem wäre es so oder so fragwürdig, eine wie auch immer definierte landschaftliche Repräsentativität anstreben zu wollen, da Fotografien nur eine von verschiedenen und eine vorwiegend kleinräumig nutzbare Quellenart darstellt. Schließlich stammen die landschaftlich gut verwertbaren Fotografien fast ausschließlich aus dem südlichen Hochland Eritreas. Und wie bei vielen zeitgenössischen Reisefotografen in Äthiopien ist die Vermutung wohl nicht unangebracht, daß die für das europäische Auge attraktivsten Landschaften abgelichtet wurden.

Das erste Bild (Abb. 1) stammt von der archäologischen Stätte von Toconda und ihrer Umgegend.

Abb. 1   Toconda (Littmann-Foto Nr. 2256.1).

Ortsangaben	Im Tal unterhalb des Dorfes Toconda (Region Kohaito), ca. 4 km S von Adi Keyh (Eritrea), ca. 2400 Meter über NN. (Übergang Weyna Dega/Dega), Blick nach SW
Aufnahmedatum	20. April 1906
Originallegende	Keine, nicht publiziert; zu Bildvariante Bild.-Nr. 2256.2: „Ruine in Tocondo. Blick von Süd-Westen"
Fotograf; Fund-/ Aufbewahrungsort	Th. von Lüpke; Aufbewahrungsort: Brandenburgisches Landesamt für Denkmalpflege und Archäologisches Landesmuseum. Meßbildarchiv, Bild-Nr. 2256.1
Bemerkungen	Einige Angaben und Ergebnisse wurden dank der ähnlichen Bildvariante unter Bild-Nr. 2256.2 (publiziert als Tafel XXII im Bd. II der DAE 1913) präzisierbar
Quellentyp	Tradition
Bildbeschreibung, Interpretation	Der Vordergrund wird von der Ruine von Toconda eingenommen (eine vorne liegende, dahinter vier stehende Säulen), von einigen Steinen (vielleicht Ruinenresten), einem vermutlich eritreischen Reisebegleiter (als Größenvergleich)

sowie einigen niedrigen Büschen. Dahinter senkt sich das Relief um wenige Meter in eine kleinere, quer zum Bild verlaufenden Talebene, die wiederum vereinzelt Buschwerk und einige ebenfalls quer zum Bild verlaufende Terrassenlinien gegen den ansteigenden Hügelzug im Hintergrund aufweist. Genau hinter den stehenden Säulen ist ein breiter, sanft nach vorne auslaufender Schuttkegel zu erkennen, auf dem sich die Mehrheit der Busch- und Baumvegetation des Mittelgrundes befindet.

Nur wenige Einzelheiten des vielleicht hundert bis zweihundert Meter hohen und ein wenig gewellten Hügelzuges im Hintergrund sind noch klar identifizierbar. Die Hänge scheinen einen Boden aufzuweisen, der wohl eher mit fest anstehendem Gestein (mesozoische Sedimente) als mit weiteren Terrassen durchsetzt ist, also unterbrochen und nur wenig tiefgründig ist. Dennoch sind an diesem Hang recht viele einzelstehende Büsche und niedrige Bäume zu sehen. Auf der Bildvariante (2256.2) sind an der höchsten Stelle des Hügelzuges wenige größere Bäume zu erkennen, aufgrund des typischen Standortes möglicherweise eine Kirche mit ihrem obligaten Kirchhain.

Die hier erkennbare, insgesamt karge Vegetation korrespondiert einigermaßen mit der eher kleinen Regenmenge der Gegend (ca. 500 mm). Diese Vegetation könnte durch den hier möglicherweise vorhandenen Karst erklärt werden (in diesem Falle geringe Bodentiefe, starke Versickerung von Bodenwasser). Der Schuttfächer in der Mitte des Bildes weist auf eine lange andauernde Bodenerosion hin. Der offenbar sehr karg bewachsene Hügelzug im Hintergrund dürfte ebenfalls Resultat eines längeren Degradationsprozesses sein. Eine präzisere zeitliche Aussage müßte mit pedologischen Methoden (z.B. C14) angestrebt werden. Physikalisch nicht verwunderlich ist die auf den Schuttkegel konzentrierte Busch- und Baumvegetation: Hier dürfte das Wasserangebot vergleichsweise gut sein, die Bodenbeschaffenheit für den Ackerbau jedoch weniger attraktiv als in der restlichen Talaue.

Terrassen, die es nach der gängigen Literatur noch nicht geben dürfte (s.o.), sind klar identifizierbar und belegen bereits existierende Boden- und Wasserkonservierungsmethoden und damit ein Bewußtsein der Einheimischen für die entsprechende Problematik. Über das Alter dieser Einrichtung kann aufgrund des Bildes nichts gesagt werden. Aufgrund der von den Kolonisatorinnen und Kolonisatoren

| | wenig veränderten Landwirtschaft Eritreas ist äußerst unwahrscheinlich, daß diese Konservierungsmethode hier erst gerade eingeführt worden wäre. |
| Weitere Verweise | - |

Nur rund zehn Kilometer von Toconda hat die DAE dieses leere Staubecken von Kohaito dokumentiert (Abb. 2):

Abb. 2   Kohaito (Littmann-Foto Nr. 2258.1).

Ortsangaben	„Kohaito", ca. 4 km E von Adi Keyh (Eritrea), ca. 2600 Meter über NN (Dega), Blick nach S (?)
Aufnahmedatum	22. oder 23. April 1906
Originallegende	„Östlicher Teil der großen Staumauer in Kohaito und rechtwinklig anschließender Flügelmauer"
Fotograf; Fund-/ Aufbewahrungsort	Th. von Lüpke; Aufbewahrungsort: Brandenburgisches Landesamt für Denkmalpflege und Archäologisches Landesmuseum. Meßbildarchiv, Bild-Nr. 2258.1
Bemerkungen	Einige Angaben und Ergebnisse wurden dank der ähnlichen Bildvariante unter Bild-Nr. 2258.2 (beide als Abb. 308 bzw. 309 publiziert im Bd. I, S. 150 der DAE 1913) und der Kartenskizze S. 149 im selben Band präzisierbar

Quellentyp	Tradition
Bildbeschreibung, Interpretation	Das Bild wird von einem leeren Staubecken mit einer nur noch teilweise intakten Staumauer aus reihenförmig aufgetürmten Steinquadern dominiert. Im Vordergrund fällt das Gelände über eine seitliche Mauer (welche nur in der Bildvariante klar erkennbar ist) rund fünf Meter in das leere, flache und von Steinen übersäte Becken von 55 m Breite (gemäß Kartenskizze). Im Becken, einige Meter vor der Mauer entfernt, steht wiederum ein vermutlich eritreischer Reisebegleiter für den Größenvergleich. Die Länge des Beckens ist zum rechten Bildrand hin etwa gleich der Breite, in Wirklichkeit sicherlich noch einige dutzend Meter länger. Die maximal etwa 5 m hohe Staumauer ist an zwei Stellen rechts und links deutlich durchbrochen, also zerstört. Im Vordergrund ist eine karge Grasvegetation mit wenigen kleinen Büschen zu sehen. Auf dem Damm und dahinter stehen viele Bäume mit Höhen bis zu 10 m. Bis zum Horizont erscheint der Hintergrund als dicht mit Bäumen durchsetztes Grasland, wobei das Gras sehr kurz ist und eher eine Vermutung darstellt, als eine sichtbare Tatsache ist. Die Sichtweite beträgt insgesamt etwa 300 bis 500 m. Außer dem alten Staubecken, welches von Littmann als alt-aksumitisch eingeschätzt wird, fehlen optisch erkennbare Hinweise auf eine alte oder um 1906 existente Landnutzung. Die Fotografie legt (irreführend, s.u.) eine heute extensiv genutzte, kaum bewohnte Gegend nahe. Das sehr kurze oder fast fehlende Gras könnte auf eine Übernutzung durch Viehwirtschaft hindeuten. Ob das Wasserbecken um 1906 noch eine, wenn auch nur sehr bescheidene Funktion hat, ist nicht erkennbar, unter anderem, weil die Aufnahme am Ende der Trockenzeit gemacht wurde.
Weitere Verweise	Gebiet wurde bereits von Schöller (1895) beschrieben, welcher 1894 mit Schweinfurth da war; vgl. auch Kartenskizze, die auf der Kartierung von Schweinfurth basiert (DAE 1913: I, 148-49, Ibid.: 24-25).

Dank der kurzen Reisebeschreibung und Angaben zur Lokalität können die aus der Fotografie gelesenen Ergebnisse noch ergänzt und relativiert werden. Zur Vegetation schrieben Littmann und von Lüpke (Deutsche Aksum-Expedition 1913: I, 24): „Die ganze Hochfläche [von Kohaito] ist von Büschen und Bäumen bewachsen und glich einem Park. Ein Anblick, der in dem baumarmen abessinischen Hochlande dem Auge besonders wohltat." Das bedeutet also, daß hier eine unüblich dichte Baumvegetation anzutreffen war. Auch im nahe gelegene Lager war kein Holzmangel: „Holz war genugsam vorhanden, meist ‚sehedi', aus dessen Harz der Weihrauch gewonnen wird" (Ibid.: I, 25).

Die menschenleere Landschaft stammte daher, daß die Bewohnerinnen und Bewohner zu der Zeit gerade im Tiefland die Winterernte einholten und erst auf die im Hochland bald beginnenden Sommerregen zum Pflügen, Säen und Ernten zurückkehrten (Ibid.: I, 24). Da der Bildausschnitt kein Areal zeigt, das man als Ackerland identifizieren würde, dürften das Ackerland außerhalb des Bildes bzw. durch die Vegetation verdeckt gelegen sein. Für die Landnutzung wird auch klar, daß in diesem Gebiet ein transhumantes System existierte, was in schwierig nutzbaren und Randgebieten der Ökumene häufig anzutreffen ist, fotografisch jedoch wiederum nicht erkennbar wird.

Auf dem Weg zu einer historischen Geographie von Eritrea

Mit diesen beiden Fallbeispielen konnten ohne größeren Aufwand einige Ergebnisse der bekannten Literatur ergänzt oder gar korrigiert werden. Verantwortlich dafür ist unter anderem das Spezifische an Fotografien, daß scheinbar Nebensächliches im Bild mittransportiert wird und für bestimmte Fragestellungen wie jenen der historischen Geographie und Umweltgeschichte von großem Wert sind, mitunter gar kleine Sensationen darstellen können (vgl. z.B. Ritler, Scheidegger 1999). Anderseits sind systemische und nur über längere Beobachtungszeiten eruierbare geographische Zusammenhänge wie z.B. die Organisation der Landnutzung manchmal nur unvollständig oder gar nicht aus Fotografien ablesbar. Erschwerend wirken auch der beschränkte Bildausschnitt und die technischen Eigenschaften bzw. Grenzen des Mediums.

Damit wird klar, daß alte Fotografien für historisch-geographische und umwelthistorische Studien zwar sehr wertvoll sein können, ihre volle Aussagekraft häufig aber erst gemeinsam mit anderen Quellen und den Methoden verschiedener Disziplinen entwickeln. Einer historischen Geographie Eritreas kann mit Hilfe von alten Fotografien demnach ein großer Dienst erwiesen werden. Für sich allein sprechend dürfen diese Quellen jedoch nicht genommen werden.

Bibliographie

Anonymous
1995 *Eritrea – National Map. Scale 1:1,000,000.* Government of the State of Eritrea Asmera, Berne.

Baatz, W.
1997 *Geschichte der Fotografie.* DuMont Schnellkurs. Köln.

Bahru Zewde
1991 *History of Modern Ethiopia, 1855-1974.* London - Athens (Ohio) - Addis Abeba.

Bairu Tafla
1981 Ethiopia and Germany. Cultural, Political and Economic Relations, 1871-1936. *Äthiopische Forschungen 5.* Wiesbaden.

Boerma, P.
1999 *Seeing the Wood for the Trees: Deforestation in the Central Highlands of Eritrea since 1890.* PhD Thesis, Oxford University.

Brognini Künzi, G.
2001 Der Sieg des Negus. Adua, 1. März 1896. In: *S. Förster, M. Pöhlmann, D. Walter, Schlachten der Weltgeschichte. Von Salamis bis Sinai.* München.

Fritzsche, B.
1996 Das Bild als historische Quelle. In: *A. Volk (Hrsg.), Vom Bild zum Text. Die Fotografiebetrachtung als Quelle sozialwissenschaftlicher Erkenntnis.* Zürich: 11-24.

Gautrand, J.-C.
1998 Spontanes Fotografieren. Schnappschüsse und Momentaufnahmen. In: *M. Frizot (Hrsg.), Neue Geschichte der Fotografie.* Köln: 232-241.

Geary, C. M.
1990 Text und Kontext: Zu Fragen der Methodik bei der quellenkritischen Auswertung historischer Fotografien aus Afrika. *Zeitschrift für Kulturaustausch 40,3:* 426-439.

Gernsheim, H.
1983 *Geschichte der Fotografie. Die ersten hundert Jahre.* Propyläen Kunstgeschichte. Frankfurt a.M. - Berlin - Wien.

318   Alfons Ritler

Häfeli, U.
1997   Rekonstruktionen historischer Landschaftsfotografien. Der Beitrag einer neu-
        en Methode zum umweltgeschichtlichen Diskurs. *Traverse 4,2:* 69-83.

Hofer, J.
1996   *Schein und Sein der Fotografie in der Geschichte. Der Umgang mit der Foto-
        grafie als historische Quelle in der Geschichtswissenschaft.* Unveröff. Lizenti-
        atsarbeit, Hist. Inst. Univ. Bern.

Hornberger, T.
1973   Die Fotografie als geographisches Arbeitsmittel. *Der Erdkundeunterricht, 16.*
        Stuttgart.

Hurni, H.
1982   Hochgebirge von Semien B Äthiopien. Vol. II. Klima und Dynamik der Hö-
        henstufung von der letzten Kaltzeit bis zur Gegenwart. *Jahrbuch der Geogra-
        phischen Gesellschaft von Bern, Beiheft 7.* Bern. auch als: *Geographica Ber-
        nensia G13.*
1986   *Soil Conservation in Ethiopia.* Guidelines for Development Agents. Addis
        Abeba.

Killion, T.
1998   Historical Dictionary of Eritrea. *African Historical Dictionaries, No. 75.* Lan-
        ham, Md. - London.

Liebi, F.
1993   *Landnutzungsstruktur und Landschaftsentwicklung im Hochland Eritreas
        1800-1952. Eine Analyse anhand des Modells der ökologischen Handlungs-
        kompetenz.* Unveröff. Lizentiatsarbeit. GIUB. Bern.

Lill, R.
1987[3] *Geschichte Italiens in der Neuzeit.* Lizenzausg. Buchclub ex libris Zürich.
        Zürich.

Littmann, E.
1913   *Deutsche Aksum-Expedition.* Hrsg. von der Generalverwaltung der Königli-
        chen Museen zu Berlin. 4 Bde. Berlin.

Littmann, E. und Krencker, D.
1906   Vorbericht der Deutschen Aksum-Expedition. *Abh. Preuss. Akad. d. Wiss.,
        Phil.-hist. Kl. 1906.* Berlin.

McCann, J. C.
1994   Historical Methods Toward a Landscape History of the Axum Region, 1500-
        1990. In: *H. G. Marcus, New Trends in Ethiopian Studies. Proc. 12^{tb} Int. Conf.
        Eth. Stud., Michigan State Univ., 2 vols. 1994. East Lansing. Vol. 1.:* 846-856.
1995   *People of the Plow: An Agricultural History of Ethiopia, 1800-1990.* Madison -
        London.
1997   The Plow and the Forest. Narratives of Deforestation in Ethiopia. 1840-1992.
        Environmental Hist. 2,2: 138-159.

Murtaza, N.
1998   *The Pillage of Sustainability in Eritrea, 1600s-1990s. Rural Communities and
        the Creeping Shadows of Hegemony.* Westport (Conn.) - London.

Nippa, A.
[1996] *Lesen in alten Fotografien aus Baalbek.* Zürich.

Opgenoorth, E.
1997^5 *Einführung in das Studium der neueren Geschichte.* UTB 1553. Paderborn,
        München, Wien, Zürich.

Pankhurst, R.
1966a   Some Factors Depressing the Standard of Living of Peasants in Traditional
        Ethiopia. *J. Eth. Stud. 4,2:* 45-98.
1966b   State and Land in Ethiopian History. *Monographs in Ethiopian Land Tenure,
        3.* Institute of Ethiopian Studies. Addis Ababa.

Pankhurst, R. and Gerard, D.
1996   *Ethiopia Photographed. Historic Photographs of the Country and Its People
        Taken between 1867 and 1935.* London - New York.

Ritler, A.
1997   Land Use, Forests and the Landscape of Ethiopia, 1699-1865. An Enquiry into
        the Historical Geography of Central-Northern Ethiopia. *Soil Conservation
        Research Report 38.* Bern, Addis Abeba.
2001   *Wald, Landnutzung und Landschaft im zentralen und nördlichen Äthiopien
        1865-1930.* Diss. phil. Universität Bern. Unveröff. Dissertation Geogr. Inst.
        Univ. Bern.

Ritler, A. und Scheidegger, D.
1999   Landschaftswandel in Äthiopien anhand historischer Fotografien. In: *Roost
        Vischer, L., Mayor, A., Henrichsen, D., (Hrgs.), Brücken und Grenzen – Pas-
        sages et frontières. Werkschau Afriakstudien – Le forum suisse des africanistes
        2. Afrikanische Studien, Bd. 13.* Hamburg: 260-278.

Rosen, Felix
1907   *Eine deutsche Gesandtschaft in Abessinien.* Leipzig.

Ryan, J. R.
1995   Imperial Landscapes: Photography, Geography and British Overseas Explora-
        tion, 1858-1872. In: *Bell, M., Butlin, R. Heffernan, M. (eds.), Geography and
        Imperialism., 1820-1940. Studies in Imperialism.* Manchester: 53-79.

Scheidegger, D.
1999   *Äthiopien rekonstruiert. Landschafts-, Landnutzungs- und Walddynamik im
        Hochland von Äthiopien zwischen 1930 und 1998 anhand von Photoverglei-
        chen.* Unveröff. Lizentiatsarbeit Geogr. Inst. Univ. Bern. (Bern.)

Schöller, M.
1895   *Mitteilungen über meine Reise in der Colonia Eritrea.* Berlin.

Steiger, R.
1997   To see or not to see. Randbedingungen zur Verwendung von historischen
        Fotografien in der Ethnologie. In: *Museumskommission der Schweizerischen
        Ethnologischen Gesellschaft (Hrsg.), 1997: L'objectif subjectif... – Das subjek-
        tive Objektiv. Sammlungen historisch-ethnographischer Fotografien in der
        Schweiz. Ethnologica Helvetica 20.* Bern: 45-53.

Stern, H. A.
1862   (repr. 1968): *Wanderings among the Falashas in Abyssinia; together with a
        Description of the Country and its Various Inhabitants.* London.

Taddia, I.
1986   *L'Eritrea-Colonia 1890-1952: Paesaggi, strutture, uomini del Colonialismo.*
        Milano.

Tekeste Negash
1987   *Italian Colonialism in Eritrea, 1882-1941. Policies, Praxis and Impact.* PhD
        Thesis University of Uppsala. Uppsala.

Theye, T. (Hrsg.)
1985   Optische Trophäen. Vom Holzschnitt zum Foto-Album: Eine Bildgeschichte
        der Wilden. In: *Wir und die Wilden. Einblicke in eine kannibalische Bezie-
        hung.* Reinbek: 18-95.
1990   Vorwort [Zu den Kongreßaufsätzen: „Über die Wichtigkeit der Bewahrung
        photographischer Kulturerzeugnisse"]. *Zeitschrift für Kulturaustausch 40, 3:*
        375-380.

Tyrrell, J. G.
1985   Observations of Environment and Vegetation by Early European Travellers in East Africa. *Geogr. Ann., ser. B, 67(1):* 29-34.

Volker-Saad, K.
2004   *Die politische Situation Eritreas und Tigrays zur Zeit der Aksum-Expedition (1905-1906).* In vorliegendem Band.

Yemane Mesghenna
1988   *Italian Colonialism: A Case Study of Eritrea, 1869-1934. Motive, Praxis and Result.* PhD Thesis University of Lund. Lund.

Yohannes Gebre Mikael
1999   The Use, Maintenance and Developmet of Soil and Water Conservation Measures by Small-Scale Farming Households in Different Agroecological Zones of Northern Shewa and Southern Wello, Ethiopia. Soil Conservation Research Programme Ethiopia, *Research Report 44.* Addis Abeba - Bern.

www.worldbank.com/data/countrydata, Stand 7.2.2002

Historical Sound Recordings from Ethiopia on Wax Cylinders

Susanne Ziegler

Introduction

The Berlin Phonogramm-Archiv, today part of the Ethnologisches Museum in Berlin, (former Museum fur Völkerkunde) houses some of the earliest sound documents of the world, that were collected with a phonograph on wax cylinders between 1893 and 1954. Due to the war and post-war politics, 90% of the famous wax cylinder collections were hardly accessible after the end of the Second World War and they were returned to the Museum of Ethnography as late as 1991. Since 1998 an ambitious project has been established with the aim to make the valuable historical recordings known and available to the world again. The early wax cylinder collections received the honour of being entered in the UNESCO register "Memory of the World" in 1999.[1]

The aim of this paper is to present the oldest sound documents that were recorded for the Berlin Phonogramm-Archiv at the Horn of Africa, in Abyssinia at the beginning of the 20th century. My intention here is to present a survey of the collections in their historical context, which is independent from a musicological analysis or a re-study carried out by specialists on Ethiopian music.[2]

The Berlin Phonogramm-Archiv was founded by Carl Stumpf (1848-1936), professor of psychology at the Berlin University, and directed from 1905-1933 by Erich Moritz von Hornbostel (1877-1935). This institution was closely linked with the Museum of Ethnography and incorporated into the Academic sphere in Berlin. In addition, the majority of the academically trained researchers were members of the interdisciplinary Society „Berliner Gesellschaft für Anthropologie, Ethnologie und Urgeschichte", founded in 1869. Felix von Luschan, director at the „Königliches Museum für Völkerkunde in Berlin" at that time, was enthused about the new phonographic technique and propagated the phonograph by his own recordings during excavations in Sendschirli (Zencirli, Turkey) in 1902. In his booklet „Anleitung für ethnographische Beobachtungen und Sammlungen in Afrika und Oceanien" of 1904 we find a strong call for collecting phonographic recordings. Besides a detailed

---

1 For more information on the history and holdings of the Berlin Phonogramm-Archiv see Simon 2000 and Ziegler 2000, 2001, 2002.
2 Timkehet Teffera, a specialist in Ethiopian music, has recently presented transcriptions and an analysis of the Kaschke collection (Teffera 2002).

description of how to handle the phonograph, recommendations are also made as to what should be recorded and what should be asked. These guidelines were obviously distributed to all scholars, missionaries, officers, and volunteers who were interested in being of services to the Archive. In a short demonstration at the Phonogramm-Archiv these persons were introduced into the technique before going into the field.

Survey

Among the more than 16,700 original wax cylinders a total of 124 stem from Abyssinia. They were recorded in different areas of Abyssinia at different times by different collectors:

Collection		Year	Amount
Felix Rosen	(Deutsche Gesandtschaft)	1905	46 cylinders
Erich Kaschke	(Aksum-Expedition)	1906	37 cylinders
Fritz Weiss	(Legationsrat)	1921-24	35 cylinders
Max Grühl	(Nil-Rudolfsee-Kaffa-Exp.)	1926	7 cylinders

This paper is concentrating on the collections of Felix Rosen, which will be discussed briefly, and focus on phonographic recordings of the German Aksum-Expedition carried out by Erich Kaschke.[3]

According to the reports of Rosen (1907) and Littmann (1913) the wax cylinders recorded in Abyssinia were given to the Museum of Ethnography as part of the ethnographical objects, the museum handed them down to the Psychological Institute of Berlin University. The primary source for the phonographic collections is the Berlin Phonogramm-Archiv, at the time of the recordings part of the Psychological Institute of Berlin University, today incorporated into the Museum of Ethnology in Berlin-Dahlem. The Phonogramm-Archiv houses the wax cylinders, together with a so called "Journal" – a list of the recordings – and the correspondence of the Phonogramm-Archiv. In addition, in the Museum of Ethnology one can still find part of the ethnographical objects as well as the respective explanatory correspondence.

Technique

The phonograph was invented by the American Thomas A. Edison in 1877 and used for ethnographic field recordings first in the United States in 1890. This machine was

---

3   During the conference some musical examples were demonstrated. A choice of recordings from both collections will be published on the forthcoming CD.

easy to carry, easy to handle and allowed recording and reproducing immediately. According to Felix von Luschan (1904) every ethnographer was asked to take a phonograph and a couple of wax cylinders on field research. Unfortunately, the soft wax originals were easily destroyed when played repeatedly. Thanks to von Hornhostel's activities the Berlin Phonogramm-Archiv became renown throughout the world by providing copies through galvanization, and many collectors sent their original cylinders to have copies made. However, the original wax cylinder is preserved only in few cases, as is the case with recordings of language. Within our project we have to produce new wax copies from more than 14,000 galvanos and to transfer them to digital sound carriers. By April 2002 we transferred more than 5500 cylinders to digital format, including the four collections from Abyssinia. They are nearly completely preserved; only broken, mouldy or scratched cylinders are missing.

Usually we have one recording in several copies in the archive, at least the original or a copper-negative (galvano) and one copy.

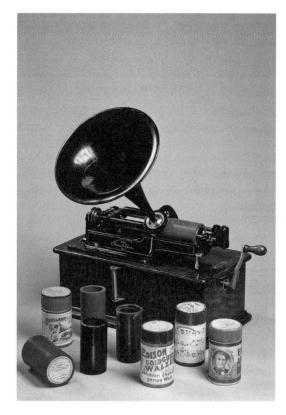

Fig. 1   Edison Home Phonograph and cylinders. Reference: Phonogramm-Archiv, Ethnologisches Museum Berlin.

1. The Rosen collection 1905

In March 1905 an official imperial German delegation was sent to Ethiopia. Leader of the delegation was the diplomat Friedrich Rosen, who requested that his brother Felix, professor of botany at Breslau University and interested in anthropology and ethnography also be included in the group. The Rudolf-Virchow-Stiftung provided 1500 German Marks for ethnographic research and acquiring ethnographical objects for the Museum of Ethnography, among them 46 wax cylinders with phonographic

recordings. The expedition began in Addis Abeba and followed the route Godjam –
Tanasee – Semien – Aksum – Adua – Massaua. Four boxes with objects, collected in
Ethiopia, arrived in Breslau much later in July 1905. Parts of the objects were given to
Berlin, parts to a museum in Stuttgart. In August 1905 Rosen came to Berlin and together with Bernhard Ankermann, assistant curator of the African collections, compiled an inventory of all objects, which included also a list of phonographic recordings. In his letter of 16.10.05 Rosen informed von Hornbostel, the director of the
Phonogramm-Archiv, that the collection of phonographic recordings was to he found
in the museum. At the same time Rosen explained, that due to the physical strain and
the manifold tasks he was unable to make as many recordings as he had originally
intended. In addition, he remarked that "the texts ... are charming; the music from all
ethnic groups we visited was very poor and primitive. Only one song is well-sound-
ing" (Letter of Rosen to von Hornbostel, 16.10.1905, cf. Appendix 1). At the end of
December 1905 the museum sent the phonographic recordings to the Psychological
Institute, with the request for galvanoplastic copies of the cylinders and a reimburse-
ment for the phonographic equipment. The collection of 46 wax cylinders was inventoried there (Inv. no. 108- 153). Today one cylinder (no. 27) is missing; all the others
have survived and are available in digital format.

While the recordings themselves present music, the supplementary documentation, the so called "Journal" supplies further information on the recorded music and
the performer (Table 1).

From the documentation it becomes clear that mostly songs have been recorded:
War songs, courting songs, girls' songs, mourning songs, songs of praise and even a
welcome song for Minister Rosen, sung by the Somali chief Scheual-Abdi (cyl. 17).
The text of this song, together with a photograph was published in Rosen 1907: 110.
The songs were performed by men as well as women. In one of his letters Rosen
mentioned that song texts were translated by his brother, some of which are published in Rosen 1907. Unfortunately no musical instruments were recorded, which is
probably due to the conviction that the music in Ethiopia is poor and primitive; however, perhaps technical difficulties were also a reason.

Irrespective of the sound quality and the lack of basic information about the performers, it should be emphasised that these are indeed the oldest recordings from
Ethiopia. Their intrinsic value will become even more apparent when the texts and
the music will be available.

2. The Kaschke collection 1906

From the introduction to Littmann's publication we have learned that Stabsarzt Dr.
Erich Kaschke took part in the Aksum-expedition as staff physician, and was also
responsible for ethnographical, zoological and phonographic collections: „Kaschke
leistete der Expedition und den Abessiniern ärztliche Hilfe, machte ethnologische
und zoologische Sammlungen und phonographische Aufnahmen von Gesängen in
tigrinischer, amharischer und arabischer Sprache sowie von Proben abessinischer
Musik" (Littmann 1913: 6). We may assume that before leaving Germany he was made

Table 1   Original documentation of the collection "Rosen 1905" (1st page).
Reference: Phonogramm-Archiv, Ethnologisches Museum Berlin.

acquainted with procedures of ethnographic collecting and phonographic recording
by von Luschan himself. Obviously Kaschke was also supplied with Luschan's booklet of recommendations. In a letter of March 12th to von Luschan he reports that he has
already made 30 recordings, and according to the "Printed Recommendation" tried to
answer all questions together with Professor Littmann. In the same letter Kaschke
noted that he had made photos of the performers („... Ihre Musikstücke habe ich
phonographisch aufgenommen und sie, wie verschiedene andere meiner
phonographischen Modelle photographieren lassen" (cf. Appendix 2)). In the official
report ethnological studies are mentioned only once: For the week February 12th–17th
we can read „Ethnologische Studien: Dr. Kaschke hat bereits eine Sammlung von
Speeren, Schilden und Gegenständen aller Art angelegt; ferner macht er
phonographische Aufnahmen von Kriegsliedern, Hochzeitsliedern, von einem
mohammedanischen Gebete, das von Kindern arabisch gesungen wurde, von einem
Posaunenkonzerte u.a.m." (Littmann 1913: 11). More detailed information on the
content of the cylinders can be gained from the notes on the cylinder boxes and the
announcements on the cylinders. Accordingly cyl. 1–6 and 37 were recorded on January 19th, cyl. 7–14 on February 6th, cyl. 15 and 16 on February 7th, cyl. 17–20 on February 11th cyl. 21–28 on March 7th, cyl. 29–31 on March 15th, cyl. 32–34 on March 27th,
and cyl. 35 and 36 on April 1st. By comparing these dates with the diary (Littmann
1913: 3ff.) one may find out the occasion and possibly time and place of the recordings. In addition, the photos taken by Kaschke at different recording sessions can
help to provide a visual impression of Kaschke's recording activities.[4]

Upon the return of the expedition in Berlin all ethnographic material was given to
the Museum of Ethnography, including objects, photos, and wax cylinders.[5] The wax
cylinders, together with documentation and 11 sheets with Abyssinian texts were
given to the Psychological Institute of the University in July 1906. Hornbostel wrote
on July 23rd: "We confirm that we received 37 Abyssinian phonograms recorded by
Dr. Kaschke; the recordings are excellent and all wax cylinders in good condition ..."
(cf. Appendix 3). From this statement it is clear that Hombostel was eager to listen to
the recordings before they were copied. Hornbostel's impatience possibly caused a
loss in the sound quality of the cylinders. Kaschke's wax cylinders were inventoried
in the Phonogramm-Archiv (Inv. numbers 367–403). By October 1906 von Luschan
asked Stumpf about the reproduction of 6 cylinder recordings on request by Dr.
Kaschke and the Museum, but received the answer that due to lack of funds nothing
had been done yet. The archive was always short of money, and especially galvanization was extremely expensive. There is no evidence when the galvanization was actually carried out.

---

4   Only part of the photos taken by Kaschke during the Aksum expedition were inventoried in
the Museum für Völkerkunde (cf. the inventory list of photos in E 1106/06). They disappeared during the Second World War. Meanwhile the whole collection has been found and will
be published by Steffen Wenig.

5   A complete list of all objects given to the museum is to be found in E 1160/06.

Since then the entire collection comprising 37 cylinders has been galvanized and is available today in digital format. The documentation is rudimentary, but an additional list provides some information. Most of the texts are available in Amharic script, which is handwritten, but obviously not by an Abyssinian scholar. In his letter of March 12th, 1906 Kaschke wrote to von Luschan that he would discuss his recordings with the Italian Resident in Adua, Capitano-medico Dr. Mozzetti who had spent 15 years in Ethiopia. Other remarks are namely due to Aleka Taje, an Abyssinian scholar who spent two years in Germany (Voigt 2001). Therefore it is not clear whether the remarks and handwritten texts are due to Littmann himself, Dr. Mozzetti, Aleka Taje, or to a performer, translator or guide (Table 2).

According to von Luschan's recommendation-booklet the collector was asked to announce the song briefly and to blow the pitch pipe (435 Hz) for adjusting the speed. The phonograph allows speed-changing within a range from 100 up to 250 rpm, so the pitch pipe indicates the right speed. On almost every cylinder one can listen to the military voice of Kaschke announcing the recording, the words clearly pronounced and disjointed, for example on cyl. 2: „Zweite Aufnahme in Axum, 19. Januar 1906", followed by the pitch pipe. A cylinder recording lasts normally about 2 ½ minutes.

The cylinder recordings of Dr. Kaschke present a variety of genres, love songs, dance songs, war songs, battle songs, hunters' songs, and wedding songs. Some song titles are roughly translated, obviously not by a German, but an English speaking person. When evaluating the recordings, one must differentiate: some recordings are most valuable historical documents; others present examples of the different genres and styles of Abyssinian music. However, the sound quality in most recordings does not correspond to the historical documentary value: it is not optimal for listening purposes.

To the first group we may assign cylinder no. 5, a song composed for the reception of diplomat Rosen and performed then; it is accompanied by trumpets and performed by the singer with a bowed instrument which is not namely mentioned in the documentation, but was in fact a *masinqo*. Unfortunately the trumpets are very loud, and the singer hardly audible; the string instrument *masinqo* cannot be identified at all. The bard (in Abyssinian *azmari*) with the *masinqo* was obviously recorded a second time, separately and of better quality. On cyl. no. 6 the *masinqo* is at least audible during the interludes. Additional remarks explain „der Barde reist von Ort zu Ort, wie auch ein christlicher Chor existiert, der an verschiedenen Orten bei Festen singt. Musikalischen Unterricht erteilen nur die Priester".

Fig. 2 Photo of the Barde; from: Littmann 1913: Abb. 6.

A photo of a bard is to be found in Littmann 1913: Abb. 6 (cf. Fig. 2).

Abessinische Phonogramme, aufgenommen von Stabsarzt Dr.Kaschke
Axum 10.I.06 - 1.IV.06

Jw. 4.°

Kal 4.

Kal 4.

404/-k.

367

1. Kriegslied „Ahai. gume" = Hol Dich der Geier. Ein Vorsänger und
   Chor von ca. 10 Knaben (Phot.)

368

2. Volkslied. Knabe mit Chor.(Erregt stets Freude und bei einer
   Stelle Gelächter.)

369

3. Gesang-Solo, dazwischen Chor.

370
371

4. Solo, Chor mit Händeklatschen.

5. Trompeten. Sänger mit Streichinstrument. 2. Empf. v. Rosen komp.

372

6. Barde mit Streichinstrumenten.   u. vorgetr.

373
374
375

7. Hochzeitslied, vorsänger, Chor, Pauke.(Berufschor. Tanzbewegungen.)
   Dies.
8. Hochzeitslied. Vorsänger, Chor, Pauke, Händeklatschen, Trillern.

9. Vorsänger (Knabe), Chor, Pauke und Händeklatschen.

376

10. Vorsänger, Chor, Pauke.

377
378

11. Vorsänger, Chor, Pauke, Händeklatschen, Trillern.

12. Vorsänger, Chor, Pauke, Händeklatschen.

379

13. Vorsänger, Chor ; mohamedanische Schüler . Sehr bekannte
    Koransure. (Phot.)

380

14.   do.   Noch bekannter wie No.13.

381

15. Schlachtgesang (Phot.)

382

16. Schlachtgesang. „König Johannes gegen die Aegypter" ges.v.
    Lidsch (Prinz) Tefferi.

383

17. Lied (sehr beliebt--) Solo (Soldat) /mit Chor?/

384
385°

18. Liebeslied /Forts.v.17/

19. Jägerlied.. Ich kille Loewen, Elephanten etc.(mit einem Kioker)
    Askari?

386

20. Ein Lidsch singt ein Lied, das er in der Schule gehört hat.

387
388

21. Ein Knabe singt ein Liebeslied. (Sehr bekannt und typisch)

22. Tanzlied. Sänger macht Juchzer und Tanzbewegungen. (Erregt
    Heiterkeit) /amharisch (traurig) A.T./

389
390
391

23. „Ich kille alles, Löwen etc." (erregt viel Freude) Gesprochen.

24. „Ich kille alle Leute, Araber, Allen". (Gesprochen).. /amharisch/

25. Tanzlied. Askari. (erregt viel Heiterkeit) Von einem Soldaten
    gesungen. /tigrisch/

392

26. Jäger-oder Soldatenlied „Ich kille alles".

Table 2   Original documentation of the collection "Kaschke 1906" and additional remarks
(3 pages). Reference: Phonogramm-Archiv, Ethnologisches Museum Berlin.

Raschke

Ju.
a
343
344   Kat. N°
395   *nach.K.*

27. Assalitsch, amharisches Mädchen. Wenn der Mann aus dem Krieg
    kommt, und alles getötet hat, singen die Mädchen so.

28.   do. Also for kill.

29.   do. For kill, wenn ein big man einen Elephanten
    gekillt hat und zurückkkehrt zur Begrüssung. (Sehr bekanntes Lied)

396   30.   do. For kill.   " Aja marigawa" - „Honig von der

397   31. (Fortsetz.v.30)   Blüte d.Gawabaumes"

398   32. Askari des Lidsch Tefferi.

399   33.   do.

400   34.   do.

401   35.   Flöte.Indur. (Kein guter Spieler)

402   36. Flöte. Indur. (Guter Spieler,) Das Oktavieren ist beabsichtigt
        (männl. u.weibl.Stimme)/

403   37. wie 1. Knabe (Vorsänger) und Chor))

V

Zu den abessinischen Phonogrammen   v.Dr.Kaschke.

Bemerkungen v.Dr.Kaschke.

ad 5) Der Barde reist von Ort zu Ort, wie auch ein christli-
        cher Chor existiert, der an verschiedenen Orten bei Festen
        singt. Musikalischen Unterricht erteilen nur die Priester.

ad 8) Das Trillern wird eigentlich nur von Frauen ausgeführt, die
        sonst als besonderer Chor abseits stehen.

ad 16) Vornehme, stets Jäger, lernen in der Familie,diese rezi-
        tativartigen Heldenerzählungen neben den religiösen Ge-
        sängen in der Schule.

ad 24) Es ist eine Schande, sich selbst so zu rühmen, wenn man
        die Taten nicht wirklich vollbracht hat.

ad 35) Der Hirte sitzt bei seiner Herde und bläst die Flöte.

Bemerkungen von Aleka Taje.

ad 27) Komm, komm Du Tapferer (Giftvoller),
        Komm, komm Du Schöner,
        Komm, komm Du guter Schütze!

Jeder Azmari (fahrender Sänger) erfindet neue Worte zu den alten
Melodieen (Sēm*a) Es gibt sehr viele Melodieen. Auch neue Melodieen werden gemacht. Zu den Baganā (10 sait.Leyer) mag es
300 verschiedene Melodieen geben. Priester singen Teile der
Bibel; der Sängerchor fällt ein. 3 Blasinstrumente sind im
Gebrauch: Indur, eine kleine 5löchrige Flöte; Imbilta, eine
grosse Flöte und Malhat, eine Art Horn.

In der Liste durch /   / gekennzeichnet.

The text is given along with the documentation and translated as follows (Tables 3, 4 and 5):

20

Table 3   Transcription of cyl. no. 5 „Barde mit masinqo" by Timkehet Teffera.

№ 124

ንደ ይ፡መንፆ፡ ንደ ይ፡መንፆም፡ጠሬም፡ማይፋሬ፡
ዮሬፆ፡ማይመሬሰው፡ጠርበሬ፡ሸይጬ፡ሸንጉሬት፡ቆንጋኝ፡

№ 5

ጀሬመን፡ይግሬው፡ ይግሬት፡መፆም፡ማይ ወሬስ፡
ከደዜት፡ጀምሬ፡ሸሰከ፡ሰሰፆን፡ ይሬስ፡
ንደመ፡ንደመ፡ ና፡ ና፡ ፅ ፋይ ፆም፡ ያሰነ፡ነበሬ፡ፋ ኋሬ፡
የኋስ፡በደሐይ፡መወጬ፡ነው፡የጻ ወጠ፡ንጬሠ፡
ጀሬመን፡መማሬን፡ሸያይሬ፡ንኋሠ፡
ክርኋ፡ሸይይሰም፡ወይ፡የጥንት፡የዒስ፡
ንጉሠ፡ማግሰኝ፡የሰኋፆን፡ሰጬ፡

№ 6

ሸዝሰበ፡ ይሰኝ፡ይቀመንፆ፡ጣፆፋ፡በሬይ፡ ይ ይሬብነፆ፡
ሸ ነመን፡በገሬ፡ ይ ተጠፆ፡ነሬ ይ ው፡በፆኝ፡ ይ ፆኝ እነቅ፡
ንፋስ፡በሰይ፡ ይ ይሬብነፆ፡ማን፡የመፆማሰት፡ሰው፡ሸሰነ፡
ሸ ኋስ፡መሬት፡ ሸጬህ፡ሸሬሬ፡ሸ ፆማጠ ይ፡የሬት፡
የሰመይ፡ እ ንደት፡ ሬህ፡ ጀሬመን፡በህሬ ሸሬ ጠ፡ወይ፡
ኤሬ፡ ነ ተ ይ፡ሸንጋሰ ው፡ ክወሬ ኋ፡ ማኝ ታ፡
ክሸ ን ማሬ ዝ፡ወፈ ኋ፡ ክሰው፡ ጋሬ፡ ጸ ጠ፡የሰኝ፡
በሰቀሰ ው፡ መማ ጬ፡ ይ ሬ ታ ፆ፡ በሰ ኝ፡በሸ ኋሬ፡ ክሬ፡ ይ ሬ ታ ፆ፡

Table 4   Original handwirtten text of cyl. nos. 4-6.
    Reference: Phonogramm-Archiv, Ethnologisches Museum Berlin.

Nr. 5

---

(1) ጀርመን:ደግነው:ደግነት:መቸም:ማይወረስ:
(2) ከዳዊት:ጀምሮ:እስከ:ሰሎሞን:ድረስ:
(3) ባደሙ:ገደሙ:ና:ና:ቀድሞም:ይለነ:ነበር:ፍካሬ: (4) የሱስ:
በጸሐይ:መውጪ (l. መውጫ):ነው:የሚመጣ:ንጉሥ:
(5) ጀርመን:መጣልን:እያዳረ:ንጉሥ:
(6) ከርሱ:አይዶለም:የጥንት:ቀሚስ:
(7) ንጉሥ:ምንልክ:የሰለሞን:ልጅ::

(1) Ğärmän dägg(ə)-näw. Dägənnätu mäčäm mayəwwåṛräs.
(2) Kä-Dawit ğämməro əskä Sälomom d(ə)räs
(3) badämu gädämu (?)[1] 'Na, na!' ḳädmo-mm yəlänä[2] näbbär fəkkare (4) Yäsus.
    Bä-ṣähay mäwča näw yämmiwåṭa nəgus.
(5) Ğärmän mäṭṭallən əyyaddärä nəgus.
(6) Kä-rsu aydolläm wäy yä-ṭənt ḳämis.
(7) Nəgus Mənələk yä-Sälåmon ləğ.

„ (1) Deutsches ist gut. Diese Güte kann nicht (von uns) ererbt sein.
(2) Denn[3] angefangen von Dawid bis Salomo
(3) seine Heiligkeit, seine Heiligkeit,[4] pflegte uns in alten Zeiten das Buch der Prophezei-
    ung Jesu[5] 'Komm, komm!' zu sagen.
(4) Im Westen (eig. Ausgang der Sonne) ist es, daß der König (heraus)kommt.
(5) Es ist (nun) - im Laufe der Zeit - ein deutscher König zu uns gekommen.
(6) Ist nicht von ihm das Ehrengewand von früher?
(7) Der König Menelikist Salomons Sohns."

Table 5   Text in original script and translation by Rainer Voigt: cf. the following chapter
           (Amharisches Lied).

Another song which is due the greatest attention is cylinder 16, performed by Lidsch (Prince) Tefferi. His song is entitled "Emperor Johannes against the Egyptians". The following remarks explain: „Vornehme, stets Jäger, lernen in der Familie diese rezitativartigen Heldenerzählungen neben den religiösen Gesängen in der Schule". It is well known that one Lidsch Tefferi later became Emperor Haile Sellasie. Unfortunately it is not mentioned in Littmann's diary that Prince Tefferi was visiting the German expedition or that he was recorded on a phonograph. Thus, we can not be sure to have a very early historical recording of Emperor Haile Selassie. The recording itself is merely a recitation than a song and the text is as follows (Table 6):

Table 6   Original text of cylinder no. 16. A translation into German is not yet available.

A second group of recordings comprise all those recordings which are of musico-logical value. An extraordinary example is cylinder no 5, the song of the bard. Besides a *masinqo* which is in fact very difficult to discover among the loud trumpets (*imbilta*). Another indigenous musical instrument that has been recorded is the flute (*induri*) (cyl. 35 and 36) (cf. Fig. 3). For cyl. 35 we find the additional remarks by Kaschke „Der Hirte sitzt bei seiner Herde und bläst die Flöte", and the commentary by Aleka Taje: /not a good player/. According to Taje the player of no. 36 was a good player who was able to differentiate the male and female voice by overblowing at the octave.

Fig. 3   Photo of the flute player.
           Reference: Brandenburgisches Landesamt für Denk-
           malpflege und Archäologisches Museum Neg. Nr.
           220.17.

Surprisingly no church music or Christian songs were recorded, but a few scores from the Koran (cylinders 13, 14), the text of which also available in Arabic handwritten script. However, after reading Littmann's diary we realise that the relationship between the expedition participants and the priests at the church was not favourable, and possibly no one in the church was willing to be recorded on the phonograph.

From Littmann's introduction we learn that Dr. Kaschke died in 1910. In connection with the wax cylinder catalogue of the Berlin Phonogramm-Archiv (in preparation) extensive research has been undertaken to compile biographies of the collectors. Erich Fritz Otto Kaschke was born 1873 in Berlin.[6] After a short military service he studied medicine and continued his military service in 1897, first as assistant, and later as staff physician. During his service among the German troops in Cameroon (1900-1901) he was affected with tropical diseases, came back to Germany and continued as a military physician in Berlin. In September 1905 he became a member of the „Kaiser-Wilhelms-Akademie für das militärärztliche Bildungswesen" and was appointed in November to accompany the official scientific expedition to Abyssinia. From 1907 onwards he suffered from tropical diseases which finally caused his untimely death in 1910. From Kaschke's biography thus it becomes clear why the correspondence with the Phonogramm-Archiv interrupted, and also explains the missing information on ethnographical objects at the museum as well as in Littmann's publication.

On the other hand one also wonders why there is not one single article by the director of the Phonogramm-Archiv, Erich M. von Hornbostel, devoted to Abyssinian music. Usually Hornbostel transcribed and analyzed the music that had been recorded by others. Though an "armchair ethnomusicologist" he is regarded as the founder of the university subject "Comparative Musicology" or "Ethnomusicology" as it is called today (cf. Ziegler 2001). Since there is no single transcription and hint to one of the Kaschke cylinder recordings in Hornbostel's articles and papers, one may assume, that the cylinders have been galvanized only later.[7]

General observations

When dealing with the early wax cylinder recordings we must bear in mind that most of the collectors were anthropologists, ethnographers, linguists, missionaries, archaeologists etc. This is also the case with the early Ethiopian recordings: Felix Rosen was a biologist, Erich Kaschke staff physician. It was assumed that natural scientists could make good recordings, since they had experience with all sorts of technical instruments. In most cases the researchers going on fieldwork were officially requested be at the Phonogramm-Archiv's services, but only few of them were really interested in

---

6   According to the research at the Military Archive in Freiburg i.Br. (Personalakte des Versorgungsamtes V Berlin, Sign. Pers 6/13410) carried out by Ingrid Bertleff, Freiburg.
7   Further information about Erich M. von Hornbostel and the Berlin Phonogramm-Archiv may be found in Ziegler 1998.

music. Probably all of them were aware of the importance of having a phonograph –
a recording machine – in their baggage. So they normally used it not only for musico-
logical research, but also for memorable events. The music they were asked to record
was quite different from European music. Thus, even if collectors were interested in
music and enthusiastic when they set off on expedition, they were most likely disappointed when they heard the actual music in the field, which was then described as
primitive and not fascinating at all.

In most cases the collector could operate the recording machine more or less, but
he had no idea about the kind of music to expect and what kind of music was worth
recording. Therefore the collectors recorded whatever they met on their way, not
being able to differentiate between typical music and non-typical, a good or a poor
performer, traditional or not. It is only by chance that we can find one or the other
example that is not only a valuable historical sound document, but also represents a
musical culture in general.

The phonographic recordings of the German Aksum-Expedition are unique historical sound documents, yet they do not present a complete picture of Abyssinian music of a hundred years ago. They can only be regarded as occasional glimpses, as
accidentally preserved minutes from the past, as parts of a puzzle where most other
parts are missing.

Future perspectives

In the course of our project a list of all collections has been published in 1995 and
again in 2000 (Ziegler 1995; 2000). The lists include information such as the name of
the collector, the region and year of the recordings, the size of the collection and
whether documentation is available or not. Since then we have gathered much more
information. A catalogue of all wax cylinder collections, including the documentation
and photos as well as short biographies of the ca. 200 collectors, is in preparation
(Ziegler forthcoming). In addition, it is our aim to produce the best recordings in a
series of CDs as soon as possible and to collaborate with the institutions involved. A
CD with a choice of the early recordings from Abyssinia (Rosen 1905; Kaschke 1906)
is in preparation, including transcriptions, song texts and photos, and a comprehensive commentary.

Despite all limitations and critical observations, these early wax cylinder recordings represent the earliest recordings of Abyssinian music.[8] In Ethiopia today they
could very well serve for comparative ethnohistorical studies carried out by specialists. Safeguarding and preserving these invaluable recordings is important not only
for archival purposes, but even more for the people of Ethiopia themselves.

---

8   Another early collection of wax cylinder recordings has been located in Sweden. This col-
    lection, recorded by the Swedish missionary Richard Sundström comprises 30 cylinders
    from about 1912. Information thanks to Mathis Boström, Svensk Visarkiv, Stockholm, April
    2002.

Bibliography

Littmann, E.
1913   *Deutsche Aksum-Expedition.* Herausgegeben von der Generalverwaltung der Königlichen Museen zu Berlin. Bd. I: Reisebericht der Expedition, Topographie und Geschichte Abessiniens. Berlin.

Luschan, F. von
1904   *Anleitung für ethnographische Beobachtungen und Sammlungen in Afrika und Ozeanien.* Königl. Museum für Völkerkunde in Berlin. 3. Aufl. L. Musik.

Rosen, F.
1907   *Eine deutsche Gesandtschaft in Abessinien.* Leipzig.

Simon, A. (Hg./Ed.)
2000   *Das Berliner Phonogramm-Archiv 1900-2000/The Berlin Phonogramm-Archiv 1900-2000.* Sammlungen der traditionellen Musik der Welt/Collections of Traditional Music of the World. Berlin.

Teffera, T.
2002   *Historische Tonaufnahmen aus Axum – Äthiopien: Sammlung Kaschke 1906.* Bd. 1: Darstellungen, Bd. 2: Anlagen. Manuskript im Phonogramm-Archiv Berlin.

Voigt, R.
2003   Äthiopistik in Berlin: das Wirken von Eugen Mittwoch und Aläqa Tayyä. In: *Voigt, R. (Hrsg.), Die äthiopischen Studien im 20. Jahrhundert/Ethiopian Studies in the Twentieth Century: Akten der internationalen äthiopischen Tagung,* Berlin Juli 2000, Berlin: 103-121.

Ziegler, S.
1995   Die Walzensammlungen des ehemaligen Berliner Phonogramm-Archivs – Erste Bestandsaufnahme nach der Rückkehr der Sammlungen 1991. *Baessler-Archiv N.F. XLIII/1:* 1-34.
1998   Erich M. von Hornbostel und das Berliner Phonogramm-Archiv. In: *Klotz, S. (Hrsg.), Vom tönenden Wirbel menschlichen Tuns. Erich M. von Hornbostel als Gestaltpsychologe, Archivar und Musikwissenschaftler,* Berlin: 146-168.
2000   Das Walzenprojekt zur Rettung der größten Sammlung alter Klangdokumente von traditioneller Musik aus aller Welt – Walzen und Schellackplatten des Berliner Phonogramm-Archivs. In: *Simon, A. (Hrsg.), Das Berliner Phonogramm-Archiv – Sammlungen der traditionellen Musik der Welt* (zweisprachig dt./engl.), Berlin: 189-202 und Liste der Walzensammlungen des Berliner Phonogramm-Archivs. Ebenda. S. 228-237.

2001   Die Sammlungen von Edisonzylindern im Berliner Phonogramm-
               Archiv. *Systematische Musikwissenschaft 7, 3:* 223-242.
2002   The Berlin Wax Cylinder Project – Recent Achievements and Aims.
               In: *Berlin, G. and Simon, A. (eds.), Music Archiving in the World.*
               Proceedings of the Conference on the Occasion of the 100th anniver-
               sary of the Berlin Phonogramm-Archiv, Berlin: 163-172.
forthcoming   Katalog der Edisonwalzen des Berliner Phonogramm-Archivs.

Sources

Ethnologisches Museum [Museum für Völkerkunde]

I/MV 732/ E 2002/04 and E 828/05 Erwerbung ethnologischer Gegenstände aus Afrika
I B 32
I/MV 737/E 688/06 and E 1160/06 Erwerbung ethnologischer Gegenstände aus Afrika
I B 37

Korrespondenz Kaschke im Phonogramm-Archiv, Ethnologisches Museum Berlin

Korrespondenz Rosen im Phonogramm-Archiv, Ethnologisches Museum Berlin

Appendix 1: Brief von Felix Rosen an von Hornbostel

(Quelle: Korrespondenzakten Rosen - Phonogramm-Archiv, Ethnologisches Museum Berlin)

Breslau IX
Marienstr. 4
16 Oct. 1905

Sehr geehrter Herr Doctor,

verzeihen Sie, daß ich Ihnen nicht schon längst Mitteilung über die Phonogramme gemacht habe; ich ersehe erst aus Ihrem werten Brief, daß Sie darüber nicht – wie ich angenommen hatte – von den Herren im Museum f. Völkerkunde informiert worden sind. Dort habe ich nämlich die Phonogramme mit allen andren aus dem Rudolf Virchow-Fonds erworbenen Gegenstände deponiert. Die Abwesenheit Prof. von Luschan's erklärt wohl, daß man Ihnen keine Mitteilung gemacht hat. Mein Journal liegt ebenfalls dort.
Viel Interessantes werden Sie, fürchte ich, unter den Aufnahmen nicht finden. Die Texte, deren mein Bruder einige aufgezeichnet und übersetzt hat, sind reizvoll, die Musik fand ich bei allen besuchten Völkern sehr ärmlich und gleich niedrigstehend. Wohllautend ist nur das nubische Liebeslied „Brief an Hassan".
Unsere forcierten Märsche und meine vielfachen, zeitraubenden Aufgaben erschwerten mir die Arbeit des Aufnehmens; der Apparat selbst functionierte sehr mäßig, da er das Schütteln beim Maultiertransport schlecht vertrug.
In der Hoffnung, Sie bei meinem nächsten Besuch in Berlin aufsuchen zu können um Ihnen eventuell noch Auskünfte zu geben, und mit der Bitte um Empfehlungen an Herrn Geheimrat Stumpf bin ich

Ihr sehr ergebener

Felix Rosen

Appendix 2: Brief Kaschke an von Luschan

(Quelle: Erwerbungsakten Afrika, Ethnologisches Museum Berlin, I/MV 737 E 688/06)

Aksum, den 12. März 1906

Sehr geehrter Herr Professor!

Gestatten Sie mir, Ihnen den Empfang der Schreiben vom 6., 7., 8. und 9. Dezember 1905 zu bestätigen, die ich erst hier erhielt.
Den Phonographen habe ich fleißig gebraucht und ca. 30 Aufnahmen gemacht, von denen ich hoffe, daß Sie Ihre Zufriedenheit finden werden; auch die übrigen Walzen werde ich bespielt mitbringen.
...
Selbstverständlich werde ich mir die größte Mühe geben Ihre Wünsche zu erfüllen.
Das Ausfüllen Ihrer gedruckten „Anleitung" besorge ich mit Professor Littmann zusammen.
Wir werden uns zur Beantwortung der von hier aus nicht zu erledigenden Punkte mit dem italienischen Residenten in Adua, Capitano-medico Dr. Mozzetti, welcher 15 Jahre lang in Abessinien gelebt hat, in Verbindung setzen.
...
Die außerordentliche Liebenswürdigkeit und Hilfsbereitschaft sowohl der italienischen Kolonialregierung als auch der abessinischen Behörden, wenn man so sagen darf, kontrastiert erheblich gegen die Fremdenfeindlichkeit der Aksumiten, welche bereits einmal unsretwegen die Sturmglocke geläutet haben. Wenn der Dedanatsih [?] (Gouverneur) Aksum verläßt, werden wir voraussichtlich vorher unsre sieben Sachen gepackt haben müssen, da dann der von der weltlichen Macht niedergehaltene gegen uns und die „Regierung" genährte Groll zur Explosion kommen dürfte.
...
Zum Schluß erlaube ich mir ein Bild beizulegen, welches eine Musikbande darstellt, die in der Zeit vor Fasten, als hier Jedermann feierte [?], ihr Wesen trieb. Ihre Musikstücke habe ich phonographisch aufgenommen u. sie, wie verschiedene andere meiner phonographischen Modelle photographieren lassen.
Indem ich für die gütigen Wünsche für unsere Reise meinen besten Dank sage, bin ich, hochverehrter Herr Professor, Ihr ergebenster

Stabsarzt Dr. Kaschke

Appendix 3: Brief von Hornbostel an von Luschan

(Quelle: Erwerbungsakten Afrika, Ethnologisches Museum, I/MV 737/E 1160/06)

Psychologisches Institut der Universität
Berlin, N.W.7, den 23.7.1906
Dorotheenstrasse 95/96 III.

An die Direktion des k. Museums für Völkerkunde, z.H. Herrn Prof. Dr. v. Luschan
Hier.

Hochgeehrter Herr Professor!

Wir bestätigen mit bestem Dank den Empfang der 37 abessynischen Phonogramme des Herrn Dr. Kaschke; die Aufnahmen sind ausgezeichnet und die Walzen sämtlich in tadellosem Zustand. Für weitere Weisungen erwarten wir den Besuch des Herrn Dr. K., bitten aber, Herrn Dr. K. darauf aufmerksam zu machen, dass das Institut Ende dieser Woche geschlossen wird.
...
Mit vorzüglicher Hochachtung
ergebenst

v. Hornbostel

Ein amharisches Lied zu Ehren des Deutschen Kaisers aus der Sammlung Kaschke

Rainer Voigt

Während seiner Teilnahme an der *Deutschen Aksum-Expedition* (1905/6) unter Leitung von Enno Littmann[1] fertigte Dr. Erich Kaschke 1906 in Aksum eine Reihe von Walzenaufnahmen an, die heute im *Ethnologischen Museum* (früher *Museum für Völkerkunde*) in Berlin verwahrt sind. Zu weiteren Informationen zu den Walzenaufnahmen siehe den voranstehenden Beitrag von Frau Dr. S. Ziegler, die mir dankenswerterweise den amharischen Text zur Veröffentlichung zur Verfügung gestellt hat.[2]

Bei dem hier vorgestellten Lied Nummer 5 aus der Sammlung der „Abessinischen Phonogramme", die von Kaschke im Frühjahr 1906 aufgenommen wurden, handelt es sich um ein Loblied auf den Deutschen Kaiser.

(1) ጀርመን፡ደግነው፡ደግነቱ፡መቾም፡ማይወረስ፡

(2) ከዳዊት፡ጀምሮ፡እስከ፡ሰለሞን፡ድረስ፡

(3) ገዳሙ፡ገዳሙ፡ና፡ና፡ቀድሞም፡ይለነ፡ነበር፡ፍካሬ፡ (4) የሱስ፡ በጸሐይ፡መውጫ፡ነው፡የሚወጣ፡ንጉሥ፡

(5) ጀርመን፡መጣልን፡እያደረ፡ንጉሥ፡

(6) ከርሱ፡አይዶለም፡ወይ፡የጠንት፡ቀሚስ፡

(7) ንጉሥ፡ምንልክ፡የሰለሞን፡ልጅ፡፡

(1) *Ğärmän dägg(ə)-näw. Däggənnätu mäčäm mayəwwårräs.*

(2) *Kä-Dawit ğämməro əskä Sälåmon d(ə)räs*

(3) *„gädamu gädamu, na na!' ḳädmo-mm yəlänä-näbbär Fəkkare* (4) *Yäsus. Bä-ṣähay mäwça nåw yämmiwåṭa nəgus.*

(5) *Ğärmän mäṭṭallən əyyaddärä nəgus.*

(6) *Kä-rsu aydolläm wäy yä-ṭənt ḳämis*

(7) *nəgus Mənələk yä-Sälåmon ləğ.*

---

1 Zu Enno Littmann s. meinen Beitrag in vorliegendem Band.

2 Ohne eine vorliegende zeitgenössische Niederschrift des Textes durch einen Äthiopier ließe sich aus der phonographischen Aufnahme der vollständige Text kaum rekonstruieren.

‚(1) Deutsches (Deutschland) ist gut. Diese Güte kann nicht ererbt sein.
(2) Denn angefangen von David bis Salomo,
(3) ‚Wohlan, wohlan! Komm, komm!' pflegte uns in alten Zeiten das Buch der Prophezeiung Jesu zu sagen.
(4) Im Osten (eig. Aufgang der Sonne) ist es, daß der König (heraus)kommt.
(5) Es ist (nun) – im Laufe der Zeit – ein deutscher König zu uns gekommen.
(6) Ist nicht das Ehrengewand von früher von ihm,
(7) dem König Menilek, Salomos Sohn?'

In dem Text sind einige sprachliche Besonderheiten festzuhalten, auf die an anderer
Stelle näher eingegangen werden soll.

Die bisher veröffentlichten amharischen bzw. altamharischen Kaiserlieder stellen
die orale Ergänzung zu den wenigen in Handschriften erhaltenen Zeugnisse der altamharischen Literatur dar. Die Gattung der fast ausschließlich mündlich überlieferten
amharischen Kaiserlieder ist nur wenig bezeugt. Einen Teil der Lieder, die in einer –
um 1600 entstandenen – Handschrift der Bodleiana erhalten sind, edierte und übersetzte Franz Praetorius in seiner *Amharischen Sprache* (1878/79: 499-502). Eine text-
kritische Ausgabe (mit Vergleich der beiden Versionen) der insgesamt zwölf Lieder,
jedoch ohne Übersetzung („in molti luoghi di queste canzoni è oscuro"), hat Ignazio
Guidi (1889: 53-66) vorgelegt. Von Enno Littmann stammt die deutsche Übersetzung
1914 (*Die altamharischen Kaiserlieder* 1914) und – die Ergebnisse zusammenfassend
– sein *Altamharisches Glossar* (1944). Mit vorliegendem Loblied läßt sich nun das
schmale Corpus der amharischen Kaiserlieder etwas erweitern.

Der Deutsche und Äthiopische Kaiser

Vergegenwärtigen wir uns die Situation 1906 in Aksum. Aus dem fernen Deutschland
sind Männer mit vielen Helfern und Gerätschaften gekommen. Sie werden am 12.
Januar 1906 vor der Stadt vom Däǧǧazmač Gäbrä-Səllase mit seinem Gefolge („einem
gewaltigen Zug von Kriegern und Posaunenbläsern") empfangen. Der Däǧǧazmač,
der in der Folge den erfolgreichen Verlauf der Kampagne in Aksum gegen den Widerstand der Priester und der Einheimischen ermöglicht hat, „begrüßte uns freundlich
und hieß uns im Namen seines Kaisers willkommen. Darauf ritten wir zusammen bis
zur Stadt."

Am nächsten Morgen wurden sie feierlich und mit großem Prunk vom Däǧǧazmač
im Kirchenbezirk von Aksum empfangen. Um die Zustimmung der Einheimischen zu
gewinnen, wird man ihnen sicherlich auch über den Freundschaftsvertrag und die
Freundschaft zwischen dem Deutschen Kaiser Wilhelm (*Gärmän nəgus* ‚deutscher
König') und dem äthiopischen Kaiser Menilek (*nəgus Mənələk*) berichtet haben, die ja
beide in unserem Lied erwähnt werden.

Zu *dägg* ‚gut' und *däggənnät* ‚Güte'

Statt einen Vergleich mit furchteinflößenden Tieren (wie dem Löwen) oder Erscheinungen (wie dem Feuer) anzustellen, wird von den persönlichen Qualitäten des Kaisers die Güte (*dägg* und *däggənnät*) erwähnt. Dies steht im Gegensatz zu der in Kaiserliedern oft geschilderten Stärke und Rücksichtslosigkeit des Kaisers und dem
Schrecken, den er hervorruft. Vgl. die Aussage: *əndi'at tastädänäggəṣ* ‚Wie sehr er-
regst du Schrecken!' (Guidi 1889: 54; Littmann 1914: 10).

Die Prophezeiung

Die genannte Schrift *Fəkkare Iyyäsus* ‚Erklärung/Auslegung Jesu' ist eine eschato-
logisch-apokalyptische altäthiopische Schrift, die im frühen 15. Jh. entstanden ist. Der
genaue Titel lautet *Fəkkare Iyyäsus wä-tənbit zä-täsə'ələwwo arda'ihu* ‚Die Erklärung
und Prophezeiung Jesus, als seine Schüler ihn befragten' (Vajnberg 1908: 1, Zä-
Mänfäs-Ḳəddus: *Ḥatäta mänafəst* 1970/71: 285). Dort prophezeit Jesus das Kommen
eines guten Herrschers mit Namen Theodor (äth. *Tewodros*). Im Synaxar wird am 29.
säne des Königs *Tewodros nəgusä Ityoṗya wäldä Dawit* ‚Theodor, König von Äthiopien, Sohn Dawits' gedacht (*Mäṣəḥafä sənkəssar* 1998/89).

David

David wird in den altamharischen Kaiserliedern verschiedentlich (insgesamt neun-
mal) erwähnt (s. Littmann 1944: 503). Sechsmal kommt *anbäsa Dawit* ‚Löwe Davids'
vor. Wichtig ist die Stelle, wo Kaiser Aṣnaf Sägäd (d.i. *Gälawdewos* ‚Claudius') von
Gott auf den Stuhl Davids gesetzt wird (Guidi 1889: 65; Littmann 1914: 32):
> *bi-yanägsəh*[3] *Ǝgzi'abəher*   ‚wenn Gott zum König dich einsetzt
> *bä-Dawit mänbär*   auf Davids Thron'
Es wird also eine historische Kontinuität von David und Salomo bis zum Deutschen
und Äthiopischen Kaiser gezogen.

---

3   Geschrieben *biyanägsək*.

Der König erscheint im Osten

Wie die Sonne im Osten aufgeht, so erscheint auch der König im Osten. In einem der Kaiserlieder wendet sich der Kaiser bei seinem Kommen gegen Westen (Guidi 1889: 55; Littmann 1914: 10). Von daher kann der Kaiser direkt mit der Sonne verglichen werden.

Das Ehrengewand

Das Ehrengewand, das der Deutsche Kaiser trägt, hat er von früher (*yä-ṭəni*), d.i. von Menilek I., dem Sohn Salomos (*yä-Sälåmon ləǧ*). Die Erwähnung von Menilek I. zielt sowohl auf die Tradition als auch auf den damals regierenden Kaiser Menilek II.

Menilek

In dem Lied wird der Deutsche Kaiser sowohl als Verheißung des *Fəkkare Iyyäsus* als auch in Kontinuität von David und Salomo gesehen. Da der Deutsche Kaiser in Wirklichkeit nicht der Herrscher Äthiopiens ist, ist es nötig, am Anfang und am Ende des Liedes einen Bezug zum gegenwärtigen Kaiser herzustellen. In einigen Kaiserliedern wird nämlich der Kaiser am Anfang und am Ende genannt. In vorliegendem Lied erscheinen David und sein Sohn Salomo, der Vater von Menilek I., in der zweiten Zeile und Menilek, Salomos Sohn, in der letzten Zeile.

Mit der Erwähnung Davids und Menileks und der besonderen Betonung der salomonischen Linie wird vorliegendes Lied auf den Deutschen Kaiser auch zu einem Loblied auf den regierenden Kaiser Menilek II.[4]

Zum Reim

Von den sieben Zeilen sechs auf Vokal + s (dreimal -*us*, zweimal -*äs* und einmal -*is*).

---

4   Eine ausführlichere Behandlung des Kaiserliedes soll in *Aethiopica* erscheinen.

Bibliographie

Anonymus
1973/74 *Fəkkare 'Iyyäsus wä-tənbitä näbiyat*. Addis Abäba 1966 a.m.
1998/89 *Mäṣaḥafä sənkəssar əm-lədätä ∃gzi'ənä Iyyäsus Krəstos*. Asmära 1991.

Basset, R.
1909   *Apocryphes éthiopiens*, vol. XI. *Fekkâré Iyasous*. Paris.

Crummey, D.
1971   The violence of Tewodros. *Journal of Ethiopian Studies*, 9, 2: 107-125.

Dässəṭa Täklä-Wäld:
1970   *Addis yamarəñña mäzgäbä-ḳalat*. Addis Abäba 1962 a.m.

Guidi, I.
1889   Le canzoni geez-amariña in onore di Re Abissini. *Rendiconti della Reale Accademia dei Lincei, cl. di scienze morali, stor. e filol., vol. V*: 53-66.
1932   *Storia della letteratura etiopica*. Rom.

Kane, T. L.
1990   *Amharic-English dictionary*. Wiesbaden.

Littmann, E.
1907   Geschichte der äthiopischen Literatur. *Geschichte der christlichen Literaturen des Orients*. Leipzig: 185-270, 277-281.
1914   *Die Altamharischen Kaiserlieder*. Straßburg.
1944   Altamharisches Glossar. *Rivista degli studi orientali 20*: 473-505.
1947   Verbesserungen zu meinem Altamharischen Glossar. *Rivista degli studi orientali 22 : 46*.

Littmann, E. unter Mitwirkung von T. von Lüpke
1913   *Reisebericht der Expedition – Topographie und Geschichte Aksums*. (Deutsche Aksum-Expedition, 1), Berlin.

Praetorius, F.
1878/79 *Die amharische Sprache*. Halle.

Rosen, F.
1907   *Eine deutsche Gesandtschaft in Abessinien*. Leipzig.

Täsämma Habtä-Mika'el:
1958/59 *Käsate bərhan täsämma – yä-amarəñña mäzgäbä-ḳalat*. Addis Abäba 1951 a.m.

Vajnberg, I.
1907 *Skazanie Iisusa – apokrif o poslědnich vremenach mira*. Pamjatniki efiopskoj pis'mennosti, 6. St. Petersburg.

Voigt, R.
2004 Enno Littmann: Leben und Werk [s. den Beitrag in vorliegendem Band].

Ziegler, S.
2004 Historical sound recordings from Ethiopia on wax cylinders. [s. den vorangehenden Beitrag in diesem Band].

Zä-Mänfäs-Ḳəddus Abrəha:
1970/71 *Ḥatäta mänafəst wä-ᶜawdä nägäst*. Addis Abäba: 1963 a.m. [Titel, Ort und Jahr nach Angaben auf dem Einband; auf dem Titelblatt teilw. verschieden].

Die politische Situation Eritreas und Tigrays zur Zeit der Aksum-Expedition (1905-1906)

Kerstin Volker-Saad

Als im Oktober 1905 die letzten Vorbereitungen für die Aksum-Expedition[1] getroffen werden, befindet sich Littmann bereits in Keren im Hochland Eritreas.[2] Er macht Notizen von der Sprache sowie den „Sitten und Gebräuchen" der Tigré (Tigray), genauer der Mensah, einer muslimischen, Tigre sprechenden Ethnie im Nordwesten des heutigen Eritrea. In Berlin bereiten sich die anderen Expeditionsteilnehmer – der Regierungsbaumeister Dr. Daniel Krencker, der Meßbildfotograf Theodor von Lüpke und der Stabsarzt Dr. Erich Kaschke – auf die Reise vor. Die Generalverwaltung der Königlichen Museen zu Berlin schreibt am 28. November 1905 einen Brief an den Expeditionsleiter, den Orientalistikprofessor Dr. Enno Littmann: „(...) Im übrigen bringen die von hier aufbrechenden Herren[3] an Geld 3000 Maria-Theresien-Thaler sowie für 2000 M. französisches Geld mit sich. Sofort nach Empfang dieses Briefes wollen Sie sich dann ferner mit unserem Geschäftsträger in Addis Abeba, Herrn von Muntius, in Verbindung setzen. Herr von Muntius ist durch das Auswärtige Amt instruiert, er wird für den Schutz der Expedition sowie für eine freundliche Aufnahme in Axum bei Menelik Sorge tragen. Er wird aber auf jeden Fall auch noch durch Sie über die Ankunftszeit, dann später über die tatsächlich erfolgte Ankunft, den Zeitpunkt des Betretens abessinischen Bodens etc. zu unterrichten sein. Auch werden ihm nachdem die Expedition ihre Tätigkeit in Axum aufgenommen hat, zweckmäßig von Zeit zu Zeit orientierende Berichte zu erstatten sein.

Außer Herrn von Muntius und durch diesen Menelik ist die italienische Regierung der Colonia Eritrea ersucht worden, der Expedition jeder Zeit Hülfe, Schutz und alle sonstigen möglichen Erleichterungen zu gewähren (...)"[4]

Die Expedition beginnt in Massawa, einer Hafenstadt der italienischen Kolonie Eritrea am Roten Meer. Der kaiserliche Gesandte Dr. Littmann notiert in seinem Tagebuch die Ankunft der „Herren" und den weiteren Reiseverlauf von Massawa bis Aksum: „Am 29. Dezember 1905 trafen alle Delegierten in Massawa zusammen, am

---

1 Für die Bezeichnung der Stadt sind alternative Schreibweisen möglich: Aksum (Littmann) als auch Axum (Königliche Museen) werden in den historischen Dokumenten verwendet. Ich schließe mich Littmanns Orthographie an.

2 Früher: Cheren.

3 Gemeint sind Dr. Krencker, von Lüpke sowie Dr. Kaschke.

4 Auszug aus dem Brief der Generalverwaltung der Königlichen Museen zu Berlin an Dr. Littmann vom 28. November 1905 (Littmann Nachlaß 245, Kasten 43).

31. Dezember wurde Asmara erreicht. Die erforderlichen Reit- und Lastentiere, zur Hälfte Maultiere zur Hälfte Kamele wurden durch einen (...) Unternehmer in Asmara gestellt. Am 6. Januar brachen wir von Asmara auf. Unser Weg führte über Debaroa (...), Adi Ugri (Mendeferra), Adi Quala, den Mareb, Daro Taele (Adua oder Adwa), Daro Täkle, Mai Kamaue nach ?? (unlesbar) wo wir am 11. Januar ankamen. Am 12. (Januar) gelangten wir dann nach Aksum, wo wir bis zum 7. April arbeiteten (...)"[5]

Massawa ist zu diesem Zeitpunkt bereits durch eine Schotterstraße mit Asmara, einem wichtigen Verkehrsknotenpunkt, Handelsplatz sowie Regierungssitz der italienischen Kolonialverwaltung, verbunden. Um die Stadt Aksum im abessinischen Hochland zu erreichen, reisen auch Littmann und seine Kollegen über diese eritreische Hafenstadt an. Die Arbeiten an der Eisenbahnstrecke laufen seit 1897 und haben bereits Ghinda erreicht. Von dort erklimmen die Reisenden mit der Postkutsche in Serpentinen die 2400 Höhenmeter bis nach Asmara.

Dieser Küstenstrich am Roten Meer hat aufgrund seiner geostrategischen Bedeutung eine wechselvolle Geschichte. Bereits die Sabäer gründeten an der afrikanischen Küste Handelsposten, die sich zu Häfen entwickelten – wie z. B. das antike Adulis, das 60 km von Massawa entfernt liegt. Bis zum 6. Jahrhundert war das Gebiet des heutigen Eritrea der Sitz des aksumitischen Königreiches (Raunig o.J.: 7f.). Als dessen Bedeutung schwindet, wird die Region von verschiedenen Herrschern regiert, bis es im 14. Jahrhundert von Bahri Negassi zu dem „Land am Meer" (Medri-Bahri) vereint werden kann (Wilson 1991: 3). Dieses Land wird durch den Mareb von Abessinien getrennt.

Im 16. Jahrhundert besetzten Türken Küstenstriche Eritreas wie z. B. die Stadt Massawa. Den Rest besetzten sudanesische Truppen. 1867 nehmen die Ägypter Massawa, Keren und das südliche Zentraleritrea ein. Mit der Öffnung des Suezkanals 1869 gewinnt das „Horn von Afrika" für außerregionale Mächte an Attraktivität. Im selben Jahr kaufen die Italiener die Bucht von Assab (Gebiet der Afar). Fast zwanzig Jahre später, 1889, nehmen Italiener im Kampf gegen Äthiopien die Stadt Asmara ein und besetzen sie. Der Ort auf dem Hochlandplateau, an dem die spätere eritreische Hauptstadt Asmara entstand, wurde bereits in der prä-aksumitischen Zeit erwähnt. Aber erst im 10. Jahrhundert n. Chr. wurde möglicherweise das christliche Kerndorf gegründet, um das sich die Stadt später entwickelte. In italienischen Quellen wird darauf hingewiesen, daß Asmara im 16. Jahrhundert bereits als eine große Stadt ausgebaut wurde, die aufgrund von sich kreuzenden Karawanen- und Pilgerrouten zu wirtschaftlichem Wohlstand kam. Die moderne Entwicklung Asmaras wurde unter Ras Alula, einem tigrayischen Herrscher, im Jahre 1884 eingeleitet, als dieser seine Residenz dorthin verlegte. Als die Italiener Eritrea 1890 zur Kolonie machten, zählte die Stadt ungefähr 2000 bis 2500 Einwohner (Killion 1998: 94ff). Nach Schoenfeld bedeutet „Asmara" auf Amharisch „guter Weideplatz" (Schoenfeld 1904: 25). Im zwi-

---

5 Littmann-Nachlaß 245, Kasten 88; Auszug aus Littmanns Feldtagebuch. Im Nachlaß gibt es ein Foto mit Littmann und Krencker (?) vor einer Kutsche, die für ihre Reise von Massawa nach Asmara vorgesehen ist.

schen Kaiser Menelik und der italienischen Regierung ausgehandelten Grenzvertrag von Wichale (Ucciale) werden 1889 die Landstriche beschrieben, die seit 1890 die italienische Kolonie Eritrea ausmachen. Die Benennung Eritreas hatte die italienische Kolonialmacht von dem altgriechischen bzw. lateinischen Namen für das Rote Meer abgeleitet.[6] Der Grenzverlauf umschließt den Lebensraum von neun verschiedenen ethnischen Gruppen, den Kebessa (heute: Tigrinya), Saho, Afar, Tigre, Baza (heute: Kunama), Baria (heute: Nara), Bogos (heute: Bilen), Beja und Rascheida, die jeweils unterschiedliche Sprachen sprechen und verschiedene Religionen ausüben.[7] Bis auf die Bogos wurden alle Bevölkerungsgruppen durch die Grenzziehung von einem Teil ihres Siedlungsgebietes abgetrennt: "As in most other colonial situations, Italy created an Eritrean territory by an act of surgery: by severing its different peoples from those with whom their past had been linked and by grafting the amputated remnants to each other under the title of Eritrean".[8]

Die Expeditionsmitglieder treffen auf ihrer Reise auf die christlichen Tigrinya, die ebenfalls um Aksum siedeln, die muslimischen Saho, möglicherweise auch auf Kunama sprechende Gruppen wie die Baza.[9] Die Tigrinya sprechende Bevölkerung, die zum größten Teil das Hochland Eritreas bewohnt, stellte die Hauptzielgruppe kolonialer Verwaltung und wirtschaftlicher Verflechtungen dar.[10]

Die italienische Expansion auf das Gebiet des nördlichen Äthiopien wurde erleichtert durch das politische und ökonomische Chaos, das 1888 und 1889 in dieser Region herrschte. Einer extremen Dürre im Jahre 1888 folgten eine große Hungersnot, die bis 1892 anhält, eine Choleraepidemie und eine bis heute unbekannte Rinderkrankheit. Des weiteren hinterläßt der Tod des abessinischen Kaisers Yohannes (März 1889) ein Machtvakuum und bewirkt den Wechsel der Zentralregierung vom Norden Äthiopiens zum Süden des Landes (Negash 1987: 2). Kaiser Menelik II., der die Regierung übernimmt, kolonisiert ausgedehnte Gebiete und Völker im Süden und Westen und steckt so die Staatsgrenzen des heutigen Äthiopien ab. Die kleine Provinz Shoa mit seiner Hauptstadt Addis Abeba avancierte zum machtvollen Zentrum und die Amharen zur dominanten Volksgruppe (Sendker 1990: 10).

Die Besetzung Eritreas durch die italienische Armee erfolgte zunächst ohne Widerstand aus der Bevölkerung. Ein Teil der eritreischen Elite aus dem Tigrinya sprechenden, christlichen Hochland hatte sich mit den Italienern verbündet, in der Hoffnung auf Unterstützung in dem Kampf gegen die muslimischen Bewegungen aus Ägypten und dem mahdistischen Sudan, die bis ins Hochland vorzudringen suchten. Ein anderer Teil der politischen Wortführer wird von den Italienern hingerichtet, um die Bevölkerung führungslos und gefügig zu machen. Als sehr nützlich für die italie-

---

6 Vgl. neugriechisch für rot: *erithros*; lateinisch: *mare erythraeum*.
7 Siehe Ethnonyme bei Tom Killion 1998 für einen knappen geschichtlichen Überblick.
8 Trevaskis 1960: 69 zitiert in Sherman 1981: 122.
9 Littmann-Nachlaß 245, Kasten 97 (Fotos), Kasten 99 (Reisebilder und Porträts Va, Vb).
10 Vgl. auch Schoenfeld 1904:25: „Zwei Dinge werden das weitere Wachstum Asmaras befördern, die Wichtigkeit seiner strategischen Lage und die Vorzüglichkeit seines Klimas."

nischen Invasionstruppen stellte sich die Verteilung von Lebensmitteln an eritreische Sympathisanten heraus, was die Folgen der Dürre abzumildern half und aus der „eritreischen Bevölkerung" loyale Verbündete machte (Negash 1987: 121). Nachdem die Italiener den bis Agordat vordringenden General Ahmed-Ali in einer blutigen Schlacht am 21. Dezember 1893 zurückgeschlagen hatten, übernahmen sie im Januar 1894 die strategisch und handelspolitisch wichtige Stadt Kassala von den mahdistischen Derwischen (Schoenfeld 1904: 76). Kassala beherrscht den Eingang in das Tal des Sabderat und damit die Einfallspforte in das eritreische Hochland. Diesen Weg müssen sowohl die Karawanenzüge nehmen, die das Meer bei Massawa aufsuchen, als auch die dorthin vordringenden Truppen (Schoenfeld 1904: 75ff). Die Italiener besetzen Kassala fast vier Jahre lang, bis sie es Weihnachten 1897 den Engländern übergeben.

Als erster Gouverneur der eritreischen Kolonie wird General Gondolfi (1890 bis 1897) eingesetzt; ihm folgt Ferdinando Martini (1897-1907), dessen Hilfe Littmann und die Expeditionsmitglieder bei der Durchreise in Anspruch nehmen. Eritrea ist zu der Zeit kein sicheres Reiseland. Die anhaltenden Landenteignungen lassen den Unmut über die italienische Willkürherrschaft stetig wachsen. Aberra, ein politischer Führer aus der Provinz Hamasien, der der italienischen Inquisition entkommt, leitet den Widerstand ein. Er versammelt seine Anhänger um sich und wartet auf die italienischen Truppen, die ihn gefangen nehmen sollten. Doch statt daß ihn die Italiener nach Asmara bringen, tötet er bei dem Zusammenstoß mit der italienischen Armee Capitano Bettini und flüchtet zuerst nach Asmara, dann nach Äthiopien (Negash 1987: 123). Kaiser Menelik lädt daraufhin Aberra zu einer Audienz nach Addis Abeba ein und belohnt ihn für seine tapferen Taten mit dem Rang eines Dejatsch in der äthiopischen Armee. Im März 1896 spielte er eine entscheidende Rolle bei der Schlacht bei Adua, in der die Truppen Kaiser Meneliks siegreich die italienische Armee abwehrten und damit verhinderten, daß die Italiener Aksum vereinnahmten.

Die Aktivitäten von den zwei anderen Widerstandskämpfern, Mohamed Nuri und Gebremedhin Hagos, machen deutlich, wie intensiv die jeweiligen politischen Bemühungen um das abessinische Hochland am Ende des 19. bzw. am Anfang des 20. Jahrhunderts waren. Nuri gehörte zu den Saho, die in der Provinz Akele-Guzay am östlichen Hochlandrand leben. Gebremedhin Hagos (Sohn von Bahta Hagos) versucht wiederholt, die Herrscher der Provinz Tigray zu überzeugen, mit ihm die Italiener aus Eritrea zu vertreiben. Ein bereits zerrüttetes Land Tigray ist jedoch nicht gewillt, sich die Italiener zum Feind zu machen. Nuri organisierte dennoch von Tigray aus beständig Überfälle auf die italienische Armee. Zwischen 1890 und 1891 erbat er die Erlaubnis von Ras Mekonnen, dem territorialen Gouverneur von Nordäthiopien, den italienischen Gouverneur Ferdinando Martini zu ermorden, was ihm aber nicht gelingt. Anfang Februar 1903 wird Nuri zeitweilig von Dejatsch Gebre Selassie in Adua interniert. Dejatsch Gebre Selassie war ein äthiopischer Verbündeter Italiens, der ein Auslieferungsabkommen mit Italien unterzeichnet hatte. Nuris gesellschaftliche Stellung und seine Verbündeten unter der äthiopischen politischen Elite bewirkten jedoch, dass Dejatsch Gebre Selassie diesem Abkommen erst entsprach, nachdem die ausdrückliche Genehmigung des äthiopischen Kaisers Menelik eingeholt worden war (die offensichtlich nicht erteilt wurde). Nuri und Gebremedhin blieben während der gesamten Regierungszeit Martinis, also bis zum Jahre 1907, an der Eritreo-Tigray-Grenze im Saho-Gebiet aktiv. Martini schrieb am 30. Juni 1900 in sein Tagebuch: "(...) desertions and armed confrontations between the colonial army and those who resisted its presence constituted the daily menu in Eritrea (...)".[11]

Littmanns Reise führt genau durch die „Unruheprovinz" Akele-Guzay in Eritrea, wo er nicht ausgraben darf. Ob dieses Grabungsverbot politisch motiviert ist, oder aus Sicherheitsgründen unterbunden wird, ist anhand der Quellen nicht zu klären. Italien und auch England und Frankreich haben kein Interesse daran, daß der deutsche Gesandte ihre politischen Ambitionen am Horn von Afrika stört. Denn Italien hat große Pläne mit seiner ersten Kolonie (*la colonia primogenita*). Die koloniale Herrschaft Italiens über Eritrea dauert bis 1941. Zur Zeit der Aksum-Expedition (1905-1906) waren die Italiener bereits fünfzehn Jahre im Land und hatten massiv begonnen, Eritrea als einen starken Nachbarn Äthiopiens auszubauen. Zunächst waren landlose süditalienische Bauern angesiedelt (1889-1895) worden, die das konfiszierte Land bewirtschafteten. Eritrea sollte außerdem als Zwischenlager für Handelsgüter aus Äthiopien und Arabien genutzt werden. Die Häfen Massawa und Assab wurden beständig als Umschlagplatz ausgebaut. Eritreische Männer dienten als Soldaten in der italienischen Armee und marschierten in Somalia (1908-1910), Libyen (1912-1931) und Äthiopien (1935-1941) ein. Bei dem Ausbau der Landwirtschaft, der Tierzucht und dem Abbau von mineralischen Rohstoffen sollten Eritreer die italienischen Zuwanderer unterstützen. Die Produktion sollte jedoch in der Hand der Italiener bleiben, die an den Eritreern lediglich als Konsumenten von italienischen Fertigprodukten interessiert waren.[12] Trotz aller kolonialen Unterdrückung und diskriminierenden Entmündigung der einheimischen Bevölkerung erfuhr Eritrea durch den Ausbau der Infrastruktur, der Häfen, der Städte, der Plantagen, der Straßen und der Eisenbahn sowie der italienischen Kolonialarmee „ein rapides wirtschaftliches Wachstum" (Eikenberg 1990: 114). Damit einher ging die Rekrutierung von eritreischen Bauern und Städtern, die in der Kleinindustrie und den Fabriken (z. B. Leder, Erfrischungsgetränke und Bier) als lohnabhängige Arbeiterinnen und Arbeiter tätig wurden. Der Aufbau eines säkularen Bildungswesen ließ in den Städten eine gebildete Mittelschicht von Verwaltungsbeamten entstehen. Neben Land- und Fabrikarbeiterinnen arbeiteten vermehrt Frauen als Hausangestellte im Dienste italienischer wie auch wohlhabender eritreischer Familien.[13] Die koloniale Gesetzgebung, besonders die sehr detailliert ausgearbeiteten Rassengesetze aus dem Jahr 1937, schaffte eine Mehrklassengesellschaft, die die eritreische Bevölkerung offen diskriminierte (Sherman 1981: 122). Richard Pankhurst kommentierte diesen Umstand wie folgt: „The Italian colony was

---

11 Zitiert aus Negash 1987:124.
12 Negash 1987: 179; vgl. auch Sherman 1981: 122.
13 Vgl. Wilson 1996:16; Wilson beschreibt ausführlich anhand von biographischen Interviews die sozialen Spannungen, Ängste und Konflikte, die durch diese neuen Arbeitsverhältnisse entstanden waren.

one of the most racist territories in Africa, and one of the few under Allied control in which anti-Semitic laws were in force." (Pankhurst 1995: 25).

Die Rassengesetze verboten (eheliche) Beziehungen zwischen italienischen Männern und eritreischen Frauen. Ferner sahen die Gesetze eine Trennung von eritreischen und italienischen Wohnvierteln, ein Lokalverbot für Eritreer in italienischen Gaststätten und die Unzulässigkeit der Beförderung von Einheimischen durch italienische Fahrer vor. Verstöße gegen das Gesetz wurden mit Haftstrafen geahndet.[14] Der soziale Wandel erfaßte alle Bereiche des täglichen Lebens, besonders in den Städten, in denen die italienische Verwaltung Zugriff hatte (Sherman 1981: 122). Dies betraf in besonderem Maße die Ansiedlungen im Hochland, die sich zu Großstädten entwickelten, und die Küstenregion mit den Häfen Massawa und Assab. Oder es betraf Hochländer, die zum Aufbau der Städte ins heiße Tiefland versetzt wurden.

Wie massiv die Bemühungen Italiens in Eritrea waren, zeigen die stetig steigenden Einwohnerzahlen von zuwandernden Italienern. Innerhalb von zehn Jahren kamen etwa 50.000 Siedler und ca. 150.000 italienische Soldaten nach Eritrea, das zu dieser Zeit nicht mehr als 700.000 indigene Einwohner zählte. Asmaras Bevölkerung wuchs in diesen Jahren stetig an. Als Littmann im Jahr 1905 dort ankam, zählte die Stadt 7.000 Eritreer und 1.500 Europäer, 1931 zählte sie bereits 20.638 Eritreer und 3.101 Europäer und im Jahre 1941 lebten 120.000 Eritreer sowie 55.000 Italiener in der Stadt (Killion 1998: 95f.) Dennoch konzentrieren sich die Italiener zunächst auf die Entwicklung des Hochlandes. Als Schoenfeld im Jahre 1903 – also nach dreizehnjähriger italienischer Kolonialzeit und zwei Jahre vor Littmann – von Kairo über Suez nach Massawa, weiter nach Asmara und von dort nach Keren durch das westliche Tiefland Eritreas bis nach Kassala im Sudan reiste, stellte er zunächst fest: „daß nur das östliche Drittel der Kolonie zwischen Massawa und Cheren [Keren] das Eindringen der italienischen Kultur zeigt und zwar hier recht sichtbar, während die Zweidrittelstrecke zwischen Cheren und Sabderat (das Gebiet der Beni-Amer im westlichen Tiefland an der Grenze zum Sudan gelegen) noch völlig unberührt von derselben daliegt" (Schoenfeld 1904: 52).

Interessanterweise korrespondierte diese Entwicklung jeweils mit der Stationierung der italienischen Truppen in den Städten Asmara, Keren und der Hafenstadt Massawa. Kurz nach der Gründung der italienischen Kolonie entwickelte General Gondolfi ein Vier-Punkte-Programm, das u. a. vorsah, keine Militärposten außerhalb der o. g. Städte aufzubauen, sondern die Ernennung einheimischer Scheichs als Lokalbehörden vorzog (Schoenfeld 1904: 64). Unter Gouverneur Martini wurde der Einflußbereich der Italiener durch die Gründung italienischer Verwaltungshauptquartiere in den Tieflandstädten Agordat, Barentu und Tessenei erweitert. Es wurde nicht nur eine moderne materielle Infrastruktur geschaffen, wie der Bau der Eisenbahn von

---

14 Kemink 1991: 6; vgl. hierzu auch den Roman von Erminia Dell'Oro, „Der Tag des Regenbogens", 1997, in dem die Autorin den qualvollen Lebensweg einer eritreischen Frau beschreibt, die ihre zwei Kinder aufgrund der rigiden Rassengesetze ohne ihren italienischen (Ehe-) Mann großziehen und für deren Lebensunterhalt sorgen muß.

Keren bis Argordat (1922-1930), sondern ein komplexer Umsiedlungsprozeß eingeleitet, der italienischen Siedlern im Tiefland Gelegenheit verschaffen sollte, das fruchtbare Land an den Flußläufen zu bewirtschaften (Nadel 1944: 15).

Als Littmann im Oktober 1905 Eritrea bereist, entfernt er sich nicht weit von der gut ausgestatteten Hauptstadt. Seine Reise vor der eigentlichen Aksum-Expedition führt ihn nicht etwa in das Herz des Tigrelandes wie z.B. nach Agordat, sondern nach Keren, das 104 km von Asmara entfernt liegt. Erst zwischen 1903 und 1906 bauen die Italiener ihre Verwaltung aus. Neben den Hochlandprovinzen Hamasien, Akele-Guzay, Seraye, werden die Tieflandprovinzen Sahel, Gash-Setit, Assab und Barka geschaffen (Negash 1987: 116).

Bei so vielen politischen Ambitionen der Italiener erscheint eine Expedition aus wissenschaftlichen Beweggründen als suspekt. Littmann und seine Kollegen spüren den Gegenwind, der ihnen auf diplomatischem Parkett entgegenweht und notiert dies in seinem Abschlußbericht: „Ferner wurde (...) berichtet, daß Italiener, Franzosen und Engländer miteinander wetteiferten, die Abessinier gegen die Deutschen aufzuhetzen. Da jene drei Nationen, oder zum mindesten manche Angehörige derselben, in der That über den deutsch-abessinischen Handelsvertrag sehr erbost sind, trat überall in der Colonia Eritrea, besonders später in Cairo hervor. Unter anderem hat der französische Gesandte in Addis Abeba, – oder sein Vertreter –, vor der Ankunft des Kaiserlichen Gesandten Dr. Rosen einen abessinischen Großen zu überreden gesucht, Kaiser Menelik zu bestimmen, die Deutschen abzuweisen; der Franzose behauptete unter anderem, die Deutschen seien schlechte und treulose Menschen, auch würde Abessinien die Freundschaft von Frankreich, Rußland, England und Italien verlieren, wenn es mit Deutschland einen Vertrag schließe (...).“[15]

Kaiser Menelik reagiert sehr souverän auf die Einmischungsversuche des französischen Gesandten und empfängt den kaiserlichen Gesandten Dr. Rosen mit besonderen Ehren und stellt die deutsche Expedition unter seinen Schutz. In Adua sowie Aksum in der Provinz Tigray stehen sie folglich unter dem Schutz des Dedschasmatsch Gebre Selassie, der sich offensichtlich sehr um die Expeditionsteilnehmer kümmert, wie aus Littmanns Abschlußbericht, der für Kaiser Menelik in Addis Abeba bestimmt ist, deutlich wird: „Und wiederum thun wir Euch kund, daß der von Euch eingesetzte Dedschasmatsch Gabre Sellase, der Gouverneur von Tigre, uns viel Gutes gethan und uns gar sehr erfreut und uns in allem geholfen hat. Und wir danken Euch und den von Euch Eingesetzten dafür, daß Ihr uns in Freundschaft aufgenommen und uns in Sicherheit im Lande Äthiopien habt wohnen lassen." [16]

Am 6. April 1906 werden die Ausgrabungen in Aksum beendet und am 7. April brechen die Expeditionsteilnehmer auf in Richtung Asmara. Littmann notiert in seinem Tagebuch: „Auf der Rückreise wurde in folgenden Orten Forschungen unternommen; auf abessinischen Gebieten konnten zur Vervollständigung unserer Untersuchungen Schürfungen vorgenommen werden, auf italienischem Gebiet waren Gra-

---

15 Littmann-Nachlaß 245, Kasten 43, Abschlußbericht.
16 Littmann Nachlaß 245, Kasten 43; Anlage C zum Abschlußbericht.

bungen durch die Regierung untersagt. Adua 2 1/2 bis 3 1/2 Tage (Aufbruch am 11. April), Yeha 2- bzw. 3 Tage, Debra Damo, Senafé – Matarra 1 1/2 Tage, Kaskasä, Adi Caie, Cohaito".[17]

Am 29. April reist die Gruppe zusammen von Asmara nach Massawa. Von dort brechen sie am 2. Mai nach Aden auf. Hier trennen sich dann die Expeditionsmitglieder. Krencker bleibt noch wenige Tage in Aden und setzt dann seine Schiffspassage nach Marseille fort. Littmann, von Lüpke und Dr. Kaschke fahren nach Ägypten und bleiben dort eine weitere Woche in Kairo.[18]

Quellen

Littmann Nachlaß, Nr.245, Kasten 43, 87, 99, 100, 101. Staatsbibliothek zu Berlin, Stiftung Preussischer Kulturbesitz, Handschriftenabteilung.

Bibliographie[19]

Anonymous
1986   *Brockhaus Enzyklopädie*. F. A. Brockhaus Mannheim.

Dell'Oro, E.
1997   *Der Tag des Regenbogens*. Eine eritreische Geschichte. Innsbruck [Erstausgabe: 1991].

Eikenberg, K.
1990   Der Eritrea-Konflikt. In: *Brüne, Stefan und Volker Matthies (Hrsg.), Krisenregion, Horn von Afrika*. Institut für Afrikakunde, Hamburg, 107-153.

17 Littmann Nachlaß 245, Kasten 43 „Die Exp. betr.".
18 Auszug aus dem Aksum-Schlußbericht, Littmann Nachlaß 245, Kasten 43.
19 Die bibliographische Erfassung von eritreischen und äthiopischen Autoren ist schwierig, da der erst genannte Name der eigentliche Nachname und der zweitgenannte Name der Vorname des Vaters ist. Dieses Problem wird von jedem Wissenschaftler und jedem Verlag unterschiedlich gelöst. Ich habe mich entschlossen, den zweiten Namen eines eritreischen/äthiopischen Autors als Referenz anzugeben und ihn in der Bibliographie an die erste Position zu stellen und durch ein Komma von dem zweiten zu trennen (Bsp.: Iyob, Ruth; Tesfagiorgis, Abeba). So verfahren auch eritreische bzw. äthiopische Wissenschaftler/innen, die sich einer international gebräuchlichen Bibliographierweise anschließen (müssen). Es ist zu beachten, daß einige Autoren in anderen Quellen auch unter ihrem „Vornamen" bibliographiert sein können (Bsp. Ruth Iyob; Abeba Tesfagiorgis).

1997   *The Eritrean Struggle for Independence. Domination, resistance, nationalism 1941-1993*. Cambridge.

Girma Fisseha
o.J.   *Bergland Äthiopien. Kunst und Kultur aus dem Hochland*. München.

Kemink, F.
1991   *Die Tegrenna-Frauen in Eritrea*. Stuttgart

Killion, T.
1998   *Historical Dictionary of Eritrea*. African Historical Dictionaries, No. 75. Lanham, Md. and London.

Littmann, E.
1910-15 *Publication of the Princeton Expedition to Abysinnia: Tales, Customs, Names and Dirges of the Tigre Tribes*. Leyden.

Nadel, S. F.
1944   *Races and Tribes of Eritrea*. British Military Administration – Eritrea, Asmara(1946): The Tenure on the Eritrean Plateau. *Journal of the International African Institute*, Vol.XVI, No.1, 1946: 1-22

Negash Tekeste
1987   *Italian Colonialism in Eritrea, 1882-1941. Policies, Praxis and Impact*. Upsala.

Pankhurst, Richard
1990   *A Social History of Ethiopia*. Addis Abeba
1995   The legal question of racism in Eritrea during the British military administration: A study of colonial attitudes and responses, 1941-1945. *NEAS* 2: 25-70.

Raunig
o.J.   Historische Einführung. In: Girma Fisseha, *Bergland Äthiopien. Kunst und Kultur aus dem Hochland*. München: 7-9.

Schoenfeld, D. E.
1904   *Erythräa und der Ägyptische Sudan*. Berlin.

Sendker, L.
1990   *Eritreische Flüchtlinge im Sudan. Zwischen Assimilation und Segregation*. Institut für Afrika-Kunde, Hamburg.

Sherman, R.
1981   The Rise of Eritrean Nationalism. *Northeast African Studies, 2, 3 (1980-81), 3, 1 (1981):* 121-129.

Trevaskis, G. K. N.
1960   *Eritrea: A Colony in Transition, 1941-52.* London.

Wilson, A.
1991   *Women and the Eritrean Revolution. The Challenge Road.* Trenton.

V. Recent Research and New Discoveries

Controversy over Local Tradition and National Ethiopian Context: Case Study of the Hadiyya[1]

Ulrich Braukämper

Some remarks on ethnic identity in the Ethiopian context

The historical conditions and the policy regarding ethnicity in Ethiopia have to some extent been different from the postcolonial nation-states of the rest of Africa. Apart from the Italian occupation from 1936 to 1941 the country was exempted from foreign rule, but two-thirds of its territory experienced an internal colonization (or a so-called endo-colonialism) by the conquests of the Christian empire in the late 19th and the early 20th centuries. However, the problems and consequences Ethiopia is facing as a multi-ethnic state with approximately seventy ethnic units, are largely comparable to those of the bulk of the continent. The country is confronted with the struggle to arrive at meaningful terms for constructing a sense of belonging, of moral and material community, in circumstances which privilege difference as well as in the endeavour to regulate sovereign borders under global political and economic conditions. It is furthermore involved in the often bitter controversies that rage as people assert various kinds of identity to make claims of entitlement and interest. It is also engaged in troubled public discourses on the proper reach of 21st century constitutions and their protection of individual rights, in controversies about corruption and its policing and in the complicated processes by which government, nongovernmental organizations, citizens acting in the name of civil society and other social fractions seek to carve out a division of political and social labour.[2]
Ethnic and national identities are on the one hand contradictory, but on the other hand closely interconnected. Since the end of the 20th century, developments on the local, regional, national and even global levels can no longer strictly be separated,

---

1 It goes without saying that Littmann, to whose memory the contributions of this volume are dedicated, was not basically concerned with scientific approaches of the kind dealt with in this paper, but rather devoted to the "classical" fields of study in philology, linguistics and archaeology. It can nevertheless be assumed that his huge range of interests regarding research on north-eastern Africa would not have neglected the topic presented here. His contributions on the folklore of the Tigray (Littmann 1913) provided an enormous treasure also for ethnology.

2 These facts have more extensively been elaborated by Jean and John Comaroff (2000: 12, passim) with particular reference to the situation in postcolonial South Africa.

although their linkages are sometimes difficult to analyse in the context of areas such as southern Ethiopia. This paper aims at revealing controversies between local cultural traditions and socio-political interests perplexing the nation state.

Four major points are to be discussed here: first, some terminological problems in historical perspective; second, an ethnographic sketch of the elected case study, the Hadiyya of southern Ethiopia; third, a presentation of certain cultural traditions which are relevant in the current discourses on the local and the national context; fourth a critical analysis of these traditions in a broader context of Ethiopian policy.

The first of these topics deals with some terms and concepts in a retrospective view. A controversy between the strata of ethnic and national priorities and loyalties has of course always existed in the history of the multi-ethnic Ethiopian nation-state since the 19th century. However, because of the highly centralistic governmental organization and ideology of the imperial and the DERG regimes, ethnic identities were not permitted to play a prominent role. For example, Amharic was the official language of the whole country and it was almost exclusively used in school education and in all important national institutions. Therefore its mastery was an absolute prerequisite for any kind of vertical social mobility within the Ethiopian state. When in the mid-1970s the term "nation" (*biheer*) for large groups such as Amhara and Oromo, "nationality" (*biheere sab*) for groups of medium size such as Hadiyya and people (*hizb*) for small groups such as the Mursi became of official use in political and administrative documents including the constitution of the country,[3] this did not cause a *de facto* change of its centralistic character. The term nationality itself and its ideological understanding were adopted from the model of the Soviet Union, where it was employed for the numerous ethnic groups of the state.[4] This meaning is usually rejected by social scientists because nationality in its ordinary sense is defined as the citizenship of a nation state. Therefore, I follow this academic tradition and prefer the terms ethnic entity, ethnic unit or ethnic group which appear to be most neutral. A differentiation according to quantitative criteria, as it has been employed in the Ethiopian political nomenclature (*biheer, biheere sab, hizb*), also seems to be problematic, because the borderlines are not clearly defined.

After the EPRDF-dominated government (IHADIG) had taken power in 1991 a dramatic change from a centralistic to a federalist pattern of administration occurred, deeply affecting the situation of minority groups in the country. After a transition period Ethiopia became a "federal democratic republic" composed of regional states which are largely based on ethnic considerations and facts. Cultural autonomy and

---

3 Already in the "Programme of the National Democratic Revolution of Ethiopia", issued in April 1976 (Section II, § 5, p. 16), the following statement was laid down: "The right to self-determination of all nationalities will be recognized and fully respected".

4 This was common from the 1920s until the present. Bromlej (1977) as one of the leading representatives of Soviet ethnography, however, preferred the term ethnos.

pluralism were granted to an extent never experienced before.[5] But, at the same time, an outbreak of ethnic particularism occurred which sometimes became unfavourable or even destructive for the co-existence of people in many parts of the country. In the new federal system the *Southern Nations, Nationalities and Peoples' Regional State* (SNNPRS) deserves particular attention because it is in many respects different from the rest of the country. It is not dominated by a particular ethnic group and named after it as it is the case for most of the other Regional States, but it is inhabited by c. 40 ethnic units (cf. map 1). Linguistic and cultural heterogeneity seems to be a defining characteristic of this administrative entity. Moreover, it is commonly perceived as the economically and culturally most "backward" part of the country. Before the ratification of the New Constitution by the government in 1994, local leaders and representatives of the ethnic minority groups (mostly from the SNNPRS) were urged by the government to eliminate "harmful" customs of their groups such as body decorations and certain burial rituals.[6]

According to the "constructivist" approach advocated, for example, by Fredrik Barth,[7] which I consider most convincing, the following essential criteria of ethnic group are listed: 1. It is largely biologically self-perpetuating; 2. it has a common territory; 3. it shares fundamental cultural patterns; 4. it possesses an outstanding consciousness of a common descent or past; 5. it embodies the concept of a distinctive identity of its members, which is also recognized by members of other categories of the same order, i.e. the phenomenon which is usually labelled ethnicity. It has to be added that in Ethiopia, although not necessarily all over the world,[8] a common language constitutes a further prerequisite for the definition of an ethnic group. Additional but not indispensably necessary criteria may be provided by a common ethnonym, a common future-orientation and a basic equilibrium of centrifugal and centripetal tendencies within the respective ethnic groups.

In an article entitled "New Configurations of Ethiopian Ethnicity: The Challenge of the South" Jon Abbink (1998) has recently contributed new stimulating ideas to this topic. He focussed on the changing politics of identity which demand an increasing sense of mutual cooperation but which is to a large extent still dominated by conflict. It can be stated that the "Southerners" are striving much more fervently to be part of the larger Ethiopian state than for example the Oromo and the Somali are. There are

5   In the new Constitution of 1995 (Art. 39.1) even the "...unrestricted right up to secession" from the nation-state is principally not excluded, although such a solution can theoretically and practically hardly be imagined. This Constitution has to some extent been influenced by Western concepts of law (cf. Scholler 1999).

6   Cf. Abbink 1998: 67f.

7   Barth 1969: 10f. The so-called primordial approach, which propagates a more or less static and ever-lasting concept of ethnic group, seems to me highly problematic. But an analysis of this problem is outside the scope of this paper.

8   For example, in a study on migration and ethnic change in the Darfur region of Sudan Republic (Braukämper 1992: 49f., 241f.) I concluded that a common language does not constitute a necessary criterion of an ethnic group.

nevertheless serious sources of potential conflict inherent in the federal structure and ethnic self-determination, in the balancing of ethnic group representation, in educational policy and in the definition of administrative borders.

The case study of Hadiyya

The Hadiyya are one of the major ethnic groups in the northern part of SNNPRS.[9] In the context of this analysis it has to be stressed that their dwelling-areas do not constitute a coherent territorial cluster (cf. map 2). The three *woreda* districts of Misha (Konteb), Leemo and Sooro constitute a compact area from which the *woreda* of the Baadawwaachcho is separated. These four administrative districts constitute the *Hadiyya Zone*. Another Hadiyya-speaking group, the Libido or Maraqo, live in the district of Masqan and Maraqo of the Gurage Zone. Hadiyyeesa, the language of the Hadiyya, belongs to the Highland East Cushitic cluster (which also includes the Qabeena, Alaaba, Kämbaata, Tembaro, Sidama, Gedeo and Burji). The Hadiyya are estimated at 1.2 million people, inhabiting one of the most densely populated regions of Ethiopia. The major part of their dwelling areas is situated west of the Rift valley between the rivers Omo and Bilate.

Leemo *woreda* is inhabited by the Hadiyya groups of the Leemo and the Shaashoogo and by a minority of people belonging to the Semitic-speaking cluster of the Gurage, the Indagayn and the Adäre (Selti, Ulbaräg, Azernet, Berbere). Leemo, besides Baadoogo and Sooro, also constitute the bulk of the Hadiyya population of Misha (Konteb) *woreda*. The Mäsmäs of this district originally belonged to the Gurage ethnic cluster, but they were completely assimilated to the Hadiyya in the 19th century.[10] The Sooro woreda is populated by Hadiyya people of the same name and by a minority of people belonging to the groups of the Dubamo, Donga and Looka. These ethnic units originally spoke the Kizinya dialect of Kämbaata, then became increasingly bilingual from the 19th century onwards and have meanwhile predominantly shifted to Hadiyyeesa.[11]

The Hadiyya represented in map 2 are commonly labelled "Hadiyya proper", but it has to be mentioned that the name Hadiyya in historical perspective is also claimed by the Qabeena and to some extent by the Alaaba and the Semitic-speaking East Gurage, who now prefer the name Adäre. This claim results from the historical tradition that all these people were once representatives of a powerful state, Hadiyya, which occupied between the 13th and the 16th centuries a vast area east of the Rift

---

9   I carried out field research among the Hadiyya in 1970-71, 1972-74 and 1999-2000. For publications resulting from these studies cf. Braukämper 1980 and 1999-2000 and Braukämper and Tilahun Mishago 1999.

10   Cf. Braukämper 1980: 202f.

11   Braukämper 1980: 210ff., Braukämper 1983: 55ff. During my field research of 1999-2000 I collected some information about the Looka which are not yet included in the hitherto published materials.

Valley in parts of present Arsi, Bale and western Chärchär which is now inhabited by Oromo-speaking groups.[12] Since the official introduction of the federalist organizational structure such reminiscences of the past have considerably increased in importance for the political consciousness of the present time. A particular pride has developed over the last two decades which refers to the powerful state that lasted until the 17th century mentioned in Ethiopian and Arabic chronicles. As already indicated, this political entity was also inhabited by the ancestors of other people of present southern Ethiopia such as the Qabeena, the Alaaba and parts of the Adäre-East Gurage. However, the legacy of the old state has been mainly usurped by the Hadiyya proper, who proudly refer to it as the creation and possession of their forebears. Obviously, this historical consciousness to some extent resulted from a feedback from recent literature.[13]

In the Hadiyya Zone, disputes of people concerning their political affiliation can be observed with regard to neighbouring groups as well as internally. The Maraqo in the Gurage Zone, for example, are strongly opting to be incorporated into the Hadiyya zone. This is also reported of Hadiyya-speaking people in the lowlands east of the Bilate River, which belong to the Regional State of Oromia. On the other hand, Gurage-speaking people in northern Hadiyyaland want to join their kinsmen either in the districts of Silte-Adäre or of the Sebat Bet, the "Seven Houses" of the western Gurage. Because people are frequently mixed in many villages and peasant associations (*kebeles*) – they have sometimes been living together since generations – it is difficult for them to reach a consensus of the diverging options.

This problem could be observed in the case of the Indagayn, a Gurage-speaking group in Hadiyya Zone.[14] As it can be evidenced by oral traditions, the interethnic relations of the Leemo-Hadiyya and the Indagayn in terms of intermarriages and mutual cultural exchanges had been very intensive since the middle of the 19th century. For example, the formerly semi-nomadic Leemo-Hadiyya agropastoralists adopted the cultivation of *Ensete ventricosum*, the most important staple food of the area, from the Indagayn. After a long period of predominantly cordial relations the question arose with an astonishing abruptness in the 1990s, which peasant associations in the border regions of the two groups had to be transferred either to the Hadiyya or to the Gurage Zone. With the growth of particularistic ethnic consciousness new constellations of political interests evolved which even resulted in violent clashes and casualties.[15]

---

12 For the historical reconstruction cf. Braukämper 1980, chapters 3.3 – 3.5. Braukämper 2002: 55-68.

13 I was recently informed in Hadiyyaland and in Addis Ababa that my own writings played a role in this development.

14 The historical and contemporary relations of the Indagayn-Gurage with the Leemo-Hadiyya were studied by Bustorf during our common research in Hadiyyaland in 1999-2000. See Bustorf 2002. We are grateful to the German Research Council for its generous support of this field research.

15 This situation also affected our research programme, because the local authorities suspected a potential interference into their respective political strategies and goals.

Similar problems could also be noted in the southern parts of the Hadiyya Zone. After the introduction of the federal system the Dubamo and Looka increasingly became aware of their non-Hadiyya origin and started demanding an administrative district of their own. This claim was vehemently rejected by the administrators of the Sooro *woreda*, who insisted that these people have always been Hadiyya and the idea of a separate sub-district would therefore be groundless.[16] The Looka started referring to historical traditions which remind those of the Dubamo in many details: seven original clans originated from the Gondar region of northern Ethiopia; a monarchic institution (*wooma*) with royal insignia; sacred objects from an ancient Christian past which had been hidden in caves during the Muslim invasion of Ahmad Grañ of the 1530s. Looka people are now scattered in some places of the Hadiyya Zone and of the Kämbaata-Alaaba-Tembaro Zone. They founded a political organization in order to pursue the aim of an administrative territory of their own. Although this organization was dissolved in 1994, the Looka are still cultivating their dream of an individual sub-district. Opposition to the regional authorities is, however, not merely restricted to more or less symbolic claims. In the late 1990s some of the Dubamo and other people stopped paying taxes to the local administrators whom they refused to acknowledge as their legitimate rulers. This act of passive resistance almost inevitably entails sanctions by the government.

Apart from interethnic disputes, which are mostly occurring in the border areas of the Hadiyya Zone, also intraethnic controversies can be observed. They result from particular socio-economic constellations and conflicts of different phases of history. Before the 1990s, the political, administrative and economic elite in Hadiyyaland, as in most other parts of southern Ethiopia conquered by emperor Menilek, mainly consisted of so-called *Näftäñña* (gun-men), i.e. military colonists of Amhara or Tigray descent. After they had been deprived of their mighty position by the IHADIG government and had mostly left for Addis Ababa or various parts of northern Ethiopia, an internal struggle for power arose among the autochthonous inhabitants of the Zone. In this situation, the historical traditions of genealogical descent and of the time depth of settlement in a particular area started playing an increasing role.

Originally, the Hadiyya were an egalitarian society vehemently rejecting all attempts to establish monarchical institutions.[17] But an internal division of clans, locally named *sulla*, according to criteria of age, reputation of certain ancestors and political strength seems to have always existed.

There was, for example, one person called Booyaamo or Booye who is consid-

---

16 Although I had no intention whatsoever to interfere in political affairs, I nevertheless became personally involved in this dispute. Hadiyya administrators blamed me for the fact that in the map of the book of 1999 the Dubamo are classified as "linguistically assimilated to the Hadiyya". A Dubamo delegation presented another map of my book on Kambata (1983: 60) to Prime Minister Meles Zenawi in order to prove their claim.

17 This is most clearly recalled by the Sooro-Hadiyya, who foiled the attempts of ambitious leaders to establish a monarchy according to the Wälaytta model during the second half of the 19th century. Cf. Braukämper 1980: 218f.

ered the ancestor of most people among the Hadiyya subgroups Sooro, Shaashoogo and Baadawwaachcho. In genealogies, which I recorded in the early 1970s, he is listed about 16 generations ago.[18] This Booyaamo is most probably identical with the Bamo of the chronicle of emperor Zarʾa Yaᶜqob (1434-68). According to the oral tradition he accompanied his father Manchichcho on his way from the east, from Raaya in Bale, to the Rift valley. Numerous versions exist of the legend how Booyaamo became a leading personality among the Hadiyya.[19] The core element can be sketched as follows: He sat in a tree with a red coat, a symbol of royalty, and waited until people called him to come down and to accept the leadership of the area. That is why his descendants, the Booyaamanna, henceforth have laid claim to be the noblest group of the Hadiyya.

When the political reshuffle occurred after 1991 the non-Booyaamanna suspected that they were being discriminated against in the power play of the Zone. As a result, a new internal discourse started among the Hadiyya on the base of genealogical descent and of the time-depth of settlement in the area. When I collected historical traditions in the 1970s, the role of Booyaamo as the noblest ancestor was undisputed. In the 1990s, however, the other Hadiyya groups vehemently started opposing the elitist position of the Booyaamanna and their allegedly privileged access to administrative jobs. In this new trend, the groups of the so-called Agara Hadiyya – *agara* means land – emphasize that they are the oldest inhabitants of the area and also constitute the majority of the population. The first mentioned claim is undisputed; the latter cannot yet be proved by demographic statistics. The dispute has verbally become very radical and will hopefully not escalate in violent actions.[20]

During my last stay, in 1999-2000, I was sometimes blamed by Hadiyya informants and intellectuals for having put too much weight on the traditions of the Booyaamanna and comparatively neglected those of the Agara Hadiyya. Representatives of this group now discovered on the basis of my own writings that Booyaamo was a "traitor", a person who supported emperor Zarʾa Yaᶜqob against rebels or, one could also say, freedom fighters, of his own people. This is indeed proven by the historical sources. In the 1970s, however, when Amharic overlords directly administered all Hadiyya, the differences of genealogical origin were by no means relevant in the sense as they appear to be now.[21] Every Hadiyya was more or less proud of heroes such as Booyaamo.

18 In this context I mainly refer to the pedigrees of my major informants such as Nammana Dilliso, Nunishe Manta and Haile Bubbamo Arficio.
19 Cf. Braukämper 1980: 82-87, 209, *passim.*
20 In 2000 I heard statements by Agara Hadiyya such as "We are going to finish the Booyaamanna".
21 By that time people in certain cases collected money to bribe the governor of Shawa Province in order to change the name of a *woreda*, for example from Tembaro to Sooro, which involved a more or less symbolic matter of ethnic prestige.

Analysis of discourses on the unity and diversity of Ethiopian culture

The case study of the Hadiyya presented here seems to be symptomatic for many parts of the SNNPRS and also other parts of Ethiopia after the introduction of the federal system. The ethnological view is basically directed to facts and events of a local sphere, but it can at least try to embark on the broader perspective of national developments. Undisputedly, the strict centralism which was employed in Ethiopian policy from the time of emperor Menilek until the fall of the DERG regime was a major root of serious socio-economic problems, particularly in the south of the country. That is why the change towards a more decentralized federalist structure was welcomed by the bulk of Ethiopian citizens (and by foreign observers). However, the dilemmas the government of Ethiopia is facing after the far-reaching political alterations are enormous. It certainly cannot satisfy all the desires of small ethnic groups regarding a more autonomous representation in their respective territorial units. Otherwise the whole nation-state would be splintered to an extent that a proper administration is hardly manageable. It takes of course time to establish a functioning equilibrium of centralism and federalism.

At the same time a process is going on in this context, which can be labelled as an "invention of tradition".[22] This is occurring, as far as I can see, in many parts of Ethiopia on the ethnic level, but it is more or less profoundly also affecting the national level. As already pointed out, representatives of various ethnic groups frequently appeal to the highest political authorities of the country in order to achieve a renaming of territorial units as well as changes of boundaries and educational or cultural institutions on the ground of historically defined claims. These are mostly derived from oral traditions, which therefore enjoy an astonishing degree of revitalisation, and to some extent also from ethnographic literature predominantly written by foreign researchers. For example, the interest, which arose among intellectual Oromo in the *Gada* age class order already in the 1960s, could be nourished in most regions only by European writings, because apart from Boränaland the system no longer existed as a living whole. When Oromo scholars sometimes glorified it as an ideal democratic institution this could consequently not be made on the base of their own empirical research.[23]

I sometimes experienced discussions with Ethiopian intellectuals who argued on the ground of place names or etymological speculations associated with them that

---

22 This topic is extensively analysed in the famous book by Hobsbawm and Ranger 1994. In this context, one could probably also talk of a "re-invention" of tradition.
23 The substantial study on the *Gada* system by Asmarom Legesse (1973) was carried out by a non-Oromo.

people of their own group settled certain historical localities.[24] However, the labels in Cushitic languages are often similar or even identical and do not necessarily prove concrete ethnic specifications in time-depth. What can furthermore be observed among many agropastoralist groups in southern Ethiopia is an outstanding nostalgia regarding affluent conditions of former times, particularly before the Amharic conquest, when cattle were abundant and enough high quality food was always available. People in those days, it is emphasized, were strong and happy, blessed by God.

What we can presently observe all over Ethiopia can be labelled an "ethnicization of political discourse". After a long period of an ideology emphasizing the unity of Ethiopian culture, which was more or less defined by the culture of the Amhara-dominated Christian state,[25] the diversity of Ethiopians in terms of ethnicity and individual cultural expressions is now propagated. Some African countries, such as the Sudan before the breakthrough of Islamic fundamentalism in the 1980s, advocated a doctrine of "unity in diversity". Principally, as we can see from numerous examples, a federal structure tends to reduce tensions within states which are not fully homogeneous in their population and their cultural orientations. Switzerland with four official languages is obviously facing less internal problems than France with its highly centralized cultural policy. Countries like Tanzania where people openly discuss their ethnic background are prospering more than for example Somalia where a citizen's mentioning of his clan group was considered a quasi-criminal act. That is why the overwhelming majority of social scientists were enthusiastic about the change from centralism to federalism in Ethiopian policy in the 1990s.[26]

However, when this change occurred it was difficult or even impossible to predict certain disadvantages which are rooted in the local traditions of people. It is indeed astonishing how vital particularistic ethnic interests have been preserved despite their having been sheltered for more than a century by the shade of a mighty pan-Ethiopian national umbrella. This does not only refer to the big ethnic clusters such as the Oromo, but also to medium-sized ones like the Hadiyya and even to groups consisting of only some thousands of individuals. Unlike in former times, ethnic priorities and aims can legally be expressed and realized now. For the IHADIG government the managing of regional diversity and the balancing of multiple ethnic interests undoubtedly became a serious problem, but it acted at the same time as an efficient means of power control. Controversial interests and aims at the level of the Regional States, the zones and the districts of course do not work in favour of a united opposition. Despite the high esteem for the treasure of diversity of Ethiopian cultures, Donald Levine's (1974) vision of an "Ethiopian synthesis" derived from the multiple ethnic

---

24 An example of this kind was my friend Haile Bubbamo Arficio, who then behaved as a "Hadiyya nationalist". I also had discussions with Mohammed Hassen on place names attributed to Oromo.

25 As a cultural anthropologist, Haberland always drew attention to "pan-Ethiopian" features of culture also in the south of the country.

26 Cf., for example, the respective statements by Asfa-Wossen Asserate 1993.

backgrounds of the country (with a particular emphasis on Amhara and Oromo) deserves a thorough reconsideration.

Historical traditions are not only revitalized or even (re)invented, but also sometimes manipulated. This has of course always been done, but field researchers can experience it in their empirical work. Thus it can happen that the naive anthropologist who does not want to interfere in political affairs is all of a sudden confronted with accusations from different lobbies of political interests. As I have explained with some examples above, results of ethnographic research are not simply considered as neutral *l'art pour l'art*, but they are exploited by political agents on the local as well as on the national level.

The desire to strengthen indigenous traditions and to introduce the local language in school education and administration is fully understandable after a long period of an almost complete denial of cultural autonomy in southern Ethiopia. But it undoubtedly has led to an overreaction, such as the temporary closing of the schools in Hadiyyaland, because many teachers were not able to teach in the local language Hadiyyeesa. The need of a *lingua franca* at the national level – and in Hadiyya and most other parts of the country this has to be Amharic for pragmatic reasons – appears to be an indispensable requirement. Compromises have to be made concerning the introduction of local dialects for educational purposes in order to avoid violent clashes as occurred in Soddo/Wälaytta in November 1999. People there refused to accept a standardized language which to some extent tried to integrate the closely related dialects of Dawro, Gofa and other regions.

It is sometimes difficult to decide what are really genuine indigenous traditions. The most common type of house in Hadiyyaland was adopted from Gurage. The typical dress of the region – as far as it is still employed beside the general European standards – corresponds to the national Ethiopian style. A return to the traditional clothes made of leather and cotton imported from Wällayta and Dorze is outside every serious consideration. The present Hadiyya are Protestants, Orthodox Christians, Roman Catholics or Muslims and nobody is interested in returning to the traditional religion *Fandaano*, which definitely became extinct in the 1990s.[27] That is why a reconsideration or even reinvention of tradition is concentrated to the field of the language and to a lesser extent to the folklore and to historical reminiscences.

In the case of the Hadiyya ethnic consciousness and pride have recently found an additional political arena in the solidarity with the officially acknowledged opposition party "Southern Ethiopia Peoples' Democratic Coalition" (SEPDC) headed by the Baadawwaachcho-Hadiyya Dr. Beyene Petros. Despite massive obstructions on the part of the ruling party, it enjoys a devoted backing by the majority of his people and to a lesser extent also by other groups in SNNPRS who thus demonstrate a regional

---

27 My own attempt at composing an analysis of this traditional socio-religious system *Fandaano* from information and observation of the early 1970s when it still existed as a functioning whole in some parts of Hadiyyaland can therefore be regarded as a kind of ethnographic archaeology.

solidarity, which exerts a notable feedback on the national level of the Ethiopian federal state.

The following table summarizes some of the opposing factors inherent in the controversy of local and national contexts which have to be balanced for the sake of a peaceful and prosperous development.

Local Ethnic Traditions	National Ethiopian Context
priority of local ethnic diversity	priority of national unity
priority of particularistic interests	priority of interests of the entire federation
demand for the use of the local language	demand for a national language
pride in individualistic ethnic prestige	demand for national egalitarianism
efforts for expansion of the area	efforts for territorial stability
claim to early settlement in the area	prevention of internal and border disputes
search for local historical roots	search for markers of national identity
revitalization of ethnic-oriented tradition	strengthening of national cultural tradition
nostalgia for a glorious past	aspiration for a common future orientation

Bibliography

Abbink, J.
1998   New Configurations of Ethiopian Ethnicity: The Challenge of the South. In: *Northeast African Studies 5, 1*: 59-81.

Asfa-Wossen Asserate
1993   *The Necessity of a Federal Structure for Ethiopia. A Paper Presented at the Symposium on "The Making of the New Ethiopian Constitution", 17[b]-21st May 1993*, Africa Hall, UN Economic Commission for Africa. Addis Ababa, Ethiopia.

Asmarom Legesse
1974   *Gada: Three Approaches to the Study of African Society*. Free Press. New York [etc.].

Barth, F.
1969   Introduction. In: *Barth, Fredrik (ed.), Ethnic Groups and Boundaries. The Social Organization of Culture Difference*. Universitets Forlaget. Bergen, Oslo: 9-38; George Allen & Unwin. London.

Braukämper, U.
1980   *Die Geschichte der Hadiya Süd-Äthiopiens - Von den Anfängen bis zur Revolution 1974*. Steiner. Wiesbaden.
1983   *Die Kambata – Geschichte und Gesellschaft eines südäthiopischen Bauernvolkes*. Steiner. Wiesbaden.
1992   *Migration und ethnischer Wandel. Untersuchungen aus der östlichen Sudanzone*. Steiner. Wiesbaden.
1999-00 Fandaano: A Vanishing Socio-Religious System of the Hadiyya in Southern Ethiopia. In: *Bulletin of the Committee on Urgent Anthropological and Ethnological Research* 40: 52-63.
2002   *Islamic History and Culture in Southern Ethiopia. Collected Essays*. LIT-Verlag. Münster [etc.].

Braukämper, U. and Tilahun Mishago
1999   *Praise and Teasing: Narrative Songs of the Hadiyya in Southern Ethiopia*. Frobenius-Institut. Frankfurt a.M.

Bromlej, J. V.
1977   *Ethnos und Ethnographie*. Akademie-Verlag. Berlin.

Bustorf, D.
2002   *Leemo-Hadiyya und Indagayn-Gurage: Zur Geschichte und Gegenwart ihrer interethnischen Beziehungen*. Universität Göttingen. (Unpubl. MA thesis).

Comaroff, J. and J.
2000   Naturing the Nation: Aliens, Apocalypse, and the Postcolonical State. *HAGAR. International Social Science Review 1, 1*: 7-40.

Hobsbawm, E. J. and Terence R. (eds)
1994   *Invention of Tradition*. Cambridge [etc.]: Cambridge University Press (Repr.).

Levine, D.
1974   *Greater Ethiopia. The Evolution of a Multiethnic Society*. University of Chicago Press. Chicago, London.

Littmann, E. et al.
1913   *Deutsche Aksum-Expedition*. 4 vols. Reimer. Berlin.

Scholler, H.
1999   La réception du droit occidental en Ethiopie. Contribution à la théorie de la Réception et de l'Implementation. In: *Verfassung und Recht in Übersee, Law and Politics in Africa, Asia and Latin America 32, 3*: 296-313.

SNNPRS - Administrative Units (Zones, Districts) 1999

Legend

Gurage

E-Z	Ezana & Wolene
K-G	Kokier Gedebano
La	Fanfero
M-M	Meakan & Mareko

Hadiya

| Ba | Badawacho |

KAT	Kembata Alaba Tembaro
An	Angacha
K-B	Kacha Bira
K-G	Kadida Gemila

Sidama

| Ar | Arbegona |

Gedeo

Bu	Bule
Ko	Kochera
We	Wenago
Y-C	Yerga Chefe

North Omo

Baa	Baaketo
B-A	Boreda Abaya
B-S	Bolesa Soro
CH	Chencha
D-D	Dita Deramalo
D-G	Damot Gale
D-W	Damot Weyde
K-K	Kindo Koyaha
M-G	Mareka Gena
S-Z	Sodo Zuriya

Map 1

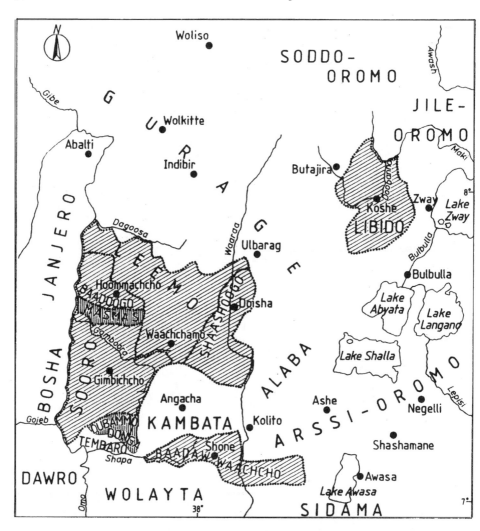

HADIYYA IN SOUTHERN ETHIOPIA

0   25   50 km

Hadiyya-speaking groups
(acc. to new system of transcription)

Groups linguistically assimilated by Hadiyya

Boundaries of Hadiyya subgroups

GURAGE Other ethnic groups

Map 2

Morgenländische Wörter im Deutschen: Die ägyptischen Lehnwörter

Francis Amadeus Karl Breyer

Vorbemerkungen

Kaum ein orientalistisches Werk ist in den Nachbarfächern in solchem Maße rezipiert worden, wie Littmanns Buch über die *Morgenländische Wörter im Deutschen* (Littmann 1920). Ein Blick in die letzte Auflage von Kluges Etymologischem Wörterbuche beispielsweise zeigt uns, daß in der Tat Littmanns Arbeit neben K. Lokotsch, *Etymologisches Wörterbuch der europäischen Wörter orientalischen Ursprungs*, das bisher einzige Referenzwerk auf diesem Gebiet geblieben ist, zumindest für die neuphilologischen Disziplinen (Lokotsch 1927).

Allerdings ist die zweite, verbesserte Auflage des Werkes immerhin bereits aus dem Jahre 1924 und obwohl sich in vielen Punkten die Lehrmeinungen nicht geändert haben werden, so gibt es doch einen Teil, bei dem sich die Grundvoraussetzungen seit den 20er Jahren erheblich verschoben haben. Es handelt sich um das erste Kapitel, das mit den altorientalischen Wörtern.

An dieser Stelle kommt auch bereits ein Punkt zum Vorschein, der Littmanns Arbeit von der Lokotschs unterscheidet. Hatte sich doch Ersterer dafür entschieden, die Etymologien nicht in alphabethischer Reihenfolge, d.h. in Wörterbuchform zu präsentieren, sondern nach Sachklassen oder Kulturkreisen geordnet in zusammenhängender Form auszuformulieren. Dabei bedient er sich eines gut lesbaren und auch für den Laien sehr klar verständlichen Stils, ja fast eines Plaudertons. Auf diese Weise ist es Littmann gelungen, nicht nur einen Hort an etymologischen Quisquilien zusammenzutragen, sondern zugleich ein schön geschriebenes und spannendes Buch zu verfassen, das sich gerade auch ein interessierter Nicht-Orientalist abends am Kaminfeuer zu Gemüte führen kann – selbst wenn das nicht oft der Fall sein wird.

Die altorientalischen Fächer standen 1924 noch sehr viel mehr als heute in den Kinderschuhen. So gab es zu dieser Zeit weder für das Ägyptische noch für das Akkadische umfassende und brauchbare Wörterbücher. Zwar bestand das ägyptologische

Großprojekt *Wörterbuch der ägyptischen Sprache* bereits seit 1897, doch erschien der erste Band erst 1926.[1]

Noch viel schlechter war die Situation in der Akkadistik (vgl. Borger 1984). Nach den im Grunde nicht zu Ende geführten Arbeiten von Delitsch und Betzold sollte noch ein halbes Jahrhundert ins Land gehen, bis mit von Sodens *Akkadischem Handwörterbuch* das erste vollständige assyrisch-babylonische Wörterbuch vorlag. Für etymologische Fragen der Nachbarfächer ist dies von großer Bedeutung, wie am Beispiel der Ugaristik als Negativbeispiel zum Vorschein kommt: allein bei der Lektüre der ersten Tafel des Baal-Zyklus wird in den verschiedenen Bearbeitungen mit beinahe einem halben Dutzend angeblich akkadischer Wörter etymologisiert, die weder im *Akkadischen Handwörterbuch* noch im *Chicago Assyrian Dicionary* zu finden sind und trotzdem innerugaristisch seit Jahrzehnten weiter tradiert werden.

Ein weiteres Teilgebiet der Altorientalistik – die Hethitologie – existierte im Grunde genommen Anfang der 20er Jahre noch gar nicht. Erst seit Beginn der Grabungen in Bogazköy 1905 wurde bis 1912 der Großteil des hethitischen Staatsarchives ausgegraben und damit Texte in größerem Umfang zugänglich gemacht. Hrozný zeigte dann 1915 und erneut 1917, daß es sich um eine indogermanische Sprache handelt und stieß damit zu Beginn auf erhebliche Ablehnung. Es bedurfte der Stimme des Indogermanisten Sommer, um ab 1920 die Anerkennung des indogermanischen Sprachbaus des Hethitischen durchzusetzen. Durch die schnelle und gediegene philologische Erschließung des Hethitischen durch J. Friedrich (1921), A. Goetz (1922), E. Forrer (1922) und H. Ehelolf (1923) konnte Delaporte dann bereits 1929 eine erste Zusammenfassung der Ergebnisse vorlegen. Obwohl mehrere verschiedene Wörterbuchprojekte existieren, ist der hethitische Wortschatz bis heute noch nicht zusammenhängend erschlossen.

Es versteht sich von selbst, daß mit den nach Littmanns Werk erschienenen Wörterbüchern die Erforschung altorientalischer Lehnwörter im Deutschen auf eine völlig neue Grundlage gestellt wird. Daß sich seither niemand mehr in vergleichbarer Art dieses Themas angenommen hat, mag zum einen nicht nur am Zeitgeist liegen (man fürchtet möglicherweise in den Verdacht der Deutschtümelei zu kommen), zum anderen schlichtweg an der Kraft der Forschergestalt Enno Littmann.

Besonders letzteres sollte nicht unterschätzt werden. Bei genauerem Hinsehen bemerkt nämlich der Fachkundige, daß die entsprechenden Passagen über akkadisches Sprachmaterial direkt von Heinrich Zimmern, *Akkadische Fremdwörter als Beweis für babylonischen Kultureinfluß* (1915), übernommen sind. Dies soll selbstredend kein Vorwurf sein, schließlich lag der Alte Orient Littmanns *etwas* ferner als die jüngeren Bereiche der Orientalistik. Die Tatsache ist einfach nur aufschlußreich vor dem Hintergrund, daß im Gegensatz zu den *„Morgenländischen Wörtern im Deutschen"* Zimmerns Buch so gut wie nicht rezipiert wurde.

---

1   A. Erman und H. Grapow (Hrg.), Wörterbuch der ägyptischen Sprache. Die Bände 1-5 erschienen zwischen 1926 und 1931, die Belegstellenbände bis 1955 bzw. 1963 der 12. Band. Fortan abgekürzt als Wb.

Nachdem ich hier einzelne Aspekte altorientalischer Lexikographie aufgezeigt habe, möchte ich im Folgenden mein Augenmerk auf einen speziellen Ausschnitt der „*Morgenländischen Wörter im Deutschen*" richten, die Wörter ägyptischen Ursprungs. Ich habe diese nicht nur gewählt, weil ich mich damit als Ägyptologe auf sicherem Terrain bewege. Als Altorientalist kann ich mit gutem Gewissen vertreten, daß der größte Teil der akkadischen bzw. sumerischen *Etyma* einer Reevaluation standhält, was bei den ägyptischen in viel weniger Fällen gesagt werden kann.

Meine Neubewertung der deutschen Wörter ägyptischer Etymologie gliedert sich in vier Abschnitte:

1. Zuerst sollen die Einträge Littmanns angerissen werden, die revidert werden sollten, wobei
   a) einige Wörter nach heutigem Stand der Dinge ganz wegfallen (*Lilie, Kuchen*),
   b) zu manchen nach der *communis opinio* immer noch eine ägyptische Etymologie aufrechterhalten wird, wenn auch eine andere, als die von Littmann angenommene (*Ägypten, Papyrus, Nil*).
2. In einem zweiten Schritt möchte ich Etymologien vorstellen, die sich bei Littmann noch nicht finden (*Pavian, Elefant*), um dann
3. unter Einbeziehung weiterer Etymologien, die seit langem unbestritten sind,
4. zuletzt den Versuch zu wagen, von einem Überblick der wahrscheinlichen ägyptischen Etyma deutscher Wörter ausgehend, ein Bild von ihren Entlehnungsprozessen zu entwerfen mit Schwerpunkt auf einer Motivationsanalyse (*Salmiak / Ammoniak, Oase, Alabaster, Natron, Gummi, Pharao*).

1. a) Besonders interessante Lexeme, die nach den derzeitigen Erkenntnissen doch nicht auf ägyptisches Sprachgut zurückgeführt werden können

Lilie:
Die Pflanzenbezeichnung „Lilie", von lat. *lilium* bzw. gr. λεῖριον ist meines Wissens sogar zuerst von Littmann in die Diskussion gebracht worden. Von ägyptologischer Seite ist die Verbindung zu Saîdisch-kopt. ϩⲣⲏⲣⲉ bzw. Fayumisch ϩⲗⲏⲗⲓ 1945 von W. H. Worell in seinen „*Coptic Sounds*" aufgegriffen worden, der die Gleichung als *striking etymology* bezeichnete (Worell 1945: 67). Frappierend ist freilich der Wechsel von /l/ und /r/ sowohl im Griechisch-Lateinischen als auch im Koptischen. Allerdings kann man beide Phänomene unabhängig voneinander erklären. So muß die Unschärfe der Liquida bei der Entlehnung ins Lateinische nicht mit dem fayumischen Lambdazismus zusammenhängen. Ebensowenig muß man aus der Tatsache, daß das dem Koptischen zugrunde liegende Wort in syllabischer Schrift geschrieben wird, folgern, daß es sich um ein semitisches, d.h. kanaanäisches Lehnwort im Ägyptischen handelt, wie dies Albright (1934) getan hat. Dieser hatte ägyptisch *ḥrrt*, syllabisch

ḫaruru gelesen und mit arab. *zahr* „Blume", he. *zohar* „Glanz" und *'ōr* „Licht", akkad. *āru* „Blume" verglichen. Gegen die Identifizierung als kanaanäisches Lehnwort spricht, daß *ḫrrt* bereits in der 18. Dynastie bestens bezeugt ist. Hauptargument gegen eine weitere Entlehnung von ägyptisch *ḫrr.t* spricht seinerseits, daß es „Blume" bedeutet und das ägyptische Wort für „Lilie" *sšš n*, kopt. ϣⲱϣⲉⲛ lautete, dessen Verbindung zu he. *šōšan, šōšanním,* fem. *šōšannā,* d.h. dem Personennamen „Susanne" auf der einen Seite und dem arab. *sawsan, sūsān* sowie gr. σοῦσον „Lilie" hinlänglich bekannt ist (DEC, 276).

Generell scheinen die Liliennamen große Entlehnungsfreudigkeit zu besitzen. So ist beispielsweise das ägypt.-arab. *bašnīn* mit Sicherheit unter Hinzunahme des koptischen Artikels ⲡⲁ übernommen worden und auch das klassisch-arab. *nīlūfar,* seinerseits Ausgangspunkt für französisch *nénuphar* „Lotus", wird meist von pers. *nīlūfar* abgeleitet. Die Herkunft von ägyptisch *nꜣ-nfr.w* ist hingegen aus lautlichen Gründen nicht möglich.[2]

Das ägyptische *ḫrrt* kann, wenn überhaupt, nur als Wanderwort gelten, das im Hethitischen auftritt (*alel, alil* „Blume, Blüte", mit prothetischem *a-*) sowie in berberischen (*alili*) und kuschitischen Sprachen (*ilili*).[3]

Kuchen:

All diejenigen, die gerne *Kuchen* essen, wird es erstaunen, bei Littmann auch das Objekt ihrer Begierde verzeichnet zu finden. In der ägyptologischen und gräzistischen Literatur ist von seiner Herleitung aus dem selten bezeugten Wort für Kuchen *ꜥkk* des öfteren zu lesen.[4] Damit verglichen wird he. *kăꜥăk* und arab. *kaꜥk* (*kaḥk* im kairener Dialekt) derselben Bedeutung. Strabon berichtet von κακεῖς, einer ägyptischen Brotsorte. W. Vycichl spricht sich deswegen in seinem *„Dictionnaire étymologique de la langue copte"* für die Richtigkeit der Herleitung aus, doch gehörte er offensichtlich auch zu den κακεῖοφιλοι, denn er referiert nicht nur die Belege und Lehrmeinungen, sondern gibt darüber hinaus noch ein vollständiges Rezept der ägyptischen *kaḥk*-Kuchen, was für etymologische Wörterbücher eher ungewöhnlich ist. Ein anderes dieser klugen Werke, *Kluges Etymologisches Wörterbuch der deutschen Sprache,*[5] geht auf die ägyptische These nicht ein, findet allerdings auch keine bessere Erklärung, ich zitiere: „Sonst (d.h. außergermanisch) ist die Herkunft dunkel. [...]." Vielleicht handelt es sich um ein kindersprachlich reduplizierendes Wort.

Soviel zu den zu streichenden Etyma.

---

2   *n˘-nafrū < n˘(ꜣ)-nāfir.ū* o.ä., vgl. *Wnn-nfr.w* (B) ⲃⲉⲛⲟϥⲉⲣ, Ὀννῶφρις, Vycichl, DEC 150. Das Abstraktum wird immer mit dem Pluralartikel gebraucht.

3   Schneider 1997: 241-267, besonders 266 mit Anm. 103, 248 mit Anm. 25.

4   Fournait 1989: 55-80, speziell hierzu 66.

5   Kluge 1999: 490 s.v. Kuchen.

1. b) Wörter, zu denen sich die *communis opinio* bezüglich ihrer ägyptischen Etymologie geändert hat

Den Anfang macht die Bezeichnung des Landes selbst.

Ägypten:
Bereits in den Linear B Texten taucht der Personenname *a-ku-pi-ti-yo* auf, der den Träger als Ägypter ausweist und so den Schluß zuläßt, daß schon zu jener Zeit die griechische Bezeichnung für Ägypten eben Αἴγυπτος war (Ventris - Chadwick 1973: 136). Littmann hält sich zwar diesbezüglich bedeckt, erwähnt allerdings auch den alten Versuch, eine Verbindung zum Toponym Koptos herzustellen, das heute auf äg.-arab. *Qifṭ* heißt, was allerdings im lokalen Dialekt als *Guft* realisiert wird (Vycichl, DEC 72). In der Ägyptologie wird heutzutage die Lehrmeinung vertreten, daß sich Αἴγυπτος von einer Bezeichnung für die Hauptstadt Memphis ableitet, von *ḥw.t-k3-Ptḥ*. Diese bedeutet ungefähr „Höchsteigene Kapelle des Ptah"[6] und ist nicht nur keilschriftlich als *URUḥi-ku-up-ta-aḥ* bezeugt, sondern auch bereits in den ugaritischen Texten eine gängige Bezeichnung für Ägypten. Man darf allerdings auch die Probleme bei der Gleichung Αἴγυπτος - *ḥw.t-k3-Ptḥ* nicht unter den Tisch kehren. Da wäre zum einen der Auslaut, der zur Zeit Assurbanipals, d.h. um 660 v. Chr., noch deutlich wiedergegeben wird. Schwerer ins Gewicht fällt die ungewöhnliche griechische Wiedergabe der Plosive *p, t* und *k*. Bei ihnen würde man nach allem, was wir wissen, eine aspirierte Wiedergabe erwarten, die auch beim Gott Ptah sonst anzutreffen ist: Φθα /*pʰtʰa*/. Auch der Anlaut erscheint doch sehr stark verkürzt, zumal sich das Element *ḥw.t* in anderen Verbindungen, etwa Hathor <*ḥw.t-Ḥr(.w)* erhalten hat.

Papyrus:
Auch bei dem Wort Papier bzw. dessen griechischer Etymologie πάπυρος, wurde schon immer ein ägyptischer Ursprung vermutet. Littmann folgt einem Vorschlag Bondis (1895), nach dem gr. πάπυρος auf äg. *p3-n-p3-ỉtr.w* „Der des Flusses" zurückginge. Die beiden Schwachpunkte dieses Ansatzes sind das Fehlen sowohl des nach Ausweis des koptischen ⲉⲓⲟⲟⲣ und hebr. *ỉeʔōr* sicher anzusetzenden Stimmabsatzes,[7] als auch das des Yod. Dieses ist in anderem Zusammenhang in griechischer Transkription erhalten geblieben, z.B. in dem Namen Ψανιῦρις *P3-šnᶜ-n(.ỉ)-ỉr*.

Wahrscheinlicher und mittlerweile allgemein akzeptiert ist eine Ansicht, die auf Seyffarth (1842) zurückgeht und in neuerer Zeit besonders von Vergote, der sich

---

6 Das Element *k3* hat in diesem Kontext die Grundbedeutung „privat, selbst".

7 Vycichl (1942: 79-93) hat sich dagegen ausgesprochen und nimmt die Graphie mit Aleph als *mater lectionis* für *ō*. Diesem Ansatz ist C. Peust (1999: 206) gefolgt. Aufgrund der keilschriftlichen Wiedergabe halte ich es für besser, die hebräische Graphie als Notation des Stimmabsatzes zu interpretieren.

eingehend mit der Problematik befaßt hat, vertreten wurde.[8] Sie geht von der Überlegung aus, daß Papyrus ein besonders wertvoller Schriftträger war und somit die Bezeichnung „Das des Pharao" recht angebracht wäre. Auf Koptisch hieße das dann auch ΠΑ ·Π·Ρ̄ΡΟ < *pȝ<-n(.ỉ)> pȝ-pr(.w)-ʿȝ .

Nil:
Das geflügelte Wort von Ägypten als Geschenk des Nils ist genauso allgegenwärtig wie der Nil in der ägyptischen Landschaft und da verwundert es nicht, wenn hinter diesem Flußnamen etwas Ägyptisches vermutet wird. Das ägyptische Wort für „Fluß" wurde bereits vorgestellt. Nun ist der Nil in Ägypten selbstredend *der* Fluß schlechthin, oder auch *der große* Fluß, was auf koptisch Π·ЄІЄΡΟ <*pȝ-ỉtr.w-ʿȝ* heißt. Das führt uns allerdings noch nicht zu gr. Νεῖλος. Dazu bedarf es der weiteren Annahme, daß sich der Nil bekanntlich in seinem Delta in mehrere Flußarme verzweigt. Auf diese Weise kommt man zum Ansatz der Pluralform ägypt. **nȝ-ỉtr.w-ʿȝ.w*> kopt. Ν·ЄІЄΡШΟΥ. Der Wechsel von *r>l* ist durch den Fayumischen Lambdazismus hinreichend erklärbar.

Eine ganz andere Hypothese hat W. Vycichl (1972: 8-18) vorgebracht. Er versucht eine Etymologie zu etablieren, die auf einer erschlossenen afroasiatischen Wurzel für Wasser o.ä. beruht. Diese Wurzel ist vertreten im akkadischen *nīlu(m)* „Fluß", ägypt. *nnw* <**nlw* „Urozean" und berber. (Djerba) *ilēl* < **a-lil*. Im Kuschitischen ist Bedja *lil* „flüssig, feucht" hinzuzustellen (Roper 1928: 212). Besonders interessant ist in diesem Zusammenhang eine Stelle bei Hesiod, in der ein libysches λίλυ mit „Wasser" übersetzt wird. Trotz der unglaublichen Fülle an Informationen, die Vycichl wie üblich bietet, spricht manches gegen seinen Ansatz. Der Vokal wird nur paradigmatisch erschlossen als *pars* vs. *pirs* (wie im akkad. *nīlu*). Hauptargument ist, daß die Wurzel im Zusammenhang mit dem Nil im Ägyptischen nicht vorkommt.

2. Nach Littmann (1920) vorgeschlagene Etymologien

Nach diesem Abriß über die Wörter, bei denen sich die Sicht der Dinge seit den Tagen Littmanns geändert hat, möchte ich nun auf Lexeme zu sprechen kommen, deren ägyptische Herkunft nach dem Erscheinen seiner Arbeit überhaupt erst vorgeschlagen wurde:

---

8 Vergote 1951: 411-416. Dort auch die älteren Etymologisierungsansätze.

Basanit/Basalt	<βασανίτης <**bsn.tỉ* „Gestein, aus dem der Grabstichel besteht" (Kammerzell 2001)
Bluse	< Πηλούσιον < *sỉn* „Festung"[9] (Lokotsch 1927: Nr. 1647)[10]
Chemie	< χημηεία < km.t, kopt. ⲕⲏⲙⲉ (Herrmann 1954)
Alaun/Aluminium	< lat. alumen < * ⸢r⸣-*ỉbnw* „Alaunkies" (Kammerzell 2002)
Labyrinth	< λαβύινθος < *r'-pr(.w) rn=ś* (Schenkel 1997a)
Pyramide	< πῦραμίς < *p3-mr* (Lang 1923/24)
Atlantik/Atlantis	< ἡ Ἀτλαντιάς νῆσος (Herodot, Historien I, 202)< *ỉw.tt-rn=ś* „die namenlose (Insel)" (Schenkel 1979)
Mythos	< μῦθος < *mṱ.t*, kopt. ⲙⲟⲩⲧⲉ (Ernštedt 1953: 55-57)[11]
Barke	< βᾶρις < *br* (Fournet 1989: 55-80, bes. 57)
Bronze	< * *bỉ3-rwč* „Hartes Metall" (Kammerzell 2002: 39-55)
Pavian	< βεβον oder βαβυς < äg. *b3by* (v. Bissing 1951; Edel 1956; Derchain 1952, 1963)
Elefant	< ἐλέφας < *3bw* (Grimm 1862; Breyer i. Druck)

Basanit/Basalt:
K. Sethe (1933: 894-909) hat den Vorschlag gemacht, das griechische βασανίτης, auf das die Bezeichnungen für das Eruptivgestein zurückgehen, von äg. *bḫn* abzuleiten. Er klärt vorab die Beziehung zwischen Basanit und Basalt, die letztlich dasselbe sind und deren Unterscheidung auf einer verderbten Textstelle bei Plinius, Nat. hist. 36, 58; 36, 147 und 36, 157 beruht. So war die falsche Lesung denn auch Ausgangspunkt für G. Agricola, welcher die Gesteinsbezeichung in der Wissenschaft etabliert hat. Das griechische βασανίτης sei, so Sethe, sicherlich die richtige Lesung, da sie sich auf die Eigenschaften des Steines beziehe, die ihn als βάσανος befähigen, d.h. als Prüfstein für Gold. Das ägyptische *bḫn* könne von einer Wurzel mit der Bedeutung „prüfen" abgeleitet werden, die auch in andere orientalische Sprachen gedrungen sei, z.B. he. *bḫn*. Ein Schwachpunkt bei der Argumentation Sethes ist, daß es zeitliche Schwierigkeiten bei dem Übergang *ḫ* > *š* gibt, die er zu überbrücken sucht, indem er davon ausgeht, er sei im anatolischen Bereich, etwa dem Lydischen, Lykischen o.ä. geschehen. Das Lexem ist dort allerdings nicht belegt. Noch viel konstruierter ist seine Erklärung des Zusammenhangs zwischen βασανίτης und βάσανος „Prüfstein", den er schon für das Altägyptische rekonstruiert. Auf einer heute in Turin befindlichen Landkarte ist im Zusammenhang mit Goldminen ein Toponym *p3 čw n(.ỉ) bḫn* „Das Grauwackengebirge" verzeichnet. Das Wort *bḫn* „Grauwacke" wird mit einem Auge determiniert, woraus Sethe auf einen Gleichklang mit einem nicht belegten Wort für

---

9 Die Herleitung aus dem Ägyptischen ist nicht ganz einfach, weil mehrere Faktoren hineinspielen. Zum einen gilt der Vater des Achill, Peleus, als Gründer der Stadt. Dies hat ihren Grund in einer volksetymologischen Verbindung von äg. *sỉn* „Lehm" mit gr. πηλός „Lehm". Dazu siehe *LÄ IV*, 925f.
10 Siehe auch W. Vycichl, DEC 164.
11 Siehe auch Peust 1999: 71.

„spähen" schließt. Damit bringt er wiederum *bḫn.t* „Pylon" in Verbindung, das seinerseits mit dem Kopf einer Antilope determiniert wird, denen „das Spähen nach Feinden" eigentümlich sei. Es dürfte klar sein, wie wenig Sethes verschlungene Argumentationskette einer eingehenden *Prüfung* standhält. So kann man getrost die Herleitung des Gesteinsnamens aus einer Bezeichnung für den „Prüfstein" als altgriechische Volksetymologie abweisen. Allerdings lenkt Plinius doch wieder auf die richtige Fährte, wenn er schreibt (Nat. hist. 36, 58): *Invenit eadem Aegyptus in Aethiopia quem vocant basaniten, ferrei coloris atque duritiae, unde et nomen ei dedit.* „Außerdem brechen die Ägypter in Äthiopien einen Stein, den sie basaniten nennen, von der Farbe und Härte des Eisens, daher gaben sie ihm auch seinen Namen." Es kommt deutlich zum Ausdruck, woher der Name des Steines zumindest nach Plinius' Ansicht kam. In neuester Zeit hat sich F. Kammerzell (2001) erneut der Problematik gewidmet und ein passendes ägyptisches Etymon gefunden. Das koptische Wort für „Schmied, Metallarbeiter" lautet ʙᴇᴄɴʜᴛ (S., B.), ʙᴇᴄɴᴀᴛ (S.) oder ʙᴀᴄɴʜᴛ (B.) (Vycichl, DEC 32). Es kann zurückgeführt werden auf äg. *bśn.t*, das im Neuägyptischen vorkommt und für welches das *Wörterbuch der ägyptischen Sprache* (Wb I, 477) aufgrund der Wendung *čꜣ̣ m bśn.t* „mit dem *bśn.t* gravieren" die Übersetzung „Grabstichel" angibt. Das koptische ʙᴇᴄɴʜᴛ ist für die ältere Sprachstufe als **bǎśnītiꝏ* anzusetzen, was der Form nach einer sogenannten reziproken Nisba entspricht. Dabei handelt es sich um Nisbe, die eine Appositiv-Relation zu ihrem Bezugswort ausdrücken und gegenüber den „normalen" Nisbe durch eine Akzentverschiebung nach vorne gekennzeichnet sind (Schenkel 1997b: 123; Osing 1976: 309-320) (vgl. **ꝏamĭꝏ-rǎʾ* „der, der sich im Mund befindet = Zunge" und **ꝏāmiꝏ-rǎʾ* „der, in dem sich der Spruch befindet = der Aufseher"). Entsprechend ist die Grundbedeutung „Der, zu dem der Grabstichel gehört". Andererseits kann davon ausgehend die nicht belegte „normale" Nisba **bǎśǎntiꝏ* „der (Stein), der zum Grabstichel gehört" rekonstruiert werden, das der Ausgangspunkt für das griechische βασανίτης bilden dürfte.

Bluse:

Die Bluse ist zuallererst nach einer Stoffart benannt. Es handelt sich um einen ganz bestimmten Stoff, der besonders in Pelusium hergestellt wurde. So bezieht sich das *pelusia* der Kreuzritter ursprünglich nur auf ein sehr spezielles Kleidungsstück, das charakteristischerweise von blauer Farbe war. Namengebend war die stärkste ägyptische Grenzfeste gegen den Sinai Πηλούσιον. Deren Name leitet sich im Prinzip ab von äg. *sìn* „Festung". Ganz so einfach ist der Fall aber doch nicht, weil mehrere andere Faktoren mit hineinspielen.[12] Zum einen gilt der Vater des Achill, *Peleus*, als Gründer der Stadt. Zum anderen hat dies seinen Grund in einer volksetymologischen Verbindung von äg. *sìn* „Lehm" mit gr. πηλός „Lehm". Alles zusammen ergibt den Etymologiebrei Πηλούσιον.

---

12 Vgl. dazu H.-J. Thissen, LÄ IV, 925f., s.v. Pelusium.

Chemie:

Bei der Chemie vermischen sich manche gleichartigen Dinge rein äußerlich – *similia similibus sulvuntur* – um in Wirklichkeit doch getrennt zu sein. Beispielsweise ist die *Alchemie* zwar in der Sache von der Chemie zu trennen, nicht aber auf der lexikalischen Ebene. Während sich die Alchemie aus dem arabischen Raum herleitet und auf arab. *al-kīmīa* zurückgeht und solchermaßen gesichert erscheint, ist der Ursprung von „Chemie" nicht restlos geklärt. Unbestritten ist die ägyptische Herkunft des Wortes. Ob sich das griechische χημηεία allerdings von äg. *km.t*, kopt. ⲕⲏⲙⲉ herleitet, wie zuletzt wieder von Herrmann (1954: 99-105) herausgearbeitet, oder im Gegenteil auf den für die Metallurgie zuständigen Zwergengott Chnum, ist umstritten.[13]

Die Gleichung gr. χημηεία - äg. *km.t* wurde zuerst von Maspero (1875: 125) aufgestellt und zuletzt besonders von Herrmann verteidigt. Hatte Maspero noch an einen Zusammenhang zur „Schwarzen Kunst" bzw. an die Beschäftigung mit dem allen Substanzen zugrundeliegenden schwarzen Urstoff gedacht, stellt Herrmann eine Verbindung zum Buch *Kemit* her. Dabei handelt es sich wahrscheinlich um eine Art Kompendium für die Schreiberausbildung, das sich großer Beliebtheit erfreute.

Alaun/Aluminium:

Das Metall Aluminium in der Reihe ägyptischer Lehnwörter zu finden, mag erstaunen, handelt es sich doch um eine relativ moderne Entdeckung. Seinen Namen hat das Aluminium von seinem Vorkommen in Alaunerde. Es konnte zwar erst 1827 isoliert werden, war allerdings bereits 1782 im Alaun vermutet worden und hatte daher schon vorher seinen neoklassischen Namen erhalten, von lat. *alumen* „Alaun". Dieses tritt seinerseits im ersten vorchristlichen Jahrhundert bei Q.C. Quadrigarius ins Blickfeld des Philologen und verbreitet sich von dort aus in den meisten indogermanischen Sprachen Europas. Es hat zwar nicht an Versuchen gefehlt, lat. *alumen* grundsprachlich anzubinden (Adams - Mallory 1997: 60) – man dachte an *$h_2$elut-* „Bier" (vgl. engl. *ale,* isl. *öl* etc.) in einer Grundbedeutung „bitteres Getränk" – doch wird dafür eher an einem anderen semantischen Strang gezogen, der zu heth. *alwanzaḫḫ-* „bezaubern" bzw. gr. ἀλύω „außer sich sein" führt (de Vries 1977: 686; Polomé 1997). Wenn man sich wieder bei Plinius kundig macht, erfährt man, daß die am höchsten geschätzte Sorte Alaun aus Ägypten geliefert wurde (Nat. hist. 35, 184): *...gigitur autem in Hispania, Aegypto...; laudatissimum in Aegypto.* Ein Blick in die ägyptologischen Wörterbücher liefert uns dann prompt ein Lexem, das als Etymon in Frage kommt (Kammerzell 2002: 44-46). In Ägypten fand Alaun, äg. *ỉbnw*, kopt. (S.) ⲟⲃⲛ, (B.) ⲱⲃⲛ vor allem als Droge und beim Färben Verwendung.[14] Obwohl es nicht in syllabischer Schrift, sondern – wenn auch spät – normalschriftlich belegt ist, handelt es sich möglicherweise im Ägyptischen selbst ebenfalls um ein Lehnwort[15] und zwar aus einer semitischen Sprache: < *ʾabn* „Stein" (vgl. akkad. *abnum*). Wie dem auch sei,

---

13 Vgl. A. Brack, LÄ I, 916f. s.v. Chemie.
14 W. Helck, LÄ I, 130, s.v. Alaun.
15 Siehe vorige Anm.; F. Kammerzell bestreitet dies; siehe Adams - Mallory 1997: 60.

die Bedeutung *Alaun* im Ägyptischen ist unbestritten. Wie im Falle des Basanits wird auch hier eine Genitivverbindung als Etymon anzusetzen sein, in Frage kommen:

1.   * *ᶜr-ỉbnw (* ᶜal-ỉằbn˜w > * ᶜalōbn > * alōmn)* „Alaunkies"
2.   * *ᶜȝ-n(.ỉ).t-ỉbnw (* ᶜaʳ-n˜t-ỉằbn˜w > * ᶜaʾnōbn> * alōmn)* „Mineral des Alauns"
3.   * *ỉnr-ỉbnw (* ỉana-ỉan˜w> * anaʾōbn> *alaōmn)* „Alaunstein"

Prinzipiell sind alle drei Möglichkeiten denkbar, als einfachste Lösung wird die erste sicherlich zu favorieren sein.

Labyrinth:

Von den antiken Reisenden Diodor, Plinius, Strabo und ganz besonders von Herodot sind uns Beschreibungen erhalten,[16] die sich auf ein riesiges und offenbar äußerst prächtiges Bauwerk beziehen: den Tempelbezirk bei der Pyramide Amenemhats III. von Hawara (Arnold 1979: 1-9). Genannt wird es λαβύινθος und war eine sehr weitverzweigte Anlage, die auf die klassischen Autoren erheblichen Eindruck gemacht hat. W. Schenkel (1997a) hat die Entstehung des Namens sehr überzeugend rekonstruiert. Demnach ist der Ursprung von λαβύινθος eine Frage Herodots nach dem Namen des Bauwerkes, das er vor sich hatte, woraufhin ihm sein Gewährsmann die äußerst simple Antwort *rʾ-pr(.w) rn=ś* „Tempel ist ihr Name" (kopt. (S.) * ⲣⲁⲛⲡⲉ̄ⲛⲧⲕ̄, (F.) * ⲉⲗⲡⲏⲉⲛⲧⲉⲥ) gab.

Was die geläufige griechische Etymologie betrifft, so muß man betonen, wann die Bezeichnung auftritt, nämlich nach Herodot im Bezug auf Kreta erst bei Callimachus im 3. Jhd. v.Chr., also nicht sehr früh. Zudem ist das Zugrundeliegende *λάβρυς „Axt" nur erschlossen und die Gleichung beruht auf der Überlegung, die Doppelaxt, die offensichtlich in Knossos als Königssymbol fungierte, habe beim minoischen Labyrinth Pate gestanden. In Wirklichkeit wird wohl der Pate Amenemhat III. sein und das ägyptische Labyrinth lexikalisches Vorbild für das minoische gewesen sein.

Pyramide:

Die landläufige Meinung, der Name für einige der größten Bauwerke der Menschheit leite sich von einem „Küchlein" ab, sorgt allenthalben für Erheiterung. Genau besehen ist die griechische Etymologie äußerst wacklig. H. Diehls sah in gr. πῦραμίς eine Zusammenziehung von πυρός „Weizen" und ᾽αμᾶν „mähen" zu „Schnittweizen" (Diehls 1916: 193ff.). Dieser stehe ähnlich wie bei κάλαμος „Rohr, Schreibrohr" auch für konische oder pyramidenförmige Kuchen aus Weizen und Honig. Viel wahrscheinlicher ist da der Vorschlag Langs (1923/24), auf die ägyptische Bezeichnung der Monumente *pȝ-mr* zurückzugreifen. Die Metathese braucht hier nicht mehr, wie Lang es tut, begründet zu werden. Auch beim arabischen *haram* dürfte dieses Phänomen vorliegen, wenn es nicht von der Wurzel √*hrm* „alt werden" abgeleitet sein sollte (Wehr 1976: 1026).

---

16 Lloyd 1970: 81-100; Lloyd 1975ff: III 120 f.

Atlantik/Atlantis:

Die Bezeichnung für den Ozean, der uns von der Neuen Welt trennt, habe ich ausgewählt, weil es doch erstaunlich ist, daß immerhin eines der Weltmeere einen ägyptischen Namen trägt. Gleichzeitig ist es ein Beispiel dafür, wie die Griechen nicht anders als heutige Esoteriker glaubten, die Ägypter hätten ein geheimnisvolles Urwissen besessen. Der Atlantische Ozean trägt seinen Namen nach dem sagenhaften versunkenen Kontinent Atlantis. Lange hat man nach einer Deutung des Namens gesucht, bis W. Schenkel festgestellt hat, daß die Suche vergeblich sein wird, weil es ihn bildlich gesprochen nicht gibt: Atlantis heißt nichts anderes als „Die Namenlose" *ỉw.tt-rn=ś*, auf Fayumisch-Koptisch ⲀⲦⲖⲀⲚⲦⳒ. Gemeint ist eine namenlose Insel. Die Inseln inmitten des Ozeans (*ỉw.w m šn-wr*) sind ein weit verbreiteter Topos in Ägypten, der offensichtlich auch Plato gefallen zu haben scheint.

Mythos:

Das *Lexikon der Ägyptologie* macht s.v. Mythos die kurze und knappe Aussage: „Eine äg. Vokabel für M(ythos) ist unbekannt...".[17] Sollte das gr. μῦθος, wie von Ernštedt (1953: 55-57)[18] vorgeschlagen, auf das ägyptische *mt.t*, kopt. ⲘⲞⲨⲦⲈ zurückzuführen sein, widerspricht sich dieser zutreffende Satz geradezu selbst. Von gräzistischer Seite wird eine ägyptische Etymologie wahrscheinlich als „Mythos" abgetan werden, doch sollte man sie nicht von vornherein abtun. Bemerkenswert ist immerhin, daß sowohl μῦθος als auch äg. *mt.t*, kopt. ⲘⲞⲨⲦⲈ „Wort, Rede" bedeuten. Beiden Lexemen ist neben dem profanen Gebrauch auch eine überhöhte Bedeutungsnuance zu eigen. Das Wort *mt.t* findet sich tausendfach an ägyptischen Tempelwänden als Einleitung der Beischriften, welche die Reden der Götter und Könige wiedergeben. Es ist davon auszugehen, daß diese Redeeinleitung *ḏt-mtw.w* „Worte-Sprechen" nicht mitgelesen wurde. Wichtiger im vorliegenden Kontext ist die Schöpferkraft, die dem Wort in Ägypten beigemessen wurde (Zandee 1964). Auf der lautlichen Ebene ist zu bemerken, wie gut die aspirierte Wiedergabe des ägyptischen Dentals im Griechischen paßt.

Barke:

Im Ägyptischen ist eine Bezeichnung für eine Art Schiff bezeugt, die *br* lautete und Ursprung des gr. βᾶρις sein soll (Fournet 1989: 57). Die Gleichung ist ziemlich eindeutig, zumal das ägyptische Lexem in syllabischer Schreibung auftritt, die eine Notation des Vokals *a* enthält. Nicht zu übersehen ist freilich, daß eben diese syllabische Schreibweise ein Hinweis auf ein Fremdwort im Ägyptischen sein kann.

---

17 E. Brunner-Traut, LÄ IV, 277, s.v. Mythos.
18 Siehe auch Peust 1999: 71.

Bronze:
Wenn in den einschlägigen etymologischen Wörterbüchern überhaupt eine Etymologie von „Bronze" < mlat. *bronzium*, ital. *bronzo* vorgeschlagen wurde, dann eine der folgenden Herleitungen (Kammerzell 2002: 39-41):

1. < ahd. *brunizzo* „bräunliches Metall" (Skeat 1884: 53)
2. < mlat. *obryzum* < gr. χρυσίον ὄβρυζον „Gold, das die Feuerprobe bestanden hat" (Lokotsch 1927: 133)
3. < mgr. βροντήσιον < lat. *aes brundisium* „Erz aus Brundisium" (Guiraud 1994: 162)
4. < arabisch. *....< neupers. *birung* „Kupfer" (Kluge 1999: 137)[19]
5. < lat. brontea „Donnerstein" (Guiraud 1994: 162-163), aber <gr. βροντή „Donner"

Alle fünf Vorschläge weisen mehr oder weniger große Schwachpunkte auf, die nicht umsonst viele Lexikographen dazu bewogen hat, die Etymologie als nicht geklärt einzustufen. Auch bei diesem Wort dürfte eine Rückführung auf das Ägyptisch-Koptische (Kammerzell 2002: 39-41) Licht ins Dunkel bringen.

Seit dem Mittleren Reich ist der Ausdruck *biȝ-rwč* „hartes Metall" in Ägypten nachweisbar (Wb I, 437, 21). Die Verbindung wird mäg. etwa *biła'-lāwič* gelautet haben, was über näg. *biła'-rāwit* zu kopt. ⲃⲁⲣⲱⲧ „Messing, Bronze" univerbiert wurde. Der semantische Rahmen des Wortes war relativ weit gefaßt, wie die spezifizierenden Zusätze ⲃⲁⲣⲱⲟⲟ ⲛⲁⲗⲁⲩ „*weiße Bronze*" und ⲃⲁⲣⲟⲧ ⲉⲧⲧⲟⲣϣ „*rote Bronze*" nahelegen, die wohl die Legierungen Weißguß bzw. Arsenbronze und Rotguß voneinander unterscheiden. Wie man sich den Entlehnungsvorgang im einzelnen vorzustellen hat, ist nicht ganz klar. Möglicherweise spielt mgr. βροντήσιον als Adjektivbildung eine Mittlerrolle, doch ist angesichts der regen Handelsbeziehungen zwischen Ägypten und italienischen Städten wie Venedig oder Genua im 14. Jahrhundert n. Chr. eine direkte Entlehnung ins Italienische nicht ausgeschlossen. Bestätigt wird ein reger Kontakt auf der Sprachebene durch ein Glossar aus dem 13. Jahrhundert, in dem altfranzösische Wörter und Phrasen koptisch transkribiert und mit arabischer Übersetzung versehen wurden (Peust 1999: 77, 93).

Es sollte an dieser Stelle nicht unerwähnt bleiben, daß auch für „Messing" eine altägyptische Etymologie vorgeschlagen wurde: * *biȝ-snk (biła'-senkiw)* „dunkles Metall" > kopt. ⲃⲁⲥⲉⲛϭ (Kammerzell 2002: 39-41). In lautlicher Hinsicht ist eine solche Etymologie durchaus denkbar, doch ist zwischen dem koptischen Wort und den Messing-Wörtern der germanischen Sprachen kein Bindeglied auszumachen. Hinzu kommen trotz anderweitiger Belege für krasse „Fehlbenennungen" bei Metallen (heth. *dankui-* „Zinn" zu heth. *dankuis* „dunkel, schwarz" [< *d^b(o)ngu-]) Bedenken

---

19 Neuperisches *birung* „Kupfer" scheint auf manichäisch mpers. *bring* zurückzugehen; im Sogdischen ist ein Wort *brynt* „Kupfer" bezeugt; es wird auch in andere Sprachen entlehnt, etwa arm. *płinj*, georg. *brindžao*, siehe Fournet 1989: 57, mit Anm. 5 und Anm. 7.

bezüglich der Semantik. Darüber hinaus existiert eine durchaus überzeugende Etymologie von Μοσσύαοικος (χαλκός) „mossynoikisches (Erz)".[20]

Pavian:

Das in den europäischen Sprachen geläufige Wort „Pavian" leitet sich von dem Namen eines Dämonen mit Namen *bꜣby*[21]ab, der mit dem Gott Seth in enger Verbindung steht und auf Griechisch βεβον oder βαβυς heißt.

Friedrich Wilhelm von Bissing, der sich erstmals näher mit dem Dämonen beschäftigt hat,[22] kommt zu dem Schluß, daß der Dämon *Bebon* als Fremdwort aus einer altafrikanischen Sprache entlehnt worden sei, was er mit der schwankenden Schreibung begründet. Aus den gleichen Sprachen wäre später das Wort als *Babuin* wieder entlehnt worden.

Fast gleichzeitig hat sich Philippe Derchain mit dem Dämonen auseinandergesetzt und seine Aspekte und sein Vorkommen in den Texten beleuchtet.[23] Er schließt sich – mit Vorbehalt – einem älteren Vorschlag Jablonskis[24] an, *Bebon* an das Wort für „Höhle, Loch" *bꜣbꜣ*[25] anzuknüpfen.[26]

Für diese These tritt dann Edel sehr bestimmt ein und verwirft zurecht den Vorschlag von Bissings,[27] bleibt jedoch reserviert, was die Gleichung *bꜣby* mit griechisch βεβον, βαβυς angeht.

Er rekonstruiert den Tonvokal als *bu̯ꜣb̆ꜣ̯w̆y* oder *bĕ̆ꜣb̆ꜣ̯w̆y* und in Analogie zu ⲭⲱⲭ <*čꜣꜣčꜣꜣ den Nachtonvokal als *bu̯ꜣbuw̆y* oder *beꜣbew̆y*. Den Vokal o in der griechischen Form erklärt er als Nachklang der Pluralform -aw, mir scheint der Vokal jedoch ganz einfach zur griechischen Nominalendung zu gehören. Dies wäre sogar ein Hinweis darauf, wie das Wort in die europäischen Sprachen, die ja alle ein -n am Ende zeigen, eingedrungen ist: über das Griechische.

Edel geht jedoch schon von wackligen Voraussetzungen aus, nimmt er doch als Beleg für die Vokalisation einfach das koptische ⲃⲏⲃ, welches nicht den Dämonen, sondern die Höhle bezeichnet. Auch wenn ein etymologischer Zusammenhang festzumachen wäre, so liegen doch sicherlich zwei homophone Lexeme vor.

20 Abgeleitet vom Nehmen eines Volkes von der Schwarzmeer-Küste, von dem eine pseudo-aristotelische Schrift (Aristoteles XIV 835 a 9-14) sagt, sie hätten ein besonders glänzendes und helles Erz.

21 E. Otto, LÄ I, 675, s.v. Bebon, Namensform gebraucht nach Plutarch, De Iside et Osiride, c. 49, 62.

22 von Bissing 1951; dort findet sich auch die ältere Literatur zusammengestellt.

23 Derchain 1952: 23-47, nach Anm. 2 bei Erscheinen des Artikels von Bissings schon im Druck.

24 Zitiert bei v. Bissing 1951: Anm 51 <non vidi>.

25 Wb I, 419, 1-5; koptisch ⲃⲏⲃ.

26 K. Sethe in: G. Wissowa, Paulys Realencyclopädie der classischen Altertumswissenschaften 2.2. München 1958-1980, s.v. Seth.

27 Edel 1956: 74-76. Ders. in: ZÄS 90, 22ff.

Nun hat sich zusätzlich in der Folgezeit ergeben, daß dieser etymologische Zusammenhang letztendlich besteht, jedoch auf einer völlig anderen Ebene. Der Bezug zur Höhle war gemacht worden, weil man von der Beobachtung ausging, daß Paviane auf Felsen übernachten und deshalb „Höhlentiere" seien.[28] Nach Störk[29] übernachten Mantelpaviane zwar auf Schlaffelsen, doch zeichnen sich diese nicht durch eine höhlenartige Beschaffenheit aus. Störk folgt einem anderen Weg, den zuvor A. Ward (1978: 91, 133ff.) aufgezeigt hatte. Es ist dies die Rolle, denen Affen[30] im Bereich der Erotik zugewiesen wurde.[31] In der ägyptischen Vorstellung spielt die sexuelle Mächtigkeit des Pavians[32] eine große Rolle, besonders im Hinblick auf die Wiedergeburt im Jenseits (Hornung - Staehelin 1976: 106ff.). Durch diese Konnotation bedingt, wird der Kanopengott Hapi und selbst Osiris paviangestaltig dargestellt.[33]

Dieser sexuelle Aspekt drückt sich in der etymologischen Verbindung des ägyptischen Affennamens *bnw/bn.t* mit der Wurzel √ *bn* aus, die in etwa „anschwellen, erigieren" bedeutet und nicht zuletzt auch mit der gemeinsemitischen Wurzel √ *bny/w* verglichen werden kann.[34] Genau so gut kann *bꜣby* mit äg. *bꜣ* „ejakulieren" verbunden werden.

Elefant:

Die Fülle der Literatur über die Herkunft des Wortes „Elefant" ist wie die Körpergröße dieses Tieres riesig. Zwar ist heute in jedem etymologischen Wörterbuch nachzulesen, daß sich „Elefant" vom koptischen ⲉⲃⲟⲩ und damit vom altägyptischen *ꜣbw* ableitet. Auch von Ägyptologen gebetsmühlenhaft wiederholt ist aber bisher noch niemandem aufgefallen, daß es das betreffende koptische Wort gar nicht gibt. Wie ich in einer Arbeit zu diesem Thema aufdecken konnte, liegt der Fehler bei den Gebrüdern Grimm, welche die in koptischen Buchstaben geschriebene Transkription ägyptischer Wörter, die Champollion in seinem *Dictionnaire Égyptienne* gibt, für genuin koptische Lexeme hielten. Zu allem Überfluß kamen sie dann noch auf die hybride Idee, das koptische ⲉⲃⲟⲩ mit dem arabischen Artikel zu *al-ebou* zu verbinden. Trotz alledem möchte ich an einer Entlehnung von äg. *ꜣbw* festhalten, wenn auch unter völlig anderen Prämissen. Wie sich in jüngerer Zeit immer stärker herauskristallisiert hat,[35] ist der Laut, den Ägyptologen traditionellerweise als *Aleph* bezeichnen, in Wirklichkeit ein Labial. Damit kann man nicht nur das ägyptische *ꜣbw* an die semitische Wur-

---

28 So auch Osing 1976: 310, 854 als Nisba.
29 L. Störk, LÄ IV, 919, Anm. 12, s.v. Pavian.
30 Sowohl Paviane als auch Meerkatzen tanzen für Hathor, die Liebesgöttin, s. Schott 1950: 80.
31 Derchain (1975: 68f.) „le singe est en Egypte suvant porteur d'une connotation érotique".
32 Der Pavian als sexuell agressives Tier: Reinisch 1972: 191.
33 L. Störk, LÄ IV, 918, s.v. Pavian.
34 Ward 1968: 66-67, II. Egyptian *bn* = Semitic *bny*.
35 Rössler 1971: 263-326, nachgedruckt bei Schneider 2001: 543-607; Loret 1945: 236-244; Hodge 1966: 40-57, Vergote 1945: 76, 109-114; ders. 1973/83: §26; Edel, Altäg. Gramm., 58, § 131; Osing 1997: 223-229; Schenkel 1990: 34, 36, 44; Loprieno 1995: 33; Peust 1999: 140; Satzinger 1994: 202-205.

zel √*pl/pr* = „Elefant" anschließen, sondern auch das bisher nicht erklärbare *l* in gr. ἐλέφας „Elefant". Besonders spannend ist die weitere Verflechtung des Elefantenwortes, denn mit der semitischen Verbindung erschöpft sich unser Wissen über diese Wurzel noch lange nicht. Gerade das Ägyptische ist eine Art lexikographischer Brückenkopf nicht nur in den Vorderen Orient und nach Griechenland, sondern insbesondere zum afrikanischen Kontinent. Dort ist die Wurzel in derselben Form wie im Ägyptischen als *lb/p* weit verbreitet, sowohl in den Berbersprachen, als auch in den kuschitischen und den Tschad-Sprachen (Breyer, i. Druck).

3. Lexeme, deren ägyptischer Ursprung als gesichert angesehen werden kann

Ibis	< Ἴβις < *hb.w* „Der Stelzende", koptisch (B) ϩⲓⲡ,(S) ϩⲓⲃⲱⲓ, (Spiegelberg 1907: 131)[36]
Natron	< arab. *an-naṭrūn* < *nčr.ỉ* „Das Göttliche, Reine" (Brugsch, Wörterbuch VI, 708)
Salmiak/Ammoniak	< Ammuns-salz *sāl ammoniâcum*, weil aus Siwa
Alabaster	< ἀλάβαστρον < *ʿ(.w) n(.ỉ) Bȝs.t.t* „Bastetnapf" (Sethe 1933)
Gummi	< gr. κόμμι < äg. *kmy.t* (kopt ⲕⲟⲙⲙⲉ) (Fournet 1989: 62)[37]
Ebenholz	< ἔβενος < *hbny* (Spiegelberg 1907: 131)[38]
Oase	< Ὄασις < *wḥȝ.t*, demot. *wḥỉ* ʿOase" vgl. äg.-arab. *wāḥ* < kopt. (B: ⲟⲩⲁϩ). (Sethe 1914: 142-144)
Pharao	< he. *fāraʿō* < äg. *pr(.w)-ʿȝ* „Großes Haus = Palast", kopt. ⲡ-ⲣ̅ⲣⲟ „König"

Ibis:
Der Ibis spielte in den religiösen Vorstellungen der Ägypter eine große Rolle. So verwundert es nicht, wenn neben dem Fabeltier *Phönix* auch der Vogelname *Ibis* über Griechenland aus Ägypten kam. Etymologisch bezieht sich der ägyptische Tiername auf eine charakteristische Eigenschaft dieser zur Gattung der sog. Stelzvögel gehörenden Tiere: *hb.w* (*hībaṷ) bedeutet „Der Stelzende", koptisch (B) ϩⲓⲡ,(S) ϩⲓⲃⲱⲓ, seinerseits im äg.-arab. *hēba* weitergeführt.

Natron:
Ursprünglich mit dem arabischen Artikel von arab. *an-naṭrūn* als *anatron* entlehnt, trägt das Salz einen wahrhaft göttlichen Namen (Peust 1999: 71). Es bedeutet nichts geringeres als „Das Göttliche". Die Erklärung für diese ungewöhnliche Erhöhung liegt

---

36 Wer die Etymologie zuerst aufgestellt hat, konnte ich nicht mehr nachvollziehen.
37 Von wem die Etymologie aufgestellt wurde, entzieht sich meiner Kenntnis.
38 Schon bei Schrader 1917: 148.

daran, daß es nicht nur bei der Mumifizierung eine erhebliche Rolle spielte, sondern der Erlangung kultischer Reinheit diente. Aus dem klassisch-ägyptischen *nč̣r.ỉ (*načī-ril)* wurde im Neuägyptischen *ntr.ỉ. (*natīri >natir* vgl.[39] mhe. *nᵉt̬ᵉr*, syr. *netrā*, ar. *naṭ-ūr, naṭrūn*). Wie früh die Vokale schon an Quantität eingebüßt haben, zeigen die Formen der akkadischen Entlehnung *nitru, nitiru.* Hauptabbaugebiet von Natron war das nicht umsonst so benannte Wadi Natrun.

Salmiak/Ammoniak:

Gleichfalls nach dem Ort der Gewinnung wurde das Ammonium bezeichnet und zwar nach der Nähe zum Heiligtum des Ammun in der Oase Siwa, das bekanntlich im Hellenismus durch das Königsorakel Alexanders des Großen zu Berühmtheit gelangte. Dieses Ammuns-salz *sāl ammoniācum* wird später zu Salmiak zusammengezogen (Kluge 1999: 343). Der Name des Gottes selbst ist innerägyptisch weiter durchschaubar. Er bedeutet *'Imn(.w)* „Der Verborgene" in später Zeit Ἄμμων[40], ⲀⲘⲟⲨⲚ vokalisiert, keilschriftlich noch *amānᵉ(w)*. Aus den allgemein für das Ägyptische angenommenen Silbenregeln[41] ist abzuleiten, daß im Auslaut noch ein Konsonant zu ergänzen ist. Wie die Götternamen *Ḥr(.w)* und *Itm(.w)* gehört *'Imn(.w)* zur Nominalbildungsklasse *śačằmuw.*[42]

Alabaster:

Der Alabaster (lat. alabaster) bzw. das ἀλάβαστρον „Alabastergefäß" (lat. *alabastrum*) scheint dahingegen eine Affinität zur Göttin Bastet zu zeigen und konnte von Sethe (1933: 887) überzeugend als äg. *ᶜ(.w) n(.ỉ) Bȝs.t.t „Bastetnapf"* erklärt werden. Dieses könnte im 6. Jahrhundert v. Chr. etwa *ᶜa-na-baste* oder *ᶜa-la-baste* gelautet haben (Sethe 1933: 889).[43] Selbstredend ist damit das Alabastron primär gemeint und die Gesteinsart wäre nur nach der Gefäßart benannt worden, da sie sich für deren Herstellung als besonders geeignet erwies. Das Alabastron war auch namensgebend für den Ortsnamen Ἀλάβαστρων (πόλιϛ) (Ptolemäus) bzw. *Alabastron* (Plinius) und nicht umgekehrt, wie manche etymologischen Wörterbücher glauben machen wollen.[44] Sethes Vorschlag hat einiges für sich. Schon die Graphie sowohl des Toponyms *Bubastis*, äg. *Bst.t.*, später *Pr(.w)-Bst.t*, gr. Βούβαστιϛ, kopt.(B.) ⲡⲟⲨⲂⲀⲤϯ, als auch

---

39 Koehler - Baumgartner 1995: 696.

40 Manetho; Herodot II, 29, 83; Plutarch, de Iside et Osiride, c. 9; Herodot verwendet die Form Ἀμοῦν für den Akkusativ, die Form Ἄμμων für den Amun von Siwa, Plutarch bezeichnet letzteres als die griechische Form des Namens und Ἄμμουν als die ägyptische, siehe dazu: E. Otto, LÄ I, 237, s.v. Amun.

41 Schenkel 1990: 67ff., anders nun Peust 1999: 175-188.

42 Zu Amun (*'Iamằn̬w*) und Atum (*'Iatằm̬w*) Osing 1976: 184; Schenkel 1983: 65f. Beide interpretieren Amun als „der Verborgene", was Schenkel auch für Atum tut (im Index, sicherlich ein Versehen), Osing etymologisiert Atum mit „der Nichtexistierende"?. Zu Horus *(Ḥắr̬w =* „der Ferne"): Osing 1976: 185 und Schenkel 1983: 89, 96.

43 Zur Vokalisation des Gottesnamens *Bst.t.* als *bū̆restit > *ū̆bĕsti* siehe Osing 1976: 855.

44 Beispielsweise Kluge 1967: 12.

des damit etymologisch verknüpften Theonyms *Bastet* werden mit dem Dreikonso-
nantenzeichen *bȝs* geschrieben, das ein Salbgefäß darstellt. Die Göttin *Bastet* ist also
„Die von Bubastis" und *Bubastis* ist „Die Salbgefäß-Stadt". Damit wird bereits eine
etymologische Richtung eingeschlagen, die Kammerzell (2001: 118) verfolgt hat. Zurecht fragt er sich, ob nicht eher dieses *bȝs* „Salbgefäß" selbst und nicht eine Ableitung
davon dem *Alabastron* zugrunde liegen müsse. Hier kommt nun wieder Plinius ins
Spiel, der bemerkt (Nat. hist. 37, 73): *Iuba auctor est smaragdum, quam chloram
vocent, in Arabia aedificiorum ornamentis includi et lapidem, quem alabastriten
Aegyptii vocent...* „Juba ist Gewährsmann, daß der Chlora genannte Smaragd in Arabien als Architekturverzierung eingelassen werde, desgleichen auch der Stein, den
die Ägypter Alabastrites nennen...". Diesen Worten kann man entnehmen, daß es im
Ägyptischen auch ein Wort für den gesagten Stein gegeben haben muß. Dessen
Nachweis bleibt Sethe jedoch schuldig. Kammerzell kann nun auf der Suche nach
einem Etymon des Vordergliedes *Ala-* mit einem solchen aufwarten, indem er das
koptische Wort für Stein ins Spiel bringt, ⲱⲛⲉ (S.), ⲱⲛⲓ (B.). In der Verbindung (B.)
ⲁⲙⲁ ⲙⲏⲓ bzw. (S.) ⲉⲛⲉⲙⲙⲉ „Edelstein, Perle" < *ỉnr-mȝꜥ.t* „Stein der Wahrheit = echter
Stein" taucht auch eine in der Genitivverbindung enttonte Form auf, die für ein postu-
liertes **ỉnr-bȝs* „Salbgefäßstein" ebenfalls in Anspruch zu nehmen wäre. Der Wechsel
von *n > l* bereitet keinerlei Schwierigkeiten, denn gerade vor Labialen ist er gut belegt
(Peust 1999: 167). Hinzu kommt die häufige Verwechslung von *ỉnr* „Stein" und *ꜥr*
„Kiesel" im Neuägyptischen.[45] Eine Frage bleibt allerdings noch zu klären – der Auslaut auf *-t.* Zu dessen Klärung kann man auf eine zeitgenössische volksetymologische
Verknüpfung von *ỉnr-bȝs (*ỉanal-bŭris>(ỉ)alabǎs)* zu *ỉnr-Bȝs.t.t* „Bubastis-Stein" *(*
ỉanal-u̯bǎsti)* verweisen.

Gummi:
Bereits bei Herodot wird das Gummi erwähnt, gr. κόμμι. Koptisch heißt es ⲕⲟⲙⲙⲉ
und altägyptisch *ḳmy.t* (W. Vycichl, DEC 80f.). Das ägyptische Lexem bezieht sich
meist auf wertvolle Harze, wie Weihrauch, Myrrhe und Ebenholzharz, d.h. auf Duft-
stoffe (Wb V, 39, 1-15). Daneben ist aber auch schon die Verwendung bei der Tintenherstellung bekannt, bei der Pigmente mit *mw n(.ỉ) ḳmy.t* „Gummiwasser" angerieben
wurden. Heute bezeichnen wir das Harz zur Tintenherstellung als *gummi arabicum*,
denn nach dem modernen Sprachgebrauch ist der Gummi ein Weiterverarbeitungs-
produkt des Kautschuks. Dieser wird auf die gleiche Weise gewonnen wie Myrrhe
und andere Balsame, insofern besteht schon eine Verbindung zwischen den Stoffen.
Im Koptischen steht ⲕⲟⲙⲙⲉ speziell für Akazienharz, das in frischer Form gegessen
wurde. So gesehen ist es berechtigt, wenn man den Ägyptern die Erfindung des Kau-
gummis zuschreibt.

---

45 Westendorf 1965-77: 292, mit Anm. 7 und Harris 1961: 26f.

Ebenholz:
Sicherlich eines der luxeriösesten Güter, die aus Schwarzafrika über Ägypten nach Europa gelangten, war neben dem Elfenbein das Ebenholz. Das ägyptische Wort dafür ist *hbn* oder *hbny.* Im Hebräischen wurde dies in der Form *hobnīm* übernommen, im Klassisch-Arabischen heißt das Holz *ʾabanūs, ʾabnūs* (W. Vycichl, DEC, 39). Vycichls Annahme (ibid.), das Wort sei über das Arabische ins Griechische gekommen, wird durch die Erwähnung bei Herodot (III, 97) widerlegt. Bestimmt aus dieser Quelle kam es hingegen zu den Tuareg, die den Stoff *yābnūs* nennen.[46] Bemerkenswerterweise haben die Araber das Wort ein zweites Mal übernommen und zwar aus dem Koptischen (ⲡ·ⲉⲃⲉⲛⲟⲥ), was wegen des Anlautes eindeutig ist, der den koptischen Artikel darstellt: *bābanūs.*

Oase:
Wenn heutige Reiseveranstalter mit dem Schlagwort „Oase des Friedens" werben, lassen sie sich kaum träumen, daß sie von einem alten Kessel sprechen. Der ägyptische Kessel heißt *wḥ3.t,* demot. *wḥỉ* "Oase", was gr. mit Αὔασις (Strabon 170) und Ὄασις (Herodot III 26) wiedergegeben wird. Die arabischen Formen *wāḥ* und *wāḥa* sind Lehnwörter aus dem Koptischen (B: ⲟⲩⲁϩ, S: ⲟⲩⲁϩⲉ).

Pharao:
Der uns aus der Bibel bekannte Titel „Pharao", he. *faraʿō* leitet sich von einem Substitut ab. Äg. *pr(.w)-ʿ3* „Großes Haus", kopt. ⲡ·ⲣ̄ⲡⲟ „König" bezeichnete zuerst den Wohnsitz des Herrschers, den Palast, und sekundär die Institution „König" ähnlich wie in unserem Sprachgebrauch vom „Weißen Haus" oder der „Hohen Pforte" die Rede ist. Der König selbst wird erst ab der 18. Dynastie auf diese Weise benannt.

4.   Zusammenfassung: Versuch einer Motivationsanalyse der Entlehnungsvorgänge

Besieht man sich all diese Lexeme in einer Gesamtschau, dann kann man sie in mehrere Gruppen unterteilen. Die ersten Gruppe bilden die Benennungen von besonderen Materialien, die vornehmlich aus Ägypten stammen oder bei denen Ägypten der wichtigste Zwischenhändler mit dem zentralafrikanischen Raum ist. Transitgüter sind Ebenholz und Gummi, sehr typisch ägyptische Produkte besonders das Papyrus und der Alabaster, aber auch Natron und Salmiak. Naturgemäß sind die Namen von Handelsgütern besonders häufige Kandidaten für Entlehnungsvorgänge, nicht zuletzt, weil durch den Handel der Sprachkontakt besonders gut gegeben ist. Oft handelt es sich zudem um Luxusgüter, bei denen der fremde Name eben auch ein gewisses Prestige mit sich bringt. Auf jeden Fall spielt dieser Aspekt beim Papyrus und dem

---

46 Siehe W. Vycichl, DEC, 39, dazu auch Duveyrier 1864: 211f.

Alabaster mit hinein. Was Natron und Salmiak betrifft, so wird rein das Vorkommen in Ägypten ausschlaggebend für die Benennung sein.

Die zweite größere Gruppe besteht aus sehr spezifischen *termini technici*, die aus der Landesnatur erwachsen. Es sind dies die Toponyme Ägypten und Oase, der Flußname Nil und nicht zuletzt der Titel Pharao. Bei ihm ist die Motivation der Benennung am besten nachzuvollziehen. Das ägyptische Herrschaftssystem wurde offenbar als so eigen empfunden, daß es notwendig erschien, den Titel unübersetzt zu lassen.

Die letzte Gruppe beinhaltet Tiernamen. In diesem Zusammenhang ist zu bemerken, daß dieselben Wörter von den Arabern bei der Eroberung Ägyptens übernommen werden. Motivation ist also nicht besonderes Prestige, Herkunftsangabe oder Sprachökonomie, sondern schlichtweg Unkenntnis. Wie den Arabern das Krokodil – arab. *timsaḥ* <ägypt. *msḥ* – nicht bekannt war, gehörten für die Griechen Tiere, wie Pavian, Ibis oder der Elefant, nicht zu den heimischen Tierarten.

Zum Schluß möchte ich Ihnen noch eine Kleinigkeit vorstellen, die demonstriert, daß bei all den knallharten Lautregeln und linguistischen Verrenkungen das Aufspüren von Lehnwörtern unglaublich spannend sein kann.

Vor ein paar Jahren erst wurde in der prädynastischen Königsnekropole von Abydos – Umm el-Qaab – im sogenannten Grab U-j Schriftfunde gemacht,[47] die um ein ganzes Stück älter sind als die bisher ältesten Bezeugungen von Schrift in Ägypten. Sie datieren etwa um 3150 v. Chr. und sind damit möglicherweise die bisher ältesten Schriftzeugnisse überhaupt. Eines der wenigen Wörter, die mit einiger Sicherheit identifiziert werden können, ist der Name der Insel Elephantine auf einem Etikett, das eine *Lieferung aus dem Heiligtum von Elephantine* bezeichnet.

Dies bedeutet, daß wir für das größte zu Lande lebende Tier heute noch dasselbe Wort verwenden, wie es zur Zeit der allerersten Aufzeichnung menschlicher Sprache der ägyptische Schreiber vor über 5000 Jahren tat. Dergestalt subsummiert diese Etymologie die wichtigsten Punkte, die unsere Betrachtungsweise über Ägypten kennzeichnet. Als Quelle von exotischen Luxusgütern steht gerade der Elefant für die Korridorstellung Ägyptens in Richtung Afrika und seine Wort-Langlebigkeit für die Kontinuität, welche die ägyptische Kultur in unseren Augen ausmacht.

---

47 Dreyer 1998: Taf 29 und S. 119, jeweils Nr. 59.

Abkürzungen

Brugsch	Wörterbuch Brugsch, H., Hieroglyphisch-demotisches Wörterbuch enthaltend in wissenschaflicher Anordnung die gebräuchlichsten Wörter der heiligen und der Volks-Sprache der alten Ägypter, Leipzig 1867-1882
DEC	W. Vycichl, Dictionnaire étymologique de la langue copte, Leuven 1983
Edel	Altäg. Gramm.Edel, E.,Altägyptische Grammatik. Pontificium Institutum Biblicum, Analecta Orientalia 34/39. 2 Bde., Rom 1955/64
GM	Göttinger Miszellen, Göttingen
LÄ	W. Helck und W. Westendorf (Hrsg.), Lexikon der Ägyptologie, 7 Bde., Wiesbaden 1975-1992
SAK	Studien zur Altägyptischen Kultur, Hamburg
Wb	A. Erman und H. Grapow (Hrg.), Wörterbuch der ägyptischen Sprache. Die Bände 1-5 erschienen zwischen 1926 und 1931, die Belegstellenbände bis 1955 bzw. 1963 der 12. Band.
ZÄS	Zeitschrift für Ägyptische Sprache und Altertumskunde, Berlin - Leipzig

Bibliographie

Adams, D. Q. und Mallory, J. P.
1997   Beer. In: *Adams, D. Q. und Mallory, J. P. (Hrsg.), Encyclopedia of Indo-European culture.* London - Chicago.

Albright, W. F.
1934   *The Vokalization of the Egyptian Syllabic Orthography.* American Oriental Series 5. New Haven.

Arnold, D.
1979   Das Labyrinth und seine Vorbilder. *Mitteilungen des Deutschen Archäologischen Instituts Abteilung Kairo 35:* 1-9.

Breyer, F. A. K.
2003   Die ägyptische Etymologie von gr. ἐλέφας „*Elephant*" und lat. *ebur* „*Elfenbein*". Sprachkontakt zwischen Island und dem Tschadsee vom Neolithikum bis zu den Türkenkriegen. In: *A. Loprieno und S. Bickel (Hrsg.), Basel Egyptological Prize 1. Junior Research in Egyptian History, Archaeology and Philology. Aegyptiaca Helvetica 17: 251-276.*

Borger, R.
1984   *Altorientalische Lexikographie. Geschichte und Probleme.* NAWG, Phil.-hist. Kl. 1984/2, Göttingen.

de Vries, J.
1977   *Altnordisches etymologisches Wörterbuch.* 3. Aufl., Leiden.

Delapotre, L.
1929   *Élements de la grammaire hittite.* Paris.

Derchain, Ph.
1952   Bébon, le dieu et les mythes: *Revue d'Égyptologie 9:* 23-47.
1963   Nouveaux documents relatifs à Bébon (*Bȝbȝwj*). *ZÄS 90:* 22-25.
1975   La perruque et le cristal. *SAK 2:* 55-74.

Diehls, H.
1916   Etymologica. *Zeitschrift für vergeichende Sprachforschung 47:* 193-209.

Dreyer, G.
1998   *Umm el-Qaab I. Das prädynastische Königsgrab U-j und seine frühen Schriftzeugnisse.* Mit Beiträgen von U. Hartung und F. Pumpenmeier und einem Anhang von F. Feindt und M. Fischer. Archäologische Veröffentlichungen 86, Mainz.

Duveyrier, H.
1864   *Les Touaregs du Nord.* Paris.

Edel, E.
1956   Beiträge zum ägyptischen Lexikon III, Nr. 15. Zur Lesung des Götternamens *bȝbj* und Varr. als *bȝbȝwj*. *ZÄS 81:* 68-76.

Ernštedt, P. V.
1953   *Egipetskie zaimstvovvanija v greèeskom jazyke.* Moskau - Leningrad.

Fournait, J.-L.
1989   Les emprunts du grec à l'égyptien. *Bulletin de la Société de Linguietique de Paris 84:* 55-80.

Guiraud, P.
1994   *Dictionnaire des étymologiques obscures.* Paris.

Harris, J. R.
1961   *Lexicographical studies in Ancient Egyptian minerals.* Berlin.

Hermann, A.
1954   Das Buch „*Kmj.t*" und die Chemie. *ZÄS 79:* 99-105.

Hodge, C. T.
1966   Hausa-Egyptian establishment. *AnthrL 8,1:* 40-57.

Hornung, E. und Staehelin, E.
1976   *Skarabäen und andere Siegelamulette aus Basler Sammlungen.* Mainz.

Hrozný, F.
1915   Die Lösung des hethitischen Problems. *Mitteilungen der Deutschen Orient Gesellschaft 56:* 17-50.
1917   *Die Sprache der Hethiter I.* Leipzig.

Kammerzell, F.
2001   Aegypto-Germanica: Ägyptischer Wortschatz in westeuropäischen Sprachen (Teil 1). In: *S. Schierholz et al. (Hrg.), Die deutsche Sprache in der Gegenwart. Festschrift für Dieter Cherubim zum 60. Geburtstag, Frankfurt a. M.:* 115-127.
2002   Aegypto-Germanica: Ägyptischer Wortschatz in westeuropäischen Sprachen (Teil 2). *Göttinger Beiträge zur Sprachwissenschaft 4:* 39-55.

Kluge, F.
1967   *Etymologisches Wörterbuch der deutschen Sprache.* 20. Auflage bearbeitet von W. Mitzka. Berlin - New York.
1999   *Etymologisches Wörterbuch der Deutschen Sprache.* 23., erweiterte Auflage, bearbeitet von E. Seebold. Berlin - New-York.

Koehler, L. und Baumgartner, L.
1995   *Hebräisches und Aramäisches Lexikon zum alten Testament.* 3. Aufl., Leiden.

Lang, K.
1923/24 Die Etymologie des Wortes „Pyramide". *Anthropos 18/29:* 551-553.

Littmann, E.
1920   *Morgenländische Wörter im Deutschen.* (2. Aufl. 1924) Tübingen.

Lloyd, A. B.
1970   The Egyptian Labyrinth. *Journal of Egyptian Archaeology 56:* 81-100.
1975ff. *Herodotus Book II,* Band I-III. Leiden.

Lokotsch, K.
1927   *Etymologisches Wörterbuch der europäischen (germanischen, romanischen, slavischen) Wörter orientalischen Ursprungs.* (2. unveränderte Aufl. 1975) Heidelberg.

Loprieno, A.
1995   *Ancient Egyptian. A linguistic introduction.* Cambridge NY.

Loret, Y.
1945   La lettre L dans l'alphabet hiéroglyphique. In: *Comptes rendus des séances de l'Academie des Inscriptions et Belles Lettres, Paris:* 236-244.

Maspero, G.
1875   *Histoire ancienne des peuples de l'Orient.* Paris.

Osing, J.
1976   *Die Nominalbildung des Ägyptischen.* Mainz.
1997   Zum Lautwert von <ꜣ> und <ꜥ>. *SAK 24:* 223-229.

Peust, C.
1999   *Egyptian Phonology.* Göttingen.

Polomé, E.C.
1997   Beer, runes and magic. *Journal of Indo-European Studies 24:* 99-105.

Reinisch, L.
1972   *Sprache von Nord-Ost-Afrika.* (Reprint) Wiesbaden.

Rössler, O.
1971   Das Ägyptische als semitische Sprache. In: *F. Altheim und R. Stiehl (Hrsg.), Christentum am Roten Meer, Bd. I, Berlin:* 263-326.

Roper, E. M.
1928   *To-Bedauye.* Hertsford.

Satzinger, H.
1994   Das ägyptische „Aleph"-Problem. In: *M. Bietak et al., Zwischen den beiden Ewigkeiten, Festschrift für Gertrud Thausing, Wien:* 202-205.

Schenkel, W.
1979   Atlantis: die „namenlose" Insel. *GM 36:* 57-60.
1983   *Zur Rekonstruktion der deverbalen Nominalbildung des Ägyptischen.* Göttinger Orientforschungen IV B 13, Wiesbaden.
1990   *Einführung in die altägyptische Sprachwissenschaft.* Darmstadt.
1997a   Wie das ägyptische Labyrinth zu seinem Namen kam. *GM 159:* 87-90.
1997b   *Tübinger Einführung in die klassisch-ägyptische Sprache und Schrift.* Tübingen.

Schneider, T.
1997   Das Schriftzeichen „Rosette" und die Göttin Seschat. *SAK 24:* 241-267.
2001   (Hrsg.) Otto Rössler. Gesammelte Schriften zur Semitohamitistik. *Alter Orient und Altes Testament 287, Münster:* 543-607.

Schott, S.
1950   *Altägyptische Liebeslieder.* Zürich.

Schrader, O.
1917   *Reallexikon der indogermanischen Altertumskunde I.* Leipzig.

Sethe, K.
1914   Koptische Etymologien II. *ZÄS 41:* 142-144.
1933   Die Bau- und Denksteine der alten Ägypter und ihre Namen. *SPAW* 19-22, 894-909.
1958-80 Seth. In: *G. Wissowa, Paulys Realencyclopadie der classischen Altertumswissenschaften.* Band 2.2. München.

Skeat, W.W.
1884   *A concise dictionary of English etymology.* Oxford.

Sommer, F.
1920   *Hethitisches I.* Boghazköi-Studien 4.

Spiegelberg, W.
1907   Ägyptische Lehnwörter in der älteren griechischen Sprache. *Zeitschrift für vergleichende Sprachwissenschaft 41:* 127-132.

Ventris, M. und Chadwick, J.
1973   *Documents in Mycenaean Greek.* Cambridge.

Vergote, J.
1945   Phonétique historique de l'Egyptien. Les consonnes, *Bibliothèque du Muséon* 19: 109-114.
1951   L'origine du mot „papier". *In: Annuaire de l'Institut de Philologie et d'Histoire Orientales et Slaves 11, Mélanges Henri Grégoire, III, Bruxelles:* 411-416.
1973/83 *Grammaire Copte, Teil Ib: Introduction, phonétique et phonologie, morphologie systhématique, partie diachronique.* Louvain/Leuven.

von Bissing, F. W.
1951   *Die altafrikanische Herkunft des Wortes Pavian = Babuin.* SBAW, Heft 3.

Vycichl, W.
1942   Ägyptische Ortsnamen in der Bibel. *ZÄS 78:* 79-93.
1972   L'origine du mot du Nil. *Aegyptus 52:* 8-18.
1983   *Dictionnaire étymologique de la langue copte.* Leuven.

Ward, W. A.
1968   Notes on Some Egypto-Semitic Roots. *ZÄS 95:* 66-67.
1978   *The four Egyptian homographic roots b-ꜣ.* Rom.

Wehr, H.
1976   *Arabic-English Dictionary.* 3. Aufl., New York.

Westendorf, W.
1965-77 *Koptisches Handwörterbuch.* Heidelberg.

Worell, W. H.
1945   *Coptic Sounds.* Ann Arbor.

Zandee, J.
1964   Das Schöpferwort im Alten Ägypten. In: *Verbum (FS Obbink), Leiden:* 33-66.

Zimmern, H.
1915   *Akkadische Fremdwörter als Beweis für babylonischen Kultureinfluß.* Leipzig.

Oriental Carpets and Textiles in Ethiopia: Evidence of Trade and Contacts

Martha H. Henze

The finding of a considerable number of quite early Turkish carpets in Ethiopian churches provides new information about Ethiopia's trade connections with its neighbors in the Mediterranean and Red Sea region between the 16th and 19th centuries.[1] Because of traditions prevailing in Ethiopian society at the time, luxury objects of foreign manufacture – predominantly textiles and metal objects – are often found in the treasuries of Orthodox churches throughout the Christianized areas of the country.

Foreign visitors as early as the 16th century have left vivid accounts of their reception in royal courts of Ethiopia and describe being honored with celebrations and feasts amid astonishingly luxurious furnishings – "layers of carpets", lavish garments of silk, and heaps of honorific gifts such as bolts of silk, the best local cotton, and imported carpets.[2] It was the custom among aristocrats to make pious gifts of carpets and textiles as well as paintings, manuscripts, crosses, drums, ewers or other metalwork to a favored religious establishment to ensure their salvation. Such donors are sometimes depicted on wall paintings or identified by inscriptions on objects.

During turbulent times, when one of the intermittent Muslim incursions threatened or when one of the many feudal princes threatened the land and wealth of a neighbor, privately owned precious objects would be sent to the church for relatively safe keeping . Depending on the outcome of the crisis, these objects might become permanent possessions of the church. In these various ways, items of luxury goods from abroad have accumulated in their treasuries.

Christianized in the 4th century, Ethiopia's Church has been formed by centuries of contact with the Eastern Churches of the Middle East. There was also extensive contact with the Byzantine Empire. Having accepted the monophysite doctrine, the Ethiopian Church's liturgy, ceremony, and furnishings most resemble those of the Eastern Christian Churches of Syria and Armenia. The first Ethiopian bishop was appointed by

---

1   In 1992 the author discovered an Anatolian Turkish kilim of classic design (c. 1800) in a church on Lake Tana. Successive trips in 1995, 1997, 1998, 1999, and 2000 resulted in the photographing and recording of an estimated 150 hand-woven oriental carpets or kilims. Half of these are of Turkish origin, predominantly tapestry-woven kilims which include the oldest and most valuable examples; the other half are mostly Persian knotted pile carpets of types woven in the late 19th century or early 20th century and a few Persian kilims.

2   Beckingham - Huntingford 1954: 92 ff.; Pearce 1980: 106, 129, 159, 194, 244.

the Roman Church of Alexandria, Egypt, thus the relation with the Coptic Christians of Egypt. Indeed, all bishops of Ethiopia until the 1930s were appointed by Alexandria, long after the power of that Church gave way to the Islamic presence in Egypt. From the earliest times, the clergy was exposed to the luxurious regalia and ceremonial traditions of the Eastern Christian Church. Syrian, Cappadocian, and Armenian churchmen translated religious texts into the Ethiopic language of Ge'ez; Ethiopian monks were sent to Jerusalem and other centers to study.[3] The Ethiopian Church naturally wished to emulate their custom of using luxurious textiles to honor their faith and adorn their sanctuaries. Fortunately, the powerful position of the Church in society and political life guaranteed that they could afford this tradition.

Although there are few formal records of trade between Ethiopia and neighboring countries before the 19th century,[4] one can glean a great deal of information from reading accounts of foreign visitors and the chronicles of Ethiopian rulers, studies of Red Sea trade at different periods and histories of the countries surrounding it. In effect, the Red Sea region was part of the Ottoman Turkish Empire from the early 16th through the 19th centuries. By the end of the first half of the 16th century, the Ottoman Turks had annexed Egypt, Syria, and Yemen and established themselves in the Muslim principalities along the Red Sea Coast of Ethiopia, occupying Massawa in 1557. After several failed attempts to gain influence in the highlands, the Turks satisfied themselves with leaving port management and protection of the trade routes from the Ethiopian interior and from India under Egyptian supervision. By the end of the 18th century, Turkish influence was no longer of much consequence in the Horn of Africa. Their primary focus was to secure a steady supply of Abyssinian non-Christian slaves who were higly desired in Muslim countries under Ottoman control, a very lucrative trade for all concerned.[5] The kings of Ethiopia and the succeeding feudal rulers traditionally received a huge share of the profits from the trade of resources within their territories. Products such as gold, incense, ivory or other animal products were certainly part of the wealth available for trade, but human slaves, usually southwestern lowland people captured or bought by foreign and domestic traders, were by far the most renewable resource. Profits from the slave trade very likely helped small princes buy costly imported luxuries like silks and carpets.

Quite a lot has been written about the trade caravans that traversed the tortuous and dangerous trails from port cities on the Mediterranean and the Red Seas to the highlands of Ethiopia. Routes existing since Aksumite times are still in use forming the outline for the modern highway network that is now developing over the country

---

3   Henze, P. 2000: 32-39, *inter alia*.

4   See Pankhurst 1968. The author includes available customs lists of imports for this period. Chapter IX, pp. 346-459, on "Trade" emphasizes the period 1800-1935 and is based on all written sources. It describes the world of markets, caravans, export and import patterns of the period, reflecting ancient patterns as well.

5   Mordechai Abir (1968: Introduction and pp. 1-8) gives a good account of the Ottoman presence in the Horn or Africa and a description of the slave trade. See also Pankhurst 1968: 73-134 (= Chapter III, "Slavery and the Slave Trade").

(Pankhurst 1968: 346-360). Many modern towns grew from the market centers where merchants left or joined the passing caravans and stopped to sell and buy new supplies. Undoubtedly, the Ottoman Turkish kilims and carpets and bolts of silk satin, velvet, and brocade that were made into garments and covers for the court and church reached the highlands in such caravans, passing from one merchant to another. There was probably no official record of such trade in Ethiopia in early centuries and only a few clues might exist in export and shipping papers at the point of origin or the offloading port, both uncertain.

Since finding the first early Turkish kilim in 1992, I have pursued several avenues of research in order to record as accurately as possible the existence and historical importance of these textiles. To establish the scope of the present study: the subject group consists of approximately 150 imported carpets/kilims. Of these, half are of Turkish origin; among them about forty of significance; the other half are from Persia and the southern Caucasus, woven in the late 19th or early 20th century. My priority has been to study the Turkish pieces which have been my field of special interest for thirty years. They are also the most important to textile studies because of their age and unusual characteristics of many of them. This half-and-half proportion, though it may not apply to the unknown numbers not yet examined,would be consistent with the fact that Ottoman Turkish power and commercial influence was strongest in the Horn of Africa in the 17th and 18th centuries, and lingered through the early 19th century. Thereafter, countries further east like India and Persia assumed the lead in textile trade with the Horn, as actual import lists of the period show. In that case, one would expect the older pieces to be from Turkey, newer pieces from Persia (Pankhurst 1968).

To verify that my identification of the kilims and their age was close to the mark, I have shown photographs of them to several scholars and collectors of old Turkish kilims. Although most did not have the advantage of examining them personally, they agreed with the one Turkish expert who accompanied me that those they saw were woven of wool dyed with natural dyes and were of designs traditional to types common in southwestern and Central Anatolia before the introduction of chemical dyes which occurred in the 1850s. The motifs used in a few of the kilims suggested to them a production date of the late 17th century, a very respectable age for Anatolian kilims. Figs 1-5 are examples of the types found to date.

Recent studies of Ottoman Turkish internal economic and social development in the period from the 15th to the 18th centuries by Prof. Halil Inalcik and Prof. Suraiya Faroqhi[6] suggest a possible explanation for the predominance in the group of kilims

---

6 See Inalcik 1993; a compendium of writings of Prof. Halil Inalcik, an outstanding historian at the Indiana University Turkish Studies Center, based to a large extent on Ottoman archives, and Faroqhi 1984; Prof. Suraiya Faroqhi, formerly at Middle East Technical University and now at the University of Munich Faculty of Near Eastern Studies and Turcology, has studied the Ottoman Turkish economy as it affected the internal trade, crafts and food production in the 16th and 17th centuries, again using archives.

from the southwestern region of Anatolian Turkey. It is widely known that the Ottoman Turks put a high priority on government-sponsored production of hand-woven carpets for export as early as the late 15th century. The industry flourished into the 18th century and after a decline experienced a strong revival in the 20th.[7] The product of this early industry was a huge quantity of hand-woven knotted pile carpets which rapidly covered floors, tables, and walls throughout Europe and the newly annexed countries of the Ottoman Empire. A small percentage of the production was sent to the great eastern markets, to such cities as Alexandria in Egypt and Aleppo in Syria. Merchants of many nationalities flocked to these centers to buy goods to satisfy their clients along the trade routes radiating from them, like Cairo or even the highlands of Ethiopia. The shipping route between Antalya and Alexandria was a very old one. Members of semi-nomadic Turkmen tribes living in the Taurus Mountain region had established a thriving business in processing wood products from the forests soon after they arrived from the East in the 12th century. They carried large quantities of lumber and charcoal to Turkey's southern ports – Antalya, Alanya, Finike – to be shipped to Egypt and Syria. These ports were also used by the Ottomans to carry pilgrims to Mecca and Medina under government protection and merchants would join the "caravan" to take products for sale at markets and fairs in the pilgrimage centers. Prof. Halil Inalcik states that Ottoman customs registers of the late 15th and 16th centuries show that Turkish carpets were exported to Egypt and a customs register in Antalya for the middle of the 16th century lists carpets as the principal goods exported from this port to Egypt (Inalcik 1993: 115). Interestingly, a Venetian handbook of weights and measures published between 1503 and 1540 is cited as stating that "Alexandria sent Constantinople spices, sugar, rice and dates; wax, silk, camlets and carpets traveled in the other direction."[8]

The reference here indicates Bursa or Constantinople as the origins of the trade. It could equally well apply to the ports adjacent to the Taurus mountains. The Turkmen pastoralists were also animal herders and the women wove from the sheep and goat wool all the utilitarian textiles needed in their tents, among them flat-woven kilims. Bee-keeping in the forest meadows was (and still is) an important occupation and source of income.

To date, only four Ottoman pile carpets of an early period have come to light in Ethiopia.[9] Perhaps they were too expensive or too heavy to transport in large num

---

7 Inalcik 1993: 116-119; Faroqhi 1984: 137; Pinner and Denny 1986: 29-38, 177-187; Raby 1986a, b.
8 Pinner and Denny 1986: 73-81; Irwin 1986.
9 Among the handful of Turkish knotted pile carpets found to date are fragments of four Medallion Ushak pieces. One of them was recorded in church inventories as a gift from a king of Gondar who ruled in 1670 and the design is consistent with the period. A second carpet is of the basic medallion design but seems considerably later. Two others show designs like the so-called "Smyrna" type which were produced for a very long period in several variations, making it difficult to estimate their age without close examination. See

(continued...)

bers. But why the less expensive, lightweight kilims appear in such numbers is part of the puzzle and the problem. Among textile specialists, it has always been thought that kilims, traditionally made for personal use by a village group, were never made for export. It may be true that kilims were not produced for export on a large scale by organized workshops. This does not preclude the possibility that a limited number of kilims were collected in weaving villages by local merchants who sold other local products to foreign traders. Weavers might well weave a few extra kilims for sale or sell one that was no longer needed. It is known that regional markets were held in Maskolur in Thessaly where wagonloads of carpets and kilims were collected for sale to long-distance traders (s. Faroqhi 1984: 138). While there is no evidence yet available, it seems likely that the enterprising Turkmen of the Taurus might well have organized such a market. Basing this speculation on a variety of sources, I would suggest that just such a circumstance could have existed in the region surrounding the ports the southern coast of Turkey that served Egypt and Syria, two major centers for trade in the Near East and northern Africa. So many of the kilims in the subject group were made in communities in the Taurus mountains or the plateau to the north and west of them that it is tempting to say that this centuries-old trading route played a role in bringing Anatolian Turkish kilims to highland Ethiopia.

The study of this important group of textiles has only begun and no one can estimate how many more of similar quality may survive in unknown churches. There is no inventory of church textiles in Ethiopia to guide a search. We were extremely lucky to come upon two formerly wealthy churches on days of high ceremony when they displayed their best carpets and used their most precious drums and crosses.

These textiles are important to textile studies because they are of types rarely found in the market today and are even scarce in museums. They are of interest to Ethiopian studies because they are tangible evidence of trade relationships of a period where little else exists and they also broaden our understanding of Ethiopian Church and secular traditions. They are aso intrinsically valuable objects of textile art. The possession and use of Oriental carpets in palaces and aristocratic dwellings as well as on the altars of Christian churches of Europe has been a widespread practice since the 16th century, a tradition we now know Ethiopia shared.

9   (...continued)
    Franses - Pinner 1984: 357-381.

Bibliography

Abir, M.
1968   *Ethiopia, the Era of the Princes*. London.

Beckingham, C. F. and Huntingford, G. W. B. (eds.),
1954   *Some Records of Ethiopia, 1593-1646*. Hakluyt Society, London.

Faroqhi, S.
1984   *Towns and Townsmen of Ottoman Anatolia, Trade, Crafts, and Food Production in an Urban Setting, 1520-1650*. Cambridge Universit Press, Cambridge.

Franses, M. and Pinner, R.
1984   The Classical Carpets of the 15th to 17th Centuries. In: *Hali Magazine, The International Journal of Oriental Carpets and Textiles*, vol. 6, No. 4: 357-381.

Henze, P. B.
2000   *Layers of Time: A History of Ethiopia*. Hurst & Company, London and St. Martin's Press, New York.

Inalcik, H.
1993   *The Middle East and the Balkans under the Ottoman Empire*. Indiana University Turkish Studies and Turkish Ministry of Culture Series, vol. 9, Bloomington, Indiana.

Irwin, R.
1986   Egypt, Syria and their Trading Partners, 1450-1550. Chapter 5. In: *R. Pinner and W. Denny (eds). Oriental Carpet and Textile Studies II*. London.

Pankhurst, R.
1968   *Economic History of Ethiopia, 1800-1935*. Haile Sellassie I University Press, Addis Ababa.

Pearce, N.
1980   *Life and Adventures in Abyssinia*. New edition in two volumens with introduction by Richard Pankhurst. Sasor Publisher, London.

Pinner, R. and Denny, W. B.
1986   *Oriental Carpet and Textile Studies II: Carpets of the Mediterranean Countries 1400-1600*. Published in association with Hali Magazine, London.

Raby, J.
1986a   Court and Export, Part I: Market Demands in Ottoman Carpets 1450-1550.
        Chapter 2. In: *R. Pinner and W. Denny (eds.), Oriental Carpet and Textile
        Studies II.* London: 29-38.
1986b   Court and Export, Part II: The Ushak Carpets. Chapter 15. In: *R. Pinner and
        W. Danny (eds.), Oriental Carpet and Textile Studies II.* London: 177-187.

Fig. 1 Interior of church in Eastern Gojjam with Kilims and drums prepared for special services.

Fig. 2 Photography Session in Churchyard, Eastern Gojjam.

Fig. 3   Kilim with anthropomarphic design of a type woven by semi-nomadic Turkmen group
          in the Taurus Mountain region north of Antalya, port city on South coast of Turkey.

Fig. 4   Assessing Kilim Fragments.

Fig. 5   A fine example of a Kilim type
          woven in sothwestern Anatolia
          c. 1800.

Scholarly Research and Publications on Islam in Ethiopia (1952-2002): An Assessment[1]

Hussein Ahmed

Why Study Islam in Ethiopia?: a Personal Account

My interest in research on Islam in Ethiopia goes back to the time of my undergradu-ate studies in the Department of History at Addis Ababa University in the 1970s. As a second-year student, I wrote a term paper on Ibn Khaldūn's *Muqaddima* which impressed the course instructor, Professor Merid Wolde Aregay who was later to become one of my intellectual mentors (the other being Professor Taddesse Tamrat under whose supervision I also wrote a paper on selected Arabic sources, in their French and Italian translations, on the mediaeval history of Ethiopia). It was Professor Merid who inspired and encouraged me to cultivate and fully develop my academic interest in the field of Islamic history by familiarizing myself with the scattered but vast literature on the subject and mastering the Arabic language. (It is also worth noting that in my minor field, English – which I was briefly tempted to specialize in – I also produced papers analysing the chief works of such luminaries as the American Herman Melville and the Nigerian Chinua Achebe, *Moby Dick* and *Things Fall Apart*, respectively).

In spite of such auspicious beginnings, however, the subject of my senior essay which I finally submitted in 1977, after frequent interruptions of my studies, was the chronicle of Emperor Menilek II (Hussein Ahmed 1977) written by *Alaqā*, later *Ṣaḥafē Te'ezāẓ*, Gabra Sellāsē. This was because the Ethiopian University Service, which was in charge of assigning third-year students to teach in high schools in the provinces for a year, turned down my request to go to Wallo where I hoped to collect material on Islam in that region. Three years later I went to the UK to work for my second degree and read the literature on Islam in Africa. However, the topic of my thesis turned out to be a partial translation and edition of the earliest version of Menilek's chronicle (Hussein Ahmed 1981), although I did manage to take and audit several courses on Islam in West Africa and to polish my Arabic. By the time of my return home, I had made the decision to abandon the study of chronicles and focus on Islamic history with special reference to Ethiopia.

---

1 A paper prepared in advance for dicussion at the First International Littmann Conference on the "Archaeology and History of the Horn of Africa" held in Munich, 2-5 May 2002.

Twenty years ago, when I made my first debut into the field of the history of Islam in Ethiopia, I had the audacity, which must not have passed unnoticed, to comment that Islam had remained for too long, and for a variety of reasons, a neglected subject in Ethiopian studies (Hussein Ahmed 1982), and to challenge the die-hard notion that Islam had always played only a negative and subversive role in the history of the country. I did not claim then (as I do not now) to have been the first to draw the attention of Ethiopianist scholars to the glaring lacuna in our knowledge of Islam[2] in Ethiopia or to note that the history of Islam was like a small, barren and isolated island in the midst of the vast and rich ocean of Ethiopian studies. It is therefore with a sense of gratification and fulfilment that I am now reporting to this august gathering of scholars that the research and literature on Islam in Ethiopia have made great advances since 1982.

Half a century of scholarly research and publications on various aspects of the history and culture of Ethiopian Muslim communities, undertaken by professional and nonspecialist Ethiopians and non-Ethiopians, have yielded a large corpus of material which has enriched our limited knowledge about the character and modes of the process of Islamization, and about the role and significance of Islam in the context of both historical and contemporary Ethiopia. The tradition of research and writing on Islam in Ethiopia was pioneered by a handful of European missionaries and Orientalist scholars beginning from the early twentieth century and continued by a young generation of indigenous and foreign students since the 1970s. This development marked the transition from the Eurocentric and Middle Eastern perspective, based on ethnographic material and archival sources, to one drawing on Ethiopian oral and documentary evidence, and from an approach which treated the history of Islam in Ethiopia as an appendage of the history of the dominant Christian polity to one analysing the independent evolution and development of the Muslim communities and states which have flourished in the region since at least the 9th century of the Christian era.

The aim of the present communication is two fold: to review a selection of the works published until the 1970s, with particular reference to their methodological and analytical strengths and weaknesses, and to assess briefly those that have appeared since then.[3] A short description will also be made of research in progress and of works which still remain unpublished in the form of theses submitted for advanced degrees in institutions of higher learning both within and outside Ethiopia. Since access to such works outside Ethiopia is very limited, this section of the paper may turn out to be less complete than would have been desirable. The present writer hopes that such a lacuna can be filled by a further survey of materials kept in Europe, the Middle East and North America in collaboration and/or partnership with researchers and scholars based there. More importantly, the establishment of an Islamic centre of

---

2   Crummey 1970: 23; 1990: 118; and Cerulli 1961: 317-329.
3   For an earlier and partial survey of the literature on Islam from the earliest period to the late 1980s, see Hussein Ahmed 1992: 15-46.

research and documentation within the Institute of Ethiopian Studies of the Addis Ababa University for coordinating research on Islam both in Ethiopia and abroad, and acquiring materials (both published and in manuscript) will provide the institutional basis for the advancement of Islamic research that will enrich and broaden the perspective of Ethiopian studies.

The Early Pioneers: Missionaries and Orientalists

While Cederquist, the Swedish missionary, chiefly responsible for the establishment of the Evangelical Lutheran presence in Addis Ababa, made the bold assertion that Islam was introduced to Ethiopia by [Imām Aḥmad b. Ibrāhīm] Grāñ (Cederquist 1912), Arnold's work, based on Arabic sources and European travellers' accounts, contains detailed information on the position of Islam in the 1880s, particularly on the impact of Emperor Yohannes IV's policy of religious coercion on the Muslims of Wallo (Arnold 1913: 321). Basset, the French translator and editor of the *Futūḥ al-Ḥabasha*, published a long article on the emirs of the city-state of Harar up to the time of the Shawān conquest (Basset 1914: 245-288). Another Swedish missionary, Iwarson (1928: 356-361) and the German national Zwemer (1936: 5-15) represent the typical missionary perspective on Islam in the country characterized by the inadequacy of sources and the tendency to make unfounded speculations. The latter made the bold assertion that the Muslim mystical orders did not exist in Ethiopia.

The Contributions of Cerulli

The Italian scholar, Enrico Cerulli, stands out as the most prolific writer on Islam in Ethiopia who systematically collected and tapped indigenous Arabic documents for the reconstruction of the dynastic and cultural history of the Muslim states which once flourished in the eastern and southern parts of the country. He can therefore rightly be considered as the real founder of scholarly research on Islam in Ethiopia and the Horn. One of his earliest studies was a short account of Ḥasan Injāmo (Cerulli 1922). The other was an article on Muslim and Christian publications (Cerulli 1928: 429-432). Cerulli was also a pioneer in the translation and edition of local histories including one on the Sultanate of Shawā (Cerulli 1941: 5-42) and has published a large collection of Arabic material on Ifāt, Awsā and Harar (Cerulli 1931; 1964).

In 1933 Cerulli included a chapter on the diffusion of Islam in southwest Ethiopia in a monograph which he edited (Cerulli 1933), and three years later produced a longer work on the literature and history of Harar (Cerulli 1936), but without discussing the links with other Muslim communities in the country.[4] In 1941 one of Cerulli's lengthy studies was published. It deals mainly with the wider issue of the spread of Islam in Ethiopia and the Horn (Cerulli 1941a). In the following year an article on the political history of Harar came out,[5] while in 1943 Cerulli wrote an article on the mediaeval history of Ethiopia on the basis of Arabic sources (Cerulli 1943).

After a pause of two decades, Cerulli turned his scholarly attention to Islamic history and produced an article in which he lamented the neglect of Islam in Ethiopia by scholars and explained the origin of the traditional image of Islam as a threat to Christian Ethiopia and the modes of its expansion in the southern and southwestern parts of the country (Cerulli 1961). In 1969 he contributed a chapter on East Africa to an edited volume in which he outlined the background to, and process of, the expansion of the mystical orders (Cerulli 1969). The last major contribution of Cerulli was a chapter on the history of Islam in Ethiopia within a wider geographical context (Cerulli 1988).

It should be noted that most of Cerulli's contributions on Islam, scattered in various journals, have been reprinted in a single volume (Cerulli 1971),[6] to the great relief of scholars. Cerulli's numerous writings on Islam represent a solid contribution to the field and testify to the breadth of his knowledge and his mastery of the sources. However, his earlier works suffer from two major shortcomings: firstly, their spatial coverage is restricted to eastern and southwestern Ethiopia, and interactions and contacts between the Muslim communities there and those in other parts of the country are hardly discussed. Secondly, they are exclusively based on written documents; oral traditions and recollections have been marginalized. Thus they do not reflect popular perceptions and views on the events described and analysed in them.

Arabic Writings on Islam in Ethiopia

a) (1908-1948)

The earliest published work is that of the Turkish officer, Ṣādiq Mu'ayyad al-'Aẓm (1908), who visited Ethiopia in the early 20th century. In 1935 Yūsuf Aḥmad, an Egyptian, wrote a short book on Islam in Ethiopia based on a few mediaeval Arabic sources and European accounts (Yūsuf Aḥmad 1935). The outbreak of the Italo-Ethiopian war was the subject of several works on Ethiopia analysed by Erlich (1994:

---

4   For a preliminary discussion of this neglected aspect, see the present writer's paper on the links between Harar and Wallo read at a workshop held in Harar in November 2001.
5   Cerulli 1942: 3-20. This is a further contribution to the history of Harar (see Cederquist 1912). Another related work on the subject was that of Wendt 1935.
6   For a short and cursory account of Cerulli's contribution, see Pankhurst 2001.

101-109).[7] The last works which appeared before the middle of the last century were a book on Ethiopia and the Arabs by 'Abd al-Majīd (1945) and an article by Ibrāhīm on the Muslim states of the mediaeval period (Ibrāhīm Ṭarkhān 1948).

b) (the 1950s to 2001)

In 1953 *Shaykh* Maḥmūd b. Sulaymān al-Tijānī wrote a biography of *Shaykh* Aḥmad b. 'Umar (1892-1953).[8] The year 1960 was an important landmark in the history of Arabic publishing on Islam in Ethiopia because an Ethiopian wrote a book on the subject for the first time ever (Abū Aḥmad al-Ithyūbī n.d.).[9] However, the new trend did not last long since throughout the 60s non-Ethiopian scholars continued to publish books. They include, among others, Zāhir Riyaḍ, (1964 and 1966) Ramzī (Ramzī Tādrus n.d.) and Fatḥī (Fatḥī Ghayth 1967).

Like their counterparts of the 1930s and 1940s, the Arabic published works of the 1960s lack adequate documentation and the approach of the authors is paternalistic. They also dwell too much on the real and imagined plight of Ethiopian Muslims and view and interpret events from a Pan-Islamic perspective, and not from that of the indigenous Muslims of the country.

The period from the early 1970s to the end of the 1990s witnessed the publication of a number of books by both Ethiopians and foreigners. In 1972 two works by Sudanese scholars on the relations between Ethiopia and the Mahdist Sudan were published.[10] In 1975 Mumtaz published a general history of Islam (Mumtāz al-'Arīf 1975).[11] Other works included a book by a Sudanese scholar ('Abd al-'Azīz 'Abd al-Ghānī Ibrāhīm 1994), a two-volume study by an Ethiopian (Muḥammad al-Ṭayyib b. Muḥammad b. Yūsuf 1996), a book by another Ethiopian ('Alī al-Shaykh Aḥmad Abu Bakr, n.d.), and still another by his compatriot (Muḥammad Tāj 'Abd al-Raḥmān

---

7   They include: 'Abdallāh al-Ḥusayn 1935; Muḥammad Luṭfi 1935; Bulus Mas'ad 1935; Salim Khayyāṭa 1937; Muḥammad Ṭāriq Bey 1937; and Muḥammad Tayāsir Zabiyān al-Kaylānī 1937. (See also Dejazmatch Zewde Gabre-Sellasie 2001. He also mentioned (p. 155) the fact that Murād Kāmil was the author of *Fī Bilād al-Najāshī* (n.d.).

8   Maḥmūd *b.* Sulaymān al-Tijānī 1953. See also Jamāl al-Dīn Muḥammad al-Annī's collection of three works: *Kitāb rawḍat al-asrār fi'l-ṣalāt 'alā nabiyy al-mukhtār, Kitāb al-tuḥfa al-rabbāniyya bi'l-ṣalāt 'alā imām al-ḥaḍra al-qudriyya*, and *miftāḥ al-madad fi'l-ṣalāt wa'l-salām 'alā rasūl Allāh al-ṣamad* (Addis Ababa: Maṭba 'at Addīs, n.d.) and Muḥammad Amīn Muḥammad *Yāsīn, Kitāb Dawā' al-qulūb fī mu 'āmalat al-'abd ma'a rabbihi al-maṭlūb* (Addis Ababa: Berhānennā Salām Printing Press, n.d.).

9   See also 'Abd al-Raḥmān al-Ḥuss 1960 and Rāshid Barāwī 1960.

10 Muḥammad Sa'īd al-Qaddāl 1972, and Muḥammad Ibrāhīm Abū Salīm - Muḥammad Sa'īd al-Qaddāl 1972. [A year later, *Al-Ḥājj* 'Umar b. Ibrāhīm 1973)].

11 See also 'Abd al-Ḥalīm Muḥammad Rajab 1985 and Muḥammad 'Abd al-Fattāḥ 'Aliyyan 1987.

1999). The latest work on Islam written in Arabic by an Ethiopian Muslim is that of
Sayid *Shaykh* Muḥammad Ṣādiq (2000).[12]

Trimingham, Cuoq, Wagner and a new generation of scholars

In 1952 J. Spencer Trimingham published the first extended study of Islam in English
(Trimingham 1952). His skilful use of Arabic, Ethiopic and European sources for the
reconstruction of the history of Islam in Ethiopia and treatment of the subject from a
wider spatial framework constitute a major contribution to the development of the
field. However, he devotes too much space to discussing the protracted struggle between the mediaeval Muslim states and the Christian kingdom,[13] and there is too little
coverage of developments in north and central Ethiopia. A more serious shortcoming
is his view that the history of Islam is an appendage to that of the Christian state.[14]

The French scholar, Father Cuoq, wrote a survey of Islam in Ethiopia from the
seventh to the sixteenth century based on Arabic sources (Cuoq 1981). Like
Trimingham and others before him, he, too, over-concentrates on Christian-Muslim
antagonism.[15]

Ewald Wagner is perhaps the true successor of Cerulli not only in terms of the area
of study (Harar) but also in his publication output (translation of Arabic texts and
many articles).[16] The only minor problem with his works is that the majority of them
were written in German and therefore not readily used by English-speaking scholars.

The Dutch scholar, van Donzel, has made immense contributions to the history of
the relations between the Muslim world and Ethiopia during the seventeenth century.[17]

Braukämper (1977a; 1977b) has considerably widened our knowledge about the
mediaeval Muslim states, while Dombrowski (1983) has contributed to the debate
over the process of Islamization in Ethiopia and the Horn.

Over the last ten years or so, anthropologists/sociologists based in Japan, the
Netherlands and Canada, and in Ethiopia, have ventured into the study of aspects of

---

12 It is worth noting that the work of Shaykh Muḥammad Tāj al-Dīn Aḥmad, *I'lām al-Aghbiyā'
    bihayāt 'Uẓamā' Ityūbiyā mina' l-'Ulamā' wa'l-Awliyā' wa'l-Salāṭīn al-Islām wa'l-Aṣfiyā*, is in
    press in Addis Ababa.
13 Edward Ullendorff regarded this as a creditable achievement of Trimingham. He wrote
    about this in a review of Trimingham's book (Ullendorff 1953).
14 For a critique of this and other stereotypical images of Islam, see Hussein Ahmed (1992:
    15-21).
15 See also his much more sober and useful chapter on Ethiopia in his *Les Musulmans en Afri-
    que* (Cuoq 1975: 358-395). For a detailed analysis of the former, see Hussein Ahmed 1985:
    353-358.
16 Among his major works are: Wagner 1973; 1974; 1974a; 1978; 1983.
17 His major works include: van Donzel 1979; 1980; 1986; 1986a.

popular, regional and contemporary Islam in Ethiopia from the perspective of their field of specialization. They include Ishihara (1997), Abbink (1998),[18] Gibb (1999), Alula Pankhurst (1994), and Kalkilachew (1997). Others who have turned their attention to the study of some aspects of Islam include Abdussamad H. Ahmad (2000: 161-172) and Ahmed Hassen Omer (2000: 147-159).

The post-1991 period witnessed an unprecedented output of indigenous literature on Islam in Ethiopia in the form of books (both original and in translation into Amharic, Oromifa and Harari), and, more importantly, weekly newspapers and occasional/regular magazines. Space does not allow us to describe and analyse the contents of these works (Hussein Ahmed 1998) but mention should be made of the translation into Amharic of a part of the *Futūḥ al-Ḥabasha*,[19] the first of its kind to appear in print. Perhaps as a reaction to this extraordinary outpouring of writings on Islam in Ethiopia, and as a manifestation of the traditional Islamophobia, two booklets in Amharic were published by Alamāyyahu and Masmara[20] which aroused Muslim public indignation and critical comments published in the leading Islamic weekly, *Ḥikma*.

In this paper the coverage of Islam in biographical/historical dictionaries and bibliographies, international conferences of Ethiopian studies held between 1959 and 1988, and in scholarly journals, is not treated because that was adequately analysed in the present writer's article (Hussein Ahmed 1992: 31-40). The proceedings of the Ethiopian conferences which took place between 1991 and 1997 contain several studies on Islam in Ethiopia. At the eleventh conference in 1991, four papers were read.[21] At the twelfth conference the same number of papers were presented and subsequently published in the proceedings.[22] At the thirteenth conference, four papers were also read.[23]

Important works published by younger scholars include those by Gori (1993; 1995 and 1995a), Pelizzari (1993), and myself (Hussein Ahmed 2001). As far as research on Islam (both completed and in progress) is concerned, it is worth mentioning the the-

18 See also Abbink 1999 and Hussein Ahmed 2002.
19 *Abashān Yamāqnāt Zamachā* (transl. 'Abdallāh Muḥammad 'Alī) (Addis Ababa: Harari National League, 2001).
20 Alamayyāhu Mogas, *Lamen Alsallamhum?* [Why I did not convert to Islam] (Addis Ababa, March/April 1998); Masmara Salomon, *Yedras Lamuslim Waganochē* [May it reach my Muslim compatriots] (Addis Ababa 1998).
21 van Donzel 1994; Wagner 1994; Hussein Ahmed 1994; A. Pankhurst 1994.
22 Hussein Ahmed 1994a; van Donzel 1994a; Ibrahim Idris 1994; Schlee 1994.
23 Abdussamad H. Ahmad 1997; Hussein Ahmed 1997; Ishihara 1997; Jacob 1997.

ses of Abbas Ahmed (1992), Muhammad Sayid,[24] Carmichael,[25] Ahmed,[26] Temam[27] and Ficquet[28]. Two book chapters by Mohammed Hassen (1992) and Kapteijns (2000) are works of synthesis and useful for both researchers and general readers.

Abbreviations

AE   Annales d'Ethiopie, Addis Ababa - Paris
Annali = Annali dell'Istituto Universitario Orientale di Napoli, Naples
JAH   Journal of African History, London
ISIM   International Institute for the Study of Islam in the Modern World, Leiden
MW   Muslim World
RSE   Rassegna di Studi Etiopici, Rome

Bibliography

Abbas Ahmed
1992   *A Historical Study of the City-State of Harar (1795-1875)*. M.A. thesis, Department of History, Addis Ababa University.

Abbink, J.
1998   An historical-anthropological approach to Islam in Ethiopia: issues of identity and politics. *Journal of African Cultural Studies 2, 2:* 109-124.
1999   Ethiopian Islam and the Challenge of Diversity. *ISIM Newsletter 4:* 24.

'Abd al-'Azīz 'Abd al-Ghānī Ibrāhīm
1994   *Ahl Bilāl: Judhūr al-Islām al-Ta'rīkhiyya fi'-Ḥabasha*. Khartoum.

24 Muhammad Sayid wrote last year an M.A. thesis in Arabic on Islam in Ethiopia in the late nineteenth and early twentieth centuries for the University of Tripoli, Libya.
25 Tim Carmichael has recently completed a thesis at Michigan State University on the response of the Harari to the establishment of Shawan administration.
26 Ahmed Hassen Omer is doing fieldwork for a Ph.D. thesis on trade and Islam in northern Shawa in the nineteenth century to be submitted to the Université de Provence.
27 Temam Haji Adem, *Islam in Arsi, Ethiopia ca. 1840-1974*. M.A. thesis just submitted to the Department of History, Addis Ababa University.
28 Eloi Ficquet completed a doctoral thesis on Christian-Muslim relations in southwest Wallo under the title "Du barbare au mystique. Anthropologie historique des recompositions identitaires et religieuses dans le Wällo (Éthiopie centrale)" (Ecole des Hautes Etudes en Sciences Sociales, Paris 2000).

'Abd al-Ḥalīm Muḥammad Rajab
1985   Al-'alāqat al-siyāsiyya bayn al-muslimī al-Zayla 'wanuṣārā al-Ḥabasha fī'l-
        'uṣūr al-wusṭā. Cairo.

'Abdallāh al-Ḥusayn
1935   Al-Mas'ala al-Ḥabashiyya min al-ta'rīkh al-qadīm ilā 'ām 1935. Cairo.

'Abd al-Majīd 'Abidīn
1945   Bayna 'l-Ḥabasha wa'l-'Arab. Cairo.

'Abd al-Raḥmān al-Ḥuss
1960   Ithyūbiyā fī 'ahd Hayla Sellāsī al-awwal. Beirut.

Abdussamad H. Ahmad
1997   Trade and Islam: Relations of the Muslims with the Court in Gondar
        1864-1941. In: Fukui, K., Kurimoto, E. and Shigeta, M. (eds.): Ethiopia in
        Broad Perspective: Papers of [the] 13th International Conference of Ethiopian
        Studies, vol. I, Kyoto: 128-137.
2000   Muslims of Gondar 1864-1941. AE 16: 161-172.

Abū Aḥmad al-Ithyūbī (pseud.),
n.d.   Al-Islām al-Jarīḥ fī'-Ḥabasha. [1960].

Ahmed Hassen Omer
2000   The Italian Impact on Ethnic Relations: a Case Study of a Regional Policy in
        Northern Shoa (Ethiopia), 1936-1941. AE 16: 147-159.

Alamayyāhu Mogas
1998   Lamen Alsallamhum? [Why I did not convert to Islam]. Addis Ababa.

'Alī al-Shaykh Aḥmad Abū Bakr
n.d.   Ma'ālim al-Hijratayn ilā arḍ al-Ḥabasha. Riyāḍ.

Arnold, T. W.
1913   The Preaching of Islam. 2nd ed., London.

Basset, R.
1914   Chronologie des rois de Harar 1637-1887. Journal Asiatique, vol. 3: 245-258.

Braukämper, U.
1977a   Islamic Principalities in south-east Ethiopia between the Thirteenth and
         Sixteenth Centuries. (Part One). *Ethiopianist Notes 1,1:* 17-56.
1977b   Islamic Principalities in south-east Ethiopia between the Thirteenth and
         Sixteenth Centuries. (Part Two). *Ethiopianist Notes 1,2:* 1-43.

Bulus Mas'ad
1935   *Al-Ḥabasha aw Ithyūbiyā fī munqalab al-ta 'rīkhihā.* Cairo.

Cederquist, K.
1912   Islam and Christianity in Abyssinia. *The Moslem World 2:* 152-156.

Cerulli, E.
1922   *The Folk-Literature of the Galla of Southern Ethiopia.* Varia Africana 3. Cam-
         bridge, Mass.
1928   Pubblicazioni recenti dei Musulmani e dei Cristiani dell'Etiopia. *Oriente
         Moderno* 8, 9: 429-432.
1931   *Documenti arabi per la storia dell'Etiopia.* Rome.
1933   La diffuzione dell'Islam nel sud- ovest etiopico. In: *Cerulli, E. (ed.), Etiopia
         occidentale, Rome:* 189-193.
1936   *La lingua e la storia di Harar.* Rome.
1941a   Il Sultanato dello Scioa nel secolo XIII secondo un nuovo documento
         storico. *RSE I, 1:* 5-42.
1941b   *L'Islam nell'Africa orientale.* Rome.
1942   Gli emiri di Harar dal secolo XVI alla conquista egiziana (1875). *RSE 2, 1:*
         3-20.
1943   L'Etiopia medievale in alcuni brani di scrittori arabi. *RSE 3, 3:* 272-294.
1961   L'Islam en Ethiopie. *Correspondance d'Orient,* 5: 317-329.
1964   La fine dell'emirato di Harar in nuovi documenti storici. *Annali dell'Istituto
         Universitario Orientale di Napoli n.s. 14, 1:* 75-82.
1969   Islam in East Africa. In: *Arberry, A.J. (ed.), Religion and the Middle East, vol.
         1,* Cambridge: 203-219.
1971   *L'Islam di ieri e di oggi.* Pubblicazioni dell'Istituto per l'Oriente 64. Rome.
1988   Ethiopia's relations with the Muslim world. In: *El Fasi, M. and Hrbek, H.
         (eds.), UNESCO General History of Africa, vol. 3.* Paris - London - Los An-
         geles: 575-585.

Crummey, D.
1970   Rev. of M. Abir, Ethiopia: the Era of the Princes, the Challenge of Islam and
         the Reunification of the Christian Empire 1769-1855. (London 1968). *JAH 11,
         2:* 280-282.
1990   Society, State and Nationality in the Recent Historiography of Ethiopia. *JAH
         31, 1:* 103-119.

Cuoq, J.
1975   *Les Musulmans en Afrique*. Paris.
1981   *L'Islam en Ethiopie des origins jusqu'au XVIe siècle*. Paris.

Dombrowski, F. A.
1983   The Growth and Consolidation of Muslim Power in the Horn of Africa: Some Observations. *Archív Orientální 51*: 55-67.

Erlich, H.
1994   *Ethiopia and the Middle East*. Boulder - London.

Fatḥī Ghayth
1967   *Al-Islām wa'l-Ḥabasha 'abr al-Ta'rīkh*. Cairo.

Gibb, C.
1999   Baraka without Borders: Integrating Communities in the City of Saints. *Journal of Religion in Africa 29, 1*: 88-108.

Gori, A.
1993   Islam in Etiopia. *RSE* 37: 45-87.
1995a   Soggiorno di studi in Eritrea ed Etiopia, brevi annotazioni bibliographiche. *RSE 39*: 81-129.
1995b   Alcuni considerazioni e precisazioni preliminari sull'origine e sulla natura delle presenze islamiche non autoctone nelle communitá musulmane d'Etiopia. *Annali 55, IV*: 406-36.

Hussein Ahmed
1977   *Some Problems of the Gabra Sellāsē Chronicle*. B.A. thesis, Department of History, Addis Ababa University (unpublished).
1981   *The Chronicle of Shawa: a Partial Translation and Annotation*. M.A. thesis, Centre of West African Studies, University of Birmingham.
1982   *Ethiopian Islam: A Review of Sources*. A paper read at the international conference on 'Ethnography and History in Ethiopian Studies', Addis Ababa, Institute of Ethiopian Studies.
1985   Rev. of J. Cuoq, Les Musulmans en Afrique (Paris 1975). *Journal of Semitic Studies 30, 2*: 353-358.
1992   The Historiography of Islam in Ethiopia. *Journal of Islamic Studies 3, 1*: 15-46.
1994a   *Al-'Alam*: The History of an Ethiopian Arabic Weekly. In: *Zewde, B., Pankhurst R. and Beyene, T. (eds.): Proceedings of the Eleventh International Conference of Ethiopian Studies, Addis Ababa, April 1-6, 1991*. Institute of Ethiopian Studies, vol. I, Addis Ababa: 155-165.

1994b   Islam and Islamic Discourse in Ethiopia (1973-1993). In: *Harold G. Marcus (ed.), New Trends in Ethiopian Studies. Papers of the 12th International Conference of Ethiopian Studies,* vol. I, Lawrenceville, N.J.: 775-801.

1997   A Brief Note on the Yemeni Arabs in Ethiopia. In: *Fukui, K., Kurimoto, E. and Shigeta, M. (eds.): Ethiopia in Broad Perspective: Papers of [the] 13th International Conference of Ethiopian Studies, vol. I,* Kyoto: 339-348.

1998   Islamic Literature and Religious Revival in Ethiopia (1991-1994). *Islam et Sociétés au sud du Sahara, 12:* 98-108.

2001   *Islam in Nineteenth-Century Wallo, Ethiopia: Revival, Reform and Reaction.* Leiden.

2002   19th-Century Islamic Revival in Wallo, Ethiopia. *ISIM Newsletter 9:* 26.

Ibrahim Idris
1994   Freedom of Religion and Secularization of State: The Legal Status of Islamic Law and Shariat Courts in Ethiopia. In: *Harold G. Marcus (ed.), New Trends in Ethiopian Studies. Papers of the 12th International Conference of Ethiopian Studies,* vol. II, Lawrenceville, N.J.: 151-156.

Ibrāhīm Ṭarkhān
1948   *"Al-Islām wa'l-mamālik al-islāmiyya bi'l-Ḥabasha,"* Majalla al-Jam 'iyya al-Miṣriyya li'l-Dirāsat al-Ta'rīkhiyya. Cairo.

Ishihara, M.
1997   The Life History of a Muslim Holyman: *Al-Faki* Ahmad Umar. In: *Fukui, K., Kurimoto, E. and Shigeta, M. (eds.): Ethiopia in Broad Perspective: Papers of [the] 13th International Conference of Ethiopian Studies, vol. II,* Kyoto: 391-402.

Iwarson, J.
1928   Islam in Eritrea and Abyssinia. *MW 18:* 356-361.

Jacob, P.
1997   La Communauté Afar et l'Islam. In: *Fukui, K., Kurimoto, E. and Shigeta, M. (eds.): Ethiopia in Broad Perspective: Papers of [the] 13th International Conference of Ethiopian Studies, vol. III,* Kyoto: 175-188.

Kalkilachew, A.
1997   *Religion, Rituals and Mutual Tolerance in Wallo: the Case of Kabe.* M.A. thesis, Department of Sociology and Social Administration, Addis Ababa University.

Kapteijns, L.
2000   Ethiopia and the Horn of Africa. In: *Levtzion, N. and Pouwels, R.L. (eds.), The History of Islam in Africa*. Athens, Ohio: 227-250.

Maḥmūd b. Sulaymān al-Tijānī
1953   *Jilā' al-Fikr fī tarjama bi 'ārif billāh Sayyid Aḥmad b. 'Umar al-Barnū al-Tijānī*. Cairo.

Masmara Salomon
1998   *Yedras Lamuslim Waganochē*. [May it reach my Muslim compatriots]. Addis Ababa.

Mohammed Hassen
1992   Islam as a Resistance Ideology among the Oromo of Ethiopia: the Wallo Case 1700-1900. In: *Said S. Samatar (ed.), In the Shadow of Conquest: Islam in Colonial Northeast Africa*, Trenton, N.J.: 75-101.

Muḥammad 'Abd al-Fattāḥ 'Aliyyan
1987   *Al-hijra ilā al-Ḥabasha wamunāqashat qaḍiyya al-najāshī*. Cairo.

Muḥammad Ibrāhīm Abū Salīm and Muḥammad Sa'īd al-Qaddāl (eds.)
1972   *Al-Ṭirāz al-manqūsh bibushrā qatl Yuḥannā malik al-Ḥubūsh*. Khartoum.

Muḥammad Luṭfi Jum'a
1935   *Bayn al-asad al-Ifrīqī wa'l-nimr al-Iṭālī*. Cairo.

Muḥammad Sa'īd al-Qaddāl
1972   *Al-Mahdiyya wa'l-Ḥabasha*. Khartoum.

Muḥammad Ṭāj 'Abd al-Raḥmān
1999   *Ta'rīkh Ithyūbiyā*, vol. I, Islamabad.

Muḥammad Ṭāriq Bey
1937   *Mudhakkirātī fī'l ḥarb al-ḥabashiyya al-īṭāliyya 1935-1936*. Damascus.

Muḥammad Tayāsir Zabiyān al-Kaylānī
1937   *Al-Ḥabasha al-muslima: mushāhadātī fī diyār al-Islām*. Damascus.

Muḥammad al-Ṭayyib b. Muḥammad b. Yūsuf al-Yūsūfī
1996   *Ithyūbiyā wa'l-'Urūba 'abr al-Ta'rīkh*. Mecca.

Mumtāz al-'Arīf
1975   *Al-Aḥbāsh bayna Ma'rib wa Aksum*. Baghdad.

Pankhurst, A.
1994   Indigenising Islam in Wallo: *Ajam*, Amharic verse written in Arabic script. In: *Zewde, B., Pankhurst, R. and Beyene, T (eds.): Proceedings of the Eleventh International Conference of Ethiopian Studies, Addis Ababa, April 1-6, 1991*. Institute of Ethiopian Studies, vol. 2. Addis Ababa: 257-273.

Pankhurst, R.
2001   Italian Scholarship on Ethiopia: a Brief Historical Introduction. *Bibliotheca nubica et aethiopica 8:* 90-91.

Pelizzari, E.
1993   L'Islam popolare in Etiopia, Il pellegrinagio di *Shaikh* Husayn. *Africa 47, 3:* 382-395.

Ramzī Tādrus
n.d.   *Kitāb Ḥādir al-Ḥabasha wamustaqbaluhā*. Cairo.

Rāshid Barāwī
1960   *Al-Ḥabasha bayn al-iqṭā' wa'l-'aṣr al-ḥadīth*. Cairo.

Ṣādiq Mu'ayyad al-'Aẓm
1908   *Riḥlat al-Ḥabasha*. Cairo.

Salim Khayyāṭa
1937   *Al-Ḥabasha al-maẓlūma*. Beirut.

Sayid Shaykh Muḥammad Ṣādiq
2000   *Manhal al-'Aṭshān fī Ta'rīkh al-Ḥubshān*. Ṣan'ā'.

Schlee, G.
1994   Islam and the Gada System as Conflict-Shaping Forces in Southern Oromia. In: *Harold G. Marcus (ed.), New Trends in Ethiopian Studies. Papers of the 12th International Conference of Ethiopian Studies,* vol. II, Lawrenceville, N.J.: 975-997.

Trimingham, J. S.
1952   *Islam in Ethiopia*. London.

Ullendorff, E.
1953   Rev. of J. S. Trimingham, Islam in Ethiopia (London 1952). *Africa 18:* 75-77.

'Umar b. Ibrāhīm, Al-Ḥājj
1973   *Jawāhir al-Dhahab al-Aḥmar fī Manāqib al-Ustādh al-Akbar al-Shaykh 'Umar b. 'Alī al-Balbalittī al-Ghalamsī*. Addis Ababa: *Maṭba 'at Addīs* (1393 A.H.).

van Donzel, E. J.
1979   *Foreign Relations of Ethiopia 1642-1700, Documents Relating to the Journeys of Khodja Murād*. Leiden - Istanbul.
1980   Fasiladas et l'Islam. In: *J. Tubiana (ed.), Modern Ethiopia from the Accession of Menilek II to the Present: Proceedings of the Fifth International Conference of Ethiopian Studies, Nice, 19-22 December 1977*, Rotterdam: A. A. Balkema 387-397.
1986a   Correspondence between Fasiladas and the Imams of Yemen. In: *G. Goldenberg (ed.), Ethiopian Studies, Proceedings of the Sixth International Conference, Tel-Aviv, 14-17 April 1980*, Rotterdam - Boston: 91-100.
1986b   *A Yemenite Embassy to Ethiopia 1647-1649*. Stuttgart.
1994a   Foreign Relations During the Reign of King Fasiladas 1632-1667. In: *Zewde, B., Pankhurst R. and Beyene, T. (eds.): Proceedings of the Eleventh International Conference of Ethiopian Studies, Addis Ababa, April 1-6, 1991*. Institute of Ethiopian Studies, vol. I, Addis Ababa: 117-122.
1994b   Fasiladas and Islam. In: *Harold G. Marcus (ed.), New Trends in Ethiopian Studies. Papers of the 12th International Conference of Ethiopian Studies*, vol. I, Lawrenceville, N.J.: 1030-1035.

Wagner, E.
1973   Eine Liste der Heiligen im Harar. *ZDMG 123:* 269-292.
1974a   Genealogien aus Harar. *Der Islam 51:* 97-117.
1974b   Three Arabic Documents on the History of Harar. *JES 12, 1:* 213-224.
1978   *Legende und Geschichte der Fatḥ Madīnat Harar von Yaḥyā Naṣrallāh*. Wiesbaden.
1983   *Harari Texte in arabischer Schrift*. Wiesbaden.
1994   The Genealogy of the Later Walashma' Sultans of Adal and Harar. In: *Zewde, B., Pankhurst R. and Beyene, T. (eds.): Proceedings of the Eleventh International Conference of Ethiopian Studies, Addis Ababa, April 1-6, 1991*. Institute of Ethiopian Studies, vol. I, Addis Ababa: 135-142.

Wendt, K.
1935   Amharische Geschichte eines Emirs von Harar im XVI. Jahrhundert. *Orientalia 4:* 484-501.

Yūsuf Aḥmad
1935   *Al-Islām wa'l-Ḥabasha*. 1st ed., Cairo.

Zāhir Riyād
1964   *Al-Islām fī Ityūbiyā fī 'uṣūr al wusṭā*. Cairo.
1966   *Ta'rīkh Ithyūbiyā*. Cairo.

Zewde Gabre-Sellasie, Dejazmatch
2001   The Contribution of non-Ethiopian Scholars to the Development of Ethio-
          pian Studies: the Role of Jerusalem and Adwa. *Bibliotheca nubica et aethio-
          pica 8:* 152-153.

Zwemer, S. M.
1936   Islam in Ethiopia and Eritrea. *MW 26, 1:* 5-15.

Rescue Excavations at Mai-Temenay

Yoseph Libseqal

The National Museum of Eritrea has carried out a rescue excavation at Mai-Temenay, north of the capital city Asmara. A cistern quarried at a depth of three meters revealed a tomb like structure. This systematic excavation has resulted in remarkable findings such as bracelets, rings, daggers of copper and bronze and golden ear-rings which gave an intriguing glimpse to the wealth of information that highly contribute to the Eritrean National Heritage. Moreover, beautifully executed pottery vases, with some multiple enclose, suggest a culture which concern with production of objects in elegance. The charcoal from the excavated site of Mai-Temenay, Level five has been dated with Carbon 14 dating, 2370B.P/400 B.C. This date of the Mai-Temenay site is particularly interesting as it places the site within the frame of the poorly known so called pre-Axumite sites in Eritrea. There is no evidence of human remains. The discovery will challenge historians and archaeologists to the development of an elaborate material culture that demands to be understood better. Such result will set the background that future research will elaborate upon.

'Persian' and 'Galla' Presence on the Afar Coast[1]

Didier Morin

Based on archeological vestiges or oral sources, Gallas and Persians are supposed to have settled on the Afar coast. In fact, the geographical center of this tradition seems to be Somalia where the French explorer Révoil (1882: 275, 295) noted that 'ancient pagans', described as Persians (Farsân) or Gallas, were said to have been the former inhabitants expelled by the local Somalis. This is repeated in the same terms by Antoine d'Abbadie (1890: 344-345).

Thanks to fresh data Cerulli (1926 and 1957: 51-71) could establish the Galla presence prior to the Somali one. I. M. Lewis (1959) has discussed and confirmed it for the Northern Somali region. It may be interesting to question the diffusion of what has become a kind of 'ethnic' novel out of the Somali territory. Despite the fact that the great *éthiopisant* made clear that it was impossible to be sure that 'Galla' meant Oromo population, Robert Lamy (1959: 178-179), among other French sources extended the story to the Afar region of Djibouti.

> 'On trouve en pays somali de nombreuses ruines ou tombes attribuées aux Galla qui auraient pu être les premiers occupants du pays; on en trouve même en Côte française des Somalis où les Danâkil auraient pris ensuite la place des Galla avant d'être partiellement refoulés par les Issa.'

When numerous Oromo toponyms, especially inside the former British Somaliland, give strong support to this thesis, their absence in the Republic of Djibouti make the diffusion of the Galla tradition out of the Somali territories, i.e. on the Afar coast highly uncertain. In fact, this equivalence 'Galla' = Oromo during the colonial period seemed to have been carried out by soldiers originating from the Somaliland who constituted the brunt of the local 'Milice indigène'. It may be noticed that it was in Dikhil, where Afar and Somali Issa communities live side by side, that the first French administrative post had been established in 1928. Dikhil became an active place where military officers and scientists began to collect informations about the interior of the colony. Apart from the rare Arab-speaking French officers who could direcly converse with Arabic-speaking Afars, none of them knew enough Afar or Somali language. They had to rely on Somali rank and file who used Arabic (or Afar) with the Afar informants. It was obvious for a Somali born in Hargeysa or Boorama that '*Galla*' meant Oromo.

---

1   *Notation:* ['] indicates a stressed syllable. [^] indicates a stressed long syllable.

Aubert de la Rüe, the first professional geologist to explore the interior of the Côte française des Somalis between Nov. 1937 and May 1938 writes (1939: 19):

'Avant les Danakil et les Issa, le pays paraît avoir été habité par les Galla qu'ils ont refoulés plus au sud-ouest dans le Harrar, pour prendre leur place. Les Galla, qui étaient des agriculteurs et des sédentaires, semblent avoir laissé dans toute la Côte française des Somalis des traces nombreuses de leur occupation, en particulier des monuments très fréquents. (...) Ces constructions, parmi lesquelles j'ai parfois relevé des enceintes avec miram [*mirhab*], qui devaient être des mosquées, paraissent faire défaut dans les régions occupées aujourd'hui par les Galla.'

This 'Galla' alleged presence is reaffirmed when discovering the ruined town of Handōgá, some six miles west of Dikhil (Aubert de la Rüe 1939: 34-35)[2]:

'(...) L'ancienne cité de Gallagota, appelée Handouga [Handōgá] a été créée jadis, il peut y avoir sept ou huit siècles de cela, par les Galla.'

Also (Aubert de la Rüe 1939: 72-73):

'Dans la vallée de Laassa [Lā'assá, North of Obock], ouverte dans le flanc d'un imposant massif en forme de table, le djebel Goutouali [Gutú'li], je découvre (...) les restes très bien conservés d'une cité galla (?), comprenant des vestiges d'habitation en gros blocs de basalte et des monuments d'un type commun dans toute la Somalie (...) Ils consistent en un monticule de pierre, haut de trois mètres, situé sur une plateforme circulaire de quinze mètres de diamètres, bordée de dalles dressées. Ces monuments, d'après les Danakil, ne sont pas des tombes.'

The French officer Péri, in charge of the post of Dikhil, created in 1928, writes in 1938:

'Le pays, d'après les traditions Danakil, a été à l'origine peuplé par les Galla (les Songo n'ont été sans doute qu'une fraction), dont on peut trouver à peu près partout de nombreuses traces (grandes enceintes en pierres de formes diverses, tombeaux). L'orientation des corps, dans les tombeaux que les indigènes reconnaissent comme Galla, semble faire remonter la présence de ces populations à une époque anté-islamique. Les dimensions de ces enceintes, leur nombre, indiquent une densité de population incompatible avec les exigences du climat actuel (...) L'emplacement et la forme des ruines permettent d'affirmer que les Galla constituaient une population d'agriculteurs ou, en tous cas, de semi-nomades possédant des boeufs.'

2   In Kern 1969 [quotes Aubert de la Rue]; Grau 1976; 1981.

The eight dwells made of stone, at Dawdáwya, North of the Ɖer 'Elwá plain, are declared 'Galla' (Bésairie 1949: 18). This interpretation is sustained by so-called local traditions (in fact inherited from Arabized circles) describing the Afar as immigrants from *barr* 'Arab (ibid.) who expelled sedentary Gallas and Songos. This tradition of a former population called Songó inhabiting the Godá mountain behind Tadjoura is mentioned by internal as external sources. Described as 'tall, stupid and Christians', the Songó, whose existence is recalled in the exact toponym Songó-g Godá 'the Songó mountain', are said to have died of thirst in the Awɖá'a plain, North-West of Tadjoura, where they were led by a sultan's slave.[3] Harris (1844) mentions the country of Hai (Ḥāy, in *wadi* Sēkaytó, where Handōgá is located) as the one of the 'Gittereza' (Gittīrissó) and of their chief Sango. Johnston (1844) indicates there circular tombs with an 'opening' to the South attributed to '*Kâfir*, former owners of the country', which he says are 'Sabean Afars (*Sabian Affahs*), common ancestors of the Somalis and Dankallis'. Other informations are found in Angoulvant and Vigneras (1902: 153) who give a Persian origin to these Songó, now located near Zeyla:

'Puis, à Tadjourah, une autre race complètement disparue, les Songo: d'après une légende, ils étaient de très haute taille et d'origine perse. On leur attribue la construction des puits de Tadjourah et de deux grandes citernes dans l'île Saad ed-Din, en face de Zeyla. Ils furent chassés du pays qu'ils occupaient et massacrés par les Ankellos [Ankālá].'

Until recently, the existence of 'Galla' vestiges has been sustained by the discovery of other sites, Guédi Allalé (Km 29 on the road to Arta), the Lāngobālé *tumuli,* north of Obock (Bouvier - Miche 1974), all including stelae and mortars which could indicate sedentary and agricultural more than strictly pastoral populations.

As a non-archeologist I will not enter the debate concerning these data, and their prehistoric or protohistoric origin.[4] I will only make three remarks based on historical facts, language and *de visu* observation, which militate against an Oromo-oriented interpretation.

First, if we accept the classical tradition which makes 'Galla' a nickname for Oromo, their expansion inside Ethiopia is not recorded prior to the 16th century. In the Awash valley, the first battles between Oromos and the Imams of Awsa are dated from 1583 (Cerulli 1931). This chronology doesn't fit the existence of tombs and empty towns discovered by the Afar Debné, when entering the area for the first time.[5] If we admit, thanks to the count of generations through genealogies that the expansion of the Debné, from their original location, the Dadár, between Godá and Mablá

---

3   The noun Songo might be of Sidamo origin (where *songo* is the elder's assembly).
4   Some sites mentioned here have been described by egyptologists in search of vestiges of the Ptolemaic period (Desanges 1978; Desanges - Reddé 1994; Labrousse 1978).
5   According to local traditions, Handōgá (13th century A.D.) was an empty town after a plague, when the Debné entered it.

mountains, North of Tadjoura, could occur during the 15th century, these vestiges cannot be Oromos' one.

Second, the Afar clearly differenciate *tumuli* (ḥawwēló, pl. ḥawwēlólá) from tombs (*kábri*), especially those called *gāllá-k kábri* 'Galla tombs'. The ordinary Muslim tomb is materialized with a circle of stones, sometimes covered with pebbles. Two stones, at the head and at the feet, called *šāhid*, a third stone in the middle for a woman, are the only ornaments, when *tumuli* have generally an hemispheric shape, different in size and structure. They can be:

- simple (between 1 to 3 or 4 meters in diameter), as in Lā'assá, north of Obock; or on the cliff near the sea shore, between Obock and *ras* Ḥagág. Some are of bigger size as the great *tumulus* at the mouth of *wadi* Barkállu covered with white seashells.
- double (Ɖaḍḍa'tó, Sagár, Wayḍéḍlu) or even triple (Barrá-w waydál), each of them on a stone-made plateform (sometimes without that base) linked by a kind of alley made of two rows of big stones.

The so-called 'Galla tombs', for instance at Waydōláli, near Ḥerkálu, West of *ras* Siyyan, also at Aburgúba near Baylûl, consist in flat rectangular terraces made of sand (H: 0.50/0.70 cm; L: 3/4 to 8 m). The long one could be collective tombs. Henri Bésairie (1949: 17) saw other 'Galla tombs' in Lā'assá made of rectangular graves 'avec de petites pierres debout (1m)' which could be stelae. In Mud'údli, near the strip of sand of *ras* Siyyan, many flat and circular tombs made of stone of 4/5 m diam. can be seen. None of them are *qibla* oriented or have any *šāhid*.[6]

Very different are the 'Songo tombs' consisting in four pilars of about one meter hight, ornated with blue stones. Until the seventies, one could be seen in Tadjoura, near the residence of the district commissioner (commandant de cercle), also in *wadi* 'Iddeytá, 3 Kms to the South of Marrâ, in the Godá mountain. Both were differenciated from the Afar tombs (the 'normal' Muslim one) as the *waydál* dedicated to warriors dead in battle.[7]

In 1980, in Rabnó area we could observe tombs with a particular shape. Their circular wall was higher near the 'entry' materialised by two pillars than at the back. These monuments were considered as tombs of unknown origin, not to be confound with the shelters built for the cattle (*áwdi, gasó*).

Third, in the Afar language, two homonymous nouns 'Galla' have to be differenciated:

---

6 Bésairie (1949) indicates a N-W or W orientation for the 'Galla tombs' of Lā'assá when Muslim tombs are more or less N-NE oriented. One will note that N-W direction is the exact opposite of what the Afar consider as the 'South', i. e. South-East, or *Gabbí 'ári* (Morin 1997: 153).

7 Non-Somali grave in Lās 'Arro (Cerulli 1957: 90) shows similarities with the Songo tombs. The Songo tomb near the adminstrator's residence was also witnessed by Chailley (1980: 66).

1. *gā̆llá* (coll.), sing. *gā̆lláytu* 'Oromo'; fém. *gā̆llaytó*.
2. *gálli*, pl. *gā̆llá*, with two meanings:
   a. 'crowd', also *galgalá: gálli-k galgala-lów mássa hínna* 'the leader of the
       crowd is not equal to everybody'; *gallí 'ansá-t* 'in public'.[8] The singular is
       used for 'people': *'afár gálli* 'the Afar people'; *gálli-k yan rásu* 'a well-popu-
       lated country'. The singular is frequently used in alternation: *gálli... gálli* 'the
       one ... the other'. Here, *gálli*, pl. *gā̆llá* opposes unit to plurality. Gallâmir
       (*gallí amir), son of Adâ'al, the leader of the Debné expansion, was nick-
       named as 'the chief of a united multi-tribal coalition': the paramount chief.
   b. 'foreign, far people': *gallí bāḍó* 'a far country': *gallí maró* 'circle of nations'
       translates 'the United Nations Organization'; *gallí ḍâgu* is 'international
       news'. 'Gallagota' (see above) could be:
       1. *Gāllá-g gútá 'revenge of (against) the foreigners', from verb *gût* 'desire of
           revenge': *gûtuh kā yōgoré* 'he beat him for revenge';
       2. ***Gāllá-g gut'á* 'the expelling of the foreigners' (gutu' 'to kick, to push out');
       3. *Gāllá-g gáta 'the foreign land (*gáta*) of the foreigners'. The noun *gáta* 'out-
           side, foreign' (*gáta-t yan* 'he is out of the tribe') is also used as a neologism:
           gatí ḥāgid-íh ministir 'Minister of Foreign Affairs';
   c. 'ordinary people, commoners' (with the derogatory meaning of 'Galla' *vs.*
       Oromo), as opposed to *modda 'í* 'of high descent'.

For these three reasons, the equivalence 'Galla' = Oromo cannot be taken for grant. In
some cases, see Aḍaytá's legend, who is said to have been captured during the wars
that the Afars waged against the Oromos, the 'Galla' origin of the latter is certain. In
other cases, especially when dealing with the collective origin of the former inhabitants, 'Galla' appears to be a political term more than an ethnic one, applied to non
united groups (including Afars, as in Gallâmir!). It could include Cushitic-speaking (?)
groups as those mentioned in the 'Amdä Ṣəyon chronicle (Perruchon 1889), which
were part of the Adal coalition (1333), but which cannot be related to any living stock
of population. Unfortunately, the chronicle list doesn't mention the Songo, so that we
still miss clues for an hypothetical Galla-Songo period prior to the 14th century.

Gálli as for 'stranger' means more exactly 'outsider' *i.e.* out of, or without, a
(united) political organization. Somali *gālo* (sg. *gāl*) has a more religious meaning
designating infidels, pagans, also quite distinct from *gālla* 'Oromo' in Northern Somali. One will note that it is the same Debne tribe which invaded (14th century) the
former 'Galla' territory from Dadár to Handōgá, and later had to fight Oromos on the
Awash river (18th century). The confusion Galla/Oromo in Afar might have its explanation here.

---

8   The noun *gálli* has a final stress in a Noun phrase.

Persian, as a political term

There seems to be more clues of a Persian presence on the Afar coast. The Persian colonization of Yaman during the 7th century in reaction to the Aksumite expansionism may have led to further expeditions on the Red Sea shores. At least, this presence is certain in the Dahlak main island where carved out citerns are attributed to *Furs* or Persians (Conti Rossini 1928: 295).[9] A local tradition among the Dammohoytá of the Bôri peninsula says that the stone-made well of Đa'ērimá at Awán, in the Bôri mountain, was built by Persians.[10] Antoine d'Abbadie (1890: 24) refers to traditions which say that they also settled at Ḥaffalé, a cape East of Mi'dír (different of the Amphilla (= Mi'dír) Bay in the European sources), and "Gammela" (Gimmâḍi), an islet to the East of 'Íddi. Interestingly, in the Afar tradition, the noun *Fursi* doesn't mean 'Persian' but 'Turk' or 'Egyptian' (Morin 1997: 61). This double meaning of *Turk* 'Ottoman' or 'Egyptian' has its parallel in the Ethiopian tradition (Bahru Zewde 1992: 26) and must go back to the capture of Massawa in 1557 by the Turks, and since then their more or less nominal occupation of the coast, before the transfer of their 'rights' to the Egyptian Khedive (1866). In Afar *Fursé* 'Persian' is the place near Lake 'Uddúmma ('*Uddummí bad*) where the Egyptian troops led by Werner Munziger 'Pacha' were defeated by the sultan of Awsa (Nov. 15, 1875). An older *Fúrsi* (written *Furzi* on Italian maps[11]), the sultan's residence, according to Nesbitt (1928: 267), precisely *Ḥanlé Fúrsi*, is located on the left bank of the Gurmuddáli canal, some 7 kms to the South-East of Aysa'íyta (Braca - Comolli 1939). There are other toponyms, as Fârísti "The Persian one", a little summit (433 m) South-West of 'Asal Lake. In the Bôri peninsula, the Ankālá tribe has a war cry (*itrô*): *anâ Fārísli* 'Persians! Courage !'[12] One can reject a derivation from verb *ftaras* 'to devore'[13], according to the bad reputation that the Ankālá acquired before being expelled by the legendary Ḥaḍal-Mâḥis 'the one near the tree in the morning'. Without entering the details of the miraculous apparition of this ancestor of the majority of the ruling Afar tribes, one must recall that oral traditions state he was of Arab or Persian origin. Another tribe, the Dúlum, not included in Ḥaḍal-Mâḥis descent, is also said to have an ancestor coming from "Dêlam", the Dailem region of Gīlān, in Persia.

---

9 A citern discovered by the French archeologist J. Barthoux (1961), since then known as 'Citerne Barthoux' is located at 'Aygí Đaḍḍa', in *wadi* 'Aygu (Labrousse 1978). A possible datation has been given between 235 and 575 A.D.

10 Many tombs are found in the vicinity with what could be the ruins of an ancient town (see Ibn Sa'īd).

11 Ex. Istituto geografico militare, 1939 (1: 100.000) sh. Aussa.

12 From Fārs, the Afar loan *Fârís* is regular (a double consonant in final position being impossible in Afar). Fārísli 'having Persia, being from Persia'.

13 Barthélémy (1950: 600). The less convincing *equestrian* (*fāres*) can also be rejected.

From these different observations, we will make two conclusions:

1. *Fúrs(i)* designates 'non Arab Muslim foreigners' coming from the East across the Red Sea and ruling the coastal area, when *gállá* is applied to non Afar inhabitants, as the Songó of the inland area; or politically non united Afars as those lead by Gallâmir. *Fúrs(i)* includes Persians, Turks or Egyptians, not the Arabs of Yaman.
2. *Fúrs(i)* is applied in Afar to those who would classify Afars as part of the *barr-'ağam*, i. e. non-Arab territories.[14] But *Fúrs(i)* as *gállá* appears to be more political than geographical or ethnical, with a possible conversion of the classical meaning of *Al-Furs* (Encycl. Islam, III: 1110):
   'L'appellation *Al-Furs* qui se trouve dans d'anciennes sources littéraires arabes désigne l'ensemble du peuple de la Perse, mais s'applique d'une façon restreinte aux Persans de l'époque pré-islamique ou aux parties de la population qui avaient conservé leurs anciennes opinions traditionnelles et religieuses. Dans ce sens, cette appellation est souvent synonyme de l'expression arabe *al-'Adjam*.'

Harris (1844) is aware of that, when he writes that the African coast is called '*Barr Adgem*', which is also 'the name given to Persia by the Arabs'. Other classical loans can be found in the Afar lexicon. Such is *dardár* which is the title of the Ad'áli sultans of Tadjoura and of the ancient Ankālá chiefs. It is a loan-word from Persian *sardār* 'who keeps the head', 'chief' *via* Persian-Arabic *zirzār*. T.W. Haig (Encycl. Islam, IV: 168) refers to a letter from a Yamani prince (1581) where *sardār* is used in the sense of 'head of the troops'. *Dardár* (*zirzār* < *sardār*), as the title of the sultans confirms its military meaning illustrated by the way the Ankālá ruled the country from which they were expelled by the Ad'áli who in their turn annihilated the Songó.

   As a conclusion, *gálli* as *Fúrsi* are part of a genuine political lexicon which deserves further investigation.

Abbreviations

Cercle Militaire de Dikkil-Gobad [Cne Péri]
15 mai 1938, Danakil Adoiamara du cercle militaire de Dikkil-Gobad, 34 p. [unpubl.].

Cerulli, Somalia *Somalia. Scritti vari editi ed inediti*. 3 Vols., Roma 1957-59.

Encycl. Islam: Encyclopédie de l'Islam, 4 T. et Suppl. Leiden: 1913-1938.

---

14 *Barr-'adjam* as opposed to *barr-'Arab*, as a local usage, is reported by colonial sources (Bésairie 1949: 18).

Bibliography

Abbadie, (D') A.
1890   *Géographie de l'Ethiopie: ce que j'ai vu faisant suite à ce que j'ai entendu.* Paris.

Aubert de la Rüe, E.
1939   *La Somalie française.* Paris.

Anfray, F.
1970   Notes archéologiques. *Annales d'Ethiopie 8:* 31-42.

Angoulvant, G. and Vigneras, S.
1902   *Djibouti, Mer Rouge.* Abyssinie.

Bahru Zewde
1992   *A History of Modern Ethiopia.* London - Addis Ababa.

Barthélèm, Y.
1950   *Dictionnaire Arabe-Français.* Paris.

Bésairie, H.
1949   *La Côte française des Somalis.* Bureau géologique. Tananarive.

Bouvier, P. and Miche, S.
1974   Enceintes, tombes et habitations anciennes en T.F.A.I. *Pount 13:* 7-22.

Braca, G. and Comolli, R.
1939   La Dancalia meridionale. *Gli Annali dell'Africa Italiana 2, 1.* Roma: 196-239.

Cerulli, E.
1926   Le popolazioni della Somalia nella tradizione storica locale. *Rendiconti R. Accademia dei Lincei (Scienze Morali).* Firenze: 150-172.
1931   Documenti arabi per la storia dell'Etiopia. *Mem. della R. Acc. Nazionale dei Lincei. Classe di Scienze Morali storiche e filologiche ser. VI, vol IV:* 37-101.

Chailley, M.
1980   *Notes sur les Afars de Tadjoura.* Paris.

Conti Rossini, C.
1928   *Storia d'Etiopia.* Bergamo.

Desanges, J.
1978   Le littoral africain du Bab el-Mandeb d'après les sources grecques et latines. *Annales d'Ethiopie 11:* 83-101.

Desanges, J. and Reddé, M.
1994   La côte africaine du Bab-el-Mandeb dans l'Antiquité. *BdE 106/3, IFAO., Le Caire:* 161-194.

Grau, R.
1976   Le site de Handoga. Fouilles archéologiques. *Pount 16:* 4-22.
1981   Le site de Handoga. *Archéologia 159:* 55.

Harris, W. Cornwallis
1844   *The Highlands of Aethiopia described during eighteen months' residence of a British Embassy at the Christian Court of Shoa.* London.

Johnston, C.
1844   *Travels in Southern Abyssinia through the country of Adals to the Kingdom of Choa during the years 1842-43.* 2 vols. London.

Kern, L.
1969   Le site de Handoga. *Pount 6:* 19-23.

Labrousse, H.
1978   Enquêtes et découvertes d'Obock à Doumeira. *Annales d'Ethiopie 11:* 75-77.

Lamy, [Ferry] R.
1959   Le destin des Somalis. In: *Mer Rouge-Afrique orientale. Cahiers de l'Afrique et de l'Asie V, Paris:* 163-212.

Lewis, I. M.
1959   The Galla in Northern Somaliland. *Rassegna di Studi Etiopici 15:* 21-38.

Morin, D.
1997   *Poésie traditionnelle des Afars.* Paris.

Perruchon, J.
1889   *Histoire des guerres de 'Amda Seyôn.* Paris.

Révoil, G.
1882   *La Vallée du Daror.* Paris.

Cultural Interactions with the Horn of Africa – a View from Early Arabia

Burkhard Vogt – Vittoria Buffa

Introduction

The geographical proximity of the cultures of the Horn of Africa and those of South-west Arabia and the well-known and later Northeast African contacts with the kingdom of Saba seem to justify the assumption of intensive cultural and even political interactions between the two areas. If scholars never questioned this view the explanation resulted from the fortuitousness of the early history of archaeological research in the two regions. Researchers often compared the cultural development of Ethiopia and Eritrea before the Axumites with the then better-known ancient cultures of 1st millennium BC South Arabia. During the last two decades a different picture started to emerge with the intensification of prehistoric research mainly, although not exclusively, in eastern Sudan. The same applies to Yemen, which witnessed an increasing scholarly interest in the predecessors, roots and the genesis of the South Arabian kingdoms. During the last ten years, different research projects have helped to define at least three distinct cultural provinces of the Bronze Age in Yemen – the Khawlan Bronze Age in the highlands, the post-Neolithic Hadramawt Megalithic Complex in the east and the so-called Sabir Culture, which is the subject of this contribution.

The Sabir Culture was defined through the field research of the Joint German-Russian Expedition. It is a cultural assemblage exclusively along the coastal plains of the Yemeni and Saudi Tihama and the Gulf of Aden littoral (Fig. 1). Its maximum extension exceeds 600 km covering an area, which extends even far beyond the sites of Sabir in the south and Sihi in the north. In addition to a few excavated sites, of which the key-site Sabir is also the largest, surveys have recorded dense clusters of respective sites for example in the Abyan oasis, the Aden hinterland, around the mouth of Wadi Surdud as well as in the Jizan area of Saudi Arabia. Most likely the nucleus of the Sabir Culture was the hinterland of Aden with a settlement density that is paralleled only by the settlement pattern of today (Vogt - Sedov 1998). Outside the coastal plains Sabir-related stray finds (i.e. pottery) have been identified only in three places, Marib, Hajar Yahar in the Wadi Marha and Dhi Sa'id in the uppermost Wadi Bana – all of these sites discovered or studied by the German and Russian archaeologists.

Supplementary excavations by our mission at Khor Umayrah, an-Nabwa and Ma'layba have helped to reconstruct ancient subsistence patterns which fall into two major groups: coastal shell midden communities with a marine-oriented economy (Amirkanov et al. 2001; Amirkhanov - Vogt 2002) and inland oasis sites, which subsisted on irrigation agriculture, animal husbandry, industrial production of different commodities and trade (Vogt - Sedov 1998). Although still lacking the graveyards of this culture, the hitherto known material evidence reflects in its later stages a stratified society characterized by the existence of very large political centres plus their satellites, infra-site spatial organisation, the construction, control and maintenance of large-scale irrigation systems, as well as intensive commerce within the catchment of the Sabir Culture.

We define the Sabir Culture by the showing of a very distinctive settlement pottery. It became clear from our field studies that the ceramics attest to a long tradition of pottery making which demonstrates on one side a strong conservativism in the range of modelling techniques, a subsequently expanding variability in shapes and ornamentation and on the other side an increasingly refined technical execution. Digging at the settlement mound of Ma'layba allowed dating early productions to the very end of the 3rd millennium BC. More recently, we could on the strength of fully developed ceramics from our soundings in the shell middens of an-Nabwa extend this date to the 24th or 23rd century BC. The earliest local roots of the Sabir pottery manufacture, however, are yet unknown. This development culminates and in fact ends with the ceramic production of the type-site Sabir, where kilns, deposits and stratified contexts produced enormous quantities also of complete vessels.

These general observations enabled us to distinguish in fact two larger chronological subdivisions of the Sabir Culture (Fig. 13) – an earlier phase 1 represented by the sites of an-Nabwa, Ma'layba and the lower cultural deposits at Sabir, and the later phase 2, which is documented by the main occupation of Sabir and the uppermost levels of Ma'layba. Each of these two phases is divided in further sub-phases, the distinction of which is based on stratigraphic observations. In terms of absolute chronology Sabir Culture phase 1 covers the time-span almost from the middle of the 3rd millennium to the 14th/13th cent. BC (Buffa 2002: 6; Vogt et al. 2002). Phase 2 dates from the 14th/13th century BC to the 9th/8th century BC but may have extended within the same cultural tradition until the 6th century BC. At Sabir a dense deflation pavement and isolated fireplaces represent the only surviving relics of this final occupation.

The entire absolute chronology of the Sabir Culture depends on radiocarbon dates. We therefore consider its phase 1 and the very beginning of phase 2 as Bronze Age contexts. Most of the occupation of phase 2 corresponds in its absolute dates to a period in the Ancient Near East commonly labelled Iron Age – a term, which for good reasons is barely used for Southwest Arabia. The stratified settlement deposits of Ma'layba and Sabir do not show a major cultural break between the two phases but rather a transition. And it was also clear from the very beginning of our research that the phase 2 inventory of the apparently illiterate Sabir Culture does in almost no way match with any other cultural horizon on the Arabian Peninsula nor with the much better known material culture of the literate South Arabian kingdoms in the interior. The formation of the latter overlapped chronologically with the final occupation of Sabir, i.e. after the 12th century BC. Regardless of the late absolute date of phase 2 we consider Sabir's material assemblage as expression of a Bronze Age tradition.

Early contacts between the Sabir Culture (phase 1) and the Horn of Africa?

3rd and 2nd millennium pottery assemblages from the Horn of Africa and Yemen's coastal Sabir culture display specific morphological and decorative characteristics that place each of them in significantly different cultural settings. We have already mentioned elsewhere that with the possible exception of the small group of "steatite-tempered cooking ware" (Buffa - Vogt 2001: 443) we consider Sabir pottery as mass-produced on the site. The Ma'layba pottery – our phase 1 – represents an earlier stage of a tradition that will later develop into the pottery of phase 2. Characteristic of this early pottery (Fig. 2) are shapes, which are not as elaborate as during phase 2; most common are bowls, jars and necked jars. Incised and impresso designs are usually combined with appliqué decorations (Figs. 3-4), handles and knobs and a carefully executed (pattern) burnishing is more frequent than in later contexts.

In terms of relative chronology Sabir Culture phase 1 is contemporary to parts of the Gash Delta sequence as illustrated by the work of Rodolfo Fattovich (1989: 121), and the early Jabal Mokram occupation of the Gash. The same is true for Asa Koma (Joussaume 1995), an inland lake site in the Gobaad Plain of Djibouti. It is one of the few studied, dated and published sites in the far south with pottery antedating the mid 2nd millennium, therefore also partly overlapping with our phase 1. Phase 1 ceramic is known only from the Gulf of Aden and unreported from the Tihama. Traces of contacts with the African coast of the Red Sea are indeed scarce. The fishermen's site of Asa Koma in Djibouti yielded a set of vessels all decorated with incisions and punctate designs – geometric decorations, which show to some extent affiliations with the Sabir Culture phase 1 ceramics from Ma'layba (Joussaume 1995: Fig. 12). Apart from a few isolated shards such as a fragment with appliqué concentric triple circles from the lowest pottery level at Ma'layba (Fig. 4) with a parallel in Mahal Teglinos, Kassala, from the end of the 3rd millennium BC (Capuano et al. 1994: 114, fig. 4: 2) similarities in decoration to published early African pottery are rather confined to general features.

Later contacts between the Sabir Culture (phase 2) and the Horn of Africa

During later periods evidence for contacts between the Yemen and its western neighbours on the Horn of Africa appear more intensive. At Sabir a large storeroom, which
is attached to a monumental building (temple?) of phase 2 produced the largest ever
collection of palaeobotanical finds from Yemen. Expectations ran high when a first
study (de Moulins et al. 2003) of different vessel contents recorded doum palm, a
native tree from Yemen, linseeds and other oil plants, *Brassicaceae* and mustard
seeds, many Ziziphus stones, flax, *Sesamum indica* (oil seed), millet and sorghum as
well as *Rottboellia cochinchinensis*. De Moulin and co-authors, however, hesitated to
positively answer the question of whether certain plants spread from Ethiopia/Eritrea
to Yemen (or vice versa?). The two areas are similar in respect to the their general
environment (geology, soils, climate etc.). Both sides of the Red Sea present the same
cultivated plants and this applies also to the natural vegetation. It prompted Zohary to
consider a common Eritreo-Arabian vegetation, which is most complex and "closely
reminiscent of that of the mountainous East Africa, both in floristic make-up and its
altitudinal zonation" (Zohary 1973: 244). Major methodological obstacles are at present the lack of quantitative and detailed analyses, the lack of systematic retrieval of
samples from longer stratigraphic sequences, the varying probability of identification,
etc. (see de Moulins et al. 2003: 225).

Hundreds of clay figurines were collected from the excavations in Sabir. Many of
these were found on the surface, the stratified examples originated exclusively from
phase 2 contexts. While purely geometric representations are rare, animal figurines of
goats, sheep and cattle (and to a much lesser extent camels) are abundant. Human
representations are almost exclusively those of naked obese females in a standing or
more frequently in a seated position (Fig. 5). The latter are characterised by multiple fat
folds and tattoo-like incisions on the thighs. As a whole this type is unknown in Arabia.
Although considerably larger, they show some striking resemblances to much earlier
productions from Northeast Africa, for example C-group contexts in Aniba (Institut du
monde arabe 1997: 55-56, #45) or finds from the eastern desert of Sudan (Bonnet -
Reinold n.d.: 26, figs. 7-8), which are dated roughly to the 2nd millennium BC.

Pottery constitutes the most eminent class of finds: Millions of shards were discovered; hundreds of complete vessels were re-assembled. Excavated kilns and refuse
heaps support our assumption of a local mass-production. Very few types had parallels
in collections from sites of the South Arabian Period and these – not surprisingly – were
restricted to the latest occupation of the Sabir sequence. Affinities to any other known
pottery production from the Arabian could not be identified. It was the general "feel" of
the Sabir pottery that – immediately after 1994 – prompted us to explain it within the
wider sphere of African productions. This was because of the shapes, which almost
exclusively showed rounded or strongly convex bases (Figs. 6-7) while flat bases make
up the bulk of contemporary (late) Bronze Age productions from the High Yemen.
Altogether we registered an extremely wide variety of shapes, decorations, applications,
and modelling techniques. Pattern burnishing (Fig. 8) and punctate and incised designs

were recurrent motifs of decoration. And from the technical point of view, the entire production was handmade making use of different modelling techniques including for example the paddle-and-anvil technique (Fig. 9). A few exotic shards (imports?) seemed to confirm our first attempts to somehow relate Sabir to the African side of the Red Sea (Figs. 10-12).

Roughly contemporary to phase 2 of the Sabir Culture is, in Eastern Sudan, the Jabal Mokram Group, a Pan Grave related assemblage. During the 1st millennium BC Ethiopia and Eritrea witness the formation and flourishing of the Pre-Axumite Culture. Regarding the scarcity of respective ^{14}C dates the Pre-Axumite chronology is based on cross dating with cultural sequences from South Arabia and the Nile valley. According to R. Fattovich (1990: 15) it can be stated with some certainty that the end of the Early Pre-Axumite Phase dates to the 9th/8th century BC, preceding the construction of the temple in Yeha. The Middle Phase dates from the 8th/7th to the 4th/3rd century BC, the Late Phase from 3rd/2nd BC to the 1st/2nd century AD. Recent excavations by the Franco-Italian Mission in the Yeha temple have confirmed the date of its construction during the 8th/7th century BC (Robin - de Maigret 1998: 778). An important contribution to the understanding of the cultural development in this area comes now from a recent publication of surveys and test excavations in Eritrea by an American mission (Schmidt - Curtis 2001: 854). This has provided the first ^{14}C dates that place the Ona Culture in the Highlands of Eritrea, in the Asmara area, between the 9th and the early 4th century BC. Since the Pre-Axumite period covers at least the entire 1st millennium BC and since we date the ultimate end of settlement activities at Sabir prior to the 6th century BC, parallels from Northeast African pottery productions are only of uncertain value for dating (!) our material from Sabir.

Before dealing with possible similarities between the later ceramic assemblages let us discuss the variability within the Sabir productions. At Sabir pattern burnishing (Fig. 8) is the most typical pottery decoration since phase 1. Carefully executed zigzag and criss-cross patterns, vertical and horizontal burnish strokes on plain surfaces (without slip) cover the upper exterior, radial patterns and wide-spaced horizontal strokes the interior. Red and/or white painted decoration in form of geometric patterns is also recorded. Incised decoration is mainly restricted to bunches of vertical lines on large pithoi. Punctate horizontal lines are present on carinated bowls. Metopae of impresso dots starting below the rim cover the upper part of vertical handles on footed bowls and on globular jars. The variety of shapes is enormous and includes, among others, convex profile bowls, footed bowls, beakers, ovoid jars with vertical rims, hole-mouth jars, frankincense burners, perforated vessels, large pithoi with inverted rim, etc.

Apart from Sabir and Ma'layba, the main corpus of published material comes from the Sihi shell-midden in the Saudi Tihama (Zarins - Zahrani 1985; Zarins - al-Badr 1986). In the Sihi assemblage a group of red ware (Zarins - Zahrani 1985: pls. 81, 82: 1-4, 7-8; 83: 1-5, 7-8) vessels is perfectly comparable with examples from Sabir phase 2, in terms of shapes and decorations, including burnishing. Considering the altogether small size of the test trenches at Sihi, the number of complete vessels is as amazing as in Sabir.

Sihi yielded also a set of black ware vessels (Zarins - Zahrani 1985: pls. 87: 1-4, 7-11, 17-19, 21-22; 88: 5-6, 8-14, 16) bearing punctate and incised decorations. The excavators regarded this as an indication of an earlier occupation suggesting direct C-Group and Kerma parallels (2500-1500 BC) from Nubia (Zarins - Zahrani 1985: 92, 96; Zarins - al-Badr 1986: 50). Nevertheless it has to be noted that no parallels with Sabir phase 1 are present at Sihi and that our phase 1 pottery does not include any possible parallels that may corroborate a typological or stylistic impact of C-Group or Kerma pottery productions. Some motifs rather recall, as we suggest, the decorative repertoire of the Jabal Mokram Group, an assemblage that came into being in the Gash Delta around 1500 BC. In Sabir on the other hand we found only very few Jabal Mokram-like elements from the Gash Delta sequence (see for example Fattovich 1989: figs. 3-6, 10).

When first publishing the Sihi excavation Zarins dated the site by means of three radiocarbon dates between 1540 and 1200 BC and by red ware parallels from 1500 BC through the South Arabian period. In this context Zarins and Zahrani (1985: 96) referred to "some obvious parallels with the South Arabian corpus at Hajar Ibn Humeid in shape and decoration" such as ring bases, trumpet feet, and low carinated vessels with ring bases. These occur only in phase 2 of the Sabir Culture indeed, but do not figure prominently in terms of percentage. By virtue of a fourth radiocarbon date Zarins and al-Badr (1986: 50) later expanded the occupational range of Sihi to 2400-1200 BC encompassing a possible period of abandonment of the site. The shell samples on which the analysis was based may explain the high readings, which may need to be lowered by several hundred years. If we accept Zarins first published chronology for the site, its approximate range matches with of our phase 2.

Closer contacts may have existed with Ethiopia and Eritrea. Again the Pre-Axumite corpus of vessels, taken as a whole, is quite far from the Sabir types and Sihi red ware types. Yet, few shapes seem to possess good parallels both in Sabir and Sihi. The large shallow bowls (Fattovich 1980: Tav. 16: 1), bowls of different size with horizontal ledges (Tav. 27: 20; 33: 7. 9), the vases on a high trumpet foot (e. g. Tav. 11: 3) and, to a certain extent, the goblets (Tringali 1978: fig. 4: 9) are relatively close to examples from both funerary (Yeha) and settlements sites of the Pre-Axumite Period and in the Ona Culture in the Highlands of Eritrea. Notwithstanding, it is rather surprising that some of these vessels come not only from the Early Pre-Axumite Phase – as it would be expected – but some also from the Middle and even the Late Axumite Phase.

The Pre-Axumite culture is also distinguished by a set of rather elaborate impresso and incised decorations. Of these the superimposed bands of impresso dots and horizontal lines of impresso triangles find parallels both in Sabir and Sihi. The rest of the geometric incised patterns remain different from examples from Sabir. Red ware vessels with bands of punctate triangles at Sihi (Zarins - Zahrani 1985: pls. 87-88) recall finds from Yeha.

In the ancient port site of Adulis, the majority of the pottery from the deepest, so-called archaic layers is a black ware with incised decorations (Paribeni 1907: Tav. III-VI). Only two shards from Sabir, one with a series of inscribed open triangles, the other with a line of impresso dots seem to recall this kind of decorations. These examples appear exotic within the Sabir assemblage and can therefore be considered as imports. No real similarities seem to exist between decoration patterns of Sihi and Adulis. The complexity of the picture is illustrated by the fact that, among the few shapes of black ware vessels documented in Adulis, two types of carinated bowls with incised decorations match sufficiently well with undecorated specimens from Sabir and in Sihi red ware.

Conclusion

Judging from our present knowledge we can no longer support the hypothesis of a cultural *koinè* from the end of the 3rd millennium to the first half of the 1st millennium BC between coastal Yemen and the Horn of Africa. This model should reflect itself in the archaeological record with a vast diffusion of pottery types that – as a matter of fact – we do not find in the areas concerned.

At the end of the 3rd millennium and during the first half of the 2nd millennium BC some contacts of unknown intensity may have existed between the Arabian coast of Gulf of Aden and the Djibouti area. The excavators of Asa Koma report two radiocarbon dates deriving from the top layers of the site with datings roughly from the first half of the 2nd millennium BC (Joussaume 1995: 32). This will indeed place the earlier occupation of the site to the very beginning of the 2nd or the end of the 3rd millennium BC. It would be very tempting to explain cultural interactions with nearby Djibouti as the first ones to occur in an area where the Sabir Culture seems to have emerged. But too little has been excavated and published from other Bronze Age sites in the Tihama to advance such a hypothesis. Very loose contacts between Northeast Africa – i.e. Eastern Sudan – and the Yemeni highlands – could have evolved already in the 3rd millennium, as R. Fattovich has pointed out, comparing two shards from the Gash Delta sequence with specimens from Khawlan sites. In this case Fattovich (1991: fig. 5: 1, 5) considers the two shards as imports from Yemen.

During phase 2 the picture is more complex. In comparing different assemblages, it seems that the diffusion of decorative ornaments and shapes follows at least partially different circuits. At Sabir only a couple of vessels show some general traits also common in productions from the Jabal Mokram Group in Eastern Sudan and from the archaic levels at Adulis. The Sabir pottery and the Sihi red ware assemblages yield some shapes that are also known from the Pre-Axumite and the Ona Culture. Despite the poor evidence cultural interactions involving an exchange of commodities are quite likely. The intensity and nature of these interactions remain as unknown as their function (storage and transport containers, "exotic" funerary vessels as symbols of prestige etc.).

Sabir, Sihi red ware and the Pre-Axumite pottery share a very limited spectrum of decorative elements associated with different shapes. The taste for incised and punctate pottery decorations and (pattern) burnishing is certainly an African one, but the directions and the way in which modelling techniques, ideas and different tastes circulated and changed, remains still unclear. At present we may assume that within the Sabir Culture different geographical locations led to privileged interactions with different areas. This seems to be true for Sihi, where the interaction with the Jabal Mokram Group was certainly more intense than in Sabir.

As long as the scope and nature of the interactions between the two areas are unknown it will be impossible to fully assess their dynamics and mechanisms. In the future we may contribute to the discussion from the Arabian side only by clearly proving the association of such distant sites like Sihi and Sabir to the same material and cultural background.

Bibliography

Amirkhanov, Kh. A. et al.
2001   Excavations of a settlement of prehistoric fishermen and mollusk gatherers in the Khor Umayra Lagoon, Gulf of Aden, Republic of Yemen. *Archaeology, Ethnology & Anthropology of Eurasia 4 (8):* 2-12.

Amirkhanov, Kh. A. and Vogt, B.
2002   An-Nabwa 2 – A settlement of ancient fishers and clam-gatherers on the Aden Gulf coast (Republic of Yemen). *Rossijskaya Archeologia 2:* 30-43 (in Russian).

Anonymous
1997   *Soudan - Royaumes sur le Nil.* Institut du monde arabe (ed.). Paris.

Bonnet, Ch. and Reinold, J.
n.d.   Deux rapports de prospection dans le desert oriental. In: *Bonnet Ch., Reinold J., Gratien B., Marcolongo B., Surian N. (eds.), Kerma – Soudan* 1991-1992 – 1992-1993.

Buffa, V.
2002   The stratigraphic sounding at Ma'layba, Lahj Province, Republic of Yemen. *ABADY IX:* 1-14. Mainz.

Buffa, V. and Vogt B.
2001   Sabir – Cultural Identity between Saba and Africa. In: *R. Eichmann, H. Parzinger (eds.), Migration und Kulturtransfer. Der Wandel vorder- und zentralasiatischer Kulturen im Umbruch vom 2. zum 1. vorchristlichen Jahrtausend.* Bonn: 437-450.

Capuano, G., Manzo, A. and Perlingieri, C.
1994   Progress Report on the Pottery from the Gash Group Settlement at Mahal Teglinos (Kassala), 3rd-2nd Mill. BC. *Études Nubiennes VI*: 109-115.

de Moulins, D., Phillips, C. and Durrani, N.
2003   The archaeobotanical record of Yemen and the question of Afro-Asian contacts. In: *K. Neumann, Butler A., Kahlheber (eds.), Food, Fuel and Fields. Progress in African Archaeobotany. Africa Praehistorica 15*. Köln: 213-228.

Fattovich, R.
1980   Materiali per lo studio della ceramica pre-aksumita etiopica. *Suppl. 25 to AION 40/4*.
1989   Ricerche archeologiche italiane nel delta del Gash (Kassala), 1980-1989: Un bilancio preliminare. *Rassegna di studi Etiopici 33*: 89-130.
1990   Remarks on the Pre-Aksumite Period in Northern Ethiopia. *Journal of Ethiopian Studies 23*: 1-33.
1991   At the periphery of the empire: the Gash Delta (Eastern Sudan). In: *W. Davies (ed.), Egypt and Africa. Nubia from prehistory to Islam*. London: 40-48.

Joussaume, R.
1995   *Tiya. L'Ethiopie des mégalithes. Du biface à l'art rupestre dans la Corne de l'Afrique*. Poitier.

Paribeni, R.
1907   Ricerche nel luogo dell'antica Adulis. *Monumenti Antichi, Reale Accademia dei Lincei, Vol. XVIII*. Rome: 438-572.

Robin, C. and de Maigret, A.
1998   Le Grand Temple de Yéha (Tigray, Éthiopie), après la première campagne de fouilles de la Mission Francaise (1998). *CRAI 1998*: 737-798.

Schmidt, P. R. and Curtis, M. C.
2001   Urban precursors in the Horn: early 1st-millennium BC communities in Eritrea. *Antiquity 75*: 849-59.

Tringali, G.
1978   Necropoli di Cascassè e oggetti sudarabici (?) dalla regione di Asmara (Eritrea). *Rassegna di studi etiopici 26 (1973-1977)*: 47-98.

Vogt, B. and Sedov, A.
1998   The Sabir Culture and coastal Yemen during the 2nd Millennium BC – The present state of discussion. *PSAS 28*: 261-270.

Vogt, B., Buffa, V. and Brunner, U.
2002　　May'layba and the Bronze Age Irrigation in Coastal Yemen. *ABADY IX*: 15-26.

Vogt, B., Sedov, A. and Buffa, V.
2002　　Zur Datierung der Sabir-Kultur, Jemen. *ABADY IX:* 27-39.

Zarins, J. and Zahrani, A.
1985　　Recent Archaeological Investigations in the Southern Tihama Plain. The sites of Athar and Sihi. *Atlal 9:* 65-107.

Zarins, J. and al-Badr, H.
1986　　Archaeological Investigations in the Southern Tihama Plain. *Atlal 10:* 65-107.

Zohary M.
1973　　*Geobotanical foundations of the Near East*. 2 vols., Stuttgart.

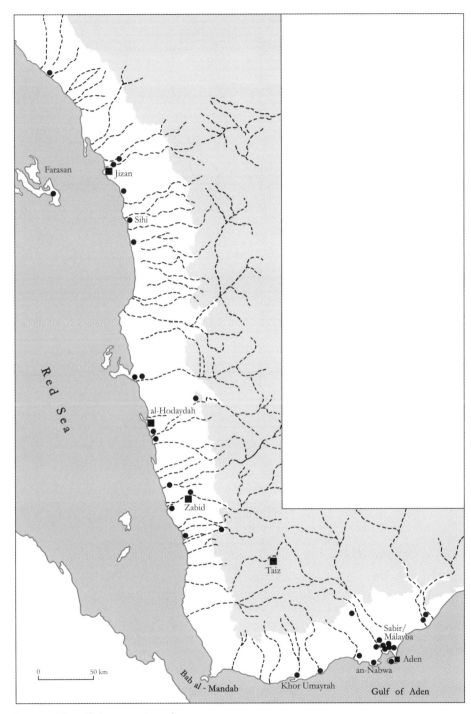

Fig. 1   Map of sites mentioned.

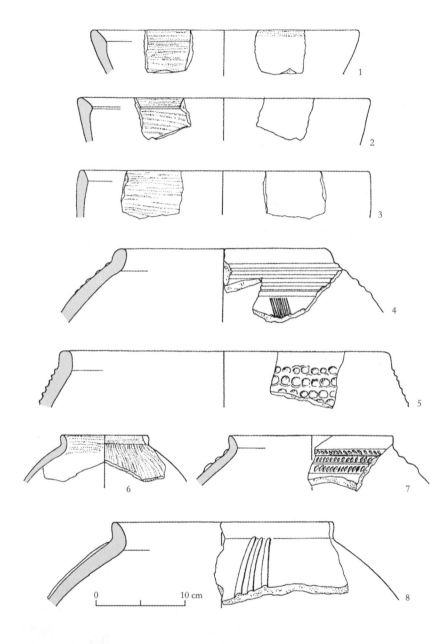

Fig. 2   Selection of potsherds typical for phase 1 of the Sabir Culture, from Ma'layba
          (Vogt et al. 203: figs. 3-4).

Fig. 3   Body shard with appliqué decoration
          from the early layers of Sabir (phase 1).

Fig. 4   Body shard with appliqué decoration
          from the deepest pottery layer (phase 1)
          in Ma'layba.

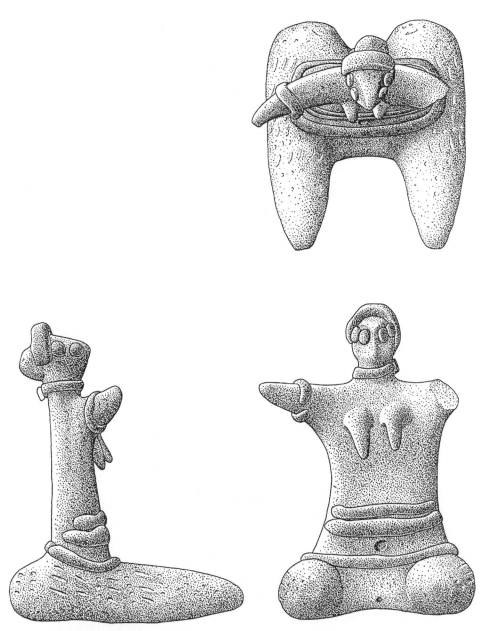

Fig. 5   Terracotta figurine of a seated female. Reconstruction from several fragments
          (drawing M. Manda).

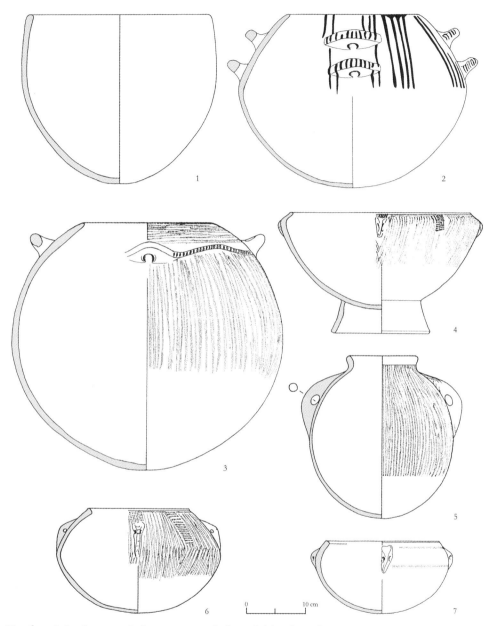

Fig. 6   Selection o typical pottery vessels from Sabir, phase 2.

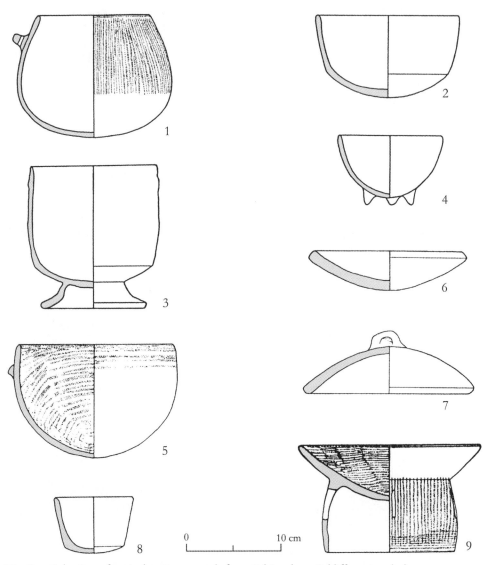

Fig. 7   Selection of typical pottery vessels from Sabir, phase 2 (different scales).

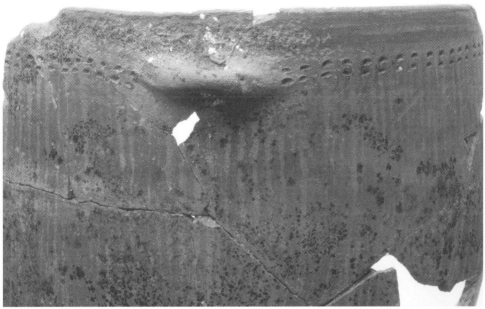

Fig. 8   Pattern burnishing. Detail of an ovoid jar from Sabir 5, around 1000 BC.

Fig. 9   Paddle-and-anvil technique on a large bowl from Sabir 5, early
         1st millennium BC.

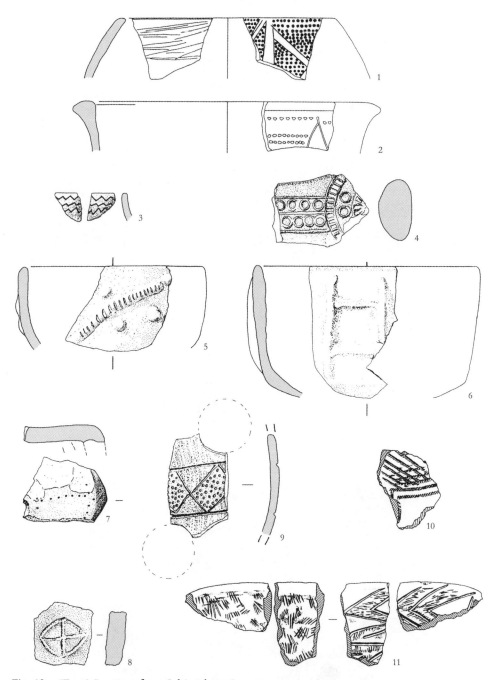

Fig. 10 "Exotic" pottery from Sabir, phase 2.

Fig. 11   Stamped pottery from Sabir, phase 2.

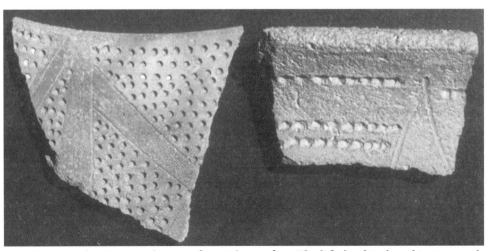

Fig. 12   Incised and stamped pottery from Sabir, surface. The left shard is also white incrusted.

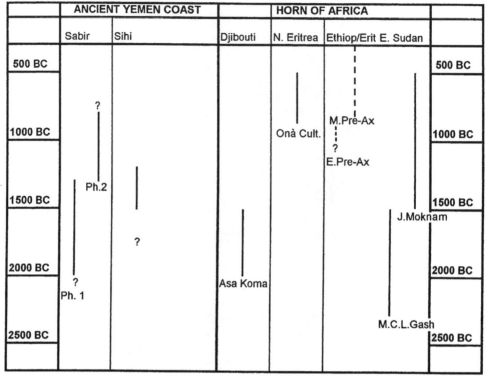

Fig. 13   Comparative chronological chart.

Meroitica

Schriften zur altsudanesischen Geschichte und Archäologie Humboldt-Universität zu Berlin

Herausgegeben von Steffen Wenig

Volume 20: Peter L. Shinnie, Julie R. Anderson (Ed.)

The Capital of Kush 2

Meroë Excavations 1973–1984

With chapters by N. B. Millet and T. Hägg, C. Näser, J. H. Robertson and E. M. Hill, J. Yellin

2004. XXXIII, 429 Seiten, 316 Abb., 15 Tafeln, gb
ISBN 3-447-04892-1
€ 128,– (D) / sFr 217,–

From 1909 to 1914 John Garstang explored Meroë, the ancient capital of the Kingdom of Kush, which is situated about 220 kilometers north of the city Khartoum in today's Sudan. He discovered 1912 the so-called *Royal Baths*. Garstang had to terminate his work because of World War I. and did not submit a comprehensive documentation of the complex of buildings. Only in the sixties of the 20th century the work was taken up again in 11 seasons under the direction of P. L. Shinnie. While the first 7 seasons were documented in volume 4 of Meroitica the present volume describes all the work carried out in the eighth to tenth seasons together with the ironworking area excavated in 1969–1970 und 1973–1974. Of the final season 1983–1984, temple M292 is reported on here, but the publication of the missing seasons will be reserved for a separate report.

Volume 21: Steffen Wenig (Hg.)

Neueste Feldforschungen im Sudan und in Eritrea

Akten des Symposiums vom 13. bis 14. Oktober 1999 in Berlin
2004. XXXVI, 233 Seiten, 102 Abb., gb
ISBN 3-447-04913-8
€ 78,– (D) / sFr 132,–

Aus Anlass des Ausscheidens von Prof. Dr. Steffen Wenig aus dem Universitätsdienst fand 1999 an der Humboldt-Universität zu Berlin ein international besetztes Symposium statt. Die Publikation enthält zehn Beiträge von Gelehrten aus sechs Ländern.

Es wird über die monumentale Inschrift des Königs Taharqa am Gebel Barkal berichtet (T. Kendall), C. Näser legt den letzten Teil der Berichte über die Feldarbeiten der Meroe Joint Excavations in Meroe-Stadt vor (1992), und H.-U. Onasch beschreibt die Arbeiten in einer Keramikwerkstatt in der Großen Anlage von Musawwarat es Sufra, deren Auffindung 1997 überraschend war. Fünf Ausgrabungsberichte, die vom Gebiet der Southern Red Hills, die Nubian Desert über die Region Dinder bis nach Kerma reichen, stammen von sudanesischen Kollegen und einem italienischen Team.

Ein Beitrag schildert die Arbeit der German Archaeological Mission to Eritrea, die erste archäologische Unternehmung im Horn von Afrika durch deutsche Archäologen seit E. Littmanns Deutscher Aksum-Expedition, die 1996 bis 1997 stattfand und überraschende Ergebnisse lieferte. Der Beitrag *Symbiosis Man – Archaeology* bietet einen konzeptionellen und methodischen Ansatz einer *Archäologischen Entwicklungshilfe*, der am Beispiel Qohaito/Eritrea exemplifiziert wird, aber mit Modifikationen auch anderswo anwendbar ist.

HARRASSOWITZ VERLAG · WIESBADEN

www.harrassowitz.de/verlag · verlag@harrassowitz.de

Siegbert Uhlig (Ed.)

Encyclopaedia Aethiopica

Volume 2: D – Ha*

(Encyclopaedia Aethiopica 2)
2005. Ca. 1150 pages, 500 ill., clothbound
ISBN 3-447-05238-4
Ca. € 78,– (D) / sFr 132,–

The encyclopaedia for the Horn of Africa treats all important terms of the history of ideas of this central region between Orient and Africa. After its completion the set will comprise five volumes – four text and one index volume with altogether more than 4000 articles. The topics range from basic data over archaeology, ethnology and anthropology, history, the languages and literatures up to the art, religion and culture. This second volume combines about 1170 articles in English language, written by approximately 250 authors with extents varying from a few lines to several pages. Approximately 250 maps and about the same number of illustrations round off this unique reference book.

More details: http://www.rrz.uni-hamburg.de/EAE/

* Volume 1: A – C. ISBN 3-447-04746-1. € 78,– (D) / sFr 132,–

Extract from a review:

«Notre collègue Uhlig a eu le mérite de donner à un certain nombre de personnes qui se sont présentées comme compétentes l'occasion de faire la preuve de leur compétence, et il faut l'en remercier et l'en féliciter. On trouve dans ce tome I les signatures de savants dont le mérite était connu, et aussi celles d'une nouvelle génération d'éthiopisants, dont on attendait impatiemment l'apparition, et qui vient de faire ses preuves.» *Joseph Tubiana (Institut National des Langues et Civilisations Orientales (INALCO), Paris) in: Aethiopica 7 (2004)*

HARRASSOWITZ VERLAG · WIESBADEN
www.harrassowitz.de/verlag · verlag@harrassowitz.de